# Lecture Notes of the Institute for Computer Sciences, Social Informatics and Telecommunications Engineering 389

More information about this series at http://www.springer.com/series/8197

Weina Fu · Shuai Liu · Jianhua Dai (Eds.)

# e-Learning, e-Education, and Online Training

## 7th EAI International Conference, eLEOT 2021
## Xinxiang, China, June 20–21, 2021
## Proceedings Part I

Springer

*Editors*
Weina Fu
Hunan Normal University
Changsha, China

Shuai Liu
Hunan Normal University
Changsha, China

Jianhua Dai
Hunan Normal University
Changsha, China

ISSN 1867-8211 ISSN 1867-822X (electronic)
Lecture Notes of the Institute for Computer Sciences, Social Informatics and Telecommunications Engineering
ISBN 978-3-030-84382-3 ISBN 978-3-030-84383-0 (eBook)
https://doi.org/10.1007/978-3-030-84383-0



This Springer imprint is published by the registered company Springer Nature Switzerland AG
The registered company address is: Gewerbestrasse 11, 6330 Cham, Switzerland

# Preface

We are delighted to introduce the proceedings of the Third European Alliance for Innovation (EAI) International Conference on e-Learning, e-Education, and Online Training (eLEOT 2021). This conference brought together researchers, developers, and practitioners from around the world who are leveraging and developing e-educational technologies as well as related learning, training, and practice methods. The theme of eLEOT 2021 was "The Educational Revolution: Opportunities and Challenges Brought by COVID-19".

The technical program of eLEOT 2021 consisted of 104 full papers, including 2 invited papers, in oral presentation sessions at the main conference tracks: Track 1 – New Trends of Teaching: Evaluation, Reform, and Practice and Track 2 – Intelligent Learning and Education. The technical program also featured two keynote speeches. "Artificial Intelligence Computing Solutions and Applications", given by Xiaochun Cheng from Middlesex University, UK, reviewed the rational, the potential, and the limitations of relevant AI computing solutions and AI applications, and discussed how new and better AI applications could be developed in the future by integrating diverse AI computing solutions.

"Blockchain-based Secure Data Sharing Platform in IoT", given by Jin Li from Guangzhou University, China, looked at a data incentive mechanism to provide data privacy and fairness measures for users in IoT, providing two different constructions of the proposed mechanism, and analyzing their performances on privacy protection and transaction efficiency.

Coordination with the steering chairs, Imrich Chlamtac, Bruno Kesler, and Giovanni Vincenti, was essential for the success of the conference. We sincerely appreciate their constant support and guidance. It was also a great pleasure to work with such an excellent organizing committee team for their hard work in organizing and supporting the conference. In particular, we are grateful to the Technical Program Committee (TPC), led by our TPC chair, Guanglu Sun, who completed the peer-review process for the technical papers and put together a high-quality technical program. We are also grateful to the conference manager, Elena Davydova, for her support and to all the authors who submitted their papers to the eLEOT 2021 conference.

We strongly believe that the eLEOT conference provides a good forum for all researchers, developers, and practitioners to discuss all science and technology aspects that are relevant to e-learning and e-education. We also expect that the future editions of the conference will be as successful and stimulating as eLEOT 2021, as indicated by the contributions presented in this volume.

July 2021

Weina Fu
Shuai Liu
Jianhua Dai

# Preface

# Organization

## Steering Committee

### Chair

| | |
|---|---|
| Imrich Chlamtac | University of Trento, Italy |

### Co-chairs

| | |
|---|---|
| Bruno Kesler | University of Trento, Italy |
| Giovanni Vincenti | University of Baltimore, USA |

## Organizing Committee

### General Chair

| | |
|---|---|
| Shuai Liu | Hunan Normal University, China |

### Technical Program Committee Chair

| | |
|---|---|
| Guanglu Sun | Harbin Univerity of Science and Technology, China |

### Special Issue Chair

| | |
|---|---|
| Gautam Srivastava | Brandon University, Canada |

### Panel Chair

| | |
|---|---|
| Arun Kumar Sangaiah | Vellore Institute of Technology, India |

### Session Chair

| | |
|---|---|
| Zeguang Lu | National Academy of Guo Ding Institute of Data Sciences, China |

### Publications Chair

| | |
|---|---|
| Khan Muhammad | Sejong University, South Korea |

### Tutorials Chair

| | |
|---|---|
| Tao Li | Hunan Normal University, China |

### Web Chair

| | |
|---|---|
| Weina Fu | Hunan Normal University, China |

**Publicity and Social Media Chair**

| | |
|---|---|
| Lei Chen | Georgia Southern University, USA |

**Local Chair**

| | |
|---|---|
| Junna Zhang | Henan Normal University, China |

## Technical Program Committee

| | |
|---|---|
| Shui-Hua Wang | Loughborough University, UK |
| Amin Taheri-Garavand | Lorestan University, Iran |
| Khan Muhammad | Sejong University, South Korea |
| Gautam Srivastava | Brandon University, Canada |
| Dang Thanh | Hue Industrial College, Vietnam |
| Thippa Reddy Gadekallu | Vellore Institute of Technology, India |
| Uttam Ghosh | Vanderbilt University, USA |
| Norbert Herencsar | Brno University of Technology, Czech Republic |
| Hari Mohan Pandey | Edge Hill University, UK |
| Jerry Chun-Wei Lin | Western Norway University of Applied Sciences, Norway |
| Ashutosh Dhar Dwivedi | Technical University of Denmark, Denmark |
| Adam Zielonka | Silesian University of Technology, Poland |
| Marcin Woźniak | Silesian University of Technology, Poland |
| Arun Kumar Sangaiah | Vellore Institute of Technology, India |
| Ping Yu | Jilin University, China |
| Mu-Yen Chen | National Cheng Kung University, Taiwan |
| Xiaochun Cheng | Middlesex University, UK |
| Fida Hussain Memon | Jeju National University, South Korea |
| Wu-xue Jiang | The Education University of Hong Kong, Hong Kong |
| Dan Zhang | Xinyang Vocational and Technical College, China |
| Dongye Liu | Inner Mongolia University, China |
| Fanyi Meng | Harbin Institute of Technology, China |
| Feng Chen | Xizang Minzu University, China |
| Fu Guang Guo | Henan Vocational College of Industry and Information Technology, China |
| Guanglu Sun | Harbin University of Science and Technology, China |
| Tenghui He | Hunan Normal University, China |
| Heng Li | Henan Finance University, China |
| Jian Feng Cui | Xiamen University of Technology, China |
| Keming Mao | Northeastern University, China |
| Lei Ma | Beijing Polytechnic, China |
| Shuai Wang | Hunan Normal University, China |
| Xiaogang Zhu | Nanchang University, China |
| Xin Chun Zhou | Baoji University of Arts and Sciences, China |

| | |
|---|---|
| Xinyu Liu | Hunan Normal University, China |
| Xuan Yue Tong | Nanyang Institute of Technology, China |
| Yan Ning Zhang | Beijing Polytechnic, China |
| Yong Jun Qin | Guilin Normal College, China |

# Contents – Part I


**Research on Design and Method of Intelligent Education System**

Study on the Curriculum Construction and Teaching of Professional Mathematics in Automobile Major for "Double High Plan" . . . . . . . . . . . . 3
*Rui-can Hao, Hua-gang Liu, Zhi-xin Feng, Shang Wang, and Guang-hui Xia*

Reform and Practice of Digital Teaching of Engineering Mechanics Course Under the Background of "Double High Program" . . . . . . . . . . . . . . 15
*Jin-ru Ma, Rui-can Hao, and Shang Wang*

Study on Modular Curriculums in Vocational Education and Training System . . . . . . . . . . . . . . . . . . . . . . . . . . . . . . . . . 23
*Rui-can Hao, Zhi-xin Feng, Hua-gang Liu, Shang Wang, and Yu-hui Wei*

Research on Human Resources Situational Teaching Model Based on Social Information Orientation . . . . . . . . . . . . . . . . . . . . . . . . . . . 32
*Huan-wei Liang and Shao-lin Liang*

Research on Internal Cost Accounting and Control of Education System Based on Activity Based Costing . . . . . . . . . . . . . . . . . . . . . . . . . . . . 43
*Li-min Zhang*

Research on Power Consumption Control Method of Online Teaching Terminal Based on IEEE 802.11 . . . . . . . . . . . . . . . . . . . . . . . . . . . . . . . . 57
*Zheng Zhang and Tian-Hui Wang*

Financial Management Course Distance Teaching Method Based on B/S Model . . . . . . . . . . . . . . . . . . . . . . . . . . . . . . . . . . . . . . . . 71
*Xi Chen and Shu-Yang Zhang*

Research on Online Teaching Method of Equation Solving Based on Transfer Learning . . . . . . . . . . . . . . . . . . . . . . . . . . . . . . . . . . . . 86
*Li An and Yan Wang*

Online Intelligent Teaching Method of Track and Field Error Avoidance Based on Multimedia Video . . . . . . . . . . . . . . . . . . . . . . . . . . . . . . 99
*Yong-ming Chen and Shu-tao Shen*

Method of Online Teaching Resource Recommendation Towards International Communication Based on.NET Platform . . . . . . . . . . . . . . . . 110
*Qian Jiang and Lin He*

Data Mining Method of English Online Learning Behavior Based on Machine Learning Technology . . . . . 122
*Yi Jiang and Yi-huo Jiang*

Intelligent Recommendation Model of Distance Education Courses Based on Facial Expression Recognition . . . . . 134
*Ying Yang, Dong-rui Li, Xiao-feng Huang, and Sheng-bin Wu*

Online Teaching Method of Conductive Characteristics of Graphene Materials Based on Big Data Mining . . . . . 146
*Tian-hui Wang, Ang Li, and Zheng Zhang*

Distance Teaching Method of Accounting Informatization Course Based on Big Data Mining . . . . . 155
*Qi-feng Wu*

University Ideological and Political Multimedia Network Teaching Based on MOOC . . . . . 167
*Hong-bing Jiang*

An Efficient Teaching Method for Physiological Basic Course of Online and Offline Integration . . . . . 181
*Lian-shi Dong, Dan Wang, and Jing-qiong Xiao*

Decision Support Model for Online Education of Logistics Management Major from the Perspective of "Credit Bank" . . . . . 194
*Jun Fu and Ming Qin*

Comprehensive Control Method of Network Teaching Data Scheduling Based on Fuzzy Mathematics . . . . . 205
*Mei-li Dai and Li An*

Design of Personal Learning Model Recognition Model for Online Teaching of Ideological and Political Theory Course . . . . . 218
*Li-tang Xu and Hong-gang Wang*

Research on the Ideological and Political Teaching Mode of Dual System Curriculum in Colleges and Universities Based on MOOC . . . . . 231
*Jiang-lin Lu*

Pattern Recognition Method of Training Japanese Talents in Online Education . . . . . 243
*Hui Sun and Yan Liu*

Research on Hybrid Learning Mode of Financial Management Course in Cloud Classroom Environment . . . . . 254
*Ling Cheng and Hui-ying Yan*

Research on Pattern Recognition Method of Online English Education Based on Feature Self Learning . . . . . . . . . . . . . . . . . . . . . . . . . . . . . 266
*Xiao-xiao Duan and Ping Duan*

Pattern Recognition Method of English Distance Online Education Based on Big Data Algorithm . . . . . . . . . . . . . . . . . . . . . . . . . . . . . . . 278
*Xiao-xiao Duan and Ping Duan*

Big Data Based Human Resources Professional Distance Training Platform . . . . . . . . . . . . . . . . . . . . . . . . . . . . . . . . . . . 289
*Cai-ming Zhang and Li Liu*

Design of Personalized Employment Guidance System for College Students Based on Big Data . . . . . . . . . . . . . . . . . . . . . . . . . . . . 301
*Mei-bin Qi and Yu-juan Zhang*

Design of Mixed Learning System of Tourism Planning Course Based on Mobile Terminal. . . . . . . . . . . . . . . . . . . . . . . . . . . . . . . . . 311
*Yu-xiang Liu and Zhi-li Sha*

Design of Digital Repair System for Damaged Cultural Relic Image in the Professional Training of Restoration . . . . . . . . . . . . . . . . . . . . . . . . . 322
*Shu-tao Shen and Yong-ming Chen*

The Design of College Ideological and Political Teaching System Based on Online and Offline Mixed Mode. . . . . . . . . . . . . . . . . . . . . . . . . . 332
*Fang Liu*

Design of Innovation and Entrepreneurship Teaching System for Ideological and Political Courses in Universities Based on Online and Offline Integration. . . . . . . . . . . . . . . . . . . . . . . . . . . . . . . . . 344
*Fang Liu*

Design of English Listening Simulation Teaching System Based on Cloud Computing . . . . . . . . . . . . . . . . . . . . . . . . . . . . . . . . . . 355
*Fa-li Mi and Jia-wei Yuan*

Design of Ideological and Political Intelligence Teaching System for Sino-German Dual System Course Based on MVC Architecture . . . . . . . 367
*Jiang-lin Lu*

Design of Virtual Simulation Experiment Teaching System for Electrical Engineering and Automation Specialty. . . . . . . . . . . . . . . . . . . . . . . . 381
*Quan -wen Chen and Ping Gong*

Design of Simulation Teaching System of Automatic Control System Course Based on MATLAB . . . . . . . . . . . . . . . . . . . . . . . . . . . . . . . 395
*Ru Yan and Chun-ni Zheng*

Design and Practice of Online and Offline Mixed Education System . . . . . . . 405
*Ying-jian Kang, Xin-yu Lv, Mei Chen, and Lei Ma*

Design of Auxiliary Teaching System for Oral English Training Based on Cloud Computing . . . . . . . 418
*Ying Lin, Ying-di Xi, and Yang-bo Wu*

Design of Computer Professional Training Teaching System Based on Big Data Under the Background of "Three Integration" . . . . . . . 430
*Jie-lan Zhang*

Design of Multimedia Intelligent Classroom Interactive Teaching System Based on Internet of Things Technology . . . . . . . 442
*Wei He, Cheng-hui Zhang, and Yang-bo Wu*

Design of Dance Action Simulation Teaching System Based on Cloud Computation . . . . . . . 453
*Yi-jia Shang and Dong-dong Suo*

Design of Enterprise Job Training Education Management System Based on J2EE . . . . . . . 464
*Yong-lan Yan and Jun-mei Li*

CAD Drawing Teaching Assistant System of Civil Engineering Based on Digital Technology . . . . . . . 476
*Yu Liu*

**Design and Development of Online Education System**

Construction of Online Open Distance Teaching Platform for Meridians and Acupoints of TCM . . . . . . . 489
*Yu-juan Zhang and Mei-bin Qi*

Design of Spoken English Distance Teaching Training System Based on Virtual Reality Technology . . . . . . . 502
*Zhi-li Sha and Yu-xiang Liu*

Design of Online Education Decision Support System Based on Machine Learning . . . . . . . 515
*Shao-lin Liang and Huan-wei Liang*

Design of Financial Management Teaching System Integrated with Online Micro Class . . . . . . . 527
*Zhen Li and Min Luo*

Design of Online Teaching System for Financial Management Course Based on Cloud Platform . . . . . . . 541
*Min Luo and Zhen Li*

Construction of Network Teaching Information Interactive Platform of Traditional Music in New Media Era . . . . . . . . . . . . . . . . . . . . . . . . . . . 553
*Jun Zhou, Liang Lu, and Yang-bo Wu*

Design and Development of Online Distance Learning System for Electrical Automation Technology Specialty . . . . . . . . . . . . . . . . . . . . . . . . . . . . 566
*Quan-wen Chen and Shan Jiang*

Design of Online Teaching Platform for Packaging and Printing Course Based on Joint Image Denoising . . . . . . . . . . . . . . . . . . . . . . . . . . . . 579
*Jia Wang and Ming Yue*

Design of Online Teaching Platform for Printing Color Course Based on Visualization Technology . . . . . . . . . . . . . . . . . . . . . . . . . . . . 592
*Jia Wang*

Design of Online Teaching System of Real Estate Operation and Management Course Based on Cloud Model . . . . . . . . . . . . . . . . . . . . 604
*Yi-pin Yan and Qian Peng*

Design of a Flipped Classroom Platform for Online Music Education in Colleges and Universities Based on the Internet . . . . . . . . . . . . . . . . . . . 617
*Hui Lin and Yang-bo Wu*

Function Design of Music Online Education Network Virtual Classroom Platform . . . . . . . . . . . . . . . . . . . . . . . . . . . . . . . . . . . . . . 631
*Yang-bo Wu, Hui Lin, and Wei-hua Zhu*

Design of Online Teaching Platform for Accounting Informatization Course Based on Cloud Computing . . . . . . . . . . . . . . . . . . . . . . . . . . . . 644
*Qi-feng Wu*

Online Video Learning Design of Civil Engineering and Architecture Education in Higher Vocational Education Based on Streaming Media Technology . . . . . . . . . . . . . . . . . . . . . . . . . . . . . . . . . . . . 657
*Yu Liu*

**Author Index** . . . . . . . . . . . . . . . . . . . . . . . . . . . . . . . . . . . . 669

# Contents – Part II

**Design and Development of Online Education System**

Design of Online Multimodule Educational Administration System Based on Time Difference Database Technology . . . . . . . . . . . . . . . . . . . . . . . . . 3
*Jun-mei Li and Yong-lan Yan*

Chemical Structure Data Retrieval Algorithm for Chemistry Online Teaching . . . . . . . . . . . . . . . . . . . . . . . . . . . . . . . . . . . . . . . 16
*Guang-min Jiang, Xin Dai, and Wei Hou*

Multi Mode Interactive Information Processing Method in Online Education System of Ideological and Political Course . . . . . . . . . . . . . . . . . 25
*Hong-gang Wang and Li-tang Xu*

Design of Online Training System for Innovative and Entrepreneurial Talents Based on Interdisciplinary Integration. . . . . . . . . . . . . . . . . . . . . . 39
*Yu-feng Men and Hong Cai*

Diversified Design of Distance Teaching Platform for Pathogenic Microorganism and Immunology. . . . . . . . . . . . . . . . . . . . . . . . . . . . . . . 50
*Dan Wang, Lian-shi Dong, and Ying Wang*

Design of Sports Dance Online Interactive Teaching System Based on Intelligent Terminal . . . . . . . . . . . . . . . . . . . . . . . . . . . . . . . . . 61
*Jing Zhao and Ya-na Tang*

Construction of Online Distance Three Dimensional Teaching Platform for Industrial Design Major in Colleges and Universities . . . . . . . . . . . . . . 75
*Ji-wei Liu and Li-na Dong*

Design of Online Visual Interactive Teaching System Based on Artificial Intelligence Technology . . . . . . . . . . . . . . . . . . . . . . . . . . . . . . . . . 90
*Jie-lan Zhang*

Design of Management Accounting Online Teaching System Based on Virtual Simulation Technology. . . . . . . . . . . . . . . . . . . . . . . . . . . . . . 103
*Shu-yang Zhang, Xi Chen, and Pei-jun Han*

The Design of Interactive English Online Education System Based on B/S Structure . . . . . . . . . . . . . . . . . . . . . . . . . . . . . . . . . . . . . . . 118
*Ying-di Xi, Ying Lin, and Yangbo Wu*

Design of Online Management System for Painting Teaching Based on Artificial Intelligence Technology . . . . . 130
*Dong-dong Suo and Yi-jia Shang*

Design of Online Teaching System for Innovation and Entrepreneurship of Finance Major Based on Big Data. . . . . 143
*Tong Sun*

Design of Economics Course Teaching System Based on Online and Offline Mixed Mode . . . . . 154
*Tong Sun*

One Belt, One Road Background, International Logistics Professional Online Training and Education System Design . . . . . 165
*Ming Qin and Jun Fu*

Online Education System for Innovation and Innovation Courses Based on Big Data from the Perspective of Rural Revitalization. . . . . 176
*Chun-ni Zheng and Ru Yan*

**Research and Application of Teaching Resources**

Design of Online Sharing System for College Writing Teaching Resources in the Media Age . . . . . 193
*Li-jun Yun and Ming-sheng Li*

Design of Online Education Resource Sharing Model Based on Blockchain Technology . . . . . 205
*Li-ting Liu, Ran Ma, and Fei Gao*

Conflict Coordination Method of Heterogeneous Educational Resources Sharing Based on Blockchain . . . . . 218
*Jiang Li, Xiao-tian Yang, and Fei Gao*

Teaching Resource Sharing System of Real Estate Management Course Based on Data Mining . . . . . 230
*Qian Peng and Yi-pin Yan*

Design of Intelligent Cloud Teaching Resource Sharing Platform for Chinese and Korean Modern Ceramic Art . . . . . 241
*Hong Cai and Yu-feng Men*

Design of Security Sharing System for Online Teaching Course Resources of Fine Arts Specialty . . . . . 252
*Li-na Dong and Ji-wei Liu*

Statistical Model of Online Educational Resource Allocation for Coordinated Development of Regional Economy . . . . . . . . . . . . . . . . . . 264
*Xin Tang and Jun-hao Qiao*

Design of Teaching Resource Integration System Based on Load Balancing Algorithm . . . . . . . . . . . . . . . . . . . . . . . . . . . . . . . . . . . . . 277
*Rou-jia Ji and Guang Tao*

A Data Mining Based Method for Identifying the Mismatch of Educational Resources in Regional Colleges and Universities. . . . . . . . . . . . . . . . . . . . . . 291
*Yan Liu, Sun Hui, and Sen-wei Wang*

Optimization and Integration of Network Teaching Resources of Ideological and Political Course Based on Big Data . . . . . . . . . . . . . . . . 303
*Ming-sheng Li and Li-jun Yun*

Research on Hybrid Recommendation Algorithm of Educational Courseware Resources Based on Heterogeneous Information Fusion . . . . . . . 313
*Sheng-bin Wu and Ying Yang*

Research on Resource Integration Method of Civil Engineering Construction Course Based on Big Data Mining . . . . . . . . . . . . . . . . . . . . . . 325
*Hong-wei Tian*

**Research on Teaching Evaluation Method**

Teaching Quality Evaluation Method of Human Resource Management Based on Big Data . . . . . . . . . . . . . . . . . . . . . . . . . . . . . . . . . . . . . . 341
*Liu Li and Cai-ming Zhang*

Evaluation Model of English Continuous Pronunciation Teaching Quality Based on Cloud Computing . . . . . . . . . . . . . . . . . . . . . . . . . . . . . . . 354
*Dan Zhao and Guang-min Jiang*

Design of Intelligent Evaluation System for Application Effect of Internet Financial Sharing Course . . . . . . . . . . . . . . . . . . . . . . . . . . . . . . . . . 365
*Hui-ying Yan and Ling Cheng*

Comprehensive Evaluation Model of MOOC Teaching Quality of Accounting Major Based on Rete Algorithm . . . . . . . . . . . . . . . . . . . . . 379
*Li-min Zhang*

Evaluation Method of Teaching Effect of Applied Logistics Management Course Based on Deep Learning . . . . . . . . . . . . . . . . . . . . . . . . . . . . . 392
*Lin He, Qi-xiang Wu, and Qian Jiang*

Evaluation Method of Online Learning Process Under the Background of Educational Big Data. . . . . . . . . . 403
*Yi- huo Jiang and Yi Jiang*

Research on Online Course Teaching Quality Evaluation Method Based on Internet of Things Technology . . . . . . . . . . 415
*Guang Tao, Jie He, and Rou-jia Ji*

Evaluation Model of Computer Education Reform Effect in Colleges and Universities Based on Improved Fuzzy Clustering Algorithm . . . . . . . . . 430
*Lu Guo, Ying Wei, and Shan Jiang*

Evaluation Model of Electrical Control Teaching Mode Reform Effect Based on Deep Convolution Neural Network . . . . . . . . . . 441
*Shan Jiang, Quan-wen Chen, and Lu Guo*

Evaluation Method of Interactive Quality of Road and Bridge Construction Course Teaching Based on Principal Component Analysis . . . . . . . . . . 452
*Hong-wei Tian*

Research on Intelligent Correction of Abnormal Data in Online Education System Based on Big Data Technology . . . . . . . . . . 465
*Yana Tang and Jing Zhao*

Monitoring Method of students' Learning Behavior in Online Education Platform Based on Data Mining . . . . . . . . . . 477
*Cheng-zhao Chen, Zheng Chen, and You-xin Li*

**Internet of Things and Collaborative Computing**

Research on the Application of CI System in the Construction of University Class Culture Under the Internet Background . . . . . . . . . . 491
*Cheng-hui Zhang, Wei He, and Yang-bo Wu*

Education Information Network Terminal Big Data Analysis Response and Monitoring System . . . . . . . . . . 502
*Lei Ma, Xin-yu Lv, and Shuai Fu*

Feature Extraction Method of Students' Ideological and Political Learning Behavior Based on Convolutional Neural Network . . . . . . . . . . 514
*Hong-bing Jiang*

Research on the Diversity of Technical Characteristics of Folk Music Classroom Teaching Based on Network Knowledge Sharing . . . . . . . . . . 527
*Liang Lu, Jun Zhou, and Yang-bo Wu*

Adaptive Parameter Determination Method of Synchronous Motor Digital PI Regulator . . . . . 538
*Jin-tian Yin, Li Liu, Jie Tang, Zhi-hua Peng, and Hui Li*

Research on the Relationship Between Volatility and Regional Economies of Scale in Cloud Computing . . . . . 550
*Jun-hao Qiao and Xin Tang*

Multimedia Resources Search Service System of Preschool Education Based on Augmented Reality Technology . . . . . 562
*Jia-wei Yuan and Fa-li Mi*

Detection Method of Machine Tool Axis Offset Distance Based on Rough Set Neural Network . . . . . 576
*Nan Qin*

Control Method of Multi Joint Snake Like Manipulator Based on Hybrid Fish Swarm Ant Colony Algorithm . . . . . 588
*Nan Qin*

Design of Step Motor Automation Control System Based on Lyaponov Stability Theory . . . . . 599
*Jin-tian Yin, Jie Tang, Li Liu, Qing-yue Luo, Xin-bo Liu, and Wei Chen*

**Author Index** . . . . . 613

# Research on Design and Method of Intelligent Education System

# Study on the Curriculum Construction and Teaching of Professional Mathematics in Automobile Major for "Double High Plan"

Rui-can Hao(✉), Hua-gang Liu, Zhi-xin Feng, Shang Wang, and Guang-hui Xia

Beijing Polytechnic, No. 9 Liangshuihe First Street, Yizhuang, Beijing, China
haoruican@bpi.edu.cn

**Abstract.** Under the policy of "Double High Plan", the quality of the vocational education should be improved and developed. In automobile major, professional mathematics course is one of the most important professional basic courses for the development of students. How to design and teach the course is a valuable question to research. The curriculum framework of professional mathematics was designed by analyzing course orientation, course objectives (including social capacities, operation abilities, and developing capacities) and course framework. The course contents were designed for students' learning by completing the projects such as typical application of professional mathematics in automobile specialty, basic operation in mathematical software, numerical analysis on characteristics of vehicle driving, analysis on mathematical model of automobile braking, and mathematical model of robot in automobile production line. The projects were designed and the 3rd project of the course was designed and listed according to the students training program. The teaching methods and evaluation of the course were designed for students to master the basic knowledge effectively.

**Keyword:** Curriculum construction · Teaching · Professional mathematics · Automobile major

## 1 Instructions

In April 2019, the Ministry of Education and the Ministry of Finance jointly issued the "opinions on the implementation of high level higher vocational schools and specialty construction plan with Chinese characteristics". It is proposed to focus on the construction of about 50 high-level vocational schools and about 150 high-level professional groups, to build a highland for the cultivation of technical talents and a platform for the innovation of technical skills [1]. Here the high level higher vocational schools and specialty construction plan with Chinese characteristics and specialty construction plan is called "Double High Plan" in Chinese.


W. Fu et al. (Eds.): eLEOT 2021, LNICST 389, pp. 3–14, 2021.
https://doi.org/10.1007/978-3-030-84383-0_1

With the developing of the automobile industry, the complex jobs related to automobile require the workers to have more comprehensive professional knowledge and adept skills. At the same time, high level higher vocational schools with Chinese characteristics and specialty construction plan requires that the vocational education should be more improved and perfect. It is proposed in Implementation Plan of National Vocational Education Reform that vocational education should be placed in a more prominent position in educational reform innovation and economically social development. In the Implementation Plan, important development goals for vocational education are put forward, including that the vocational education and training system should be improved, the directions should be changed from pursuing the scale expansion to improving the quality of education, and so on [2].

Under the guidance of this policy, to cultivate students with high quality, the curriculum construction for teaching is top priority. How to design and teach a course is a valuable research subject for a teacher to achieve a more satisfactory effect.

## 2 Professional Mathematics in Automobile Specialty

Automobile industry is a comprehensive enterprise developed on the basis of many related industries and technologies. The products of many departments are used in automobile, and all kinds of processing technologies are needed from blank processing to vehicle assembly. Car parts include thousands of different parts ranging from flooring to screws. The automobile production process includes the assembly of engine, transmission, axle, car body, tires, glass, electrical appliances, car body interior parts and other small parts [3].

Professional mathematics (PM) is one of the most important courses for students' development in career designing, and it is the first professional basic course in the process of learning courses in major [4–6]. For example, automobile assembly sequence optimization is the key and difficult content in the course of "automobile manufacturing process basis", and it is also a basic skill that the students majoring automobile must master. The problem requires students to solve it by analyzing the process requirements of color, configuration and power on the assembly line, establishing the LP model meeting 20 constraints, and solving it by related software. The algorithm also requires students to have strong understanding ability and programming ability [7–9].

For another example, the teaching fields of automobile major include sales, maintenance, design and other specific categories, many of which are similar to "cylinder diameter" and "piston stroke" closely related to the function relationship, curve trend and monotony knowledge points in higher mathematics. In this regard, teachers should stand in the perspective of automobile professional teaching, to classify and summarize some knowledge points, and combine with the teaching plan of higher mathematics. As the builder and leader of knowledge system, teachers should actively guide students to find the correct direction of learning mathematics, so that students can understand the relevant skills and application of automobile professional learning in the process of learning mathematics knowledge, and effectively improve their professional practice ability [10, 11].

The designed quality and teaching effect of Professional mathematics directly affect students to master and absorb the knowledges of professional courses in the later stage, and may even affect students' performance and career development in specific work in the future. So how to design and how to teach the course is deserved to research.

## 3 Curriculum Framework Construction

### 3.1 Course Orientation

Professional mathematics is a compulsory technical basic course for students majoring in automobile manufacturing and assembly technology.

Based on the original knowledge of higher mathematics, the course adopts the method of combining theoretical teaching with practical application, and combines with some typical cases to lead the students to learn the basic theory of automobile mathematics. Through these methods, students could be familiar with the basic operation of mathematical modeling software, improve the ability of logical reasoning and mathematical induction, and master the ability of mathematical modeling and model calculation and analysis, so as to lay a good foundation for students' subsequent professional courses.

In the course designing plan, the integration, connection and cooperation with professional courses was proposed, the connection between curriculum content and professional courses was strengthened, and practical education was highlighted. The course is not only a supplement to the previous course "higher mathematics", but also a foundation for the related mathematical knowledge in the following courses "industrial robot technology application", "vehicle assembly and debugging", "welding robot operation and operation and maintenance", "production line operation and monitoring".

Table 1 shows the technical basic courses for specialty group designed in the students training program majoring in automobile manufacturing and assembly technology [12]. It is shown that the course of Professional mathematics designed is offered in the second semester of the second academic year for students. It is an integrated course of theory and practice whose class practice teaching accounts for about 50% of the total class hours.

In the students training program, the concept of learning time was put forward for the first time. The learning time of students includes not only the length of time for students in class, but also the corresponding learning and consolidation time under the guidance of teachers after class.

For the course of Professional mathematics, the total teaching time is 32 h and total learning time is 64 h. It means that students need to complete 32 extra hours of study after class under the guidance of the teacher.

### 3.2 Course Objectives

Through the study of this course, students should master the basic operation of mathematical calculation and drawing software, and master the knowledge of differential and integral of one variable function, extreme value of function, data fitting, matrix, and its operation in a calculating software. Students should understand the theory of

**Table 1.** Technical Basic Courses for Specialty Group

| | Courses | Class hours | After class hours | Learning hours | Semester |
|---|---|---|---|---|---|
| 1 | Engineering Graphics | 64 | 64 | 128 | 1 |
| 2 | Engineering Mechanics | 64 | 64 | 128 | 1 |
| 3 | Mechanical Design | 64 | 96 | 160 | 2 |
| 4 | **Professional Mathematics** | **32** | **32** | **80** | **4** |
| 5 | Electrical and Electronic Technology | 64 | 64 | 128 | 3 |
| 6 | Automobile Structure | 64 | 96 | 160 | 3 |

vehicle driving dynamics, and master the method of using software to calculate the dynamic factor speed equation to solve the speed threshold. Students can understand the influence factors of vehicle braking distance, and master the method of solving the braking distance threshold by using software to calculate the braking balance equation. Students could understand the kinematics equation of robot arm in automobile manufacturing, and master the method of coordinate transformation using related software. Students can also be able to use the advanced mathematics and automobile professional knowledge to solve the related practical engineering problems, and have the ability of preliminary mathematical modeling and result analysis after learning the course. The specific objectives of the course to develop the abilities for students are shown in Fig. 1 as follows.

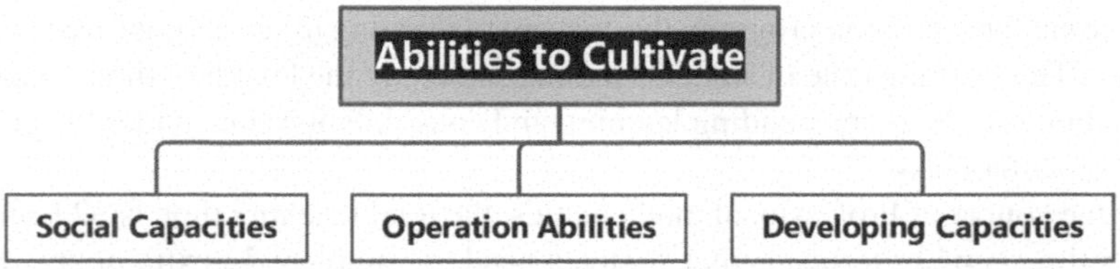


**Fig. 1.** The abilities to cultivate in specific objectives of professional mathematics.

**Social Capacities.** Our teaching design should take the following methods to help students to achieve the social capabilities. (1) Carry forward the socialist core values and establish the world outlook of dialectical materialism. (2) Establish the ideal and belief of innovation, cultivate the craftsman spirit and the professional spirit of continuous improvement, and cultivate the students' sense of responsibility, self-discipline and the spirit of hardship. (3) Enhance students' executive ability and communication ability, and cultivate students' team cooperation ability. (4) Cultivate students' ability of self-study, literature review and summary, and improve their ability of using mathematical knowledge to analyze and solve practical problems.

**Operation Abilities.** Our teaching design should take the following methods to help students to develop students' operation skills. (1) Understand the basic concept of function, master the commonly used dynamic calculation and analysis methods, so as to solve the problems of vehicle power calculation and performance factor analysis, to improve the ability of solving problems. (2) Be proficient in curve fitting of discrete points with the software. (3) Master the concept of derivative and extremum in mathematics, be able to solve the calculation problems in vehicle motion and braking by combining kinematics and dynamics theory and using relevant mathematical knowledge. (4) Master the basic concepts of array and matrix, master the contents of linear equations and related matrix transformation, and skillfully use software to calculate matrix. (5) Be able to apply the knowledge of matrix analysis to solve the problems of industrial robot motion and its positive and negative solutions. (6) Master the basic operation of the related mathematical software, be able to use software to establish the mathematical model of automobile driving, braking and robot kinematics of automobile production line, and carry out simulation calculation. (7) Be able to analyze the mathematical logic of the research object and its influencing factors based on the results of simulation calculation.

**Developing Capacities.** The teaching design should help students to achieve the developing capabilities which are designed to include logical reasoning ability, analysis ability and preliminary mathematical modeling ability.

*Logical Reasoning Ability.* Facing to the problems in the processing of learning, students can use the achieved knowledge to analyze reasoning related problems and get mathematical laws for solving the kind of problems.

*Analysis Ability.* Students could be able to calculate with related software and analyze the results of the calculations. For example, for automobile, the steel panel part will deform after being stressed. By modeling, the deformation will be calculated and displayed in the software to help students to analyze the forces and materials being stressed. Figure 2 shows the deformation in the example.

*Mathematical Modeling Ability.* After analyzing on the problem, by mathematical modeling software, students could master the relationship between the objects and the mathematical models. For example, the plot drawing with software was taken into the teaching to help students to establish mathematical models. Fig. 3 and Fig. 4 show the plot models for students' practicing.

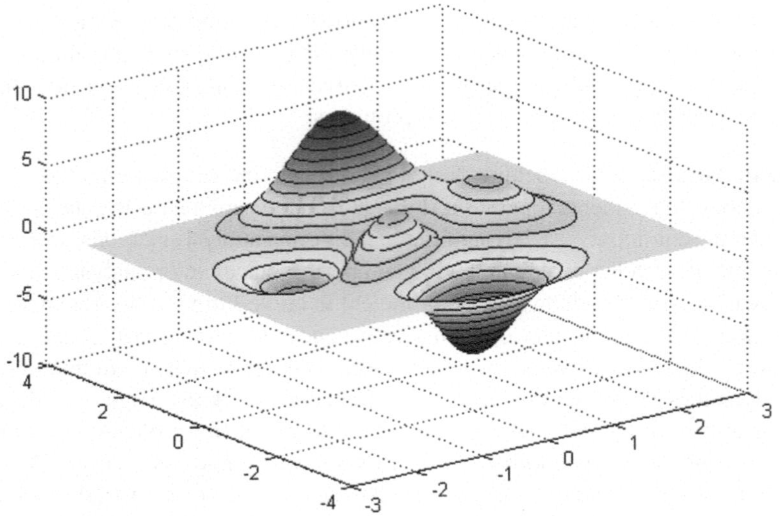


**Fig. 2.** Deformation model and analysis in professional mathematics.

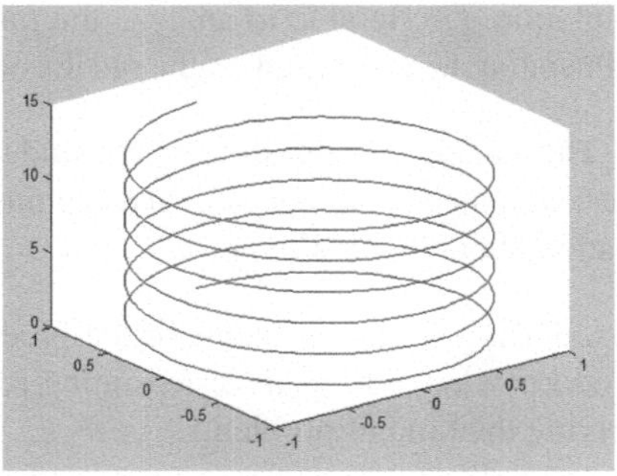

**Fig. 3.** A drawing example in professional mathematics.

# 4 Course Contents Design

## 4.1 Modular Projects Design

Based on the study and supplement of advanced mathematics and applied mathematics, combined with the automobile assembly and manufacturing technology related majors, mathematical calculation software was applied to design the relevant mathematical models and calculation problems of automobile in driving, braking, production and other projects. Students could solve the related problems in the automobile industry through learning mathematical knowledge, building models and software calculation. These problems were summarized into several kinds of related modular projects shown in Fig. 5.

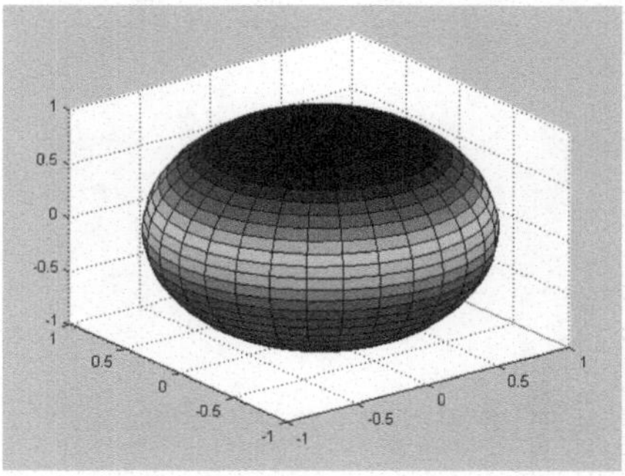

**Fig. 4.** The plot drawing in professional mathematics.

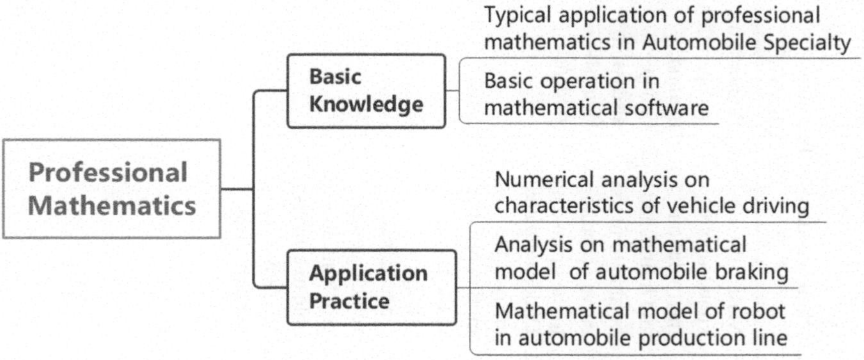


**Fig. 5.** Modular projects designed in professional mathematics.

### 4.2 Course Contents Design

The course contents were designed and summarized into five modular projects including typical application of professional mathematics in automobile specialty, basic operation in mathematical software, numerical analysis on characteristics of vehicle driving, analysis on mathematical model of automobile braking, and mathematical model of robot in automobile production line. For example, the specific contents of 3rd part of projects are designed and shown in Table 2.

**Table 2.** The specific contents of the 3rd project designed.

| Projects | Learning models | Contents | Teaching standards | Teaching methods | Evaluation content | Learning hours |
|---|---|---|---|---|---|---|
| 3. Numerical analysis on characteristics of vehicle driving | In Class | 1. Interpolation and fitting<br>2. Motion analysis in the process of driving<br>3. Vehicle power analysis and modeling | 1. Master the knowledge of interpolation and fitting, and be able to fit the curve according to the given data<br>2. Understand and analyze the motion problems in the process of driving<br>3. Understand vehicle power problems and be able to establish relevant mathematical models | 1. Demonstrate the operation method<br>2. Group discussion<br>3. Heuristic guidance | 1. Attendance and answering questions in class<br>2. Class notes and exercises in class<br>3. Case analysis | 6 |

(continued)

**Table 2.** *(continued)*

| Projects | Learning models | Contents | Teaching standards | Teaching methods | Evaluation content | Learning hours |
|---|---|---|---|---|---|---|
| | After Class | 1. Interpolation and fitting exercises<br>2. Consult materials to understand and summarize the problems of motion and power in driving<br>3. Case analysis, using MATLAB software to model and analyze the problem | 1. Be able to use interpolation and fitting knowledge to solve problems<br>2. Be able to use MATLAB software to analyze and calculate relevant models | 1. self-directed learning<br>2. Group discussion<br>3. Practice the problem driven method | 1. Study notes<br>2. Group discussion<br>3. Research Report or professional mathematics essay | 9 |

## 5 Teaching and Evaluation

### 5.1 Teaching Methods and Devices

The teaching mode of professional mathematics course should highlight students' subjectivity, strengthen the interaction between students in teaching activities, and mobilize students' learning enthusiasm to the maximum extent. Affirm the progress of students in learning in time, strengthen the role of motivation, so that students can establish self-confidence. At the same time, we should pay attention to the trinity of knowledge, ability and attitude.

**Teaching Methods.** In terms of teaching methods, case driven, demonstration and group learning are the main methods. Combining mathematical knowledge and specialty, using mathematical modeling to deal with professional problems, the importance of the course was stated, so as to stimulate students' enthusiasm for knowledge, and mobilizes students' subjective initiative. In the teaching mode, we should reduce and prevent the simple explanation teaching, emphasize the students as the main body, give students more space for practical activities, actively carry out the interaction and multimedia teaching suitable for students, and make full use of the network resource platform. We should establish a new teaching mode of "taking learning as the center, taking students as the main body and teachers as the leading role", and pay attention to the Trinity training of knowledge, ability and quality in teaching objectives.

**Teaching Devices.** In classroom teaching, students should complete the project through learning. Multimedia teaching and broadcasting system, multimedia teaching website, network classroom, animation demonstration and other auxiliary teaching methods are adopted. The most time in class should be spent on students' completing the projects on their own initiatively. Its rich and diverse information bearing forms, flexible and convenient interactive features, which is easy for students to understand and master, increase students' interest in the course. When operating on the computer, software is necessary to train students to establish and analyze the mathematical model of the relevant problems encountered in professional learning.

### 5.2 Evaluation

"N + 2" evaluation pattern is adopted. The evaluation system includes mid-term test (10%), summary report (15%), case analysis report (15%), special research report (10%), Notes (10%) and module end test (40%), which is shown in Fig. 6.

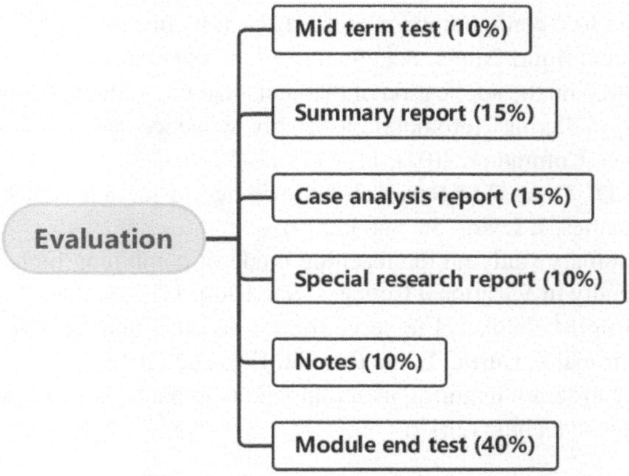


**Fig. 6.** Evaluation system.

## 6 Summary

Professional mathematics is an important basic course for students majoring in automobile. The framework of professional mathematics was designed by analyzing course orientation, course objectives (including social capacities, operation abilities, and developing capacities), and course framework. The course contents were designed into five projects whose contents and teaching methods were designed. The 3$^{rd}$ project of the course was shown in paper. The teaching methods and evaluation of the course were designed for students to master the basic knowledge effectively. The constructions of the curriculums under the background of the "Double High Plan" will push the development of vocational education in China forward.

**Acknowledgments.** Thanks to the fund and support from Beijing Education Science Planning in the 13th Five Year (CCDB2020135) and Beijing Polytechnic (2020Z041-SXZ2020Z003-039-SXZ).

## References

1. Opinions on the implementation of high level higher vocational school and specialty construction plan with Chinese characteristics (2019)
2. Implementation plan of national vocational education reform (2019)
3. Zhao, G., Yang, N.: Automobile manufacturing technology, no. 1. Peking University Press (2008)
4. Gu, Q.: Exploring a new mode of mathematics teaching in Higher Vocational Colleges with specialty orientation. Knowl. Base **24**, 79–80 (2020)
5. Wei, X.: The construction and practice of modular curriculum system for preschool education. Int. J. Educ. Econ. **3**(4) (2020)
6. Liu, M.: Empirical analysis on the demand for mathematical knowledge of automobile majors in Higher Vocational Colleges. Intern. Combust. Engine Accessories **20**, 265–266 (2019)

7. Wang, C.: Research on configuration model of LP automobile assembly line based on discrete optimization. China Build. Mater. Sci. Technol. **4**, 87–89 (2019)
8. Wang, X.: Research on the application of mathematical modeling in Higher Vocational Automobile Specialty – Taking Automobile assembly sequence optimization as an example. J. Wuhan Tech. Coll. Commun. **22**(02), 113–117 (2020)
9. Zhang, J., Dan, D., Dong, M.: Research and practice of modular teaching construction of Applied Mathematics. J. Learn. **36**, 5–6 (2020)
10. Shi, B.: A preliminary study on the teaching mode of combining higher mathematics with automobile specialty in Vocational Colleges. Sci. Chin. **17**, 238–239 (2017)
11. Xie, H.: Exploring Mathematics to serve the classroom teaching of secondary vocational automobile repair major. Curric. Educ. Res. **32**, 199–202 (2018)
12. Students training program majoring in automobile manufacturing and assembly technology, pp. 5–7. Beijing Polytechnic (2019)

# Reform and Practice of Digital Teaching of Engineering Mechanics Course Under the Background of "Double High Program"

Jin-ru Ma[1,2](✉), Rui-can Hao[1,2], and Shang Wang[1,2]

[1] Beijing Polytechnic, Beijing 100176, China
[2] Beijing Polytechnic, No. 9 Liangshuihe First Street, Yizhuang, Beijing, China

**Abstract.** At present, higher vocational education is in a very important period of change, especially the "Double High Program" launched in 2019. Combining with our own reality, we should promote the curriculum construction around the goals, tasks and requirements of the "Double High Plan". Digital curriculum is an important content of teaching construction in various colleges and universities at present. And it is the foundation of education and teaching informationization. Taking the course of engineering mechanics as an example, the construction of digital course is carried out. In most engineering majors, such as mechanical engineering, engineering mechanics is an important professional basic course, which is a bridge from basic course to professional course. Engineering mechanics course is characterized by many concepts, many theorems, many formulas, many calculations, strong theory, etc., the course is difficult, backward teaching methods and insufficient experimental equipment. In this Paper, digital construction of engineering mechanics course from the following aspects: build a virtual simulation practice teaching platform, the establishment of digital teaching re-sources, choose a suitable e-learning platform, scientific research work of data statistics. It has been proved by practice that compared with traditional teaching classes, the teaching effect of students' learning enthusiasm and academic achievements has been significantly improved.

**Keywords:** Higher vocational education · "Double High Plan" · Engineering mechanics · Digital course

## 1 The Importance of Constructing Digital Curriculum

After the promulgation of the National Vocational Education Reform Implementation Plan in January, 2019, the Ministry of Education and the Ministry of Finance promptly launched the high-level vocational schools with Chinese characteristics and professional construction plan (referred to as the "Double High Plan"), which placed higher vocational education in a more prominent position in building a modern vocational education system and promoting educational reform and innovation, and entrusted higher vocational schools with the historical responsibility of deepening educational reform, exploring


W. Fu et al. (Eds.): eLEOT 2021, LNICST 389, pp. 15–22, 2021.
https://doi.org/10.1007/978-3-030-84383-0_2

the laws of type education and promoting the high-quality development of vocational education. The "Double-high Plan" puts forward the standard requirements of "Chinese characteristics and world level", shows the expected goal of "significantly improving school-running level, service ability and international influence", plans the construction path of "one strengthening, four building and five upgrading", and depicts the blueprint for the development of higher vocational education in China [1]. At present, under the guidance of Xi Jinping's thought of socialism with Chinese characteristics, our school is studying in depth the important deployment of vocational education reform in China, combining with its own reality, and doing a good job in the construction of our school around the goals, tasks and requirements of the "Double High Plan". In the process of work, we deeply realize that the "double high plan" is a great opportunity to promote the construction of school curriculum.

With the advent of the "digital" era, great changes are taking place in students' learning methods, and the integration of information technology and education and teaching has become an inevitable choice for educational informationization. The digital curriculum draws lessons from the open educational concept and uses the support of information infrastructure to digitally process and produce various professional teaching resources for learners to learn. Digital curriculum can create an environment of "autonomy", "intersection", "universality" and "immediacy", and improve learning efficiency through new learning methods, which has important guiding significance for students in higher vocational colleges.

## 2 The Present Situation and Existing Problems of Engineering Mechanics Teaching

### 2.1 The Course Is Difficult

Engineering mechanics is a technical core basic course with strong theory and close connection with practical engineering application. Its theorems, laws and conclusions are widely used in engineering technology of all walks of life, which is an important basis for solving practical engineering problems. This course has many abstract theoretical knowledge points and limited teaching hours, resulting in unsatisfactory teaching effect. In addition, the contents of the teaching materials are not updated in time, lacking social practicability and professional pertinence, which virtually increases the difficulty of the course.

### 2.2 Students Have Poor Foundation and Low Enthusiasm for Learning

Engineering mechanics course is characterized by many concepts, many theorems, many formulas, many calculations, strong theory, etc. In addition, students in higher vocational colleges have weak foundation in mathematical physics, most of them have no good study habits, lack confidence and enthusiasm in learning, and most of them have weak imagination and sense of space, which makes it difficult to understand the structural stress state and stress distribution in "engineering mechanics". In the course teaching, there are few engineering cases, so students lack motivation and enthusiasm for the course of engineering mechanics, which makes engineering mechanics one of the courses with high make-up and re-examination rate every semester.

### 2.3 Backward Teaching Methods and Insufficient Experimental Equipment

In most engineering majors, such as mechanical engineering, engineering mechanics is an important professional basic course, which is a bridge from basic course to professional course, The practical teaching of engineering mechanics can deepen students' understanding of the movement law of components and their understanding of material properties and engineering safety. Practical teaching is an important organic part of the curriculum. For a long time, the experimental module of engineering mechanics has been a difficult point in vocational college teaching. The related experimental equipment has many capital investment, large area, high experimental cost and danger. Students are generally not interested in experimental teaching, and the teaching quality is poor.

## 3 Digital Construction of Engineering Mechanics Course from the Following Aspects

### 3.1 Build a Virtual Simulation Practice Teaching Platform

Practical teaching is an important organic part of the curriculum. Developing digital courses in the form of virtual simulation is the future development direction, which can reduce school capital investment, effectively avoid safety accidents and improve students' learning enthusiasm.

Taking the classical mechanics experimental teaching in engineering mechanics course as the research subject, our school develops digital software, and carries out tensile, compression, bending and torsion tests on metal samples of various materials to obtain rich experimental data, and records the video of the experimental process at the experimental site, taking pictures before and after the experiment; Combined with experimental data, set mathematical model and running program, and develop digital

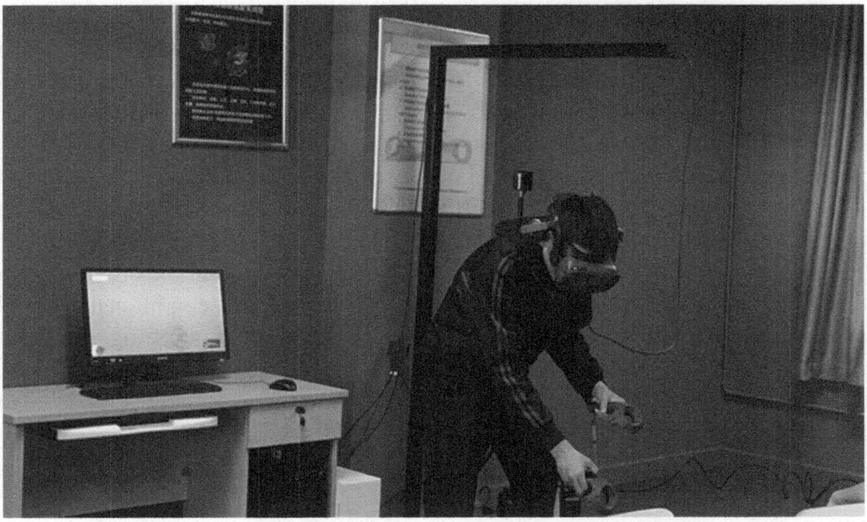

**Fig. 1.** Virtual simulation practice.

teaching software. The virtual simulation technology is applied to the practical teaching of engineering mechanics. The virtual simulation practice process of students (see Fig. 1).

In the process of virtual simulation, students can freely choose the speed of experimental animation on the experimental platform, pause the stretching process at any time and observe the force deformation curve; Secondly, students can also choose different loading speeds and loading methods to observe the performance changes of specimens under different stress environments; Finally, with the support of a large number of experimental data samples in the database, students can observe the deformation process and damage of specimens of various materials and shapes in the limited teaching hours, which greatly improves the learning effect. It can be seen that after the application of virtual simulation technology in practical teaching, the teaching process can be liberated from the traditional fixed experimental process, and students can get more operation direction, background knowledge, trial and error space and detailed data through the virtual simulation experimental platform [2].

### 3.2 The Establishment of Digital Teaching Resources

Digital teaching requires students to learn actively through the Internet, provided that the teaching resources are rich enough. The construction of digital teaching resource database is an important work for the success of digital teaching. Based on the existing teaching resources, the course teaching resource base integrates, expands and improves excellent teaching resources, and provides a platform for teachers and students to acquire knowledge and train. Specifically, teaching resources mainly include: media materials, test questions, test papers, courseware, study cases, course contents, experimental instructions, teaching videos, course development, literature materials, answers to common questions, resource directory index and online courses.

The teaching materials include mainly includes micro-lesson videos, teaching courseware, teaching plans, pictures, animations, simulations, curriculum standards, exercises and tests, test question banks and so on. The microlesson video of engineering mechanics course is fragmented, and a micro-lesson video is made for a knowledge point. The video duration is generally 5–10 min, which can ensure that students have patience to watch the complete video and complete the knowledge point before students become bored. Learning; The design of exercises and test questions is to ensure that students can study purposefully and with tasks in digital learning, and guide and help students to understand and master relevant knowledge. In a word, the construction of digital teaching resource library is a task with a heavy workload in the digital teaching reform of engineering mechanics course, and it is also a necessary condition that must be established before carrying out digital teaching. The establishment of digital teaching resource library is not static. With the changes of curriculum standards and technological development, the resources of teaching resource library should be updated and supplemented at any time.

### 3.3 Choose a Suitable Elearning Platform

Adopt the teaching platform-Superstar Learning Communication. This learning platform is based on a mobile App developed by Superstar Company, which integrates resources, courses, learning, evaluation and interaction. Based on the deep integration of informationization and teaching, it is a mobile online teaching platform for mobile terminals (smart phones or tablet computers), and the mobile phone and computer terminals of the online teaching platform of Engineering Mechanics are established. On the computer side of Superstar Learning, teachers create courses, publish tasks and organize teaching activities on the platform; Students actively respond to and complete the tasks issued by teachers on the mobile side, and interact with teachers anytime and anywhere. At the same time, teachers can check students' learning situation in real time according to the statistical data of the platform, and adjust the offline teaching content in time according to the online learning situation of students. This mixed teaching method has realized many teaching ideas and effects that traditional teaching can't achieve at all, and provided students with a brand-new autonomous learning model [3].

### 3.4 Scientific Research Work of Data Statistics

Compared with traditional teaching, digital teaching software can provide a large amount of data, and the statistics and research of these data can better feedback and optimize classroom education, improve teaching quality and students' participation, and form a closed-loop teaching. Based on the field experimental data, software programs, students' experimental data and so on, a digital teaching mathematical model is established. Furthermore, the A/B teaching scheme is adopted to optimize the teaching mathematical model from the aspects of teaching time allocation, students' participation and examination results. The digital teaching mathematical model developed in this course is universal and provides theoretical support for the digital construction of other courses shows the statistical work (see Fig. 2).

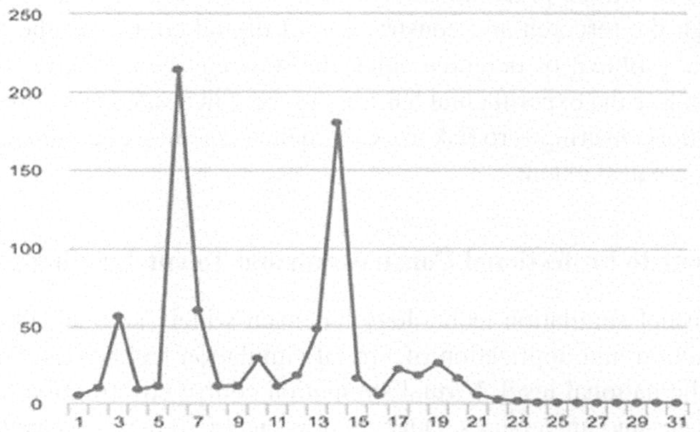


**Fig. 2.** Work of data statistics.

## 4 Advantages of Digital Teaching Course Development of Engineering Mechanics Course

### 4.1 Innovative Teaching Mode and Concept of Engineering Mechanics Course

At present, the teaching of engineering mechanics still adopts the traditional classroom teaching mode, and the teaching materials are only in the form of teaching materials and courseware, so the teaching effect is seriously limited. Developing the digital course of engineering mechanics based on virtual simulation technology is a great innovation to the existing conventional teaching mode and concept, an important step and inevitable choice for the scientific, informational and digital teaching mode of engineering mechanics course, and also a step exploration for the construction of "double high program".

### 4.2 Significant Savings in Teaching Costs

In the standard engineering mechanics course, the basic mechanics experiment teaching link is essential, and it is an essential link to cultivate students' practical ability and help students understand the course. However, the cost of purchasing and maintaining experimental equipment and consumables is very high. If we only spend a lot of money to purchase experimental equipment and materials for this course, the cost is huge and the utilization rate is low. This problem can be effectively solved by building a digital course of virtual simulation. Students can learn and simulate the mechanical experiment process through simulation software, which not only avoids the lack of experimental links, but also saves a lot of hardware costs.

### 4.3 Avoid Potential Safety Hazards

In recent years, school laboratory safety accidents have occurred frequently, causing irreparable losses to both schools and students' families. There are certain dangers in related experiments in engineering mechanics course, and even strict management measures can only minimize potential safety hazards, which cannot be completely eliminated. Through the research and construction of digital courses in the form of virtual simulation, the problem of potential safety hazards can be perfectly solved, and students can complete the experimental learning process in a safe and controlled computer environment, thus ensuring zero risk in experimental teaching of engineering mechanics courses to the greatest extent.

### 4.4 Contribute to Professional Construction and Talent Training of Teachers

At present, virtual simulation technology has been widely recognized by the society, and the promotion and application of virtual simulation technology are also actively promoted at the national level. Virtual simulation course construction is being carried out in all colleges and universities. Our school is one of 10 tier-A colleges and universities listed in the List of Construction Units of High-level Higher Vocational Schools and Specialty Construction Plans with Chinese Characteristics published by the Ministry of Education and the Ministry of Finance. Among them, the automobile manufacturing and assembly technology major is the key professional group, and will focus on supporting the first development in the next five years. Engineering mechanics course is an important professional basic course in the new talent training program of automobile manufacturing and assembly major, and the construction of engineering mechanics course should keep pace with the times. Through the construction of digital course module, virtual simulation technology and digital technology can effectively help the development and progress of engineering mechanics courses. At the same time, in the process of digital curriculum module construction, through the development of relevant research work, it can also train a group of teachers who master virtual simulation technology and digital technology for schools, and lay a talent foundation for the subsequent "double high program" construction and future curriculum construction.

## 5 Conclusion

To sum up, college education follows the development trend of digital curriculum, and the concepts of changing roles, free learning and instant learning are gradually becoming the core concepts of talent training in new colleges and universities in the 21st century. Under the impetus of "double high" construction, the digital course construction of engineering mechanics is carried out. By constructing the digital course of virtual simulation, the problems of students' learning difficulty, high school input cost and potential safety hazards in practice can be effectively solved. Students can learn and simulate the mechanical experiment process through simulation software, which not only avoids the lack of experimental links, but also saves a lot of hardware costs. Give full play to the advantages of a series of teaching allocation such as advanced teaching resources, teaching concepts and service facilities, and provide students with a broader learning space and meet the needs of socialized learning; Students are encouraged to keep pace with the times, change their methods and study independently, so as to cultivate new talents with high qualification, high quality and high technology to meet the requirements of future social development.

**Acknowledgement.** Thanks to the fund and support from the program of Beijing Polytechnic Polytechnic (NO. 2020Z025-KXZ).

## References

1. Cheng, J.Z.: Ministry of Education, Ministry of Finance. Opinions on the implementation of highlevel vocational schools and professional construction plans with Chinese characteristics, no. 5 [A].2019/03/29 [2019]
2. Liu, C.: Application of Web3D virtual simulation technology in mechanical practice teaching. Agric. Mech. Using Maint. **9**(12), 112–113 (2020)
3. Wang, Z.: Reform of blended teaching mode of comprehensive English based on superstar learning. J. Liaoning Univ. **3**(6), 121–126 (2018)
4. He, X.: Exploring the evaluation system of modern higher education with Chinese characteristics to comprehensively improve the quality of personnel training. China High. Educ. Res. **10**(12), 1–5 (2018)

5. Liu, S.: Engineering Mechanics, 4th edn., pp. 1–10. Mechanical Industry Press, Beijing (2019)
6. Yang, J., Ying, Z.: Application of flip classroom mode in engineering mechanics teaching. New Curric. Res. **12**(12), 96–98 (2015)
7. Lu, R.: Discussion on the teaching and experimental reform mode of engineering mechanic. Educ. Teach. Forum **29**(52), 102–103 (2015)
8. Li, S., Mo, Q., Liu, J.: Exploration on the reform of teaching mode of "engineering mechanics" based on micro-lesson. Asia-Pac. Educ. **25**(36), 56 (2015)
9. Hu, T., Zhou, X.: Present situation analysis and development countermeasure research of university micro course construction. Mod. Educ. Technol. **2**(24), 5–13 (2014)
10. He, C.: To explore the modern higher education evaluation system with Chinese characteristics improve personnel training quality in an all-round way. China High. Educ. Res. **10**(12), 1–5 (2018)
11. .Bai, Q.: Rethinking the reform and development of Chinese higher education in the new era. J. Tongren Univ. 3(21), 40–48 (2019)
12. Tang, J., Fan, Q.: Exploration of research-based teaching method of basic mechanics course. Mech. Eng. **4**(6), 89–90 (2008)
13. Zang, Y.: Development status and integration path of digital curriculum resources sharing. J. Teach. Manag. **33**(36), 78–81 (2020)
14. Yue, X., He, X.: Application of virtual simulation technology to practical teaching of surveying and mapping engineering. Eng. Surv. Mapp. **1**(30), 76–80 (2021)

# Study on Modular Curriculums in Vocational Education and Training System

Rui-can Hao(✉), Zhi-xin Feng, Hua-gang Liu, Shang Wang, and Yu-hui Wei

Beijing Polytechnic, No. 9 Liangshuihe First Street, Yizhuang, Beijing, China
haoruican@bpi.edu.cn

**Abstract.** With the development policies and plans for vocational education appearing, modular curriculum in improving the vocational education and training system is more important to improve the education quality. The concept of module was introduced in the paper. The modular curriculum was explained by the analogy with the system which is composed of modules with different functions and characteristics. The characteristics of modular curriculum including functionality, interchangeability, flexibility and applicability were introduced and discussed. Taking automobile major as an example, the modules of the curriculums were studied and divided. The background and the career analysis of the students were investigated and researched on automobile engineering. Especially, the professional course modules were studied according to professional background and career analysis of the students. Curriculums in the professional modules were divided into four parts including Basic technology courses for specialty group, Vocational and technical skills courses, Professional comprehensive modular courses, and Innovative practical modular courses. Among the course modules, the professional comprehensive modular courses and the innovative practical modular courses are designed and divided into specific courses, and the specific courses were firstly designed with the type of micro lectures.

**Keywords:** Modular curriculum · Vocational education · Vocational training

## 1 Introductions

With the development of vocational education, especially with several important policies and plans from the government appearance, the vocational education enters a new developing stage in China. Vocational education stands side by side with general education for the first time in China. It is proposed in Implementation Plan of National Vocational Education Reform that vocational education should be placed in a more prominent position in educational reform innovation and economically social development. In the Implementation Plan, important development goals for vocational education are put forward, including that the vocational education and training system should be improved, the directions should be changed from pursuing the scale expansion to improving the quality of education, and so on [1].


W. Fu et al. (Eds.): eLEOT 2021, LNICST 389, pp. 23–31, 2021.
https://doi.org/10.1007/978-3-030-84383-0_3

At the Symposium of experts on education, culture, health and sports held on September 22$^{nd}$ in 2020, it was emphasized that the vocational education and training should be developed energetically, and lifelong learning system should be built [2]. With the lifelong learning being emphasized gradually, more and more social personnel have participated in vocational training. At the same time, our education objects have expanded from students to different kinds of people including students, company staff, migrant workers and other groups.

However, for different education objects, different curriculum forms and contents should be researched and designed to meet different work requirements to achieve good teaching and learning effects. No matter which type of students they are, the final learning goal and ability level they achieved are the same. Then challenges are brought for teachers in preparing lessons and teaching students. So how to organize the course materials to satisfy different requirements, is a new challenging work for teachers to reform the vocational education and training system.

## 2 Modular Curriculum

Due to the different kinds of students, different teaching methods and different teaching contents and form are required. Modular curriculum is an inevitable education reform mode on the curriculum for different kinds of students, facing the integration reform of vocational education and training system.

### 2.1 Module

Module is a typical general unit which can be combined into a system and has certain functions and interface structure. There are 4 characteristics for module including independence, abstractness, interchangeability, and flexibility [3]. The independence of the module refers to that not only the function of the module in a system is independent, but also the process of the designing, manufacturing and debugging module is independent in a system. The abstractness of the module refers to that it is not necessary to understand the internal structure and characteristics of the module fully. Even people who do not possess the knowledge about how to design the mode can design the whole system according to the function and interface of the module. The interchangeability of the module refers to that the module could be substituted by another one according to another parameter and target. The flexibility of the module refers to that the convenience for substitute some old modules with new ones in the system to update the characteristics and functions of the system.

Modularization is a way to deal with the decomposition of complex systems into better manageable modules [4]. The relationship between the module and the system is applied into the relationship between the curriculum unit and the curriculum constructions. Then the modular curriculum is produced.

### 2.2 Modular Curriculum

The module of a course is an independent unit designed in a course which could be flexibly substituted with another independent unit to construct a new course for another group of students with different skill background.

Modular curriculum refers to the curriculum which is composed of independent module units suitable to build any curriculum related to the professional background. Modular curriculum is the product from the development of the lifelong learning system which grows for improving the vocational education and training systems.

As shown in Fig. 1, the characteristics of modular curriculum include functionality, interchangeability, flexibility and applicability [3, 5, 6].

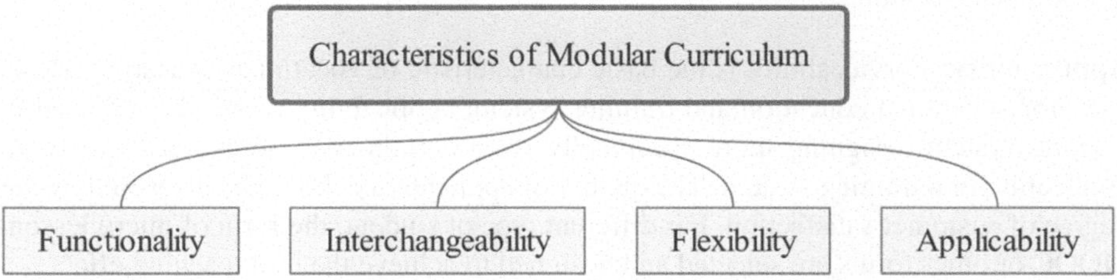


**Fig. 1.** Characteristics of modular curriculum

**Functionality.** Curriculum function is the role and utility of curriculum. John D. McNeil, an American curriculum scientist, summed up the recognized and typical functions of curriculum in his book. The first function is the common function or general education function, which aims to enable learners to participate in community public affairs, master the minimum ability necessary for health, welfare and protection, and become responsible people or citizens. The second function is the function of compensation or supplement, specially designed for individual defects or unique talents, is an individual course, which is opposite to ordinary (common) courses. The third function is the function of inquiry, which provides students with the opportunity to discover and develop their personal interests, so that learners can find out whether they have the ability and enthusiasm to engage in certain types of activities. The fourth function is the professional function, which requires learners to master the skills necessary for skilled workers and scholars, in order to meet the standards required by a certain industry, occupation or academic research [7].

The functionality of modular curriculum in vocational education and training system is reflected in that it could meet many different kinds of students' requirements more professionally besides common skill needs, knowledge defects compensation with a definite aim for a determined occupation worker and focused inquiry.

**Interchangeability.** Generally, interchangeability refers that for a machine, in a batch of parts (or components) with unified specifications, any one of them can be installed on the machine to meet the specified functional requirements without selection, repair or adjustment. For a modular curriculum, any module combined in the curriculum could be changed with another one to meet the specified functional requirements for another education project or training program. For a training system, a modular curriculum could be substituted by another one designed for the specified requirements of the education or training system.

**Flexibility.** By analogy with the flexibility of the module in a system, the modular curriculum possesses flexibility. The flexibility of the modular curriculum refers not only the contents of the course are flexible to be chosen, but also the association of courses are flexible to be designed. Due to the interchangeability of modular curriculum, the curriculum system composed of modules designed according to the specified requirements is flexible to adapt to every related system in one hand. On the other hand, learners could choose the suitable modular curriculum flexibly according to their own career development planning.

**Applicability.** Serviceability is the basic characteristic of vocational education. However, for vocational education and training system, applicability should be reflected in training system designing more specifically for a certain type of students and more applicably for a training system. The quality of applicability should be measured by the degree of customer satisfaction. For different type of student, the form of micro lesson, MOOC or other forms are selected and designed to achieve the best teaching effect.

Comparing with the common single and stable curriculum structures, modular curriculum could meet the students' interests in learning goal definitely and improve the enthusiasm in learning. Then the learning effect could be achieved and the skills of the students are developed more comprehensively.

# 3 Constructions of Modular Curriculum

The overall goal of modular curriculum construction is to optimize the contents of the curriculums by reconstructing the curriculum content system and refining the knowledge module and skill module in the course [8]. On the basis of optimizing the teaching contents, it is meaningful to construct a teaching mode that meets the needs of society and students so as to realize the effective teaching of modular curriculum.

Taking automobile majors as an example, the module analysis and curriculum design are very important works.

## 3.1 Career Analysis for Curriculum Constructions

For the major of automobile manufacturing and assembly technology in vocational education, the professional background and career analysis of the students were researched. Because the curriculums are designed for students who are working in the automobile related enterprises or who will work in the related companies, the career analysis is the necessary prerequisite work.

A statistical analysis on the common positions and job requirements of the graduates from the major of automobile manufacturing and assembly technology was made. According to the content and degree of social ability, operation ability and development ability required by typical jobs, and according to the theory of vocational education classification system, the typical job groups are divided into six levels [9]. For example, the contents of the $4^{th}$ level job are summarized and shown in Table 1. And the typical tasks and ability requirements of the fourth level job are shown in Table 2.

**Table 1.** The contents of the $4^{th}$ level job

| Production operators | Equipment maintenance personnel | Quality inspectors |
|---|---|---|
| Assembly, welding and gluing of BIW assembly | Inspection and maintenance of production line | Inspection and repair on the appearance defects of stamping parts |
| Engine sub assembly and whole machine assembly | Robot operation and maintenance | Inspection and repair on BIW body defects |
| Static assembly and debugging of finished vehicle | Fundamentals of PLC operation | Quality control of assembly and welding process |
| General maintenance and emergency disposal of equipment | | |

**Table 2.** The typical tasks and ability requirements of the fourth level job

| | Corresponding position | Typical tasks |
|---|---|---|
| 1 | Assembly, welding and gluing of BIW assembly | ① Welding and gluing of side panel assembly;<br>② Front end assembly, main floor assembly and rear end assembly welded and glued;<br>③ Welding and gluing of body in white lower body assembly;<br>④ BIW assembly welding and gluing |
| 2 | Engine sub assembly and whole machine assembly | ① Assembly of crank connecting structure;<br>② Assembly of valve train;<br>③ Assembly of cooling system;<br>④ Assembly of lubrication system;<br>⑤ Assembly of fuel supply system |
| 3 | Static assembly and debugging of finished vehicle | ① Assembly of interior and exterior ornaments;<br>② Assembly of four doors;<br>③ Assembly of chassis;<br>④ Assembly of power train |
| 4 | General maintenance and emergency disposal of equipment | ① Production line equipment inspection and daily maintenance;<br>② Process equipment operation and parameter adjustment;<br>③ Fixture inspection and maintenance;<br>④ Check and maintenance of transmission equipment;<br>⑤ Robot emergency stop reset operation and point-to-point programming |

(*continued*)

**Table 2.** (*continued*)

| | Corresponding position | Typical tasks |
|---|---|---|
| 5 | Inspection and maintenance of production line | ① Inspection and maintenance of water supply system;<br>② Check and maintenance of power supply system;<br>③ Check and maintenance of compressed gas system;<br>④ Machining of simple mechanical parts |
| 6 | Robot operation and maintenance | ① Robot debugging operation, parameter setting and tooling tool switching;<br>② Mechanical system fault diagnosis and maintenance of robot workstation;<br>③ Electrical system fault diagnosis and maintenance of robot workstation;<br>④ Control system fault diagnosis and maintenance of robot workstation |
| 7 | Fundamentals of PLC operation | ① PLC network and communication;<br>② PLC control system;<br>③ PLC programming foundation;<br>④ PLC common instructions |
| 8 | Inspection and repair on the appearance defects of stamping parts | ① Judge and release the visual defects of stamping appearance parts;<br>② Find and judge invisible defects of stamping appearance parts;<br>③ Use sheet metal repair tools and equipment to repair damaged and non-destructive parts |
| 9 | Inspection and repair on BIW body defects | ① Assembly precision and debugging of four doors and two covers;<br>② Discovery, judgment and repair of appearance defects;<br>③ Torque adjustment;<br>④ Residual glue cleaning |
| 10 | Quality control of assembly and welding process | ① Quality inspection of resistance spot welding;<br>② Connection quality inspection of physical connection points;<br>③ Appearance quality inspection;<br>④ Torque quality inspection;<br>⑤ Assembly accuracy inspection of four doors and two covers |

### 3.2 Curriculum Design

Taking automobile majors as an example, since the major of automobile manufacturing and assembly technology was the core major in the national "double high" specialty group, the curriculums were designed and divided into several modules such as basic modules, professional modules, improvement modules and expansion modules, as shown in Fig. 2. The construction of curriculum system, especially in the modular curriculum development, adopts the way that one specialty leads other specialties to construct the specialty compound and innovative practice curriculum module, which creates conditions for the automobile manufacturing and assembly technology specialty to adapt to the transformation and upgrading of automobile manufacturing industry, and meets the requirements of enterprises for the cultivation of the specialty compound ability and innovation ability of higher vocational graduates. Students can choose their own career development path to achieve individualized teaching and individualized training.

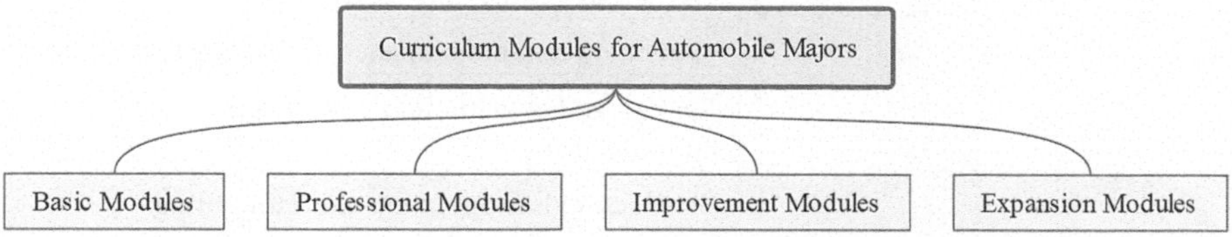


**Fig. 2.** The divided curriculum modules for automobile majors

In the automobile majors in Beijing Polytechnic, the curriculums in the professional modules were designed and divided into basic technology courses for specialty group, vocational and technical skills courses, modular courses for professional comprehensive students, and modular courses for innovative and practical students. Figure 3 shows the compositions of the curriculums in professional modules.

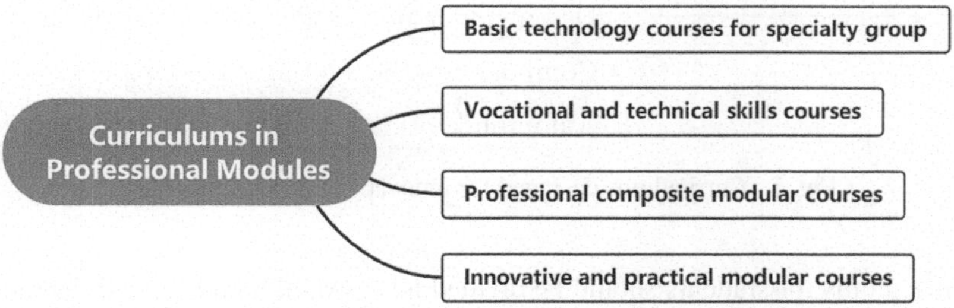


**Fig. 3.** Curriculums modules in professional modules

For example, in detail, the specific courses designed for professional comprehensive module in Beijing Polytechnic are shown in Fig. 4. The specific courses designed for innovative practical module are shown in Fig. 5. The courses designed for the professional comprehensive type students mainly includes Inspection and repair of BIW, Inspection and maintenance of electrical appliances in production line, Assembly and online diagnosis of industrial robot, Engine assembly and debugging, Vehicle assembly and debugging, Operation and maintenance of welding robot, Design and construction of intelligent manufacturing cell, Production line operation and monitoring. The courses designed for the innovative and practical type students mainly includes Intelligent assembly of automobile body, Robot operation and maintenance based on Integra 6 standard, Practice of automobile quality management system, Design and manufacture of students' racing car, Composite manufacturing of auto parts, and Automobile off line detection and debugging [9].

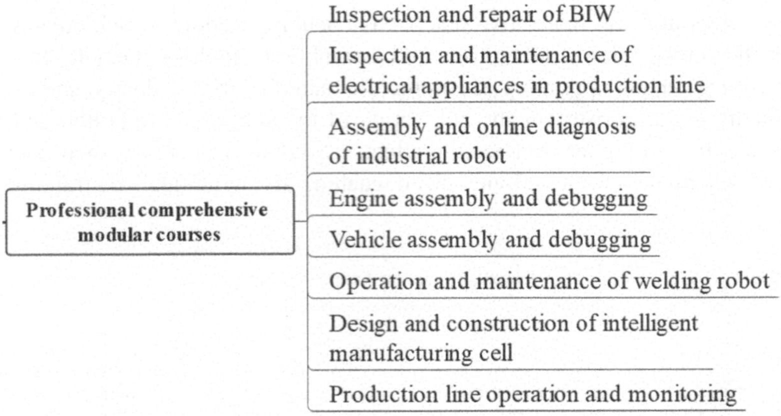


**Fig. 4.** Curriculums designed for professional comprehensive modules

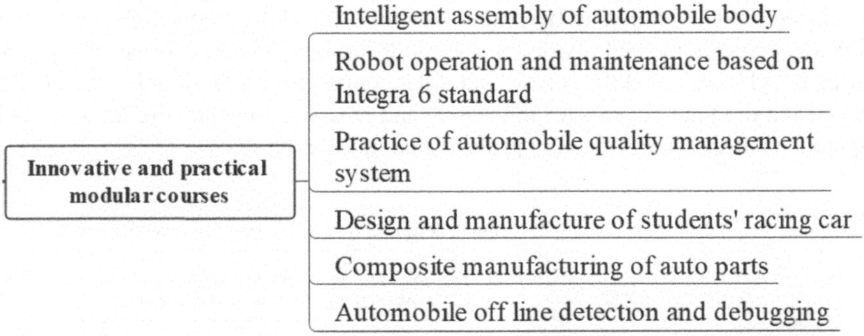


**Fig. 5.** Curriculums designed for innovative practical modules

Curriculums for students should be divided into several modules, and the modules should be designed in the form of more modules. Then a course should be designed into modules such as micro lectures, and every micro lecture could be designed several forms for different types of students [10, 11].

The most important work is that for every certain type of students, the specific contents of a certain course should be designed into different types to attract the attention of students and to make up the disadvantage of students. Then the teachers' team and the teaching methods should be the next important research objects.

## 4 Summary

The modular curriculum is more and more important in the developing of the vocational education and vocational training system with the lifelong learning and education development in China. In the paper, the modular curriculum was introduced, then the relationship between the modules and the curriculums were studied based on the career analysis and the contents of jobs related to the automobile majors. The curriculums in the professional modules were designed and divided into specific modular courses. The specific courses should be designed according to the specific type of the students and considering the work contents of the students. Especially the designing of the micro-lectures is the important recommended.

**Acknowledgments.** Thanks to the fund and support from Beijing Education Science Planning in the 13th Five Year (CCDB2020135) and Beijing Polytechnic (2020Z041-SXZ2020Z003-039-SXZ).

## References

1. Implementation plan of national vocational education reform, pp. 1–3 (2019)
2. Xi, J.: Speech at the Symposium of experts on education, culture, health and sports, 22 September 2020
3. Lu, C.: Modularization theory of curriculum structure in Vocational Education. Res. Contin. Educ. **4**, 125–128 (2015)
4. Knoernschild, K.: Java application architecture: modularity patterns with examples using OSGi. ACM SIGSOFT Softw. Eng. Notes **38**(1), 1–55 (2013)
5. Kong, F.: Research of female secondary vocational education modular curriculum. J. Adult Educ. Hebei Univ. **17**(3), 65–67 (2015)
6. Zhang, X.: Research and exploration of modular teaching mode in Higher Vocational Education (in Chinese). Sci. Technol. Vis. 287–288 (2015)
7. McNeil, J.D.: Contemporary curriculum. In: Thought and Action, no. 10, p. 384. Jossey Bass An Imprint of Wiley (2005)
8. Lu, S.: Research on the modular curriculum construction on "international Chinese teaching ability" for undergraduate students of Chinese to speakers of other languages (in Chinese). Theoret. Res. Pract. Innov. Entrepreneurship **24**, 89–92 (2020)
9. Talent training program of automobile manufacturing and assembly technology, pp. 5–7. Beijing Polytechnic (2019)
10. Shu, W.: Composition of modern apprenticeship "modular" curriculum system in Vocational Education (in Chinese), vol. 9, pp. 101–105 (2018)
11. Wei, X.: The construction and practice of modular curriculum system for preschool education. Int. J. Educ. Econ. **3**(4) (2020)

# Research on Human Resources Situational Teaching Model Based on Social Information Orientation

Huan-wei Liang[1] and Shao-lin Liang[2](✉)

[1] Huali College Guangdong University of Technology, Guangzhou 511325, China
[2] College of Mathematics, Sichuan University of Arts and Science, Dazhou 635000, China
jhuysdf7498@sina.com

**Abstract.** With the deepening of the economic system transition, the importance of human resource management in enterprises is increasing. Therefore, in order to further optimize the human resources situational teaching model, the human resources situational teaching model oriented to social information is designed. Using VR technology to build a virtual teaching platform, and set the hardware parameters of the platform. Determine the teaching content, clear teaching objectives, the use of the form of group division, the completion of situational teaching process. Using the analytic hierarchy process to evaluate the results of classroom teaching content design, to ensure the effectiveness of teaching. So far, the design of human resources situational teaching mode based on social information-oriented has been completed. Compared with the traditional teaching mode, the teaching mode designed in this paper can promote the improvement of students' comprehensive learning ability.

**Keywords:** Social information-oriented · Human resources curriculum · Teaching model · VR platform

## 1 Introduction

In recent years, with the rapid development of China's economy, with the deepening of cultural and economic exchanges at home and abroad, more and more large joint ventures have been set up in China, and the implementation of efficient personnel management has become the goal of enterprises. Therefore, higher requirements have been put forward for human resources management [1, 2]. Human resource management is the overall allocation of labor resources within a certain scope, and realizes the optimal allocation and maximum utilization of labor resources by certain principles. In our country each big enterprise establishes a personnel resources management department, enhances the human resources efficiency as the goal, and introduces the specialized talented people to enrich the strength positively. This specialized talented person's demand is also increases with the tide. In recent years, colleges and universities have set up human resources management major, aiming at training high-quality talents, and continuously providing


W. Fu et al. (Eds.): eLEOT 2021, LNICST 389, pp. 32–42, 2021.
https://doi.org/10.1007/978-3-030-84383-0_4

high-quality personnel management talents through the implementation of high-quality teaching mode. Schools should pay attention to the integration of theory with practice in the teaching of human resources, rely on the theoretical basis, and understand and absorb all kinds of knowledge learned through carrying out simulation exercises. For example, students should be involved in the main steps in the process of simulation recruitment, so as to lay a good foundation for future adaptation. As the designer of human resource course, human resource teaching should focus on the characteristic teaching mode on the premise of carrying out the educational policy of "practicality, practicality and sufficiency". At present, many researchers and educators have actively explored how to integrate situational teaching into human resources teaching, but seldom involved in the use of situational teaching in human resources teaching.

Situational teaching refers to a cognitive method that enables the educatees to understand the teaching content by simulating or reproducing the environment and process of the occurrence and development of events or things so as to improve their abilities in a short time [3, 4]. In the process of personal experience, the students can understand the connotations of knowledge, improve their ability and form their own values. Situational teaching can help students improve their thinking ability in images, realize the status, situation and working essentials of some roles, and enhance their ability to predict and deal with practical problems.

Most schools adopt the traditional, boring and cramming teaching methods, and pay little attention to arousing students' interest and motivation in human resource management, which makes them unable to express themselves freely. Some students are as mechanical as reciting texts in the process of human resource management, others lack fluency and accuracy in their expressions because of their lack of confidence, and still others are unable to use the human resource theories they have learned. These invalid expressions are often repeated mechanically in the classroom and are not corrected in a timely manner. Therefore, in this study, the design of the social information-oriented human resources situational teaching model to improve students' learning ability and the application of knowledge.

## 2 Research on Human Resources Situational Teaching Model

In order to ensure the rationality of the design of HR situational teaching model, the design process is described as follows (Fig. 1):

Using the above design process, the situational teaching group teacher gives the theory and operation training according to the basic theory that the students should understand. Teachers and students plan and prepare the process of rehearsal according to the teaching content and goal. In the process of implementing situational teaching, students are the main body of teaching.

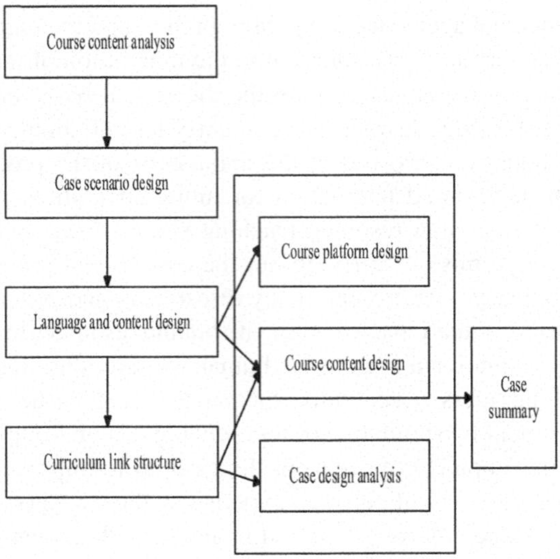


**Fig. 1.** Human resources situational teaching model

### 2.1 Construction of Situational Teaching Platform

In order to improve the authenticity of situational teaching, it is necessary to build a corresponding situational teaching platform. In this study, the platform is set up as a virtual reality teaching system based on VR technology and applied in multiple platforms. As a result, five pieces of software have been selected for the technical architecture of the teaching system, namely Autodesk Maya, Adobe Photoshop, Final Cut Pro, Adobe Premiere, Unity3D [5, 6].

When the pre-preparation is completed, then according to the content, text and images generated by the Photoshop editing layout into a display board map. Maya is responsible for presenting the design of the exhibition hall as a model. Final Cut Pro, Premiere, edits human resources instructional content for video and audio materials, and so on. The above four software content, respectively, into the integration of Unity3D, and then add interaction and lighting and other rendering. Finally, the optimized output is the executable version.

The human resources VR teaching platform's demonstration scene altogether divides into an initial introduction interface and three main content interfaces. The exhibition design of each interface should not only show the different styles and feelings of each case, but also let the students understand the content and situation of the case clearly. In the initial design of the interface, consider that this scenario is the first scenario in which the student enters the case. First impressions tend to dominate the viewer's mind and to a large extent determine whether a case is appealing. Therefore, the design should not only let people have the feeling of immersion, but also have a realistic experience. In order to ensure the effect of VR platform, the hardware requirements of the situational teaching platform are set as follows (Table 1).

**Table 1.** Hardware requirements of situational teaching platform

| Direction of use | Device name | Parameter |
|---|---|---|
| Control terminal | Video card | 64 MB |
| | Memory | 16 GB |
| | CPU | Intel CPU&"Leopard" 10.5 |
| | Operating System | Windows 10 |
| | Database | MY SQL 2016 |
| | Macintosh | Intel 64-bit processor |
| Client | Video card | NVIDIA GeFore GTX560 |
| | Memory | 1 GB |
| | CPU | Intel Core Duo |
| | Operating System | Mac OS X 10.5 |
| | Database | MY SQL 2016 |

According to the hardware parameters, the platform is constructed, and the required course content is introduced into the platform as the basis of situational teaching, providing a hardware basis for its vivid classroom teaching.

### 2.2 Design of Classroom Teaching Content

The creation of human resources teaching is a process. Compared with the conventional teaching mode, situational teaching is difficult. From the initial determination of teaching content, clear teaching objectives, to the creation of the situation, the introduction of the situation, and finally, to guide students to actively build knowledge, it can not be completed in the classroom temporarily. The teacher must analyze the teaching content carefully before class.

First of all, to determine the content of teaching, clear teaching objectives. Clarifying specific teaching objectives in combination with social information [7]. The goal of knowledge is to make the students understand the composition of human resources, the goal of emotion is to stimulate the students' love for the courses of human resources, and the goal of ability is to cultivate the students' ability to independent inquiry and cooperative learning, to improve the ability of language expression and the ability of high-level thinking. In the process of teaching, we insist on the principle of combining theory with practice. That is, in the process of teaching, we should teach professional knowledge, professional skills and combine theory with practice to improve the students' theoretical level and practical ability.

In the class, the students participate in the group to explain, actively reveal their ideas, discuss and communicate with the group members, and the other members of the group to supplement and improve the materials. Through active observation, association, comparison and generalization, meaningful knowledge transfer learning is conducted on the basis of learning from each other's strong points to offset their weaknesses.

In the design of the teaching model, teaching methods are more diverse. Situational teaching method and cooperative inquiry teaching method are mainly used to carry out situational teaching of human resources. Situational teaching method is to put students in a series of rich teaching situations, the teaching content and the real situation, so that students in meditation in search of their own answers. The cooperative inquiry method is a teaching method in which the selected problems are discussed and analyzed in the way of group cooperation, student-student cooperation and collective cooperation, and the final research conclusion is obtained through joint efforts [8, 9]. This method fully embodies the leading role of teachers and the principal position of students. In human resources teaching, teachers do not give ready-made answers to students, but let them explore the answers. At the same time, it also emphasizes the setting of problem situation, which makes students enter the situation naturally and inspires students' study enthusiasm. The thought of cooperation and interaction runs through the whole of teaching, inspires students to connect with life practice and constructs a meaningful connection with learning knowledge.

## 2.3 Teaching Context Design Evaluation

In order to ensure the reasonableness of the situation design, the author evaluates the result of the situational teaching of human resources. First of all, define the problem of situational teaching and analysis of human resources. According to the nature of the problem and the overall goal to be achieved, the complex problem is decomposed into component factors, which are divided into different groups according to their attributes, thus forming different levels [10, 11]. All the elements in the same layer dominate some or all the elements in the next layer while all the elements in the next layer dominate the same layer, which constructs a hierarchical structure reflecting the essential attributes and internal relations of the system.

The hierarchical structure can be generally divided into: the target layer, that is, the highest level, in which there is only one element, which is the overall goal or ideal result to be achieved for the problem; the intermediate level is the criterion layer, also known as the sub-objective layer, factor layer, indicator layer, criterion layer, etc., the measures and criteria to be adopted by the elements in the layer, which can be divided into the criterion layer and sub-criterion layer according to the size and complexity of the problem; the lowest level is the scheme layer, measure layer or reason layer, which is composed of alternative schemes, corresponding measures or the most basic risk factors to achieve the goal [12, 13]. Based on the hierarchical structure model, starting from the second layer, a judgment matrix $X$ is constructed by pairing the relative importance of the elements of the same layer that belong to each criterion in the next layer and combining with the 1–9 scaling method proposed by T. L. Saaty. Assuming that there are $n$ elements $X_1, X_2, ..., X_n$ in a layer $H$ subordinate to some judgment criterion in the next layer, If $X_i$ is compared with $X_j$, $x_{ij}$ is obtained, then $X_i$ is compared with $X_j$, $x_{ij} = 1/x_{ij}$ is obtained, thus $n$ order judgment $X = (x_{ij})_{n*n}$ can be obtained. The matrix has the following properties: $x_{ii} = 1, x_{ij} > 0, x_{ij} = 1/x_{ij}x_{ij} = x_{ik}x_{jk}$. The corresponding judgment matrix can be obtained by this setting as shown below (Table 2).

The relative weights of the elements to be compared are calculated by the judgment matrix, that is, the weights in single order of hierarchy. First, the maximum eigenvalue

**Table 2.** Situation teaching design effect judgment matrix

| $H$ | $X_1$ | $X_2$ | ... | $X_n$ |
|---|---|---|---|---|
| $X_1$ | $x_{11}$ | $x_{12}$ | ... | $x_{1n}$ |
| $X_2$ | $x_{21}$ | $x_{22}$ | ... | $x_{2n}$ |
| ... | ... | ... | ... | ... |
| $X_n$ | $x_{n1}$ | $x_{n2}$ | ... | $x_{nn}$ |

$\alpha_{\max}$ of the matrix $X$ is calculated, then the eigenvector $V$ is obtained by using the eigenequation $X = \alpha_{\max}$. Then the $n$ components of the vector are the weights of the corresponding $n$ elements after $V$ normalization [14, 15]. When the precision is not high, the ranking weight vector can be calculated by approximate eigenvalue methods such as sum method and square root method. In addition, the use of MATLAB software can also be very convenient for accurate calculation.

First normalize the column vectors of the matrix $X$ to get the matrix $F = (f_{ij})_{n*n}$. Then sum the elements in F row by row, that is:

$$v_i = \sum_{j=1}^{n} f_{ij} \tag{1}$$

Among them,

$$f_{ij} = x_{ij} / \sum_{j=1}^{n} x_{kj} \tag{2}$$

Finally, $V$ should be normalized as a weight vector [16]. The maximum eigenvalue $\alpha_{\max}$ of the matrix $X$ can be approximately calculated from the following formula:

$$\alpha_{\max} = \frac{1}{n} \sum_{i=1}^{n} \frac{(XV)_i}{v_i} \tag{3}$$

In an expression, $(XV)_i$ represents the $i$ element of a vector $XV$. Using the above formula to evaluate the effect of situational teaching design, in order to ensure the effectiveness of teaching model. The above design content is integrated, so far, based on the social information-oriented human resources situational teaching model design is completed.

# 3 Experimental Analysis

## 3.1 Experimental Environment Settings

In this part, I will carry on the teaching practice to test the validity of the teaching model, analyze the questionnaire, interview survey and the academic achievement analysis, and draw the conclusion, in order to provide one kind of strong implementation teaching model for the human resources curriculum, help the student to understand the science essence, promote the science accomplishment.

This practice research is mainly based on questionnaires, supplemented by interviews. The experimental class and the control class are selected as the experimental subjects, and the control class is taught in the integrated mode of situational teaching. The experiment lasts for one semester.

In this experimental study, the situational teaching model of human resources is independent variable, and the learning interest, human resources management ability and level of students in experimental class and control class are dependent variables. The experiment proves that the situational teaching mode of human resources can enhance students' interest in learning and improve their communicative competence and level.

The subjects of this study are 400 students of public administration at a normal university. Two classes are selected as the experimenters in each grade. Class A is the experimental class and Class B is the control class. Questionnaires were distributed to both classes, and the response rate was 100%.

### 3.2 Experimental Procedure Setup

In the preparation stage of the experiment, questionnaires and pre-experiment tests were carried out in the experimental class and the control class to find out the students' interest and attitude towards the human resources management course, and to analyze the pre-test scores of the two classes; interviews were conducted with the teachers who listened to the lectures to find out the students' enthusiasm for learning the human resources course and their performance in the class.

In the experimental stage, the situational teaching model of human resources was used in the experimental class for 18 weeks, while the traditional teaching model was still used in the control class. At the 8th and 18th week, the middle and late tests were carried out and the results of experimental class and control class were analyzed. At the end of the experiment, the students were investigated by questionnaires and the results were analyzed. Both oral test and paper test are included in the experiment. The test results are graded on a percentage basis. Among them, oral test results account for 60%, and written test results 40%. At the same time, it analyzes the students' ability to understand the knowledge of human resources and the ability to manage human resources, in order to achieve the design of teaching model in-depth study.

### 3.3 Analysis of Experimental Results

Through the above results, we can see that the teaching model designed in this paper plays a certain role in improving students' HR course examination results. Through comparison, we can see that the average score of the designed teaching mode is higher than the original teaching mode. And the design of teaching model for freshmen who have just come into contact with human resources management courses more useful. It can be seen that the design of teaching model has the corresponding scientific nature (Table 3).

**Table 3.** Comparison of mean scores of students in human resources courses

| Grade | The average score of the design teaching model | Average score of original teaching mode |
|---|---|---|
| Freshman year | 95.1 | 93.5 |
| Sophomore | 94.5 | 92.15 |
| Junior year | 95.5 | 90.0 |
| Senior year | 92.7 | 88.5 |

In order to get the influence of design pattern and original pattern on students' learning achievement, the change of students' learning attitude will be reflected in the form of images. Students' HR courses are divided into four parts: excellent, good, qualified and unqualified, and the differences between the original model and the design model are compared (Fig. 2).

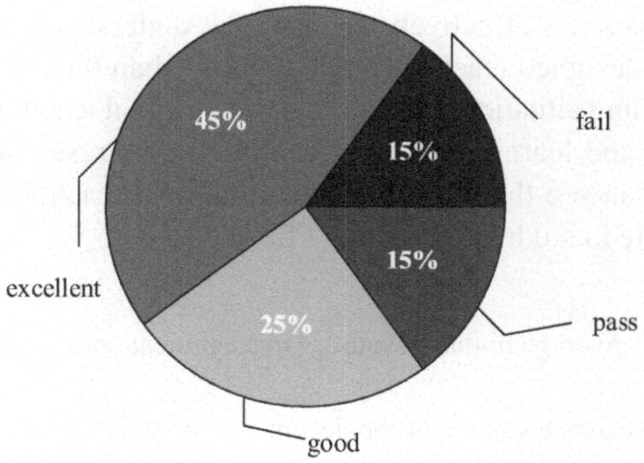


(a) Results of the use of design patterns in the text

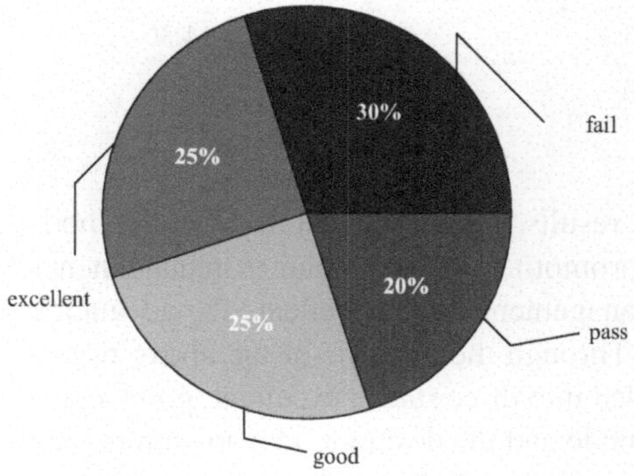


(b) Results of use of the original model

**Fig. 2.** Student HR achievement chart

Through the above research results, we can see that the teaching effect of the design model is better, using this model can effectively improve students' learning attitude, and effectively enhance students' HR exam results, and enhance students' learning enthusiasm (Table 4).

**Table 4.** Average human resources knowledge comprehension ability score

| Grade | The average score of the design teaching model | Average score of original teaching mode |
|---|---|---|
| Freshman year | 4.35 | 4.05 |
| Sophomore | 4.25 | 3.64 |
| Junior year | 4.10 | 3.58 |
| Senior year | 4.10 | 3.55 |

Through the above research results can be seen, the design of teaching model in the use of human resources effectively enhance the understanding of knowledge. The average score of the designed teaching mode is better than that of the original teaching mode. Therefore, adding situational teaching to the original teaching mode can enhance students' perception and learning ability. Combining this result with the above investigation results, we can see that the designed situational teaching of human resources plays an auxiliary role in students' learning (Table 5).

**Table 5.** Average human resources management competency score

| Grade | The average score of the design teaching model | Average score of original teaching mode |
|---|---|---|
| Freshman year | 4.05 | 3.95 |
| Sophomore | 4.25 | 4.25 |
| Junior year | 4.25 | 4.30 |
| Senior year | 4.50 | 4.30 |

Through the above results, we can see that the teaching model designed in this paper plays a certain role in promoting human resources management ability. Students' ability of human resource management directly reflects the advantages and disadvantages of educational methods. Through the analysis of the above research results, the comprehensive ability is divided into three states: excellent, good and poor, and the differences between the original mode and the design model are compared (Fig. 3).

Through the above research results can be seen, the design of teaching model in the use of better results, can effectively enhance the comprehensive learning ability of human resources courses. After using the original teaching mode, the students' comprehensive ability is obviously lower than the teaching mode designed in the text. Through the above

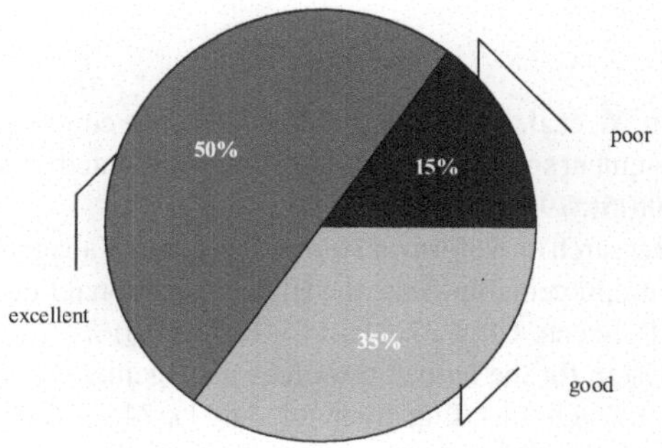


(a) Results of the use of design patterns in the text

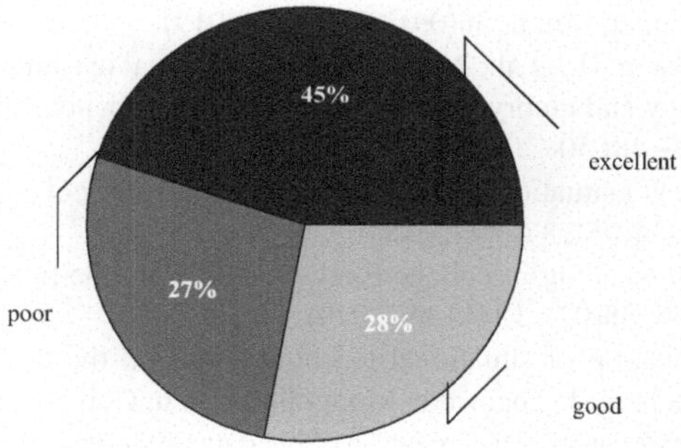


(b) Results of use of the original model

**Fig. 3.** Embodiment of students' human resource management ability

research results can be seen, the design of teaching model in the use of human resources can achieve the current teaching objectives. Applying the teaching mode of design in this paper to the real life can effectively improve the teaching effect and achievement of human resources course.

## 4 Conclusion

The application of the teaching model in this study provides advanced means for human resources teaching, ensures and improves the quality of professional teaching, and enhances the pertinence and practicability. On the background that many enterprises integrate mobile application into human resource management, the follow-up development of teaching mode can focus on this aspect, and realize the necessary links of human resource management in enterprises. Teachers and students complete part of learning tasks through the mobile terminal, which can improve the convenience of teaching mode and improve students' understanding of human resource management.

## References


1. Li, L., Huang, H., Xu, Y., et al.: Research and practice on the course group of human construction resources management specialization in application-oriented undergraduates. J. Xiangnan Univ. (Med. Sci.) **40**(05), 79–82 (2019)
2. Zhang, Q., Liu, L.: Research on Reform of Human Resource Management from the perspective of innovation and entrepreneurship–Take the Higher Vocational Logistics Management as an example. J. Wuhan Polytech. Univ. **37**(01), 115–120 (2018)
3. Li, N.: Curricular design for the human resources management specialty based on students' core qualities. J. Jilin Teach. Inst. Eng. Technol. **34**(11), 74–77 (2018)
4. Wang, K.: Research on the reform of human resource course teaching mode based on scenario simulation and practical experience. J. Beijing Inst. Econ. Manag. **34**(02), 65–69 (2019)
5. Cui, R.: A construction study base on STEAM education for innovative practice teaching model of human resources management major – base on the course of "organization design and job analysis." J. Mudanjiang Univ. **29**(03), 105–109 (2020)
6. Yao, L., Shao, X., Jiang, X.: Research of virtual reality training system of cooking specialty based on unity. Comput. Simul. **36**(09), 371–375 (2019)
7. Lv, Y., Wang, H., Wang, H., et al.: Application of situational teaching method in experimental teaching of histology and embryology for international students. J. Hebei North Univ. (Nat. Sci. Ed.) **34**(08), 46–48+50 (2018)
8. Zhu, S.: Application of situational approach to the teaching of college Chinese. J. Jilin Teach. Inst. Eng. Technol. **34**(05), 37–39 (2018)
9. Long, C.: Situation teaching in college English class from the perspective of humanism. J. Liuzhou Teach. Coll. **35**(02), 134–136 (2020)
10. Yan, C.: The application of situational teaching based on the theory of constructivism in college English teaching. J. Zhaowuda Mongolian Teach. Coll. **39**(02), 155–157 (2018)
11. Fu, W., Liu, S., Srivastava, G.: Optimization of big data scheduling in social networks. Entropy **21**(9), 902 (2019)
12. Liu, S., Bai, W., Zeng, N., et al.: A fast fractal based compression for MRI images. IEEE Access **7**(3), 62412–62420 (2019)
13. Liu, S., Li, Z., Zhang, Y., et al.: Introduction of key problems in long-distance learning and training. Mob. Netw. Appl. **24**(1), 1–4 (2019)
14. Navy, S.L., Nixon, R.S., Luft, J.A., et al.: Accessed or latent resources? Exploring new secondary science teachers' networks of resources. J. Res. Sci. Teach. **57**(2), 184–208 (2020)
15. Wonah, F.A.: Human resource management practices and quality of teaching in private secondary schools in cross river state, Nigeria. Int. J. Educ. Res. **5**(5), 78–89 (2019)
16. L'Ecuyer, F., Raymond, L., Fabi, B., et al.: Strategic alignment of IT and human resources management in manufacturing SMEs: empirical test of a mediation model. Empl. Relat. **41**(5), 830–850 (2019)

# Research on Internal Cost Accounting and Control of Education System Based on Activity Based Costing

Li-min Zhang(✉)

School of Economics and Management, Shenyang Institute of Technology,
Shenfu Demonstration Zone, Shenyang 113112, China

**Abstract.** In recent years, the competition among universities has become more and more fierce, and major changes have taken place in the operating environment of universities. By analyzing the problems and causes of internal cost accounting in universities, an internal cost accounting model based on activity-based costing has been established, and cost accounting has been defined. To determine the cost driver rate and operating costs, ensure that the internal cost accounting results of universities can accurately reflect the educational costs of universities, enhance the value-added ability of educational resources and the awareness of cost control in universities, and aim to continuously reduce the internal costs of universities.

**Keywords:** Activity based costing · Education system · Cost accounting · Cost control

## 1 Introduction

Cost accounting is an important part of corporate accounting work; correct cost information is an important basis for corporate decision-making. But today, in actual work, most companies make major decisions such as pricing, product mix, and process technology selection based on distorted cost information. To make matters worse, there is almost no other information that can make the management aware of the serious distortion of product costs, and only after the profitability and competitiveness have declined, the company found out that there was a problem.

Since the reform and opening up, the state has increased investment in education, especially in higher education, which has made China's higher education develop rapidly. In particular, the implementation of the strategy of "rejuvenating the country through science and education" has provided a good opportunity for the development of higher education. Due to the transformation of China's planned economy to market economy, the establishment of independent legal person status of independent colleges and universities, colleges and universities have changed from a planned economy to a market economy Relying solely on government funding has been transformed into a multi-channel financing pattern dominated by government funding [1]. If colleges and universities want


W. Fu et al. (Eds.): eLEOT 2021, LNICST 389, pp. 43–56, 2021.
https://doi.org/10.1007/978-3-030-84383-0_5

to survive and develop in the tide of market economy, they must "open source" and "reduce expenditure" simultaneously. On the one hand, it is necessary to expand the sources of funds, improve the quality of teaching and ensure good social benefits; on the other hand, it is necessary to implement strict economy, carry out education cost accounting and strengthen management, and control unreasonable expenditures to reduce costs and improve school running efficiency.

This article establishes an internal cost accounting model based on activity-based costing, and defines cost accounting. Determine cost drivers and operating costs to ensure that the university's internal cost accounting results accurately reflect the university's educational costs, enhance the value-added capabilities of educational resources and the university's cost control awareness, and strive to continuously reduce the university's internal costs.

## 2 A Survey of Internal Cost Accounting and Control in Education System

At present, the internal cost accounting system of colleges and universities is the cost accounting system of institutions. China's colleges and universities are non-profit institutions, and their teaching activities are not aimed at profit [2]. Therefore, at this stage, the internal cost accounting system of colleges and universities does not fully analyze the impact of cost factors on Colleges and universities. For example, the lack of education cost accounting system is the reflection of the internal cost accounting problems of colleges and universities. The evaluation index of the cost assessment system in Colleges and universities needs to be improved, which is also a prominent problem in the internal cost accounting of colleges and universities.

At present, the education cost assessment system formulated by the national and local education authorities mainly focuses on the following contents: first, the total amount of education investment index; second, the teaching quality index. The economic benefit of colleges and universities mainly refers to the amount of teaching resources input under the same teaching quality [3]. In the case of the lack of attention to the economic benefit cost index in the evaluation index, colleges and universities will show the problem of ignoring the cost in teaching management. In the case of weak cost awareness and insufficient attention to the importance of cost management in Colleges and universities, some colleges and universities may have the problem of insufficient funds, and some colleges and universities will show serious waste.

College education cost management system is not perfect, financial management lags behind. The role of the financial management department of colleges and universities is only to calculate the balance of revenue and expenditure of colleges and universities. So far, China's colleges and universities have not established a set of systematic and reasonable university cost management system, nor have they established a control system for the prior, in-process and after event management of university education cost. As a result, there is a waste phenomenon in many links of teaching and scientific research management in Colleges and universities, which increases the operation cost of colleges and universities. At the same time, the capital management level of colleges and universities is generally low Low [4, 5]. There is no standard to measure the internal cost control of higher education. There is no internal cost control standard issued by the state and universities, and it is not easy to establish a unified cost control standard implemented by all universities in the country because of the different school running concepts, school running levels and school running conditions.

The responsibility of cost management is not in place. The internal cost control of higher education is a complex system engineering, involving the management and control of each department. From the perspective of the overall management mechanism and current situation of China's colleges and universities, there are still problems in the implementation of management responsibilities [6, 7]. For example, in the administrative management, there are overstaffed organizations, overlapping functions, no clear scope of responsibility between various departments, no accountability for unreasonable and inaction phenomenon, resulting in low management efficiency; in the personnel management, the post setting is repeated, the responsibility sharing is not clear, and the work efficiency is low. These problems have increased the difficulty of university education cost management to varying degrees.

## 2.1 Control Algorithm of Internal Cost Accounting in Education System

Combined with the activity-based costing, this paper optimizes the internal cost accounting control algorithm of the education system, establishes n student training centers according to the current situation of college specialty setting in Colleges and universities, selects the resource drivers, and apportions the resource consumption to the student training center according to the resource drivers, so as to form the cost of the cost library. Set the cost matrix of the cost base of the student training center as $\mathrm{C}_0$, as shown in the formula.

$$\mathrm{C}_0 = [\mathrm{C}_1, \mathrm{C}_2, \cdots, \mathrm{C}_\mathrm{n}] \tag{1}$$

The cost of the cost base of the student training center is divided into fixed and variable parts:

$$\Delta\mathrm{C}_0 = \mathrm{C}_\mathrm{f} + \mathrm{C}_\mathrm{v} \tag{2}$$

Where: $\mathrm{C}_0$ is the student training cost of the cost library of the student training center; $\mathrm{C}_\mathrm{f}$ is the fixed cost of the cost library of the student training center; $\mathrm{C}_\mathrm{v}$ is the variable cost of the cost library of the student training center. Let the matrix of cost drivers of student training be MD, as follows:

$$MD = [md_1, md_2, \cdots, md_n] \tag{3}$$

The calculation formula of cost driver rate of J cost base of student training center is as follows:

$$\mathrm{M}R = [\mathrm{m}r_1, mr_2, \cdots, mr_n] \tag{4}$$

The calculation formula of cost driver rate of J cost base of student training center is as follows:

$$\mathrm{S} = \frac{\mathrm{C}_0 - \mathrm{m}_\mathrm{r} * \mathrm{n}}{\Delta\mathrm{C}_0\mathrm{d}(MR - MD)} \tag{5}$$

Where: c is the student training cost of the cost library of the student training center; $m_r$ is the cost driver rate of the student training center; d is the amount of the student training driver. The cost of cultivating students in Colleges and universities is the cost of each student training center, which is the product of the quantity of resources consumed by the student training center and the price of resources. Suppose that the cost matrix of cultivating students in Colleges and universities is GC, the motivation matrix is D, and the diagonal cost motivation rate matrix is DR, then the calculation of GC is as follows:

$$GC = GC - S^*DR = [d_i]^*\text{diag}\,[r_1, \cdots, r] \tag{6}$$

Where: $d_i$ is the activity cost of student training center, r is the consumption cost driver, diag is the consumption cost driver rate. Suppose that the cost matrix of the materials consumed by the university training is L, the labor cost of the staff is P, and the indirect cost of the university operation is OH, then the calculation method of the cost CC of the university training students is as follows:

$$CC = L + P + OH \tag{7}$$

The organizational structure of colleges and universities is usually composed of several secondary colleges, which are further divided into several specialties. When calculating the internal cost of colleges and universities, each major can first calculate the cost of cultivating students according to their own actual situation, and then summarize it to the school by the secondary college [8, 9]. Adopting multi-level cost accounting from bottom to top can not only provide relatively accurate data information for school management, but also enable managers at all levels to distinguish value-added work and non value-added work, which is conducive to reducing invalid work, reducing internal costs, improving core competitiveness of colleges and universities, and making rational and efficient allocation and use of educational and scientific research resources in Colleges and universities .

## 2.2 Optimization of Internal Cost Accounting System in Education System

The methods of educational cost accounting in Colleges and universities include the measurement and calculation methods of educational cost accounting. It is mainly based on the financial data of colleges and universities to calculate the education cost of colleges and universities. In order to make the measurement process easier, to a certain extent, it refers to the enterprise accounting method and uses accounting means to calculate, that is, the accounting adjustment method [10, 11]. In the calculation process, considering the causes of different cost items, according to different motives and beneficiaries, according to a certain standard, they are allocated to each college, so that they can be finally allocated to each cost accounting object. College education cost project is set up according to the specific situation of colleges and universities, which is used to collect various expenditures of colleges and universities, so as to calculate the cost of college education conveniently [12]. Cost items can be set according to the situation and Department of University expenses, which can simplify the accounting process of university education cost to a certain extent and provide beneficial support for the establishment of university education cost accounting [13]. To optimize the internal cost accounting system of education system, the specific system structure is shown in the Fig. 1 below:

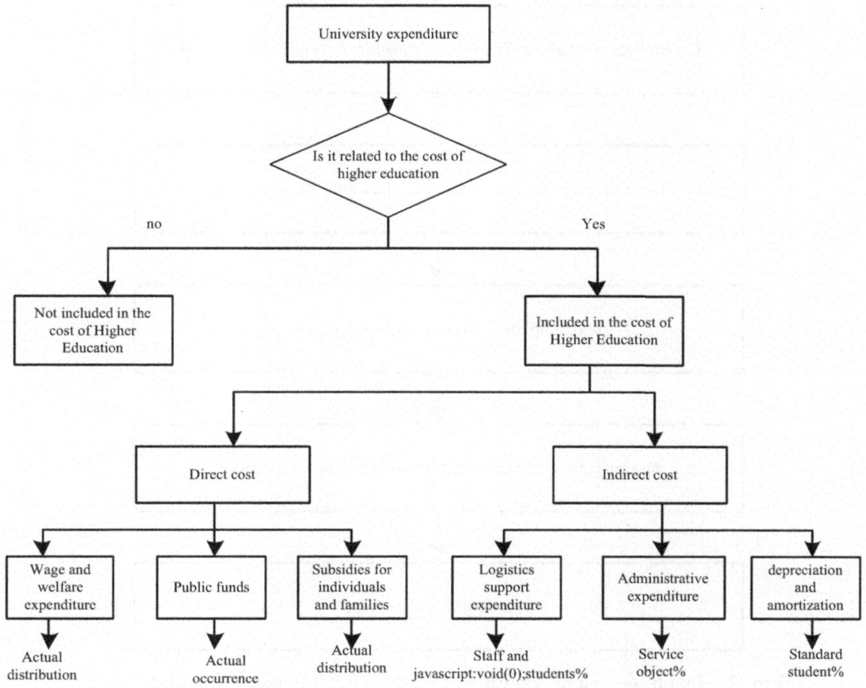


**Fig. 1.** Internal cost accounting system of education system

Because the purpose of educational cost accounting in Colleges and universities is to meet the relevant needs of the government, colleges and Society for educational cost information, it is considered that under the current conditions, the choice of accounting method for the measurement of educational cost in Colleges and universities is more valuable [14]. Under this method, China's colleges and universities should, in accordance with the principle of accrual basis, take the current accounting data of institutions of higher learning as the basis, and according to the requirements of education cost accounting, set up separate cost accounting accounts and accounting subjects to carry forward various business expenditures, so as to carry out education cost accounting continuously, systematically and completely [15]. In order to carry out education cost accounting and provide reliable education cost information for relevant users, we must set up a set of standardized procedures, so that education cost accounting can be carried out in full accordance with the set procedures, so as to ensure the reliability of the provided cost information [16]. Referring to the enterprise cost accounting procedure, the general procedure of education cost accounting in Colleges and universities is divided into the following steps: obtaining the financial and non-financial information required by education cost accounting, determining the object and period of cost accounting, setting up cost accounting subjects, recording, collecting, distributing and accounting education cost, and compiling education cost statements. The specific process is shown in the Fig. 2 below:

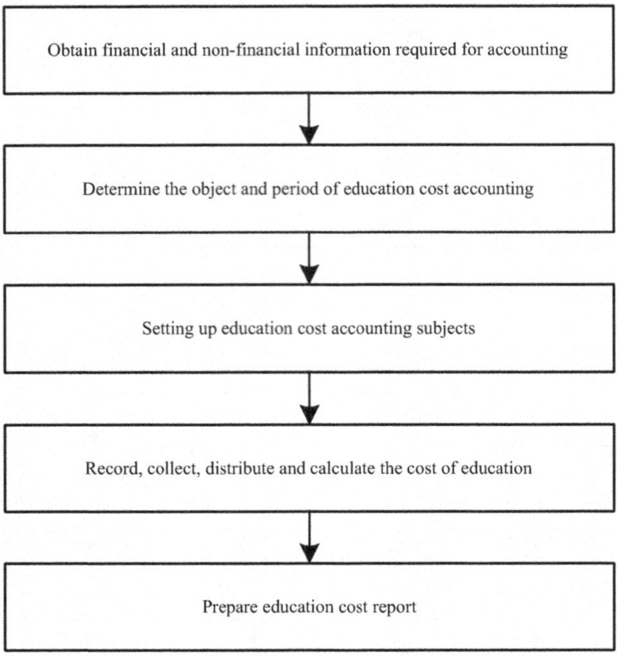


**Fig. 2.** Teaching cost accounting procedure in Colleges and Universities

In the case that the cost accounting system of colleges and universities needs to be improved and the compensation mechanism needs to be optimized, the basis for carrying out the education cost sharing work of colleges and universities needs to be improved . The problem of indiscriminate and high charges in Colleges and universities is criticized by the society. Under the influence of the above factors, the optimization of internal cost accounting system and cost sharing mechanism has become an inevitable choice for colleges and universities to improve the efficiency of capital use and ensure the

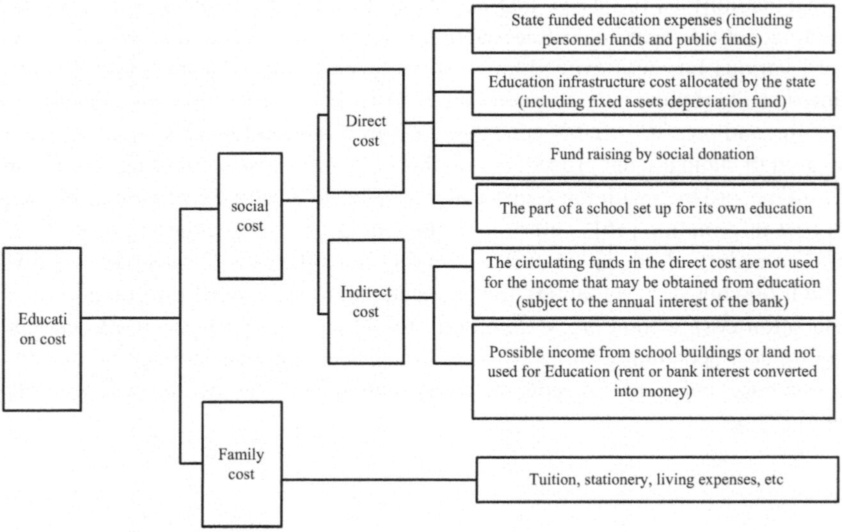


**Fig. 3.** Classification of education cost

quality of teaching. Education cost is divided into family cost and institution cost, but education cost is not equal to the sum of family cost and institution cost. Because there are overlapping contents between family cost and institution cost, such as tuition fees in family cost, as the income of school, can be used for capital investment or recurrent expenditure of school, thus forming a part of institution cost (Fig. 3).

Through the above classification, it is possible to distinguish educational activity expenditures and non-educational activity expenditures, and group educational activities into "career expenditures". In this way, "operating expenditures", "appropriation of funds", "subsidy expenditures to affiliated units", "carryover self-financing infrastructure", etc., are classified as non-educational expenditures that are not related to educational activities. This more accurately reflects the accounting scope of education costs. Among them, teaching cost refers to all kinds of expenses related to the educational services provided by colleges and universities, which is basically the same as the teaching expenses in Colleges and universities. However, it does not include non academic education and other aspects of teaching expenditure, because such education does not belong to the scope of higher education cost accounting, but should belong to the expenditure not included in the education cost.

## 2.3 Construction of Internal Cost Control Model in Colleges and Universities

At present, the financial software used by colleges and universities in our country is not unified, and the calculation method of cost accounting in Colleges and universities is not the same, so the cost accounting in Colleges and universities has not been effectively carried out nationwide. With the deepening of the reform of financial management in Colleges and universities, the financial information of colleges and universities will gradually be open to social supervision, and colleges and universities urgently need to establish internal cost accounting model suitable for their own situation. The internal cost control model of colleges and universities is established based on activity-based costing (Fig. 4):

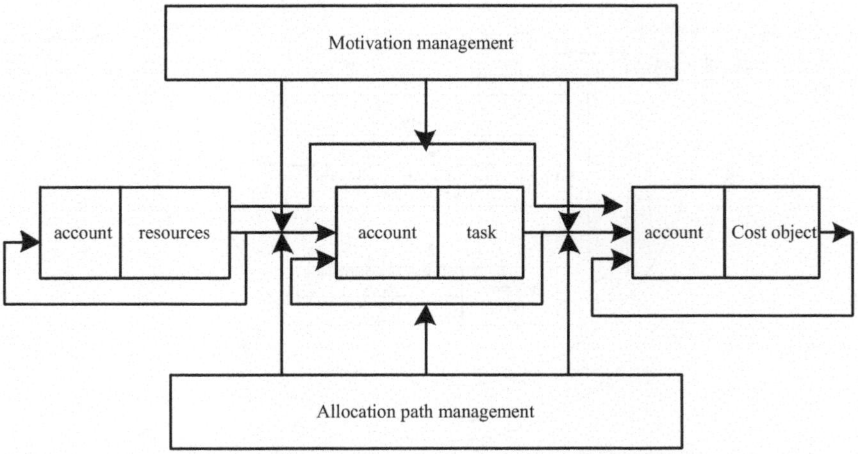


**Fig. 4.** Internal cost control model of colleges and Universities

To establish the cost control model of colleges and Universities Based on activity-based costing, we need five elements: resources, activities, cost objects, cost drivers and distribution path, as well as accounting period and organizational structure. The resources in the internal cost accounting of colleges and universities refer to the expenses for cultivating students, mainly including staff expenses, teaching expenses, management expenses, part of scientific research expenses, intangible assets investment, depreciation of fixed assets, etc. The resource account of colleges and universities is a series of resource sets with hierarchical structure. It realizes multiple allocation by subdividing the resource account to increase the accuracy of resource cost allocation.

Based on the theory of cost control system, combined with the production characteristics and cost management needs of colleges and universities, this paper takes the sustainable and healthy development of colleges and universities as the goal, takes the principles of "strategic orientation, full participation, equal rights and responsibilities, cost-effectiveness, and continuous improvement", takes the Education Cost Management Committee of colleges and universities as the main body, and according to the development strategy of colleges and universities, from the macro management system, cost-effectiveness, and so on In order to improve the cost control of higher education, a long-term mechanism system should be built to realize the effective and healthy operation of the cost control of higher education. The cost control mechanism of higher education is shown in the Fig. 5.

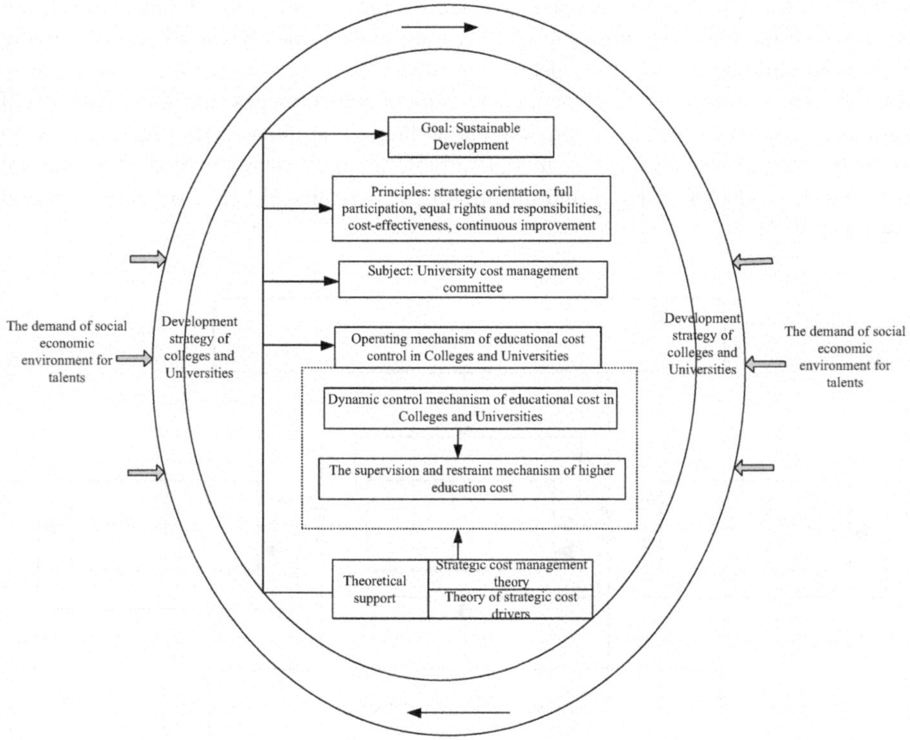


**Fig. 5.** Education cost control mechanism

In order to effectively control the same period, we should decompose the cost control standard determined according to the different characteristics of budget, project and operation to each department, each post, each stage and each link, so that the leaders of each department and all staff can make clear its significance, and link the cost control with their interests, so as to encourage everyone to take measures consciously and actively to control the cost. Through the effective supervision system and information communication channels, timely and accurately find out and understand the deviation in the process of education cost operation in each stage, and carry out difference analysis. The deviation should be corrected on the basis of difference analysis. There are usually two ways to correct the deviation: one is to correct the deviation by changing the objective, the other is to improve the system control ability by appropriately changing the quality and quantity of input, as well as the human, financial, material, information and system structure, so that the output can meet the target cost requirements as soon as possible. The correction of education cost deviation in Colleges and universities also includes the construction of effective information communication channels, strengthening the contact of various departments, realizing the sharing of resources and improving the utilization rate of resources. The cost control process is shown in the Fig. 6.

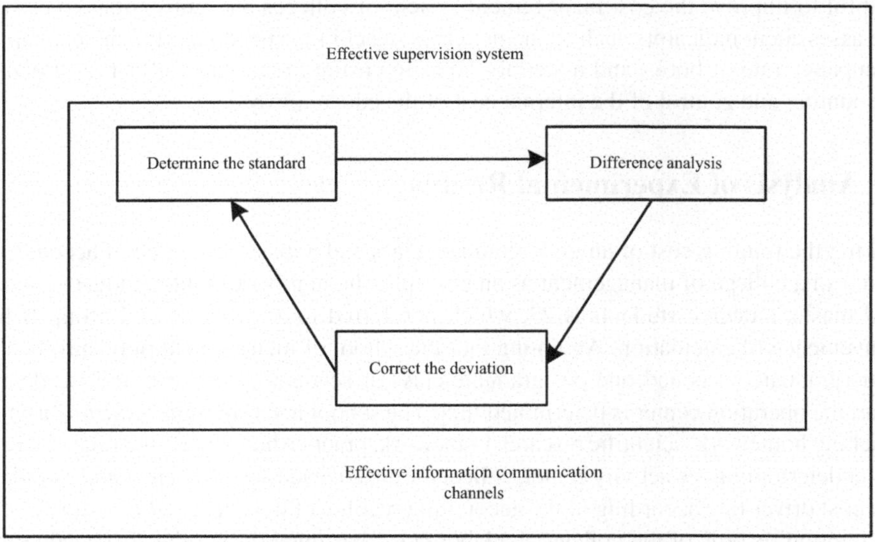


**Fig. 6.** Internal cost control process of education system

Teaching activities belong to the basic activities of colleges and universities. Teaching cost can reflect the level of teaching cost in the process of providing education services, and can analyze the level of resource consumption in teaching activities (Fig. 7).

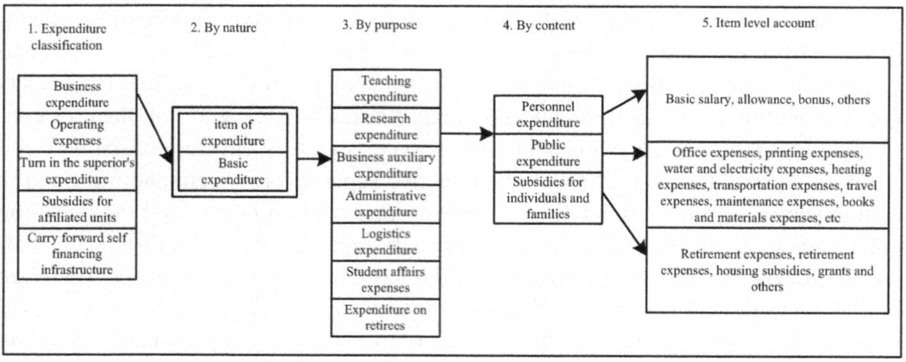


**Fig. 7.** Control level of University expenditure accounting

The construction of cost management evaluation system is also an important content in the process of cost management system construction. In the process of constructing the teaching evaluation system, colleges and universities can adopt the assessment system of carrying out cost assessment according to departments and departments. It is also helpful to improve the cost management system of colleges and universities to clarify the assessment indicators such as the per capita teaching expenditure and the per capita occupancy rate of books and materials, so as to ensure the research effect of effective accounting and control of the internal cost of the education system.

## 3 Analysis of Experimental Results

Taking the training cost of an undergraduate class and a master's degree of accounting major in a college of management as an example, the number of undergraduate classes and master's degree students is 23, which is referred to as group A and group B for convenience of calculation. Assuming that the school of management only enrolls one undergraduate class and one postgraduate class of accounting major in this academic year, the operation center is determined first. The school needs to train students through teaching homework, scientific research homework, practice homework and related work. After determining the activity center, collect the cost of each activity center and calculate the cost driver rate according to the accounting records of the college. According to the accounting records of the college, the labor cost consumed during the cost accounting period is 176000 yuan, the depreciation cost is 124000 yuan, the material cost is 64000 yuan, and the management cost is 36000 yuan. In order to simplify the calculation, financial expenses are included in the management expenses. Taking teaching assignments as an example, teaching assignments consume three kinds of resources: Teachers' labor, teaching materials and depreciation of assets and equipment. The management cost of the college is 25000 yuan, the wage cost is 35000 yuan, the depreciation of assets and equipment is 25000 yuan, and the material cost is 16000 yuan. The list of teaching activity cost is as follows (Table 1):

**Table 1.** Internal teaching activity cost accounting sheet

| Cost classification | Cost element | Resource driver | Amount (ten thousand yuan) |
|---|---|---|---|
| Fixed cost | Management expenses | 3.33% | 0.60 |
| | Depreciation of assets and equipment | 33.33% | 6.00 |
| Variable cost | Labor, materials | 63.33% | 11.40 |
| Total cost library | – | – | 18.00 |

According to the same method to calculate the cost sheet of scientific research, practice and study, the total cost of each activity cost library is 140000 yuan, 60000 yuan and 20000 yuan respectively. According to the calculated cost sheet, determine the cost driver and cost driver quantity of each activity, and calculate the cost driver rate of each activity, as shown in the Table 2:

**Table 2.** Internal cost base and control factors of education system

| j | Nature of operation | Cost driver | Cv | Cf | Cj | mdj | mrj |
|---|---|---|---|---|---|---|---|
| Teaching assignments | Batch level | Frequency | 11.4 | 6.6 | 18.0 | 50 | 0.36 |
| Scientific research work | Unit level | Frequency | 9.8 | 4.2 | 14.0 | 50 | 0.28 |
| Internship assignment | Batch level | Frequency | 1.2 | 4.8 | 6.0 | 4 | 1.50 |
| Study and work | Unit level | Frequency | 1.60 | 0.40 | 2.00 | 4 | 0.50 |
| Total | – | – | – | – | 40.00 | – | – |

After further listing the cost list and calculating the cost driver rate, the activity driver rate of each assignment is counted, and the education cost of each group A and B is calculated (Table 3).

**Table 3.** Comparison of educational expenses allocation accounting and control

| j | mrj | Group A (i1) | | Group B(i2) | |
|---|---|---|---|---|---|
| | | d1j | gc1j | d2j | gc2j |
| Teaching assignments | 0.36 | 20.00 | 7.20 | 10.00 | 3.60 |
| Scientific research work | 0.28 | 5.00 | 1.40 | 60.00 | 16.80 |
| Internship assignment | 1.50 | 2.00 | 3.00 | 4.00 | 6.00 |
| Study and work | 0.50 | 3.00 | 1.50 | 1.00 | 0.50 |
| Total | | | 13.10 | | 26.90 |

According to the traditional cost accounting method, the education cost of group A and group B is the same, that is, when calculating the education cost, the unit education cost is obtained by dividing the total education expenditure of colleges and universities by the number of students on campus, while ignoring the need to invest different staff labor costs and scientific research material costs when cultivating students with different academic degrees, which makes the education cost can not be reversed truthfully Reflect the actual situation. Based on the cost accounting model of activity-based costing, it is concluded that the education cost of students with different degrees is quite different, as shown in the Table 4 below:

**Table 4.** Comparison of activity-based costing and traditional methods in education cost control

| Law of costs | Amortization expenses of undergraduates (10000 yuan) | Amortization expenses of postgraduates (10000 yuan) |
|---|---|---|
| Traditional method | 20 | 20 |
| Activity based costing | 13.1 | 26.9 |
| Difference rate | 34.50% | −34.50% |

Based on the above table, we can see that in the actual operation and control process of internal cost accounting in Colleges and universities, we should pay attention to avoid increasing too much workload for financial personnel in order to obtain accurate data, or the obvious increase of management cost due to too complex internal cost accounting process. It is suggested that colleges and universities should calculate the training cost of students with different degrees according to their own situation, so as to increase the accuracy of cost information and avoid excessive increase in the workload of financial personnel.

## 4 Suggestions on Internal Cost Accounting and Control of Higher Education

In order to reduce the cost of education successfully, colleges and universities must set up the concept of cost management among all the staff, let the staff have the sense of cost at any time, continuously innovate the teaching and management methods, improve the quality of education products, and reduce the cost of education. With the deepening of the reform of higher education system, the level of higher education cost has a direct bearing on the survival and development of the school, and on the salary and welfare of the whole school staff. A large number of colleges and universities have different degrees of funding shortage. This requires the whole school staff to change their ideas and establish a correct sense of cost.

According to the internal and external actual situation, colleges and universities should weigh the objective needs and subjective possibilities, and put forward the specific cost objectives that colleges and universities need to achieve in a certain period of time in the future through scientific prediction. That is to say, colleges and universities should set up in advance the project cost of cultivating a college student, as the goal of the whole school staff's efforts and the measure of actual cost saving or overspending, so as to realize the prior control of education cost. All expense budgets can only be paid after the application and approval procedures before spending. Even if it is stipulated in the original plan, it also needs to be applied and approved. This is conducive to the further study of all expenses before they will occur. According to the new changes, the rationality of expenses will be determined again, so as to ensure the use effect of all expenses. To reduce the cost of higher education, we must tap the potential of existing houses and equipment, improve the utilization rate of houses and equipment, and reduce the unit depreciation. The instruments and equipment of a school are all for teaching, scientific research and production. All colleges (departments) and departments should coordinate with each other and give full play to their due role. In recent years, many colleges and universities have merged similar laboratories, especially basic laboratories, unified management, coordinated use of instruments and equipment, and achieved good results, which is worthy of reference for colleges and universities across the country.

Education cost management is divided into pre-, during and post-management. In the process of incurring educational costs, rationally controlling various educational expenditures, and striving to save various teaching and management expenses without affecting the normal order of teaching work, is a direct way to reduce educational costs. After the education cost occurs, summing up experience and lessons, revising the budget for the coming year is a remedial measure to reduce the long-term education cost, and reducing the education cost should also be forward-looking and preventive. For example, when introducing talents, it is important to consider whether the school has the basic conditions for talents to carry out work and exert their expertise, and consider the cost of brain drain caused by this. Before constructing various projects and purchasing various teaching equipment, feasibility analysis and opportunity cost analysis should be carried out. When conducting demonstrations of new majors and selection of old majors, the professional life cycle and the total cost in the life cycle should be considered. In a word, reducing the cost of education is a long-term and complex systematic project. Only by taking the system as the starting point, careful research and continuous exploration, can we really find an effective way to reduce the cost of education.

## 5 Concluding Remarks

Cost control is a big topic, and colleges and universities are more complex, so it is difficult to carry out cost control. To carry out the research on the cost control in Colleges and universities, it can not be completed overnight. There is a lot of detailed work to do. The theory and practice of internal cost control in Colleges and universities are not mature in China, and it will be a long-term exploration work. Therefore, this paper studies the internal cost accounting and control method of education system based on activity-based costing. With the deepening of the research, the problems of internal cost control of higher education will be solved one by one, and the efficiency of running a school will be gradually improved.

## Reference

1. Gui, F., Ren, S., Zhao, Y., et al.: Activity-based allocation and optimization for carbon footprint and cost in product lifecycle. J. Clean. Prod. **236**(10), 117627 (2019)
2. Ostadi, B., Daloie, R.M., Sepehri, M.M.: A combined modelling of fuzzy logic and Time-Driven Activity-based Costing (TDABC) for hospital services costing under uncertainty. J. Biomed. Inform. **89**(11), 11–28 (2019)
3. Martinek, R., Brablik, J., Kolarik, J., et al.: A low-cost system for seismocardiography-based cardiac triggering: a practical solution for cardiovascular magnetic resonance imaging at 3 tesla. IEEE Access **7**, 118608–118629 (2019)
4. Zhu, T., Liu, C., Tan, X., et al.: Se-incorporating stabilizes and activates metastable MoS2 for efficient and cost-effective water gas shift reaction. ACS Nano **2019**(10), 11303–11309 (2019)
5. Tonta, M.M., Sezer, U.A., Olmez, H., et al.: Cost-effective synthesis of polyricinoleate: investigation of coating characteristics, in vitro degradation, and antibacterial activity. J. Appl. Polym. Sci. **136**(44), 48172 (2019)
6. Lacher, R.M., Vasconcelos, F., Williams, N.R., et al.: Nonrigid reconstruction of 3D breast surfaces with a low-cost RGBD camera for surgical planning and aesthetic evaluation. Med. Image Anal. **53**(11), 11–25 (2019)
7. Togan, V., Eirgash, M.A.: Time-cost trade-off optimization of construction projects using teaching learning based optimization. KSCE J. Civ. Eng. **23**(1), 10–20 (2019)
8. Andrada, A., Murdocca, R.M., Dondo, J., et al.: Didactic prototype for teaching the MQTT protocol based on free hardware boards and Node-RED. IEEE Lat. Am. Trans. **18**(2), 376–382 (2020)
9. Xue, R., Wu, Z., et al.: A survey of application and classification on teaching-learning-based optimization algorithm. IEEE Access **8**(4), 1062–1079 (2019)
10. Reznik, A., Kissinger, M., Alfasi, N.: Real-data-based high-resolution GHG emissions accounting of urban residents private transportation. Int. J. Sustain. Transp. **13**(1–5), 235–244 (2019)
11. Lai, H., Harun, N.F., Tucker, D., Adams II, T.A.: Design and eco-techno-economic analyses of SOFC/Gas turbine hybrid systems accounting for long-term degradation. Comput. Aided Chem. Eng. **48**, 415–420 (2020)
12. Li, F., Fan, Z.P., Cao, B.B., et al.: Logistics service mode selection for last mile delivery: an analysis method considering customer utility and delivery service cost. Sustainability **13**(1), 284 (2020)
13. Lakew, D.M., Musa, M.G.: Assessment of undergraduate accounting and finance education in Ethiopia. Int. J. Bus. Soc. Res. **9**, 21–37 (2019)
14. Samaduzzaman, M.: Blockchain: future of accounting education. Asian J. Finance Acc. **12**(2), 14 (2020)
15. Utama, A.: Design of agro-education tourism accounting information system. South Asian J. Eng. Technol. **2**(6), 54–61 (2020)
16. Tilahun, M.: A review on determinants of accounting information system adoption. Sci. J. Bus, Manag. **7**(1), 17 (2019)

# Research on Power Consumption Control Method of Online Teaching Terminal Based on IEEE 802.11

Zheng Zhang[1](✉) and Tian-Hui Wang[2]

[1] Nanyang Institute of Technology, Nanyang 47300, China
[2] Zhuhai College of Jilin University, Zhuhai 519041, China

**Abstract.** The online teaching terminal of Internet of things platform has a huge amount of information transmission, and power consumption has become one of the important factors restricting the development of mobile Internet of things teaching platform. In order to ensure the good operation of online teaching terminal, a power consumption control method of online teaching terminal based on IEEE802.11 is proposed. Collect power consumption characteristic data, optimize the power control protocol of online teaching terminal according to different application scenarios of mobile Internet of things platform, reduce the average power consumption of online teaching terminal without changing the hardware of mobile network and online teaching terminal, so as to achieve the low-power operation state of online teaching terminal of mobile Internet of things platform.

**Keywords:** IEEE802.11 · Internet of things platform · Online teaching terminal · Power consumption control

## 1 Introduction

With the continuous expansion of the application scale of the online teaching platform of the Internet of Things, the power consumption of the online teaching terminal of the platform of the Internet of Things is getting higher and higher. The low-power design of the online teaching terminal of the Internet of Things platform is a research hotspot. The online teaching terminal node of the Internet of Things platform contains high-performance modules, such as baseband processing, signal processing and RF power control, etc., with high power consumption. In the operation process, the online teaching terminal nodes of the Internet of Things platform drive multiple online teaching terminals of the Internet of Things platform, collect and transmit the data of the online teaching terminal of the Internet of Things platform, process and analyze the data, fix the wireless digital baseband, network formation, and drive the RADIO frequency to send information, which all need to consume a large amount of current [1].

The current power consumption control technology has limited power, so it is difficult to make the online teaching terminal node of Internet of Things platform work for a long time. Internet online teaching platform terminal nodes need to work continuously for


W. Fu et al. (Eds.): eLEOT 2021, LNICST 389, pp. 57–70, 2021.
https://doi.org/10.1007/978-3-030-84383-0_6

one year and do not need to change, power consumption in recent years, the node online teaching terminal of the low power design is very important, most of the time, only the Internet of things platform online teaching terminal and its drive peripheral equipment to keep working, and the central processor and some high-performance power control module in the idle state [2]. Therefore, only a small part of the online teaching terminal nodes of the Internet of Things platform need to keep working during most of the time. If most of the other idle modules can be shut down or turned off, the dynamic and static power consumption of the Internet of Things platform will be significantly reduced.

In the traditional online teaching terminal power control method of the Internet of Things platform, all terminals control their working state accordingly according to the sequence information. In order to reduce the collision probability of the competing channel, the response competition window is introduced. When there is no data grouping in an access point (AP), the AP broadcasts the GAS frame and activates the idle timer. All terminals go to sleep until the idle timer expires [3]. However, the method neglects the collection of power characteristic data, which leads to a large error in power control.

For this reason, an IoT terminal power control method based on IEEE802.11 is proposed. According to the different application scenarios of the mobile Internet of Things, the terminal power control protocol is optimized, and the average power consumption of the terminal is reduced without changing the mobile network and terminal hardware, so as to improve the service time of the terminal power consumption of the mobile Internet of Things.

## 2 Power Consumption Control Method of Online Teaching Terminal of Internet of Things Platform

### 2.1 Power Characteristic Data Acquisition

Most of the online teaching terminal data of the Internet of Things platform are stored in the acquisition and sensing layer, and the information is transmitted to the network transport layer. Although the equipment can be maintained to work all the time in the power consumption life cycle of the online teaching terminal of the Internet of Things platform, the defects are obvious at the same time. The charging controller of the online teaching terminal equipment of the Internet of Things platform takes up the investment cost, and the installation is complicated, which requires a special bracket to fix the solar power consumption board, and the power consumption is also limited by charging times. Generally, the charging period is about 400 to 600 cycles, and it needs to be replaced after running for about 2 years [3]. With the development of modern technology, more and more low-power Internet of Things platforms are launched, and the power control technology is becoming more and more mature, which makes the power consumption capacity of the same information storage capacity gradually increase. The wireless channel of the online teaching terminal of the Internet of Things platform refers to the propagation path of the electromagnetic wave signal of the online teaching terminal of the Internet of Things platform between the transmitting end and the receiving end. A linear band-pass model is used to describe the wireless channel to construct the structure of the online teaching terminal of the Internet of Things platform, as shown in the Fig. 1.

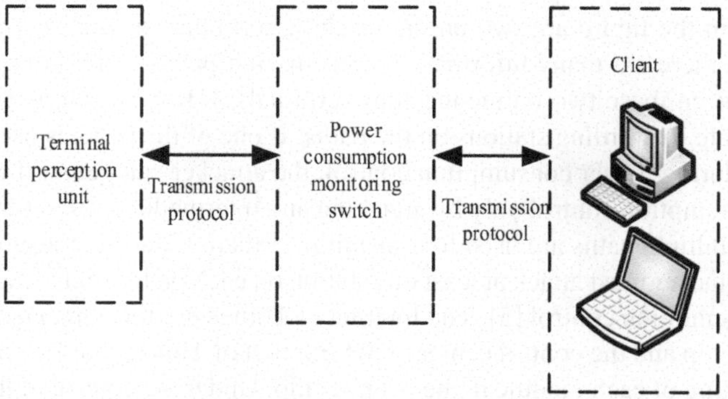


**Fig. 1.** Internet of things platform online teaching terminal wireless channel structure composition

Internet of Things platform online teaching terminal data acquisition telemetry Online teaching terminal should realize the data acquisition of various online teaching terminals on the site of Internet of Things platform. Acquisition signals can be divided into three types: analog signals, digital signals and Internet of Things platform interface signals. Among them, the analog quantity is mainly 4–20 mA current or 0–5 V voltage, the digital quantity signal is mainly switching quantity and pulse quantity signal, and the interface signal of the Internet of Things platform is mainly RS232 and RS485 interface. The wireless Internet of things platform of data acquisition and telemetry online teaching terminal adopts GPRS mode. Using the SIM900A Platform module of the Internet of Things, the establishment of the platform link of the Internet of Things and the sending and receiving of data are completed through AT instruction [4]. The principle of the multi-channel transmission model under the Internet of Things platform is to determine the information output path according to the stability of the two-party network controlled by power consumption and the processing of the system's online teaching terminal. The subsequent multiplexing key and the process of multiplexing should follow this principle to select the path. Figure 2 shows the multi-channel transmission model under the Internet of Things platform environment.

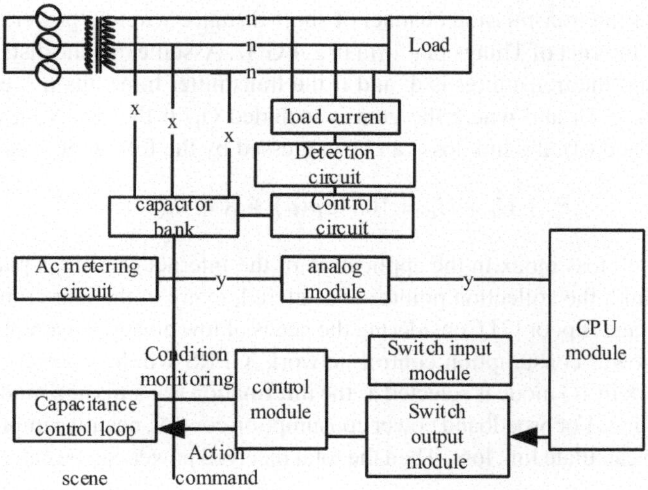


**Fig. 2.** Power transmission model in the environment of Internet of things

X and Y in the figure are two online teaching terminals of the Internet of Things platform, and there are many information transmission paths of the Internet of Things platform between these two online teaching terminals. N1, N2... Ni + 1 in the figure are intermediate forwarding stations on the paths. If one of the paths is used to transmit information during power consumption control, the attacker can get all the information of power consumption control only by attacking any intermediate forwarding station on this path. If multiple paths are used to transmit information during power consumption control, the attacker must attack at least one station on each path to get some information of power consumption control [5]. The Internet of Things platform manager is the clock of the whole chip and the control center of the Internet of Things platform. Clock gating and power gating of each module in the control chip. Under the control of the Internet of Things platform manager, general peripheral modules can enter three modes: working mode, sleep mode and deep sleep mode. In addition to these three modes, the CPU can also enter the backup mode. In the transmission process of its Internet of Things platform, a series of vector $\delta$ of signal components after varying degrees of attenuation h, delay and phase shift arrive at the receiving end due to multipath effect. The discrete time-domain multipath model is described as a linear bandpass filter, and its equivalent baseband pulse effect X is shown in formula.

$$\mathrm{X} = \sum_{l=0}^{N(\mathrm{d,t})-1} \alpha_l(\mathrm{d,\,t})e^{-j} \cdot (\tau - \tau_l(\mathrm{d,\,t})) - lh(\mathrm{d,\,t,}\,\tau) \tag{1}$$

Where $l$ represents the resolvable path component of the $l$, N(d, t) is the spacing between the terminals d, the number of resolvable multipath components at observation time t, where $\tau_l(\mathrm{d, t})$ represents the arrival path relative to the first, The arrival delay of path $l.\alpha_1(\mathrm{d, t})\mathrm{e}^{-j}$ is the component of article $l$ when the distance d and the observation time t are measured. The amplitude and phase of the $l$ path component in the delay time $\tau_l(\mathrm{d, t})$. The multipath channel time domain model is constructed under the fixed distance between the transceiver and the wireless power control node. Among them, link loss is not only related to the coverage of wireless power control, but also related to the link budget, which is the most important large-scale fading parameter [6]. A link loss model is proposed for the transmission channel of short-distance wireless power consumption control on the Internet of Things platform in 2.4 GHz. Assume that the distance between the receiver and the transmitter is d, and if the transmitter transmits power $\mathrm{P_t}$, the test gain is known as $\mathrm{G_t}$ and where the gain is included $\mathrm{G_r}$, if the receiving power at the receiving end is p (d), the link loss can be expressed by the following formula.

$$P_t + G_t + G_r = 10n\lg p(d) + \mathrm{X} + lh(\mathrm{d,\,t,}\,\tau) \tag{2}$$

Where, n is path loss index.In the application of the Internet of Things platform, especially in the field, the collection points are scattered, many of them are remote, and the network coverage is poor [7].Considering the needs of low power consumption and wide coverage of power consumption control network, GPRS wireless power consumption control network in 4G mode is selected as the information transmission mode of wireless Internet of Things. For broadband power consumption control, negative impulse response can be used to calculate link loss. Then the total received power can be calculated, which can be expressed as the formula:

$$P_r(d,t) = \sum_{l=0}^{M(d,t)-1} \alpha_1^2(d,t)/P_t + G_t + G_r \tag{3}$$

Where, M is the number of multipath components. $\alpha_1^2$ is shadow fading.

Assuming that a total of K points are tested around the distance d point, the total received power can be expressed as formula:

$$P_t(d,t) = 1/\sum_{K=0}^{K-1} K \sum_{l=0}^{N(d,t)-1} \alpha_1^2(d,t) \tag{4}$$

The algorithm is very important in the software design of the online teaching terminal of the Internet of Things platform. To solve the information problem under normal circumstances, the formula can be used to express:

$$W(a)_{\min} = \sum_{i=1}^{n} \lambda_i[\left(K_i^t \alpha_1^2\right) + KP_r(d,t)]P_t(d,t) \tag{5}$$

The function of online teaching terminal information collection can be expressed by formula:

$$W(b)_{\min} = \sum_{i=1}^{m} \lambda_i(-b_i)t - \delta y\left(\frac{1}{\delta}\sum_{i=1}^{m} k_i b_i\right) \tag{6}$$

Where, $k_1, \cdots, k_m \in 2^m$ is a vector of m pieces of information; $\lambda_1, \cdots, \lambda_m$ is the amount of information loss; y represents the coefficient of the function; $\delta$ stands for conjugate function; b represents the variable of the fault information function.

$t \geq 0$ is the function parameter. Each information variable $c_i$ corresponds to a stored variable. The constraint software function model can be obtained from the above formula:

$$f(a)_{\min} = \|Fa - r\|_3^3 + z\left\|a\lambda_i\left(c_i^t a\right)\right\|_2 \tag{7}$$

Where, $F$ belongs to the matrix of $n$ items of fault information; z is the parameter of information constraint.

## 2.2 Power Consumption Control Algorithm of Online Teaching Terminal of Internet of Things Platform

The low-power design of wireless Internet of Things platform online teaching terminal network software can be divided into different levels according to the network protocol stack, that is, the physical layer, the MAC layer, the network layer and the application layer. The emphasis is on the research, design and implementation of the physical layer and the MAC layer. The online teaching terminal of the Internet of Things platform only performs power control at a fixed time point or specified time point, and does not perform power control at other times [8]. The samples from the established learning and training sample set are input into the neural network structure for learning and training. The process is as follows:

Input fault sample (xi) to the input layer of BP neural network. In the input layer, when the following constraints are satisfied, namely, the formula, output and input into the hidden layer.

$$\mathrm{A} = \sum_{i=1}^{1} \sqrt{\mathrm{BC}} - \frac{\mathrm{d}}{2}\mathrm{e} \tag{8}$$

Where, A is the target output; B and C are the output functions of each neuron between the input layer and the hidden layer; d is the initial value of the weight; e is the threshold. Input the ith neuron from the input layer into the hidden layer according to formula (9) below.

$$u1 = \sum_{i=1}^{N} w \cdot x \tag{9}$$

In the formula, w is the weight. The output result of the hidden layer is as follows:

$$y1 = f\left[\sum_{i=1}^{N} w \cdot x\right] \tag{10}$$

In the formula, f is the number of alternations. Input the output of the hidden layer into the output layer as follows.

$$u2 = \sum_{i=1}^{N} w \cdot y1 \tag{11}$$

Output results of the output layer are obtained:

$$y2 = f\left[\sum_{i=1}^{N} w \cdot y1\right] \tag{12}$$

5) Output layer error $g$ is:

$$g = m - y^2 \tag{13}$$

In the formula, $m$ is the expected output value and $g = m - y^2$ is the actual output value output layer. Judge whether the error value g meets the termination condition. If it meets the termination condition, it ends. If it does not, it needs to carry out back-propagation to adjust the connection weight W between neurons in each layer, so that the weights can be infinitely connected with the expected value after the output of the transfer function. Then the weights of each neuron after the correction of the weights are calculated, and the results are compared with the expected values again When the results meet the conditions, the sample training is finished [9]. According to the working mode, the online teaching terminal of mobile Internet of things platform is divided into three states: null, standby and connected. The main principle of online teaching terminal power control is to make the online teaching terminal as low power consumption as possible. Power optimization is based on the Internet of things platform [10–12]. The three-layer neural network structure, namely neural network, is adopted, as shown in Fig. 3.

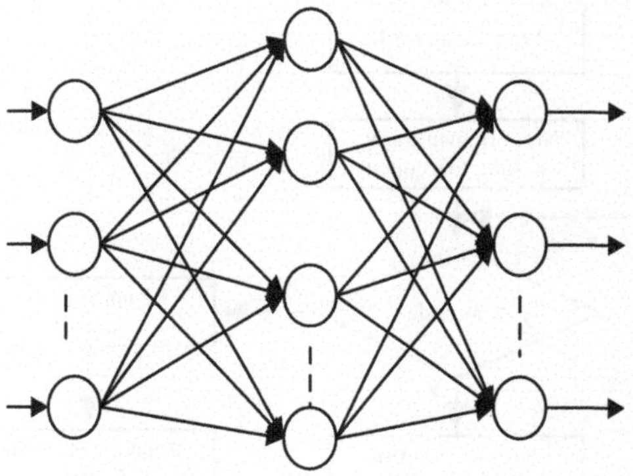

**Fig. 3.** Control layer structure of neural network

Neural network control operation direction can be divided into two types: forward propagation, that is, fault samples are input into the input layer, and then into the hidden layer. After the hidden layer processing, the final output results are output through the output layer, and each layer of neurons only works on the next layer of neurons; reverse transmission: when the output of the output layer is not accurate, it needs to reverse (output layer → hidden layer → Input layer) modify the connection weight of each layer (which can be modified for many times) to obtain the most accurate fault diagnosis results. Online teaching terminals are in fixed or low mobility application scenarios. Many Internet of things platforms online teaching terminals are in fixed or low-speed mobile application scenarios [13].

### 2.3 Realization of Power Consumption Control of Online Teaching Terminal on Internet of Things Platform

The protocol stack is initialized; then the idle channel is selected to construct the network environment, and finally the channel is found. If the appropriate channel is found, the coordinator will have the pan identification, which can represent the whole network information monitoring situation. Therefore, it is necessary to select pan identification. If there is information missing at the node, intelligent scanning should be carried out to find out whether there is a coordinator in the surrounding environment, and then the beacon should be monitored within the scanning limit to obtain the relevant information of the coordinator and send a connection request. Finally, the coordinator node is assigned a short address, which contains the new address and the instruction of the successful connection state, so that the information power consumption can be controlled. The specific process is shown in the figure (Fig. 4).

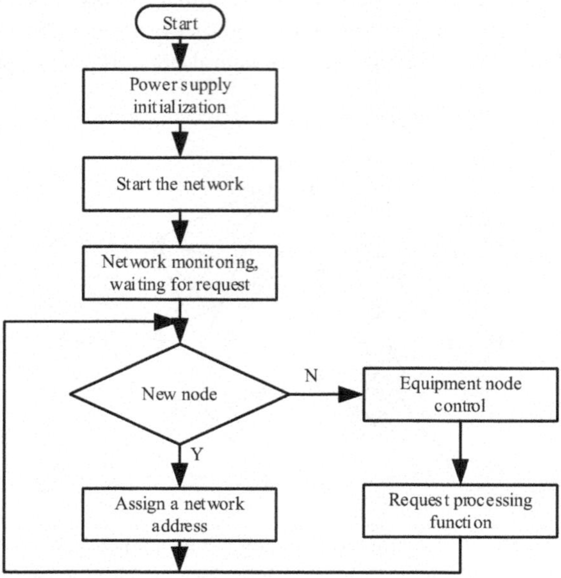


**Fig. 4.** Power consumsption control flow of online teaching terminal on internet of things platform

As the network master node in the Internet of Things platform environment, the wireless power consumption control technology coordinator node can exchange the old address and the new address in real time. This kind of online teaching terminal does not need to move or only moves at low speed. The principle of power consumption optimization is to reduce the power consumption in low Standby state and Connected state by reducing the mobility management process. The specific implementation method is a protocol optimization process that reduces power consumption and location area update frequency by optimizing periodic location/routing area update process, reducing the number and frequency of service and neighbor cell measurements in Standby state and reducing the number and frequency of service and neighbor cell measurements in Connected state. If T3212 timer is set to 30 min, it takes 250 ms to update the location area or routing area once, that is, every 30 min, which can save the working power consumption of 54 TDMA frames. Optimize the protocol control flow of measurement frequency and cell number to reduce power consumption. After optimization design, if there are 102 TDMA in a paging cycle, it saves 2 TDMA frames for measurement, reception and calculation, and reduces the average standby power consumption. Based on this, the energy consumption control state of the online teaching terminal of the Internet of Things platform is optimized, as shown in Fig. 5:

After building the energy consumption control platform of the online teaching terminal of the Internet of Things platform, the functional optimization is carried out. In the process of functional optimization, it is necessary to verify whether the functions of the

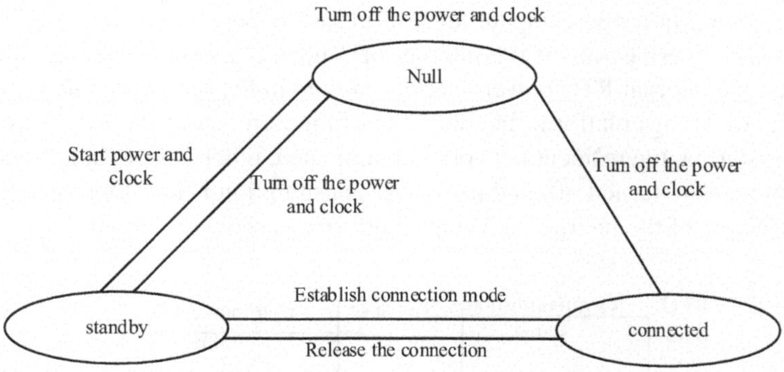


**Fig. 5.** Energy consumption control status of online teaching terminal of internet of things platform

online teaching terminal of the Internet of Things platform meet the design requirements. The following aspects need to be optimized in functional testing:

1) Whether the receiving module can receive the power consumption data of the online teaching terminal of the Internet of Things platform is verified whether the functions of the Internet of Things platform are normal.
2) Verify whether the platform and data processing function of the Internet of Things are normal through the analysis of the received operation data.
3) Through analysis, the data values of online teaching terminals of the Internet of Things platform are obtained, and compared with the actual output of online teaching terminals of the Internet of Things platform or the simulated value of instruments and meters, to verify whether the data collection function is normal.
4) By setting the time interval of certain timing startup, the observation of equipment operation and data reception is consistent with the set time interval. It can judge whether the response of the online teaching terminal of the Internet of Things is normal.
5) By triggering the associated external triggers, the collection and sending functions of the device are started to check the running state of the device and the condition of the data receiving end.
6) Use serial port to connect with the computer, use the setting software to set the parameters, and verify whether the setting function of the online teaching terminal is normal. At the same time, the setup software is used to read the internal Flash area of the online teaching terminal and check whether the data control function is normal.

Compared with the common online teaching terminals on the Internet of things platform, the power consumption in the non-power control state is reduced from 5 mA to less than 100 A level after optimization. Optimization in two situations: one kind is when the Internet of things online teaching platform terminal peripherals with RTC, RTC power overflow, peripherals to start the iot terminal online teaching platform, hosted network, power control, power control, instructs the peripherals to start the timer values of the next boot, peripherals to close the terminal iot online teaching platform, online teaching terminal in a microampere level of ultra-low power consumption; The other is that when the peripherals of the Internet of Things platform are not equipped with RTC, when the internal RTC power overflow occurs in the online teaching terminal of the Internet of Things platform, the online teaching terminal of the Internet of Things platform is started, the resident network is maintained, other power sources and clocks of the terminals are turned off, and the power consumption is low. Optimize the power control principle of the Internet of Things platform, as shown in Fig. 6:

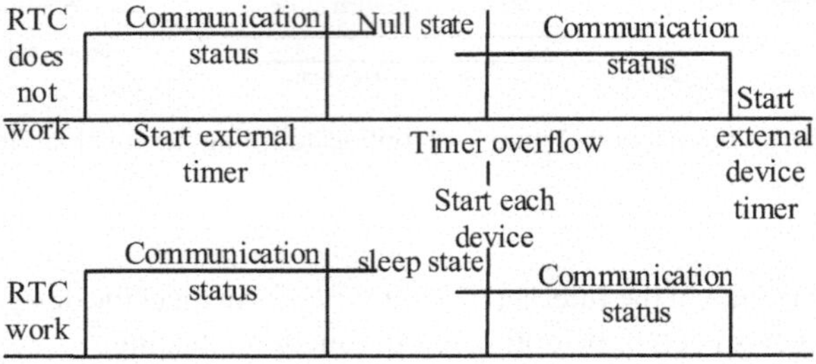


**Fig. 6.** Power consumption control principle of internet of things platform

Iot online teaching platform terminal nodes on the introduction of the Internet of things platform manager, can according to the Internet of things platform of each module in the idle state, in the wake of time and save the power to make a compromise between, to select the most appropriate for each of the Internet of things platform domain sleep sleep depth, significantly save a iot of online teaching platform terminal node power consumption, but at the cost of the Internet of things platform manager itself in the Internet of things platform, therefore, the Internet of things platform manager's power consumption on a piece of very important in the design of low power consumption. The iot platform manager has one core manager and four APB managers. The entire IOT platform manager is located at SMIC 130 nm. The power consumption of 1.08 V and 32 kHz is shown in Table 1.

**Table 1.** Power consumption of online teaching terminal module of Internet of Things platform

| Submodule | Core Power Manager | Single APB power management | Total power |
|---|---|---|---|
| Dynamic power consumption | 0.046 | 0.008 | 0.063 |
| Static power consumption | 0.678 | 0.341 | 1.050 |
| Total power consumption | 0.751 | 0.329 | 2.034 |

This paper briefly introduces the requirements, structure, hardware composition and embedded software structure of the data acquisition telemetry online teaching terminal.

This paper introduces the structure of information acquisition and data processing on the platform of Internet of Things, and analyzes the position and function of the online teaching terminal of data acquisition and telemetry in the platform of Internet of Things. The design idea and overall design principle of the data acquisition telemetry online teaching terminal are described from the perspective of the equipment components, and the design framework is given. The definition of software function module and function division of several tasks are given. To realize the research goal of effectively controlling the power consumption of online teaching terminals on the Internet of Things platform.

## 3 Analysis of Experimental Results

In order to verify the power consumption control method of Internet of things platform online teaching terminal based on IEEE802.11, MATLAB software is used to fit the test data according to logarithmic distance path loss model and improved model. The experimental simulation platform of Internet of things platform is constructed in matlab7.0 environment. The network simulator is used as information transmission simulator, and C++ language is used as network protocol Results: the standardized experimental platform tools are shown in Table 2.

**Table 2.** Experimental tool parameters

| Type | Tool name |
|---|---|
| Development system | Windows 2013 |
| Development platform | ASP.NET + IIS5.0 |
| Data access | Data access class library set (ADO.NET) |
| Using tools | Photoshop, Dreamwever |
| Programming languages | SQL, HTML |
| Database server | SQL Server 2014 |

The log distance path loss model parameters of the scene under different operating frequencies are shown in Table 3, and the modified model parameters are shown in Table 3.

**Table 3.** Improving model parameters

| **Frequency** | Path loss index | Attenuation factor |
|---|---|---|
| Power index | 2405 | 2480 |
| The path loss index | 70.26 | 72.16 |
| Long distance transfer factor | 2153 | 2100 |
| Short distance transmission factor | −9.45 | −8.95 |

In order to better reflect the accuracy of the power control method of the online teaching terminal of the Internet of things platform based on IEEE802.11, this paper compared the traditional control method and added gupl model to verify the three parameter models, and compared the root mean square error (RMSE). If the root mean square error is smaller, the accuracy of the corresponding model will be higher, and the more accurate description of the Internet of things platform will be Wireless transmission channel characteristics. Among them, the measured values are measured in the experimental environment, and the predicted values are predicted in the experimental environment when the predicted values are different models.

$$RMSE = \sqrt{\frac{\sum_{n=1}^{N} |f(n) - f'(n)|^2}{n}} \tag{14}$$

The specific experimental results of the root mean square error of the traditional method and the proposed method are as follows (Fig. 7):

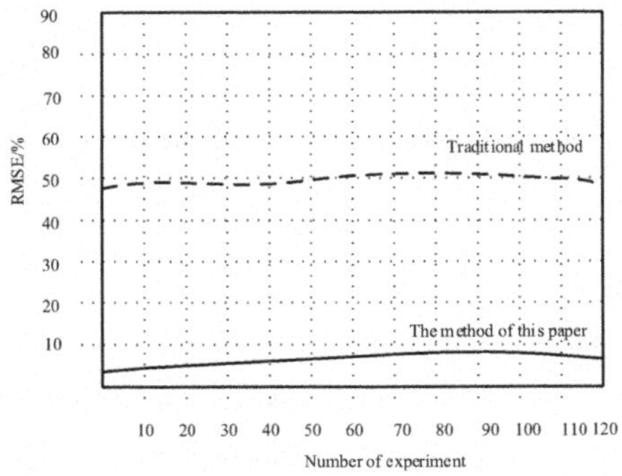


**Fig. 7.** Comparison of experimental detection results

According to the experimental results in the figure above, compared with the traditional method, the proposed online teaching terminal power control method has a lower root mean square error. In 120 experimental iterations, its mean square error has been less than 10%, while the traditional method has a root mean square error of about 50%. The above data show that the proposed method is more applicable.

The measured data are exported, and the mean value is calculated according to the sequence of distance, and the mean value of path loss measurement is plotted. With the help of the improved model, the mean value of the measured data was fitted, and the fitting curve of the improved model was drawn. As shown in the figure. It can be seen from the figure that the improved model can better predict the path loss at three measurement frequencies (Fig. 8).

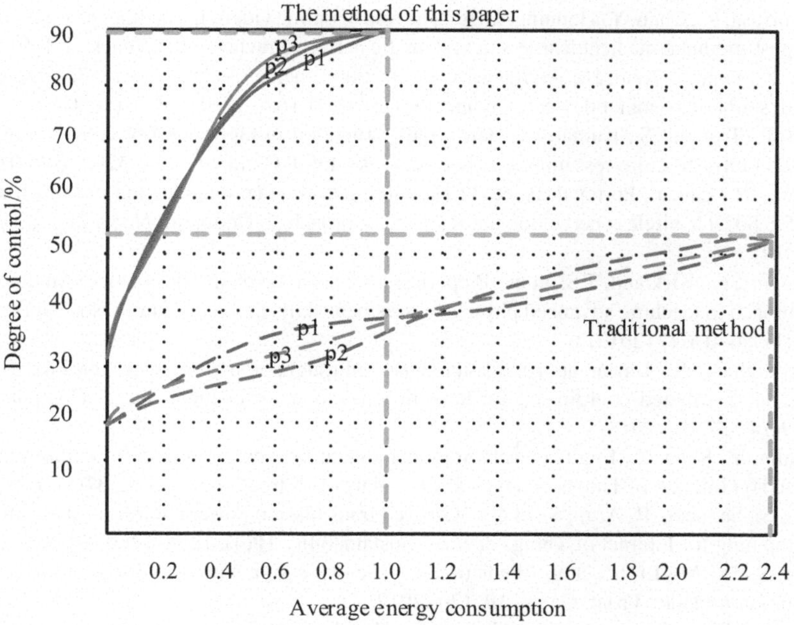


**Fig. 8.** Compare the test results

Based on the above figure, compared with the traditional control methods, the proposed power consumption control method of the Internet of things platform online teaching terminal based on IEEE802.11 in the actual application process, the control accuracy is obviously better than the traditional method, and the power consumption is relatively lower, which fully meets the research requirements.

## 4 Conclusion

In side don't need to modify the network control protocol (TCP) power consumption and terminal side equipment under the premise of online teaching based on Internet of things platform online teaching business application characteristics of the dynamic optimization process and parameters, terminal power consumption control agreement to make the Internet of things platform terminal in the connection state of online teaching have significantly lower power consumption, and decrease the cost of the Internet of things platform online teaching the use of the terminal.

## References

1. Khanouche, M.E., Atmani, N., Cherifi, A.: Improved teaching learning-based QoS-aware services composition for Internet of Things. IEEE Syst. J. **99**, 1–10 (2020)
2. Yan, L.: Design of piano teaching system based on Internet of Things technology. J. Intell. Fuzzy Syst. **37**(5), 5905–5913 (2019)

3. Srinivasa, K., Chen, Y., Henning, M.A.: The role of online videos in teaching procedural skills to post-graduate medical learners: a systematic narrative review. Med. Teach. **6**, 1–9 (2020)
4. Lu, X., Pan, Z., Xian, H.: An integrity verification scheme of cloud storage for internet-of-things mobile terminal devices. Comput. Secur. **92**, 101686.1–101686.8. (2020)
5. Pal, P., Tripathi, S., Kumar, C.: Bandwidth estimation in high mobility scenarios of IEEE 802.11 infrastructure-less mobile ad hoc networks. Int. J. Commun. Syst. **32**(1), e4080 (2019)
6. Costa, R., Lau, J., Portugal, P., et al.: Handling real-time communication in infrastructured IEEE 802.11 wireless networks: the RT-WiFi approach. J. Commun. Netw. **21**(3), 319–334 (2019)
7. Higgins, K., Kirkland, T.S., et al.: Preparing students to be ready for practice: An innovative approach to teaching advanced physical assessment skills online. J. Am. Assoc. Nurse Pract. **31**(11), 640–647 (2019)
8. Abdulghani, S.: Linear approximation model throughput performance analysis of IEEE 802.11 distributed coordinated function in wireless lossy channel. Int. J. Comput. Appl. **179**(14), 37–44 (2018)
9. Linlin, Y., Song, Z.: English teaching model and cultivation of students' speculative ability based on Internet of Things and typical case analysis. J. Intell. Fuzzy Syst. **37**(5), 1–9 (2019)
10. Ali, S., Sandeep, P., Arun, S., et al.: 5G-based transmission power control mechanism in fog computing for Internet of Things devices. Sustainability **10**(4), 1258–1260 (2018)
11. Liu, S., Lu, M., Li, H., et al.: Prediction of gene expression patterns with generalized linear regression model. Front. Genet. **10**, 120 (2019)
12. Fu, W., Liu, S., Srivastava, G.: Optimization of big data scheduling in social networks. Entropy **21**(9), 902 (2019)
13. Liu, S., Bai, W., Zeng, N., et al.: A fast fractal based compression for MRI images. IEEE Access **7**, 62412–62420 (2019)

# Financial Management Course Distance Teaching Method Based on B/S Model

Xi Chen(✉) and Shu-Yang Zhang

SIAS University, Zhengzhou 451150, China

**Abstract.** In view of the low efficiency of traditional teaching methods, this paper puts forward the financial management course distance teaching method based on B/S mode. This paper analyzes the teaching environment and platform of financial management, constructs the remote teaching platform based on B/S mode, designs the financial management platform module from four aspects: financial voucher management, financial account management, financial statement management and user management, and analyzes the specific content of the remote teaching of financial management course in detail from three aspects: preparation before class, classroom analysis and discussion, summary and evaluation and writing report. The test results show that the teaching method is high and has a good teaching effect.

**Keywords:** B/S model · Financial management · Courses · Distance learning

## 1 Introduction

Along with our country joins WTO and the financial system reform gradually thorough, our country enterprise is facing the unprecedented competition pressure [1]. Under such circumstances, enterprises all over the world have made use of various advanced information technologies, especially the computer network technology based on Internet technology, to actively promote the construction of enterprise informationization, so as to realize remote processing, resource information sharing and centralized management, decentralized operation and improve work efficiency, so as to obtain advantages in the fierce competition and make the enterprises grow and develop continuously [2]. At the same time, the traditional business model and management model is not suitable for today's network information age development needs. Enterprise financial management is an important part of enterprise management, and plays an important role in enterprise management [3]. At present, most of the students in vocational schools have poor cultural foundation, no enthusiasm for learning, lack of interest in learning and poor autonomy in learning [4]. Under this background of students, when traditional teaching methods are adopted, class becomes a synonym for "pain". The phenomenon of skipping class occurs from time to time. In class, a common headache for teachers often appears: students are forced to sit in the classroom, sleep, play with mobile phones and talk, plagiarize homework collectively after class, and live for 60 points in the exam [5]. This


W. Fu et al. (Eds.): eLEOT 2021, LNICST 389, pp. 71–85, 2021.
https://doi.org/10.1007/978-3-030-84383-0_7

kind of learning state not only makes teachers distressed, but also makes students miserable, and the enthusiasm of teachers and students is hit. In order to arouse the interest of learning, the B/S model is introduced, the content of financial management course is decomposed into several specific learning tasks, and the distance teaching method of financial management course based on B/S model is proposed to guide students to use the rich resources of the world university town space to explore and study independently and complete the task. In this way, students are no longer "passive learning", but "active learning", teaching becomes easier and more effective, students in the process of completing the task also exercise the practical ability and innovation ability.

## 2 Financial Management Teaching Environment and Platform Construction Content

### 2.1 Financial Management Teaching Environment

Since the reform and opening up, our country's political and economic environment has changed with each passing day. Entering the new century, the socialist economic and political system reform has been deeply promoted, which has a far-reaching impact on the teaching of financial management. To sum up, it is mainly reflected in the following aspects:

First, in terms of enterprise organization, with the deepening of the reform of the state-owned enterprise system, a large number of state-owned enterprises have been restructured into companies and listed companies, and the modern enterprise system has been implemented in most state-owned enterprises. At the same time, due to the strong support of the Party and the government, the quantity and quality of private enterprises have developed rapidly.

Secondly, in the capital market, with the reform of the RMB exchange rate, the RMB has taken a big step in the direction of free convertibility; the institutions and business scope of international financial institutions conducting business in China are becoming larger and larger; the bond market is gradually opening up, and the share-trading reform in the stock market is proceeding smoothly. All of these will make our capital market develop in an efficient, normative and healthy way, and become an important guarantee for the healthy development of enterprise financial management.

Third, in terms of opening up to the outside world, with the deepening of opening-up policies and the strengthening of efforts to attract foreign investment, more and more transnational companies have set up branches or invested in enterprises in our country; and with the development of opening up to the outside world, more and more domestic enterprises go abroad to participate in global economic competition [6].

Fourthly, in terms of fiscal and tax policies, in order to fulfill China's commitment to join the WTO, we have intensified institutional reforms, such as the reform of the customs tax system, enterprise income tax and individual income tax, so as to ensure that each subject enjoys national treatment and fair competition in the market economy.

Fifthly, with regard to education reform, in order to raise the level of education, especially higher education, and train high-quality talents, the State has put forward new requirements for the objectives and tasks of higher education and the quality of education.

In particular, the documents No.4 and No.5 issued by the Ministry of Education in 2004 have exerted great influence on the reform and development of higher education [7].

### 2.2 Content of Financial Management Teaching Platform

This paper studies the enterprise financial data management system, analyzes, designs and realizes the enterprise financial data management system by using the structure technology of data layer, business application layer and data access layer, and tests the main functions of the system. Storing data in SQL database, programming business functions and data management functions, and establishing the software architecture of enterprise financial data management system [8].

According to the functional requirements of the enterprise financial data management system, the financial data management system is divided into several modules: system initialization, system setup, account management, voucher management, financial data management, account book management and financial statement management. The system can manage the financial data of the enterprise in an all-round way, so that the financial data management personnel of the enterprise can grasp the state of the financial data of the enterprise and the operation situation of the data in real time. All of these work are carried out on the Internet, which realizes paperless office, ensures the smooth progress of the financial data management of the enterprise and reduces the pressure of the staff [9]. The design of the system needs to collect and collect the data involved in the financial data management business accurately. The accurate data collection information will improve the system's operability, and make the designed system meet the needs of the manager and the user more, and make the data analysis and management of the financial data management system in a reasonable state.

## 3 Distance Teaching Method of Financial Management Course Based on B/S Mode

### 3.1 Construction of Distance Learning Platform Based on B/S Mode

The distance teaching platform of financial management course based on B/S mode is user-centered. Its service object is students, teachers and managers. The core is to provide personalized service. But the traditional network teaching method's center usually is the resources, the primary goal provides the sharing resources, the user cannot obtain the personalized service [10]. Distance education platform based on B/S model can provide users with learning programs, the platform can save the user's learning programs, so that users can obtain personalized information. Traditional teaching methods seldom record the user's learning log, or do not record directly, so users can not get personalized information. In the courseware, direct on-demand learning content is to play the whole process, without personalized interaction, the platform can not track the user's watching process, can not give instructive teaching suggestions. But based on B/S model, the interaction frequency between user and system is large, users can directly use the system to achieve user interactive transmission, improve user experience has an important impact.

The distance teaching platform of financial management course based on B/S mode is shown in Fig. 1.

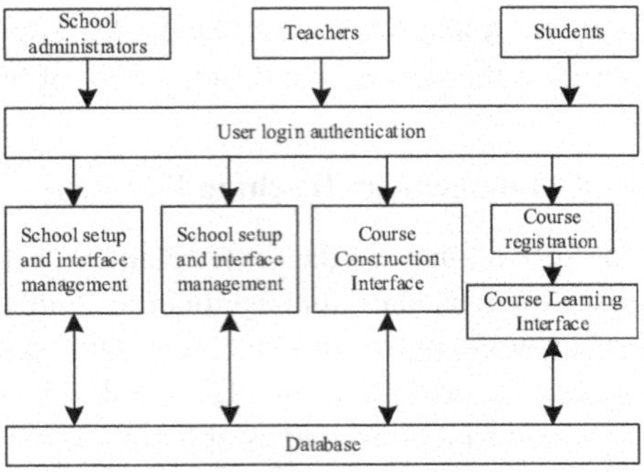


**Fig. 1.** Remote teaching platform of financial management course based on B/S mode

Along with our country joins WTO and the financial system reform gradually thorough, our country enterprise is facing the unprecedented competition pressure. Under such circumstances, enterprises all over the world have made use of various advanced information technologies, especially the computer network technology based on Internet technology, to actively promote the construction of enterprise informationization, so as to realize remote processing, resource information sharing and centralized management, decentralized operation and improve work efficiency, so as to obtain advantages in the fierce competition and make the enterprises grow and develop continuously. At the same time, the traditional business model and management model is not suitable for today's network information age development needs. Enterprise financial management is an important part of enterprise management, and plays an important role in enterprise management. At present, most of the students in vocational schools have poor cultural foundation, no enthusiasm for learning, lack of interest in learning and poor autonomy in learning. In this context, the use of traditional teaching methods, class has become a "pain" synonym, the phenomenon of truancy occurs from time to time, the classroom is often a common headache for teachers: students are forced to sit in the classroom, sleep, play cell phone, talk, homework, collective plagiarism, examination 600,000. This kind of study condition not only lets the teacher distress, also lets the student be miserable, teacher and student's enthusiasm receives the blow. In order to arouse students' interest, B/S model is introduced, and the financial management course is divided into several specific learning tasks to guide students to explore independently and complete the task. In this way, students are no longer "passive learning", but "active learning", teaching will become more relaxed, more effective, students in the process of completing the task also exercise the practical ability and innovation ability.

## 3.2 Financial Management Teaching Environment and Platform Construction Content

### 3.2.1 Financial Management Teaching Environment

Since the reform and opening up, our country's political and economic environment has changed with each passing day. Entering the new century, the socialist economic and political system reform has been deeply promoted, which has a far-reaching impact on the teaching of financial management. To sum up, it is mainly reflected in the following aspects:

First, in terms of enterprise organization, with the deepening of the reform of the state-owned enterprise system, a large number of state-owned enterprises have been restructured into companies and listed companies, and the modern enterprise system has been implemented in most state-owned enterprises. At the same time, due to the strong support of the Party and the government, the quantity and quality of private enterprises have developed rapidly.

Secondly, in the capital market, with the reform of the RMB exchange rate, the RMB has taken a big step in the direction of free convertibility; the institutions and business scope of international financial institutions conducting business in China are becoming larger and larger; the bond market is gradually opening up, and the share-trading reform in the stock market is proceeding smoothly. All of these will make our capital market develop in an efficient, normative and healthy way, and become an important guarantee for the healthy development of enterprise financial management.

Third, in terms of opening up to the outside world, with the deepening of opening-up policies and the strengthening of efforts to attract foreign investment, more and more transnational companies have set up branches or invested in enterprises in our country; and with the development of opening up to the outside world, more and more domestic enterprises go abroad to participate in global economic competition.

Fourthly, in terms of fiscal and tax policies, in order to fulfill China's commitment to join the WTO, we have intensified institutional reforms, such as the reform of the customs tax system, enterprise income tax and individual income tax, so as to ensure that each subject enjoys national treatment and fair competition in the market economy.

Fifthly, with regard to education reform, in order to raise the level of education, especially higher education, and train high-quality talents, the State has put forward new requirements for the objectives and tasks of higher education and the quality of education. In particular, the documents No.4 and No.5 issued by the Ministry of Education in 2004 have exerted great influence on the reform and development of higher education.

### 3.2.2 Content of Financial Management Teaching Platform

This paper studies the enterprise financial data management system, analyzes, designs and realizes the enterprise financial data management system by using the structure technology of data layer, business application layer and data access layer, and tests the main functions of the system. Storing data in SQL database, programming business functions and data management functions, and establishing the software architecture of enterprise financial data management system.

According to the functional requirements of the enterprise financial data management system, the financial data management system is divided into several modules: system initialization, system setup, account management, voucher management, financial data management, account book management and financial statement management. The system can manage the financial data of the enterprise in an all-round way, so that the financial data management personnel of the enterprise can grasp the state of the financial data of the enterprise and the operation situation of the data in real time. All of these work are carried out on the Internet, which realizes paperless office, ensures the smooth progress of the financial data management of the enterprise and reduces the pressure of the staff. The design of the system needs to collect and collect the data involved in the financial data management business accurately. The accurate data collection information will improve the system's operability, and make the designed system meet the needs of the manager and the user more, and make the data analysis and management of the financial data management system in a reasonable state.

### 3.3 Financial Management Platform Module Design

The financial management platform is composed of modules, which are logically divided into three modules: management module, teacher module and student module. Management module for system administrator maintenance and management; The teacher module is used by the system teacher, which is used to assist the teacher to impart knowledge, preside over discussion, examination, and manage the classroom, etc. The student module is used for students to study by themselves, answer questions, take examinations and participate in discussions. The entire logic module is shown in Fig. 2.

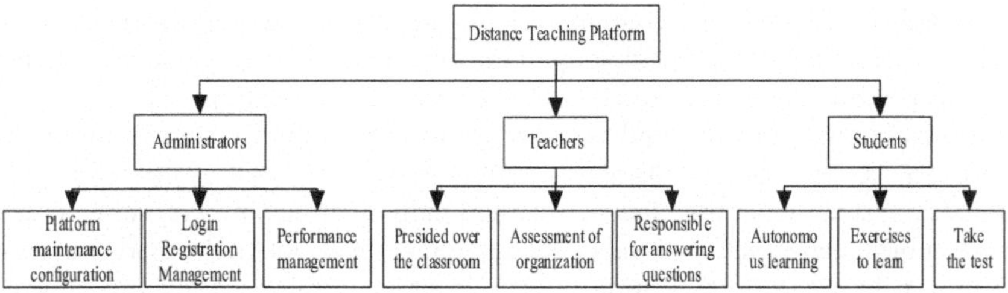


**Fig. 2.** Logic function module diagram of financial management platform

#### 3.3.1 Financial Voucher Management Module

Sequence diagrams can show different business objects, and the design of a sequence diagram can be treated as a requirement file in addition to recording the current events of an organization in order to realize the future delivery requirements of a system. Sequence diagrams in the design of the same organization, the financial management platform of financial voucher data query, financial voucher data design of the main query function, Sequence diagram is to achieve a system requirements. The financial voucher management module is shown in Fig. 3.

Voucher management is an important part of financial information management, which is related to the records of financial flow. Voucher management module is divided into three parts, voucher entry, voucher center and voucher bookkeeping design. The system provides many functions to input the voucher conveniently and efficiently, select the voucher management, click the voucher input, enter the voucher input interface, and enter the voucher input function. After the month is selected, the system automatically determines the input number, voucher word and voucher number, calls the journal entry of the duplicated voucher, and pops up the new interface, where the voucher interface appears and the user saves the confirmation after modification.

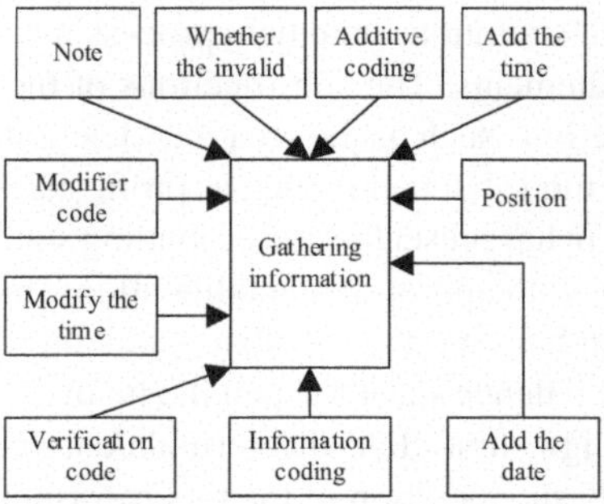


**Fig. 3.** Financial voucher management module

### 3.3.2 Financial Accounts Management Module

The management of financial accounts is divided into two parts, namely, the management of beginning data and the management of ending data. The management of beginning data includes the entry of beginning data of subjects, the entry of beginning data of auxiliary projects and the entry of beginning data of cash flow. The management of ending data includes the interface operation functions of carrying forward profits and losses, closing accounts at the end of a month, carrying forward accounts to the next year and automatic transfer accounts. Financial account management business function, to classify the financial accounts and documents and verify the relevant information. Then, the obsolete financial account information is cleaned up, and the deletion operation sequence of financial account is designed. Design "carry forward profit and loss" wizard interface, choose the end of processing a carry forward profit and loss, transfer processing operation function. You can also manually make vouchers to carry forward profit and loss. Bookkeeping vouchers shall be automatically generated to automatically transfer all the current balances of all profit and loss accounts to the profit account or profit distribution account of the current year, and the carry-over profit and loss function provided by the system shall reflect the total profits or losses realized by the enterprise in an accounting period, transfer the balance of profit and loss adjustment of previous years to the "profit distribution" account, and the balance of all profit and loss accounts shall be transferred to the "profit of the current year" account.

### 3.3.3 Financial Statement Management Module

The client of the system will receive the information of the financial statements sent by the financial management platform, and the sequence of receiving the information of the statements. The management module of the client of the system will receive the information of the statements sent by the financial management platform in the network, and the management module of the client of the system will start to receive the data of the statements, and display the information of the financial statements received on the interface of the client of the system. Completed the system client to receive financial statements information operation design.

The management of financial statements is the core of the financial data management system. The design of the management of financial statements is divided into several modules such as file operation, statement processing, statement formula and the preparation of common statements. The sub-functions of the management of financial statements include the functions such as the creation, deletion and editing of statements and the preparation of common statements such as profit statements and balance sheets.

The balance sheet system has preset the corresponding statements such as the balance sheet, and can be used only with appropriate modifications. In the menu bar, click Open in the file or click the Open button on the toolbar. Click on the balance sheet and click OK, or double-click on the balance sheet to open the financial statements. Double-click the cell to modify the design, first click the formula/data conversion button into the formula state, modify the basic operation of the report formula.

### 3.3.4 User Management

In the administrator pipeline function module, its function is to submit the instructions issued by the system, for users to manage, this part includes the Web site to publish the latest information, teachers and students use the system to use accounts, top, delete posts and other permissions. The main functions of administrators are as follows:

Administrator space → access system → input user name, password → match → system announcement user management, educational management, forum management → exit system; Administrator space → access system → input user name, password → end of the mismatch.

User management module is used for the current user consent management, which can modify and update the information. The user management object is transferred to the add user interface after logging in, then submits the user information to the user list, and returns the information successfully. As shown in Fig. 4.

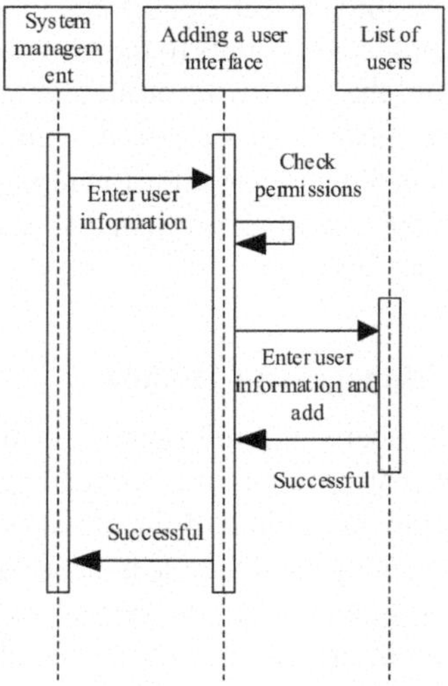


**Fig. 4.** Order of adding users

After the administrator opens the new interface, enter the user number, name and address information, confirmed to be correct, submit to save, and display the saved user list in the interface.

## 3.4 Contents of Distance Teaching of Financial Management

The distance teaching platform based on B/S model is designed to model the real situation and form a case for students to think, analyze and make a decision.

### 3.4.1 Preparation Before Class is the Premise of Case Teaching

To carry out case teaching, first of all, we should carefully prepare before class. Preparation before class mainly carries on the case the choice, the revision and the design. In the process of case selection, we should consider the situation of students' knowledge storage, and choose appropriate cases according to the teaching objectives of financial management course. If necessary, the original cases shall be modified and adjusted, and the relevant cases of newspapers, periodicals and books may be rewritten, or the cases may be rewritten according to the actual economic business in the process of enterprise investigation. Also should carry on the case the design, the design level case question, guides the student to ponder positively. In order to familiarize students with the case, for more complex cases, the case materials and discussion outlines should be distributed in advance to prepare for class discussion and analysis.

### 3.4.2 Classroom Analysis and Discussion as the Main Link of Case Teaching

Case teaching in the classroom teaching process, teachers should change the teaching concept, so that students become the main body of teaching, teachers play a supporting and guiding role. Specifically, including the following aspects: First, the introduction of the case, through text, video, audio, multimedia, teacher narrative, role playing and other forms of the case into the financial management teaching of each link. Second, case analysis, can be taken to guide the analysis and thematic analysis, the analysis process should be clear about the sequence of events and the thread of the problem, combined with financial management curriculum project analysis. Third, the case discussion, the case discussion is the case teaching most main link, in the discussion process the teacher must play the guiding role. According to the details of the case materials provided by the teacher, the case discussion can be divided into three forms: discussion, debate, discussion, discussion is the most commonly used way. Students can be grouped into small groups, or group thinking of the whole class discussion, but also according to the students generally respond to the difficulties of the thematic discussion. In the process of analysis and discussion, it is helpful for students to improve their abilities of language organization, expression and adaptability.

### 3.4.3 Summary and Evaluation and Writing Reports Are the Final Goal of Case Teaching

After the case discussion, the teacher should summarize and evaluate the whole discussion process. The contents of summary and evaluation include whether the students' analysis ideas are correct, whether the analysis methods are appropriate, and whether the conclusions are feasible. It is important to note that case teaching does not provide standard answers, but rather gives students room to think about how to analyze and deal with problems in a given situation. Teachers can also assign students to write case analysis reports, case report writing can improve the ability of students to express in words, lay the foundation for writing papers later.

## 4 Testing

In order to verify the rationality of the distance teaching method of financial management course based on B/S model, the experiment test analysis is carried out.

### 4.1 Experimental Platform

Considering the function of the experiment platform, the teacher is used as the LAN, the students can choose the courses by themselves. The experiment platform is shown in Fig. 5.

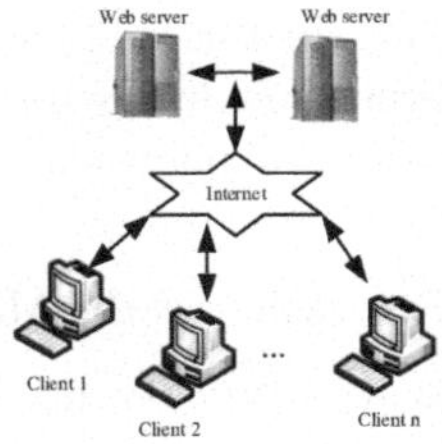


**Fig. 5.** Experimental platform

The experimental navigation table is shown in Table 1.

**Table 1.** Experimental navigation table

| Name | Remarks |
|---|---|
| Home page | Return |
| Personal data | Personal center |
| Courseware upload center | Courseware upload |
| Learning center | Download learning materials |
| Video course | Participation in teaching video |
| Press release | Press release |
| Manage users | Management of teachers and students |
| Answering question | Enter the system |

## 4.2 Experimental Results and Analysis

The experimental test is mainly a black box test, and the black box test is mainly for the corresponding operation of the research methods and traditional teaching methods. The application black box test content is shown in Table 2.

**Table 2.** Black box test content

| Serial number | Test content |
|---|---|
| 1 | Registration module test |
| 2 | Export student registration information |
| 3 | Using the system without login |
| 4 | The maximum length of the course is 30 min |

The black box test contents are as follows:

50 students were selected for the test, with 45 correct information and 5 wrong information.

(1) The wrong information appeared is the wrong ID number.
(2) Using JavaScript functions, submit the form for judgment.

After the actual user requirements, the test results of the two systems are shown in Table 3.

According to the test results in Table 3, most of the test results of traditional teaching methods failed, and the application of the methods was not stable. The test results of the design based on B/S research method are all passed, and the application of the method is relatively stable, meeting the teaching needs of students and teachers, and reaching the expected goal.

In order to further verify the high efficiency of teaching based on B / S mode, it is necessary to compare and analyze the teaching efficiency of traditional teaching method and this method, and the comparison results are shown in Fig. 6.

**Table 3.** Test results of two methods

| Serial number | Function point | Traditional teaching methods | Research methods |
|---|---|---|---|
| 1 | Page setup | Failed | Adopt |
| 2 | Students add message information | Adopt | Adopt |
| 3 | Students sign up online | Failed | Adopt |
| 4 | Student learning survey | Failed | Adopt |
| 5 | Browse the course video | Failed | Adopt |
| 6 | Browse online help | Failed | Adopt |
| 7 | System background settings | Adopt | Adopt |
| 8 | Manage message information | Failed | Adopt |
| 9 | Manage registration information | Adopt | Adopt |
| 10 | Management of teaching evaluation information | Failed | Adopt |

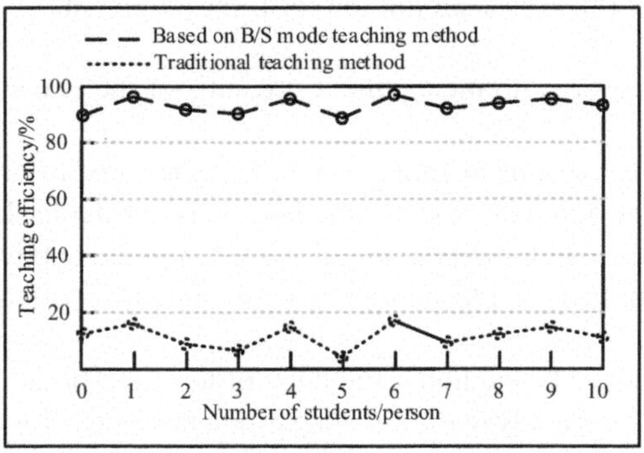


**Fig. 6.** Comparative analysis of teaching efficiency of different methods

As can be seen from Fig. 6, the teaching efficiency using traditional teaching methods is the highest at 18% and the lowest at 5%. The teaching efficiency based on B/S mode is 99% at the highest and 89% at the lowest. Compared with traditional teaching methods, the proposed teaching method based on B/S model has higher teaching efficiency and higher value and significance in practical application.

### 4.3 Suggestions for Optimizing Teaching Methods

According to the teaching task of financial management in the new era, combined with the problems existing in the current financial management teaching, the optimization of financial management teaching methods can be started from the following aspects:

First, strengthen the combination of theory and practice, optimize the link of practice education. From the education of modern financial management, there are more or less problems in the practice education of financial management in colleges and universities. Mainly in: First, the lack of a stable practice base, student practice in the status of continuous transfer. This is not conducive to summing up the experience of practice education, but also conducive to the establishment of good links with the employer to improve the effectiveness of practice education. Secondly, the employers are in the motive of protecting trade secrets, so it is difficult for the students to have a real understanding of the practice of financial management. Third, the lack of strict control system of the practice link. Many schools lack the grading standard of practice link, practice content, practice progress, instructor's guidance method and system, which make the practice link teaching in a loose state. To this end, schools may make improvements from the following aspects: on the one hand, they may establish financial supervision internship bases to maintain long-term good cooperation with employers; on the other hand, they may establish and improve the education system for the internship stage, including the control measures for the requirements of instructors, internship contents, internship progress and other aspects; and, on the other hand, they may establish financial management scenario simulation laboratories to enable students to personally understand the working process and basic working methods of financial management.

Second, change the "cramming" education, cultivate students' ability to learn independently. At present, in the teaching of financial management, teachers pay too much attention to the imparting of book knowledge, but often neglect the cultivation of students' innovation and learning ability. In order to change this situation, teachers should make full use of the advantages of information resources, encourage students to study independently and innovate learning fields and methods. For example, after the students have mastered the method of collecting network resources, they can be guided to collect the data of capital structure and dividend payment of some international large enterprises as the basis of analysis; they can also understand the specific management methods of capital structure and dividend policy of western enterprises, and analyze the differences among them with the combination of theoretical knowledge. In this way, students not only master the knowledge of books, but also cultivate the ability of independent learning, which has a better foundation for future work and adapt to the new environment.

Third, the use of case teaching, training students the ability to integrate theory with practice. Case teaching is an enlightening, practical teaching method that can improve students' comprehensive analysis ability and creativity. It can also increase students' interest in learning and improve learning effect. In case teaching, the teacher should make careful preparation, be familiar with the details and background knowledge of the case, effectively control the process of case discussion, pay attention to enlightening students, be good at summing up students' creativity, and be able to combine the background knowledge of the case with the book knowledge to summarize, so as to enable students to deepen the understanding of theoretical knowledge and achieve active learning.

Fourth, bilingual teaching should be adopted to cultivate students' ability to learn advanced western theories. In the teaching of financial management, it is very important to cultivate students' ability to read foreign documents and classical teaching materials, which is an important channel for students to learn advanced financial management theory and method. Therefore, the qualified colleges and universities should promptly carry out bilingual teaching. To improve students' ability to learn advanced western financial management theory. In bilingual teaching, attention shall be paid to the selection of teaching materials (classical teaching materials and the latest teaching materials), the training of teachers and the combination of bilingual teaching and financial management in China.

Fifth, pay attention to the use of situational teaching, simulation experiments and other teaching methods to improve students' understanding of capital market operation, financial decision-making process. In financial management, such as the operation of capital market, financial decision-making process is very complex, if the traditional classroom teaching, it is difficult for students to immediately understand, more difficult to form an effective memory. Therefore, if we can set up a simulation lab of stock exchange or financial decision, let the students operate according to the operation order of capital market or the financial decision order, we can really experience the process, deepen the understanding and understanding.

## 5 Concluding Remarks

The enterprise financial data management platform will connect with the department network information center, and communicate with all units within the enterprise. Financial data management system will provide the necessary technical means for the financial data management, information disclosure and management of enterprises. Enterprise financial data management platform, the maximum realization of enterprise financial demand data management specialization, centralization and large- scale, can quickly apply network data to the actual financial information services to play a role. The design and research of enterprise financial data management platform and the digitization and networking of financial data management will improve the efficiency of enterprise financial management, and have some practical value. For future work, we can strengthen the combination of theory and practice; Change the "cramming" education, cultivate students' ability of independent learning; Using case teaching, training students' ability to connect theory with practice and other aspects of a more in-depth study.

## References

1. Mauer, M.A.D., Sring, D., Stanczus, B., et al.: A 2-year follow-up MRI study for the evaluation of an age estimation method based on knee bone development. Int. J. Legal Med. **133**(1), 205–215 (2019)
2. Wang, C., Yang, X., Gu, B., et al.: Sensitive and simultaneous detection of SARS-CoV-2-specific IgM/IgG using lateral flow immunoassay based on dual-mode quantum dot nanobeads. Anal. Chem. **92**(23), 15542–15549 (2020)
3. Roberts, R., Campillo, A., Schmitt, M.: Prediction and management of CAD risk based on genetic stratification. Trends Cardiovasc. Med. **30**(6), 328–334 (2020)

4. Fouladi, E., Baghaee, H.R., Bagheri, M., et al.: Power management of microgrids including PHEVs based on maximum employment of renewable energy resources. IEEE Trans. Ind. Appl. **12**(99), 1–10 (2020)
5. Wang, B., Fang, G., Liang, J., et al.: Efficient multiscale analysis method for the compressive progressive damage of 3D braided composites based on FFT. Acta Mech. **231**(15), 1–15 (2020)
6. Muthukumar, N., Srinivasan, S., Subathra, B., et al.: Teaching industrial Internet-of-Things-based model-predictive controller. IEEE Trans. Educ. **6**(99), 1–9 (2020)
7. Kanoun, A.A., Kanoun, M.B., Merad, A.E., et al.: Toward development of high-performance perovskite solar cells based on CH3NH3GeI3 using computational approach. Sol. Energy **182**(4), 237–244 (2019)
8. Liu, S., Bai, W., Zeng, N., et al.: A fast fractal based compression for MRI images. IEEE Access **7**, 62412–62420 (2019)
9. Breen, C., Zhu, T., Bond, R., et al.: The evaluation of an open source online training system for teaching 12 lead electrocardiographic interpretation. J. Electrocardiol. **2**(3), 454–461 (2016)
10. Jianqiu, L.: Construction of real-time interactive mode-based online course live broadcast teaching platform for physical training. Int. J. Emerg. Technol. Learn. **13**(06), 73–80 (2018)

# Research on Online Teaching Method of Equation Solving Based on Transfer Learning

Li An(✉) and Yan Wang

Rizhao Polytechnic, Rizhao 276800, China

**Abstract.** In order to improve the online teaching effect of equation solving, an online teaching method of equation solving based on transfer learning is designed. First of all, integrate the online teaching resources in the Internet, then the data conversion and classification processing, and finally build the learner behavior and knowledge resources relationship model, to recommend the relevant teaching content to learners, so as to achieve online teaching. The experimental results show that the online teaching method of equation solving based on transfer learning has high accuracy, short classification time and high student performance. It is proved that the online teaching method in this study can effectively improve the online teaching effect.

**Keywords:** Transfer learning · Online teaching · Data flow classification · Knowledge resource modeling

## 1 Introduction

With the advent of the information age, how to make better use of computer technology to assist classroom teaching has become a hot issue in the teaching reform of various courses. Equation solving is a basic course of Mathematics for information and computing science, which plays an important role in the whole professional system [1]. Because of the combination of theory and practice, through the teaching of this course, students can not only learn professional theoretical knowledge, but also improve their ability to solve practical problems by using mathematical knowledge, and cultivate their insight, creativity and imagination. Therefore, in order to improve the efficiency of classroom teaching, the design of the online teaching method of equation solving has become a hot issue in the teaching reform of constant equation [2].

In the face of the great challenges in the era of big data, the core technologies of intelligent fields such as data mining and machine learning have been widely concerned and developed rapidly. Therefore, the online teaching method of equation solving can be improved by using machine learning. However, the limitations of traditional machine learning methods begin to show. Among them, the most important problems include: the source of training and test data is inconsistent; the distribution of training data and test data is different; the training task and test task change [3]. Traditional machine learning can achieve good results. The main premise is to avoid the emergence of the


W. Fu et al. (Eds.): eLEOT 2021, LNICST 389, pp. 86–98, 2021.
https://doi.org/10.1007/978-3-030-84383-0_8

above three situations, but in practical application, this premise is difficult to meet. In order to effectively solve a series of problems faced by traditional machine learning, transfer learning came into being. The core technology of transfer learning is to build bridges between different fields, so as to realize the cross domain transfer of knowledge and skills. Based on the idea of transfer learning, an online teaching method of equation solving based on transfer learning is designed. On the basis of data integration of teaching resources, the data in the original data table are standardized and classified according to the purification rules. By constructing the association model between learners' behavior and network resources, transfer learning is used to provide relevant teaching resources to learners. So as to realize the online teaching of equation solving.

## 2 Integration of Online Teaching Resources

With the increasing popularity of the Internet, the Internet can be closely linked with the teaching and learning activities of the Internet, including the increasing relationship with the Internet and the use of Internet technology. Equation solving course can make use of network resources for teaching, make classroom teaching more in line with the requirements of the times, and improve the quality of online teaching. The use of modern education means and internet teaching can broaden the channels of students' learning knowledge, expand the space–time scope of traditional teaching, and effectively solve the innovation of teaching methods. The Internet effectively strengthens the effect of network teaching, makes students easily understand and master knowledge, guides students from passively accepting knowledge to actively exploring knowledge, and effectively improves the learning effect.

Firstly, the mobile learning method is used to allocate the database resources in the network, and the parameters in the database are graded under the support of the mobile learning architecture. The following is the specific calculation process.

step1: According to the average number of database requests per second, it can be divided into three types: large, medium and small;
step2: Mobile learning is used to manage and schedule a large number of network connected computing resources [4]. According to the key factors affecting the consumption of database load resources, the request complexity is calculated.

$$\mathrm{Km} = \frac{\mathrm{p} \to \mathrm{o}}{\sum_{\mathrm{m}} \mathrm{j} \times \mathrm{m}} \tag{1}$$

In formula (1), $\mathrm{p} \to \mathrm{o}$ represents that p and o request a teaching resource at the same time, j represents the database request complexity, m represents the consumed database resources, and Km represents the request complexity level.

- step3: Check the corresponding time of the database, and view the time required from the submission of the request to the completion of the execution and return to the client;

- step4: The number of database connections, which represents the maximum number of connections established when a user makes a request.

According to the type of physical resources to be allocated. According to the amount of user access resources and the amount of resources available in the database, select the server to allocate resources [5]. Suppose there are m system databases on server i in the ideological and political resources, The number of connections available to the k system database is $SDGH_j(j \in 1, m)$, The database schema that can be assigned to users is $AADG_j(j \in 1, m)$, There is a q system mode in the j system database, Then the data assigned to users in the n database is expressed as $ASA^j_{qm}(n \in 1, q)$; The problem to be solved is to select which server to allocate database resources for users according to the amount of database resources required by users and the available resources of servers. When the database object to be allocated is a database schema [4], formula (2) is used to represent the number of modes that can be allocated to the database.

$$S = \sum_{k=1}^{i} ak \times V \tag{2}$$

In formula (2), S is the system database traffic, a is the number of connections accessed by users, and V is the database object to be allocated.

According to the above process, the data integration of online equation solving teaching resources is completed.

## 3 Data Stream Classification of Online Teaching Resources Based on Equation Solving

Because the data formats excavated are different, the data in the database needs to be converted to extensible markup language (eXtensible Markup Language, XML) documents, while the received XML documents are converted to the data in the database for data exchange between virtual data centers and heterogeneous databases. When the database corresponds to different application systems, the corresponding data representation methods should be different. Therefore, in the face of heterogeneous data from different data sources, we must transform the corresponding data format. XML, a heterogeneous data exchange model based on XML, can not only describe irregular data, but also include data from multiple applications in the same XML file, so as to integrate different source data. In terms of the field name and specification type of the attribute value, the data in the virtual data table is different from that in the original data table. Therefore, the data in the original data table should be normalized according to the purification rules, as shown in Fig. 1.

After the process data transformation in Fig. 1, the resources are obtained according to the user's needs, and the resources in the library database are integrated on the unified platform. Local accuracy is often used in dynamic classification selection methods. This method assumes that the classification accuracy of each base classifier is different around the samples to be classified, so the base classifier with the highest local accuracy

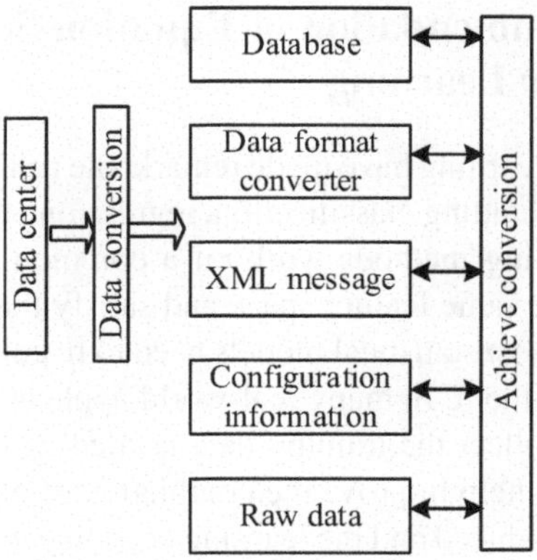


**Fig. 1.** Data conversion process

is selected, and the output of the classifier is taken as the output of the whole classifier combination system. At present, local precision can be divided into category independent and category dependent methods. The index proposed in this paper is based on the category independent method and its definition is shown in formula (3).

$$L = \sum_{i=1}^{k} \frac{I(f_j \times \text{pritect}(x_i) = y_i)}{e} \tag{3}$$

In formula (3), $x_i$ is the feature of the classified sample, k is the number of samples in its field, and $f_j$ is the feature and real class of the i th sample in the field.

On this basis, the distance between the sample and the classification sample is analyzed, and the Euclidean distance is used for processing. The processing formula (4) is.

$$I(x) = \begin{cases} 1x = \mathit{true} \\ 0x = \mathit{false} \end{cases} \tag{4}$$

In formula (4), I(x) is the indicator function.

On this basis, the classifier is selected and updated.

$$f : y = \text{sign}\left(\alpha_1 \prod\left(w_s^T x_t\right) + \alpha_{3t} \prod\left(w_s^T x_t\right) - \frac{1}{2}\right) \tag{5}$$

In formula (5), $\alpha_1$ and $\alpha_{3t}$ are the weights of the source domain classifier and the target domain classifier, respectively,f stands for weighted combined component class, $x_t$ represents the new sample, $w_s^T$ represents the weight vector of the classifier with the highest local classification accuracy selected from the classifier set, and $\prod$ is a compression function.

Based on the above process, the teaching content of equation solving is discretized and reorganized, and all contents are grouped according to the degree of difficulty or content relevance.

# 4 Knowledge Recommendation of Equation Solving Learning Based on Transfer Learning

Data mining and machine learning have made remarkable achievements in many knowledge engineering fields, including classification, regression, clustering and so on. However, many machine learning methods work on a common assumption: training and testing data come from the same feature space and satisfy the same distribution. When the distribution changes, most statistical models need to re collect training data from the beginning and reconstruct them. In many real-world applications, the cost is expensive or it is impossible to re collect the training data needed. If the processed data can be used in other task fields to help improve the completion of other tasks, the cost of data collection will be greatly reduced and the learning accuracy will be improved [6]. In this case, knowledge transfer between domains will play a significant role. The differences and connections between transfer learning and traditional machine learning are shown in Fig. 2.

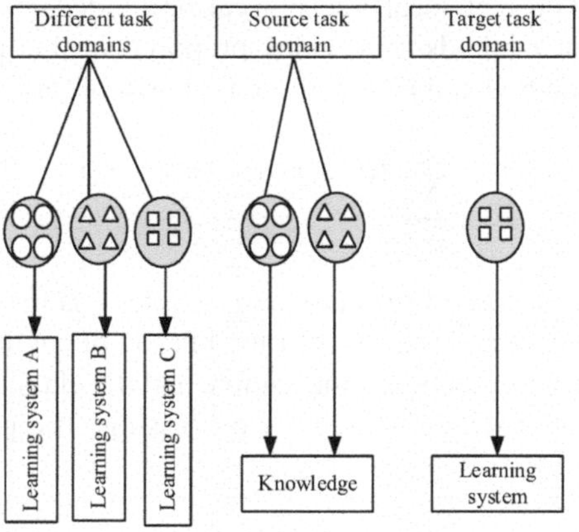


**Fig. 2.** Transfer learning

With the knowledge knowlege of the Internet, there are many resources such as topics, videos and handouts. Knowledge resources belong to a number of different feature domains, the better recommendation effect will be obtained by dividing the knowledge resources into domains and then recommending knowledge according to the fields [7]. However, learners' learning behavior patterns in one domain can also be applied to other similar domains to a great extent. And because human learning behavior itself has the ability to "transfer" and "draw inferences from one instance". It is also very important to use the transfer learning method to use its learning characteristics in one field to help learn knowledge in other fields.

## 4.1 Internet Knowledge Resource Modeling

Based on the above analysis, in order to solve the problem of disorderly and uneven quality of knowledge resources in the field of knowledge learning, and to prepare for the next step of knowledge recommendation, the first problem to be solved is the construction of learner model, knowledge resource model and the model of relationship between learners and knowledge resources.

1) Feature selection of learners and knowledge resources: by analyzing the basic information filled in by learners and the learning records of learners, the characteristics used to construct the learner model and knowledge resource model are selected. The characteristics of this part include two aspects. One is the explicit characteristics such as learning time and homework completion On the other hand, it is difficult to get the level of the current learners directly from the hidden characteristics of learners [8–10].
2) Quantifying the selected features, constructing learner model and knowledge resource model: after completing the feature selection of learners and knowledge resources, it is necessary to quantify the selected features, because the influence of each feature on learners' learning behavior is different. It is necessary to establish a model by using features, and use the model to represent the learning behavior pattern and knowledge resources of learners.
3) The construction of the relationship model between learners and knowledge resources: learners and knowledge resources are closely related. After the construction of the learner model and knowledge resource model, the relationship model between learners and knowledge resources is constructed, which can be the evaluation matrix of learners on knowledge resources. The bipartite graph model for learners to learn knowledge resources can also be a more complex Bayesian belief network model. The construction of the relationship model between learners and knowledge resources plays an important role in the following knowledge recommendation methods.

At present, in the Internet learning environment, learners and the organization of knowledge resources are chaotic. Only through these data, we can not determine the learners' preferences, the current level of learning and learning behavior patterns. Therefore, before knowledge recommendation, it is necessary to preprocess the learners' past learning records and knowledge resources [11].The process of constructing the relationship model between learners and knowledge resources is shown in Fig. 3.

The construction of learner model: Learners' learning preference, learning behavior often with certain characteristics. Before knowledge recommendation, it is necessary to model learners. The feature vector of learners mainly includes four aspects: Learners' basic information, learners' learning preferences in various fields, learners' learning feature sets in specific learning fields and learners' current learning level sets in various fields. These four aspects and their construction methods are described in detail below.

(1) The basic information about learners includes the learners' age, gender, hobbies, major and current educational background, and more basic information can be covered according to actual needs. Learners' basic information generally reflects learners' learning level and learning tendency at the present stage. This part of information is often obtained by the way of active filling in by learners, and learners may default the part of information, so it should only play an auxiliary role in the process of knowledge recommendation.

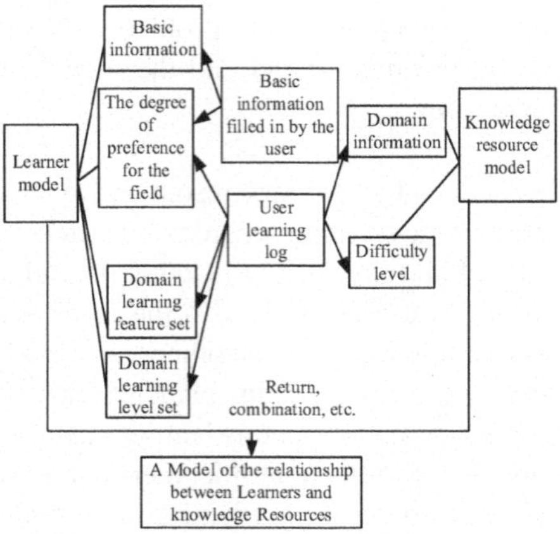


**Fig. 3.** The relationship model between learner behavior and knowledge resources

(2) At present, the knowledge in the Internet learning environment includes the knowledge of various fields and disciplines. However, the degree of learners' learning preference in different fields is quite different, which is closely related to the feature selection of knowledge resources. This part of information can be provided by learners, and more importantly, it can be obtained by analyzing learners' past learning records and quantifying them.

(3) Learners in various learning areas of learning characteristics set [12], learners will invest a lot of time and energy in their preferred learning field, the learning characteristics of learners in this field is particularly important. On the one hand, it can provide some more easily acquired features, such as learning time, visiting times, learning feedback and so on. In addition, there are many hidden features that can not be directly obtained, so the unsupervised learning method in feature selection field can be used for feature selection. Since learners may be interested in multiple learning fields, learners' learning characteristics in specific learning areas will form a set to represent the learning characteristics of learners in various fields.

(4) The collection of learners' learning level in various fields at the present stage is mainly obtained through the level of knowledge resources learned by learners and learning feedback. Define the function $h(x) \rightarrow R$.(R) as an ordered set, such as a nonnegative integer, or a range of real numbers) for two learners. If $h(x_i) \geq h(x_j)$ indicates that $x_i$'s current level of learning in a given field is higher than that of $x_j$. If the learners have learned the knowledge resources at a high level in a certain field, and give positive learning feedback, it can be considered that the learners' learning level in this field is high at the present stage. Learners' learning level in various fields is changing with their learning situation.

The construction of knowledge resource model: the characteristics of knowledge resources are closely related to learners' knowledge learning process. Learners are very interested in a certain field, so the possibility of learning knowledge resources related to this field is much higher than that of other fields. Therefore, the corresponding characteristics of knowledge resources will be combined in the process of knowledge recommendation. Therefore, the feature selection of knowledge resources is equally important. The characteristics of knowledge resources mainly include two aspects: domain information and difficulty. The following two aspects and their construction methods are described in detail.

(1) Domain information, domain information is the basic information of knowledge resources, including the subject field, subject direction, number of learners, learning duration and so on. The domain information of knowledge resources can be selected by manually marking a part of knowledge resources [13]. Automatic classification is performed by supervised learning domain classification methods such as linear classification, vector space model, word structure representation and semantic based representation.
(2) The degree of difficulty and the difficulty of knowledge resources are closely related to whether they are suitable to be recommended to a learner [14]. It is necessary to combine the level of learners and the difficulty of knowledge resources for knowledge recommendation to achieve good results. In this paper, we define a function $g(x) \rightarrow R.(R)$ as an ordered set. If $g(x_i) \geq g(x_j)$, the difficulty level of $x_i$ is not lower. On the one hand, the definition of this function is related to the number of learners and learning time of knowledge resources, and also related to the learning order and learning feedback of learners.

## 4.2 The Construction of the Relationship Model between Learners and Knowledge Resources

The model of the relationship between learners and knowledge resources is an important model to reflect learners' learning behavior patterns [5]. Through the construction of the relationship model between learners and knowledge resources, we can get the learning interest of learners and the current learning situation of learners. Reasonable relational model will greatly simplify the difficulty of knowledge recommendation in the next stage [15]. There are two main models of the relationship between learners and knowledge resources.

(1) Evaluation matrix model, evaluation matrix model is to synthesize the characteristic information of learners. The evaluation matrix R and $R_{u,j}$ obtained from the characteristic information of knowledge resources indicate the comprehensive evaluation of knowledge resources i by learners u. the higher the evaluation value, the more suitable for learning.
(2) The bipartite graph model uses the form of bipartite graph to represent the relationship between learners and knowledge resources [16]. U is the learner set, I is the set of knowledge resources. If learner u has learned knowledge resource i, there is an edge $E_{ui}$ between u and i.

### 4.3 Learning Knowledge Recommendation

The knowledge recommendation of collaborative filtering is based on the common learning behavior of other learners similar to learners [17–19]. The expression (6) is as follows:

$$\mathrm{sim}(x, y) = \frac{\sum_{s \in S_{xy}} \left(r_{x,s} - \bar{r}_y\right)\left(r_{y,s} - \bar{r}_y\right)}{\sqrt{\sum_{s \in S_y} \left(r_{x,s} - \bar{r}_x\right)} \sqrt{\sum_{s \in S_{yj}} \left(r_{y,s} - \bar{r}_y\right)^2}} \tag{6}$$

In formula (6), $S_{xy}$ represents the knowledge resources that learner x and learner y have learned together.

In general, the feature space of learners is large in the knowledge recommendation problem. In order to make the algorithm run more effectively, formula (7) is used to deal with the similarity calculation between learners.

$$u(c, s) = \alpha \bar{r}_c + \beta \frac{\sum_{x \in c_y} \mathrm{sim}(u, x) \times \left(r_{x,s} - \bar{r}_x\right)}{\sum_{x \in c_N} \mathrm{sim}(u, x)} \tag{7}$$

In formula (7), $\alpha$ and $\beta$ are adjustable parameters, s represents knowledge resources and c represents learners. Based on the streaming of teaching resource data and the construction of the relationship model between learners and knowledge resources based on transfer learning, the online teaching of equation solving is improved.

## 5 Experimental Comparison

In order to verify the effectiveness of the online teaching method of equation solving based on transfer learning, the experimental comparison is carried out. In order to ensure the preciseness of the experiment, the traditional online teaching method (reference [3] method) is compared with the teaching method of this study. In this paper, the experiment is carried out on the dataset, which is the real mathematics test scores of a school for many times in succession, including 1340 students, 92 test questions, 28 knowledge points and 291 scoring data. Online learning behavior data: login time, browsing teaching resources, forum data, online notes, homework completion and online test results. 80% of the data set is used as training data set, and 20% of the data set is divided into target training data set and test data set. In the experiment, we select the accuracy of knowledge splitting, classification time and test scores as indicators to compare the online learning effect of the traditional method and this method.

### 5.1 Accuracy Comparison of Learning Knowledge Classification

In this process, five kinds of teaching resources (text resources, image resources, audio resources, video resources, integrated resources) are classified, and the classification accuracy is shown in Fig. 4.

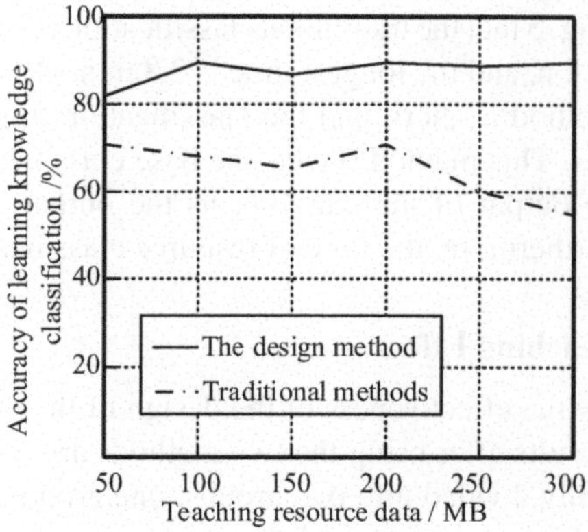


**Fig. 4.** Comparison of learning knowledge classification accuracy

It can be seen from Fig. 4 that in the experiments with different amounts of data, the classification accuracy of the online teaching method of equation solving based on transfer learning is 80% in dividing five types of teaching resources, which is less affected by the number of classification events. However, the accuracy of traditional learning knowledge classification is poor. With the increase of classification data, the classification accuracy generally shows a downward trend, and the classification accuracy rate is lower than 73%. Because this method normalizes the data in the original data table before classification, so it improves the classification accuracy of the method.

## 5.2 Comparison of Classification Time

The online teaching method based on transfer learning and the traditional online teaching method are respectively used to classify the data. Data is divided into six types: text resource (1321 data), image resource (529 data), audio resource (762 data), video resource (566 data) and integrated resource (872 data). The comparison results are shown in Fig. 5.

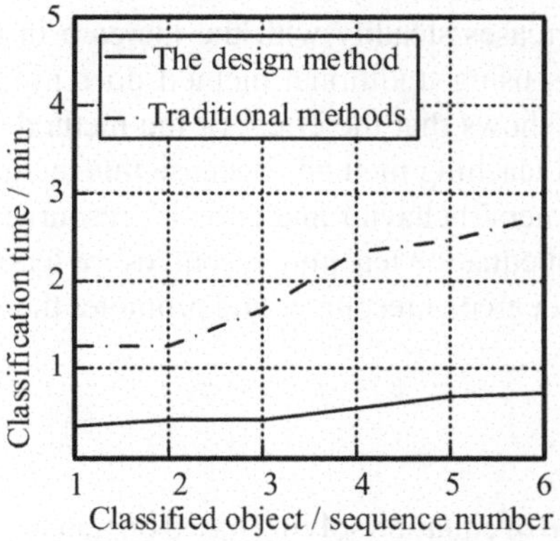


**Fig. 5.** Comparison of classification time

It can be seen from Fig. 5 that the traditional classification method takes a long time to classify related information, and the longest time is 2.8 min. However, the classification time of this research method is short, and the classification time is less than 1 min in the experimental process. This method selects the base classifier with the highest local accuracy, and takes the output of the classifier as the output of the whole classifier combination system. Furthermore, the time of resource classification is shortened.

### 5.3 Comparison of Teaching Effect

In order to further verify the effectiveness of the design of the online teaching method, the students' learning results after using the two methods are tested. 40 students in the same grade were randomly divided into two groups, one group accepted the traditional teaching method, the other group accepted the teaching method of this design. After learning, six tests were conducted with one day interval. The results of teaching effect comparison are shown in Fig. 6.

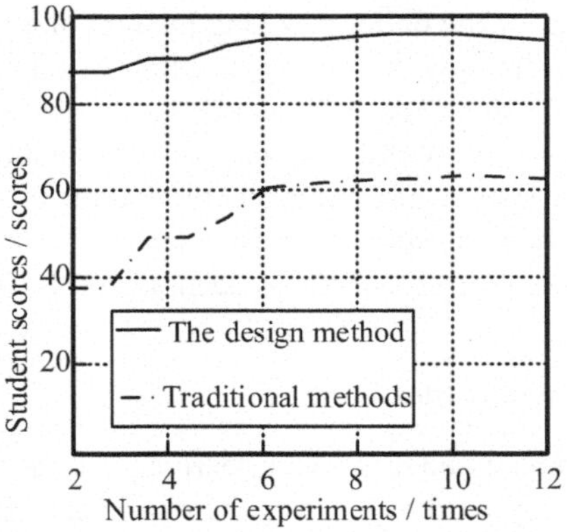


**Fig. 6.** Comparison of teaching effect

The analysis of Fig. 6 shows that after learning the online teaching method of equation solving based on transfer learning, the average score of students is higher than 80 points, and the score increases steadily with the increase in test times. However, the average score of students using traditional method does not reach the pass level (60 points). The comparison shows that the effect of the method designed in this paper is better than the traditional teaching method. Because this method constructs the association model between learners' behavior and network resources. Then transfer learning is used to provide relevant equation teaching resources for learners, which improves the recommended hardcover degree of resources and promotes the improvement of learners' academic performance.

## 6 Conclusion

An online teaching method of equation solving based on transfer learning is designed, and the effectiveness of the research method is verified by experiments. Through this research method can improve the teaching effect of students, and improve the classification effect of learning resources. However, due to the limitation of research time, there are still some deficiencies in the online teaching method of this study, and further research is needed in the follow-up study to solve the existing problems. The data show that the design method can meet the personalized learning needs of students, effectively guide students to learn knowledge in accordance with their own characteristics, and has a certain guiding and promoting role. Therefore, it is of great theoretical significance and research value to deeply analyze the guiding role of learning style in online learning guidance system, design specific algorithm and function model, and develop online learning system with strong recommendation and guidance function.

In the future research, expand the number of users of this method. In the later stage, we should constantly enrich learning resources, shorten the update time of design method resources, publicize and promote the system through multi-channel and multi-channel, and constantly collect users' suggestions on the method, and strive to improve.

## References


1. Karbalayghareh, A., Qian, X., Dougherty, E.R.: Optimal bayesian transfer learning. IEEE Trans. Signal Process. **66**(14), 3724–3739 (2018)
2. Jiang, M., Huang, Z., Qiu, L., et al.: Transfer learning based dynamic multiobjective optimization algorithms. IEEE Trans. Evol. Comput. **22**(4), 501–514 (2017)
3. Paiva, R.C., Ferreira, M.S., Frade, M.M.: Intelligent tutorial system based on personalized system of instruction to teach or remind mathematical concepts. J. Comput. Assist. Learn. **33**(4), 370–381 (2017)
4. Diasse, A., Li, Z.: Multi-view deep unsupervised transfer leaning via joint auto-encoder coupled with dictionary learning. Intell. Data Anal. **23**(3), 555–571 (2019)
5. Raffel, C., Shazeer, N., Roberts, A., et al.: Exploring the limits of transfer learning with a unified text-to-text transformer (2019). arXiv:1910.10683
6. Da Silva, F.L., Costa, A.H.R.: A survey on transfer learning for multiagent reinforcement learning systems. J. Artif. Intell. Res. **64**, 645–703 (2019)
7. Xu, J.: A study of extension strategies of multimedia online teaching platform in sports teaching of Universities. J. Comput. Theor. Nanosci. **14**(1), 94–98 (2017)
8. Dey, B., Kundu, M.K.: Turning video data into traffic data: an application to urban intersection analysis using transfer learning. IET Image Proc. **13**(4), 673–679 (2019)
9. Xia, L., Zhang, J., et al.: Transfer learning assisted deep neural network for OSNR estimation. Opt. Express **27**(14), 19398–19406 (2019)
10. Chandra, R., Kapoor, A.: Bayesian neural multi-source transfer learning. Neurocomputing **378**(22), 54–64 (2020)
11. Liu, S., Glowatz, M., Zappatore, M., et al. (eds.): E-Learning, E-Education, and Online Training, pp. 1–374. Springer International Publishing (2018). https://doi.org/10.1007/978-3-319-49625-2
12. Liu, S., Li, Z., Zhang, Y., et al.: Introduction of key problems in long-distance learning and training. Mob. Netw. Appl. **24**(1), 1–4 (2019)
13. Liu, S., Liu, D., Srivastava, G., et al.: Overview and methods of correlation filter algorithms in object tracking. Complex Intell. Syst. (2020). https://doi.org/10.1007/s40747-020-00161-4
14. Deng, L., Li, D., Yao, X., et al.: Mobile network intrusion detection for IoT system based on transfer learning algorithm. Clust. Comput. **22**(4), 9889–9904 (2019)

15. Golub, D., Huang, P.S., He, X., et al.: Two-stage synthesis networks for transfer learning in machine comprehension (2017). arXiv:1706.09789
16. Min, S., Seo, M., Hajishirzi, H.: Question answering through transfer learning from large fine-grained supervision data (2017). arXiv:1702.02171
17. Shao, K., Zhu, Y., Zhao, D.: Starcraft micromanagement with reinforcement learning and curriculum transfer learning. IEEE Trans. Emerg. Top. Comput. Intell. **3**(1), 73–84 (2018)
18. Tang S, Zhang N, Zhang J, et al.: NITE: A neural inductive teaching framework for domain specific NER. In: Proceedings of the 2017 Conference on Empirical Methods in Natural Language Processing, pp. 2652-2657 (2017)
19. Kumar, A., Ithapu, V.A.: Sequential self teaching approach for improving generalization in sound event recognition. In: International Conference on Machine Learning. PMLR, pp. 5447–5457 (2020)

# Online Intelligent Teaching Method of Track and Field Error Avoidance Based on Multimedia Video

Yong-ming Chen[1(✉)] and Shu-tao Shen[2]

[1] Huali College Guangdong University of Technology, Guangzhou 511325, China
[2] School of Information Science and Technology, Tibet University, Lhasa 850000, China

**Abstract.** The traditional teaching method adopts the unified teaching method, which can not fully pay attention to the students' differences in learning track and field movements, which leads to students' errors in learning track and field movements and affects the teaching effect. Therefore, this paper studies the online intelligent teaching method of track and field error avoidance based on multimedia video. After the multimedia video image is collected and processed, the 3D contour feature of track and field action is used to reconstruct and decompose. The gray-scale contour model is used to detect the track and field wrong actions in the image. By analyzing the causes of the wrong actions, the teaching of avoiding the wrong movements in track and field is completed. A case study in a university proves that the teaching method can improve the standard of students' movements and the teaching effect is better.

**Keywords:** Multimedia video · Track and field wrong action · Wrong action evasion · Online intelligent teaching

## 1 Introduction

Track and field, as a major subject of physical education in primary and secondary schools, is the key content of physical education curriculum. Good study of track and field can effectively improve students' physique, cultivate their strength and resilience, and promote their physical and mental health. The new national curriculum requires students to care about their physical and mental health, cherish life, improve their psychological quality, build up a strong and healthy body through physical training, cultivate team spirit, and learn how to learn and do things. Now in the technical teaching of track and field sports, the teaching method is mainly fixed class as a unit, in this model, teaching is the teacher's explanation demonstration [1]. However, in the technical items of track and field, the professional requirements of each track and field movement are very high. It is difficult for the students to observe the composition of the movement completely under the teacher's demonstration action, understand the key and heavy difficulty of the track and field movement, and the problems in the technical study can not be fed back to the students in time, so that the students can form the correct movement concept,


W. Fu et al. (Eds.): eLEOT 2021, LNICST 389, pp. 99–109, 2021.
https://doi.org/10.1007/978-3-030-84383-0_9

and the students are easy to make mistakes, so that it is difficult to achieve satisfactory teaching effect [2]. The traditional teaching method is easy to cause the difference between the students with higher physical ability level and the students with lower physical ability level under the same teaching schedule. So some students are easy to lose their enthusiasm for learning and can't keep up with the teaching schedule of other students. The traditional teaching method is difficult to meet the needs of training talents in the new era. Therefore, it is necessary to reform the teaching of track and field courses for physical education majors in colleges and universities. When teaching track and field, it is very important to correct and adjust students' wrong actions in time. Wrong track and field movements will not only affect the results of track and field sports, long time to maintain the wrong posture will affect the health of students [3].

Based on the above analysis, this paper will study the multi-media video based on the track and field error movement to avoid online intelligent teaching methods. After the multimedia video images are collected and processed, the 3D contour features of track and field movements are used to reconstruct and decompose the images. The gray scale contour model is used to detect the wrong motion in the track and field images. By analyzing the causes of the wrong motion, the teaching of avoiding the wrong motion in track and field is completed. The designed online intelligent teaching method based on multimedia video can improve the standard of students' track and field movements, and the teaching effect is more ideal. The innovation of this paper is the use of multimedia video technology, the maturity of the technology to promote the modern curriculum reform provides great convenience, the use of multimedia technology can improve the efficiency of modern teaching, improve students' learning enthusiasm.

## 2 Research on Intelligent Teaching Method of Wrong Track and Field Motion Evasion Based on Multimedia Video

### 2.1 Multimedia Video Image Acquisition and Processing

In sports training, visual recognition technology is used, mainly through the decomposition of three-dimensional contour features to complete the wrong action recognition. For example, in the hurdle movement, the site is fixed, assuming that the starting point angle of the site is the origin, and the length, width and height directions are respectively x-axis, Y-axis and z-axis [4]. The field length $x_0$, width $y_0$, and the highest $z_0$ of the athlete's flight are 14 m, 8 m and 5 m respectively, and the three-dimensional coordinate system is established. The three-dimensional coordinate system is shown in Fig. 1.

By confirming the coordinates of the shoulder, hand, toe and other important parts of the athletes, the outline of the athletes can be drawn. For example, when an athlete makes a leap in the air, he can determine whether there is any error in the movement such as swinging his legs or feet according to the difference between the toes and shoulders on the z axis. But it is easy to be affected by the environment disturbance when the contour feature is extracted according to this method, which leads to high error rate of error detection. Using 3D modeling and detection technology to realize motion image processing, it can complete image feature decomposition and detection through image processing, and check the integrity of the wrong action.

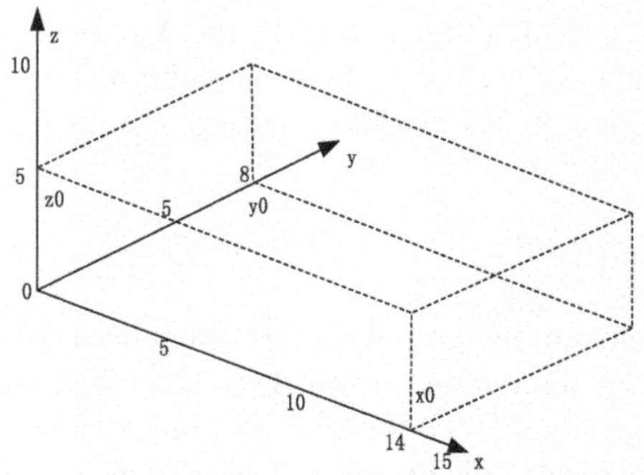


**Fig. 1.** Three-dimensional coordinate system of track and field

In accordance with the above ideas, in the use of three-dimensional visual scanning and tracking recognition technology to complete sports training in the wrong action image acquisition. For image preprocessing, we need to take into account the random distribution of images with irregular attributes [5]. If any point is regarded as the initial value of data acquisition, the attenuation coefficient must be set and the image row replacement must be performed. Combined with the wrong motion image sequence, corner marker and 3D template can be matched to reconstruct the image and calibrate the contour. On the basis of image localization, the differential feature of the image can be obtained by compensating the difference of moving frames. Using the parallax function, the image pixel features can be weighted, the shape model can be solved, and the error motion distribution domain can be obtained. By decomposing the related pixel features, the tracking parallax can be obtained and the contour features can be determined [6]. Using the weight of intersection points to cover each interval information, the feature can be determined to extract data items and complete pixel estimation. In practice, when the feature sampling points and the model match, the gray stage quantization decomposition is needed to obtain the image fuzzy vector set:

$$E^{CV}(c_1, c_2) = \mu L(C) + v \cdot A(in(C)) + \lambda_1 \int_{in(C)} |I - c_1|^2 dxdy + \lambda_2 \int_{in(C)} |I - c_2|^2 dxdy \tag{1}$$

In formula (1), $c_1$ is the reconstruction target of error action image; $c_2$ is the feature distribution primitive of error action image reconstruction, $\mu$, $v$, $\lambda_1$ and $\lambda_2$ refer to the sampling weight coefficients of multimedia video images, which are all constants greater than 0, and $L(C)$ is the length of image reconstruction contour; $A(in(C))$ is the brightness of the reconstructed pixel. Through gradient decomposition, the image is scanned from the spatial dimension, and the 3D image reconstruction can be realized.

## 2.2 Image Decomposition and Reconstruction

According to the above idea, motion feature extraction is needed in the process of image pixel decomposition to estimate the edge feature of wrong motion contour. According to the motion attitude space vector, motion elements can be introduced into the closed curve. The active region can be represented by time-delay function, and the wavelet multidimensional scaling coefficients can be obtained by referring to the set of background graph rules [7]. For the modeled image module, block matching can be implemented, and the differential matching of moving frames can be realized by multi-dimensional decomposition. In practice, in 3D modeling testing, the contour of the reconstructed image is obtained:

$$E = \theta E^{LBF} + (1 - \theta)E^{LGF} + vL(\phi) + \mu P(\phi) \tag{2}$$

In formula (2), $\theta$ refers to the gray weight coefficient of the neighborhood of each error action pixel. In the three-dimensional data field, there are two regions, as the sampling point matching field, $E^{LBF}$ is the local gray information of track and field action in the image, $E^{LGF}$ is the local gradient energy item of track and field action in the image, $L(\phi)$ is the constraint term of the edge contour length of the track and field action in the image, and $P(\phi)$ is the regular term of the edge contour length of the track and field action in the image. Through smoothing filtering, the model definition can be completed, and the local gradient feature decomposition can be realized by using quantitative information, and the correct and wrong actions in the image can be distinguished. In the case of centralized distribution of moving image pixels, the gray value of neighborhood error action image reconstruction has correlation, which can be used for image segmentation, extract the information of image 3D data field, and complete the reconstruction of action 3D coordinate system [8]. According to the detection results, it can match the contour model of the wrong action, complete the corner marking of the image sequence, and determine the Gaussian distribution of the error action in the image:

$$P(\phi) = \int \frac{1}{2}(|\nabla \phi| - 1)^2 dx \tag{3}$$

According to the Gaussian distribution of the error motion in the image, the error track and field motion in the multimedia video image is detected.

## 2.3 Wrong Track and Field Motion Detection

According to the gray-scale contour model, the 3D motion modeling and detection can be completed by combining the wrong motion rules. Concretely speaking, it is to match the motion correlation in the wavelet kernel space and complete the construction of motion mapping function. In the region boundary position, the acquired image template value can be analyzed and the moving frame coordinate of the image feature can be obtained according to the ray direction. In error motion modeling and detection, the intersection coordinates of feature moving frames need to be solved, and the corresponding 3D data field can be obtained by minimizing the reconstruction gray value [9, 10]. When the external disturbance is not fixed, it is necessary to decompose the contour features of the athlete's body to enhance the visual recognition component estimation. Region-pixel information can be obtained by traversing addressing, information collection and reconstruction of feature database using local binary fitting:

$$L = J(w, e) - \sum_{i=1}^{N} a_i \left\{ w^T \phi(x_i) + b + e_i + y_i \right\} \tag{4}$$

In formula (4), $J(w, e)$ refers to the repeated pixels in the moving position; $x_i$ and $y_i$ are the correct and wrong action eigenvectors of the $i$ Gaussian unit, $a_i$ is the standard action configuration sequence, and $\phi(x_i)$ is the contour feature distribution function. Through the analysis, we can extract the three-dimensional feature of the wrong action, and complete the action detection through decomposition.

Through 3D modeling and detection, the feature quantity of wrong movement can be extracted, but there is a great difference in position between different sports. In order to meet the requirements of sports training guidance, it is necessary to extract all position information, and then realize vector normalization by summing. For any motion, it is necessary to extract spatiotemporal features, do a good job in direction gradient and boundary selection, so as to accurately depict the motion. When the action features are combined, it can be seen that the images collected by machine vision contain 30–960-dimensional information, which makes the feature dimension far exceed the training samples. In order to ensure the efficiency of the method, dimensionality reduction is needed to reduce the computational complexity while preserving the important features.

Based on the acquisition of action video, the Gaussian mixture model is used to complete the feature extraction, and then the high-dimensional feature is obtained by fusion. Using the model to select the important features, the support vector machine for action classification can be obtained. In the application of the algorithm, we can know that the feature vector $X_1 = [x_1, x_2, \ldots, x_{Ti}]^T$ is extracted from the video, and the high-dimensional matrix is $X_1 = [x_1, x_2, \ldots, x_m]^T$. Projection in the low-dimensional space can get the reduced dimensional motion feature set $V^{RP} = \left[v_i \in R^d\right]$, $d$ refers to the reduced dimension, $R^d$ refers to the low-dimensional space, and $R^d$ refers to the reduced motion features [11, 12]. The probability of motion features obtained by dimension reduction in Gaussian element is estimated, and the estimation formula is as follows:

$$r(i) = \frac{w_i p_i - v_i}{\sum_{i=1}^{k} w_i p_i(v_i)} \tag{5}$$

In formula (5), $p_i$ refers to the probability assigned to the $i$ Gaussian cell, and $w_i$ is the mixing weight, according to the model parameters and the gradient vector, the gradient values can be cascaded to get the motion feature vector set after dimension reduction. Using the reduced dimension set to train the support vector machine, identify the correct and wrong action feature vectors, and complete the output of action category value, and get the detection results of wrong track and field actions.

## 2.4 Implementation of Evasive Correction of Wrong Track Movements

According to the above process, the causes of students' wrong track and field movements are analyzed and corrected after the transformation of students' wrong track and field movements.

First, make sure that the students have a correct idea of the technology. Secondly, find the reason from the physical quality. If the practice students have the correct concept of technology, but still can not correctly complete the movements, we should know about the physical condition of students [13, 14]. Then, find the reason from psychological factors.

Some people in a separate operation, can better complete the action, in the presence of many people or teachers, because of tension and can not complete the action. Some people in a large number of occasions full of energy, can better complete the action, when the quality of action is not high, and even the wrong action [15]. Still others are afraid to run because of the uneven ground. Bad weather will also lead to the wrong action. Finally, look for the reason from the whole factor of action [16]. Every part of any track and field skill is an organic and inseparable whole, and there is an internal connection between the movements, and the emergence of any movement is not isolated [17]. Therefore, in the search for the cause of the error, but also from the overall technical starting point, check the previous stage of action or action related to the action of other problems. In addition, we should consider students' technical proficiency. In the teaching process, the technical action which the student learns, must achieve the skilled degree, needs certain time. In the beginning stage of technology is not consolidated, this or that kind of wrong action is unavoidable, can not be overly demanding, act too hastily [18].

In view of the above analysis of the causes of students' wrong track and field movements, action correction [19]. When correcting the wrong action caused by unclear technical concept, we should further explain the technical essentials, and with the correct demonstration or see the picture, so that students have a correct understanding of the technology. When correcting the wrong actions caused by poor physical quality, we should change the conditions and requirements of teaching in class so as to realize and master more correct techniques. When correcting the wrong actions caused by psychological reasons, we should give psychological guidance to the students, explain the aim and significance of learning, enhance ideological understanding, eliminate ideological concerns, and educate them to cultivate their own bravery and tenacity and overcome difficulties [20, 21]. At the same time, we should improve the conditions of teaching and practice. From the overall technical point of view, from the most important aspects. Once the primary error is corrected, its subordinate errors can be resolved [22, 23]. If the wrong action is caused by an incomplete or imperfect previous action, it can be corrected by improving the previous action. For example, in the long jump can not jump up, the movement performance is too forward, which is the run-up the last few steps too forward and the cause of the last step is too small. According to this situation, correct the last few steps of running posture and running method, you can solve the above mistakes. For the technical unskilled and the wrong action, do not start to correct, the practice to emphasize its correct approach, repeated many times can be gradually resolved.

Through the above content, this paper completes the research on the teaching method of track and field error motion avoidance based on multimedia video.

## 3 Experimental Results

### 3.1 Experimental Preparation

In this case study, the experimental group is based on the multimedia video, and the experimental group is based on the existing teaching methods of track and field. By comparing the two groups of subjects in the verification cycle after the end of the standard level of track and field movements to evaluate the effectiveness of the two teaching methods.

The research objects are the students of the physical education college of a university. A total of 40 students are selected from Class 2 and Class 3 of the male sports training major class of the university in 2017. Before the experiment, the two groups of students were tested for the difference of body shape and physical quality. During teaching, the two groups were consistent in the number of students, teaching content and practice amount. In the last class, experts will test the standards, skills and theories, and check and ratify according to the relevant track and field action assessment standards. From two parallel classes, 20 students from Class 2 were selected as the control group, and 20 students from Class 3 were selected as the experimental group. According to the syllabus of the School of Physical Education of the university, the teaching was carried out according to the teaching schedule. The experiment period was 4 weeks, with 2 classes per week and 4 class hours, a total of 16 class hours. In the last class, the students were tested for reaching the standard, technical evaluation and theoretical knowledge.

Before the experiment: Carries on the experiment two groups of schoolmates to carry on the body shape and the physical quality pre-test examination. The Table 1 shows the test results of the subjects before the teaching begins.

**Table 1.** Analysis table of test results of physical form and physical fitness indexes of students before the experiment (n = 40)

| Groups | Numbers | Height/m | Weight/kg | 30 m/s | The standing long jump/m | Forward shot put/m |
|---|---|---|---|---|---|---|
| | | $\bar{x} \pm s$ | $\bar{x} \pm s$ | $\bar{x} \pm s$ | $\bar{x} \pm s$ | $\bar{x} \pm s$ |
| Experimental group | 20 | 177.4 ± 5.50 | 68.19 ± 6.36 | 4.15 ± 0.22 | 2.79 ± 0.07 | 9.00 ± 1.12 |
| Control group | 20 | 175.4 ± 4.558 | 65.275 ± 5.11 | 4.34 ± 0.37 | 2.79 ± 0.07 | 8.815 ± 1.1 |
| $t$ | – | 1.251 | 1.611 | 1.962 | 0.064 | 0.515 |
| $p$ | – | 0.22 | 0.12 | 0.06 | 0.95 | 0.61 |

Table 1 The results of the test show that there is no significant difference between the two classes in the body shape and main body quality indexes ($P > 0.05$). The experiment is suitable for this subject, which ensures the high validity of the experiment.

In the experiment, the experimental group and the control group were both taught by the same person. The teaching progress, teaching hours, exercise intensity and practice amount of the two groups were consistent.

After the experiment, the students were tested for reaching the goal of track and field action, skill evaluation and teaching technique theory knowledge, and the data of control group and experimental group were tested statistically. Analyze the experimental data and draw corresponding conclusions.

### 3.2 Results

After the experiment in the first teaching stage, the results of the experimental group and the control group were analyzed as Table 2:

**Table 2.** Comparison and analysis table of the scores of the experiment group and the control group (n = 40)

| Groups | Attaining result | Performance evaluation (score) |
|---|---|---|
| | $\overline{x} \pm s$ | $\overline{x} \pm s$ |
| Experimental group | 19.95 ± 2.585 | 68.95 ± 5.346 |
| Control group | 18.80 ± 1.795 | 69.70 ± 6.071 |
| $t$ | 1.634 | 0.415 |
| $p$ | 0.110 | 0.681 |

Table 2 shows the comparison between the two groups of students after the 2nd class, which shows that the average score of the experimental group is 19.95 and the standard deviation is 2.585. The average score of the control group was 18.80, the standard deviation was 1.795, the average score of the experimental group was 68.95, and the standard deviation was 5.346. The average score of the control group was 68.70, and the standard deviation was 6.071, $P > 0.05$. There was no significant difference between the control group and the experimental group.

After the experiment in the second teaching stage, the results of the experimental group and the control group were analyzed as Table 3:

**Table 3.** Comparison and analysis table of the scores of the experiment group and the control group after the 5th class (n = 40)

| Groups | Attaining result | Performance evaluation (score) |
|---|---|---|
| | $\overline{x} \pm s$ | $\overline{x} \pm s$ |
| Experimental group | 32.35 ± 3.760 | 77.15 ± 5.122 |
| Control group | 28.40 ± 2.664 | 72.40 ± 3.202 |
| $t$ | 3.834 | 3.516 |
| $p$ | 0.015 | 0.021 |

The results showed that the average scores of the two groups were 32.35, the standard deviation was 3.760, the average scores of the control group was 28.40, the standard deviation was 2.664, the average scores of the experimental group was 77.15, the standard deviation was 5.122. The average score of control group was 72.40, and the standard deviation was 3.202. Judging from the results of the second stage, the control group in the track and field reached the standard and technical evaluation results are lower than the experimental group. There were significant differences in experimental data. The results showed that the use of multimedia video in motor skill learning had an impact on the prevention and correction of motor skills, and the students in the experimental group had obvious progress.

After the experiment in the third stage, the students in the experimental group and the control group had the following results and analysis:

**Table 4.** Comparison and analysis table of the scores of the experimental group and the control group after the 8th class (n = 40)

| Groups | Attaining result | Performance evaluation (score) |
|---|---|---|
| | $\bar{x} \pm s$ | $\bar{x} \pm s$ |
| Experimental group | $40.15 \pm 4.120$ | $83.55 \pm 5.155$ |
| Control group | $31.70 \pm 3.197$ | $78.40 \pm 3.604$ |
| $t$ | 7.246 | 3.662 |
| $p$ | 0.017 | 0.010 |

Table 4 shows the comparison and analysis of the results of reaching the standard of track and field movements and technical evaluation after the course, we can see that the average score of the experimental group is 40.15, the standard deviation is 4.120, the average score of the control group is 31.70, the standard deviation is 3.197, the average score of the experimental group is 83.55, the standard deviation is 5.155, the average score of the control group is 78.40, the standard deviation is 3.604. The results of the experimental group were significantly better than those of the control group. The experimental data showed that the multimedia video teaching method was better than the conventional teaching method.

To sum up, the online intelligent teaching method of track and field error avoidance based on multimedia video studied in this paper can effectively improve the standard degree of students' track and field movements when applied to teaching, and obtain better teaching effect.

## 4 Conclusions

Traditional teaching method can not meet the needs of modern track and field teaching. In order to correct and avoid students' wrong track and field actions in time, this paper studies the intelligent teaching method of track and field actions avoiding online based on multimedia video. Compared with the traditional teaching method, the method of this paper can effectively improve the accuracy of students' track and field movements, ensure the standard of students' track and field movements, and achieve better teaching results.

## References


1. Bezodis, N.E., Willwacher, S., Salo, A.: The biomechanics of the track and field sprint start: a narrative review. Sports Med. **49**(9), 1345–1364 (2019)
2. Jacobsson, J., Ekberg, J., Timpka, T., et al.: Developing web-based health guidance for coaches and parents in child athletics (track and field). Scand. J. Med. Sci. Sports **30**(7), 1248–1255 (2020)
3. Wang, P.: Analysis and design of applying artificial intelligence in educational video. E-educ. Res. **41**(03), 93–100+121 (2020)
4. Li, J.: Computer course teaching mode based on multimedia mobile platform. Modern Informationn Technology 4(02):162–163+166 (2020)
5. Guo, R.: On innovation of multimedia teaching model based on WebRTC technology. J. Daqing Normal Univ. **39**(06), 70-75 (2019)
6. Zhang, S., Lan, S., Bu, Qi., et al.: A survey of action recognition based on deep learning. J. Commun. Univ. Chin. Sci. Technol. **26**(05), 43–49 (2019)
7. Ma, J.: Design of multimedia sharing system for multi-node networked intelligent teaching. Mod. Electron. Tech. **42**(14), 157–160+164 (2019)
8. Zhao, Z.: Application countermeasures of demonstration method in track and field teaching in higher vocational education. Contemp. Sports Technol. **10**(13), 69+71 (2020)
9. Macdonald, B., Mcaleer, S., Kelly, S., et al.: Hamstring rehabilitation in elite track and field athletes: applying the British athletics muscle injury classification in clinical practice. Br. J. Sports Med. **53**(23), 71–85 (2019)
10. Fu, W., Liu, S., Srivastava, G.: Optimization of big data scheduling in social networks. Entropy **21**(9), 902–908 (2019)
11. Liu, S., Bai, W., Zeng, N., et al.: A fast fractal based compression for MRI images. IEEE Access **7**(1), 62412–62420 (2019)
12. Liu, S., Li, Z., Zhang, Y., et al.: Introduction of key problems in long-distance learning and training. Mob. Netw. Appl. **24**(1), 1–4 (2019)
13. Sánchez-Nielsen, E., Chávez-Gutiérrez, F., Lorenzo-Navarro J.: A semantic parliamentary multimedia approach for retrieval of video clips with content understanding. Multimedia Syst. **25**(3), 337–354 (2019)
14. Liu, Y., Dhakal, S., Hao, B.: Multimedia image and video retrieval based on an improved HMM. Multimedia Syst. **3**, 45–52 (2020)
15. Zaimi, I., Boushaba, A., Houssaini, Z.S., et al.: A fuzzy geographical routing approach to support real-time multimedia transmission for vehicular ad hoc networks. Wirel. Netw. **25**(3), 1289–1311 (2019)
16. West, L., Srivastava, D., Goldberg, L.H., et al.: Multimedia technology used to supplement patient consent for mohs micrographic surgery. Dermatol. Surg. **46**(12), 15–23 (2020)
17. Omrani, T., Becheikh, R., Rhouma, R.: Towards a real-time image/video cryptosystem: problems, analysis and recommendations. Multimedia Syst. **26**(2), 339–362 (2020)
18. Ullah, H., Islam, I.U., Ullah, M., et al.: Multi-feature-based crowd video modeling for visual event detection. Multimedia Syst. **5**, 15–21 (2020)
19. Zhang, Y.: Interactive intelligent teaching and automatic composition scoring system based on linear regression machine learning algorithm. J. Intell. Fuzzy Syst. **40**(2), 2069–2081 (2021)
20. He, H., Yan, H., Liu, W.: Intelligent teaching ability of contemporary college talents based on BP neural network and fuzzy mathematical model. J. Intell. Fuzzy Syst. **39**(9), 1–11 (2020)
21. Dong, S.: Intelligent English teaching prediction system based on SVM and heterogeneous multimodal target recognition. J. Intell. Fuzzy Syst. **38**(153), 1–10 (2020)

22. Wirthmüller, F., Schlechtriemen, J., Hipp, J., et al.: Teaching vehicles to anticipate: a systematic study on probabilistic behavior prediction using large data sets. IEEE Trans. Intell. Transp. Syst. **14**(12), 1–16 (2020)
23. Yahyaabadi, M., Aslani, F., Vahidi, B.: A novel hybrid method based on teaching–learning algorithm and leader progression model for evaluating the lightning performance of launch sites and experimental tests. Electr. Eng. **101**(4), 619–633 (2019)

# Method of Online Teaching Resource Recommendation Towards International Communication Based on.NET Platform

Qian Jiang[1(✉)] and Lin He[2]

[1] International Cooperation Exchange Center, Chongqing Vocational College of Transportation, Chongqing 402260, China

[2] College of Information Engineering, Fuyang Normal University, Fuyang 236041, China

**Abstract.** According to the status quo of personalized recommendation of education and teaching resources, combined with the current main recommendation model, and according to the characteristics of education and teaching resources, a recommendation model of international exchange online teaching resources based on the .NET platform is constructed. First obtain user data, then use the frequency of user use of tags and the time factor of user use of tags to mine user interests and preferences, and then conduct unified management and classification of teaching resources, build teaching resource models, and finally implement user-based collaborative recommendation algorithms Teaching resource recommendation. The results show that compared with the recommendation model based on association rules and content, under the application of the established recommendation model, the MAE is lower, the accuracy and the recall rate are higher, which proves the recommendation quality of the model.

**Keywords:** NET platform · Teaching resources · Collaborative recommendation · Internet+ · Education

## 1 Introduction

Nowadays, when network technology and information technology are highly developed and popularized, online teaching of international exchanges has become an important way to cultivate talents and promote the development of scientific research and education [1]. However, to make the network and information technology really serve the teaching and realize the optimization of the teaching process and teaching resources, it must be supported by rich teaching resources. Therefore, the prerequisite for our development of distance teaching is to build a complete and substantial network teaching resource system [2]. Most of the current international exchange online teaching resource database systems only provide the functions of uploading, querying and downloading teaching resources. They still stay at the level of 'material-oriented' and fail to reflect the 'people-oriented' idea, a particularly prominent problem It is that most of the current teaching


W. Fu et al. (Eds.): eLEOT 2021, LNICST 389, pp. 110–121, 2021.
https://doi.org/10.1007/978-3-030-84383-0_10

resource database systems do not have the characteristics of individualization and intelligence, which has led to the contradiction between the massive teaching resources and the individual needs of users, which has become a microcosm of 'the lack of knowledge in the information explosion era' [3]. The long-term existence of this contradiction not only greatly reduces the effective utilization of teaching resources, but also creates huge difficulties for users to find and use required teaching resources, and directly hinders the role of international exchange online teaching resources in teaching. In this era, the personalized recommendation system came into being. It is currently one of the most effective tools to solve the problem of 'information overload'. It uses existing users by establishing a binary relationship between users and information products. Behavioral information and some similarity relationships to mine each user's potentially interested objects, and then make personalized recommendations for them, is essentially a process of information filtering. Personalized recommendation technology and recommendation system provide the possibility to fundamentally solve the contradiction between massive resources and the personalized needs of users. To this end, based on the NET platform, research, design and implement a feasible international exchange online teaching resource recommendation model to improve the personalization and intelligence of the teaching resource library system, and to a certain extent solve the user's difficulty in finding the required teaching resources. The problem of low utilization.

## 2 Recommendation Model of Online Teaching Resources for International Exchanges

The rapid development of the Internet and computer software and hardware technology has brought huge development space to the education field. The rapid rise of remote online teaching breaks the limitations of traditional learning methods in terms of time, space, and environment, and sharing learning resources has become a powerful supplement to traditional teaching methods [4]. Therefore, an online teaching platform for international exchange based on NET was designed. NET is Microsoft's new generation technology platform, that is, the Microsoft ML Web services platform. It can be used to agilely build standards-based, interconnected, stable and high-performance interconnected application systems that adapt to changes. XML. Web services allow applications to communicate and share data via the Internet, regardless of the operating system, device, or programming language used. The Microsoft .NET platform provides what is needed to create WML Web services and integrate these services together. From a technical point of view, a .NET application is an application running on the .NET Framework. (To be more precise, a .NET application is an application written using the .NET Framework class library and running on the Common Language Runtime).

The design and application of the NET-based international exchange online teaching platform can easily add and modify courseware subjects and content, thus avoiding repeated development, not only saving manpower and material resources, but also bringing greater convenience to the production and upgrading of online courseware. However, there is also a big problem, that is, the lack of some personalized and intelligent functional design, which brings many problems and inconveniences to the management and use of teaching resources. Because learners have individual differences in learning starting points, styles, expectations, etc., the contradiction between massive teaching resources and the individual needs of users has prevailed. The long-term existence of this contradiction not only greatly reduces the effective utilization of teaching resources, but also brings great difficulties for users to find and use the required teaching resources.

## 2.1 User Data Collection

User models are generally completed in two stages: user data collection and model characterization. The user data frequently used can be roughly divided into two categories:

**Explicit Data**
Explicit data refers to the fact that users directly give out their preference information for the project according to the guidance of the system. Such data can be directly stored in the database as the basis for the next user modeling. The advantage of explicit data input is that it can simplify the data preprocessing process, and the data obtained is highly reliable and usable, which can improve the operating efficiency of the system; but obtaining explicit data requires user intervention, and the degree of automation of the system is not high. In addition, the data is obviously subjective and lacks judgment standards, so the data has accuracy and authenticity problems. At present, the commonly used explicit data includes that the system requires the user to actively fill in the pre-set questions to submit the part of interest to the system, but the system cannot track and understand the changes in user interest [5]. In addition, the user's rating data for items is often used as explicit data input in the modeling of collaborative filtering systems. Because explicit data input can quickly obtain user preference information for items, most recommendation systems use explicit data as System input.

**Implicit Data**
Modeling users' interests is also a learning process, and constantly clarifying the needs of users. The user's demand information will be reflected in the browsing behavior when interacting with the system. The implicit data is to use information technology to find the user's various activity clues in an indirect way, and transform it into the user's interest and preference data. For example, the combination of pages that users frequently visit, the user's click stream, favorite records, browsing time, and the number of times the scroll bar is pulled up and down. The research conclusions of behavioral science prove that this kind of data often reflects the current interests of users, and plays a very critical guiding role in online recommendation. In the traditional e-commerce recommendation system, the user's historical transaction data is also used as implicit data. It is believed that every customer who has purchased a product represents the user's interest in the product, which is an estimate of historical preference. The advantage of implicit data is that the data is automatically obtained, and the user does not need additional work when accessing the system, but the process of data preprocessing is more complicated, and the data is noisy.

The collection of user data is the process of obtaining relevant information that can reflect user characteristics, preferences and needs. According to different data sources, it can be roughly divided into explicit collection methods and implicit collection methods. The display collection is mainly through the questioning requirements presented manually, and directly obtains the user's rating, options, and clear statement evaluation information. This method collects Data has obvious pertinence and is relatively easy in reality. It has been widely used in collaborative filtering recommendation technology. However, a single display collection method has problems with the authenticity of the data, and even negative data may be generated due to subjective factors and privacy reasons.

The invisible collection method mainly refers to the process of collecting Log signs and various Web resources from the system's Web server. The data acquisition process actually uses Web mining methods, among which Web content mining and Web usage mining are the main methods for data preprocessing. Web content mining involves characterizing Web pages and extracting knowledge from page content; Web application mining can discover user access patterns and provide a reliable basis for the next step of mining users' potential interests. The main techniques included are path analysis., Association rules, sequence patterns and clustering techniques. Since the invisible collection method can obtain the user's current interest preferences and reflect the timeliness of information needs, some Web recommendation systems use the log log of the user's access to the server to analyze and predict the user's pages of interest to form recommendations, such as Recommendation systems for large websites such as LOGSUM, SUGGEST 3.0 and WebPersonalizer [6].

## 2.2 User Interest Model

User interest is the core step of personalized recommendation. To recommend personalized resources that meet their interests and needs for people with different backgrounds, different needs, and different preferences, we must first accurately perceive and express user interests. User interest modeling is the process of mining and acquiring knowledge related to user interests, needs and usage habits, and generating a user interest model that can express the user's specific background knowledge and hobbies is the final result of user interest modeling. A good user interest model should not only be able to obtain, express, and store user interest preferences, but also understand user characteristics and user categories, capture users' long- and short-term interests, and understand the different needs of users in different periods [7]. From this point of view, user interest modeling should include two aspects: user interest mining and user interest expression. In the social tagging system, the tags used by users when tagging resources express users' interests. For example, the higher the frequency of tag usage, the more users like the resources related to the tag; the usage time of the tag also reflects the user's interest. Long-term and short-term interests, the tags recently used by users can reflect the user's recent interests; considering that in reality, user interests change dynamically over time, the user's interest is mined by combining the frequency and time factors of the user's use of tags. In terms of user interest model representation, according to the results of the tag network clustering, the final user interest model is represented by the user's preference vector for tag clusters.

The user's interest preference is mined by comprehensively considering the frequency of the user's use of tags and the time factor of the user's use of the tags, that is, the user's interest preferences are mined through the combination of frequency-weighted label preferences and time-weighted label preferences, and after calculating the user's interest preferences for tags, Then according to the tag clusters generated by the tag clustering, calculate the user's interest preference for each tag cluster, and finally express the user interest model in the form of an n-dimensional vector. Each component of the vector is the user's interest preference for each tag cluster [8]. As shown in Fig. 1:

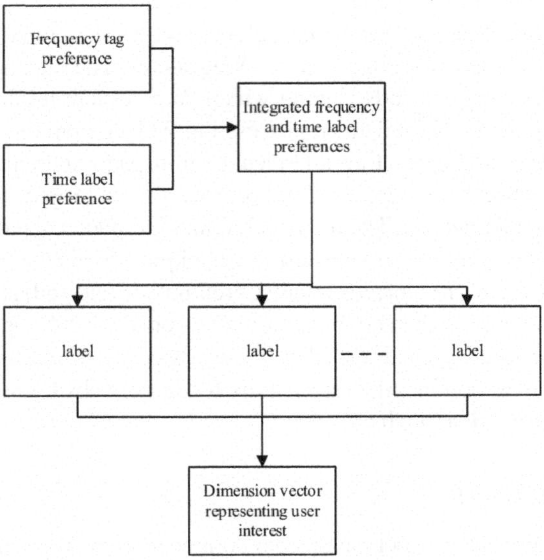


**Fig. 1.** User interest model

The vector space model was originally proposed by Gerard Msalton and others in the 1970s and was successfully used in the field of information retrieval. The basic idea of the space vector model is to express resources or search content in the form of feature vectors, thereby converting the processing of text data into matrix vector operations in the vector space, and using the similarity of vectors to reflect the similarity between resources. Usually the TFIDF value represents the feature weight, and the cosine function is used to measure the similarity between vectors.

## 2.3 Construction of Teaching Resource Model

Teaching resources refer to all resources used by users for teaching in the intelligent teaching system and E-learning environment, including information, personnel, materials, equipment, and technology. Learning resources can be divided into hardware resources and software resources according to their different forms of performance. Hardware resources mainly refer to equipment resources used for teaching design; software resources refer to multimedia resources for online teaching design, such as textbooks and videos., Audio teaching materials, etc. With the development of education informatization, the emerging online learning communities, education blogs, and online teaching platforms for learning resources have shared and reused learning resources online, breaking the traditional teaching. Therefore, the unified management and classification of teaching resources and the semantic relationship between teaching resources, subject knowledge and knowledge points are the main work of this chapter [9].

In view of the characteristics of teaching development at this stage, before personalized teaching resource recommendation, the resources must be classified first, which can improve the accuracy of teaching resource recommendation and better provide users with personalized learning services. In the mobile autonomous school, the teaching resource classification strategy is divided into: subject classification, grade classification, content classification and knowledge point classification strategies. These classifications are in a progressive relationship.

Subject classification: At present, the application of subject classification in actual teaching has been very mature, and the subject classification of teaching resources is distinguished by coding.

Grade classification: According to the different levels of knowledge and level of learning in different grades, learning resources need to be classified according to the syllabus and grade information. Teachers have a strong ability to control educational resources. Teachers can classify resources based on teaching experience and user development requirements. In the self-developed mobile autonomous school platform, learning resources are mainly classified from the teaching stage.

Content type classification: Teaching resources are presented in a variety of forms. The teaching resources are classified according to different formats, and finally resources of text, video, audio, courseware, animation and other types are obtained.

Knowledge point classification: mainly analyze the content of teaching resources, extract the attribute characteristics of the content, and build the knowledge point ontology. Knowledge point classification is a further decomposition and refinement of learning resources, so that users can search for teaching resources more accurately.

By analyzing the construction of the teaching resource model, it mainly includes several modules such as learning resource classification, classification coding, classification coding binding, and resource use subject.

## 2.4 Teaching Resource Recommendation Algorithm

Personalized recommendation refers to those who can first analyze and identify user interest preferences based on the user's background information and historical behavior, and then match user interests with resource characteristics through certain recommendation models and algorithms, and then actively meet user needs and interests A system that recommends information resources to users to meet the individual needs of each person [10]. Such a system not only enables users to easily obtain high-quality information resources, but also greatly reduces the time and energy cost of users to obtain information [11]. Due to the academic value and practical value of personalized recommendation, personalized recommendation has become a research hotspot in the fields of information science, computer science, and data mining. Teaching resource recommendation generally includes six steps:

Step 1: Data collection, see chapter 1.1.

Step2: Learning data analysis: Use educational data mining technology to analyze user data, perform data preprocessing, data cleaning, data integration and data specification. In order to achieve accurate recommendations, it is necessary to filter missing data, noise data, and redundant data.

Step3: By analyzing the user's behavior data in the learning process, extracting the three characteristic attributes of the user's knowledge level, cognitive ability and learning preference to construct the user model; among them, in order to realize the accurate recommendation of personalized teaching resources, the focus is on the user For preference information, use ontology technology to establish semantic relationships between user preferences, and use OWL ontology description language to describe user preference models.

Step4: Construction of learning resource model: through online editing by users, online creation by teachers, and semantic representation of the media form of the resource and learning content, using ontology and knowledge structure diagrams to represent the structure of teaching resources, and using Ontology to build knowledge of resources, courses, and chapters The relationship between points.

Step5: Personalized teaching resource recommendation: After the user model and the learning resource model are successfully constructed, a recommendation algorithm is selected to recommend high-quality educational resources, courses, knowledge points and similar user partners for the target users.

Step6: Multi-format presentation: After the personalized teaching resources are formed, they will be adaptively presented to users in multiple formats, so that users can accurately match resources no matter they use smart terminals such as pc, ipda or iphone, which can perform high Effective learning.

Finally, after accurately matching the teaching resources, the user automatically updates the teaching method, and re-does the teaching diagnosis and evaluation. In this way, a Step 1-Step 2-Step 3-Step 4-Steps-Step 1…continuous cycle process is formed. The user generates data and again According to the analysis results, the teaching enthusiasm and learning efficiency can be improved, so that the data in the model can be updated iteratively.

Recommendation algorithm is the core module of the recommendation system, which directly affects the efficiency and quality of recommendation. Researchers have proposed various recommendation algorithms based on the characteristics of recommendation systems in different fields. Many of these methods combine research results in the field of data mining. The mainstream recommendation algorithms currently in use include: association rules, content-based recommendation algorithms, and collaborative filtering recommendation algorithms [12].

Among the three methods, the most widely studied and applied is the collaborative filtering algorithm, so the collaborative filtering algorithm is selected for resource recommendation. Recommendation based on collaborative filtering is the earliest recommendation method proposed. Different from content-based recommendation, the main point of collaborative filtering is to generate recommendations for new users through the understanding of existing users. In this process, some of the existing users Past behavior records will be of great help to recommendations, not just a study of new users' behavior and preferences. Its main idea lies in collaboration, which is more reflected in the role of the group. The recommendation based on collaborative filtering mainly uses the nearest neighbor technology to calculate the distance through some historical preferences of the user, and then uses the weighted evaluation value of the target user's nearest neighbor user to evaluate the teaching resource to add the target user's preference for the specific teaching resource It is expected to recommend teaching resources to target users. According to the different recommended principles, they are divided into two categories:

**Based on User Recommendations**
Finding neighbor users with the same preference of the target user, recommend the target user according to some preference information of the neighbor users.

**Project-Based Recommendations**
Mainly focus on the relationship between information, match and associate resources between resources for a single user, and push resources and projects with a high degree of correlation to users. Collect all users' evaluations of resources or projects, analyze based on users' overall preference characteristics, calculate the similarity between resources or projects, and recommend corresponding resources or projects with high similarity to current users.

The specific process of user-based recommendation: Based on the user's preference vector for the tag cluster, construct the user's tag cluster-interest matrix, replace the user's scoring matrix for the item with the tag cluster-preference matrix, and perform personalized recommendation through collaborative filtering [13]. Collaborative filtering recommendation includes three basic steps: the construction of the user's tag cluster-preference matrix, the search for similar neighbors, and the generation of personalized recommendation resources.

(1) Construction of user interest matrix.
    User interest is the basis of personalized recommendation. Only by understanding the user's interest can we recommend resources that meet the user's interest. This article builds a user interest matrix based on the user's interest vector for tag clusters that integrates frequency and time factors, also called It is the user's tag cluster-interest degree relationship matrix [14].
(2) Neighboring user set construction.
    The selection of neighbor users is the core step of the collaborative filtering recommendation algorithm based on users. The construction of the neighbor user set mainly includes two steps: the calculation of user similarity and the selection of neighbor users.
    Calculation of user similarity. User similarity calculation refers to calculating the similarity degree of user interest through a certain similarity calculation method according to the user's tag cluster and interest degree relationship. Commonly used user similarity calculation methods mainly include cosine similarity, Pearson similarity and Jaccard coefficient method [15].
    Selection of neighbor users. The selection of neighbor users refers to selecting a set of users with the same or similar interests as the target user based on the calculation result of the similarity between users in the previous step. There are two main methods currently selected: Threshold setting method and K nearest

neighbor method (KNN). This paper uses the K nearest neighbor method to select neighbor users. This method sorts the similarity between the target user U0 and all other users Sim (U0, U1) in order from high to low, and selects the top K users. That is, the K users with the highest similarity to the target user U0 are regarded as the set of neighbor users. The value of K will affect the effect of the recommendation. Therefore, the selection of the K value generally has to go through many trials. Neighbor users who are not very similar will bring 'noise' to the prediction and affect the accuracy of the system recommendation. When K is too small, the number of prediction items will be too small, which will affect the recall rate of the recommendation system.

(3) Generation of personalized recommendations.
The result of tag clustering is to group tags with similar semantics into a cluster. These different clusters represent different themes. Therefore, using tag clusters as an intermediary can more clearly reflect the interests of users and the themes of resources. The resources collected by the neighbor users of the target user are used as the basic resource collection, and the user's interest in these resources is calculated using the tag cluster as an intermediary according to the user's interest in the tag cluster and the correlation between the resource and the tag cluster. Among them, the user's tag cluster-interest degree relationship matrix has indicated the user's interest in the tag cluster; and the correlation between the resource and the tag cluster can be calculated based on the tag set used by all users to label the same resource; finally, the tag cluster is Intermediary, which calculates the degree of interest of specific users in specific resources. The user's interest in resources is predicted based on the resources collected and marked by neighbor users and the correlation between resources and tag clusters.

The correlation between the resource and the tag cluster is equal to the ratio of the frequency of all users using tags in the tag cluster to annotate the resource to the frequency of users using tags in all tag clusters to annotate the resource, as shown in formula (1):

$$R_{jk} = \frac{\sum_{T_l \in C_k} \mathrm{Count}(RT_{jl})}{\sum_{T_l \in T} \mathrm{Count}(RT_{jl})} \tag{1}$$

Indicates the degree of relevance between the resource $R_j$ and the tag cluster $C_k$, $C_k$ represents the tag set in the $k$ tag cluster, $C_k(RT_{jl})$ indicates the number of times that all users use the tag $T_l$ to mark the resource $R_j$, and $T$ indicates the tag set used when the resource $R_j$ is marked by all users.

The user's interest in resources is equal to the sum of the user's interest in each cluster multiplied by the relevance of the resource to the corresponding cluster. As shown in formula (2), $n$ represents the number of label clusters after clustering.

$$I_{ij} = \sum_{k=1}^{n} U_{ik} \times R_{jk} \tag{2}$$

In formula (2), $U_{ik}$ represents the user $U_i$'s interest in the tag cluster $C_k$.

Finally, the user's interest in the resources in the basic resource set is sorted from largest to smallest, and the top N resources are recommended to the user, namely TOP-N.

## 3 Simulation Experiment Analysis

Randomly select 100 users as target users, analyze the average recommendation effect for these 100 users, and number the selected 100 target users from 1 to 10. The data in the selected data set is divided into five parts, and the five-fold cross-validation method is adopted for the experiment. 20% of each is used as the test set, and the remaining 80% is used as the experimental data to implement the recommended algorithm. In order to reflect the superiority of the recommended model studied, the recommendation model based on association rules and content is used as a comparison method. The experiment process is divided into three parts: database establishment, preference model establishment, learning model establishment, and algorithm evaluation.

### 3.1 Experimental Environment

The experimental operating system is Windows Microsoft SQL Server 2010, Windows10, CPU frequency is 2.79GHz, 8G memory, the development environment is Eclipse, and the programming language is JAVA.

### 3.2 Evaluation Criteria

Aiming at the recommendation performance of learning resources, the average absolute deviation MAE (Mean Absolute Error), which is commonly used in statistical accuracy measurement methods, is used as the metric to evaluate the recommendation quality of the recommendation system to intuitively measure the recommendation quality. The calculation formula is defined as:

$$MEA = \frac{\sum_{j=1}^{N} \left| P_{ij} - R_{ij} \right|}{N} \tag{3}$$

Among them, $N$ is the number of resources that the target user has learned in the recommendation result set, $R_{ij}$ is the user's actual score for teaching, and $P_{ij}$ is the recommendation degree between the resource and the user predicted by the recommendation algorithm.

In addition, in order to better compare and evaluate the accuracy and accuracy of the recommended results, recall and precision are used as evaluation indicators for comparative analysis. Since the data set has been divided into the training set and the test set for comparison during system testing, the intersection of the calculated recommendation result and the training set can be used as the data result for calculation. This calculation method can also be used for accuracy. Formulas such as (4), (5):

$$\text{Precision} = \frac{1}{M} \sum_{n} \frac{|R_u \cap T_u|}{R_u} \tag{4}$$

$$\text{Recall} = \frac{1}{M}\sum_{n}\frac{|R_u \cap T_u|}{|T_u|} \tag{5}$$

In formula (4) and formula (5), $M$ is the number of users in the test case, $R_u$ is the recommended list of teaching resources, and $T_u$ is the set of teaching resources actually selected by the user in the recommended list.

### 3.3 Result Analysis

**Table 1.** Recommended quality comparison table

| Method | Mean absolute deviation | Accuracy rate/% | Recall rate/% |
|---|---|---|---|
| Research method | 0.85 | 96.55 | 93.50 |
| Recommendation model based on association rules | 1.26 | 88.36 | 81.23 |
| Content-based recommendation model | 1.54 | 90.54 | 82.58 |

It can be seen from Table 1 that the researched NET platform-based international exchange online teaching resource recommendation model shows a better recommendation effect. The average absolute error of the prediction score MAE is significantly lower than the other two comparison recommendations, while the precision and recall rates are Relatively high, proving the effectiveness of the research.

## 4 Conclusion

With the rapid development of information technology and data science, as well as the 'Internet +' innovative concept, the pace of development of education informatization has been accelerated. The development of education informatization has accumulated a large amount of teaching resources, and users cannot accurately find information that suits them when facing these resources. Therefore, personalized learning in the online learning environment has become an important issue of current research. The research on personalized teaching resource recommendation model has solved the problem of inaccurate resource recommendation to a large extent, and achieved good results, but there are still many shortcomings:

In the process of constructing the user preference model, the method of obtaining content preference and media preference information is further studied, and experimental verification is performed.

The application of personalized teaching resource recommendation model is further explored.

**Fund Projects.** Jiangsu Province Tong Brand Professional Construction Project (Z215015002).

## References


1. Liu, S., Sun, G., Fu, W. (eds.): eLEOT 2020. LNICSSITE, vol. 339. Springer, Cham (2020). https://doi.org/10.1007/978-3-030-63952-5
2. Zhu, T.: Empirical research on the application of online teaching in chinese colleges and universities under the situation of novel coronavirus pneumonia prevention and control. Int. J. Emerg. Technol. Learn. (iJET) **15**(11), 119 (2020)
3. Liu, S., Li, Z., Zhang, Y., et al.: Introduction of key problems in long-distance learning and training. Mobile Netw. Appl. **24**(1), 1–4 (2019)
4. Harlow, S.: Online teaching and learning: a practical guide for librarians. Tech. Serv. Q. **35**(4), 412–413 (2018)
5. Gupta, M., Kumar, P.: Recommendation generation using personalized weight of meta-paths in heterogeneous information networks. European J. Oper. Res. **284**(2), 660–674 (2020)
6. Shi, C., Liu, J., Zhang, Y., et al.: MFPR: a personalized ranking recommendation with multiple feedback. ACM Trans. Soc. Comput. **1**(2), 1–22 (2018)
7. Le, D.D., Lauw, H.W.: Stochastically robust personalized ranking for lsh recommendation retrieval. Proc. AAAI Conf. Artif. Intell. **34**(4), 4594–4601 (2020)
8. Liu, T., Liao, J., Wang, Y., et al.: Collaborative tensor–topic factorization model for personalized activity recommendation. Multimedia Tools Appl. **78**(12), 16923–16943 (2019)
9. Xiao, H., Lukas, F., Karsten, B.: Kernelized rank learning for personalized drug recommendation. Bioinformatics **34**(16), 2808–2816 (2018)
10. Li, H.J., Yang, L., Zhang, P.W.: Method of online learning resource recommendation based on multi-objective optimization strategy. Pattern Recognit. Artif. Intell. **32**(04), 306–316 (2019)
11. Balasubramanian, C., Sekar, J.R., Devi, M.S.: A personalized user recommendation based on attributes clustering and score matrix. Int. J. Pure Appl. Math. **119**(12), 13751–13756 (2018)
12. Wang, C.Y., Wang, Y.C., Chou, S.C.T.: A context and emotion aware system for personalized music recommendation. J. Internet Technol. **19**(3), 765–779 (2018)
13. Aliannejadi, M., Crestani, F.: Personalized context-aware point of interest recommendation. ACM Trans. Info. Syst. **36**(4), 1–28 (2018)
14. Bingzhuan, P.: Intercultural communicative competence teaching and assessment based on modern information technology. Int. J. Emerg. Technol. Learn. (iJET) **16**(7), 175 (2021)
15. Zhao, Y., Luo, Y.: Autonomous learning mode based on a four-element teaching design for visual communication course. Int. J. Emerg. Technol. Learn. (iJET) **15**(19), 66 (2020)

# Data Mining Method of English Online Learning Behavior Based on Machine Learning Technology

Yi Jiang[1](✉) and Yi-huo Jiang[2]

[1] Department of General Knowledge, Fujian Chuanzheng Communications College, Fuzhou 350202, China

[2] Fuzhou University of International Studies and Trade, Fuzhou 350202, China

**Abstract.** In the current application process of learning behavior data mining, the poor classification of data model training problems leads to long data mining time and affects accuracy. Therefore, a data mining method for English online learning behavior based on machine learning technology is proposed. First, set up the set of association items and establish behavior association rules. Cluster student behaviors based on association rules. And according to the clustering set, construct a learning object model, and use machine learning technology to train the model. After training, decision tree is used to mine data. In order to verify whether the design method meets the original intention of the design, the experimental analysis is carried out. The literature method and the designed data mining method are used to mine the students' behavior data in the English online learning platform of a university. The experimental results show that the designed data mining method has shorter time-consuming and higher accuracy, and achieves the original design intention.

**Keywords:** Data mining · Association rules · Machine learning · Clustering set

## 1 Introduction

Data mining has achieved effective application in many industries and fields, and its application in education is more and more extensive, but its application in English online learning is less in China, and many researches on English online learning do not mention data mining [1–3]. With the increasing popularity of English online learning, a large number of online learning data have been accumulated. It is very necessary to apply data mining technology to online learning. Foreign online learning learners research is mainly reflected in learning support services, through providing various services to learners, can meet the needs of learners, and improve online learning quality [4–6]. These support services are provided after a detailed analysis of learners. In China, the development of online learning started late, and the quality of online learning platform is uneven. From the current situation of online learning in China, there are mainly two forms of academic education and non academic education. The theoretical research


W. Fu et al. (Eds.): eLEOT 2021, LNICST 389, pp. 122–133, 2021.
https://doi.org/10.1007/978-3-030-84383-0_11

of learning support service is paid more attention than the practical research. Many domestic scholars and researchers attach great importance to the study of learners' learning support service [7, 8]. However, due to the traditional English online learning behavior data mining method, there is a problem of mining accuracy and long mining time. This paper proposes the English online learning behavior data mining method based on machine learning technology. By setting the association entry, establish a behavioral relationship rule, Based on the association item of the students in English learning, based on clustering results, build a learning object model, using machine learning technology to train this model, combined with data mining methods to explore online online learning behavior data, implement English online learning Digging of behavioral data. Through simulation experiments, it verifies that this method is shorter than the time of English online learning behavior data mining, and the excavation accuracy is high, and it has laid the foundation for improving online learning quality.

## 2 Design of Data Mining Method for English Online Learning Behavior Based on Machine Learning Technology

The data mining method designed in this paper uses machine learning technology for data model training Fig. 1. The specific process is as follows:

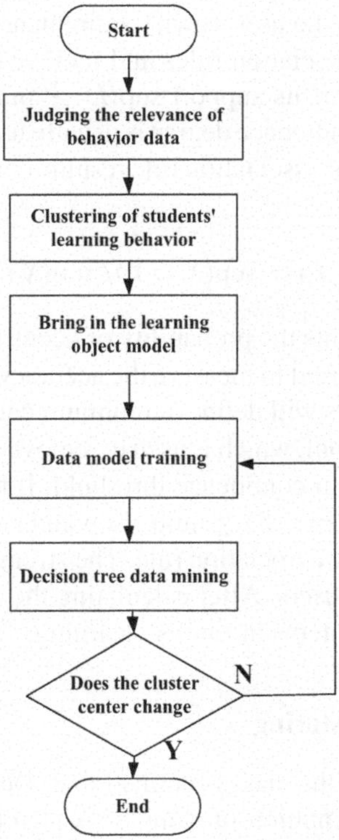


**Fig. 1.** Flow chart of online learning behavior data mining method

### 2.1 Behavioral Association Rules

Association rules can get the implicit association information between data, it can dig out the deep-level relationship between data and get the connection and law between them through analysis [9]. In the calculation of the behavior association rules, set the number of items included in the associated item set $I = \{I\ [1],\ I[2], ......I[k]\}$ as $k$, and call $I$ the $k-$ item set. The association rule of English learning behavior is generally expressed as $X\ => $ Y, which reflects the concomitant relationship of item set $X$ and item set Y, where $X \subseteq T$, $Y \subseteq T$, and $X \cap Y = \phi$, and $X$ is used as the generation condition of the association rule, and $Y$ represents the association rule As a result, it also reflects the rule that Y appears when itemset $X$ appears. Usually, the support degree is used to measure the importance of association rules. The support degree of association rule $X$ = >Y can be expressed as itemset $X$ and itemset Y The probability of simultaneous occurrence in all itemsets, namely:

$$\sup(X => Y) = \sup(X \cup Y) = P(X \cup Y) \tag{1}$$

The formula in (1) can also be expressed as (number of transactions including $X$ and Y / total number of transactions) x 100%. $P$ stands for the support rate. The greater the support, the greater the frequency and importance of association rules. In practical application, a minimum support degree is defined in min_ Sup. Minimum support is a threshold defined according to the user's own requirements to measure the support. It is used to filter the generated association rules and remove some unimportant or useless rules. For a certain itemset $I$, if its support $\sup(I) \geq \min\_\sup$, then the itemset $I$ is called frequent itemset. The confidence degree is usually used to describe the conditional probability of the occurrence of association rule results, denoted as $conf(X => Y)$, and its expression is as follows:

$$conf(X => Y) = \sup(X \cup Y)/\sup(X) = P(Y|X) \tag{2}$$

Confidence degree represents the probability of occurrence of item set $Y$ when item set $X$ occurs, and is generally used to measure the accuracy of association rules. In practical applications, general users will define a minimum confidence level by themselves, which is represented by min_conf, which is used to remove association rules whose accuracy is lower than the minimum confidence threshold. If the association rule $X => Y$ satisfies the conditions $\sup(X => Y) \geq \min\_\sup$ and $conf(X => Y) \geq \min\_conf$, then $X => Y$ is called a strong association rule. The strong association rule is generally useful information needed by users. After calculating the code rules, the cluster can be made according to the related items in English learning.

### 2.2 Learning Behavior Clustering

Before clustering the data set, the class is defined first. Due to the difference of sample things themselves, the representation of samples is also different, which leads to the difference in the definition of class [10]. Here are some definitions of classes. Firstly, the behavior data set is set as $D$, which contains sample $n$, $S_i$ represents a certain sample, $C$ and $V$ represent the preset values of the sample. If any data $S_i$ and $S_j \in D$ have

$d(S_i, S_j) \leq C$, then $D$ is a class. If $S_i \in D$ in each data, then we can get the following results:

$$\frac{1}{n-1}\sum_{j=1} d(S_i, S_j) \leq C \tag{3}$$

In the formula (3), $C$ represents the maximum number of samples in the sample set. And for any $S_i$, $S_j \in D$ can be obtained:

$$\frac{1}{n \times (n-1)}\sum_{i}\sum_{j} d(S_i, S_j) \leq V \tag{4}$$

If a, then D is $d(S_i, S_j) \leq V$ class. In order to make the clustering accurate, on the basis of completing the behavior association, we classify the data by similarity. In this paper, we choose the distance measurement method. If the data in the data set has $t$ attributes, we can take each data point as a point in the $t$ latitude space to judge the similarity of the data in the data set. Generally, we judge the similarity through the distance. If the distance between samples is small, the higher the similarity is, the smaller the difference is. On the contrary, the difference between data is larger. According to Mahalanobis formula, it can be concluded that:

$$D(X, Y) = (X - Y)^T \times \sum\nolimits^{-1}(X - Y) \tag{5}$$

In (5), $T$ represents the reference value of the Mahalanobis distance formula. In the teaching of English learning behaviors, the five aspects of English listening, speaking, reading, writing and overall ability can correspond to the score intervals of different levels of courses. This paper divides the clustering results into:

**Table 1.** Classification of cluster learning scores

| Category | Preliminary | Beginner level | Qualified level | Master level | Proficiency | Proficiency |
|---|---|---|---|---|---|---|
| Listen | [0,46] | (46,67] | (67,75] | (75,79] | (79,83] | (83,100] |
| Say | [0,42] | (42,67] | (67,77] | (77,79] | (79,84] | (84,100] |
| Read | [0,42] | (42,62] | (62,69] | (69,82] | (82,85] | (85,100] |
| Write | [0,55] | (55,76] | (76,77] | (77,85] | (85,86] | (86,100] |
| Overall | [0,45] | (45,68] | (68,72] | (72,76] | (76,83] | (83,100] |

According to the above Table 1, student samples can be specifically clustered and classified by their grades.

## 2.3 Construction of Learning Object Model

Personal E-learning behavior is a process of cognition and mastery of personal e-learning resources. However, due to the lack of supervision during personal online learning, the requirements for the self-consciousness and control ability of individual online learners are higher, and the quantity and variety of personal online learning resources are also a test of learners' information choice. In order to obtain higher learning efficiency, it is necessary to classify or formulate learning resources systematically. According to the degree of encapsulation, learning objects can be divided into compound type and atomic type. The reusability of learning objects is affected by the partition degree. The greater the partition degree is, the smaller the reusability will be, and the smaller the arc partition degree will be, the greater the reusability will be. It is also considered that the two types of learning objects are related and can be converted to each other under certain conditions. The atomic learning object mainly refers to the minimum segmentation unit that is achieved when the relevant knowledge is divided into the frame structure of the learning object. The division of atomic objects is based on the information block areas established according to the learning goals of different learners. Each information area contains a series of knowledge points. The atomic learning object is the most basic form of expression of the content of the smallest teaching unit. Among all learning objects, it has the best reusability. Atomic learning objects usually consist of a variety of learning materials, which have multiple formats, such as text, pictures, or other multimedia materials. When the learner is learning the course, the text description is usually used to logically explain the content of the course, and learners prefer non-text materials, such as images, videos, sounds, etc. available for personal online learning. Come for a better experience and increase the fun of learning (Fig. 2). The atomic learning object is shown below:

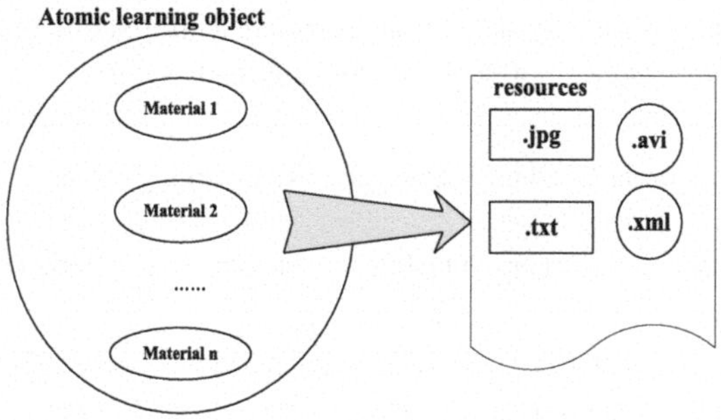


**Fig. 2.** Atomic learning objects

Compound learning object refers to a way of presenting the content, framework or internal relationship of specific learning resources. It can generally meet a variety of learning needs, and is usually composed of a variety of complex types of learning objects. Its main composition is shown in the Fig. 3.

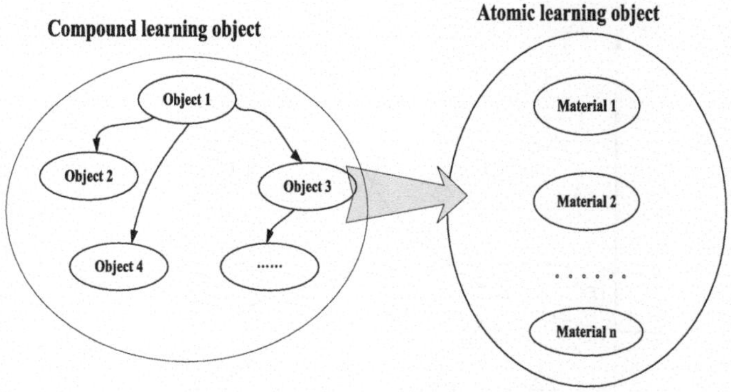


**Fig. 3.** Compound learning objects

According to the arrangement of the course content and the learning order of individual network learners, the relationship between the objects contained in the compound object can be divided into the following: 1. Antecedent relationship two objects. If the learning priority of one object is prior to the other, the former object is called the latter object.

The antecedent object of. 2. Similarly, for two objects, if the learning priority of one object is after the other, the latter object is said to be the successor of the previous object.

## 2.4 Machine Learning Technology to Achieve Model Training

After the learning object model is established, multiple separation problems often occur during data set training, and machine learning technology is required for model training. For multi-classification problems, that is, when the sample points in the training set to be classified belong to more than two categories, the two-class machine learning algorithm needs to be extended. The one-category reclassification method transforms the multi-classification problem into multiple two-classification problems, where each two-classification problem takes a certain class in the multi-classification problem as the positive class in the two-class classification, and all the rest in the multi-classification problem Class as the negative class in the two-classification problem, and then use the two-class support vector machine to construct multiple division functions. If a certain division function takes a positive value during classification, it means that the corresponding two-class support vector machine judges the sample The point belongs to the positive class of the classifier, that is, a certain class in the multi-classification problem. If the division function uses a negative value, it means that the corresponding two-level support vector machine determines whether the sample point belongs to the classifier, that is, it does not belong to the class in the multi-class problem. The way to solve the multi-classification problem by using the one-to-remainder method is shown in the figure below:

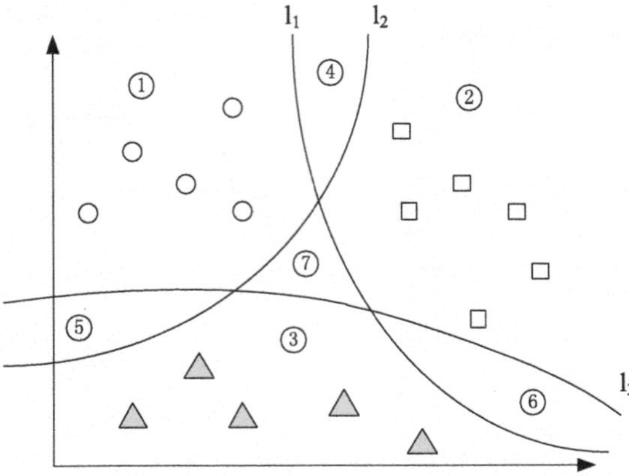


**Fig. 4.** Example of multi classification problem processing

In Fig. 4, the existence of rectangles, circles, and triangles represent three types of sample points, while l1, l2, and l3 respectively represent the three reticle curves obtained by solving the two-class support vector machine. When classifying, just substitute the feature vector of the sample point into the corresponding function of the three curves, and then make a decision based on the function value.

## 2.5 Decision Tree Data Mining

After completing the data clustering and the establishment of the learning object model, use it as a database. The database is set to $D = \{d_1, d_2, ..., d_n\}$, where $d_i =< d_{il}, ..., d_{ih} >$, the database contains the following attributes $\{A_1, A_2, ..., A_h\}$, and the point category set $L = \{L_1, ..., L_m\}$. For database $D$, the decision tree contains the following properties. Each internal node corresponds to an attribute Ai, each arc is used to judge the parent node, and the direction of decision-making is judged according to the attribute value corresponding to the parent node. Each leaf node is a completely divided Class, all the leaf nodes constitute all the classification of the sample data. The tree starts with a single node representing the training sample. If the sample is in the same type, the node becomes a leaf node and is labeled with this class. Otherwise, the algorithm uses the entropy measure called information gain as the heuristic information, and selects the attribute that can best classify the samples, which becomes the test or decision attribute of the node. Create a branch for each known value of the test property and divide the sample accordingly. The algorithm uses a similar method to recursively form the sample decision tree on each partition. Once an attribute appears on a node, it is not necessary to consider the attribute on the descendants of that node. On each node of the tree, information gain measure is used to select test attributes, which is also called attribute selection measure. By selecting the attribute with the highest information gain as the test attribute of the current node, the amount of information needed to classify the sample in the result division is minimized, thereby ensuring the simplest decision tree generated. Suppose $B$ is a collection of $b$ data samples, and there are $m$ category attributes with different values, and $m$ different classes $C_i(i = 1, ....., m)$ are defined at the same time. If $s_i$ is the number of samples in class $C_i$, then it is necessary to classify a given sample The expected value is:

$$I(s_1, s_2, ..., s_m) = -\sum_{i=1}^{m} p_i \log_2(p_i) \tag{6}$$

In (6), $p_i$ is the probability that any sample belongs to $C_i$. the logarithm function of $p_i = s_i/S$, $S = s_1 + s_2 + ... + s_m$ is based on 2, because the computer information is encoded by binary code. Let $A$ have $v$ different discrete attribute values $\{a_1, a_2, ...a_v\}$. The set $S$ can be divided into $v$ subsets $\{S_1, S_2, ...S_v\}$ by using attribute $A$, where $S_j$ contains the data samples with $a_j$ value taken by attribute $A$ in $S$ set. If attribute $A$ is selected as test attribute, the current sample set is divided by attribute $A$. Let $S_{ij}$ be the number of samples belonging to class $C_i$ in subset $S_j$. The subset Di divided by $A$ is obtained by the following formula:

$$E(A) = -\sum_{i=1}^{v} \frac{s_{1j} + s_{2j} + ... + s_{mj}}{s} I\left(s_{ij}, s_{2j}, ..., s_{mj}\right) \tag{7}$$

When the categories in the divided subsets are more unified, the direct value is smaller. Finally, from the formulas (6) and (7), the attribute can be used as the information gain value of test attribute $A$:

$$Gain(A) = I(s_1, s_2, ..., s_m) - E(A) \tag{8}$$

In the selection of attributes, the maximum information gain value is selected as the test attribute. At the same time, data mining is guaranteed by decision tree.

## 3 Experimental Demonstration Analysis

In order to verify the feasibility of the proposed method. In this paper, the data mining method in literature [2] and literature [10] is used for data mining of English online learning platform of a university.

### 3.1 Learning Platform Environment

The English online learning platform of a different grade of different grades in the experiment is the environment topology, Fig. 5 and the structure is as follows:

The operating system of the platform is Windows7, the IDE environment is MyEclipse10, the web server is JDK1.7 + Tomcat7, the programming language is JAVA + JSP, and the database is Oracle11g (Table 2). The hardware environment of the platform is as follows:

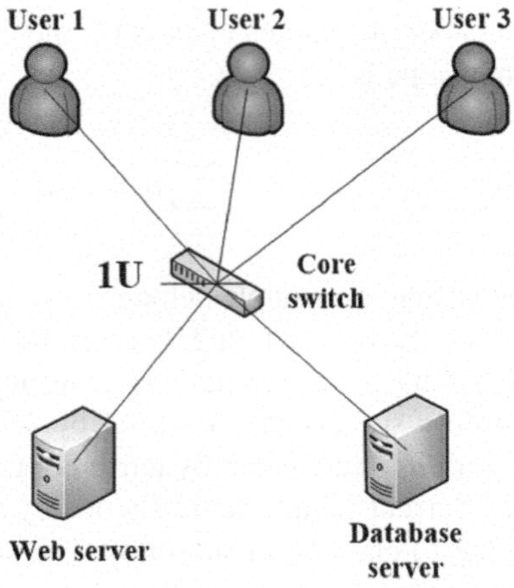


**Fig. 5.** Topology diagram of learning platform

**Table 2.** Hardware environment of experimental platform

| Equipment | Model | CPU | Memory | Network bandwidth |
|---|---|---|---|---|
| Controller | HP ProDesk 498 G2 MT | Intel(R)Core(TM) I7–4790 CPU@3.60GHz | 16 GB | 100 Mbps |
| Calculate node | HP ProDesk 498 G2 MT | Intel(R)Core(TM) I7–4790 CPU@3.60GHz | 16 GB | 100 Mbps |
| Client | HP ProDesk 498 G2 MT | HP ProDesk 498 G2 MT | 16 GB | 100 Mbps |

## 3.2 Experimental Data Situation

The data used in the experiment are the learning behavior data of the students in the above platform, and the experimental parameters are set as follows: the difference threshold is 0.01. The minimum number of samples is 2. In the experiment, the samples are divided into 10 samples, 9 of which are used as training set and the other as test set. The average accuracy was obtained by three experiments (Table 3) The sample dataset information is as follows:

**Table 3.** Experimental data set information

| Data set | Data size | Number of attributes | Number of categories |
|---|---|---|---|
| Zoo | 101 | 17 | 7 |
| Banding | 138 | 29 | 2 |
| Monk1 | 124 | 6 | 2 |
| Monk2 | 169 | 6 | 2 |
| Vote | 300 | 16 | 2 |
| Crx | 490 | 15 | 2 |
| Soybean | 683 | 35 | 19 |
| Anneal | 898 | 38 | 6 |
| Hypo | 2514 | 29 | 5 |
| Letter | 20000 | 16 | 26 |

## 3.3 Experimental Results

The data mining history of the experimental data set is shown in the following table:

**Table 4.** Data set mining operation table

| Data set | Time consumption (MS) | | | Accuracy rate (%) | | |
|---|---|---|---|---|---|---|
| | Method 1 | Method 2 | Method 3 | Method 1 | Method 2 | Method 3 |
| Zoo | 87 | 89 | 99 | 100 | 99.4 | 100 |
| Banding | 138 | 144 | 165 | 99.6 | 89.4 | 97.3 |
| Monk1 | 98 | 102 | 133 | 99.8 | 89.8 | 96.8 |
| Monk2 | 96 | 118 | 145 | 97.5 | 83.4 | 88.5 |
| Vote | 111 | 127 | 156 | 95.4 | 80.2 | 87.5 |
| CrX | 145 | 162 | 178 | 94.3 | 79.4 | 84.4 |
| Soybean | 277 | 335 | 387 | 93.4 | 77.4 | 81.5 |
| Anneal | 343 | 368 | 388 | 97.5 | 92.1 | 94.5 |
| Hypo | 397 | 408 | 465 | 94.3 | 90.2 | 91.5 |
| Letter | 14531 | 15442 | 21813 | 92.1 | 88.4 | 90.1 |

In the above table, method one is the method used in this article, method two is the method in literature [2], and method three is the method in literature [10]. It can be seen from the above table that the data mining method designed in this paper takes less time than the other two methods when mining the data set, and has a higher accuracy rate.

In order to further prove the effectiveness of the method, an incremental operation is performed on the data set, and the experimental results obtained are as follows:

**Table 5.** Data set incremental mining operation table

| Data set | Incremental scale | Time consumption (MS) | | | Accuracy rate (%) | | |
|---|---|---|---|---|---|---|---|
| | | Method 1 | Method 2 | Method 3 | Method 1 | Method 2 | Method 3 |
| Zoo | 25% | 54 | 69 | 63 | 99.8 | 97.4 | 93.2 |
| Banding | 35% | 77 | 79 | 85 | 94.5 | 90.2 | 89.5 |
| Monk1 | 30% | 66 | 78 | 91 | 98.4 | 93.5 | 92.1 |
| Monk2 | 40% | 70 | 82 | 89 | 94.6 | 91.2 | 90.2 |
| Vote | 35% | 61 | 73 | 82 | 99.6 | 92.1 | 94.5 |
| Crx | 50% | 94 | 115 | 143 | 94.2 | 93.5 | 91.1 |
| Soybean | 30% | 94 | 221 | 154 | 92.4 | 91.6 | 88.5 |
| Anneal | 20% | 214 | 336 | 298 | 99.2 | 85.4 | 92.1 |
| Hypo | 30% | 184 | 218 | 305 | 96.4 | 82.5 | 79.3 |
| Letter | 20% | 5964 | 13541 | 13481 | 96.4 | 90.1 | 88.2 |

The experiments in Table 4 and Table 5 prove that the data mining method of English online learning behavior designed in this paper has higher accuracy and lower time-consuming. The design method is feasible.

## 4 Conclusion

This paper uses machine learning technology to train data mining methods, reducing the time-consuming and improving accuracy of data mining methods. However, there are still shortcomings in the research. The amount of data for data mining is relatively small. In the follow-up research, the selection of data sources should be expanded to further prove the research conclusions.

## References

1. Zhu, J., Gong, C., Zhang, S., Zhao, M., et al.: Foundation study on wireless big data: concept, mining, learning and practices. China Commun. **15**(12), 1–15 (2018)
2. Ma, X.L., Zhai, X., Liu, J.W., et al.: Study on the biological basis of hypertension and syndrome with liver-fire hyperactivity based on data mining technology World. J. Tradit. Chin. Med. **4**(04), 176–180 (2018)
3. Cai, G., Lee, K., Lee, I.: Mining semantic trajectory patterns from geo-tagged data. J. Comput. Sci. Technol. **33**(4), 849–862 (2018)

4. Terrazas-Arellanes, F.E., Gallard, A.J.M., Strycker, L.A., et al.: Impact of interactive online units on learning science among students with learning disabilities and English learners. Int. J. Sci. Educ. **40**(5), 498–518 (2018)
5. Müller, A., Son, J.-B., Nozawa, K., et al.: Learning english idioms with a web-based educational game. J. Educ. Comput. Res. **56**(6), 848–865 (2018)
6. Liu, S., Lu, M., Li, H., et al.: Prediction of gene expression patterns with generalized linear regression model. Front. Genet. **10**, 120 (2019)
7. Liu, S., Li, Z., Zhang, Y., et al.: Introduction of key problems in long-distance learning and training. Mobile Netw. Appl. **24**(1), 1–4 (2019)
8. Liu, S., Glowatz, M., Zappatore, M., Gao, H., Jia, B., Bucciero, A. (eds.): eLEOT 2018. LNICSSITE, vol. 243. Springer, Cham (2018). https://doi.org/10.1007/978-3-319-93719-9
9. Wang, J.: A new system for distributed machine learning. Nat. Sci. Rev. **5**(03), 303–304 (2018)
10. Su, H., Li, Y., Zhang, X.: Data mining simulation of logistics frequent path based on radio frequency identification. Comput. Simul. **36**(09), 357–360–384 (2019)

# Intelligent Recommendation Model of Distance Education Courses Based on Facial Expression Recognition

Ying Yang[1], Dong-rui Li[1](✉), Xiao-feng Huang[1], and Sheng-bin Wu[2]

[1] School of Computer, Guangdong AIB Polytechnic College, Guangzhou 510507, China
[2] College of Information Engineering, Changsha Medical University, Changsha 410219, China

**Abstract.** Aiming at the lack of individualization of current course resources in distance education, an intelligent recommendation model for distance education courses based on facial expression recognition is designed. Extract data that can represent the characteristics of the resource, such as title, subject, category, path, source, author, date, keywords, description information, etc., and represent the resource in the form of learning object metadata under the LOM specification. Use Reload Edtior 2.5.5 to edit metadata and package course content. Through the establishment of learning resource model, the structure of resources is more obvious, which is convenient for resource sharing and searching. Using the modeling method of requirement tree, the user requirement model is constructed based on ontology. Based on facial expression recognition, the framework of Intelligent Recommendation Model of distance education course is built, and the intelligent recommendation model of distance education course is constructed. Through comparative experiments, it is verified that the recommendation accuracy of Intelligent Recommendation Model Based on facial expression recognition is higher than the other two recommendation models, and it has high practicability.

**Keywords:** Facial expression recognition · Distance education · Curriculum intelligent recommendation model · Metadata

## 1 Introduction

With the advancement of information technology, the popularity of 4G/5G network, wireless network and smart phone, people's quality of life and work have undergone tremendous changes. Through the network, people can use the distance education platform to learn, download network resources and related learning courseware, so that it is no longer limited to time or space, but also can carry out supplementary learning of relevant knowledge, effectively improving the learning efficiency of students [1]. Students can understand, learn, interact, upload assignments and download teaching materials through the online education platform; teachers can upload learning materials and videos and answer questions online.Since 1998, my country has developed distance


W. Fu et al. (Eds.): eLEOT 2021, LNICST 389, pp. 134–145, 2021.
https://doi.org/10.1007/978-3-030-84383-0_12

education. Up to now, it has experienced several stages including correspondence education, electronic distance, multimedia and interactive network teaching methods. With the continuous promotion of information technology, users in recent years The scale has grown rapidly [2]. According to the "Statistical Report on China's Internet Development Status" released by CNNIC, by December 2018, the number of online education users in my country had reached 201 million, an increase of 46.05 million from the previous year; and the number of online education users The utilization rate reached 24.3%, an increase of 4.2% compared to the previous year. At the same time, the number of online education users using mobile phones reached 194 million, an increase of 75.26 million compared to the previous year; and the utilization rate of mobile phone online education users reached 23.8%, an increase of 8% compared to the previous year.However, due to the online education platform only displays the offline related course content and resources, to a certain extent, due to the space and time constraints of distance education, the interaction between teachers and students is poor, and the learning efficiency is not high; at the same time, all students are taught in the same mode, which fails to reflect the personalization and is difficult to achieve To the purpose of online education to improve learning efficiency. Therefore, this paper studies the intelligent recommendation model of distance education courses, and proposes an intelligent recommendation model of distance education courses based on facial expression recognition. Firstly, metadata processing is carried out for distance education curriculum resources. Then, according to the processing results, metadata is edited and curriculum resources are packaged. According to different learning object levels, learning resource model is established to obtain user needs. Based on the needs, intelligent recommendation model for distance education curriculum is constructed, Complete the intelligent recommendation model of distance education course based on facial expression recognition.

## 2 Design an Intelligent Recommendation Model for Distance Education Courses Based on Facial Expression Recognition

### 2.1 Metadata of Curriculum Resources

Metadata refers to information used to describe elements, data sets, etc. Simply put, it is the data describing the data. Due to too many types of educational resources in the network, these resources must be collected after basic processing [3]. First, extract the data that can represent the characteristics of the resource, such as title, subject, category, path, source, author, date, keywords, description information, etc., and at the same time represent the resource in the form of learning object metadata under the LOM specification. After the collection of basic data elements based on LOM standard, it is necessary to design a metadata model according to the design requirements of the actual resources and the actual situation, complete the XML document under the syntax requirements of XML schema, and then further create the user's own metadata instance [4]. Table 1 below is a reference table of metadata information in some LOM standards, and Table 2 is a table of educational resource information that represents the basic characteristics of resources in the process of collecting educational resources.

**Table 1.** Metadata information table

| Numbering | LOM metadata | Explanation |
|---|---|---|
| 1 | General | Some general information about the learning object |
| 1.1 | General. Title | The name of the learning object |
| 1.2 | General. Keyword | Keywords describing the subject of the learning object |
| 1.3 | General.Catalogentry | The label of the learning object (unique) |
| 1.4 | General. Language | The main language used by the learning object |
| 1.5 | General. Description | Description of the content of the learning object |
| 2 | Lifecycle | The state of the learning object and the entities that act on it |
| 2.1 | Lifecycle. Contribute | Entities that contribute to the development of learning objects |
| 3 | Metametadata | Metadata itself |
| 3.1 | Metametadata.Contribute | Entities that contribute to the development of metadata |
| 3.2 | Metametadata.Language | The language used to describe metadata |
| 4 | Technical | Technical requirements and related characteristics of learning objects |
| 4.1 | Technical. Format | Data type of learning object |
| 4.2 | Technical. Size | The size of digital learning objects |
| 4.3 | Technical. Location | String used to indicate how to obtain the learning object |

**Table 2.** Educational resource information table

| Serial number | Resources | Message name |
|---|---|---|
| 1 | Title | Title |
| 2 | Theme | Subject |
| 3 | Category | Class |
| 4 | Path | Path |
| 5 | Source | Source |
| 6 | Author | Author |
| 7 | Date | Date |
| 8 | Keyword | Keyword |
| 9 | Description | Description |

## 2.2 Metadata Editing and Course Resource Packaging

It uses reload editor2.5.5 to edit metadata and package course content. It is a software that integrates different digital teaching media to conform to SCORM format [5]. Among the standards followed by reload editor, the content package supports IMS 1.1 and SCORM 1.2 standards.

The main function of Reload Editor 2.5.5 is to edit the attributes in the metadata, while creating, inserting, editing and exporting course packages containing metadata for our use.

Before using this software, you need to install javasetup 6u30, and then click reload-editor.jar You can enter the interface. The specific operation methods of metadata editing and course resource packaging are as follows: first, store the learning resources of the course in a folder (note that the name of the folder where the learning resources are stored cannot be Chinese), and the hierarchical structure of the resources in the file should be clear.In the course content packaging, first import the target course resources into the resources (Resources) panel of the software; secondly, add the organizational structure of the course in the structure function (under Organizations) in the display (Manifest) panel, and add the course resources to the course project ((Items), finally add metadata or import metadata files, and package them [6].

In the use of the software, special attention should be paid to:

1. Chinese Directory needs to pay attention to the deletion of spaces.
2. The course structure should meet the needs of packaging design.
3. There are two ways to create a directory. One is to drag, the other is to right-click and drag again.
4. The name of the hard disk where reload endtior is stored cannot be Chinese.
5. The name of the folder where learning resources are stored cannot be Chinese.

## 2.3 Establishment of Learning Resource Model

After metadata processing, educational resources will be divided according to different levels of learning objects, and the description of metadata will be obtained and stored in the education resource database, as shown in Fig. 1 [7]. There will be one to many, many to one and one to one relationships between educational resources and learning objects at different levels. According to the different learning needs and the design requirements of educational resources, the detailed division of learning objects is determined. Therefore, after metadata, we must establish the learning resource model to make the structure of resources more obvious, which is convenient for sharing and searching resources, and has an immeasurable effect on the optimization of online courses.

In the constructed learning resource model, the learning resources are described based on the LOM specification. By importing the LOM metadata, the metadata in the LOM standard is corresponding to the corresponding keywords, and then the important keywords are extracted as modeling the conditions [8]. The expressions extracted from key words are:

$$\alpha_n = \sum_{i=1}^{n} s_n w \tag{1}$$

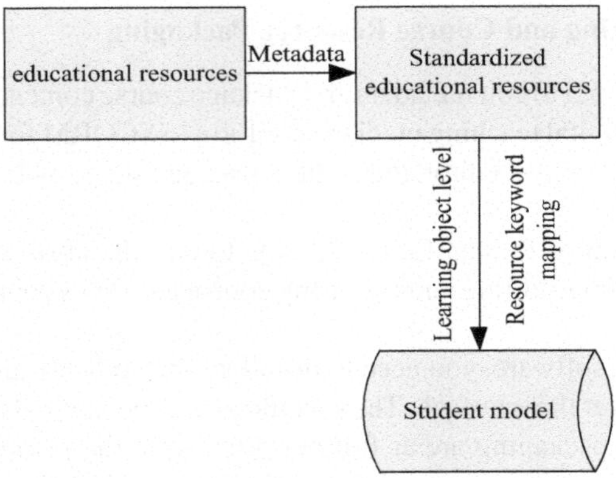


**Fig. 1.** Construction of educational resource model

The mapping relationship between descriptions and keywords is shown in Table 3.

**Table 3.** Keyword mapping table

| Numbering | Key words | LOM metadata | For example |
|---|---|---|---|
| 1 | Author | LifeCycle.Contribute.role | Fang Min, Wang Yaping |
| 2 | Keyword | General. Keyword | Operating system, computer |
| 3 | Language | General. Language | Zh |
| 4 | Media format | Technical. Format | PPT/TXT |
| 5 | Resource ID | General.Entry | 132 |
| 6 | Resource path | Technical. Location | E:\Computer OS\... |
| 7 | Educational situation | Educational.Context | Higher education |
| 8 | User role | Educational.IntendedEndUserRole | Learner/resource builder |
| 9 | Subject classification | Classification. taxon | Computer |
| 10 | date | LifeCycle.Contribute.data | year 2011 |
| 11 | Class hours | Education. Typical Learning Time | 50 h |
| 12 | relationship | Relation.kind.Value | ISPartOf |

## 2.4 Building User Demand Model

Using the modeling method of demand tree, build user demand model based on ontology. Mainly by using the conceptual relationship in the domain ontology theory to conceptualize the user demand model, and to select the same-level relationship and the relationship between the upper and lower levels in the model, which can form a tree-like "demand tree" Structure of user demand model.

There are two main functional modules in the user demand model: establishment and modification. Among them, there are two ways to establish the module: explicit and implicit. Explicit is to collect students' information, that is, students select the required knowledge points by manual operation. Students can manually select the knowledge point concepts they need and enter their information into the corresponding demand tree. Therefore, when a student logs in to the model, the model will automatically check whether the manual operation demand tree has been set up completely. If not, a new demand tree with missing content needs to be created for the student immediately; if so, it will Return directly to the demand tree that it has established.The other is to collect data in a recessive way, that is, to excavate students' behavior deeply and find out the corresponding information. In the case of no impact on the behavior of students, through this way, the model will automatically conduct in-depth mining of their behavior, find out which knowledge points the student needs, and fill it into the student demand tree [9].

The modification function module in the user demand model is mainly composed of two components: demand update and automatic recommendation. The update function required by students also includes manual and automatic methods. The reason for manual update is that there will inevitably be differences between the model recommendation and the students' rational choices. Therefore, in order to reduce this deviation, it is necessary to manually modify the student's demand tree, which includes the concept of adding and deleting knowledge points, and The evaluation weight of knowledge point needs is modified and deleted, or short-term learning needs are added. The automatic update means that the model automatically updates the content by accessing the information recently browsed by the students and filtering. The recommendation function in the model is to recommend through the knowledge points in the student demand tree. If the recommended information can be adopted by the students, it indicates that the recommendation provided by the model is more effective.If it is not adopted by students, it shows that the result recommended by the model is not the best. At this time, it is necessary to modify the demand tree to meet the needs of students for knowledge points of the course.

The constructed user demand model is shown in Fig. 2.

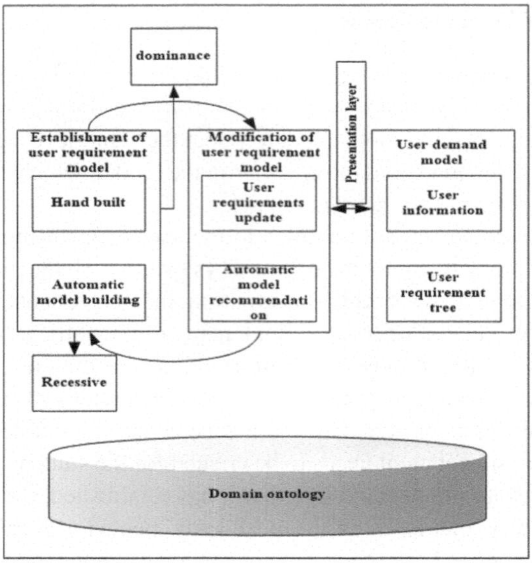


**Fig. 2.** Constructed user demand model

## 2.5 Constructing an Intelligent Recommendation Model of Distance Education Courses

Based on facial expression recognition, the framework of Intelligent Recommendation Model for distance education courses is constructed. Among them, the backstage management unit of the framework is developed by using spring boot server framework and mybatis persistence layer framework. The front end uses HTML5 and JavaScript language, adopts a set of general background management template system charisma, which is based on facial expression recognition technology. It is convenient, simple and has good compatibility, and uses postman to do interface test. In the aspect of database, MySQL is chosen as the data-driven source. The interface test recommendation engine algorithm module is written in Python and deployed independently, which can realize offline calculation [10–12]. After the recommendation results calculated by the recommendation engine are stored in the database, the recommendation model can be processed again according to the configuration information, and finally provide calling services for the master station in the form of an interface.

The intelligent recommendation model of distance education course can be divided into user interest recommendation module, similar course recommendation module and background management service module.

Among them, the main function of the user interest recommendation module is to provide courses recommendation interface services in line with their interests for the students in the main station such as the cadre network education and training platform. The recommended list of each student in the model has been calculated by the recommendation engine, so this interface only needs to query the corresponding data from the corresponding data table through the passed student ID when it is called and return it to the student. When the main station student logs in to the personal center, the browser triggers a JS script to send an Ajax request to the user interest recommendation service to obtain personalized recommendation results.

The specific processing flow of the system after receiving the Ajax request is as follows:

Step 1: after receiving the Ajax request, go to the listbyuser method in the recommendcontroller according to the request address.

Step 2: judge whether the student ID in the request parameter is empty in the listbyuser method. If it is empty, an error code is returned. If not, the selectcoursebyuser method of recommendcourseservice is called to obtain the recommended candidate set.

Step 3: after obtaining the list of recommended candidates, if there are recommended courses specified by the system, such as compulsory courses, the two methods will be fused, and finally the recommendation results will be returned to the students in JSON format.

The main function of the similar course recommendation module is to recommend courses similar to the course when the students browse the detailed information of a course. If a student is looking for course resources of interest, there is a difference between the course developed and the target course, and the course needs to be searched again. In order to avoid this problem and improve the student experience, the recommendation module is designed to provide similar recommendation services for existing courses. All courses in the model have been calculated by the recommendation engine and the results have been stored in the data table. Therefore, the interface service of this module only needs to query the corresponding data from the corresponding data table through the passed course ID when it is called and return it to the students..

When the students of the main station browse the detailed interface of the course, the browser will send the Ajax request to this module to obtain the recommended list of similar courses from JS script. The specific processing flow of the model after receiving the Ajax request is as follows:

Step 1: after receiving the Ajax request, the system will go to the corresponding processing function (listbycourse method in recommendcontroller) according to the request address.

Step 2: judge whether the course ID in the request parameter is empty in the listbycourse method. If it is empty, an error code is returned. If not, the selectcoursebycourse method of recommendcourseservice is called to obtain the recommended candidate set.

Step 3: after obtaining the recommended candidate list, filter the candidate set according to the setting information, and finally return the recommendation result to the students in JSON format.

The background management service module is the management platform of the whole recommendation model, and its main functions include login, account management, designated course setting, recommendation configuration and so on.

# 3 Experimental Verification of Intelligent Recommendation for Distance Education Courses

## 3.1 Experimental Design

The experimental environment configuration is shown in Table 4.

**Table 4.** Experimental environment configuration

| Serial number | Configuration | Data |
|---|---|---|
| 1 | Computer hardware configuration | CPU: AMD Athlon (TM) II X4 640<br>Main frequency:3. O1 GHz<br>RAM:3. 25GB |
| 2 | operating system | Microsoft Windows XP |
| 3 | Metadata editing and course content packaging | Reload Editor 2.5.5 |
| 4 | Low-level software | Xampp1.7.7 Java |
| 5 | testing platform | Joomla 1.7.3 |
| 6 | Use templates | schoolnerdfree-1. 0. 0 |
| 7 | Use plugin | Google Analytics |

The experimental network topology is shown in Fig. 3.

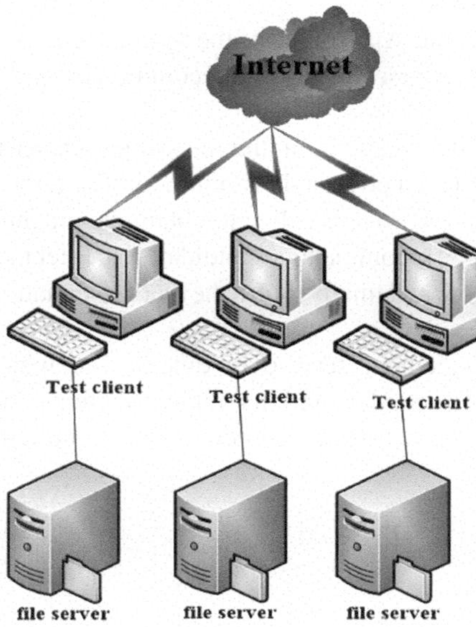


**Fig. 3.** Experimental network topology

Based on the experimental environment, the intelligent recommendation model of distance education courses based on facial expression recognition is carried out. The analysis data used in the experiment is mainly from Beijing 101 online school, which has opened more than 90 courses with a wide coverage, and the number of online students has reached more than 10000. The data obtained by using crawlers include all the basic information of students, behavior retrieval browsing, collection information, and the relevant information and knowledge point evaluation of each mathematical knowledge point. Therefore, through the use of the network school data for research, will make the recommendation results more accurate and more reliable.

In the experiment, 3563 pieces of student scoring data on the knowledge points of middle school mathematics were extracted to build a data set, which contains 3316 students' scores for 26 knowledge units of middle school mathematics, and each student's score for the knowledge unit must be 10. And above, the scoring value is set to all integers from 0 to 100. In addition, the higher the students' scores for knowledge points, the more they are eager for knowledge points.

Use accuracy to evaluate the intelligent recommendation model of distance education courses based on facial expression recognition. The average absolute deviation MAE can effectively measure the deviation between the predicted score value and the actual score value, calculate the deviation, and then measure the accuracy of the prediction. The smaller the value of MAE, the better the recommended results.

In order to make the experimental results more comparative, the two original intelligent recommendation models of distance education courses are taken as the comparison models, including the intelligent recommendation model of distance education courses based on collaborative filtering and time weighted algorithm. The MAE experimental data of three intelligent recommendation models of distance education courses were compared.

### 3.2 Analysis of Results

The MAE comparison experiment data of distance education course intelligent recommendation model based on facial expression recognition and distance education course intelligent recommendation model based on collaborative filtering and time weighted algorithm are shown in Table 5.

According to the MAE comparison experimental data in Table 5, the average absolute deviation of the distance education course intelligent recommendation model based on facial expression recognition is smaller than that of the distance education course intelligent recommendation model based on collaborative filtering and time-weighted algorithm, that is, based on facial expression recognition The recommendation accuracy of the intelligent recommendation model for distance education courses is higher than that of the other two recommendation models.

**Table 5.** MAE comparative experimental data

| Nearest neighbor student users | Recommendation model based on facial expression recognition | Recommendation model based on collaborative filtering | Recommendation model based on time weighted algorithm |
|---|---|---|---|
| | Mae average | | |
| 50 | 0.720 | 0.792 | 0.852 |
| 100 | 0.710 | 0.781 | 0.835 |
| 150 | 0.704 | 0.774 | 0.816 |
| 200 | 0.692 | 0.761 | 0.805 |
| 250 | 0.685 | 0.756 | 0.793 |
| 300 | 0.671 | 0.752 | 0.782 |
| 350 | 0.665 | 0.741 | 0.771 |
| 400 | 0.652 | 0.730 | 0.761 |
| 450 | 0.641 | 0.721 | 0.758 |
| 500 | 0.632 | 0.701 | 0.749 |
| 550 | 0.620 | 0.700 | 0.732 |
| 600 | 0.610 | 0.692 | 0.721 |
| 650 | 0.605 | 0.682 | 0.710 |
| 700 | 0.601 | 0.671 | 0.705 |
| 750 | 0.592 | 0.668 | 0.692 |
| 800 | 0.582 | 0.652 | 0.682 |
| 850 | 0.571 | 0.647 | 0.671 |
| 900 | 0.569 | 0.638 | 0.661 |
| 950 | 0.554 | 0.624 | 0.654 |
| 1000 | 0.541 | 0.617 | 0.641 |

## 4 Concluding Remarks

The current distance education platform should pay more attention to students' development and demand preference. Therefore, an intelligent recommendation model of distance education course based on facial expression recognition is designed to obtain metadata based distance education course resources, edit and package them, divide learning resources according to different learning object levels, and construct user demand model, Realize intelligent recommendation of distance education courses.. The intelligent recommendation model of distance education course based on facial expression recognition improves the accuracy of recommendation, and can solve the problems of various course recommendation, unclear purpose and noise data in many education platforms. It can provide students with more scientific and reasonable knowledge.

**Fund Projects.** By the Key Platform and Scientific Research Project of Guangdong Provincial Department of Education in 2017 - Youth Innovative Talents Project (Natural Science), Project No. 2017GkQNCX041.

## References

1. Cipryan, L., Plews, D.J., Ferretti, A., et al.: Effects of a 4-Week Very Low-Carbohydrate Diet on High-Intensity Interval Training Responses. J. Sports Sci. Med. **17**(2), 259–268 (2018)
2. Laganà, P., Votano, L., Caruso, G., Azzaro, M., Lo Giudice, A., Delia, S.: Bacterial isolates from the Arctic region (Pasvik River, Norway): assessment of biofilm production and antibiotic susceptibility profiles. Environ. Sci. Pollut. Res. **25**(2), 1089–1102 (2017). https://doi.org/10.1007/s11356-017-0485-1
3. Valentim, F.D.O., Oliveira, C.C., Amante, M.H.: Case for diagnosis. Primary cutaneous CD4+ small/medium T-cell lymphoproliferative disorder. Anais Brasileiros De Dermatologia, 94(1), 99–101 (2019)
4. Ruiz, G.J.C., Cunha Karen de Almeida Pinto Fernandes da, Silva M J R D , et al. Nasal-type extranodal T-cell/NK lymphoma in association with hemophagocytic syndrome. Anais Brasileiros De Dermatologia, 93(3), 422–425 (2018)
5. Tamar, H., Vianna, G.J.R., Hanifin, J.M.: New and developing therapies for atopic dermatitis. An. Bras. Dermatol. **93**(1), 104–107 (2018)
6. Schwalbe, F.: The importance of student leagues on medical training in neurosurgery and residency choice. Arquivos Brasilros De Neurocirurgia Brazilian Neurosurgery **37**(1), 13–18 (2018)
7. Peres, L.P., Oliveira, F.B., Cartell, A., et al.: Density of mast cells and intensity of pruritus in psoriasis vulgaris: a cross sectional study. Anais brasilros de dermatologia **93**(3), 368–372 (2018)
8. Liu, S., Lu, M., Li, H., et al.: Prediction of gene expression patterns with generalized linear regression model. Front. Genet. **10**, 120 (2019)
9. Liu, S., Li, Z., Zhang, Y., et al.: Introduction of key problems in long-distance learning and training. Mobile Netw. Appl. **24**(1), 1–4 (2019)
10. Vincenti, G., Bucciero, A., Vaz de Carvalho, C. (eds.): eLEOT 2014. LNICSSITE, vol. 138. Springer, Cham (2014). https://doi.org/10.1007/978-3-319-13293-8
11. Sundari, M.R., Shreya, G., Jawahar, T.: Course recommendation system. Int. J. Comput. Appl. **175**(29), 13–16 (2020)
12. Thanh, D.T., Sang, L.H., Hai, N.T., et al.: Course recommendation with deep learning approach. Commun. Comput. Info. Sci. **1306**, 63–77 (2020)

# Online Teaching Method of Conductive Characteristics of Graphene Materials Based on Big Data Mining

Tian-hui Wang[1(✉)], Ang Li[1], and Zheng Zhang[2]

[1] Zhuhai College of Jilin University, Zhuhai 519041, China
[2] Nanyang Institute of Technology, Nanyang 47300, China

**Abstract.** In view of the low effectiveness of traditional online teaching method based on principal component analysis and multilayer perceptron neural network, an online teaching method based on big data mining is proposed. Firstly, the conductive characteristics of graphene materials are extracted, and on this basis, the big data mining technology is used to construct the charge accumulation teaching model, and the online teaching of charge accumulation characteristics is completed through the teaching model. The experimental results show that the proposed method can effectively complete the online teaching of graphene material conductivity characteristics, and has high effectiveness.

**Keywords:** Big data mining · Graphene conductive materials · Conductive characteristics · Online teaching

## 1 Introduction

With the rapid development of information technology, people increasingly rely on computer technology to solve problems [1]. People's ability to produce, collect, store, and process information and data is constantly increasing. People's current data operations can no longer meet their needs. They hope to dig out valuable information from the current large amount of data. The same is true for the education industry [2]. The current online teaching database system can not meet this demand. On this basis, data mining emerges as the times require. As a new information processing technology, the process of extracting, transforming, analyzing and other modeling processing of a large number of data in the database is its main feature [3]. At the same time, data mining in multiple fields can extract the data that is very important for project decision-making. The essence of data mining is to carry out algorithm operation from a large number of noisy, uncertain and fuzzy real business data, and finally discover the data knowledge that has not been recognized or can not be clearly recognized and has a certain practical meaning.

The form of data analysis results obtained by data mining is not conventional. The form of results can be mathematical expressions with strong logic, or visual display results that can be easily understood by ordinary users. The application fields of data


W. Fu et al. (Eds.): eLEOT 2021, LNICST 389, pp. 146–154, 2021.
https://doi.org/10.1007/978-3-030-84383-0_13

mining are also very extensive, especially in the fields of market analysis, scientific research, social research and so on. In the process of development, data mining has been applied more and more in many fields, which also shows the importance of data mining technology. The current popular clustering ensemble learning algorithm has defects, that is, it can not give the appropriate processing scheme according to the different characteristics of different data sets. The traditional ensemble learning algorithm has the defect that it can not classify according to the characteristics of data. Traditional online teaching methods, such as principal component analysis and multi-layer perceptron neural network, are inefficient.

Aiming at the problems of these algorithms, a novel online teaching method based on big data mining for conductive characteristics of graphene materials is proposed:

(1) The conductive characteristics of graphene materials are extracted, and the charge accumulation teaching model is constructed by using big data mining technology.
(2) Based on the charge accumulation teaching model, the online teaching of charge accumulation characteristics of graphene conductive materials was completed.
(3) Experimental verification.

## 2 Extraction of Conductive Characteristics of Graphene Materials

Traditional online teaching methods of conductive characteristics of graphene materials, such as principal component analysis and multilayer perceptron neural network, are inefficient and easy to fall into local optimal solution. The online teaching method of conductive characteristics of graphene materials based on big data mining has better teaching effect, has important theoretical and practical value, and has broad development prospects.

The goal of conducting feature mining of graphene materials is to maximize the distance between different classes and minimize the within class distance. The mining process is divided into two stages: the first stage maximizes the distance between different classes; the second stage minimizes the intra class distance while ensuring the low space and time complexity of the algorithm

$$\begin{aligned} S_b = H_b H_b^t S_w = H_w H_w^t S_t = H_t H_t^t \\ H_t = A - me^t \in R^{d \times n} \end{aligned} \tag{1}$$

In formula (1), $S_b$ is the inter class matrix, $S_w$ is the intra class matrix, and $S_t$ is the overall dispersion matrix. $m$ is the global mean, $d$ is the $d$-dimensional vector space; $A$ is the data matrix, and each $a$ is a $d$-dimensional data space.

$$e^i = (1, \ldots, 1)^t \in R^{n \times l}; \cdot e = (1, \ldots, 1)^t \in R^{n \times l} \tag{2}$$

In formula (2), $n$ is the number of rows in the matrix, $l$ is a column value, and $t$ is a constant.

$$H_b = \left\lfloor \sqrt{N_1}(m_1 - m), \ldots, \sqrt{N_c}(m_c - m) \right\rfloor \in R^{d \times c} \tag{3}$$

In formula (3), $N$ is the column of the matrix.

$$H_w = A - \lfloor m_1 e_1^t, ..., m_c e_c^t \rfloor \in R^{d \times n} \quad (4)$$

The goal of this algorithm is to solve the following optimization problems:

$$G = \arg \max_{G'G=1} trace(G', S_b, G) \quad (5)$$

The objective of optimization problem (5) is to maximize the distance between classes. The solution of (5) can be obtained by solving the eigenvalues of $S_b$ or by $QR$ decomposition of the central matrix $C$. the specific calculation process is to make $C = QR$, that is, to solve $C$ by $QR$, where $Q \in R^{n \times c}$ and each column is orthogonal. If $Q \in R^{n \times c}$ is an upper triangular matrix, then $G = QV$, $V$ is an arbitrary orthogonal matrix. Among them:

$$C = \lfloor m_1, m_2, ..., m_c \rfloor \quad (6)$$

In formula (6), $C$ represents the center ID. By determining the center ID, the conductive characteristics of graphene can be extracted.

## 3 Online Teaching Model of Conductive Characteristics Based on Big Data Mining

According to the conductive characteristics of the graphene material extracted above, an online teaching model is constructed. Data mining is a process of extracting potentially useful information and knowledge from a large amount of, incomplete, noisy, fuzzy, and random data that are hidden in it, people do not know in advance, but are potentially useful [4, 5]. To define data mining from the perspective of the database, data mining technology is the process of sorting and categorizing a large amount of data in the database to create hidden valuable information. The overall process of data mining is shown in Fig. 1.

The common data mining technology is fuzzy set method, that is to use fuzzy set theory to carry out fuzzy evaluation, fuzzy decision-making, fuzzy pattern recognition and fuzzy clustering analysis on practical problems [6]. The higher the complexity of the system, the stronger the fuzziness. Generally, fuzzy set theory uses the degree of membership to describe the fuzzy things and the other [7]. In the case of given sample variables, it directly obtains the deprived index according to the membership function defined for each variable, and uses the obtained value to reflect the relative degree of individual deprivation, instead of using the values of upper and lower limits to determine whether an individual meets the criteria [8]. Therefore, the method is not only completely fuzzy, but also relative.

A set $A$ on the domain of fuzzy set $U$ makes elements in u not absolutely belong to set $A$, that is to say, there are elements belonging to or not belonging to set $A$ in different degrees. This set $A$ is called fuzzy set. The establishment method of fuzzy membership function is fuzzy statistical method. The membership function is determined by experimental statistical method [9, 10]. Suppose the universe $U$, $u \in U$, how to

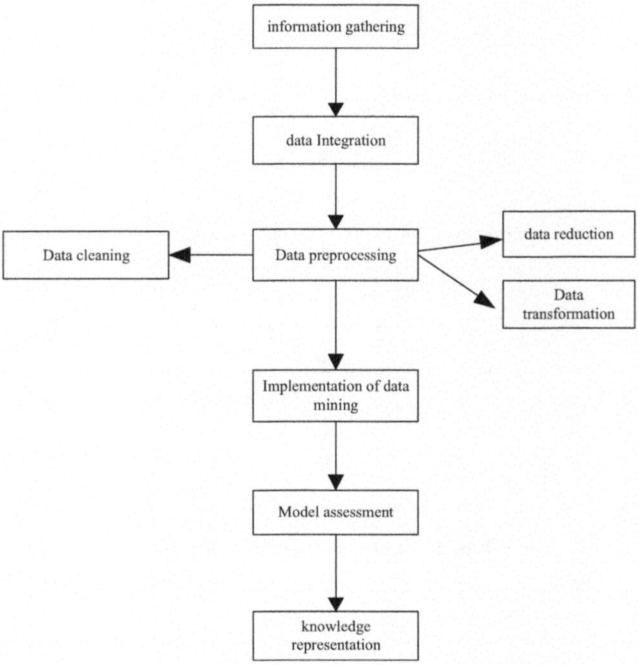


**Fig. 1.** Overall process of data mining

determine the membership degree of $u$ to set $A$ is as follows: there are $n$The electric field strength experimental results, in which $m$ times $u \in A$, $m/n$ is the membership frequency of $u$ to $A$. With the increase of $n$, the membership frequency will be stable, and the number of this stability is the membership degree of $u$ to $A$ [11–13]. The flow chart of fuzzy set induction is shown in Fig. 2.

The conductive characteristic is a time-varying process, and the change rate of the characteristic decreases with time. The surface charge accumulation of insulator is a dynamic process, which gradually reaches saturation state with the increase of pressurization time. First of all, the effect of surface charge accumulation on insulator surface is investigated when the effect of surface charge accumulation on insulator is investigated. The main sources of surface charge are: insulator body conduction, gas side space charge accumulation and insulator surface conduction. For a long time, on-line teaching staff of conductive characteristics usually teach based on macroscopic insulator body conductivity, gas conductivity and insulator surface conductivity. In fact, the accumulation of space charge on the gas side is carried out through the micro mechanism of the generation, recombination, migration and diffusion of space ions. The gas conductivity is only the overall performance of the above micro mechanism. The micro mechanism instead of the macro gas conductivity can recognize the conductive characteristics in essence.

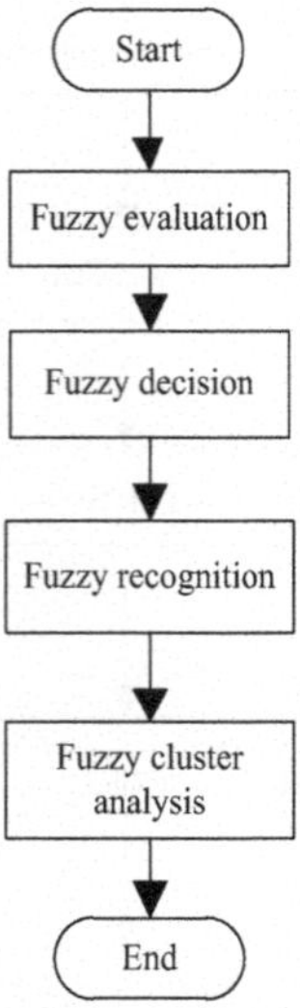


**Fig. 2.** Fuzzy set induction process

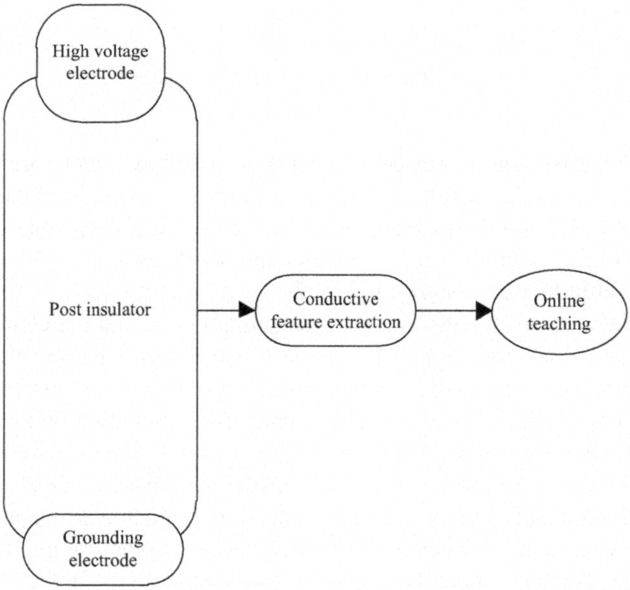


**Fig. 3.** Online teaching model

In order to realize the online teaching of conductive characteristics of graphene materials, the online teaching model of conductive characteristics was established. The main effects of conductive particles on the surface charge of insulator are attached to the surface of insulator and suspended near the insulator. For the conductive particles attached to the insulator surface, the research shows that the conductive particles always locate on the flashover path along the insulator surface. In order to realize the online teaching of conductive characteristics of graphene materials, the online teaching model of conductive characteristics was established. The main effects of conductive particles on the surface charge of insulator are attached to the surface of insulator and suspended near the insulator. For the conductive particles attached to the insulator surface, the research shows that the conductive particles always locate on the flashover path along the insulator surface Fig. 3.

The online teaching model can effectively realize the online teaching of conductive characteristics of graphene materials.

# 4 Experiment

## 4.1 Experimental Background

In order to verify the effectiveness of the proposed teaching methods, comparative verification is carried out. The experiment verified the accuracy and efficiency of charge accumulation feature extraction of online teaching method based on big data mining. It is carried out under the electric field intensity of +800 kV and −800 kV respectively.

## 4.2 Comparison of Feature Extraction Accuracy

(1) The electric field intensity is +800 kV.
At +800 kV, the experimental results of the proposed method and the actual graphene materials are shown in Fig. 4.

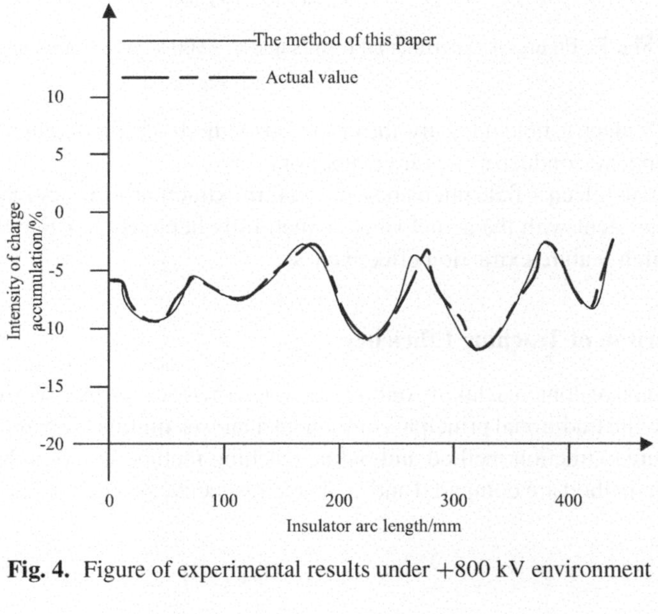


**Fig. 4.** Figure of experimental results under +800 kV environment

Under the electric field intensity of +800 kV, the extraction accuracy of conductive characteristics of graphene materials by the proposed method is basically consistent with the actual extraction value. Therefore, it fully shows that the proposed method can extract the conductive characteristics of graphene materials with high accuracy.

(2) The electric field strength is −800 kV.
Similarly, when the applied voltage is −800 kV, the experimental diagram of the extraction results and actual values of graphene material conductivity characteristics of the proposed method is shown in Fig. 5.

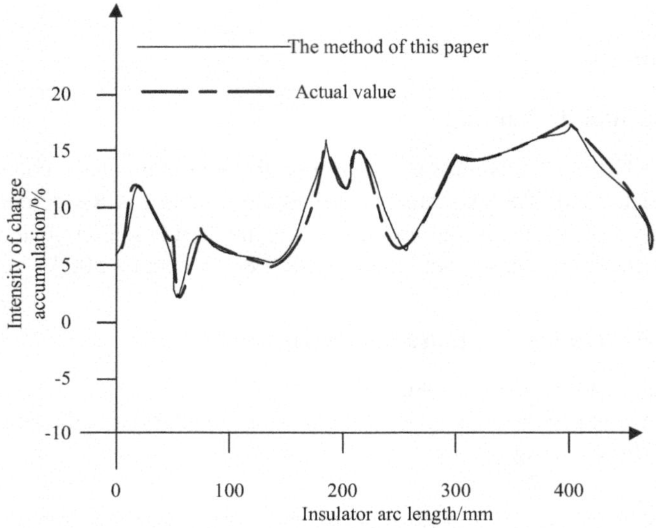


**Fig. 5.** Figure of experimental results under −800 kV environment

At -800 kV electric field intensity, the proposed method can still obtain more accurate results of graphene conductive feature extraction.

Under the two electric field intensities, the feature extraction accuracy of the proposed method is consistent with the actual value, which fully demonstrates that the proposed method has high feature extraction effectiveness.

## 4.3 Comparison of Teaching Efficiency

Based on the above contents, taking online teaching efficiency as the experimental comparison index, the traditional principal component analysis, multilayer perceptron neural network feature extraction method and online teaching method based on big data mining extraction method are compared and analyzed respectively. The results are shown in Table 1.

**Table 1.** Comparison results of teaching efficiency of three methods

| Time/min | Teaching efficiency /% | | |
|---|---|---|---|
| | Principal component analysis | Multilayer perceptron neural network | Based on big data mining |
| 10 | 42 | 78 | 95 |
| 20 | 41 | 70 | 90 |
| 30 | 58 | 65 | 91 |
| 40 | 50 | 69 | 95 |
| 50 | 49 | 62 | 90 |

It can be seen from Table 1 that the online teaching efficiency of kernel principal component analysis method is always lower than 60%, while that of multilayer perceptron neural network method is between 60% and 80%. Using the online teaching method based on big data mining, the teaching efficiency is higher than 90%, which has higher teaching efficiency.

## 5 Conclusion

In order to solve the problem of low teaching efficiency in traditional online teaching method of graphene material conductive characteristics, an online teaching method based on big data mining is proposed. The performance of the method is verified from both theoretical and experimental aspects. The method has high extraction accuracy and teaching efficiency in online teaching of conductive characteristics of graphene materials. Therefore, the proposed online teaching method is highly effective.

**Fund Projects.** Teaching Quality and Teaching Reform Project of Guangdong Undergraduate Colleges and Universities: Construction Project of Experiment Demonstration Center (2017002).

## References

1. Tseng, S.S., Yeh, H.C.: Integrating reciprocal teaching in an online environment with an annotation feature to enhance low-achieving students English reading comprehension. Interact. Learn. Environ. **26**(8), 789–802 (2018)
2. Khamparia, A., Pandey, B.: SVM and PCA based learning feature classification approaches for e-learning system. Int. J. Web Based Learn. Teach. Technol. 13(2), 32–45 (2018)
3. Wang, Y., Talim, J.: Online mobile teaching methods based on android in the 5G environment. Int. J. Continuing Eng. Educ. Life Long Learn. 30(2), 133 (2020)
4. Liu, Y.H., Yu, F.Y.: Supporting active learning and formative evaluation via teaching-by-questioning in classrooms: design, development, and preliminary evaluation of an online learning system. Interact. Learn. Environ. **27**(8), 841–855 (2019)
5. Yu-Hsin, L., Fu-Yun, Y.: Supporting active learning and formative evaluation via teaching-by-questioning in classrooms: design, development, and preliminary evaluation of an online learning system. Interact. Learn. Environ. **25**(3), 1–15 (2018)

6. Lobato, J., Walker, C.: How viewers orient toward student dialogue in online math videos. J. Comput. Math. Sci. Teach. **38**(2), 177–200 (2019)
7. Moffitt, R.L., Padgett, C., Grieve, R.: Accessibility and emotionality of online assessment feedback: using emoticons to enhance student perceptions of marker competence and warmth. Comput. Educ. 143, 103654.1–103654.11 (2020)
8. Magnifico, A.M., Woodard, R., Mccarthey, S.: Teachers as co-authors of student writing: How teachers' initiating texts influence response and revision in an online space. Comput. Compos. **52**, 107–131 (2019)
9. Shu, L., Juzhi, S.: Current situation and future development of online learning platform video interactive environment. China Educ. Technol. (2019)
10. Wu, J., Chen, B.: English vocabulary online teaching based on machine learning recognition and target visual detection. J. Intell. Fuzzy Syst. **5**, 1–12 (2020)
11. Fu, W., Liu, S., Srivastava, G.: Optimization of big data scheduling in social networks. Entropy **21**(9), 902 (2019)
12. Liu, S., Li, Z., Zhang, Y., et al.: Introduction of key problems in long-distance learning and training. Mobile Netw. Appl. **24**(1), 1–4 (2019)
13. Liu, S., Lu, M., Li, H., et al.: Prediction of gene expression patterns with generalized linear regression model. Front. Genet. **10**(8), 120 (2019)

# Distance Teaching Method of Accounting Informatization Course Based on Big Data Mining

Qi-feng Wu(✉)

Guangxi Science and Technology Normal University, Laibin 546199, China

**Abstract.** In order to maximize the practical teaching application value of accounting informatization course, a distance teaching method of accounting informatization course based on big data mining is proposed. This paper analyzes the practical value of big data mining technology in accounting information teaching from three angles of students' learning autonomy, knowledge digestibility and teaching quality. On this basis, the B/S architecture is established, and with the help of. NET dynamic development technology, the identity of the accessed teaching objects is authenticated, so as to realize the smooth application of the distance teaching method of accounting informatization course based on big data mining. The comparative experiment results show that compared with the traditional teaching system, after applying the above-mentioned distance teaching method, students can better accept the course of accounting informatization, understand and comprehend its basic knowledge, and give full play to the teaching application value of this practical course.

**Keywords:** Big data mining · Accounting informatization · Distance education · Enthusiasm for learning · Digestibility · Teaching quality · B/S architecture · Object identity

## 1 Introduction

Large data mining is a process of searching hidden information from a large amount of data by algorithms. Big data mining is usually related to computer science, and achieves this goal through statistics, online analysis and processing, information retrieval, machine learning, expert systems (relying on past rules of thumb), and pattern recognition. Large data mining is a hot topic in the field of artificial intelligence and database research. Data mining is a nontrivial process that uncovers hidden, previously unknown and potentially valuable information from a large amount of data in a database [1]. Data mining is a decision support process, which is mainly based on artificial intelligence, machine learning, pattern recognition, statistics, database, visualization technology, etc., to analyze the data of enterprises automatically, to make inductive reasoning, to mine out potential patterns, to help decision-makers adjust their market strategies, to reduce risks and to make correct decisions. The process of knowledge discovery consists of the following three


W. Fu et al. (Eds.): eLEOT 2021, LNICST 389, pp. 155–166, 2021.
https://doi.org/10.1007/978-3-030-84383-0_14

stages: (1) data preparation; (2) data mining; (3) result expression and interpretation. Data mining can interact with users or knowledge bases.

Accounting informationization is the combination of accounting and information technology. It is a new requirement for financial information management in the information society, and a necessary measure for enterprise accounting to comply with the tide of informationization. It is the main channel for enterprise leaders to obtain information under the network environment, which helps to enhance the competitiveness of enterprises, solve the "island" phenomenon of accounting computerization, and improve the decision-making ability of accounting management and the level of enterprise management. Looking at the development of accounting informationization in China over the past 20 years, although the function of information system has been enhanced and its application has become more and more popular, especially the large and medium-sized enterprises have realized accounting informationization to some extent and applied accounting software, but on the whole, China's accounting informationization is still in the process of development and there are many problems to be solved urgently. Information technology, through the network system, make business processing highly automated, information sharing, can actively and real-time reporting of accounting information. It is not only a change of information technology applied to accounting, but also a new accounting thought adapted to the environment of modern information technology. [2]. This point of view is also a deductive reasoning logic conclusion, that the goal of accounting information is to establish a modern accounting information system, will lead to a new accounting thinking. At the same time, it is pointed out that accounting informationization should restructure the traditional accounting mode, and that the characteristics of accounting informationization are highly automatic, fully open, highly shared and real-time reporting.

## 2 The Value of Big Data Mining in Accounting Informatization Teaching

Firstly, it analyzes the value of big data mining in accounting informatization teaching, cultivates students' learning enthusiasm and autonomy, constructs the B/S architecture of accounting informatization course, uses net dynamic development technology to verify the identity of the object, uses accounting virtual reality teaching mode, and with the support of big data mining technology, It realizes the smooth application of distance teaching method of accounting information course.

### 2.1 Mobilize Students' Enthusiasm and Autonomy in Learning

With the rapid development of information technology, words, pictures, sounds, videos, animations and so on can be perfectly presented with the help of information technology, and are fused into a whole, bringing strong stimulation to users in terms of vision and hearing. In the process of accounting teaching, the information technology can show the abstract and boring words in books in a vivid, vivid and novel way, bring strong stimulation to students' senses, can arouse students' enthusiasm and motivation for learning, and the efficiency and effect of classroom learning have been improved obviously. Compared with traditional oral lectures by teachers, the use of multimedia technology enriches the learning experience of students, not only audibly and visually satisfies them, but also conveys the learning content in a more diversified form to students, with learning efficiency and learning quality exceeding expectations [3]. In addition, the majority of teachers and students can log on to relevant learning websites, campus libraries and other learning centers through the Internet, using the above rich learning resources, self-learning. Students in the network learning, have more freedom and autonomy, according to their own learning ability and learning level, choose their own learning materials, in view of their own learning deficiencies to carry out purposeful leak detection and compensation learning. Such personalized learning, not only suitable for each student's actual learning situation, students' learning absorption rate is higher, but also the students' learning efficiency and learning effect is unexpected.

### 2.2 Improve Students' Knowledge Digestibility and Absorption Rate

Informationized teaching is to use modern information technology to present the abstract and difficult knowledge in various forms. Students can carry out personalized learning according to their actual learning conditions and needs, and can deepen the understanding and grasp of knowledge in repeated learning to meet the diversified learning needs. For example, in the "Basic Accounting" teaching content, including the "accounting procedures" and "accounting methods" two important knowledge learning content. Using the traditional teaching method, the teacher can only explain and impart the relevant content of the textbook by oral teaching, which is not only boring, but also difficult for the students to understand and use flexibly. In the modern information teaching environment, multimedia technology will play a role, boring and difficult to understand the abstract knowledge, in the form of pictures, animation, small video presented to students, so that the original more complex knowledge points, can be explained to students in a vivid form, not only to help students understand the knowledge, but also deepen the memory of students, students' learning ability and learning efficiency have been greatly improved.

### 2.3 Improving the Teaching Quality of Accounting Informatization Course

Using Internet technology, teachers can surf the Internet to find some high-quality teaching resources, advanced learning methods, and teach students to apply in practical teaching, and strive to improve the quality of teaching. Teachers can go to the Internet to find high-quality teaching courseware, students can go to the Internet to search for relevant learning materials to make up for their lack of learning. In addition, the use of multimedia technology saves a lot of time on the blackboard, increases the teaching time and teacher-student interaction time, greatly improve the classroom teaching efficiency.

Generally speaking, in the school official network construction, the hardware construction is less difficult, as long as a reasonable design and planning, organization, use some construction funds, you can normal operation. In the construction of the school education platform, the hardware construction is the key point, and the information points of the website cover the whole campus, which needs to be equipped with proxy server, optical disk mirror and DNS, etc., and also includes some office equipment such as computers and printers [5]. Make sure that every computer in the school can be connected to the educational platform to prepare for distance learning.

In order to achieve the goal of multi-media teaching, it is necessary to construct the teaching information resources of accounting education website and develop related teaching software. Teachers' teaching material base mainly involves electronic teaching plan base, multimedia teaching courseware base, teaching video, etc. The emphasis of building teachers' teaching material base is multimedia teaching courseware. The making of multimedia courseware needs the support of multimedia software. Teachers can use multimedia software to make the accounting content into teaching courseware that combines text, image, sound, video and other resources. The design and making of multimedia teaching courseware needs many steps: First, the overall design of multimedia teaching courseware. Teachers should strengthen the analysis and summary of accounting curriculum and teaching characteristics, and reasonably choose multimedia software and courseware development. In the development of multimedia teaching courseware, it is necessary to reasonably plan teaching strategies and teaching schemes to lay a foundation for making multimedia teaching courseware. Second, the multimedia courseware content planning [6]. According to the characteristics of accounting curriculum content planning multimedia courseware content, clear multimedia courseware structure and courseware arrangement. Teachers can reasonably plan the multimedia courseware content according to the teaching objectives, teaching requirements, the degree of knowledge difficulty and teaching methods. Third, the preparation of multimedia courseware script. The quality of multimedia teaching courseware script will directly affect the effect of multimedia teaching courseware. Therefore, teachers should make sure that the courseware script involves concrete teaching content, arranges the multimedia teaching courseware reasonably according to time and teaching order. Teachers and software staff should discuss how to write the multimedia courseware script.

## 3 Distance Teaching Method of Accounting Informatization Course

### 3.1 B/S Architecture

The most basic hierarchical model is a three-tier model, including presentation layer, logic layer and data layer. The presentation layer is a message channel, the logic layer should provide a real image, and the data layer provides the measurement of the real system. The logic model of the application system also reflects such characteristics, which includes a large level of display, data and application logic. Generally speaking, the layers of typical information systems are data layer, data maintenance layer, data semantic layer, link communication layer, application logic layer, presentation logic layer and presentation layer from bottom to top [7]. This is a complete hierarchical structure, and calls are generally not made between layers. This system reflects the flexibility and stability of the hierarchical model. The architecture of the hierarchical model is shown in Fig. 1.

There is no doubt that all the necessary data and all the forms of distance learning are stored here. The data layer mainly uses the database to save and manage the data. Relational database is suitable for storing structured data; XML file is a hierarchical

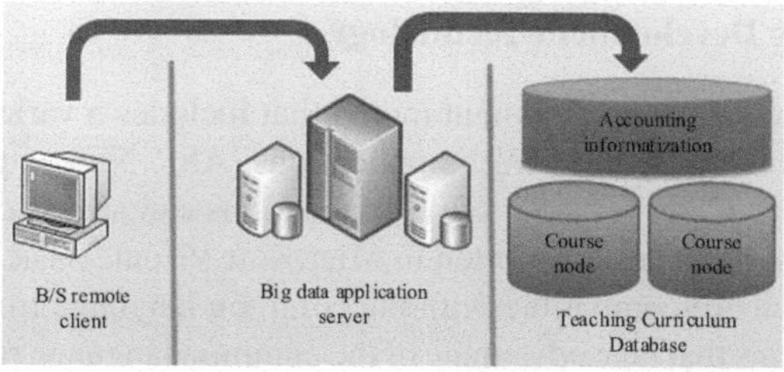


**Fig. 1.** B/S Architecture of accounting informatization course

model of self-describing information; directory service is a kind of distributed storage and management of information, which can provide higher query efficiency; file system is an operating system level data storage; registry is mainly used for software running on Windows system, which provides special API access, or it can be regarded as a directory service storage environment. In a word, the main problems of data storage layer are where the data is stored, how to access it, operation efficiency, operation security, data encryption and so on.

The data maintenance layer is based on the data layer. Its main function is to ensure the correct access to data and maintain the correct state of data. A more common implementation is the use of database stored procedures and triggers. For an object database system that holds persistent objects, the object properties process can do a similar job. The semantic layer is a very important layer of information systems [8]. At this level, the changes are numerous, constantly changing parts of the state; it is also a working information system, constantly reflecting changes in the real system. Here the communication layer is responsible for providing communication services, that is, interfaces between information systems and other systems. Because complex systems often support distributed computing systems, it is necessary to encapsulate the functions of communication for information transfer and synchronization control between systems. At the same time, this layer can be separated to facilitate the control and deployment of the whole distributed system. In this layer can be added to the system monitoring, load balancing and other functions. At the same time, a distributed message and event mechanism is often deployed in this layer, so that the transparent access to the functional modules can be achieved for the upper modules.

The Application Logic layer is where the really active system functional modules work. Here, the operating logic of true preservation is the primary focus of the system analysis. At this level, each module is in a different state, collaborating by calling each other, or by messages. The so-called presentation logic is mainly to manage the completion of the information presentation agreement. For example, what kind of information a user can see in what state. The presentation logic layer holds the various constants defined in the presentation interface, such as window size and style. In addition, this layer also includes customization and modification of the presentation interface. The presentation layer is mainly responsible for dealing with users, displaying system information, and accepting orders from users. This is the part of interacting with the user and the part of the information system that changes frequently. Specialized presentation layers are primarily used to present and interact with the look and feel of the components.

### 3.2 NET Dynamic Development Technology

ASP. NET is a unified Web development model that includes a variety of services necessary to generate enterprise-class Web applications. ASP. NET is provided as part of the. NET Framework. Code for ASP. NET applications can access classes in the. NET Framework, code for applications written in Microsoft Visual, Basic, C#, JScript. NET, and J# languages that are compatible with the common language runtime, and develop ASP. NET applications that take advantage of the common language runtime, type safety, inheritance, and more.

ASP. NET includes: Pages and Control Framework, ASP. NET Compiler, Security Infrastructure, State Management Capabilities, Application Configuration, Health Monitoring and Performance Capabilities, Debugging Support, XML Web Services Framework, Extensible Hosting Environment and Application Lifecycle Management, Extensible Designer Environments, and more. ASP. NET instructional web pages are completely object oriented. In ASP. NET Web pages, you can use properties, methods, and events to handle HTML elements. The ASP. NET Page Framework provides a unified model for responding to client-side events in code running on the server, eliminating the need to consider the implementation details of client and server isolation inherent in Web-based applications. The framework also automatically maintains the state of the page and the controls on that page during the page processing life cycle.

Using ASP. NET pages and control frameworks, you can also encapsulate commonly used UI functions into easy-to-use and reusable controls. Control can be written once for many pages and integrated into an ASP. NET Web page. These controls are placed in ASP. NET Web pages during rendering.

ASP. NET pages and control frameworks also provide features that allow you to control the overall look and feel of your Web site through themes and skins. You can define themes and skins first, and then apply them at the page or control level. In addition to themes, you can define master pages so that the pages in your application have a consistent layout. An Master Page defines the layout and standard behavior that you want for all pages (or groups of pages) in your application. You can then create individual content pages that contain the page specific content to display. When a user requests a content page, these content pages are merged with the master page to produce output that combines the layout of the master page with the content in the content page (Fig. 2).

Students' online learning database mainly involves online electronic textbooks and learning reference materials. Students' online learning database can provide students with learning materials other than teaching materials, which is of great significance to improve students' learning effect. With the gradual deepening of China's accounting reform, the original accounting teaching materials can no longer meet the requirements of accounting personnel training, so it is necessary to publish the relevant information and achievements of accounting reform in a timely manner on the accounting teaching website. Students' electronic homework system mainly involves interactive homework support system, homework question bank and homework e-mail. Students can search for learning materials according to their own learning situation and learning needs, which is beneficial to improving students' learning effect. The student electronic operation system has the following functions: First, automatically generate test questions [9]. Students' electronic homework system can automatically form and match test questions according

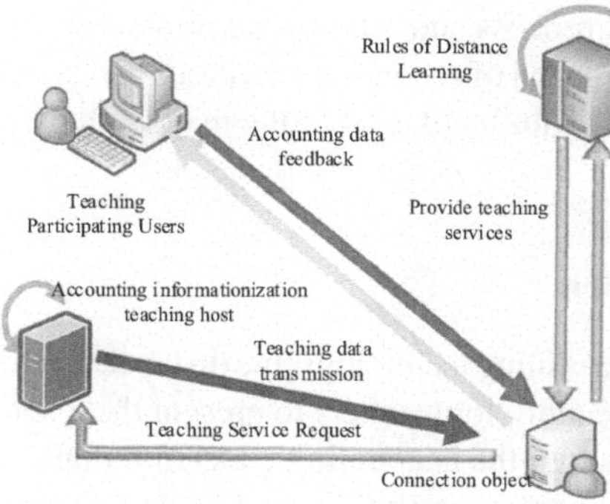


**Fig. 2.** NET dynamic development technology application flow chart

to teachers' setting requirements, teaching materials and teachers' requirements for homework difficulty. Students can automatically extract test questions from the question bank and automatically form test papers. Second, electronic testing. Students can use the student electronic operation system to answer test questions. Students' electronic operation system can automatically roll up according to the test time set by teachers. When the test time set by the teacher is reached, students are not allowed to continue answering questions. In the whole test process, if students encounter problems, the students' electronic operation system can help them. Third, automatic marking. After the students' electronic operation system is automatically rolled up, it can automatically compare the standard answers with the students' answers and score them automatically. For some subjective topics, teachers can review and give feedback by mail, and for topics with high student error rate, teachers can communicate with students through communication platform.

With the gradual development of science and technology and the popularization of computerized accounting, accountants need to use accounting software to complete bookkeeping, accounting and reimbursement, and use accounting software to do a good job of analyzing the whole financial process. Accounting information system has become a system that accounting students must skillfully use. In order to improve the practical ability of accounting majors, it is necessary to actively build accounting experimental software system and experimental case database. At present, China has developed and popularized a variety of commercialized accounting software, such as UFIDA financial and enterprise management software M8.x, UFIDA U8 series, etc. By combining commercialized accounting software with accounting education websites, students can download and install commercialized accounting software according to their own needs, and simulate corresponding accounting cases according to the experimental cases provided by the experimental case database of accounting education websites. Students independently complete accounting analysis, preparation of accounting statements, financial treatment, salary calculation, fixed assets accounting, etc. After the experiment is completed, the experimental account data formed by students in the whole experiment will be collected by the experimental operation database and evaluated by teachers. Students can use the accounting experiment software system to review related knowledge in their spare time, which can not only improve students' understanding of the basic principles of accounting, accounting process and accounting affairs management knowledge, but also improve students' cognition of accounting methods and accounting data processing, and improve the professional ability of accounting majors, thus laying a solid foundation for future development.

### 3.3 Object Authentication

With the support of big data mining technology, the distance teaching mode of accounting informatization course is mainly for teachers to present the teaching content to students through the big screen through the accounting education platform, so as to achieve the teaching purpose. Accounting demonstration teaching includes static demonstration and dynamic demonstration. Static demonstration is easy to understand, that is, putting the teaching content on the big screen. Dynamic demonstration is to show the key and difficult teaching contents to students in a dynamic form with the help of computer technology, which is more vivid and concrete. Dynamic and static demonstration methods can improve the teaching effect of accounting demonstration, and teachers should choose demonstration methods reasonably according to the teaching situation.

This teaching mode is mainly in the information technology environment. The school is equipped with a complete teaching system, through which students ask their own questions in time, and teachers answer questions for students in time on the computer. This communication mode between teachers and students breaks through the limitation of time and space, which is beneficial to improve learning efficiency and learning effect. Accounting virtual reality teaching mode refers to a kind of teaching mode which uses computer software to simulate the practical problems in accounting work and solve these problems [10, 11]. Under the indoctrination teaching mode, due to the high complexity of some accounting problems and less teaching hours, accounting students can't fully understand these knowledge and solve accounting problems with knowledge in a short time. In classroom teaching, teachers mostly explain the basic knowledge and principles of accounting to students, but they do not explain how to use accounting knowledge to solve practical problems.

Using accounting virtual reality teaching mode [12, 13], students can download accounting related data and information in accounting teaching website, and complete accounting experiments according to their own knowledge. In addition, students can also use role-playing to give full play to their subjective initiative, so as to ensure that students can correctly recognize the differences between classroom teaching and accounting work while participating in the actual accounting work, thus achieving the purpose of improving students' analytical ability and problem-solving ability. This teaching mode mainly uses the Internet and local area network to realize the long-distance transmission of courses and achieve the goal of cross-regional teaching. Because the accounting distance teaching mode has the characteristics of two-way, real-time and interactivity, and the accounting professional teaching knowledge system is relatively stable and complete, the distance teaching mode is suitable for accounting professional teaching. Let $D_{\max}$ represent Maximum interference authority of big data mining technology, $\xi_{\max}$ represent the maximum teaching application value of accounting informatization course, and $\xi_{\min}$ represent the minimum teaching application value of accounting informatization course.

Combining the above physical quantities, the object identity authentication conditions of the course distance teaching method can be defined as:

$$L = \frac{D_{\max}}{2}\sqrt{\frac{f(\xi_{\max} - \xi_{\min})^2}{n \times (e_n^2 - e_1^2)}} \tag{1}$$

In the above formula, $e_1$ represents the object identity mining processing authority at the first teaching node, $e_n$ represents the object identity mining processing authority at the $n$ teaching node, and $f$ represents the general application coefficient of accounting informatization course. At this point, the calculation and processing of various physical coefficient indexes have been completed, and with the support of big data mining technology, the smooth application of the distance teaching method of accounting informatization course has been realized.

## 4 Analysis of Experimental Results

To verify the practical application value of the distance teaching method of accounting informatization course based on big data mining, the following comparative experiments are designed. In the course implementation environment shown in Fig. 3, the same number of students are selected as the research objects of the experimental group and the control group respectively, in which the hosts used by the experimental group are equipped with the distance teaching method of accounting informatization course based on big data mining, while the hosts used by the control group are equipped with the traditional distance teaching system, and the specific changes of each experimental index are recorded under the same experimental environment.

**Fig. 3.** Application environment of distance education course implementation

TTR index can reflect students' actual acceptance of accounting informatization course. The purpose is to construct the function of technical analysis and other technical transaction rules in R. Its function is moving average Trend detection and intensity Shock indicators Volatility indicators and Volume analysis, the advantages are (1) flexible;

Support multiple temporal data formats; The index calculation methods are various (2) The calculation speed is relatively fast (3) It can process high frequency data.In general, the greater the TTR index, the higher the students' acceptance of accounting informatization course, and vice versa. The following table records the actual changes of TTR index values of experimental group and control group.

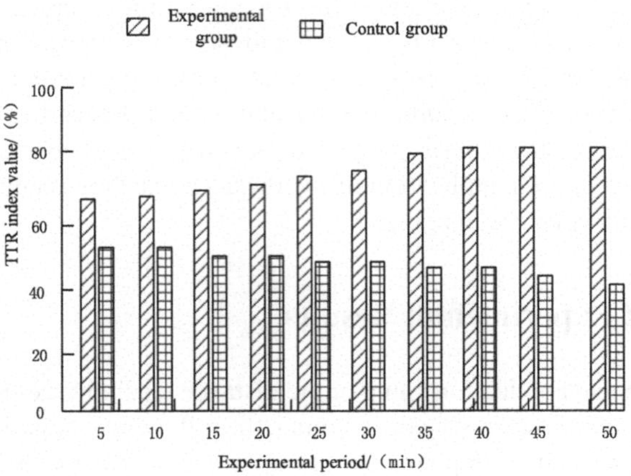


**Fig. 4.** TTR index numerical comparison figure

According to the analysis of Fig. 4, with the extension of the experimental time, the TTR index in the experimental group keeps the numerical change trend of first rising and then stabilizing, and the maximum numerical result in the whole experimental process reaches 81.6%, which is 6.8% higher than the initial numerical value of 74.8%. The TTR index in the control group began to show a continuous decline after a step-by-step downward trend. The maximum value in the whole experimental process only reached 55.1%, which was 26.5% lower than the maximum value in the experimental group. To sum up, with the application of the distance teaching method of accounting informatization course based on big data mining, the TTR index value has obviously increased, which can promote students' learning and acceptance level of accounting informatization course from the practical point of view.

STR index represents students' ability to understand and comprehend the basic knowledge of accounting informatization course. In general, the greater the STR index, the stronger the students' ability to understand and comprehend the basic knowledge of accounting informatization course, and the weaker the opposite. The following table records the specific changes of STR index values in experimental group and control group.

According to the analysis of Fig. 5, with the extension of the experimental time, the STR index in the experimental group began to decline gradually after a stable state for a period of time, and finally began to rise continuously, and the maximum numerical result in the whole experimental process reached 80.4%. In the control group, the STR index keeps a decreasing trend, but the decreasing range in the later stage of the experiment is obviously higher than that in the early stage of the experiment. The maximum value

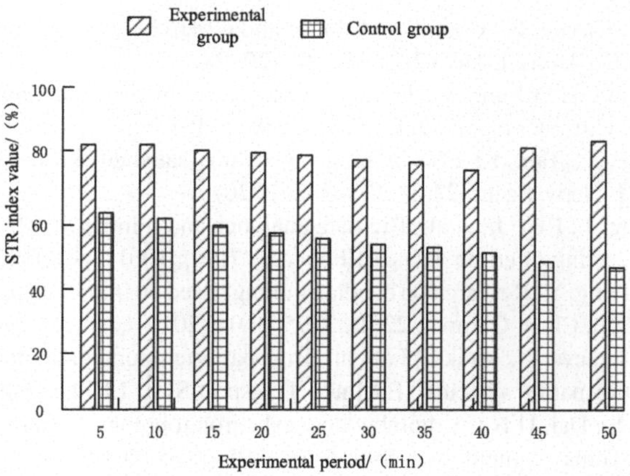


**Fig. 5.** Comparison figure of STR index values

in the whole experiment process can only reach 63.2%, which is 17.2% lower than the maximum value in the experimental group. To sum up, with the application of the distance teaching method of accounting informatization course based on big data mining, STR index also shows an obvious upward trend of numerical change, which can greatly enhance students' practical understanding and comprehension ability of the basic knowledge of accounting informatization course.This is because the role of net dynamic development technology in B/S architecture can mobilize students' learning enthusiasm and autonomy.

## 5 Conclusion

Compared with the traditional distance teaching system, the distance teaching method of accounting informatization course based on big data mining combined with. This paper establishes the B/S architecture of distance teaching method, uses net dynamic development technology to authenticate the identity of the visited teaching objects, and presents the teaching content to students with the support of big data mining technology.NET dynamic development technology under the action of B/S architecture can not only improve the actual teaching quality of accounting informatization course, but also fully mobilize students' learning enthusiasm and autonomy. From the practical point of view, the improvement of TTR index and STR index can greatly enhance students' practical understanding and comprehension ability of the basic knowledge of accounting informatization course, and meet the application demand of maximizing the practical teaching application value of accounting informatization course.

## References

1. Wen, J., Zhang, W., Shu, W.: A cognitive learning model in distance education of higher education institutions based on chaos optimization in big data environment. J. Supercomput. **75**(2), 719–731 (2019)

2. Tamburri, D.A., Casale, G.: Cognitive distance and research output in computing education: a case-study. IEEE Trans. Educ. **62**(2), 99–107 (2019)
3. Song, C.-W., Jung, H., Chung, K.: Development of a medical big-data mining process using topic modeling. Clust. Comput. **22**(1), 1949–1958 (2019)
4. Wang, J., Dong, J., Tan, Y.: Role mining algorithms satisfied the permission cardinality constraint. Int. J. Netw. Secur. **22**(3), 373–382 (2020)
5. Feng, M., Zheng, J., Ren, J., et al.: Big data analytics and mining for effective visualization and trends forecasting of crime data. IEEE Access **7**(99), 106111–106123 (2019)
6. Zhu, L., Li, H., Feng, Y.: Research on big data mining based on improved parallel collaborative filtering algorithm. Clust. Comput. **22**(2), 3595–3604 (2019)
7. Dagaeva, M., Garaeva, A., Anikin, I., et al.: Big spatio-temporal data mining for emergency management information systems. IET Intel. Transport Syst. **13**(11), 1649–1657 (2019)
8. Wang, H., Ma, S., Dai, H.N.: A rhombic dodecahedron topology for human-centric banking big data. IEEE Trans. Comput. Soc. Syst. **6**(5), 1095–1105 (2019)
9. Wibisono, A., Sarwinda, D.: Average Restrain Divider of Evaluation Value (ARDEV) in data stream algorithm for big data prediction. Knowl. Based Syst. **176**, 29–39 (2019)
10. Zhang, C., Wu, X., Yan, W., et al.: Attribute-aware graph recurrent networks for scholarly friend recommendation based on internet of scholars in scholarly big data. IEEE Trans. Industr. Inf. **16**(4), 2707–2715 (2020)
11. Liu, S., Liu, D., Srivastava, G., Połap, D., Woźniak, M.: Overview and methods of correlation filter algorithms in object tracking. Complex Intell. Syst. (2020). https://doi.org/10.1007/s40747-020-00161-4
12. Liu, S., Lu, M., Li, H., et al.: Prediction of gene expression patterns with generalized linear regression model. Front. Genet. **10**, 120 (2019)
13. Fu, W., Liu, S., Srivastava, G.: Optimization of big data scheduling in social networks. Entropy **21**(9), 902 (2019)

# University Ideological and Political Multimedia Network Teaching Based on MOOC

Hong-bing Jiang(✉)

School of Road Bridge and Architecture, Chongqing Vocational College of Transportation, Chongqing 402247, China

**Abstract.** The past, the accuracy of information retrieval based on P2P technology is low, which leads to poor students' ability to master knowledge and students' performance is not high. In order to solve this problem, this paper designs the University Ideological and political multimedia network teaching based on MOOC. According to the MOOC based College Ideological and political multimedia network teaching module, teaching resources are shared from the user end, student learning information storage, online examination, user management and function. The "3 + 2" mode is used for basic teaching, and the weighted average method is used to minimize the loss of resource allocation. The personalized recommendation model is constructed, and the interference data are eliminated by the collaborative filtering operator to complete the personalized recommendation. Under the support of network teaching mode. The experimental results show that the teaching method has high retrieval accuracy, students' ability to master knowledge is firm, and students' highest learning score reaches full score, which has good teaching effect.

**Keywords:** MOOC · University ideology and politics · Multimedia technology · Network teaching

## 1 Introduction

With the continuous updating of modern educational technology and educational concept, multimedia assisted teaching with network as the core is more and more applied to teaching work, which is the main development trend of Education Science [1]. As a subject with strong ideas and advanced scientific concepts, ideological and political course not only transfers important knowledge to students, but also plays an important role in the process of students' growth [2]. The application of multimedia technology in the process of ideological and political education and the full use of modern information technology are conducive to improving the effectiveness of ideological and political education. In the conventional teaching, the information source is very limited, influenced by the traditional teaching ideas, many teachers' teaching methods are often a blackboard, a piece of chalk, a book, which is difficult to stimulate students' learning enthusiasm [3]. The traditional teaching model with teachers as the center and students


W. Fu et al. (Eds.): eLEOT 2021, LNICST 389, pp. 167–180, 2021.
https://doi.org/10.1007/978-3-030-84383-0_15

as the object, although it maintains the authority of teachers to a certain extent, cannot reflect the status of students' cognitive subjects. To a certain extent, the teaching effect is too dependent on the teacher's personal knowledge reserve and skill level, ignoring the interaction between the two parties in the teaching activities, which has a certain negative impact on the teaching efficiency. In the past, an ideological and political classroom automatic assistance platform designed based on P2P technology was used to use the entire network node calculations to fully tap the space resources that exist on the network. Although this method has high resource utilization, the information retrieval function is poor, resulting in dissatisfaction with platform auxiliary effects. In response to this problem, design MOOC-based university ideological and political multimedia network teaching system. Based on the user-end module, the student learning information storage module, online test module and user management and function module design based on MOOC-based university ideological and political multimedia network teaching module, under the MOOC-based university ideological and political multimedia network teaching module, realize university ideological and political teaching Innovation of Models, complete the design of MOOC-based university ideological and political multimedia network teaching system. The MOOC teaching mode breaks the inherent teaching method, and it is popular among the teachers in the university.

## 2 Multi Media Network Teaching Module of University Ideological and Political Education Based on MOOC

The introduction of multimedia technology has changed the traditional teaching mode in college teaching practice. In the MOOC teaching mode, professional teachers can use multimedia technology, combine scientific and technological elements, and use text, pictures, video and other methods to conduct strict ideological and political knowledge and logical thinking on students Lively explain [4]. Give full play to the functional effects of hearing and vision, and change the interactive learning mode between subjects. MOOC teaching mode based on multimedia technology provides a convenient and efficient information exchange channel for collaborative learning. For example, through the cloud service, you can share teaching resources everywhere, teachers can participate in the entire process of students learning, thus improving students' thinking ability and thinking in class [5]. The design of College Ideological and political multimedia network teaching module based on MOOC is shown in Fig. 1.

As shown in Fig. 1, the platform can be independent of network teaching resources, effectively integrate scattered resources, and provide convenience for the acquisition and full use of teaching resources. Cloud storage in a multimedia environment has strong security storage capabilities. Teachers and students can save a lot of cloud storage resources and provide users with stable and safe services. Using the network teaching environment provided by multimedia technology, teachers can access public teaching tools, use existing teaching resources, and teachers can teach online in real time, which is convenient for students to learn [6].

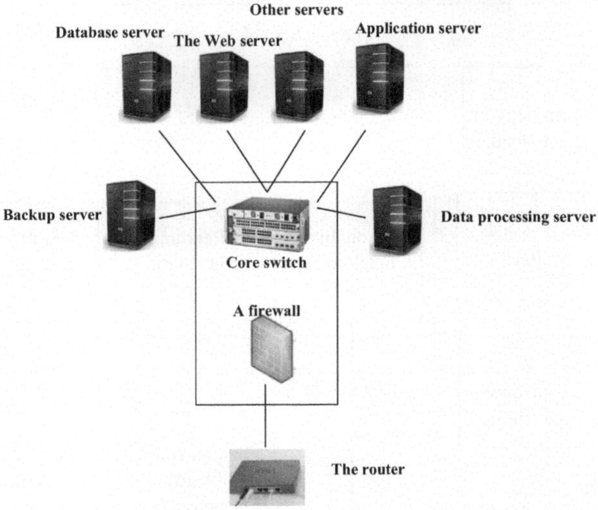


**Fig. 1.** University ideological and political multimedia network teaching module based on MOOC

## 2.1 Client Module

The client of the MOOC-based multimedia network teaching module of university ideology and politics is mainly students and teachers. In the classroom, the two parties interact through the network, while the interaction outside the class is only the student and the network. The user end module is shown as in Fig. 2.

The teacher stores all teaching content in the resource library according to the user-side module shown in Fig. 2. In the classroom, the interaction between teachers and students can supplement student knowledge at any time [7]. Students use personalized data collection methods to add teacher-student interaction information on the basis of the basic content of the basic courseware displayed by the teacher, which can be stored in personalized notes after the students themselves supplement it [8].

## 2.2 Student Learning Information Storage Module

After students add relevant knowledge points, they are stored in personalized notes. This process requires memory to store massive amounts of information. The memory can store binary data under the MOOC-based university ideological and political multimedia network teaching module, and form a storage function circuit with physical form in the integrated circuit, such as a memory stick [9]. The memory installed in the computer can be divided into memory and external memory according to its purpose. External memory is usually a magnetic medium, which can store information for a long time. Memory is a storage component on the motherboard that can be used to store the currently executing program for temporary use. Store programs and data. The student learning information storage module is shown in Fig. 3.

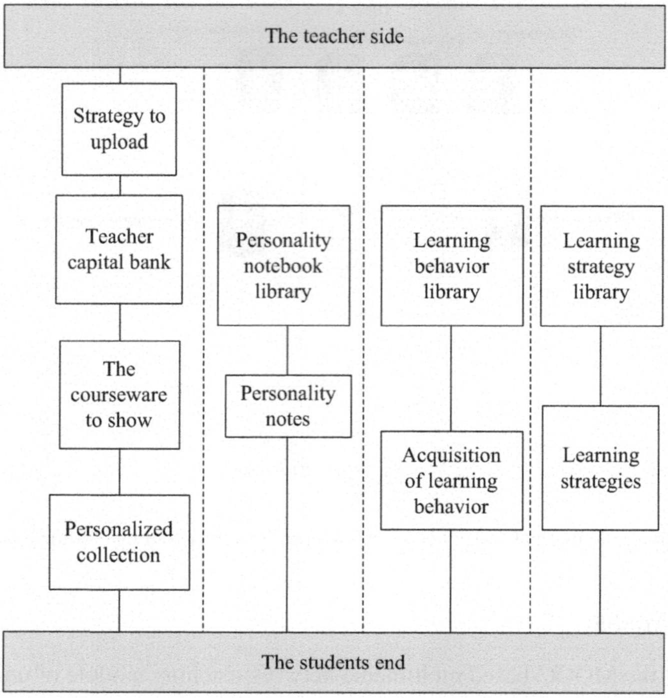


**Fig. 2.** Client module

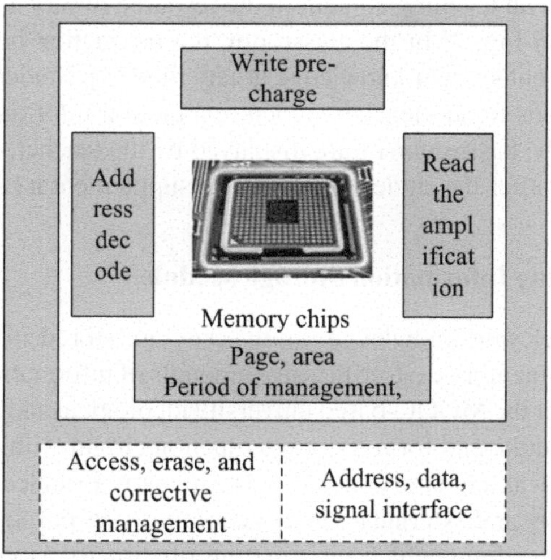


**Fig. 3.** Student learning information storage module

The storage strategy management mode is composed of a large number of memory cells, together with address decoding and read-write control circuit, forming a memory chip. Memory chip, control chip and power module integrated circuit board form a storage product, from the storage unit to the storage integrated circuit is to achieve information storage.

## 2.3 Online Exam Module

The main function of the online examination module is that after students log into the examination system, a group of test papers for each student are randomly generated. The difficulty of each test paper is the same, and the difficulty is determined by the teacher. After the end of the examination, the paper will be directly handed to the server. After logging in the system, the teacher can operate the test paper, grade and enter the student's score [10–12]. Students can log in the background management to query personal test results. Figure 4 shows the sequence diagram of the whole detection process.

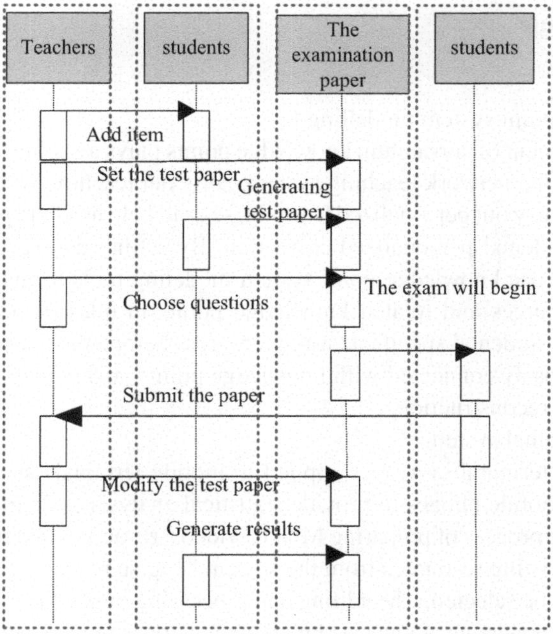


**Fig. 4.** Sequence diagram of online exam

## 2.4 User Management and Function Module

In the administrator management function module, its function is to submit the instructions issued by the system and manage the users. This part includes publishing the latest dynamic information on the website, assigning the system account number of teachers and students, setting the top, deleting post permissions, etc.

**User Management Module**

The main function flow of the administrator is as follows:

Administrator space → access system → input user name and password → match → system announcement user management, educational administration management, forum management → exit system; administrator space → access system → input user name and password → end of mismatch.

The user management module is used for current user consent management, which can realize information modification and update. After logging in, the user management object is transferred to the add user interface, and the user information is entered and submitted to the user list, and the information is successfully returned.

After the administrator opens the new interface, input the user number, name and address information. After confirmation, the administrator submits the saved user list and displays the saved user list in the interface.

**Functional Module**

(1) Knowledge point system modelling tool

The arrangement of curriculum knowledge points plays a leading role in the course. It integrates the network teaching system, sorts out teaching resources and guides students to carry out personalized learning, so as to help teachers push resources and complete students' personalized correction. By setting course knowledge points, teachers can use knowledge point system modeling tools to match and push curriculum resources and related knowledge points in question database resources according to students' specific learning progress before class, so as to form a set of resources closely connected with knowledge points, and realize knowledge points filtering and reconstruction.

(2) Teacher terminal system

The teacher terminal system is applied to mobile terminals such as mainframes, tablets and mobile phones to provide statistical analysis tools for classroom interaction. In the process of preparing MOOC videos, resources and materials, teachers can select existing resources from the system "course resources" and push the targets that can be selected. The editing and processing of teaching resources requires the use of knowledge point system modeling tools to accurately push teaching resources. In the classroom, the student terminal system provides interactive tools to meet the interaction between teachers and students in the classroom.

(3) MOOC classroom interactive system

In the design process of MOOC classroom interaction system, data analysis is mainly in-depth interaction, timely analysis of classroom data, and the interactive system functions are concentrated in the most commonly used functions in classroom teaching, discarding fragmentary functions, so that the communication between teachers and students is more convenient.

## 3 A MOOC-Based Multimedia Network Teaching Mode of University Ideology and Politics

The traditional teaching mode usually adopts the teaching method of teachers, but with the continuous improvement of ideological and political level, the introduction of MOOC university ideological and political basic courses, and according to my country's university teaching standards, the mode has become more detailed. Under the MOOC-based university ideological and political multimedia network teaching module, the innovation of university ideological and political teaching mode is realized, fully mobilizing students' enthusiasm for ideological and political learning, and improving students' ideological and political quality and practical operation ability.

### 3.1 Basic Teaching Mode

For university ideological and political course education, MOOC teaching mode is adopted, with the help of inter-school cooperation resources, the introduction of excellent teaching methods from other schools, and the use of MOOC-based university ideological and political multimedia network teaching modules to establish their own unique courses, students can set free course selection passwords Enter the multimedia network system for course learning. In MOOC courses, the introduction of learning and updating resources, and corresponding teaching arrangements and course notifications according to the actual situation of the school, to meet the individual needs of the university's ideological and political MOOC teaching mode.

In the practical application of College Ideological and political education, the "3 + 2" mode is adopted for ideological and political teaching. Among them, "3" is the three key stages of teaching, which are before class, in class and after class; "2" is the two key factors of teaching mode, which are online and offline respectively. In one semester, the University Ideological and political multimedia network teaching process based on MOOC is as follows (Fig. 5).

Through the courses based on the university's MOOC platform, students can choose real-name courses through the course selection password, and once the course selection is successful, they can obtain all relevant course materials through online inspection. In this teaching model, students need to improve their self-learning awareness and group collaborative learning ability. For this reason, relevant teaching activities are arranged during the pre-class, in-class, and after-class phases of learning, and they are successively launched online and offline.

(1) In the pre class stage, teachers need to refine the content of the course, and analyze the development trend of computer system. Different groups focus on discussing the difficulties encountered by the group in carrying out tasks, and communicate with other groups. The successful completion of each task includes two parts: autonomous learning and collaborative learning. Therefore, students should actively complete the online MOOC video learning task in the discussion area, students can exchange their learning experience under the line to help them complete the task.

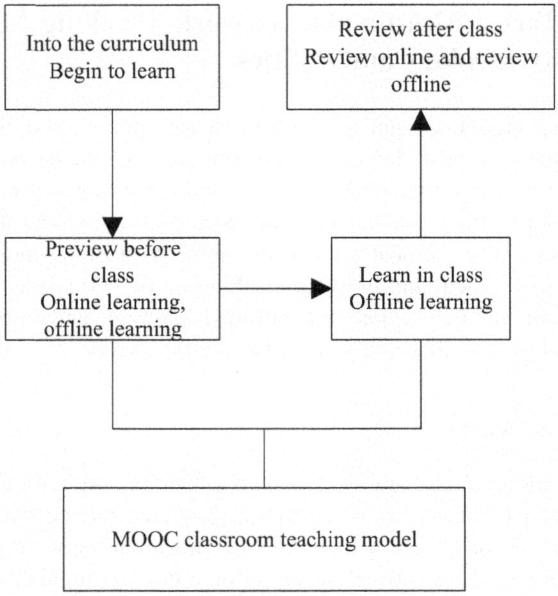


**Fig. 5.** University ideological and political multimedia network teaching process based on MOOC

(2) The classroom stage is the core part of this stage. Based on the MOOC classroom concept, students are the main speakers. Each group needs to select a group representative to report on the learning results, and other group members can supplement after the report. Teachers can help students when they are unable to answer the questions. According to the reports of each group, teachers propose central discussion topics, guide students to engage in active discussions, engage in thinking collisions, and consolidate learning. The teacher summarizes the class and completes offline learning.

(3) The after-school stage is to evaluate the entire teaching process, using staged evaluation and summative evaluation to test students' learning effects. Staged evaluation is done through online discussion and offline homework; summative evaluation needs to use staged testing methods to test students to help students check for knowledge gaps.

### 3.2 Personalized Recommendation Teaching Mode

The mobile multimedia aided teaching platform of University Ideological and political course is a mobile learning system based on client. The website provides a large number of learning materials and supports users to share learning materials. For massive database, users can learn through the mobile teaching assistant client through teacher recommendation, and the platform can also recommend learning materials according to their own recommendation methods. Recommendation based on chart model is also an important method. The algorithm of chart model is to establish different two-dimensional relationship models for different users and projects. If the user selects the course, the binary file of user and course will be formed.

Assuming that $A, B, C, D \cdots$ is the user and $a, b, c, d \cdots$ is the resource of Ideological and political class, the bipartite graph and resource allocation process are constructed.

Assuming that there are $U$ users and $G$ courses, if a single user chooses a course, then there is a relational edge in the graph model recommendation. If other users also select the item, then the value is assigned 1, otherwise it is 0. The algorithm recommendation process mainly has two steps, namely:

Step 1: According to the current user preferences, select the ideological and political classroom resources that users like;

Step 2: select courses according to the target users, obtain the resource values, and then assign the user preferred resources to the associated objects according to the selection relationship.

Assuming that there are $i$ tasks and j resources are shared, the final implementation of the resource allocation is in a non-negative $i * j$ matrix, which is:

$$0\sum_{j=1}^{i} \phi_j = 1 \tag{1}$$

In formula (1), $\phi_j$ represents resources, and the cloud service evaluation index of information interaction process is as follows:

$$R_{ij}^{(t)} = \sum_{j=1}^{i} \phi_j q_m \tag{2}$$

In formula (2), $q_m$ represents the evaluation index. When there are multiple tasks with a negative global utility loss value, in order to make the goal fair, the weighted average method is used to minimize the resource allocation loss. The autonomous auxiliary platform built with multimedia technology can help teachers teach better and students learn better, build communication channels between teachers and students, and improve teaching efficiency.

According to the above analysis, the cloud service evaluation index of information interaction process has heterogeneous influence on potential factors. Testing the feedback results obtained is an important step to verify the quality of information exchange. Taking accuracy as the standard to measure the accuracy of personalized recommendation results, the personalized recommendation model is constructed as follows:

$$\mathrm{P} = \frac{|m_a \cap T|}{|m_a|} \times 100\% \tag{3}$$

In formula (3): $m_a$ represents user recommendation results; $T$ represents a set of courses that users have rated high. In the process of accurate measurement, the higher the score and the higher the correlation, the more accurate the personalized recommendation will be, thereby completing the personalized recommendation of the teaching mode.

Due to the existence of interference data in the personalized recommendation process, it is necessary to eliminate the interference data with the help of collaborative filtering operator.

$$\lambda'_{iz} = \frac{\exp(\lambda_{iz})}{\sum_{z=C(i)} \exp(\lambda_{iz})} \tag{4}$$

In formula (4), $\lambda_{iz}$ represents the collaborative filtering operator. Formula (4) can be used to obtain the collaborative filtering operator after the interference data is eliminated, and then substituting the operator into formula (5) to accurately describe the heterogeneous impact of the interaction between different users on potential factors.

$$Q_i = \mu\left(\omega \cdot \left\{\sum_{z=c(i)} \lambda_{iz} u_{iz}\right\} + s\right) \tag{5}$$

In formula (5), $\mu$ is the activation function; $s$ is the deviation; $u_{iz}$ vector is the preference feature between the user and the course; $\omega$ is the preference parameter.

By constructing a preprocessing data set consisting of a bag of words data set, the set contains a bag of words data set and corresponding things data set, and according to collaborative filtering, all interest patterns are added to the interest pattern set to complete the elimination of interference data.

### 3.3 Assessment Mode

In order to ensure that students can complete online and offline learning in a timely manner, facing the investigation characteristics under the mixed teaching mode, from the perspective of stimulating MOOC, the traditional assessment mode is changed to make students pay more attention to the learning process and improve their active participation. The specific assessment mode is as follows:

(1) Before the next discussion, teachers need to publicize the offline discussion mechanism of computer thinking to students, and feedback student performance to individuals in real time, which is convenient for motivating and warning students' learning attitude.
(2) When conducting on-site discussions, save the entire video recording so that teachers and students can review after class, consolidate knowledge, and ensure the fairness and openness of the assessment.

Students' final scores are composed of online and offline parts, as shown in Table 1. Through the data provided by the course platform, online activities such as watching videos, completing online assignments, and conducting online discussions can be carried out online; offline scores mainly depend on students' reports and final scores.

**Table 1.** Performance assessment

| Basic score/100 | | | | | | |
|---|---|---|---|---|---|---|
| Part one | Basic capabilities 45% | | | | | |
| | check work attendance 50% | Video viewing 20% | Homework performance 30% | Mid term results 60% | | |
| Part two | Network thinking ability 55% | | | | | |
| | Online performance 50% | | | Offline performance 50% | | |
| | MOOC video viewing 50% | Online performance 30% | Results of online discussion 20% | Discussion results 30% | Participation achievements 30% | Final assessment 40% |

# 4 Experiment

In order to verify the effectiveness of MOOC based College Ideological and political multimedia network teaching, experimental tests are needed.

## 4.1 Test Content Settings

A black box test was done. In the course of MOOC-based university ideological and political multimedia network teaching, the content of the black box test is shown in Table 2.

**Table 2.** Black box test content

| Serial number | Test content |
|---|---|
| 1 | Ideological and Political Course Information Retrieval |
| 2 | Export student information |
| 3 | Student information mastery |
| 4 | Student's result |

## 4.2 Ideological and Political Course Information Retrieval Test

Two teaching modes are used to test the information retrieval situation of ideological and political courses, and the comparison results are shown in Fig. 6.

It can be seen from Fig. 6 that as the number of people retrieved using P2P-based technology increases, the accuracy of retrieval also decreases. When the number of retrieved people is 70, the retrieval accuracy reaches a minimum of 50%; the use of multimedia-based technology increases with the number of retrieved people. The search

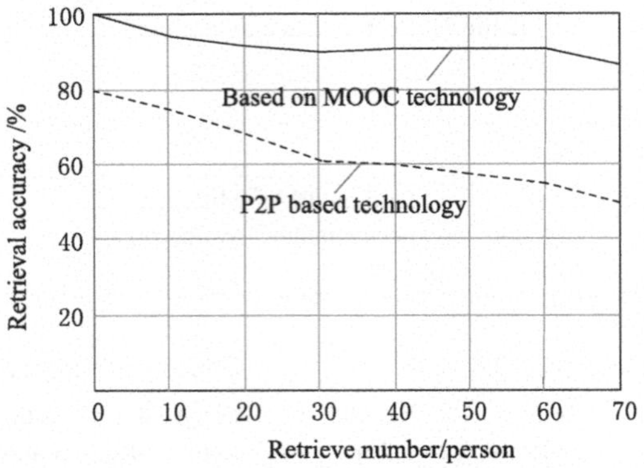


**Fig. 6.** Comparative analysis of information retrieval accuracy of Ideological and political courses of two teaching methods

accuracy has also changed. When the number of searchers is 70, the search accuracy is at least 88%. It can be seen that the accuracy of information retrieval using this technology is high.

### 4.3 Test Students' Ability to Master Knowledge

The P2P-based technology teaching method and the certification-based MOOC teaching method were used to compare and analyze the students' knowledge mastery ability. The test results are shown in Table 3.

**Table 3.** Comparison results of two teaching methods on students' knowledge mastery ability

| Project | | Teaching method based on P2P technology | Based on MOOC teaching method |
|---|---|---|---|
| Teaching schedule or not | Interaction between teachers and students | Mastering ability /% | Mastering ability /% |
| No | Yes | 41 | 81 |
| Yes | No | 32 | 79 |
| Yes | Yes | 60 | 85 |
| No | No | 25 | 75 |

It can be seen from Table 3 that in the absence of teaching time arrangement, there is a 40% difference in students' ability to master knowledge; in the absence of interaction between teachers and students, the difference is 47%; in the case of both, the difference is 25%; in the absence of both, the difference is 50%. It can be seen that the improvement of teachers' teaching methods based on MOOC teaching method can improve students' ability to master knowledge.

### 4.4 Student Achievement Test

With a full score of 100, the P2P technology-based teaching method and the MOOC-based teaching method were used to compare and analyze student performance. The test results are shown in Table 4.

**Table 4.** Comparative analysis of the results of the two teaching methods on student performance testing

| Number of students/person | Teaching method based on P2P technology | Based on MOOC teaching method |
|---|---|---|
| 2 | 130 min | 200 min |
| 4 | 342 min | 398 min |
| 6 | 628 min | 695 min |
| 8 | 735 min | 795 min |
| 10 | 943 min | 996 min |
| 12 | 1158 min | 1196 min |

It can be seen from Table 4 that students using P2P-based teaching methods have lower scores, while those using MOOC-based teaching methods have higher scores, close to full marks.

Through the above analysis results, the use of a MOOC teaching method network teaching system has a large academic performance of students, and the teaching effect is better.

## 5 Concluding Remarks

MOOC is a new teaching method which is popular all over the world. It has a great impact on the teaching of information technology in our country. Therefore, this paper proposes a multimedia network teaching based on MOOC in university ideological and political teaching. We should continue to promote the integration of teaching resources, improve the teaching quality and the use efficiency of network information, so as to expand the teaching benefit area.

Although the teaching method has basically achieved the needs of functional objectives, it is still in the preliminary research stage, and its application in real teaching is not mature, so it needs many improvements. In order to obtain more detailed data information, it is necessary to improve the multimedia network teaching mode.

(1) Strengthen course modules and interactive functions
The mobile teaching auxiliary platform is an important platform for college ideological and political teachers to integrate excellent teaching resources, and the function of webcasting courses should be actively expanded. At the same time,

mobile phone-assisted teaching systems should adopt open participation and interactive communication methods to further highlight the characteristics and thinking of ideological and political theory courses in the information age.

(2) Realize continuous operation of the platform
The normal use of the mobile teaching auxiliary system for ideological and political courses requires the normal operation of the client system. However, customer maintenance usually requires a powerful technical maintenance team, lacks research and writing process, and more power needs to be integrated to achieve continuous platform operations.

## References


1. Wang, J., Liu, D., Lu, H.: Design of online course teaching system in network environment. Mod. Electron. Techniq. **40**(22), 69–71 (2017)
2. Liu, D., Wang, J.: Design of internet online auxiliary teaching system based on web. Modern Electron. Techniq. **40**(20), 28–30 (2017)
3. Wang, L., Wang, Y., Zheng, J.: The exploration and practice of innovating the MOOC teaching mode in local colleges and Universities — Taking the blended teaching reform of "University Computer Foundation" in Southwest Petroleum University as an example. China Univ. Teach. **15**(12), 80–95 (2016)
4. Zhao, M.: Teaching practice and effect of "MOOC + flipped classroom" in computer graphics. High. Educ. Explorat. **11**(s1), 54–55 (2016)
5. Wei, W., Tan, Z.: Deep integration of information technology and experimental teaching under the background of MOOC. China High. Educ. **18**(7), 54–56 (2017)
6. Guo, B., Sun, X., Wu, J.: Thinking about the teaching reform of engineering surveying under background of MOOC. Bull. Survey. Mapp. **23**(3), 145–148 (2017)
7. Shang, W.: Construction of hierarchical and mixed teaching mode in college classroom under the background of MOOC. Heilongjiang Animal Sci. Vet. Med. **16**(1), 269–270 (2017)
8. Liu, S., Bai, W., Zeng, N., et al.: A fast fractal based compression for MRI images. IEEE Access **7**, 62412–62420 (2019)
9. Liu, S., Li, Z., Zhang, Y., et al.: Introduction of key problems in long-distance learning and training. Mob. Netw. Appl. **24**(1), 1–4 (2019)
10. Liu, S., Glowatz, M., Zappatore, M., Gao, H., Jia, B., Bucciero, A. (eds.): eLEOT 2018. LNICSSITE, vol. 243. Springer, Cham (2018). https://doi.org/10.1007/978-3-319-93719-9
11. Hu, L.: The exploration of college English teaching mode based on multimedia network technology. J. Zhangjiakou Voc. Tech. Coll. **32**(1), 67–69 (2019)
12. Kostolansk, L., Ebo, M., Tomková, V.: The Preparation of Teachers in the Field of Multimedia Education, pp. 1477–1483. Palma, Luis Gómez Chova (2019)

# An Efficient Teaching Method for Physiological Basic Course of Online and Offline Integration

Lian-shi Dong, Dan Wang(✉), and Jing-qiong Xiao

Medical and Nursing Branch, Panjin Vocational and Technical College, Panjin 124000, China

**Abstract.** High efficiency teaching method of traditional physiology basic course, and students' interest in learning gray relevance, and online teaching resources utilization rate is low. Therefore, an efficient teaching method for physiological foundation course of online and offline integration is proposed. In this paper, the basic principles of high efficiency teaching evaluation and index system are set up, the factors of teaching efficiency index are extracted, the weight set of index is calculated, the teaching effect of high efficiency is evaluated, and the teaching method with high comprehensive evaluation result is selected to carry out course teaching. Compared with the traditional methods, the results show that the design method can improve the grey relational degree with students' interest in learning, and the utilization rate of online teaching resources.

**Keywords:** Online and offline fusion · Physiology foundation · High efficiency teaching · Teaching evaluation

## 1 Introduction

In the era of knowledge-based economy, digital technology has gradually penetrated into every stage of education, especially in the traditional teaching mode. Therefore, the high-efficiency teaching mode of online and offline integration emerges at the historic moment, and promotes the generation and development of students' wisdom. A series of new changes have taken place in the teaching reform. The Ten-Year Development Plan for Education Informatization (2011–2020) points out that it is necessary to promote the integration of information technology and teaching in the reform of basic education, and explore and establish a new mode of high-efficiency teaching centered on learners. In this era of education informatization, the traditional teaching mode with knowledge teaching as the core can not meet the needs of the current teaching reform, and the traditional teaching mode needs to be changed, while the high-efficiency teaching with online and offline integration can promote the deep integration of information technology and classroom teaching, and provide a new idea for the cultivation of intelligent talents.

The study of teaching methods mainly centers on nine themes: teaching evaluation indicators, teaching evaluation methods, teaching mode reform, teaching evaluation system, student evaluation, significance of teaching evaluation, curriculum evaluation, teacher evaluation, teaching process and elements. Efficient teaching methods include


W. Fu et al. (Eds.): eLEOT 2021, LNICST 389, pp. 181–193, 2021.
https://doi.org/10.1007/978-3-030-84383-0_16

the cultural values based on the knowledge-based and competency-based concepts, and can promote students' development in an all-round way. Teaching evaluation mainly shows its own value from students, teachers and teaching activities of both sides, and equates teaching evaluation with student evaluation. It holds that teaching evaluation is the study and development of students' knowledge, skills, emotions, values and other aspects in teaching, and student evaluation is the collection, processing and analysis of students' information and data in a comprehensive and scientific manner, while making value judgments and factual judgments on students' development and changes [1]. Some scholars put forward the online and offline hybrid instructional design method based on Rasch model, evaluated 32 online and offline hybrid instructional design schemes of X University through self-made quality evaluation tools, analyzed data by using Rasch model, and found the difficulties in five aspects of current hybrid instructional design: goal design, evaluation design, content design, method design and resource design. On this basis, it was proposed that hybrid instructional design should have reverse thinking. It runs through the whole process and builds a support for learning. Some scholars put forward a mixed online and offline teaching mode based on deep learning strategy, and studied the design and practice of deep learning mode based on online evaluation system, mainly including the organization of classroom teaching under the mixed online and offline teaching mode, the design of test question bank and the realization of online evaluation teaching platform. On the basis of the above theories, this paper puts forward an efficient teaching method of online and offline integration for physiology basic courses. By setting up multi-level evaluation index, using fuzzy judgment matrix to calculate the weight value of the index, and checking the consistency of the matrix, the evaluation of curriculum teaching is realized.

## 2 Design of Efficient Teaching Method for Physiological Basic Course of Online and Offline Integration

### 2.1 Sorting Out the Efficient Teaching Process of Basic Physiology Course

In order to sort out the efficient teaching process of the basic physiology courses, in the preparation stage before class, teachers need to analyze and define the teaching three-dimensional objectives according to the teaching syllabus, and before the teaching mode of online and offline integration, teachers need to carry out clear analysis of teaching objectives, such as what contents need to be taught in an exploratory teaching mode, what contents need to be taught directly, establish clear teaching objectives, and optimize the teaching process so as to achieve the best teaching effect. During the teaching process, students can complete the internalization and acquisition of pre-class knowledge by watching the teaching video released by teachers, and how to collect and edit better teaching video is the focus of the basic physiology courses, and the editing of the video shall be completed according to the students' personality, needs and teaching objectives. The good video can be edited and released by teachers through the school website, QQ group sharing, DVD recording and other tools for students to study [2]. At the stage of internalization of students' knowledge, students can, according to their own actual learning situation, learn independently through the videos released by teachers before class, which can avoid the waste of classroom time to a certain extent. Students can take notes where they do not understand in the process of watching videos, so as to master the pace of their own learning. After the end, students can, according to their own notes, sort out and internalize the knowledge, draw the framework of the knowledge points in online teaching, and list the contents that have not been mastered yet, so as to facilitate the exchanges and questions in class. After students have watched the videos, they need to complete the targeted classroom exercises arranged by teachers. Teachers need to complete reasonable pre-class tests according to the difficulty of online videos and teaching objectives, guide students to complete the integration of new and old knowledge, and more in-depth understanding of basic knowledge of physiology. In addition, teachers need to understand the doubts encountered in the students' pre-class learning process through QQ, blog, teaching platform and other tools, and fully prepare for the solution of puzzles in class at any time. Thus, the efficient teaching process of physiology basic course has been sorted out.

## 2.2 Basic Principles of Constructing Efficient Teaching Evaluation

Objective to evaluate the efficient teaching methods of physiology basic course and construct the basic principles of evaluation. In order to change the fixed and absolute shortcomings of the previous standards, the basic principle is to be able to reasonably evaluate the majority of students, but also to reflect the development trend and level of different individuals. Therefore, the teaching evaluation should start from a broader perspective and follow the following principles: effectiveness principle: in the classroom teaching of basic physiology course Students are a group with different personalities and different ability levels, and they have different degrees of learning video materials and knowledge before class. Therefore, in the classroom teaching of basic physiology course, we can not use the only standard to evaluate, we need to reflect the actual situation of each student and pay attention to the learning situation of each student, so as to make the students more efficient Teaching, to carry out to every student, teaching methods need to be diversified, by stimulating students' interest in learning, to promote their autonomous learning, so that students at different levels can be promoted and developed; the principle of diversity: in the information environment, constantly break through the inherent thinking, realize the diversity of training purpose and content, not only pay attention to basic knowledge We should pay more attention to the education of personality, emotion, values and so on. In the process of formulating the teaching content, we need to consider the cultivation of students' comprehensive quality, and diversified evaluation is the necessary requirement at present. The feasibility principle: to formulate an evaluation system that can comprehensively evaluate students, each index should be comprehensible by students, convenient for teachers to implement, and need to be systematic In order to play the role of the evaluation system, we should consider the students' acceptance ability and the existing knowledge level. The principle of grading system: the traditional hundred point evaluation system not only increases the students' learning pressure and causes polarization, but also restricts the teachers' play, This kind of assessment method also needs to pay attention to students, such as the mastery of knowledge and skills, emotional values and other aspects, and pay attention to the usual learning performance, and finally make a comprehensive evaluation of students; pay attention to the process principle: follow the learning situation and results of students in the learning process Tracking observation, starting from the accurate and comprehensive detailed evaluation index, focuses on the learning process, the performance of students' group exploration, as well as self-evaluation and mutual evaluation [3]. So far, we have completed the construction of the basic principles of efficient teaching evaluation of basic physiology course.

### 2.3 Construction of Efficient Teaching Evaluation Index System

Confirms the high efficiency teaching appraisal target construction mentality, extracts the high efficiency teaching appraisal target. First of all, the construction principle of the index system is determined: the principle of overall integrity and objectivity [4, 5]: the evaluation index should include the performance of teachers and students in teaching activities in detail, and at the same time, it should be able to systematically reflect the individual and overall evaluation results. The principle of objectivity is to use the index to make an objective evaluation of the specific situation of teachers and students in the teaching process [6]. That is, indicators can fully reflect the accurate development of the whole, the upper indicators as an important part should form a sufficient and necessary relationship, while the lower indicators should achieve the goals and requirements required by the upper indicators; the directional principle: the goal of high-efficiency teaching should be more detailed, so that the teaching of basic physiology can be more specific and purposeful, the principle of operability: as an objective basis for the behavior and concretization of the evaluation object, it should have the conditions of easy operation and wide range of application. It should reflect its operability, be easy to understand, and play a guiding role in reality, The evaluation results should also be clearly observed and understood; the principle of mutual independence of indicators at the same level: there should be no dependency relationship between indicators at the same level, each indicator should be isolated, there should be no index structure that can produce chain effect, this indicator can not be used as the cause or result of another indicator, there should be no inclusion relationship, there should be no dependency, In order to ensure the independence of an index, we should pay attention to the relationship of cross and equality [7].

On the basis of the above principles, consult the files of efficient teaching of basic physiology courses, and in the databases of Wanfang, CBM, CNKI, Pubmed, etc., take basic physiology courses, efficient teaching, online and offline integration as key words, look up the relevant literature on factors affecting teaching efficiency, delete records of incomplete or repeated information, retain the literature information data of complete titles and abstracts, and select the indicators with high frequency [8]. The process is shown in Fig. 1:

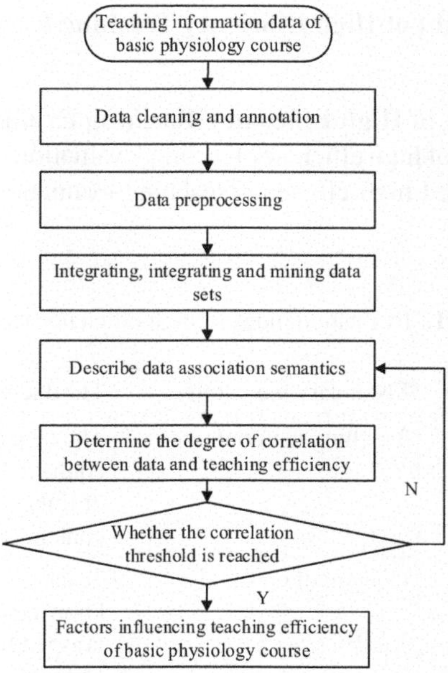


**Fig. 1.** Extraction process of teaching efficiency index factors

To preprocess the historical data related to the efficient teaching of basic physiology course, set the sample data as 1, then the sample average value of the original data is 2

$$\bar{t} = \frac{1}{n}\sum_{i=1}^{n} t_i \tag{1}$$

The residual error calculation formula of original data $u_i$ is as follows:

$$u_i = t_i - \bar{t} \tag{2}$$

According to Bessel formula, the root mean square deviation of the data is obtained as follows

$$\gamma = \sqrt{\sum u_i^2 \Big/ n - 1} \tag{3}$$

Calculate the difference between sample data $t_i$ and $\bar{t}$. When the difference is greater than $\gamma$, the information data will be eliminated, otherwise it will be retained [9, 10]. To judge the extracted data, select the data that can deal with a large amount of data, different data structures, multi-dimensional data, and multi-level data as the evaluation index of efficient teaching of basic physiology course. So far, the construction of efficient teaching evaluation index system has been completed.

## 2.4 Calculate the Weight of High Efficiency Teaching Evaluation Index

**Quantitative Processing of High Efficiency Teaching Evaluation Index**
Standardized processing of high efficiency teaching evaluation index, calculate the index weight [11]. The extracted high efficiency teaching evaluation indexes are as follows (Table 1):

**Table 1.** Evaluation index of high efficiency teaching

| First level indicators | Secondary indicators | Third level indicators |
|---|---|---|
| Teaching design of basic physiology course | Teaching materials | The materials of the courseware conform to the syllabus, the length of time is suitable, and the teaching content is highlighted; |
| | Content of courses | Teaching objectives are clear; key knowledge points should be grasped for teaching; development and integration of teaching resources should be emphasized |
| Teaching process of basic physiology course | Teacher behavior | Clear teaching ideas; accurate teaching language; encourage students to learn independently; cultivate students' understanding ability; teach students in accordance with their aptitude; accurate teaching language |
| | Teaching method | The combination of teaching and training; avoid rigid teaching methods, with flexibility |
| | Student activities | Changeable characteristics; on-the-spot training; appropriate use of information means |
| Teaching effect of basic physiology course | Affective education | Students actively participate in teaching activities, complete individual learning independently, and actively share what they have learned |
| | Teaching and education | Good classroom atmosphere; pay close attention to students' interests; achieve teaching objectives |
| | Teaching personality | The classroom atmosphere is active, and the teaching knowledge has an appropriate amount of information |

The first level index is regarded as the target layer, the second level index as the criterion layer, and the third level index as the sub standard layer. Then the fuzzy judgment matrix is constructed to transform the index from qualitative evaluation to quantitative evaluation.

**Get the Weight Set of High Efficiency Teaching Evaluation Index**
Through the hierarchical structure and judgment matrix, the weight set of high efficiency teaching evaluation index is obtained [12]. Set the weight coefficient of judgment matrix to 0.5, and the scale of judgment matrix is shown in Table 2.

**Table 2.** Meaning of judgment matrix scale

| Scale | Meaning | Scale | Meaning |
|---|---|---|---|
| 0.1 | Both indicators are equally important | 0.2 | One indicator is slightly more important than the other |
| 0.3 | One index is more important than the other | 0.4 | One indicator is far more important than the other |
| 0.5 | One indicator is more important than the other | 0.6+ | Inverse comparison of two indicators |

When the scale is reciprocal, it indicates the importance comparison of the opposite two indicators [13, 14]. If the evaluation indexes are compared by the scale shown in the table above, the calculation formula of the judgment matrix of the indexes at each level is as follows:

$$A=\begin{pmatrix} a_{11} & \cdots & a_{1m} \\ \cdots & \cdots & \cdots \\ a_{m1} & \cdots & a_{mm} \end{pmatrix} \tag{4}$$

Where $m$ is the order of judgment matrix $A$, and $(a_{11}, \cdots, a_{mm})$ is the element of judgment matrix $A$, which indicates the importance of one index relative to another index in the same layer. Calculate the product $B_I$ of elements in each row of matrix $A$, and the formula is as follows:

$$B_I = \Pi_{j=1}^{m} A_{ij} (I, j = 1, \cdots, m) \tag{5}$$

$I$ is any index in the index set, $j$ is the number of columns of the judgment matrix $A$ [15, 16]. Calculate the square root of $B_I$ and normalize the vector to get the weight coefficient $w_I$ of each index:

$$\mathrm{w}_I = \frac{\sqrt[\mathrm{m}]{B_I}}{\sum_{I=1}^{\mathrm{m}} \sqrt[\mathrm{m}]{B_I}} \tag{6}$$

In order to ensure the accuracy of importance judgment, the consistency of $A$ is checked. The maximum eigenvalue $\varphi$ of the judgment matrix is calculated

$$\varphi=\frac{1}{\mathrm{m}} \sum_{I=1}^{\mathrm{m}} \frac{A\mathrm{w}_I^T}{\mathrm{w}_I} \tag{7}$$

$T$ is matrix transpose [17]. Then the calculation formula of metric compatibility $C$ is as follows:

$$C = \frac{\varphi - \mathrm{m}}{\mathrm{m} - 1} \tag{8}$$

According to Thomas' statistical analysis, the consistency coefficient of the judgment matrix is defined as follows: select the scale 0.1, the consistency coefficient is 0.01, the scale 0.2 coefficient is 0.01, the scale 0.3 coefficient is 0.41, the scale 0.4 coefficient is 0.87, the scale 0.5 coefficient is 1.11, the scale 0.6 coefficient is 1.21, the scale 0.7 coefficient is 1.31, the scale 0.8 coefficient is 1.42, and the scale 0.9 coefficient is 1.32. Then the formula for calculating the random consistency ratio of the judgment matrix is as follows:

$$M = C/L \tag{9}$$

$L$ is the consistency coefficient of the judgment matrix. If the consistency ratio is greater than 0.1, the consistency matrix is judged to be inconsistent, and the matrix is modified to recalculate the index weight, otherwise the consistency matrix is judged to pass the consistency test. So far, the weight calculation of high efficiency teaching evaluation index is completed.

### 2.5 Evaluate the High Efficiency Teaching Effect of Basic Physiology Course

Calculate the evaluation value of high efficiency teaching and evaluate the effect of high efficiency teaching. The evaluation index set F = {F1, F2, F3, F4, F5} is established, which means that the teaching effect is good, good, general, poor, and poor, with a total of 5 grades [18]. The expert scoring method is adopted, and the score of the evaluation set is defined as {10, 20, 30, 40, 50}. Then define the judgment basis of the membership degree of each grade in the comment set, use the fuzzy multi value evaluation method to describe the degree of the evaluation index in each grade, and get the evaluation result set of the evaluation index, so as to realize the fuzzy evaluation of each index [19, 20]. The calculation formula $I$ of the score value $E_I$ of the second evaluation index is as follows:

$$E_I = 10G_1 + 20G_2 + 30G_3 + 40G_4 + 50G_5 \tag{10}$$

$G_1$–$G_5$ is the membership of F1–F5. The final evaluation result of the evaluation model is obtained by summarizing the evaluation result set and weight set

$$N = \sum_{I=1}^{\mathrm{m}} E_I \mathrm{w}_I \tag{11}$$

The teaching effect is divided into 1–5 levels, as shown in Table 3.

According to the final evaluation results, the effective and efficient teaching methods are selected to teach the basic physiology course, so as to complete the evaluation of the efficient teaching effect of the basic physiology course. So far, we have completed the design of efficient teaching method of physiology basic course based on online and offline integration.

**Table 3.** Classification of high efficiency teaching effect

| Final evaluation value | Grade | Meaning |
|---|---|---|
| 0–20 | 1 | High efficiency and good teaching effect of basic physiology course |
| 20–40 | 2 | The teaching effect of basic physiology is better than that of high efficiency |
| 40–60 | 3 | The teaching effect of physiology basic course is general |
| 60–80 | 4 | The teaching effect of physiology basic course is poor |
| 80–100 | 5 | The teaching effect of physiology basic course is poor |

## 3 Experiment and Analysis

The design method is recorded as experimental group A, the online and offline hybrid teaching design method based on Rasch model is recorded as experimental group B, and the online and offline integration teaching method based on deep learning is recorded as experimental group C.

### 3.1 Experimental Preparation

The subjects of the experiment are the students of a certain university with a master's degree. The course is the basic course of physiology. Seven groups are set up with 500 members. The teachers use three efficient teaching methods to teach the students of seven groups. The topology of online network is shown in Fig. 2

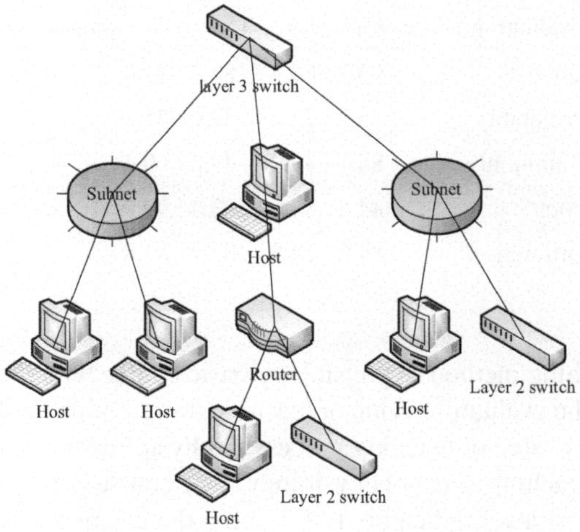


**Fig. 2.** Network topology on line

In group A, the teaching technology and teaching mode of basic physiology were searched and evaluated

$$A = \begin{bmatrix} 0.164, 0.318, 0.422, 0.076, 0.021 \\ 0.248, 0.476, 0.249, 0.256, 0.039 \\ 0.201, 0.392, 0.132, 0.209, 0.066 \end{bmatrix} \quad (12)$$

Set the first level indicators as U1–U3, compare the first level evaluation indicators, and test their consistency. The specific results are shown in Table 4.

**Table 4.** First level index weight and consistency test

| | U1 | U2 | U3 |
|---|---|---|---|
| U1 | 1/2 | 1 | 1/3 |
| U2 | 1/2 | 1 | 1/3 |
| U3 | 1/5 | 1/4 | 1/4 |
| Weight | 0.382 | 0.192 | 0.426 |

The consistency test index and average random consistency index are 0.0122 and 0.0211 respectively. The judgment matrix meets the consistency test, and the weight distribution is reasonable. By calculating the membership coefficient, the specific score values are shown in Table 5.

**Table 5.** Index score

| Evaluation grade | $U_1$ | $U_2$ | $U_3$ | Comprehensive |
|---|---|---|---|---|
| Good | 93.2 | 89.4 | 87.5 | 90.0 |
| Preferably | 78.2 | 75.4 | 59.6 | 71.1 |
| Commonly | 84.1 | 49.2 | 47.3 | 60.1 |
| Poor | 84.5 | 84.9 | 103.4 | 90.9 |
| Difference | 84.2 | 74.9 | 104.2 | 87.8 |

Finally, the teaching method of physiology basic course with the highest evaluation value is obtained. The evaluation value of teaching design of physiology basic course is 97.26, the evaluation value of teaching process of physiology basic course is 98.44, the evaluation value of teaching effect of physiology basic course is 96.91, and the evaluation grade of the three first level indicators is 1. Taking the average value of the evaluation result set, the comprehensive evaluation value of the selected teaching method can be calculated 54, and the evaluation level was 1. In group A, the teaching method of basic physiology course was selected, and the teachers were asked to teach the students.

### 3.2 Experimental Results

**Experimental Results of the First Group**

Calculate the grey correlation degree of three groups of teaching methods and students' learning interest. The greater the grey correlation degree is, the greater the correlation degree between teaching methods and students' learning interest is, and the more students' learning interest can be stimulated. The experimental results are shown in Fig. 3

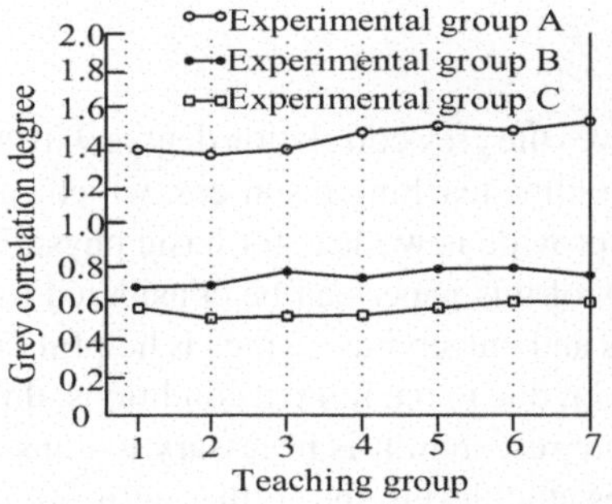


**Fig. 3.** Comparison results of the first group of experiments

As can be seen from the above figure, the average grey correlation degree of group A is 1.404, and that of group B and group C are 0.692 and 0.584 respectively. Compared with group B and group C, the grey correlation degree of group A is increased by 0.712 and 0.820 respectively.

**Results of the Second Group**

The utilization rate of online teaching resources of the three groups of teaching methods is compared, and the experimental results are shown in Fig. 4

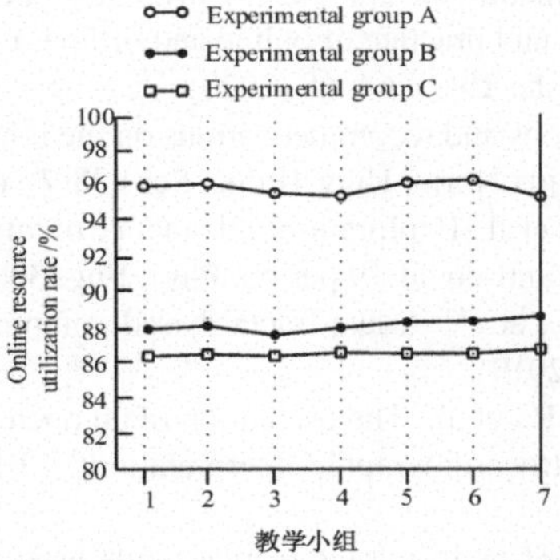


**Fig. 4.** Comparison results of the second group of experiments

As can be seen from Fig. 4, the average utilization rate of online teaching resources in experimental group A is 95.782%, and the average utilization rates of online teaching resources in experimental group B and experimental group C are 88.062% and 86.145% respectively. Compared with experimental group B and group C, the utilization rate of online teaching resources in group A is increased by 7.720% and 9.637% respectively. To sum up, compared with the traditional teaching method of physiology basic course, this design method improves the gray correlation degree with students' learning interest and the utilization rate of online teaching resources, which can fully stimulate students' learning interest and make full use of online teaching resources.

## 4 Conclusion

This design method improves the grey correlation degree with students' learning interest, and the utilization rate of online teaching resources, which can promote the generation of students' wisdom, and provide new ideas for basic physiology courses in many colleges. The research results of this paper can be considered to be applied in online and offline teaching in colleges and universities, which is helpful to the development of basic physiology course. However, due to the limited conditions, this study is only carried out in one college. In the future research, it is necessary to consider the teaching situation of colleges and universities at all levels and further optimize the design method.

## References


1. Li, H.: MOOCs of ideological and political education under the background of enrollment expansion in higher vocational colleges. J. Liaon. Agricult. Coll. **23**(1), 33–35 (2021)
2. Gao, Y.: An exploration of blended teaching model based on CBI: taking the teaching practice of international logistics as an example. J. Zhejiang Wanli Univ. **34**(1), 82–88 (2021)
3. Liu, Y., Zhang, D., Huang, J., et al.: Research and practice on blended teaching design of introduction to general practice course based on small private online course curriculum. Chin. Gen. Pract. **24**(1), 84–87 (2021)
4. Ma, X., Ma, Y., Tian, Y., et al.: Practice and thinking of "Full Online" remote hybrid teaching under novel coronavirus pneumonia epidemic. Univ. Chem. **35**(5), 29–32 (2020)
5. Chen, J., Qi, S.: Research and practice of online and offline mixed teaching model based on cloud classroom. Zhiye Jishu **19**(2), 64–68 (2020)
6. Xue, C., Guo, Y.: Reflections and recommendations on the reform of online teaching reform in Universities. J. East China Norm. Univ. (Educ. Sci.) **38**(7), 65–74 (2020)
7. Hou, D., Liu, Q., Yang, H., et al.: Exploration and practice of improving online college physics teaching effect during the anti-covid-19 period. Phys. Eng. **30**(3), 11–15 (2020)
8. Liu, S., Bai, W., Zeng, N., et al.: A fast fractal based compression for MRI images. IEEE Access **7**, 62412–62420 (2019)
9. Breen, C., Zhu, T., Bond, R., et al.: The evaluation of an open source online training system for teaching 12 lead electrocardiographic interpretation. J. Electrocardiol. **02**(3), 454–461 (2016)
10. Jianqiu, L.: Construction of real-time interactive mode-based online course live broadcast teaching platform for physical training. Int. J. Emerg. Technol. Learn. (iJET) **13**(06), 73 (2018)
11. Mnguni, L., Mokiwa, H.: The integration of online teaching and learning in stem education as a response to the COVID-19 pandemic. J. Balt. Sci. Educ. **19**(6A), 1040–1042 (2020)

12. Coman, C., Ru, L.G., Mesean-Schmitz, L., Stanciu, C., Bularca, M.C.: Online teaching and learning in higher education during the coronavirus pandemic: students' perspective. Sustainability **12**(24), 10367 (2020)
13. Scherer, R., Howard, S.K., Tondeur, J., et al.: Profiling teachers' readiness for online teaching and learning in higher education: who's ready? Comput. Hum. Behav. **118**, 106675 (2020)
14. Hofer, S., Nistor, N., Scheibenzuber, C.: Online teaching and learning in higher education: lessons learned in crisis situations. Comput. Hum. Behav. **121**, 106789 (2021)
15. Truzoli, R., Pirola, V., Conte, S.: The impact of risk and protective factors on online teaching experience in high school Italian teachers during the COVID-19 pandemic. J. Comput. Assist. Learn. **37**(4), 940–952 (2021)
16. Hamann, K., Glazier, R.A., Wilson, B.M., Pollock, P.H.: Online teaching, student success, and retention in political science courses. Eur. Polit. Sci. (2020). https://doi.org/10.1057/s41304-020-00282-x
17. Wang, Y., Liu, Q.: Effects of online teaching presence on students' interactions and collaborative knowledge construction. J. Comput. Assist. Learn. **36**(3), 370–382 (2019)
18. Garza, J.: Meditations in a pandemic: what i feared and learned about teaching online. J. Adolesc. Health. **64**(2), 215–220 (2020)
19. Monsivais, D.B., Olson, C.M.: Partnering to develop online teaching skills for master of science in nursing education students. J. Nurs. Educ. **58**(4), 240–242 (2019)
20. Powell, B., Jardine, K.D., Steed, M., et al.: Enhanced nursing self-awareness and pharmacotherapy knowledge-base: peer-teaching and nursing/pharmacy interprofessional education. Med. Educ. Online **25**(1), 1814551 (2020)

# Decision Support Model for Online Education of Logistics Management Major from the Perspective of "Credit Bank"

Jun Fu(✉) and Ming Qin

School of Economics and Management, Jiangxi Tourism and Commerce Vocational College, Nancang 330114, China
fujun123654@yeah.net

**Abstract.** For the logistics management major from the perspective of "credit bank", the traditional online education decision support model has poor reliability due to the lack of data analysis and processing ability. Therefore, this paper proposes a decision support model for online education of logistics management major from the perspective of "credit bank". Based on the actual needs of online education of logistics management, the basic framework of the model is built; the relevant database required by the model is designed, and the data is classified and standardized before data storage; the designed data path is taken as the support of the model, and the credit settlement in the credit bank is taken as the ultimate goal, and the objective function and related constraints of the model are designed, so as to realize the logistics management Decision support for online education of management major. The experimental results show that the model is more reliable than the traditional decision support model because of its low parameter correlation and high data integrity.

**Keywords:** Credit bank · Logistics management · Online education · Decision support

## 1 Introduction

The rapid development of computer, network and communication technology has laid the foundation for online education, and domestic online education is advancing towards popularization and internationalization. Various problems of online education have also been debated, and the most important one is the quality assurance of online education [1]. Online education is essentially different from traditional education. It is mainly based on media teaching, separated from teaching and learning. It is an open learning, emphasizing students' autonomy and individual learning. Quality assurance is a common problem of all kinds of education and an eternal theme [2]. Due to the essential difference between online education and traditional education, the support system for traditional education is no longer applicable. This is an urgent need to establish an effective quality assurance


W. Fu et al. (Eds.): eLEOT 2021, LNICST 389, pp. 194–204, 2021.
https://doi.org/10.1007/978-3-030-84383-0_17

support system for online education, so as to ensure the vitality of online education and play its due role in education for all [3].

Especially for the logistics management major, logistics is a major that keeps pace with the times and is changing with the construction of information technology. With the help of information technology, the construction of online education decision support model and the implementation of online education and learning is an important part of the current online education quality assurance system [4]. In the process of decision support, a large number of data and materials are needed to be processed, and these data and materials are analyzed and judged, and finally decision-making is made, which will consume a lot of time and energy. Therefore, an effective information means is needed to achieve efficient and accurate decision-making.

The traditional university system has a distinct shadow of planned economy. The development of the university is completely led by the government. The university has no autonomy, and everything is subject to the management of the government. In the administration of colleges and universities, there is a serious "government" style, and the administration is serious. Modern society is a market economy system, and colleges and universities have the right to run their own schools. Society and the market have increasingly strong expectations and demands for colleges and universities [5]. It is of great significance to build a management system that meets the needs of modern social development and conforms to the law of university development. The urgency of social demand for talents and education researchers deeply feel that only by taking the modern university system which is most in line with its own development law and education reality, can universities be more competitive [6].

"Credit bank" system can provide system guarantee for the individualization of educational goal and process. The original intention and characteristics of the credit bank system determine that it is the institutional guarantee of personalized education service [7]. The purpose of "credit bank" is to provide learning services for all kinds of learners. There are many types of students, which can only be unified on the basis of ensuring their personality. The system is very inclusive for all kinds of learners. The "credit bank" system includes a flexible educational system that can be shortened and extended by choosing courses independently according to their own time, place and preferences. The achievement and progress of learners are measured by credits [8]. It provides the most inclusive system for students to plan and manage their own learning process and activities. This has a positive effect on enhancing learners' creativity in learning activities.

The research of decision support theory and technology has been quite mature at home and abroad, and has been widely used in various fields. This paper aims to provide an effective decision support model for online education of logistics management major from the perspective of "credit bank", and solve some problems existing in the traditional decision support model, so as to assist logistics management major to achieve better online education. The specific research ideas are as follows:

First, the paper analyzes the actual needs of online education for logistics management students and constructs the basic framework of decision support model;

Secondly, the relevant database is designed to classify and standardize the data before data storage;

Then, taking the credit settlement in the credit bank as the final goal, the model objective function and related constraints are designed, so as to realize the decision support for online education of logistics management specialty;

Finally, summarize the full text.

# 2 Design of Online Education Decision Support Model for Logistics Management Major from the Perspective of "Credit Bank"

## 2.1 Model Architecture Design

The three component structure of DSS includes dialogue component, data component and model component, as shown in Fig. 1.

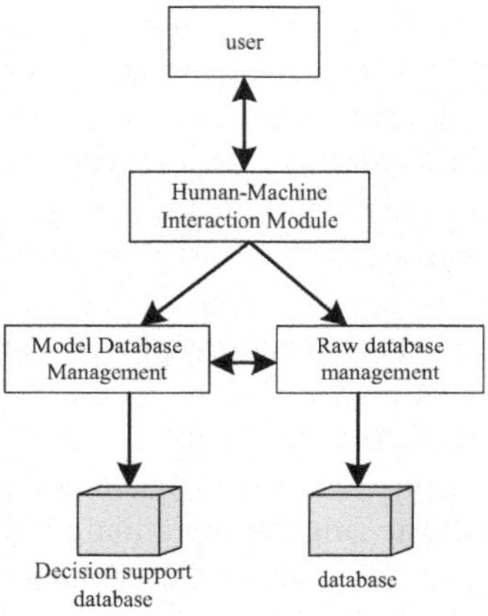


**Fig. 1.** Infrastructure of decision support model

The human-computer interaction part is also the interface of input and output, which is the interface component of the model. Receive the information input by the user, and output the processing results, to provide users with rich and colorful display and dialogue forms, such as graphics, images, sound and so on [9]. The model base is used to store models, which are expressed in the form of a computer program and can be run in a certain way for input, output, calculation and other processing; the model base management system should call out the existing basic models in the system according to the problems raised by users, and the model management part should have the functions of storage and dynamic modeling. The database is used to store a large amount of data, which is generally organized into a form easy to operate a large amount of data; the database is managed and maintained by the database management system, including the establishment, deletion, modification, retrieval, sorting and index of the database.

## 2.2 Database Design

The decision support basis of logistics management major mainly includes data information of learning and online platform, questionnaire survey results, investigation records, document information, etc. These data from different sources, in different forms into the system, must be strictly classified data, can be stored in the database. There are three ways to obtain the evaluation basis data: questionnaire survey, data collection, on-site investigation and so on [10–12]. Questionnaire survey method: students, teachers, management personnel, technical personnel and social personnel are investigated by issuing questionnaires from the Internet, and the survey results are returned to the database. The data formation process is shown in Fig. 2.

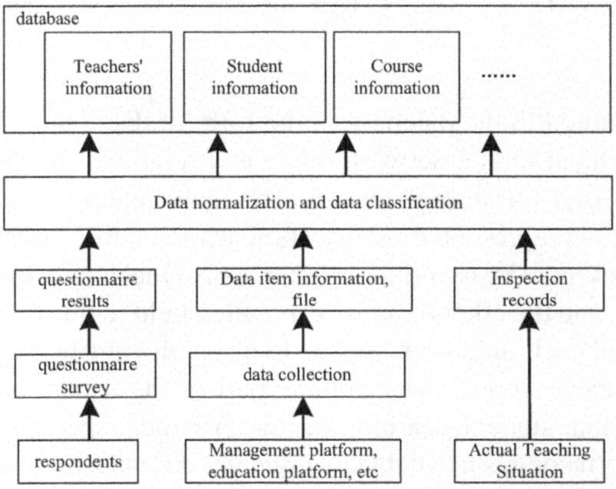


**Fig. 2.** Data formation process of decision basis

After obtaining the evaluation basis information through various ways, due to different data sources, data with the same meaning will have different representations. Therefore, these data need to be standardized to make the data complete, legal, consistent, suitable for statistics and analysis. The data items with the same meaning are transformed into a unified name, and the unified definition specification is used. Then, the data describing a kind of things are organized together by certain association, and distinguished by class name. For example, the data of teachers' name, age, gender and professional title are collectively referred to as teacher information; the course code, course name and credit are referred to as course information. In order to facilitate statistical analysis, query and decision-making.

After normalization and classification, the data has two parts, one is in the form of file, the other is in the form of data item. In the form of file, the storage is organized in the form of file directory; in the form of data item, the database is stored in the form of relational schema. Files are classified and stored in the hard disk by directory structure, and subdirectories are established according to different types. At the same time, index tables are established in the database to retrieve files. As shown in Fig. 1.

A file is identified by file number, file name, file type, upload time, storage path, etc. When you want to use a file, you can find the storage path of the corresponding file through the index table, and then transfer the file from the hard disk to the memory (Table 1).

**Table 1.** File index table

| Serial number | Field name | Data type | Length | Explain |
|---|---|---|---|---|
| 1 | F_NUMBER | VARCHAR | 50 | Document number |
| 2 | F_TITLE | VARCHAR | 100 | File name |
| 3 | F_TYPE | NUMBER | 10 | File type |
| 4 | U_TIME | VARCHAR | 20 | Upload time |
| 5 | S_PATH | VARCHAR | 200 | Storage path |

Data items are stored in the database in the form of data table. The main modes of database are hierarchical mode, network mode and relational mode. In this paper, the relational model is used for storage design. The main feature of relational schema is that not only the data is represented by two-dimensional table, but also the relationship between data is represented by two-dimensional table. One dimension of the relationship is called tuple (row), and the other dimension is called field (column). Tuple is equivalent to logical record, and each field corresponds to a specific attribute, which is equivalent to a data item in logical record. For example, part of the data storage structure based on student information, student, learning center, province, specialty, level is an entity, each entity object corresponds to a data table, there is a connection between entities, this connection makes the relevant information aggregate together, easy to query and call.

At the same time, in order to facilitate the management and query, the index table should also be established for the storage of data items, which is called user-defined data dictionary. It is used to describe the evaluation basis objects in the system, and to centralize the contact information between them for management. Data dictionary records the details of data table and data item definition in the system, including data table name, field name and field attributes (such as length, nullability, type, etc.). Through the data dictionary, we can quickly find the information about the object, which is convenient for the model to call the system data.

### 2.3 The Realization of Decision Support in Credit Bank System

Credit bank system includes credit identification, credit storage, credit transfer, credit exchange and credit settlement, in which credit settlement is an important part of academic certification or qualification certificate. It is set as the ultimate goal of the decision support model

$$F = \sum_{i \in N} \sum_{j \in M} s_i t_{ij} y_{ij} \tag{1}$$

The constraints of the objective function are as follows

$$\sum_{j \in M} y_{ij} = 1, i \in N \tag{2}$$

$$\sum_{j \in M} x_j = w \tag{3}$$

$$\begin{cases} y_{ij} \leq x_j, i \in N, j \in M \\ x_j \in \{0, 1\}, j \in M \\ y_{ij} \in \{0, 1\}, i \in N, j \in M \end{cases} \tag{4}$$

Where: $N$ is the number of courses in logistics management major, $M$ is the credit type in credit bank, $s_i$ is the demand of the $i$ course, $t_{ij}$ is the credit data required from the $i$ course to the $j$ course, $y_{ij}$ is whether the courses selected by users are satisfied, when satisfied, the value is 1, on the contrary, it is 0, $x_j$ is whether the courses exist, on the contrary, it is 1, on the contrary, it is 0. Formula 1 represents the objective function, which represents the credit settlement result of online education of logistics management major; constraint formula 2 represents that only one credit of each course can meet its service; formula 3 limits the total number of courses to $w$; constraint formula represents that the credit demand will not be met when the courses are lack. It can be seen from the above model that once the course is determined, the corresponding credits will be included, and then the most reasonable summary of different credits for each user will be determined. With the support of the above contents, the decision-making sequence diagram of the user in the decision-making process is shown in Fig. 3.

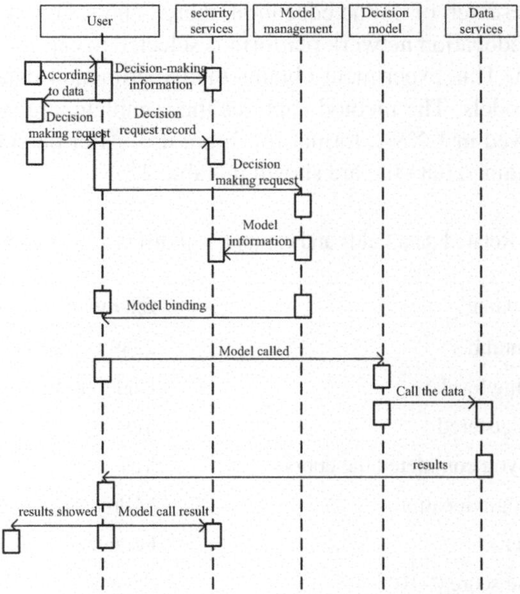


**Fig. 3.** Decision sequence diagram

The decision-making user first enters the user name and password through the browser to log in to the online education platform. This process requires the user to provide the login authentication check information, and the information provided will be checked by the security service module. There are usually two kinds of login results. One is that if the user passes the authentication, the information rented by the customer will be displayed in the decision-making interface, that is, the browser layer the other is to log out of the platform if the login fails.

The information required by the decision support is input and submitted through the prompt interface of the browser, and then the submitted information will be transferred to the management unit and the resource monitoring unit responsible for security. In the model management unit, if there is a decision model needed by the user, the binding information of the decision model will be sent to the terminal browser of the decision user.

The client of decision support can call the required model by binding it. The operation of some decision models needs the supporting data required by the model. This kind of data is mainly provided by calling the data service. Based on these data, the decision model can return the results to the browser and finally display them to the decision users. Finally, the online education decision support for logistics management specialty is realized.

## 3 Experimental Study

### 3.1 Experimental Preparation

At present, in the research of online education, there is no standard data for testing. In general, the online education network platform is selected to capture the data for experimental verification. This experiment obtains the experimental data through different decision support models. The method captures the complete and structured data. The extracted data is saved in * XML format for future use. After parsing, some fields and examples of the obtained data file are shown in Table 2.

**Table 2.** Related data fields and examples of distance education courses

| Number | Field name | Examples |
|---|---|---|
| 1 | User number | 2349****6147 |
| 2 | Training level | Undergraduate |
| 3 | Is it registered | Yes |
| 4 | Have you completed the course | Yes |
| 5 | Last login location | **Province |
| 6 | Gender | Female |
| 7 | Course score 0–10 | Seven |
| 8 | Days of interaction with courses | 5 Days |
| 9 | Number of times to watch the course video | 7 Times |
| 10 | Browsing records: Institutions | University A, University B and University C |
| 11 | Major | Physical distribution management |

Taking the information in the table as an example, 436 effective user information of distance education platform is collected and used as the model training set.

Using the data in the model training set, the traditional decision support model based on deep learning and OLAP are compared with the proposed model. Randomly select the similar user data of the course for comparative experiments, and analyze the actual performance of three different decision support models.

### 3.2 Experimental Results and Analysis of Decision Support Model Fitting

In the model evaluation experiment, the linear regression analysis evaluation method is used to verify the best approximation regression of the quantitative analysis model. The closer the fitting slope is to 1, the higher the set degree is, and the more complete the data is. The experimental results are shown in Fig. 4.

Compared with the results in the figure, from the perspective of data regression distribution, the data in figure a is distributed in the upper part with a slope greater than 1; the data in Figure B is distributed in the lower part with a loose distribution on both sides of the line with a slope less than 1; the data in Figure C is relatively concentrated with a uniform distribution along the line with a slope of 1. Therefore, the designed online education decision support model of logistics management major from the perspective of credit bank has higher fitting level and more complete data.

### 3.3 Experimental Results and Analysis of Parameter Correlation

Referring to the previous research results, a group of parameters which have the greatest impact on the model output results are selected as the target parameters. On the premise of keeping other parameters unchanged and a certain range of values, the target parameters are increased or decreased by 10% on the basis of the original value, and then the correlation index of the model output is calculated by using the calculation formula.

$$\chi = \frac{(A_2 - A_1)}{A_{12}} \bigg/ \frac{(B_2 - B_1)}{B_{12}} \tag{5}$$

Where: $\chi$ is the correlation index, $B_1$ and $B_2$ are the minimum and maximum values of input parameters, $A_1$ and $A_2$ are the model outputs corresponding to $B_1$ and $B_2$, $B_{12}$ is the average value of $B_1$ and $B_2$, and $A_{12}$ is the average value of $A_1$ and $A_2$. When $\chi$ is close to 0, the correlation is very low; when $\chi$ is between 0.5 and 1.0, the correlation tends to be in the middle; when $\chi$ is greater than 1, the correlation is relatively high. Based on the above calculation methods, the results of different decision support models are shown in Table 3.

It can be seen from the results in the table that for the data of different attributes in the model, the correlation of the parameters of the proposed decision support model is relatively low. In contrast, the correlation of the parameters of the two traditional decision support models is relatively high, which indicates that the change of parameters has a greater impact on the effect of decision support in practical application. This is because this method restricts the objective function and normalizes the data, which improves the reliability of educational decision support.

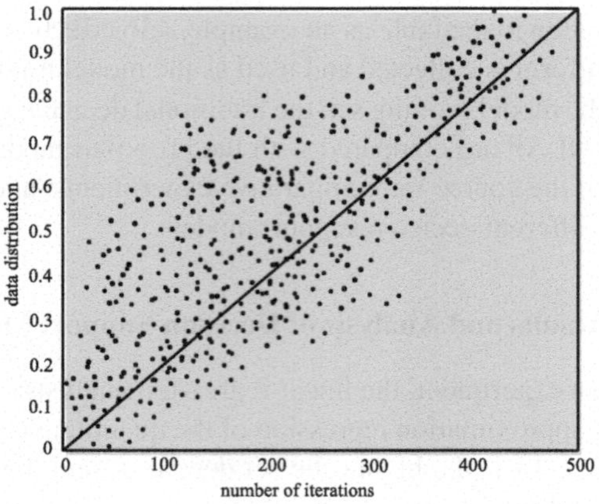


(a) Deep learning based decision support model fitting experimental results

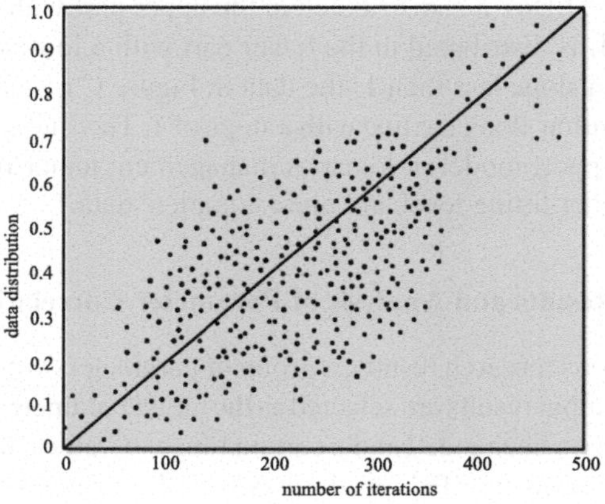


(b) OLAP Based Decision support model fitting experimental results

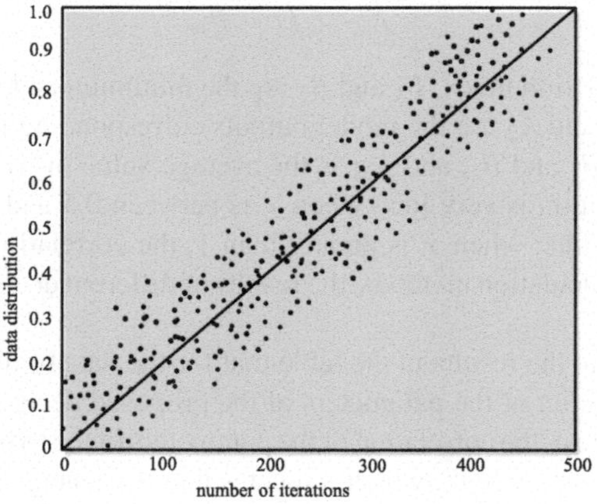


(c) The proposed decision support model fits the experimental results

**Fig. 4.** Experimental results of different decision support models

**Table 3.** Experimental results of parameter correlation of different decision support models

| | Relational parameters | Defined parameters |
|---|---|---|
| Decision support model based on deep learning | 1.62 | 0.54 |
| Decision support model based on OLAP | 1.87 | 0.68 |
| A decision support model is proposed | 0.23 | 0.19 |

## 4 Concluding Remarks

With the rapid development of society and the development of network technology, colleges and universities will face more education and teaching problems, need more and more decision-making services, and need to solve more complex decision-making problems. The traditional decision-making support model can not meet the needs of online education for decision-making support at this stage. At the same time, for different decision-making users, the demand for decision-making system is not satisfied. However, there is no decision support model for the mechanism of "credit bank". This paper takes the influence of "credit bank" on students' learning style as the research object. This paper designs the decision support model of logistics management online education from the perspective of "credit bank". After the model is designed, a large number of comparative experiments verify the reliability of the designed decision support model. However, due to time constraints, there are still some problems to be solved in the design of decision support model, such as the design of personalized service. In the follow-up research, we should expand the design of decision support model, expand the application scope of decision support model, and provide better technical support for online education from the perspective of "credit bank".

## References

1. Liu, S., Li, Z., Zhang, Y., et al.: Introduction of key problems in long-distance learning and training. Mob. Netw. Appl. **24**(1), 1–4 (2019)
2. Li, M.: Personalized appeal and resources optimization of online education in the era of big data. Theory Pract. Educ. **40**(04), 30–34 (2020)
3. Peng, F.: The mechanism of action and stimulation model of online learning participation. Adult Educ. **40**(01), 18–23 (2020)
4. Liang, Q., Zhang, G.: Research on blockchain model and realization mechanism of online learning achievement certification integrated with course quality. E-educ. Res. **41**(04), 49-54+61 (2020)
5. Huang, Q., Chen, A., Gong, L., et al.: On construction subject and promotion strategy of national credit bank of vocational education. Voc. Tech. Educ. **41**(18), 19–23 (2020)
6. Tang, X., Chen, H., Lu, Y.: Research on university data analysis and decision-making support system based on OLAP. Mod. Electr. Tech. **42**(02), 155–158 (2019)
7. Zhan, J., Li, T., Li, C.: Decision support system of adaptability evaluation for TBM selection based on artificial intelligence. J. China Coal Soc. **44**(10), 3258–3271 (2019)
8. Liu, S., Liu, D., Srivastava, G., Połap, D., Woźniak, M.: Overview and methods of correlation filter algorithms in object tracking. Complex Intell. Syst. (2020). https://doi.org/10.1007/s40747-020-00161-4

9. Qin, Q., Ke, Q., Ding, S.: An empirical study on readability calculation and application of Chinese online health education information — a case study of food safety. Mod. Inf. **40**(05), 111–121 (2020)
10. Fu, W., Liu, S., Srivastava, G.: Optimization of big data scheduling in social networks. Entropy **21**(9), 902–916 (2019)
11. Acevedo, Y., Díaz, V.G., Marín, C.E.M., et al.: Usage of machine learning for strategic decision making at higher educational institutions. IEEE Access **7**(1), 75007–75017 (2019)
12. Torrents, D., Troiano, H.: Estimated risk in educational decision-making and differences by family educational background in higher education choices (English version). Reis **174**(2), 147–168 (2021)

# Comprehensive Control Method of Network Teaching Data Scheduling Based on Fuzzy Mathematics

Mei-li Dai(✉) and Li An

Rizhao Polytechnic, Rizhao 276800, China

**Abstract.** Aiming at the problem of dividing and scheduling network teaching resources in the network environment, a more complete fuzzy mathematics theory and an example are used to introduce a method of dividing and scheduling teaching resources in detail. The main methods used during this period are: the introduction of data standardization methods to eliminate the influence of dimensions; a method of comprehensively considering various indicators and then processing them separately, in order to avoid the "barrel effect"; For some articles only relying on the error of using fuzzy similarity matrix to divide teaching resources has been corrected, and the final division should use fuzzy equivalent matrix.

**Keywords:** Teaching resources · Fuzzy clustering analysis · Barrel effect · Data standardization · Transitive closure · Fuzzy equivalent matrix

## 1 Introduction

Teaching data scheduling refers to making full use of the network teaching information resources in different time and space, using computer technology to automatically analyze, synthesize, distribute and use the network teaching information obtained according to the time sequence under certain criteria, so as to obtain the consistent description and interpretation of the tested object, so as to complete the required decision-making and estimation tasks, and make the teaching system obtain its components More superior performance [1]. The existing network teaching data scheduling methods include the least square method based on nonlinear optimization class and the method based on Kalman filter. However, the measurement of U1 can not be based on the measurement of various factors such as Kalman filter equation, which is based on the observation of various factors. However, the least square method based on nonlinear optimization class has great difficulties in the implementation of the algorithm due to the uncertainty of the available measurement elements and the need for iterative solution, which can not meet the requirements of real-time scheduling calculation [2, 3]. How to take a simple and effective method to schedule network teaching information is the key to improve the accuracy and efficiency of network data processing.

As an eye-catching next-generation network system, the grid has its own distinctive features, and thus has created its powerful functions. Simply put, the grid is the use of


W. Fu et al. (Eds.): eLEOT 2021, LNICST 389, pp. 205–217, 2021.
https://doi.org/10.1007/978-3-030-84383-0_18

all the massive and available connections on the Internet (i.e. Idle) resources (mainly including computing resources and data storage resources) are integrated into a super virtual computer. The user does not need to understand or even understand its background operation (that is, transparent to the user), just through a relatively simple user interface, This super virtual computer can be used to quickly and efficiently complete tasks such as massive data operations, massive data storage management, and massive information search [4].

Aiming at the above problems, this paper proposes a network teaching data scheduling method which combines fuzzy mathematics and non negative eigenvector theory. First of all, the method of data standardization is used to eliminate the influence of data dimension. Secondly, considering the influence of each index, fuzzy mathematics method is used to schedule and control the network teaching data. Finally, the effectiveness of the method is verified by practical application, and a better scheduling effect is obtained.

## 2 Network Teaching Resources

In a broad sense, network teaching resources are all kinds of teaching resources that are connected to the Internet, and all kinds of educational software resources installed on it. Users can get corresponding network teaching resources and resources according to their different needs and user rights service.

Through the above analysis, it can be seen that the scope of online teaching resources is very large, and the specific performance of each resource is not the same. In order to achieve effective management and efficient use to meet the needs of different students and users, a very critical step is to Division and scheduling of teaching resources. In view of the characteristics of the above teaching network resources, it can be found that applying the fuzzy clustering analysis method in fuzzy mathematics theory can solve the above problems well.

## 3 Fuzzy Cluster Analysis

Fuzzy equivalent matrix is a classical fuzzy clustering method, which combines the standard residual error with the measurement difference of adjacent time to calculate the fuzzy eigenvalue fuzzy clustering, and find the best calculation threshold. According to the data results of individual data, the clustering of target data is completed. Fuzzy equivalent matrix clustering can effectively avoid residual pollution and residual inundation, and can flexibly select clustering results to improve the effectiveness of clustering.

In ordinary cluster analysis, given objects and their characteristics can be classified according to the inherent similarity of the data. The mathematical method of classifying the researched objects according to certain standards is called cluster analysis. This is a classification method of multivariate statistics "things gather together". However, in the network teaching data, there are many types of data that are not clearly divided, the boundaries are fuzzy, and the relationship between them is more fuzzy. Therefore, fuzzy mathematics methods should be used to classify network teaching data. The cluster analysis using fuzzy mathematics method is called fuzzy cluster analysis [5, 6].

The object of this paper - network teaching resources, which can not be clearly divided between each other, the boundary is fuzzy, so it is feasible to use fuzzy mathematics to analyze it.

The following steps of fuzzy analysis are introduced

The first step is to standardize the data. ① Write out the data matrix; ② Standardize the data. Network teaching resources have many characteristics, each of which has a different dimension. In order to compare the data of network teaching resources with different dimensions, it is usually necessary to properly transform the original data to obtain a new sample. Standardization matrix. In this paper, the translation and standard deviation transformation method is used, and the new standard sample network teaching data obtained in the first step is used to eliminate the influence of dimensions, and a fuzzy matrix representing the fuzzy relationship between each network teaching data is established.

The second step is calibration (building a fuzzy similarity matrix). In order to classify network teaching data quantitatively, some quantitative indicators for classification must be determined, and some quantitative indicators that can indicate the degree of similarity between samples (or variables) are introduced, which are called cluster statistics.

The determined cluster statistics $r_{ij} = R(x_i, x_j)$ and $\underline{R}(x, y)$ are called membership function or membership degree, and their values represent the correlation degree of binary relationship $(x, y)$ with fuzzy relation $R$, where $R$ represents fuzzy similar relation, and the calculation methods mainly include similarity coefficient method and distance method. In this paper, Hamming distance method is used. A fuzzy matrix $R$ with $r_{ij}$ as its element can be obtained.

The third step is the clustering of online teaching resources. There are many clustering methods. Here we mainly introduce the clustering method based on fuzzy equivalence matrix—transitive closure method. When classifying network teaching resources according to fuzzy relations, the fuzzy relations must be fuzzy equivalence relations, which are reflexive, symmetrical and transitive [7].

According to the calibration, the fuzzy matrix is only a fuzzy similar matrix, and the fuzzy similar matrix only has reflexivity and symmetry, but it does not necessarily have transitivity, that is, $R$ is not necessarily a fuzzy equivalent matrix (fuzzy equivalent matrix has reflexivity, symmetry and transitivity). In order to classify network teaching resources, $R$ needs to be transformed into fuzzy equivalent matrix $R''$.

By finding the transitive closure $t(R)$, the fuzzy similarity matrix can be transformed into a fuzzy equivalent matrix, which is transitive, while retaining reflexivity and symmetry. Here is a practical simple method-the square method, seeking transitive closure $t(R)$.

Starting from the fuzzy similar matrix, the square is calculated in turn

$$R \to R^2 \to R^4 \to \cdots \to R^{2^4} \to \cdots, (i = 1, 2, 3, \cdots) \tag{1}$$

When $R^k \cdot R^k = R^{2k}$ appears for the first time (indicating that $R^k$ is transitive!), $R^k$ is the required transitive closure $t(R)$, which is the required fuzzy equivalent matrix $R^*$, namely $t(R) = R^*$. Then, take a fixed value $\lambda$ of [0, 1] and specify:

For any two elements $x_i$ and $y_i$ in the universe, if:

$$r_{ij} \geq \lambda \tag{2}$$

Then $x_i$ and $y_i$ belong to the same class; otherwise, they do not belong to the same class [8].

## 4 Network Teaching Data Fusion Method Based on Fuzzy Closeness

Using the real-time network teaching data processing process of positioning smoothing and filtering, the three-dimensional processing results of group $n$ are obtained:

$$e_i = (x_i, y_i, z_i), i = 1 \ldots n \tag{3}$$

According to the decision level fusion structure model, the distance between any two positioning results is calculated. The relative distance between the $i$ positioning result and the $j$ positioning result is as follows:

$$d_{ij} = \sqrt{(x_i - x_j)^2 + (y_i - y_j)^2 + (z_i - z_j)^2} \tag{4}$$

The authenticity of the $i$ th positioning result can be determined by the relative distance $d_{ij}$ between the $i$-th positioning result and the positioning result of the $j$-th measuring device: the smaller the $d_{ij}$, the higher the authenticity of the $i$-th positioning result. Conversely, the larger the $d_{ij}$, the lower the authenticity of the $i$-th positioning result, and the fuzzy closeness function $a_{ij}(k)$ between the $i$-th positioning result and the $j$-th positioning result at different spatial positions at time $k$ can be defined.

Network teaching data fusion is shown in Fig. 1.

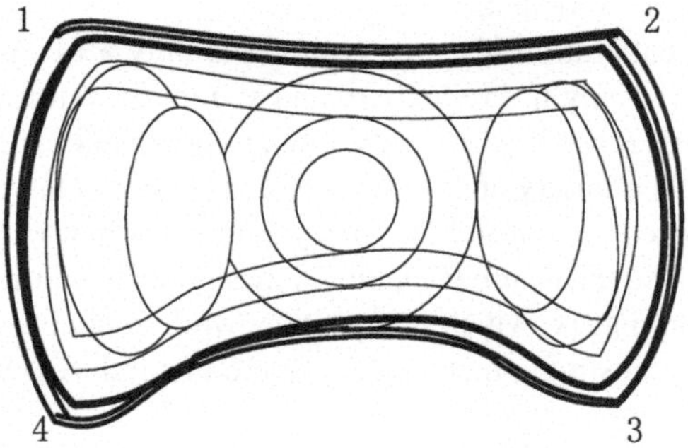


**Fig. 1.** Network teaching data fusion process

The definition of fuzzy closeness function should satisfy:

(1) When the relative distance between the two positioning results is larger, their fuzzy closeness is smaller, and the relative distance between the two positioning results is smaller, the mutual closeness between the data is greater, that is, $a_{ij}(k)$ should be proportional to the relative distance Inverse relationship

(2) If the relative distance of the data to itself is zero, the fuzzy closeness of the data to itself is 1;

(3) $a_{ij}(k) \in (0, 1)$, enabling data processing to take advantage of the membership function in fuzzy set theory, avoiding the absoluteization of fuzzy closeness between data. Therefore:

$$a_{ij} = \frac{1}{1 + d_{ij}} = \frac{1}{1 + \sqrt{(x_i - x_j)^2 + (y_i - y_j)^2 + (z_i - z_j)^2}} \tag{5}$$

It can be seen that the definition form of formula (5) satisfies the properties of fuzzy closeness function, and this definition form of satisfying fuzzy closeness function $a_{ij}(k)$ is more in line with the reality of practical problems, and is convenient for specific implementation, so that the result of network teaching resource integration is more accurate and stable [9, 10].

Through the above method, we can get the fuzzy closeness degree of arbitrary positioning results at time $k$, and then obtain a fuzzy closeness matrix $A(k)$:

$$A(k) = \begin{bmatrix} a_{11}(k)\, a_{12}(k) \ldots a_{1n}(k) \\ a_{21}(k)\, a_{22}(k) \ldots a_{2n}(k) \\ \vdots \\ a_{n1}(k)\, a_{n2}(k) \ldots a_{nn}(k) \end{bmatrix} \tag{6}$$

According to the matrix $A(k)$, the comprehensive fuzzy closeness $u_{i(k)}$ of a certain positioning result $(x_i y_i z_i)$ and other positioning results is obtained, and a set of non-negative numbers is required from the theory of probability source merger:

$$b_1(k), b_2(k), \ldots b_n(k) \tag{7}$$

Make:

$$u_i(k) = b_1(k)a_{i1}(k) + b_2(k)a_{i2}(k) + \ldots + b_n(k)a_{in}(k) \quad i = 1, 2 \ldots, n \tag{8}$$

Make:

$$\begin{aligned} U(k) &= [u_1(k), u_2(k), \ldots, u_n(k)]^r \\ B(k) &= [b_1(k), b_2(k), \ldots b_n(k)]^T \end{aligned} \tag{9}$$

Then formula (9) can be written as the following matrix form:

$$U(k) = A(k)B(k) \tag{10}$$

Because of $a_{ij} \geq 0$, $A(k)$ is a non-negative symmetric matrix. According to the properties of the non-negative symmetric matrix, it can be seen that $A(k)$ has a maximum fuzzy eigenvalue $\lambda(\lambda > 0)$, and only the eigenvector corresponding to the eigenvalue is positive, and $A(k) = \lambda B(k)$ is used to obtain the eigenvector $B(k)$, which is substituted into Eq. (10) as the fuzzy positioning result Proximity [11–13]. Expanding matrix (10), the $i$ fuzzy closeness is:

$$u_i(k) = b_2(k)a_{i2}(k) + \ldots b_n(k)a_{in}(k) \tag{11}$$

Where $b_i(k)$ is the $i$ th element of the eigenvector $B(k)$.

In the actual network teaching data fusion process, different positioning results need to be given different weights. The teaching system with better stability and higher reliability has greater weight. According to the previous discussion, the reliability and stability of the equipment with large fuzzy proximity degree are higher, and the weight should be greater, otherwise, the weight should be smaller. Therefore, fuzzy closeness can be used to represent the weight of the sensor. The clustering data is shown in Fig. 2:

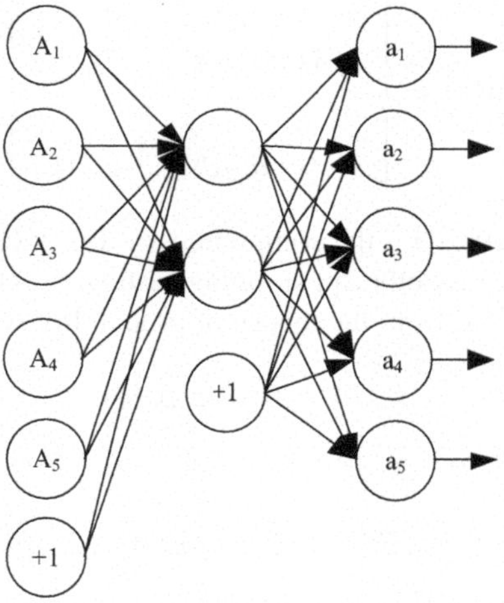


**Fig. 2.** Clustering data

Because in the rectangular coordinate system, the abnormal data sample and the normal data sample are inconsistent, so this paper completes the network teaching data processing work by establishing the rectangular coordinate system. Randomly select $n$ data as the basic sample, draw the ROC curve through MATLAB software, judge the accurate value of the data, and then repeat this operation. Other samples are sampled to calculate the offset between the standard data and the measured data, the overlapped network teaching data are stored, and the different network teaching data are re integrated until the ROC curve is a coincidence line. The established rectangular coordinate system is shown in Fig. 3.

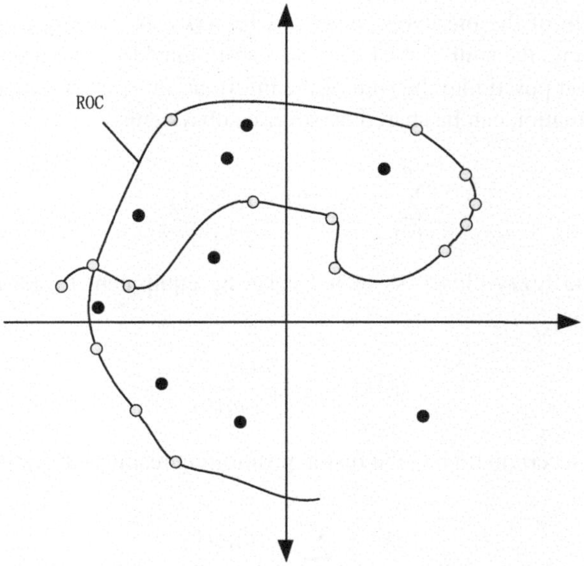


**Fig. 3.** Data processing rectangular coordinate system

The vertical axis direction of ROC curve represents the detection probability, and the horizontal direction represents the false alarm rate. According to the change of the curve, the higher the threshold value, the higher the accuracy of the system, and the stronger the self identification ability. If the ROC is not a smooth curve, it is necessary to divide the ROC curve into several sections to form a number of small trapezoids, and calculate the accurate value of each trapezoid area data. Through the addition of several trapezoid areas, the number of data is subtracted from the number of normal data, and the false alarm rate of abnormal data is obtained. The best working point is found in the ROC curve, and the positive likelihood ratio and Youden index are used to distinguish the error detection rate and false alarm rate.

After the discrete attribute data is obtained, the original network teaching data is mapped to the three-dimensional space by constructing a new linear function, and then divided in the space. The matrix is used to find the heterogeneous data, and the optimal solution is obtained. The cloud detection method mainly depends on the simulation database. If there is no normal data in the simulation database, the attack data cannot be detected. If the real-time coding of abnormal data and the normal data exceed a certain threshold, the normal data will also be attacked. The whole data is analyzed and processed to show the non-linear relationship between normal data and abnormal data. The data is compared by random sampling, and HMM model is established. Using the detection function of HMM model, different data can be identified through cloud test, so as to realize information distribution processing and increase the adaptability of processing process.

Let the weight of the measured value of $i$ be $w(k)$. According to the principle of information sharing, the sum of the information estimated by the optimal fusion can be equivalently decomposed into the sum of the information of several measurement data, that is, one information can be shared by several subsystems.

$$\sum_{i=1}^{n} w_i = 1(0 \leq w_i \leq 1) \tag{12}$$

Normalize the fuzzy closeness of $n$ measuring equipment to get their respective relative weights:

$$w_i(k) = \frac{u_i(k)}{\sum_{i=1}^{n} u_i(k)} \tag{13}$$

Therefore, at a certain time $k$, the fusion positioning result of the target is as follows:

$$e(k) = \sum_{i=1}^{n} w_i(k) e_i(k) \tag{14}$$

## 5 Using Fuzzy Cluster Analysis Method to Dispatch and Control Network Teaching Resources

Different from the previous method of considering a single index one by one, the example presented here uses two comprehensive indicators of machine computing performance and communication performance to divide machines at the beginning, which can avoid the "barrel effect" in advance and meet the real-time application requirements most concerned by ordinary users. The so-called "barrel effect" refers to the amount of water contained in a barrel, which ultimately depends on the shortest of the boards used to make the bucket. In this case, it refers to two "boards" of "computing performance" and "communication performance".

Step 1: Data standardization.

(1) Data matrix

Suppose domain $U = \{x_1, x_2, \cdots, x_{10}\}$ represents a network teaching system with 10 nodes. Each node uses two indicators of computing performance and communication performance to represent its characteristics, namely $x_i = (x_{i1}, x_{i2})$. The original data is shown in Table 1:

**Table 1.** Raw data

| Node | Index | |
|---|---|---|
| | Computational performance | Communication performance |
| $x_1$ | 0.6 | 50 |
| $x_2$ | 1.0 | 40 |
| $x_3$ | 2.0 | 60 |
| $x_4$ | 4.0 | 55 |
| $x_5$ | 2.5 | 30 |
| $x_6$ | 3.0 | 100 |
| $x_7$ | 54.0 | 20 |
| $x_8$ | 45.0 | 100 |
| $x_9$ | 20.5 | 50 |
| $x_{10}$ | 15.0 | 120 |

Therefore, the transposition matrix of the original data matrix is obtained, and the clustering results of different network teaching data are shown in Fig. 4 below:

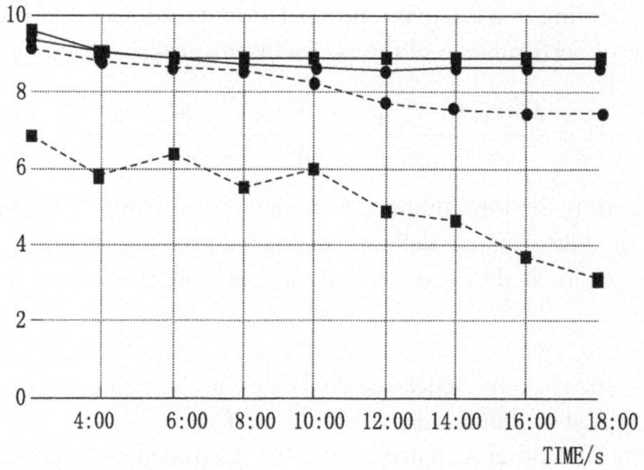


**Fig. 4.** Clustering results of different network teaching data

So far, the classification of network teaching resources has been basically completed. It can be seen that through $\lambda \in [0, 1]$ clustering from large to small, for different parameter $\lambda$, grid resources are clustered into different groups, and the nodes in each group can be regarded as nodes with similar comprehensive characteristics under the current parameter $\lambda$. Users can adjust the value of $\lambda$ according to their needs. For larger application problems, by reducing the value of $\lambda$, the "logical groups with adjacent performance" can be merged into a large logical group. When $\lambda$ is taken as 0, all nodes will form a logical group, and the scheduler will schedule the application decomposition tasks to all computing nodes as much as possible.

After successful grouping, according to the formula:

$$V = \frac{1}{M}\sum_{k=1}^{N} C_k \tag{15}$$

Calculate the cluster center value (or mean) $V$ of the computing performance of each group and the cluster center value (or mean) $V$ of the communication performance, where: $M$ is the total number of nodes in the group; $C_k$ is each node in the group Calculated performance value or communication performance value.

If the parameter $\lambda$ is 0.911, the computational performance cluster center value of the first (i.e. the first class) $\{x_1, x_3, x_4, x_2, x_5\}$ of the group (class) is 0.911:

$$V_1 = \frac{1}{5}\sum_{i=1}^{5}(6.0 + 2.0 + 4.0 + 1.0 + 2.5) = 3.1 \tag{16}$$

Communication performance cluster center value:

$$V_2 = \frac{1}{5}\sum_{i=1}^{5}(50 + 60 + 55 + 40 + 30) = 47 \tag{17}$$

It is also worth noting that the maximum performance deviation ratio $D$ can indicate the similar degree of performance of the nodes in this group

$$D = \frac{Max((Max_{k=0}^{n} C_h - V), (V - Min_{k=0} C_k))}{V} \tag{18}$$

Among them: $M$ is the total number of nodes in the group. Obviously, the smaller the $D$, the closer the performance data of the nodes in the group.

So far, we can get a scheduling control algorithm that can network teaching resource data, and its steps are:

(1) Calculate the fuzzy equivalence matrix based on the comprehensive indicators of all computing nodes, that is, the closeness matrix;
(2) Determine the first-order $\lambda$ matrix of the fuzzy equivalent matrix according to the value of $\lambda$ and refer to the maximum performance deviation rate $D$;
(3) Obtain several logical groups of machines according to the $\lambda$ order matrix;
(4) For problems of different scales and requirements, suitable or user-specified logical groups can be selected for scheduling according to the cluster center value.

## 6 Simulation Calculation

Assuming that the initial position of the network teaching data is (0, 0, 0), the scheduling movement is performed in the YOZ plane, sampling is performed at a period of 50 ms, and the data of 5 s is continuously simulated, and the fuzzy closeness formula is used to calculate the value of any two network teaching data. The fuzzy closeness degree is formed to form a fuzzy closeness degree matrix, the maximum eigenvalue of the matrix and its corresponding positive eigenvector are calculated, and then the comprehensive fuzzy closeness degree is obtained as the weight, and the weighted fusion calculation of network teaching data is performed.

Compare the actual scheduling results with the positioning results of the network teaching data scheduling method proposed in this paper. The graphs comparing the scheduling and positioning results of the two methods in the X direction, Y direction, and Z direction are respectively given, as shown in the figure below (Figs. 5, 6 and 7).

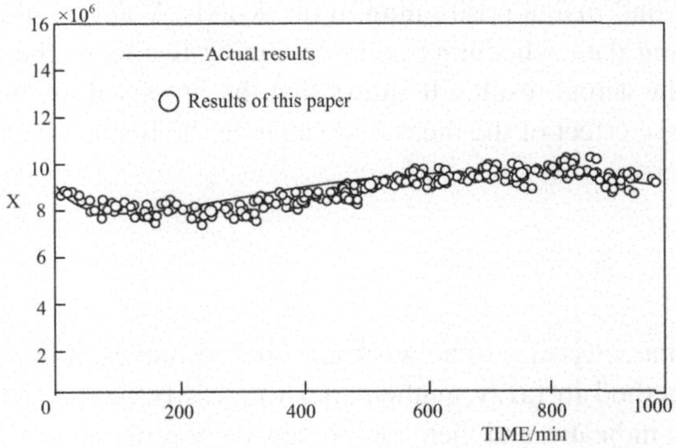


**Fig. 5.** T-X curve of dispatching positioning data

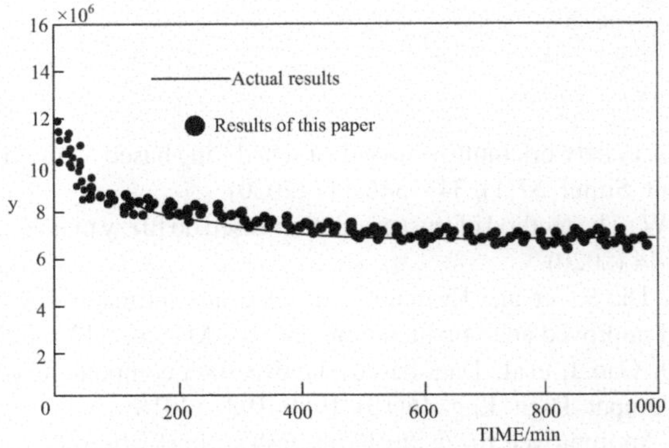


**Fig. 6.** T-Y curve of dispatch positioning data

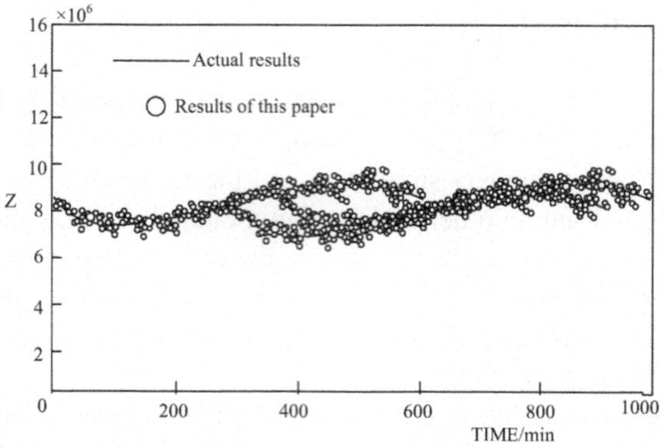


**Fig. 7.** T-Z curve of dispatching positioning data

It can be seen from the simulation results that, by comparing the results of intersection scheduling and fusion positioning in the X-axis, Y-axis, and Z-axis directions, the network teaching data scheduling and positioning results of the proposed method are very close to the actual results. It shows that the proposed method can effectively eliminate the adverse effect of the measured value on the fusion result and improve the processing accuracy.

## 7 Conclusion

According to the characteristics of network teaching resources, it is very suitable to use fuzzy clustering method in fuzzy mathematics to classify them. The early method of processing a single indicator and then comprehensively processing is more suitable for users who have special needs for grids. The method in this article is suitable for mass users who have general needs for network teaching resources and are more concerned about comprehensive performance.

## References

1. Du, P.: Simulation of network multi-source data scheduling based on multi-goal mathematical planning. Comput. Simul. **37**(1), 343–346,447 (2020)
2. Hong, T., Gong, W.: The method of trust evaluation based on fuzzy mathematics. Tech. Autom. Appl. **39**(2), 41–44 (2020)
3. Yu, W., Jia, C., Di, S., et al.: Evaluation of seawater intrusion degree based on fuzzy mathematics and improved analytic hierarchy process. Mar. Sci. **42**(6), 21–31 (2018)
4. Liu, L., Zhang, Q., Gao, J., et al.: Data-based adaptive fuzzy comprehensive evaluation method well selection. Comput. Digit. Eng. **46**(10), 1980–1983 (2018)
5. Liu, G., Shi, X.: An improved fuzzy clustering fastest time pattern of cloud computing task scheduling scheme. Control Eng. China **25**(11), 2092–2096 (2018)
6. Qian, K., Qin, M., Song, Y., et al.: Multi-objective optimal scheduling based on fuzzy membership for electric bus charging station. Electr. Power Constr. **41**(2), 118–124 (2020)

7. Deng, C., Zhang, S., Yang, W., et al.: Real-time scheduling technology of photovoltaic-battery generation system based on intelligent fuzzy logic control. Power Syst. Technol. **42**(10), 3227–3233 (2018)
8. Xu, L., Xiong, M., Xiao, Y.: On-line prediction of application runtime using schedule historical data. Appl. Res. Comput. **37**(3), 763–767 (2020)
9. Fu, W., Liu, S., Srivastava, G.: Optimization of big data scheduling in social networks. Entropy **21**(9), 902 (2019)
10. Li, W., Qi, H., Xu, R., et al.: Data center network flow scheduling progress and trends. Chin. J. Comput. **43**(4), 600–617 (2020)
11. Dang, C., Liu, Y.: Research on network priority scheduling optimization method based on TRDP. Electron. Meas. Technol. **43**(2), 59–64 (2020)
12. Liu, S., Li, Z., Zhang, Y., et al.: Introduction of key problems in long-distance learning and training. Mob. Netw. Appl. **24**(1), 1–4 (2019)
13. Liu, S., Lu, M., Li, H., et al.: Prediction of gene expression patterns with generalized linear regression model. Front. Genet. **10**(8), 120 (2019)

# Design of Personal Learning Model Recognition Model for Online Teaching of Ideological and Political Theory Course

Li-tang Xu(✉) and Hong-gang Wang

School of Marxism, Fuyang Normal University, Fuyang 236037, China

**Abstract.** Accurate identification of students' learning modes in online teaching of ideological and political theory courses is helpful to improve students' concentration in the learning process and enhance the effect of online teaching of ideological and political theory courses. To this end, this paper designed a personal learning pattern recognition model, set the identification criteria for the matching rules of personal learning pattern type and behavior purpose, collected students' learning data according to the teaching video browsing situation, and analyzed their learning behavior trajectory and the degree of attention in the learning process. By comparing the analysis results with the preset identification criteria, the quantitative identification results of online learning modes of ideological and political courses are obtained. The experimental study shows that the recognition results of the model in this paper are close to the actual online learning types of students in ideological and political courses, and after the application of this model, the test scores of students in ideological and political courses have been significantly improved, which proves that this model has a high promotion value.

**Keywords:** Ideological and political theory course · Online teaching · Personal learning mode · Pattern recognition model

## 1 Introduction

Ideological and political theory courses aim at guiding students to set up correct outlook on life, values, world outlook, cultural outlook and moral outlook, focusing on guiding students to set up correct learning goals in life, and it is also one of the key courses to carry out the fundamental task of cultivating people through virtue. Through the study of ideological and political theories, students can closely combine the development of their own quality with the process of the country and society, and make students understand that study is not only for exams, but also for improving their own quality and broadening their horizons, so as to discover their significance to the society and try their best to realize their own value. It can be said that the course of ideological and political theory is a very practical course of social significance. However, it is not difficult to see from the classroom teaching of traditional ideological and political theory course that many students are not interested in this course, or even tired of it. The main reason lies in


W. Fu et al. (Eds.): eLEOT 2021, LNICST 389, pp. 218–230, 2021.
https://doi.org/10.1007/978-3-030-84383-0_19

that most teachers mainly teach theory, the teaching form is monotonous, the content is single, resulting in students' lack of interest, the teaching quality is low [1].

In order to truly and effectively realize the value of ideological and political theory course, we should change the traditional teaching method and design the online teaching mode in combination with the background of "Internet+" in the new era. Online teaching mode can break the limitation of course teaching in time and space and provide a more scientific and convenient platform for students to learn.

Individual learning behavior is the social behavior in the classroom context and the external embodiment of classroom concentration. Students' classroom behavior reflects students' learning state and learning efficiency and is closely related to the quality of classroom teaching. Online learning behavior is based on the concept derived from online learning, which is the learning behavior occurring in the network environment. Through the identification of the personal learning mode of the online teaching of ideological and political theory courses, the basic learning rules of students can be summed up, so as to adjust the wrong learning methods and learning modes.

At present, there are some research results about learning pattern at home and abroad, including learning pattern recognition method based on network teaching platform, learning pattern recognition method based on random forest and learning pattern recognition method based on data mining. However, the traditional recognition methods have the problem of insufficient recognition accuracy, which is difficult to provide reference value analysis data for students' Ideological and political theory course learning, resulting in its poor application. In order to solve the shortcomings of traditional recognition methods, this study comprehensively analyzes students' web browsing behavior and online video learning behavior, and realizes the optimization design of personal learning pattern recognition model for online teaching of Ideological and political theory course, so as to improve the recognition accuracy and application value of the model.

## 2 Personal Learning Pattern Recognition Model Design

Personal learning pattern recognition model collects data about online learning behavior and learning style, and uses correlation analysis to explore the relationship between learners' learning style and online learning behavior. Then the decision tree algorithm is used to build the learning style prediction model, and all online learning behavior features are added to the training process [2]. After pruning the decision tree model, the prediction model of learning style of each dimension is obtained. Through four learning style prediction models, learners' learning patterns can be automatically identified by analyzing learners' online learning behavior data. The specific identification process is shown in Fig. 1.

In the process of personal learning pattern recognition designed in this paper, the basic recognition process in Fig. 1 is used to make a specific analysis of students' classroom behavior and network browsing behavior in the learning process, so as to ensure the accuracy of the final recognition results. Among them, classroom performance behavior mainly refers to the degree of activity and concentration of students in online class. It mainly uses the camera equipment on the remote computer to collect the video information of students' learning. On this basis, combined with the video image processing and

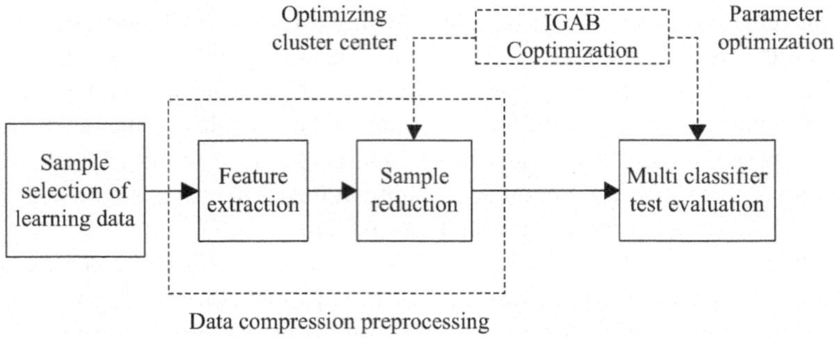


**Fig. 1.** Flow chart of personal learning pattern recognition

analysis technology, the learning behavior recognition results of students' classroom performance are obtained. The browsing behavior of students is mainly the browsing data of students, including browsing behavior data, searching behavior data, downloading behavior data and so on. Based on the above two parts, a comprehensive identification result of personal learning mode in online teaching of ideological and political theory courses is obtained.

## 2.1 Matching of Personal Learning Model Types and Behavior Items

In order to make the research results universal, this study only uses the behavior items of the most commonly used function modules in the learning management system to predict the learning style. Common function modules include discussion area, homework and online test. On the basis of literature review and platform data analysis, the dimensions of e-learning style model and behavior items are matched, which is used as the standard of personal learning pattern recognition in online teaching of Ideological and political theory course. Among them, behavioral items used to identify information processing dimensions include: number of posts, number of replies, number of posts read, number of posts read and time to submit homework, etc.

Active learners are better at using learning resources to assist in learning, and like to communicate with others. Use the discussion area in the learning platform to communicate with others through post, reply and other forms, and cooperate to complete tasks [3, 4]. Generally speaking, in the discussion area, active learners are more proactive in speaking and discussing than contemplative learners, and generally there are more posts and replies. Pensive learners like to solve problems on their own, and tend to think carefully before making decisions or taking actions. In contrast, dependent learners' learning attitude is not positive enough, they only complete the curriculum tasks required by the teacher, and rely on the teacher to give detailed and clear guidance. Therefore, dependent learners view more teacher posts, and pay less attention to other people's discussions or content that is not related to the task to be completed. After finishing the homework, dependent learners rarely check their homework for inspection and reflection. Due to the poor ability to complete tasks independently, it generally takes a long time to complete the homework. Independent learners are confident in their learning abilities and prefer to learn what they think is important. Compared with dependent learners, they are less dependent on the teacher's guidance, pay more attention to themselves or what they are interested in, and complete their homework faster. In addition, combining the maintenance time and start time of the student's course concentration, as well as the student's browsing data, can get the student's learning habits, which can summarize the student's individual learning behavior law, and get the corresponding individual learning pattern recognition results.

## 2.2 Collect Online Personal Learning Behavior Data of Ideological and Political Courses

User browsing behavior acquisition is the process of extracting user browsing action information, and the captured information is the data source of the whole process of behavior analysis. The specific user behavior acquisition process can be shown in Fig. 2.

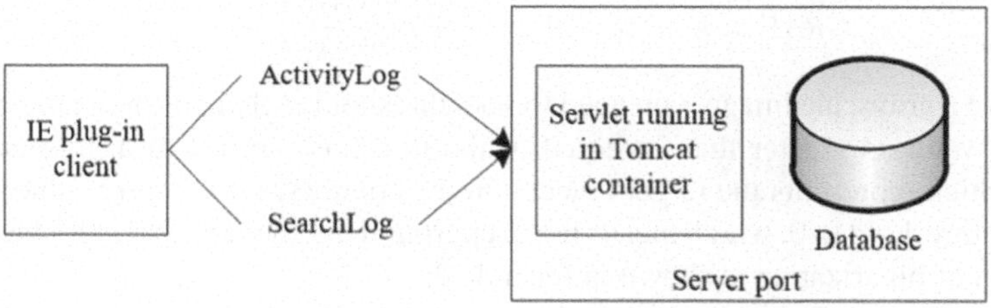


**Fig. 2.** Process diagram of user behavior acquisition

BHO technology is used to obtain the user's action information such as window events in the search process. The captured information includes action information and search web page information. This information can be uploaded to the server running in the container by the user in the form of logs. The process of users using search engines to find interesting information is a process of continuous interaction with search engines. Usually, the user enters a query keyword in the query box, and after analysis and processing inside the search engine, hundreds or even tens of thousands of related records are obtained. These records are sorted according to relevance to fix a number of records, usually one result. Page, presented to the user.

In each result page, each record usually contains the title, time, location identification, content summary and other information of the web page, representing the entrance of a web page. User interest information is obtained by combining four kinds of user browsing behaviors, such as page stay time, mouse click times, page access times and slider sliding times [5, 6]. Page dwell time belongs to window behavior, page access times belongs to repetition behavior, mouse click times and slider slide times belong to operation behavior. The user browsing behaviors collected by the browser plug-in are described in the form of basic behavior events and stored in the memory module of the recognition model.

The video data is recorded by the HD camera of the remote computer at the speed of 30 frames per second. The height of the camera is about the same as the eye height of the subject, about 25 cm away from the subject. Set the duration and interval of video data acquisition, start the video data acquisition program immediately after the students start the video courseware in the online teaching platform, and close the acquisition program one minute after the video is closed. All the video acquisition results are stored in the recognition model in chronological order.

### 2.3 Personal Learning Behavior Video Data Preprocessing

Every picture in the video stream collected by the camera is a three channel RGB color image. Each pixel in the image is composed of R, G and B components, and the value possibility of each component is 255. Therefore, the original image contains a lot of information, and a pixel has 255 × 255 × 255 values. In order to reduce the amount of original image data and subsequent calculation, it is necessary to gray the image. In this study, the average value method is selected to carry out gray conversion for each pixel in the initial video image, and the gray processing results obtained can be expressed as:

$$GRAY = R = G = B = \frac{R(i.j) + G(i.j) + B(i.j)}{3} \tag{1}$$

To binarize a grayscale image, you need to set a threshold. All pixels in the image whose grayscale value is greater than or equal to the threshold are set to a grayscale value of 255, which represents the target object. On the contrary, set the gray value of pixels below the threshold to 0, which means the background or other areas [7–9]. The concrete realization of binarization is shown in formula 2:

$$f(x, y) = \begin{cases} 255, f(x, y) \geq \lambda \\ 0, f(x, y) < \lambda \end{cases} \tag{2}$$

Among them, $(x, y)$ represents the coordinate value of a pixel, $f(x, y)$ represents the gray value of the coordinate point, and $\lambda$ is the set threshold. On this basis, bilateral filtering is used to de noise the video image. Bilateral filtering is to segment the neighborhood according to the size of the pixel value of each point in the filtered image, then assign the relatively high weight to the category of the pixel value of the point, and then carry out the domain weighted sum to get the final bilateral filtering result. In the process of filtering, the mathematical expression to define the Gaussian function in the spatial domain is:

$$d(i, j, k, l) = \exp\left(-\frac{(i-k)^2 + (j-l)^2}{2\sigma_d^2}\right) \tag{3}$$

Then the mathematical expression of Gaussian kernel function of gray distance range is as follows:

$$r(i, j, k, l) = \exp\left(-\frac{\left|f(i, j)^2 - f(k, l)^2\right|}{2\sigma_r^2}\right) \tag{4}$$

Multiply the above formula 3 and formula 4 to obtain the weight function of bilateral filtering:

$$w(i, j, k, l) = \exp\left(-\frac{(i-k)^2 + (j-l)^2}{2\sigma_d^2} - \frac{\left|f(i, j)^2 - f(k, l)^2\right|}{2\sigma_r^2}\right) \tag{5}$$

The product of the weight $w$ and the pixel $f$ obtained by the above formula is added and divided by the sum of the weight $w$, and finally the pixel value $g(i, j)$ at the point $(i, j)$ is obtained. The expression is shown in formula (6):

$$g(i,j) = \frac{\sigma \sum_{k,l} f(k,l) w(i,j,k,l)}{\sum_{k,l} w(i,j,k,l)} \tag{6}$$

In the above formulas, $(i, j)$ and $(k, l)$ are the output point and input point coordinates respectively, $\exp(*)$ represents the exponential function in mathematics, and the mathematical symbol $\sigma$ represents the standard deviation of the space domain.

## 2.4 Extracting Behavior Features of Video Frame

When performing target detection on an image, the image contour is important to extract information. Contour detection is actually the process of hollowing out the pixels inside the closed edge lines of the image and retaining the closed contour shape. By traversing the contour points of the closed contour in turn, data such as coordinate points, contour area, and number of contours are obtained to infer the subject of the image The characteristics of the target. To determine the subject's behavior in classroom teaching videos, it is necessary to study the changes of the video frame images, mainly to detect and calculate the subject's motion amplitude in the frame images before and after the video, so as to infer the current learning behavior of students [10]. This process consists of two parts: first call the similar frame images of the two videos, make the difference between them, and get the difference binary image; then the difference binary image is obtained for the detection and area calculation of the connected domain, and the integrated video image The contour feature in, the feature extraction result of the subject's motion amplitude is obtained.

In addition to the above video features, according to the process of Fig. 3, select other feature indicators in the process of personal learning of online teaching of Ideological and political theory course, and carry out feature extraction according to the above process.

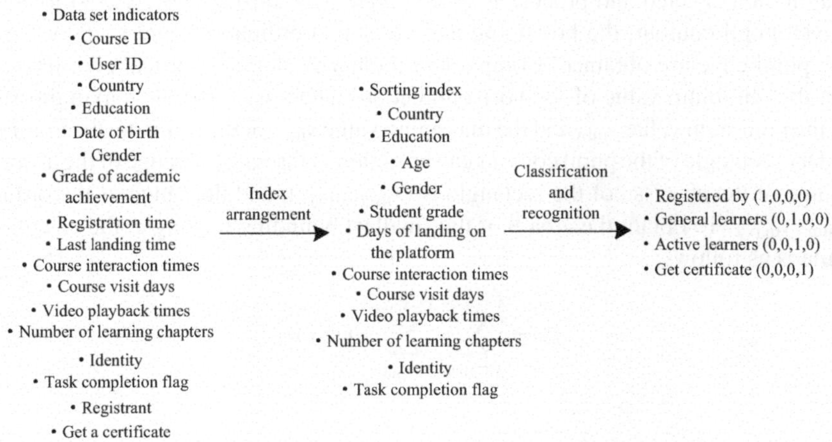


**Fig. 3.** Selection of individual learning characteristic indicators for online teaching

Finally, all the extracted learning behavior features are fused to obtain the final comprehensive feature extraction result.

## 2.5 Testing the Concentration of Online Teaching and Learning of Ideological and Political Theory Courses

According to the students' eye opening degree in class and the students' posture, expression, action and other characteristics in the classroom, the probability of students' class concentration is predicted. The judgment process of students' class concentration is shown in Fig. 4.

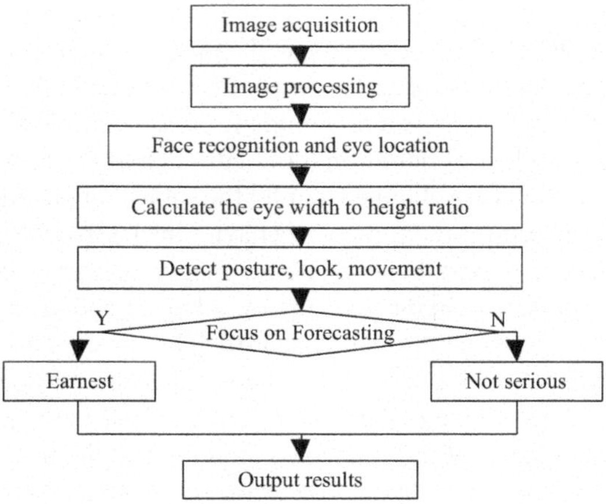


**Fig. 4.** Flow chart of individual learning concentration judgment

**Pupil Location**

Based on the collected and processed video image data, through coarse positioning of the given pupil contour, the horizontal and vertical coordinates x and y of each point on the pupil edge are obtained. Compare all the horizontal and vertical coordinates to obtain the minimum value of the horizontal coordinates. $x_{min}$ and the maximum value $x_{max}$, the minimum value $y_{min}$ and the maximum value $y_{max}$ of the ordinate, the minimum boundary rectangle of the pupil contour can be obtained through the range of the abscissa, the range of the abscissa of the rectangle is $(x_{min}, x_{max})$, and the range of the ordinate is $(y_{min}, y_{max})$. To obtain the area S of the smallest bounding rectangle, the calculation formula is as follows:

$$S = \sum_{y=y_{min}}^{y=y_{max}} \sum_{x=x_{min}}^{x=x_{max}} g(x, y) \tag{7}$$

The expression of the center of mass of the pupil contour is:

$$\begin{cases} X = \frac{1}{S} \sum_{y=y_{\min}}^{y=y_{\max}} \sum_{x=x_{\min}}^{x=x_{\max}} g(x, y) \times x \\ Y = \frac{1}{S} \sum_{y=y_{\min}}^{y=y_{\max}} \sum_{x=x_{\min}}^{x=x_{\max}} g(x, y) \times y \end{cases} \tag{8}$$

The precise position of the pupil center can be obtained by the centroid method, as shown in Fig. 5.

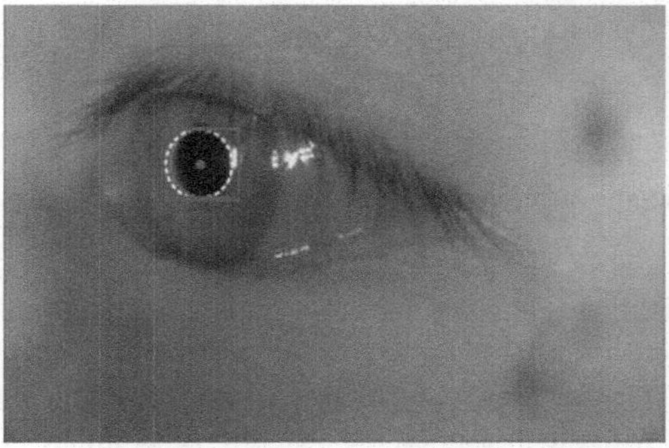

**Fig. 5.** Pupil positioning results

**Fixation Point Trajectory Calibration**

The fixation position can be obtained by eye movement video, and the fixation position can be substituted into the mapping relationship as a known condition, then the corresponding fixation position on the screen can be obtained. According to the mapping model, the fixation point mapping function is obtained. Through this function, the coordinates of the calibration point and all fixation points can be described in the image coordinate system, that is, the mapping position image of the calibration point [11, 12]. The results of individual learning fixation trajectory annotation are shown in Fig. 6.

In Fig. 6, the "+" in red indicates the position of the calibration point obtained from the reverse mapping relationship, and the "·" in blue indicates the position of the fixation point obtained from the mapping relationship.

**Blink Detection**

Blinking is the process of upper eyelid from open state to closed state, and then from closed state to open state. In this process, the main change is the position of the upper eyelid. Due to the occlusion of the upper eyelid on the pupil, the pupil size first changes from large to small and then from small to large. Therefore, only the pupil size and eyelid height of each frame in the video image sequence are required to detect the blink [13].

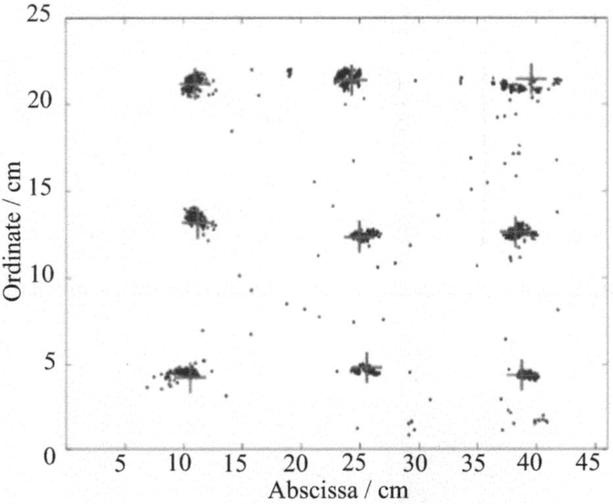


**Fig. 6.** Mapping position image of calibration point (Color figure online)

Blink detection is mainly divided into two steps: blink start position detection and blink end position detection. Firstly, the absolute value of the gray difference between the current frame and the previous frame in the video image is calculated, and a threshold is set. By comparing with the threshold, the absolute value image of the gray difference obtained before is converted into a binary image. The eye structure of eyelid can be obtained by processing the binary image. There will be small gaps and isolated points in the direct binary image of eyelid. A new threshold is set in advance, and the starting position of blink is determined by comparing the position of eyelids and the change of the width of eyelids in two adjacent frames. Find the frame with the largest eyelid width. In this frame, if the ratio of the width of the eyelid to the width of the whole eye image is greater than or equal to the previously set threshold, and the difference of the eyelid position is the largest, the frame is considered as the starting image of blinking.

With the start of blinking, the pupil area begins to decrease and the position begins to decrease until it disappears. When the eyes are opened again, the pupil area begins to enlarge and the position rises gradually. A pupil threshold is set in advance, and the position of blink termination is determined by comparing the pupil size and height of two adjacent frames. When the height of the pupil remains unchanged, the height is greater than or equal to the threshold of the pupil threshold, the ratio of the pupil width to height in the frame is between 0.3 and 3, and the ratio of the pupil size to the whole eye image is greater than or equal to the standard ratio, the frame is considered as the end image of blinking.

Combined with the above test results, the final conclusion is that Guo Chenzhong's concentration is as follows:

$$ZKD = \left(\frac{ZKDarea}{ZKDarea_{\max}}\right) \times 100\% \tag{9}$$

In the formula, $ZKDarea$ and $ZKDarea_{\max}$ respectively represent the current student's eye opening and maximum opening. When the value of the tested target ZKD is greater than 20%, it can be judged that the probability of class concentration in the class is higher. When the value of the tested target ZKD is less than 20%, it can be judged that the probability of class concentration in the class is low.

### 2.6 Analysis of Individual Learning Action Trajectory

Set the page dwell time, the number of mouse clicks, the number of page revisits, and the number of slider movements as the constituent indicators of the personal learning behavior trajectory. The page dwell time is the time when the individual browses the online teaching webpage of the ideological and political theory course. Browse to the time to perform the close action to leave the page. The mouse click is defined as the sum of the number of clicks of the left mouse button and the right mouse button. Every time a user opens a new website page, it will be recorded. When a user opens the same page multiple times, the visit volume value increases, that is, the number of times the page is viewed [14, 15]. The sliding times of the slider is the sum of all basic events related to scrolling the webpage. Arrange the above-mentioned indicator data in chronological order to obtain the analysis result of individual learning action trajectory.

### 2.7 Realize Personal Learning Pattern Recognition

Based on the analysis results of two kinds of behavior data in online teaching of Ideological and political theory course, it is output in the form of feature vector, and compared with the matching standard of the individual learning mode type and behavior item. Through qualitative comparison and quantitative calculation, the final result of personal learning pattern recognition in online teaching of Ideological and political theory course is obtained.

## 3 Comparative Experimental Analysis

In order to test the recognition function and application performance of the personal learning pattern recognition model designed above, the following comparative experiments are designed. The contrast groups in the experiment are the traditional learning pattern recognition model based on random forest and the learning pattern recognition model based on data mining.

The hardware configuration of the workstation is i7-6700 CPU, 32 g memory and GTX 1080ti graphics accelerator. The software is developed based on Python 3.6 and python 1.0. The learning pattern recognition model applied in the experiment is adjusted by grid search method. In addition, the online teaching platform of Ideological and political theory course in a university is selected as the operation platform of the identification model.

In the experimental environment to collect personal learning mode data, the video data collection needs to ensure that the classroom in the real state of shooting, effectively recording the status of students in class, according to the light intensity of the shooting scene to adjust the aperture coefficient, to ensure that the image is clear, in the recording, students are in a normal and relaxed learning state. The reference data set is set in the experimental environment to provide a comparative reference for the operation of the recognition model.

The recognition accuracy and application performance of the personal learning model are respectively set as the two evaluation indicators of the experiment. Among them, the recognition accuracy is mainly to set the actual personal learning mode of the students in the classroom, and to indicate the convenience of comparison with the recognition results in the form of numbers. In addition, the application performance test is to apply the recognition model to the actual online teaching work of ideological and political theory courses. After a period of application, analyze the students' ideological and political theory course test scores under different recognition models.

After statistics of relevant data, the test results of the recognition model are obtained, and the test results of the recognition accuracy are shown in Table 1.

**Table 1.** Accuracy test results of the recognition model

| Research object number | Research object number | Output result of learning pattern recognition model based on random forest | Output result of learning pattern recognition model based on data mining | The output results of this model |
|---|---|---|---|---|
| 1 | Autonomous learning-1 | Inquiry learning-2 | Autonomous learning-1 | Autonomous learning-1 |
| 2 | Autonomous learning-1 | Autonomous learning-1 | Autonomous learning-1 | Autonomous learning-1 |
| 3 | Cooperative learning-3 | Cooperative learning-3 | Cooperative learning-3 | Cooperative learning-3 |
| 4 | Inquiry learning-2 | Inquiry learning-2 | Cooperative learning-3 | Inquiry learning-2 |
| 5 | Inquiry learning-2 | Cooperative learning-3 | Inquiry learning-2 | Inquiry learning-2 |
| 6 | Cooperative learning-3 | Cooperative learning-3 | Cooperative learning-3 | Cooperative learning-3 |

It can be seen from Table 1 that, compared with the two comparison models, the output result of the recognition model designed in this paper is closer to the set personal learning mode without any misidentification, which indicates that the recognition model designed in this paper has a higher recognition accuracy.

On this basis, the identification model designed in this paper is applied to the actual teaching work of ideological and political theory courses, and 6 students are randomly selected as the research objects, and the scores of the most recent course examinations of the research objects are collected for comparison. During the application of the identification model Combine the recognition results to adjust the student's learning mode, and after a period of study, obtain the student's test score data after applying the recognition model. The comparison of the student's performance before and after the recognition model is applied to prove the application performance of the recognition method and test results as shown in Table 2.

**Table 2.** Application performance test results of identification model

| Research object number | Students' ideological and political theory course grades/points before the recognition model is applied | Students' ideological and political theory course grades/points after the recognition model is applied |
|---|---|---|
| 1 | 76 | 87 |
| 2 | 84 | 95 |
| 3 | 82 | 93 |
| 4 | 79 | 89 |
| 5 | 85 | 91 |
| 6 | 77 | 94 |

As can be seen from Table 2, before the application of the recognition model designed in this paper, the average score of students in ideological and political theory course is 80.5. After applying the recognition model designed in this paper, the average score of students' ideological and political theory course is 91.5 points. By comparison, we can see that the recognition model designed in this paper can effectively improve students' achievement in ideological and political theory. It can be shown that the learning pattern recognition method designed in this paper can effectively guide students' learning patterns to the right direction and has high application value.

## 4 Conclusion

This study provides an effective auxiliary tool for online teaching through the optimization design of personal learning pattern recognition model of online teaching of Ideological and political theory course, which can indirectly improve the quality and effect of online teaching of Ideological and political theory course. However, due to the design of the recognition model mainly from two aspects of video data and behavior data for specific analysis and recognition, it needs to consume more recognition time, hoping to be optimized and improved in the future work.

**Fund Project.** In 2019, Anhui Province Philosophy and Social Science Planning Project "Research on the Construction of Mainstream Ideology Discourse Power in Colleges and Universities in the "Micro-Communication" Era" (project number: AHSKY2019D052).

## References

1. Chung, C.-C., Huang, S.-L., Cheng, Y.-M., Lou, S.-J.: Using an iSTEAM project-based learning model for technology senior high school students: design, development, and evaluation. Int. J. Technol. Des. Educ. **55**(3), 1–37 (2020). https://doi.org/10.1007/s10798-020-09643-5
2. Taufik, H., Yustina: Motivation and skills of science teachers' online teaching through online learning training in the covid-19 period in Pekanbaru Indonesia. J. Phys.: Conf. Ser. **16**(1), 12–22 (2020)
3. Chen, W., Tang, X., Mou, T.: Course design and teaching practice in STEAM education at distance via an interactive e-learning platform: a case study. Asian Assoc. Open Univ. J. **15**(7), 37–46 (2019)
4. Xu, Z., Zhao, J., Yu, Y., et al.: Improved 1D-CNNs for behavior recognition using wearable sensor network. Comput. Commun. **15**(1), 165–171 (2020)
5. Nguyen, N.G., Phan, D., Lumbanraja, F.R., et al.: Applying deep learning models to mouse behavior recognition. J. Biomed. Sci. Eng. **12**(2), 183–196 (2019)
6. Xu, K., Zeng, Y., Zhang, Q., et al.: Online probabilistic goal recognition and its application in dynamic shortest-path local network interdiction. Eng. Appl. Artif. Intell. **85**(10), 57–71 (2019)
7. Tan, Z., Xu, L., Zhong, W., et al.: Online activity recognition and daily habit modeling for solitary elderly through indoor position-based stigmergy. Eng. Appl. Artif. Intell. **76**(9), 214–226 (2018)
8. Fu, W., Liu, S., Srivastava, G.: Optimization of big data scheduling in social networks. Entropy **21**(9), 902 (2019)
9. Liu, S., Glowatz, M., Zappatore, M., et al. (eds.): E-Learning, E-Education, and Online Training. Springer, Heidelberg, pp. 1–374 (2018). https://doi.org/10.1007/978-3-319-49625-2
10. Liu, S., Li, Z., Zhang, Y., et al.: Introduction of key problems in long-distance learning and training. Mob. Netw. Appl. **24**(1), 1–4 (2019)
11. Ling, X.P., Zhang, R.J., Yan, Y.F.: Research on online and offline mixed teaching mode of ideological and political course in colleges and universities. Party Build Ideol. Educ Sch. **25**(10), 46–49 (2020)
12. Liu, Q., Chen, E.H., Zhu, T.Y.: Research on educational data mining for online intelligent learning. Pattern Recognit. Artif. Intell. **31**(01), 77–90 (2018)
13. Chen, J.F., Zhu, J.: Efficient learning algorithm for maximum entropy discrimination topic models. Pattern Recognit. Artif. Intell. **32**(08), 736–745 (2019)
14. Chen, J.Y., Wang, Z., Chen, J.Y.: Design and research on intelligent teaching system based on deep learning. Comput. Sci. **46**(S1), 550–554+576 (2019)
15. Tan, Z., Jiang, X.: Interaction design of e-learning platform based on the fogg's behavior model. Packag. Eng. **41**(04), 189–194 (2020)

# Research on the Ideological and Political Teaching Mode of Dual System Curriculum in Colleges and Universities Based on MOOC

Jiang-lin Lu(✉)

College of Intelligent Manufacturing and Automobile,
Chongqing Vocational College of Transportation, Chongqing 402247, China

**Abstract.** In order to accurately study the existing application mode of ideological and political education in colleges and universities and cultivate a batch of excellent college graduates, this paper studies the dual system curriculum ideological and political education mode based on MOOC in colleges and universities. With the focus of professional quality training, the basic ideological and political curriculum should be set up and its form should be determined so as to realize the initial orientation of curriculum ideological and political teaching and complete the analysis of the differences between the educational ideas of the dual system of China and Germany. On this basis, the characteristics of Germany's "dual system" ideological and political education mode are analyzed, and the current Germany's "dual system" and domestic universities' ideological and political education mode are perfected by using efficient ideological and political education teaching methods, so as to realize the research on the ideological and political education mode of Chinese and German dual system curriculum based on MOOC. The result of the case study shows that with the application of the teaching mode of ideological and political education in Sino-German dual system, the actual employment rate of college graduates begins to increase, which can effectively meet the practical needs of the society in the application of all-round education talents.

**Keywords:** Sino-German dual system · Curriculum ideology · Teaching mode · Professional quality · Curriculum trend · Graduates · Employment rate

## 1 Introduction

Mu-class is a large-scale open online courses, is the "Internet education" product. Massive Open Online Course is a new model of online course development. MOOC is based on the theory of connectionism and the open pedagogy of e-learning. These courses, like traditional college courses, progressively enable students to grow from beginner to advanced [1]. The scope of the course covers not only a wide range of science and technology disciplines, such as mathematics, statistics, computer science, natural science and engineering, but also social science and humanities. MU courses do not offer credit,


W. Fu et al. (Eds.): eLEOT 2021, LNICST 389, pp. 231–242, 2021.
https://doi.org/10.1007/978-3-030-84383-0_20

nor do they count towards undergraduate or graduate degrees. Most of the classes are free.

Some of Coursera's courses offer a fee-based service called "Signature Track," which lets you choose whether or not to buy them. You can also take courses with this service for free and get a certificate. A course is not a collection, but rather a way of connecting lecturers and learners from all over the world through a common topic or topic. Although there is usually no specific requirement for the learner, all classes provide a general timetable in the form of weekly discussion topics, and the rest of the class structure is minimal, usually consisting of weekly lectures, discussion questions, and reading suggestions.

The innovation of this paper is that the ideological and political education is a social practice in which the society or social groups exert purposeful, planned and organized influence on its members with certain ideological concepts, political views and moral norms, so that they can form the ideological and moral character that meets the requirements of a certain society. It is also a lifelong learning course in Chinese literature. Ideological and political education is the primary content of China's spiritual civilization construction, and also one of the main ways to solve social contradictions and problems. Ideological and political education is very important, but also very difficult to do, especially in the market economy, China's Ideological and political work is relatively weak, it does not meet the requirements of modern social development [2]. There are many reasons for the ineffectiveness of ideological and political work, but one of the main reasons is that we have neglected personality education and cultivation for a long time.

## 2 Clarification of Educational Concept of Dual System Between China and Germany

### 2.1 Focusing on the Cultivation of Professional Quality

In order to study German "dual system" vocational education, we should get rid of its ideological connotation, learn its essence of educational method, and form our own characteristic vocational education idea. First, the core idea of quality education. Quality education is a fundamental and directive problem in school education. Broadly speaking, the goal of quality education in vocational schools includes not only the professional knowledge, skills and professional ethics necessary for engaging in a certain profession, but also the broader goals of political consciousness education, ideological education and ethical and moral education, which are the unity of the elements of the professional outlook, political outlook, world outlook, outlook on life and moral outlook of the people that are pursued and shaped by the quality education in schools, and the interdependence and restriction among the elements, thus forming a complete system with definite aims. This is an interrelated multi-level quality education target system. Among them, the overall goal of quality education determines and restricts the educational goal of each constituent element, and the educational goal of each constituent element, no matter how many levels, is subject to serving the overall goal.

Under the current circumstances, the motivation of quality education should be changed from political function to legal consciousness, from political function to economic function, from unified indoctrination of quality education to the combination of unity and separation, and from commonness and individuality, so as to realize the systematization, individualization, legalization and modernization of quality education working mode. Secondly, the operation of quality education. Quality education should be operated from three aspects, namely, implementing Quality education curriculum, attaching importance to daily life quality and improving professional practice ability. Among them, the vocational curriculum for quality education includes the orientation of instilling professional ethics, culture and spirit in vocational knowledge and skills [3]. The quality of daily life should attach importance to the cultivation of students' ideology, morality, behavior, norms and so on. Improve professional practice ability distribution in each specialty basic course, specialty course and each specialty practice, especially attach importance to the offering of vocational practice course.

In a word, the core position of quality education should be embodied in all social practice activities and permeated in all courses, whether explicit basic courses, professional basic courses, professional courses or professional practical courses, or hidden courses.

## 2.2 Establishment and Trend of Basic Ideological and Political Curriculum

Since entering the 21st century, the German federal and state ministries of culture and education reached a consensus: the future society should be a learning society. In order to make the young people enter the future learning society confidently, the German state departments of culture and education began to implement a series of curriculum reforms. Among them, the emphasis on general education of students is attached great importance to vocational education of students, because they realize that society on the one hand needs high-level academic researchers, on the other hand, society on the future also needs high-level engineers and technicians and skilled workers, especially different service industries need various capable staff. An important reason for this is the low enrolment rates in German high schools.

In Germany, where the "dual system" education mode is the main body of vocational education, the cultural basic courses including mathematics courses are in a relatively weak position. From the definition of the first chapter we know that the "dual system" vocational education model can be understood as: time, place, people, tasks, the results of change, see Table 1.

**Table 1.** Teaching hours of politics

| Curriculum classification | Course title | Class hours | Teaching week, hours allocation | | | |
|---|---|---|---|---|---|---|
| | | | 1 | 2 | 3 | 4 |
| | | | 20 weeks | 20 weeks | 10 weeks | 10 weeks |
| Public foundation course | Language politics | 240 | 4 | 4 | 4 | 4 |
| | Mathematics Politics | 240 | 4 | 4 | 4 | 4 |

(*continued*)

**Table 1.** (*continued*)

| Curriculum classification | Course title | Class hours | Teaching week, hours allocation | | | |
|---|---|---|---|---|---|---|
| | | | 1 | 2 | 3 | 4 |
| | | | 20 weeks | 20 weeks | 10 weeks | 10 weeks |
| | English politics | 240 | 4 | 4 | 4 | 4 |
| | Moral education and politics | 140 | 2 | 2 | 2 | 2 |
| | Career planning | 40 | 3 | 3 | 3 | 3 |
| | Sports politics | 240 | 3 | 3 | 3 | 3 |
| | Subtotal | 1140 (30.5%) | | | | |

Although the "dual system" of vocational education is intended to emphasize the equal status between enterprise training and vocational school education, under the "dual system" curriculum system, the curriculum focuses on acquiring useful professional skills and practical experience in professional fields, and under the influence of pragmatism, inevitably weakens the cultural basic curriculum, while regarding the cultural basic knowledge, what is needed to learn. At the same time, German vocational education attaches great importance to the cultivation of students' practical ability, increasing the proportion of specialized courses and reducing the proportion of common culture courses, which inevitably results in the incoordination of the proportion of common culture courses and specialized courses.

## 2.3 Orientation of Ideological and Political Education

Curriculum reform is the core of today's education reform, while the reform of mathematics curriculum is a comprehensive and systematic process because of its special nature. Curriculum objective is the basic element of curriculum. It directs the development direction of curriculum, decides the selection and organization of curriculum content and guides the teaching evaluation. Correct understanding and scientific grasp of curriculum objectives is the key to improve the quality of education and achieve the goals of school education [4]. From the perspective of ideological and political thought, cultivating students' good personality quality is the key to quality education, the need to build the ideological and political learning center, and the guarantee for students to learn ideological and political courses well. The ideological and political course is an important course in higher education, which is different from the corresponding courses offered by ordinary colleges and universities. It has distinct vocational characteristics.

Another main function of college public basic curriculum function is the need of citizen quality cultivation. Thinking and politics is an important part of modern culture. Thinking and politics permeate into all fields. The application of thinking and politics is paid more and more attention by the society. It is an important measure to use the knowledge to solve practical problems and make students have the ability of thinking and politics. This is an important measure to transfer the dual system education to the track of improving citizen quality education. At present, most of the students are weak in practice ability and application consciousness. In the long run, learning will be useless, unable to adapt to the needs of social development. Therefore, it is particularly important in ideological and political education to cultivate students' consciousness of ideological and political application and improve their ability to solve problems.

The orientation of ideological and political education in secondary vocational schools should be to cultivate students' developmental comprehensive accomplishment and their learning ability. Vocational education for sustainable development mainly refers to the continuous development of human resources through high-quality education and training to enhance the ability of sustainable development of workers, so as to serve social and economic sustainable development. Vocational education, which takes the development of human resources as its own duty, is no longer limited to pre-service education and training, but to extend to the whole career (Fig. 1).

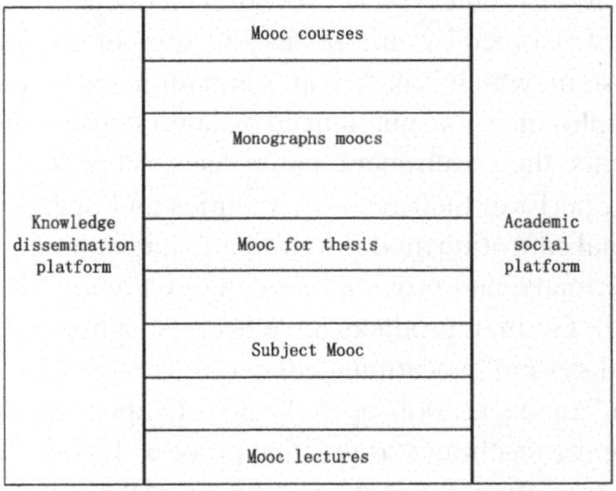


**Fig. 1.** MOOC application model

Since the reform and opening up, with the rapid development of economy and high technology, the demand for science and technology and talents has been increasing day by day. The training goal of MOOC is to train technical and skilled talents with professional quality and ability, which fits in with the demand of regional economic development for higher education. A large number of domestic and foreign -funded enterprises are expanding in different places of our country, and the transfer of capital, technology and product markets is unable to realize the transfer of highly-skilled human resources at the same time. Domestic and foreign -funded enterprises with generally high technological content need our educational institutions, especially higher education, to be able to respond quickly and provide them with sufficient and high-quality human resources [5]. Under the background of rapid development, the regional economic society has put forward higher requirements for the quantity and quality of ideological and political education personnel training. Ideological and political education can train laborers with modern quality and ability, effectively improve the comprehensive ability of laborers, provide reliable human resources for economic development, effectively enhance regional economic competitiveness, and promote sustainable and rapid development of regional economy. Vocational education provides intellectual and technical support for the sound and rapid development of regional economic industry, and is an effective guarantee for the sustainable development of regional economic industry.

## 3 Localization Practice of "Dual System" Ideological and Political Teaching Mode

### 3.1 Characteristics of German "Dual System" Ideological and Political Education Mode

German "dual system" vocational education originated from the training method of "master with apprentice" in German medieval handicraft industry. It is a vocational education mode combining school education with enterprise training, emphasizing the integration of learning and doing, and complementary advantages. Compared with school-based vocational education, "dual system" vocational education pays more attention to practical skills, so it is welcomed by enterprises and apprentices. The "dual system" is a kind of educational system, which is based on occupation, led by enterprise, centered by students, guided by employment and guaranteed by law. Focusing on the educational goal of training skilled talents, the government, enterprises, schools and associations have a clear division of labor, perform their respective duties and operate effectively. German "dual system" vocational education mode has trained a large number of high-quality technical personnel for Germany, and provided a strong guarantee for Germany's post-war rapid economic growth. German products have become synonymous with high quality in the world, and "dual system" vocational education is one of its "secret weapons".

In the "dual system" mode, schools open the door to open schools, and enterprises or employers to complete the teaching and practice process. It ensured the close combination of education and production. Students spend most of their time in enterprises, where they are trained in practical skills and exposed to the most advanced equipment and technology. At the same time, the school is closely linked with the community, enterprises, students in school learning at the same time, have the opportunity to practice production [6]. To a great extent, productive labor can reduce the cost and improve the learning goal, so that students can not only learn basic theoretical knowledge, but also master practical skills and help students to put into work immediately after finishing their studies.

### 3.2 Effective Teaching Methods of Ideological and Political Education

At present, the employment situation of college graduates in our country is becoming more and more severe. On the one hand, students can't find ideal jobs, and the phenomenon of employment becomes more and more serious. The main reason is that school education is divorced from the needs of enterprises, schools are divorced from enterprises, vocational education is facing the difficult situation of "no talent schools needed by enterprises and no students and enterprises trained by schools", so the reform of vocational education mode is the key [7]. Under the framework of the concept of lifelong education and the learning-oriented society, ponder over the lifelong and socialization of vocational education, embody the characteristics of vocational education such as diversity and professionalism, aim at serving the local economic and social development, adjust measures to local conditions, highlight characteristics, borrow the advanced experience of foreign countries, and borrow the stone of other countries to go its own way.

German "dual system" mode, that is, enterprises and schools jointly undertake the task of training unscrupulous people, according to the requirements of enterprises for unscrupulous people to organize teaching and on-the- job training, students can work on the job after graduation. This kind of pattern has the very good instruction function to China's vocational education, moreover can satisfy the current China social economy development the demand. The "dual system" emphasizes the combination of work and study, which is to closely combine higher education with social needs and the needs of enterprises, and to closely combine the application research and technology development carried out in cooperation with enterprises, so as to enable enterprises to participate in the reform and development of schools while sharing the advantages of school resources, so as to innovate the mode of personnel training in school-enterprise cooperation, realize the win-win cooperation between schools and enterprises, and effectively solve the unprecedented employment pressure that our country is currently facing.

Marxist theory on the all-round development of man holds that "human development is consistent with the development of social production." The old-fashioned division of labour has resulted in the one-sided development of man, and the production of large industrial machinery requires the all-round development of man and provides a material basis for his all-round development. The fundamental way to achieve his all-round development is to combine education with productive labour." The theory of all-round development of this person is an important theoretical basis for the purpose of education, which points out the direction of ideological and political education. Karl Marx and Karl Marx Sigus demonstrated that the development of industrial production requires the all-round development of human beings, and on this basis, pointed out that the future society will cultivate new people with all-round development through education. According to Karl Marx and Karl Marx Sigus, people who are fully developed are those who are fully free to develop intellectually and physically, and those who combine mental and physical labor. Call this "person who has the ability in all aspects, that is, the person who knows the whole production system" a person of all-round development. This fully developed person will be fully free in physical and mental development and use, "according to the needs of society or their own hobbies, from one production sector to another in turn." Although the theory of man's all-round development is a part of the theory system of political economy, it is also of great significance to ideological and political education. It has established the modern vocational education take the human as the main body, has established the raise comprehensive development modern professional person's rationale.

First of all, the educational goal of humanistic learning theory is to stimulate learners' learning motivation, develop their potential and positive self, and train students to learn to learn, so that learners can educate themselves and finally achieve self-realization. Secondly, humanistic learning theory advocates students' subject status in education, emphasizes keeping students curious in the process of teaching, explores any unknown field with the guidance of their own interests, and realizes that everything is changing and developing [8]. The primary task of teachers as facilitators is not to "teach" but to "promote", allowing students to learn independently and satisfy their own curiosity. Humanistic Learning Theory Advocates and Teaches the Value of Human Being.

The core of the purpose of education. This is consistent with the current people-oriented, student-centered educational thinking.

With the rapid development of dual curriculum and the integration of international information exchange, the demand for talents has gradually shifted from singleness to pluralism, i. e. paying more attention to people's creativity and innovation while paying more attention to knowledge and skills. As far as the goal of talent cultivation is concerned, students should be trained to be "people who learn how to learn" and "people who learn how to adapt to change". In the process of personnel training, we should pay attention to the training of learning, mobilize the students' initiative to learn to the maximum, and cultivate positive, adapting to the changes of the times. In the training methods of talents, it advocates the learner-centered and harmonious teacher-student relationship. Humanistic Learning Theory Model for Current Talents Training.

Type of reform has a certain guidance, reference role, especially for the positioning of modern professionals can well meet this demand.

### 3.3 "Dual System" in Germany and Ideological and Political Mode in Domestic Universities

The dual system in Germany is set up scientifically to cultivate professionals according to the market demand, which provides a reference for the transformation of higher vocational education in our country. The goal of higher vocational education determines the characteristics of its talent training must be market-oriented. Both at home and abroad, the talents trained by higher vocational education should be recognized and welcomed by the society [9]. Therefore, vocational education in China must be market- oriented, based on the premise of the market, to the needs of society as the center, the society needs what talent, higher vocational training on what talent, what new profession, the corresponding opening of what profession [10]. Our country higher vocational education personnel training pattern studies Germany "the dual system" the experience, pays great attention to the practice study to practice, the implementation teaching and the production labor unifies. Schools and factories and enterprises to cooperate, the enterprise as a vocational and technical students to produce labor and teaching places. This not only carried out teaching, but also enable students to participate in the labor exercise, improve the vocational ability. Schools and enterprises to cooperate, not only play their own advantages, but also make up for their own shortcomings, students have been trained in both theory and practice. At the same time, our higher vocational education must pay attention to the cultivation of students' ability [11]. Ability training is the core of higher vocational education. Ability is not only operating skills, but also a kind of professional ability. Germany's "dual system" is aimed at students to carry out this ability, so that the overall quality of students have been comprehensively improved, enhance the advantages of higher vocational education.

Of course, in the process of learning Germany's "dual system", there are still some gaps in China's talent training model [12]. Germany's "dual system" mode of practical teaching is mainly completed in enterprises, rather than in schools, practical teaching is mainly undertaken by enterprises. But our country higher vocational education practice teaching link nearly has in the school but is not in the enterprise. Vocational education in Germany is becoming more and more general and vocational [13]. Vocational education and general education are infiltrating each other. In order to cultivate the talents who can meet the needs of the development of modern society, the "dual system" combines the academic courses with the vocational courses in the curriculum setting. But there are two tendencies in our country's vocational education: one is to pay too much attention to theoretical study, and the proportion of practical teaching is obviously low; The students thus trained are either too narrow in their knowledge or too simple in their vocational skills, which imperceptibly limits their choice of posts and their adaptation to society." Coupled with the lack of national investment in higher vocational education, social understanding of vocational education and other reasons, vocational college students' self-identity is very low.

## 4 Results

Take J university as the research object, designs the following example application experiment. Since its establishment, J School has taken the lead in introducing the concept of "MOOC" into students' work, and gradually expanded it to the purpose of "Ideological and Political Teaching Mode of Sino-German Dual System Courses in Colleges and Universities", so as to create an educational atmosphere with modern vocational education characteristics. As J School students strive to become modern professionals, the college's good social image has been highlighted, the leading role of local social and economic development is gradually highlighted, and the graduate employment rate has been among the highest in the province for several years (Figs. 2 and 3).

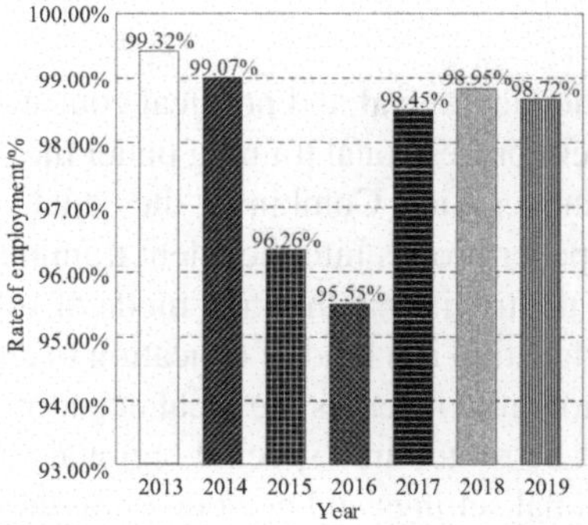


**Fig. 2.** J School graduate employment data for 2013–2019

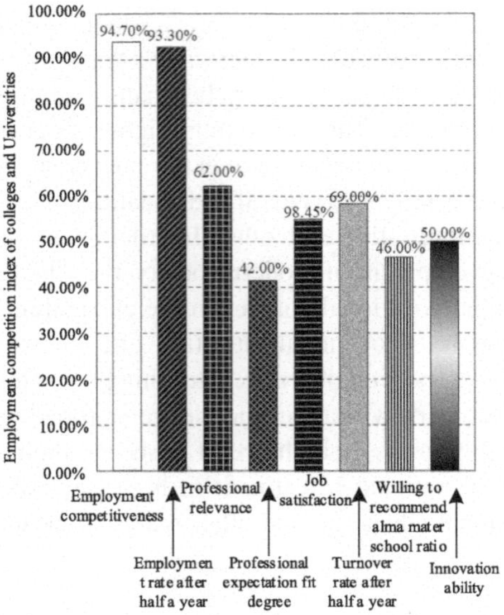


**Fig. 3.** J School graduates 2013–2019

The above two pictures are the graduate employment status of J School in 2018, 2019 follow-up survey. According to the 2019 Employment Report, J School ranks fourth out of 55 public vocational colleges in the province in 2017, while the graduates of 2018 rank third in terms of employment competitiveness. After six months, the monthly income of college graduates is 2,934 yuan, 152 yuan higher than the average in the province. The employment rate exceeded 95% for seven consecutive years from 2013 to 2019. Therefore, the modern professionals trained by J School can quickly integrate into the society, adapt to the requirements of enterprises and have strong employment competitiveness.

# 5 Conclusions

It is a brand-new idea in the ideological and political education field in recent years to probe into the path of modern professional training under the "dual system" talent training mode in colleges and universities. Combining the "dual system" with the "modern professional person", this paper probes into the talent training in colleges and universities, which breaks through the traditional thinking mode of studying the two separately. Ideological and political education is a kind of education to cultivate talents of different levels in the field of vocation, and it serves the local economic and social development directly. Therefore, it must be rooted in a specific regional economy, with strong local characteristics, its professional settings and personnel training should be adapted to the local economy and industrial structure.

MOOC thinking method has penetrated into all areas of people's lives, thinking has become an important part of social civilization. Ideological and political teaching in colleges and universities should serve not only the professional service but also the sustainable development of students so that they can become social citizens with good quality. The content of ideological and political education in colleges and universities should adhere to the principle of "making ideological and political education a tool of study and a means of solving problems and constructing a platform for the development of students' personality at different levels". In teaching practice, students should master the methods of solving practical problems, cultivate the ability of applying ideology and politics, so as to make students experience the humanistic value of mathematics, lay a foundation for them to go to the society and study for their whole life, and improve their interest in mathematics.

One of the main functions of college public basic courses is to serve professional teaching, but the actual situation is not so. In view of the recent situation, the knowledge points in the public basic courses in colleges and universities are far beyond the needs of professional knowledge learning, and most cultural knowledge is difficult to find usability in professional courses, even if there is one. The teaching requirements of college public basic courses are far from meeting the needs of professional learning, and do not meet the needs of professional teaching. Education in colleges and universities is a systematic project. A certain course can not be positioned from one's own point of view. The overall goal should be taken into account.

For the future work content, we can improve the data management system, strengthen the construction of campus spiritual civilization, and change the traditional teaching concept in the ideological and political teaching mode of Chinese German Dual System Course in Colleges and universities. The era of big data brings new opportunities and challenges to the ideological and political teaching mode of dual system curriculum in China and Germany. In order to meet the big data age better, college teachers should actively innovate teaching ideas and improve their own quality. Teachers should constantly change their teaching ideas and improve their ability to master data, so as to ensure the efficiency of Ideological and political education. Universities can improve students' initiative in learning through big data platform, better carry out the dual system curriculum ideological and political teaching mode between China and Germany, provide students with good ideological and political courses, and promote the development of innovative mode of Ideological and political education in the era of big data.

## References


1. Dafouz, E.: English-medium instruction and teacher education programmes in higher education: ideological forces and imagined identities at work. Int. J. Biling. Educ. Biling. **21**(6), 540–552 (2018)
2. Comarr, E.A., et al.: Extremity fractures of patients with spinal cord injuries. Top. Spinal Cord Inj. Rehabil. **11**(1), 1–10 (2005)
3. Deepa, S.R., Thenmozhi, R.: A study on motivation among teaching staff of academy of maritime education and training, Chennai. Int. J. Civ. Eng. Technol. **9**(1), 346–357 (2018)
4. Banu, Y., Egemen, A., Sinan, N., et al.: Estimating suspended sediment load with multivariate adaptive regression spline, teaching-learning based optimization, and artificial bee colony models. Sci. Total Environ. **639**(15), 826–840 (2018)
5. Johnstone, K., Marquis, E., Puri, V.: Public pedagogy and representations of higher education in popular film: new ground for the scholarship of teaching and learning. Teach. Learn Inquiry ISSOTL J. **6**(1), 25–37 (2018)

6. Neck, H.M., et al.: The scholarship of teaching and learning entrepreneurship. Entrep. Educ. Pedagog. **1**(1), 8–41 (2018)
7. Mohammadi, M.: Recast and metalinguistic feedback in teaching and learning L2 writing: a comparative study. J. Asia TEFL **6**(3), 227–244 (2018)
8. Stains, M., Harshman, J., Barker, M.K., et al.: Anatomy of STEM teaching in North American universities. Science **359**(6383), 1468–1470 (2018)
9. Vasiljevic, Z.: Using conceptual metaphors and L1 definitions in teaching idioms to non-native speakers. J. Asia TEFL **8**(3), 135–160 (2018)
10. Fu, W., Liu, S., Srivastava, G.: Optimization of big data scheduling in social networks. Entropy **21**(9), 902 (2019)
11. Liu, S., Bai, W., Zeng, N., et al.: A fast fractal based compression for MRI images. IEEE Access **7**, 62412–62420 (2019)
12. Liu, S., Li, Z., Zhang, Y., et al.: Introduction of key problems in long-distance learning and training. Mob. Netw Appl. **24**(1), 1–4 (2019)
13. Suyidno, N.M., Yuanita, L., et al.: Effectiveness of creative responsibility based teaching (CRBT) model on basic physics learning to increase student's scientific creativity and responsibility. J. Balt. Sci. Educ. **17**(1), 136–151 (2018)

# Pattern Recognition Method of Training Japanese Talents in Online Education

Hui Sun(✉) and Yan Liu

Dalian University of Science and Technology, Dalian 116052, China

**Abstract.** Aiming at the problem of poor recognition accuracy and poor recognition sensitivity caused by the poor feature extraction effect of the traditional talent training pattern recognition model. This paper proposes a method to identify the training pattern of Japanese talents in colleges and universities in online education. The principle of separability is used in the process of extracting the target feature quantity. Based on the extracted feature wavelet neural network architecture is constructed. The parameters of the neural network are trained to obtain the optimal parameters. Construct a talent training pattern recognition model through optimal parameters to realize the recognition of talent training patterns. The experimental results show that the accuracy of the recognition method is 92.93% on average, and it can obtain better talent training effect in application.

**Keywords:** Online education · College education · Talent training mode · Pattern recognition

## 1 Introduction

College education is a professional education based on ability, and talent training should highlight the ability requirements. With the rapid development of modern society, the practical application ability of students is highly required [1]. The training mode of professional talents in Colleges and universities affects the employment choice and employment prospect of students to a certain extent [2]. Japanese is a basic course in language learning, which is second only to English. The traditional teaching mode has been unable to meet the teaching needs of the Internet era [3]. Under the background of the rapid development of online education, how to make full use of existing teaching resources and improve classroom efficiency is of great significance to the reform and development of College Japanese teaching. Traditional education takes the form of classroom teaching, so it is difficult for teachers to teach students in accordance with their aptitude according to the characteristics of each student [4]. In the classroom, teachers teach mainly, so students' subjective initiative can not be fully mobilized. In addition, the traditional education uses paper teaching materials as the main classroom materials, which has great limitations and is not rich enough. Compared with the traditional education, online education is more convenient and abundant, and it is promoted and developed in Colleges and universities.


W. Fu et al. (Eds.): eLEOT 2021, LNICST 389, pp. 243–253, 2021.
https://doi.org/10.1007/978-3-030-84383-0_21

Online education means "large scale open network course", which is the latest form of network teaching. Under the background of the rapid development and popularization of Internet technology, online education, which spans time and space, uses Internet technology and applied information technology for content dissemination and learning, so that excellent educational resources can be shared, which attracts worldwide attention. It has the functions of recording, discussing, teaching and so on. These functions make online teaching content and form more colorful. As the consolidation and supplement of the new teaching content, as well as stimulating the desire of students' autonomous learning, it plays an irreplaceable role. Professional network teaching platform and public teaching resource platform are also very convenient, not only convenient for students to learn, test and so on [5, 6]. In view of the different ways and methods of online education, the online Japanese talent training mode in Colleges and universities is also different. In order to achieve the optimal effect of talent training, it is necessary to identify the talent training mode. Traditional talent training pattern recognition methods use shallow information for recognition. Because of the problems of inaccurate pattern feature extraction and low classification recognition rate of classifiers, the accuracy and sensitivity of recognition methods are poor. Based on the above analysis, in order to improve the training effect of online Japanese education, this paper will study the pattern recognition method of College Japanese talent training in online education. First, the hierarchical relationship between attributes is used to determine the attributes of the Japanese talent training model. Based on the known attributes of the Japanese talent training model, the characteristics of the talent training model are extracted. An adaptive algorithm is used to adjust the learning rate of the neural network. In this way, the recognition of talent training mode can be realized.

## 2 Pattern Recognition Method of Japanese Talents Training in Colleges and Universities in Online Education

### 2.1 Determine the Attribute of Japanese Talent Training Mode

In this paper, rule space model is used to distinguish the attributes of Japanese talent training mode. The rule space model does not have a unified definition of attributes. It is generally believed that attributes are the cognitive processing, skills or knowledge that the subjects need to complete a certain work successfully, and are the procedural and specific knowledge required for a specific field of work [7]. Attributes can be independent of each other without association, or they can have a certain hierarchical relationship, that is to say, there is a certain logical or psychological order among the attributes is needed in a test item. If attribute $A2$ is mastered, first master the attribute $A1$. To master the attribute $A1$ is a prerequisite for mastering attribute $AZ$, otherwise, $A2$ cannot be mastered. This hierarchical relationship between attributes is obtained through qualitative logical analysis.

The rule space model assumes that the performance of subjects on test items depends on a set of specific skills or abilities called attributes. Only when the subjects master these attributes can they correctly answer these items. The first step of the rule space model is to determine the attributes needed to answer the test items and the position of the attributes in the hierarchical relationship. There are many ways to determine the attributes of a test. This paper chooses to make clear what specific cognitive skills the attributes and the relationship between attributes are needed to solve a series of problems in the field of Japanese talent training before compiling the test If test items are compiled before the hierarchical relationship between attributes is determined, these items may not reflect the hierarchical relationship between attributes to be tested by the diagnostic test. The measurement validity of a test also depends on the ability of curriculum experts and test makers to correctly determine the attributes needed to solve specific content domain problems, clarify the relationship between attributes, and develop test items to measure these attributes purposefully and systematically.

The relationship between attributes in the regular space model is characterized by the binary connection matrix $A$ of $K \times K$ ($K$ refers to the number of attributes). The connection matrix only reflects the direct logical relationship between attributes. It indicates that one attribute has or has no direct logical relationship with another. There are only two values of 0 and 1 in the matrix. 0 indicates that there is no direct logical relationship between the two attributes, and 1 indicates that there is a direct one-way logical relationship between the two attributes. As shown in Fig. 1, there are direct unidirectional logical relationships between attributes $A1$ and $AZ$, Al and $A4$, $AZ$ and $A3$ respectively [8].

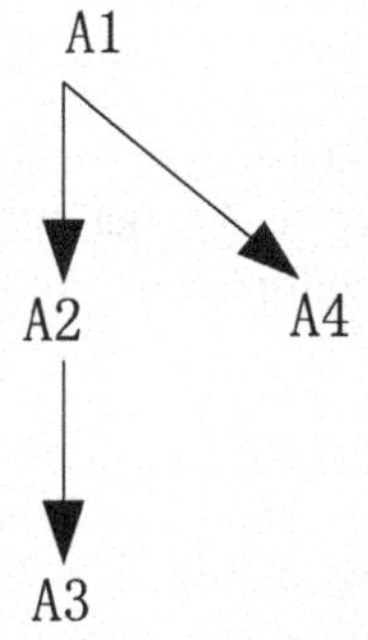


**Fig. 1.** Hierarchical relationship between attributes

In connection matrix $A$ (see Table 1), it can be seen that the one-way logical relations between $A1$ and $A2$, $A4$, $A2$ and $A3$ are represented by 1, and the rest are represented by 0.

The connection matrix only reflects the direct relationship between attributes, but not the indirect relationship between attributes. Tatsuoka uses reachability matrix $R$ of $K \times K$ to describe the direct and indirect relationships between attributes ($K$ is the number of attributes, 1 indicates that there is a relationship between attributes, and 0 indicates that there is no relationship between attributes). The reachability matrix $R$ of Fig. 1 is shown in Table 2 [9].

**Table 1.** Connection matrix A

| Attribute | Attribute | | | |
|---|---|---|---|---|
| | A1 | A2 | A3 | A4 |
| A1 | 0 | 1 | 0 | 1 |
| A2 | 0 | 0 | 1 | 0 |
| A3 | 0 | 0 | 0 | 0 |
| A4 | 0 | 0 | 0 | 0 |

**Table 2.** Attainable matrix R

| Attribute | Attribute | | | |
|---|---|---|---|---|
| | A1 | A2 | A3 | A4 |
| A1 | 1 | 1 | 1 | 1 |
| A2 | 0 | 1 | 1 | 0 |
| A3 | 0 | 0 | 1 | 0 |
| A4 | 0 | 0 | 0 | 0 |

From the first row of Table 2, it can be seen that attribute A1 is related to all attributes, and in the second row, *A*2 is related to *A*3, but not to *A*4. The reachable matrix *R* is obtained by Boolean addition and multiplication of the connection matrix according to the following formula.

$$R = (A + I)^n \tag{1}$$

In the above formula, $I$ is the identity matrix; $n = 1$. When N changes and $R$ no longer changes, the attainable matrix $R$ is obtained. $R$ the diagonal elements of a matrix are all $I$, indicating the fact that an attribute is related to itself. After determining the attributes of Japanese talent training mode, the characteristics of Japanese talent training mode are extracted.

### 2.2 Feature Extraction of Online Japanese Talent Training Mode

In general, the number of original features obtained by analyzing the actual online education data is relatively large. Assuming that all the features are used as classification features, this will not only make the structure of the recognizer more complex and the amount of calculation increase, but also will not make the classification effect better. Generally, there are $m$ methods to reduce the $n$ number of features: $m < n$, feature extraction and feature selection. The extraction of feature quantity can follow the separability criterion of category. It is assumed that the feature selection is to select the two most effective $n$ values from one feature, while for feature selection, $C_n^m$ of the $m$ features are selected, with a total of 6 combinations. However, it is impossible to determine which is the best classification effect, so a standard is set $m$. Similarly, for feature extraction, it is difficult to know which transformation is the most effective for classification, so a metric is needed. Generally, the error probability of the classifier is used as the criterion, that is, the group with the least error probability is the most effective feature vector. The greater the distance between the samples, the greater the separability of classes:

$$P_{ij} = \frac{1}{2}\sum_{i=1}^{c} P_i \sum_{j=1}^{c} P_j \frac{1}{N_i N_j} \sum_{x^{ij}\in\omega_i} \sum_{x^j\in\omega_j} D\left(x^i, x^j\right) \quad (2)$$

In the above formula, $c$ is the number of categories; $N_i$ is the number of samples in $\omega_i$ categories; $N_j$ is the number of samples in $\omega_j$ categories; $P_i$ and $P_j$ are the corresponding categories and prior probability [10, 11]; $D\left(x^i, x^j\right)$ is the distance between samples.

European distance [12, 13] is adopted, namely:

$$D\left(x^i, x^j\right) = \left(x^i - x^j\right)^T \left(x^i - x^j\right) \quad (3)$$

The $m_i$ mean vector representing the sample set of the $i$ kind is used

$$m_i = \frac{1}{N_i} \sum_{x^j\in\omega_j} x^i \quad (4)$$

$m$ is the total average vector of various samples, and the calculation formula is as follows:

$$m = \sum_{i=1}^{c} P_i m_i \quad (5)$$

In the process of talent training pattern recognition, firstly, the separability criterion $P$ is selected, and the criterion value of each feature is calculated, and the feature with the highest criterion value is selected, and the hypothesis is $x_1$. All the two-dimensional vectors including $x_1$ are selected and the criterion value of each two-dimensional vector is calculated, and then the two-dimensional vector with the highest criterion value is selected. And so on until the required combination of feature vector dimensions is selected. According to the characteristics of talent training mode extracted above, neural network is used to identify.

### 2.3 Adjustment of Neural Network Learning Rate

In the process of network initialization, the learning rate will directly affect the convergence speed of the network. Usually, the adaptive method can be used to select the learning rate to improve the convergence speed of the network. The general method is: first a random learning rate is set. After one iteration, the error function $\Delta E > 0$ is multiplied by the learning rate $\eta$ by a number less than $n$. If $\Delta E < 0$, multiply learning rate $\eta$ by a number greater than 1. Multiply and continue to iterate. Although this can adjust the learning rate, there are too many temporary data to save when writing code, which makes the whole process very troublesome. In this paper, specific steps for learning rate selection: if $\Delta E > 0$ is iterated for $\eta$ times, the constant α less than 1 is multiplied by learning rate $\eta$; if $\Delta E < 0$ is iterated for $n$ times, the constant $\beta$ greater than 1 is multiplied by learning rate $\eta$. In general, when the error function value increases, the new learning rate does not need to be recalculated along the original direction. Because the direction of the parameter adjustment vector $\Delta\vec{r} = -\eta\Delta E$, that is, $\Delta\vec{r}$, of the error function is the same as that of the negative gradient of the error function, even if the error function increases after iteration, the learning rate decreases, and there is no need to recalculate along the original direction. The direction of the corresponding learning vector is consistent with the direction of the negative gradient, and the error function can ensure that the direction of the negative gradient continues to decrease. The selection of the parameters $\alpha$ and $\beta$ of the neural network can directly affect the convergence speed of the network. Generally speaking, $\alpha$ is slightly less than 1 and $\beta$ is slightly greater than 1. Using the training sample set to train the parameters of neural network, so as to realize the recognition of talent training mode.

## 2.4 Realize Talent Training Pattern Recognition

In this paper, wavelet neural network is used to identify the talent training mode. The number of neurons in the input layer is 9, the number of neurons in the output layer is 5, and the number of neurons in the hidden layer is 15. $x_1, x_2, \ldots, x_9$ represents the input parameters, $y_1, y_2, \ldots, y_5$ represents the output parameters, and $\omega$ represents the network weight. In the wavelet neural network [14, 15] with multiple input variables and multiple output variables, the relationship between input and output is as follows:

$$y_j^P(x) = f\left[\sum_{h=1}^{15} \omega_{jh}\psi\left(\frac{\left(\sum_{i=1}^{9} \omega_{hi}x_i^p + b1_h\right) - b_h}{a_h}\right)\right] + b2_j \tag{6}$$

Where, $x_i^p$ is the input component of the $i$ input neuron of the $p$ sample in the input layer; $y_j^P$ is the actual output value of the $j$ output neuron in the output layer under the $p$ mode sample; $b1_h$ is the threshold of the $h$ hidden layer neuron; $b2_j$ is the threshold of the $j$ output neuron; $a_h$ is the output value of the fifth output neuron in the output layer Is the stretching coefficient of the $h$ hidden layer neuron; $b_h$ is the translation coefficient of the $h$ hidden layer neuron; $\omega_{hi}$ is the weight connecting the hidden layer neuron and the input neuron; $\omega_{jh}$ is the weight connecting the hidden layer neuron and the output neuron. After the network is initialized, the network is trained by the training sample set, and the network parameters are adjusted by correcting the output error. The network with definite parameters is used for pattern recognition. Through the above contents, this paper has completed the research on the pattern recognition method of College Japanese talents training in online education, and the feasibility of this method will be verified below.

## 3 Experimental Verification and Analysis

Online education is a new attempt for talent training. This section will verify the feasibility and effectiveness of the identification method proposed above through experiments.

### 3.1 Experimental Content

In order to ensure the validity of the experimental results, this experiment adopts the form of comparative experiment. This paper studies the online education in College Japanese talent training pattern recognition method as the verification group, the traditional talent training pattern feature extraction pattern recognition method as the control group. The performance of the two recognition methods is evaluated by comparing the recognition accuracy, recognition efficiency and the number of iterations in the feature extraction process.

### 3.2 Experimental Preparation and Process

Experiment 1: in the simulation experiment, the training sample set is used to test the recognition accuracy, recognition sensitivity and iteration times of the two groups of pattern recognition methods. The experimental data set is input into two computer simulation platforms with identical configuration, and the experimental images are extracted and recognized by verification group and control group method. Record the experimental data corresponding to each contrast item, and use the data processing software configured in the simulation platform to process the recorded experimental data. The final conclusion of this experiment is obtained by analyzing the experimental data, and the experimental verification is completed.

Experiment 2: 300 Japanese major students in a university were selected as the object of case verification, and the students were divided into two groups. One group of students used the training mode identified by the method in this paper for teaching and training, and the group was marked as the experimental group; the other group of students adopted the talent training mode identified by traditional methods,

The group was labeled as control group. The indicators of all the validation objects before validation were in line with the standard, with statistical significance. In the process of validation, all validation objects were the same except for the different cultivation mode. After the training process is completed according to the training mode of the experimental group and the control group, the experts in the major of the training object are invited to score the application-oriented ability of the verification object, and the ability of all the verification objects is scored. The formula for calculating the ability score s of a single student is as follows.

$$S = \frac{\sum_{j=1}^{n} g_j}{j} \tag{7}$$

In formula (7), $j$ is the number of items of a certain ability score, and $g_j$ is the score of each item of the ability of the student. Mathematical processing software is used to process the scores of all case objects, and according to the data processing results, the application-oriented ability histogram of two groups of case verification objects is drawn. Analysis of the experimental results, draw a conclusion of example verification.

### 3.3 Experimental Data and Analysis

Two methods are used to extract the characteristics of talent training mode. The comparison results are shown in Fig. 2. The relationship between the curves in the diagram is analyzed.

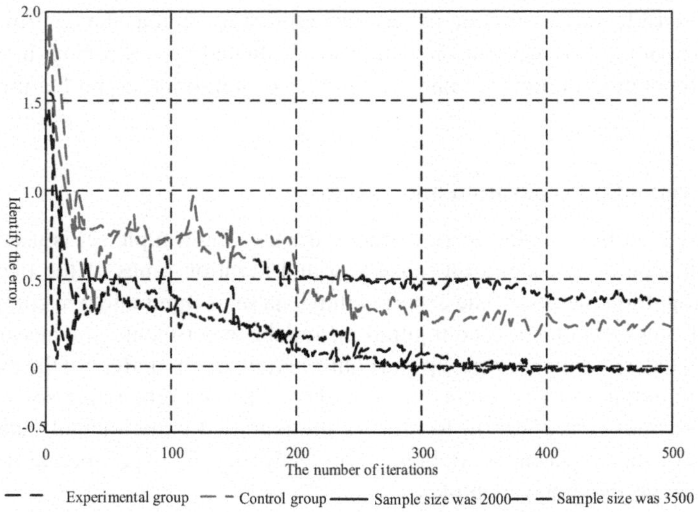


**Fig. 2.** Comparison of pattern recognition iterations

Analysis of the above figure shows that when the number of experimental samples is 2000, the control group method needs more iterations to achieve the minimum recognition error, and the iteration curve fluctuation of the control group method is more severe than that of the verification group. When the number of samples is 3500, the iterative curve of the two methods is similar to that of 2000. With the increase of the number of experimental samples, the verification group method still needs less iterations to achieve smaller recognition error. The above results show that the verification group method has less iterations and better feature extraction effect.

According to the extracted characteristics of talent training mode, the verification group and the control group are applied to recognize the talent training pattern. The recognition accuracy and efficiency of the two methods are shown in Table 3.

The results show that the recognition rate of the whole group is less than that of the control group, and the time required to verify the method is much shorter than that of the control group. The minimum time difference between the validation group method and the control group method was 26.7 Ms. The average recognition accuracy of the verification group method was 92.93%, and that of the control group was 78.70%, which

**Table 3.** Comparison of accuracy and recognition efficiency of talent training pattern recognition methods

| Serial number | Validation group | | | Control group | | |
|---|---|---|---|---|---|---|
| | Accuracy/% | Sensitivity/% | Recognition tim /MS | Accuracy/% | Sensitivity/% | Recognition time/MS |
| 1 | 92.7 | 93.2 | 18.8 | 77.4 | 73.6 | 49.9 |
| 2 | 94.2 | 89.4 | 20.9 | 79.6 | 69.5 | 58.7 |
| 3 | 95.3 | 93.6 | 18.2 | 78.9 | 72.3 | 61.4 |
| 4 | 94.7 | 93.5 | 18.2 | 77.2 | 71.7 | 55.3 |
| 5 | 93.1 | 88.9 | 18.2 | 80.1 | 69.8 | 47.9 |
| 6 | 92.5 | 91.6 | 21.0 | 76.2 | 73.4 | 55.5 |
| 7 | 91.6 | 90.8 | 20.8 | 80.4 | 71.8 | 59.6 |
| 8 | 92.4 | 91.5 | 19.6 | 75.5 | 72.6 | 53.4 |
| 9 | 94.3 | 91.1 | 19.7 | 78.9 | 70.2 | 52.7 |
| 10 | 91.8 | 93.0 | 21.1 | 77.7 | 72.1 | 60.8 |
| 11 | 95.2 | 89.7 | 20.1 | 80.8 | 71.7 | 61.2 |
| 12 | 91.0 | 89.5 | 21.2 | 78.6 | 73.4 | 58.6 |
| 13 | 91.5 | 91.0 | 21.5 | 77.6 | 71.5 | 58.6 |
| 14 | 92.2 | 91.5 | 20.9 | 78.3 | 71.4 | 59.8 |
| 15 | 93.5 | 90.9 | 21.0 | 78.5 | 71.3 | 59.7 |
| 16 | 94.4 | 92.3 | 20.7 | 79.1 | 71.5 | 58.5 |
| 17 | 92.3 | 91.1 | 19.3 | 80.2 | 72.8 | 60.2 |
| 18 | 91.2 | 90.8 | 19.4 | 79.6 | 70.4 | 60.1 |
| 19 | 91.0 | 89.7 | 19.5 | 80.1 | 73.6 | 59.3 |
| 20 | 93.8 | 92.5 | 19.6 | 79.4 | 72.1 | 60.0 |

was about 1/6 higher than that of the control group. The higher the sensitivity of the identification method, the better the stability of the identification method. According to the analysis of Fig. 2, the verification group method can obtain the minimum recognition error with the minimum number of iterations. That is to say, the pattern recognition method of College Japanese talent training in this paper has the advantages of high recognition accuracy and short time-consuming, and its performance is superior to the traditional recognition method.

The result of example verification is shown in Fig. 3, and the conclusion is drawn by analyzing the figure below.

Analysis of Fig. 3 shows that the ability scores of the control group are lower than those of the experimental group. In terms of international vision and knowledge and skills, the score of the control group was much lower than that of the experimental group. In terms of academic knowledge, there was no significant difference between the two

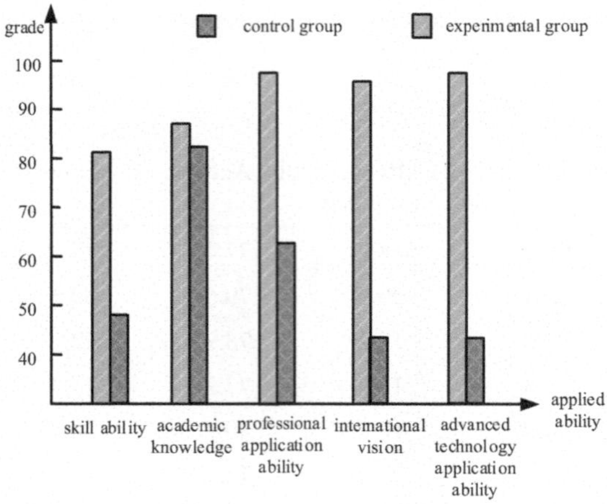


**Fig. 3.** Example verification results

groups, but the score of the experimental group was slightly higher than that of the control group. According to the scores of all applied abilities, the scores of the experimental group are more balanced than those of the control group, which indicates that the talents trained by the talent training mode identified by this method have more application-oriented abilities. To sum up, the talent training mode identified by the Japanese talent training pattern recognition method in online education studied in this paper can cultivate more balanced talents with application-oriented ability, and has more advantages.

## 4 Conclusion

In the era of online education, the traditional college Japanese teaching has been unable to meet the actual needs, the traditional teaching methods are mainly through teaching materials, offline classroom and recitation based exam oriented education. However, online education provides students with rich resources and broad space, so that students have the opportunity to choose their own course content or even choose their own teachers. By accepting Japanese knowledge from different channels, the independence and autonomy of Japanese learning will be greatly improved. In order to improve the training effect of Japanese talents in online education, this paper studies the pattern recognition method of Japanese talents training in online education. The effectiveness of the research method is proved by the combination of simulation and example verification.

## References

1. Liu, F.: Research on the training path of Japanese compound talents based on the integration of instrumental value and humanistic value. J. Liaoning Med. Univ. (Soc. Sci Ed.) **18**(04), 94–96 (2020)
2. Cai, Y., Wang, Z.: The research method of pattern recognition framework based on the distribution. J. Shandong Agric. Univ. (Nat. Sci. Ed.) **51**(02), 266–268 (2020)

3. Wang, P.: Research on the training strategy of application-oriented talents of Japanese major in private colleges and universities under the guidance of the new "national standard." Comp. Study Cult. Innov. **4**(11), 79–80 (2020)
4. Liang, Q.: Evaluation and optimization of personnel training mode in colleges and universities from the perspective of data mining technology. J. Dalian Natl. Univ. **22**(01), 92–96 (2020)
5. Xiao, L.: Research on the optimization of business administration undergraduate talent training mode in universities from the perspective of ecosystem. Mod. Educ. Sci. **10**(09), 70–75 (2019)
6. Jianqiu, L.: Construction of real-time interactive mode-based online course live broadcast teaching platform for physical training. Int. J. Emerg. Technol. Learn. (iJET) **13**(06), 73 (2018)
7. Fu, W., Liu, S., Srivastava, G.: Optimization of big data scheduling in social networks. Entropy **21**(9), 902 (2019)
8. Liu, S., Bai, W., Zeng, N., et al.: A fast fractal based compression for MRI images. IEEE Access **7**, 62412–62420 (2019)
9. Zhang, L.: Thoughts on the reform of undergraduate pattern recognition course for college students' innovation and entrepreneurship ability cultivation. Guide Sci. Educ. **05**(10), 25–27 (2018)
10. Li, X., Wang, M.: Construction and research of the teaching model of using automatic speech recognition app in simultaneous interpreting training course—a case study of voice note as an auxiliary tool. Comput.-Assist. Foreign Lang. Educ. China **1**(01), 12–18 (2018)
11. Jiang, Y., Li, X.: Intelligent online education system based on speech recognition with specialized analysis on quality of service. Int. J. Speech Technol. **23**(3), 489–497 (2020). https://doi.org/10.1007/s10772-020-09723-w
12. Caballe, S.: A computer science methodology for online education research. Int. J. Eng. Educ. **35**(2), 548–562 (2019)
13. Cao, X., Guo, S., Lin, J., et al.: Online tracking of ants based on deep association metrics: method, dataset and evaluation. Pattern Recognit. **103**(11), 107233 (2020)
14. Xu, K., Zeng, Y., Zhang, Q., et al.: Online probabilistic goal recognition and its application in dynamic shortest-path local network interdiction. Eng. Appl. Artif. Intell. **85**, 57–71 (2019)
15. Yang, Y.: The evaluation of online education course performance using decision tree mining algorithm. Complexity **2021**(7), 1–13 (2021)

# Research on Hybrid Learning Mode of Financial Management Course in Cloud Classroom Environment

Ling Cheng(✉) and Hui-ying Yan

NanChang JiaoTong Institute Business School, Nanchang 330000, China

**Abstract.** In order to realize the practical application value of the blended learning model and establish a more complete practical environment for financial management courses, this research focuses on the blended learning model of financial management courses in the cloud classroom environment. Realize the specific connotation conditions of blended learning by defining blended learning, and then clarify the theoretical support content of blended learning. On this basis, the B/S system structure is established, and after designing the blended learning design process, the activity system theory of blended learning is verified, so as to realize the smooth application of the blended learning model of financial management courses in the cloud classroom environment. Based on this, this study combined with the development status of the blended learning model in the university environment to verify the practical application value of the above learning model.

**Keywords:** Cloud classroom environment · Financial management course · Hybrid learning mode · B/S architecture

## 1 Introduction

With the development of educational technology, traditional classroom is gradually being replaced by blended learning. The use of computer and other high-tech equipment can help learners to achieve the optimal learning effect [1, 2]. The so-called blended learning is to combine the advantages of traditional learning methods with the advantages of network learning. That is to say, teachers should not only play the leading role of guiding, inspiring and monitoring the teaching process, but also fully reflect the initiative, enthusiasm and creativity of students as the main body of the learning process.

Blended learning can be summarized into the following aspects: the mixing of learning theories, learning resources, learning environments and learning styles. This study focuses on the blended learning mode of financial management courses under the cloud classroom environment, in order to better promote the development of financial management course education. In this paper, first of all, the specific connotation conditions of blended learning are analyzed, and the theoretical support content of blended learning is clarified. Then the B/S architecture is established and the hybrid learning process is designed.


W. Fu et al. (Eds.): eLEOT 2021, LNICST 389, pp. 254–265, 2021.
https://doi.org/10.1007/978-3-030-84383-0_22

# 2 Theoretical Basis of Blended Learning in Cloud Classroom Environment

## 2.1 The Definition of Blended Learning

Blended learning has experienced more than ten years of development since it was proposed. Due to the rich content involved, domestic and foreign scholars still do not have a unified and authoritative definition of this. Different experts and scholars have given different definitions of blended learning due to the different focus of research or the constraints of the research conditions at the time.

Blended learning is supported by brand-new ideas. According to the characteristics of the teaching process, the instructor or scheme designer divides it into several stages, and optimizes the teaching of each stage, so as to realize the learners' understanding and mastery of the whole. Some people also think that "blended learning" should be defined as a learning mode, including real-time online learning, face-to-face learning and self-designed pace learning [3, 4]. In addition, most of the time, blended learning is also considered as a hybrid application of various technical support, including intelligent learning tutor, e-learning, electronic performance support (EPSS) and knowledge management practice. Relevant scholars believe that blended learning should be regarded as a kind of ability, and explained from the perspective of learners, teachers or instructional designers and teaching managers. This ability includes the ability of learners to choose suitable learning resources, the ability of teachers to organize and flexibly use teaching equipment and teaching tools, and the ability of teaching managers to manage and distribute teaching equipment, teaching media and teaching materials.

Domestic scholars believe that the so-called "blended learning" is to combine the advantages of traditional classroom teaching with the advantages of online learning, that is to say, it is necessary to give play to the leading role of teachers in the teaching process, and to fully embody students as learning The initiative and creativity of the subject. Only when the two are combined to realize their complementary advantages can the best learning effect be expected. "Blend learning" means "integrated learning", which focuses on optimizing the combination of teaching media, teaching methods, and teaching strategies. The reasonable use of teachers and students in the process of teaching practice ultimately achieves the purpose of optimizing teaching and promoting students' learning.

The main idea of "blended learning" is to integrate face-to-face classroom teaching and online learning, so as to reduce teaching costs and improve teaching efficiency. In form, it is a mixture of face-to-face learning and online learning. In essence, it contains a mixture of different teaching theories, different teaching environments and different teaching media.

In summary, although the definitions of blended learning by domestic and foreign scholars are not the same in terms of description, there is no substantial difference in the deep level. By summarizing it, this research summarizes blended learning as: blended learning is a new teaching mode that combines traditional teaching and online teaching. Teachers can flexibly choose different teaching environments and teaching according to the type of knowledge and teaching goals. In this way, students choose different learning and communication methods according to their personal cognitive characteristics and knowledge mastery in order to optimize the teaching effect.

### 2.2 The Connotation of Blended Learning

Based on the research of domestic and foreign scholars, this research deeply analyzes the connotation of blended learning, and it is summarized as follows:

(1) Blending of learning environment: Blended learning combines the real classroom teaching environment with the virtual network teaching environment, and gives full play to the advantages of the two teaching environments. In real classroom teaching, students do it themselves and personally participate in practice to provide environmental support. Teachers organize and monitor the entire teaching process and play a leading role. Through face-to-face communication, they can provide timely help to students and help good teachers. The establishment of student relationship; in the virtual network teaching environment, students can study at their own pace, giving full play to the subjectivity of students and stimulating their enthusiasm for learning. Through the mixing of learning environment, the coexistence of classroom teaching and network teaching, and the coexistence of synchronous learning and asynchronous learning are finally achieved.
(2) The mixture of learning theory: learning theory includes many schools, such as behaviorism, cognitivism, humanism and constructivism in later development. Each learning theory has its own advantages and limitations. Therefore, we should not rely on a certain learning theory to guide all teaching and learning activities. In order to adapt to different learners and learning environments, blended learning cannot do without the support and guidance of a variety of learning theories [5, 6].
(3) Mixing of learning methods: Learning methods mainly include independent learning and mutual collaborative learning. Learners can conduct independent learning at their own pace in the online course according to their own situation or conduct collaborative learning with their learning partners through the online teaching platform anytime and anywhere. Learners can also carry out networked autonomous learning in traditional classroom teaching or through face-to-face knowledge exchange and sharing between peers, so as to realize collaborative learning.
(4) The mixing of evaluation methods: because a variety of learning methods and learning environment are comprehensively used in blended learning, there are more than one evaluation method, mainly including formative evaluation, summative evaluation and self-evaluation. Through the network teaching platform, with the help of related technologies, teachers can easily count the students' daily submitted homework, the completion of the work and the positive situation of participating in learning activities, so as to give students a fair and just formative evaluation. Through the mid-term and final examination organized by the school, the students can be evaluated in stages. Students can also make self-evaluation according to their homework, participation in activities and their understanding and mastery of knowledge.

Teaching activities are a complex process. In addition to the mixture of the above factors, blended learning also includes a mixture of other factors, a mixture of multiple learning resources, a mixture of formal and informal learning, and a mixture of different learning styles.

### 2.3 Theoretical Support of Blended Learning

Constructivist learning theory believes that the acquisition of knowledge is not the process of knowledge directly transferred from the outside to the brain, but the learner applies the existing knowledge to the external environment and constructs it through meaning on the basis of interaction (assimilation, adaptation) Way to get the process. This theory was first proposed by the Swiss psychologist Piaget on the basis of studying children's cognitive development. Later, with the further development of Vygotsky and others, this theory has been enriched and perfected and a unique learning outlook has been formed. Knowledge view, teaching view. From the perspective of learning, the theory believes that learning is not a process in which teachers directly transfer knowledge to students, but a process in which students construct their own knowledge under the interaction of new and old experiences. In the view of knowledge, the theory emphasizes the dynamic nature of knowledge, and emphasizes that the understanding of knowledge is constructed by individual students based on rich and unique experiences in specific situations [7]. In the view of teaching, constructivism believes that teaching is no longer the transmission of objective and definite existing knowledge, but to create an ideal learning situation for students to stimulate their original relevant knowledge and experience, promote the "growth" of knowledge, and promote students Knowledge construction.

In fact, in the early stage of the development of constructivism, because of the constraints of the teaching conditions at that time, it was difficult to implement the teaching methods advocated by constructivism. Since the 1990s, the development of computer and other related technologies has provided a reliable guarantee for the application of constructivism learning theory in the field of education and teaching. Under the guidance of constructivism learning theory, blended learning will optimize the combination of teaching elements, promote the meaning construction of personal knowledge, so as to improve learning efficiency and enhance learning effect.

## 3 Establishing a Blended Learning Model of Financial Management Courses Based on the B/S System Structure

### 3.1 B/S Architecture

Browser/Serve mode is a calculation method developed from the traditional C/S. The C/S mode is loosely coupled. The dialogue between the server and the client needs to rely on the message transfer mechanism. First, the client sends a dialogue request to the server. The server receives the request and processes it accordingly, and then sends it back through the transfer mechanism. Client. Different from the C/S model, the B/S model further decomposes the server side into a Web server and multiple database servers. In addition, the B/S model simplifies the client side and only retains the client's presentation function. The computing function is moved to the decomposed Web server, thus becoming a three-tier distributed structure consisting of a presentation layer, a function layer and a database service layer. The B/S system structure consists of three parts:

(1) Client. The client is in the presentation layer of the mixed learning mode of financial management course. The main task of the client is to guide the interface, accept the user's input, send out the service request from the web server, and display the processing results.
(2) Application server. The application server is in the business logic layer and integrates the two parts of web server application server through middleware. It is mainly used to execute business logic and send to database.
(3) Database server. The database server is in the data storage layer, which is mainly used to execute data logic, run SQL stored procedures, and save the attributes of business objects permanently.

The application mode of B/S architecture is shown in Fig. 1.

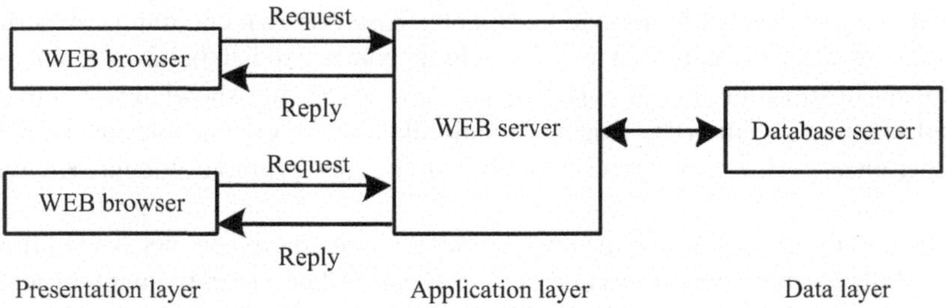


**Fig. 1.** Application mode diagram of B/S architecture

The complexity and mode of mathematical model and theoretical model of financial management decision are too high, and human's computational ability is limited. If it is too difficult to calculate simply by manual means, few people really use the financial model, thus reducing students' understanding and application of the model [8–10]. By embedding the complex financial management model into the system, students can easily use the complex model with a click of the mouse, which can reduce the amount of calculation in the application of the model, and enhance the students' understanding and application ability of the model.

### 3.2 Design Process Analysis of Blended Learning

After years of development, relevant scholars have conducted in-depth research on blended learning, and now select the research results of several representative scholars to analyze, in order to provide reference for designing the blended learning model of the cloud classroom environment.

Josh Bersin blended learning is summarized and divided into four steps, namely:

Step 1: identify and define learning needs;
Step 2: according to the characteristics of learners, make learning plans and design measurement strategies;
Step 3: select the learning content according to the existing basic conditions of blended learning;
Step 4: organize the implementation according to the plan, observe the learning process and evaluate the results.

Based on the analysis of the four basic steps of Josh Bersin's blended learning, related scholars further detailed the process of blended learning in the article "Principles and Application Models of Blended Learning", which is mainly divided into 7 links, as shown in Fig. 2 Shown.

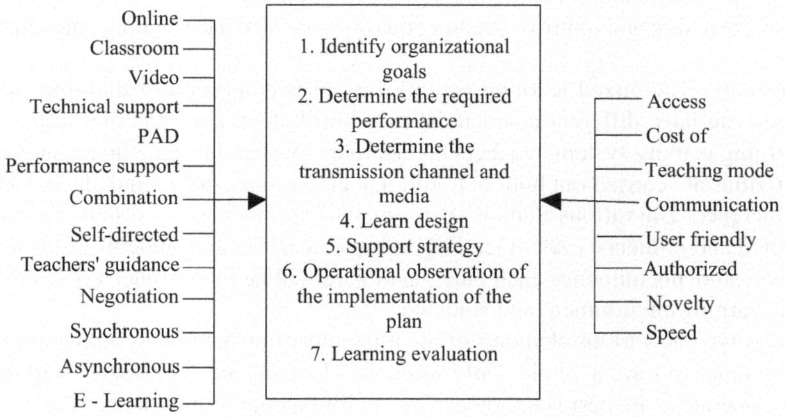


**Fig. 2.** Design steps of hybrid learning

Constructivism pointed out in the theory of learning that the learner should be regarded as the subject of learning and development in the first place when designing the curriculum. This requires us to focus on the needs of learners. Therefore, in the process of designing blended learning courses, we must insist on taking the learner as the center, fully mobilizing students' enthusiasm, stimulating students' interest in learning, and all serving students [11, 12]. At the same time, the leading role of teachers should not be ignored. Teachers, as important organizers and facilitators of the entire teaching process, should actively guide teaching activities, fully communicate with students, and complete teaching tasks in the collision of thinking.

As the carrier of knowledge transfer, curriculum resources are very important to the development of teaching activities. Various forms of resource design can attract students' interest and achieve twice the result with half the effort. However, students with different learning styles have different sensitivities to different kinds of teaching resources, and their demands for different kinds of resources are also different. Some of them like the audio-visual materials and some like the static text materials. Therefore, in the process of blended learning, teachers should consider the personalized needs of students as much as possible when selecting teaching resources Different types of resources can also be developed in combination with specific teaching content, so that students of different styles can find their own satisfactory material resources, so as to facilitate the development of learning.

### 3.3 Blended Learning Activity System Theory

When designing the blended learning activity system, it is necessary to consider the mixture of multiple learning methods (autonomous learning, collaborative learning, communication and discussion), learning theory (behaviorism, constructivism, cognitivism, humanism, etc.), teaching media (audio-visual, pictures, text, interactive media), learning environment (real physical environment, virtual network environment). As a kind of system, hybrid learning activity system has the general characteristics of generalized system [13]. At the same time, the main purpose of blended learning activity system is to improve teaching and improve teaching quality, so it also has teaching characteristics.

(1) Diversity: The mixed learning activity system is composed of multiple elements (they can have different characteristics or attributes). For example, in the mixed learning activity system, teachers and learners exist at the same time, and learning activities are carried out both in traditional classrooms and virtual classrooms.
(2) Coherence: The various elements in the mixed learning activity system are interconnected and influence each other. For example, teachers and students influence each other, students influence each other, and there will be interference effects between the learning environment and students.
(3) Integrity: The various elements of the mixed learning activity system complement each other to form a whole. Only when the elements are coordinated will the system operate at its best state, otherwise it will be counterproductive. For example, setting up a lot of online learning activities can deepen students' understanding of knowledge, but they may also take up too much time and increase the burden of learning.
(4) Dynamic: The mixed learning activity system is dynamically changing. For example, with the progress of the learning process, students' understanding of the learning content, familiarity between teachers and students, etc. will cause dynamic changes in the operation of the system [14, 15].
(5) Controllability: The operation of the blended learning activity system can be controlled by external means. For example, if too many online learning activities are set up, the students' learning enthusiasm decreases and their satisfaction decreases, the teacher can appropriately reduce the online learning activities.

Assume that $\dot{p}$ represents the set index of active application coefficient in the mixed learning system, and its calculation process is as follows:

$$\dot{p} = (e_1 + e_2)\kappa \tag{1}$$

Among them, $e_1$ and $e_2$ respectively represent two different financial management course implementation and application indicators in the cloud classroom environment, and $\kappa$ represents the applied fuzzy coefficient.

On this basis, if $\lambda_0$ represents the minimum diversity coefficient related to financial management courses in the cloud classroom environment and $\lambda_1$ represents the maximum diversity coefficient related to financial management courses in the cloud classroom environment, then the blended learning mode of financial management courses can be defined as:

$$J = \frac{\left| \dot{p} - \beta \sum_{\lambda_0}^{\lambda_1} e_1^{\sqrt{i_1^2 + i_2^2}} \right|}{\sum_{\lambda_0}^{\lambda_1} e_2^2} \tag{2}$$

Among them, $\beta$ represents the curriculum design coefficient under the mixed learning mode, $e_1$ and $e_2$ represent two different financial management curriculum implementation application indicators under the cloud classroom environment, and $i_1$ and $i_2$ represent two different power coefficient application conditions respectively. So far, the calculation and processing of coefficient index parameters are completed, and the smooth application of hybrid learning mode of financial management course is realized under the support of cloud classroom environment.

## 4 Model Application Ability Detection

In order to verify the practical application value of hybrid learning mode of financial management course in cloud classroom environment, the following experimental links are designed. According to the results of front-end analysis of learning mode, specific learning activities are designed as shown in Table 1.

**Table 1.** Learning activity design

| Title | Blended learning stack organization for financial management courses |
|---|---|
| Activity goal | Know the characteristics of the blended learning stack of financial management courses and its abstract data types;<br>Understand the implementation of the blended learning stack of financial management courses;<br>Able to perform basic operations on the blended learning stack of financial management courses;<br>Know what is function recursion;<br>Understand the role of financial management course blended learning stack in function recursion;<br>Able to compare and analyze sequential stacks and chain stacks |

*(continued)*

**Table 1.** (*continued*)

| Title | Blended learning stack organization for financial management courses |
|---|---|
| Activities | Teachers publish learning tasks through class discussion groups;<br>Students learn the relevant theoretical knowledge of the stack through the cloud classroom;<br>Teachers organize "problem solving" activities, requiring students to be able to perform basic operations on the stack;<br>Students work in groups to collect relevant information, summarize and organize them, and summarize the difference between sequential stack and chain stack |
| Event organization | Activity form: independent learning + classroom teaching + problem solving + data collection + discussion and exchange;<br>Role assignment: Heterogeneous grouping according to students' understanding of the stack;<br>Achievement form: data collection report, problem solving situation; |
| Activity evaluation | In-class test on the blended learning platform;<br>Teacher evaluation (students' performance in the classroom);<br>Student mutual evaluation (student's performance in the group) |

Financial course management requires students to master the relevant knowledge of the stack, which is theoretical. First of all, the teacher asked the students to discuss the related learning tasks in the class. Then according to the students' online course test and the problems reflected in the discussion group, the teacher re explained the key and difficult points in the form of classroom teaching, especially the knowledge point of function recursion, which was difficult for most students to understand, and the teacher explained through examples according to students' life and learning experience. The basic operation of the stack (press into the top of the stack, pop up from the top of the stack), stack application and other knowledge points are explained in the form of "classroom Professor + PPT", and then the students are tested whether they master it in the form of problem solving.

Finally, the students were divided into heterogeneous groupings, and the students collected and summarized relevant information. Each group finally reported the difference between sequential stack and chain stack in the form of a report. Subsequently, the teacher promptly encouraged and praised the good group. It can be seen from the report that students have basically mastered the related knowledge points of sequential stack and chain stack. After the learning activities, the students' learning effects were evaluated by means of teacher evaluation (for students' performance in the classroom), student mutual evaluation (for students' performance in groups), and in-class tests on the blended learning platform. The evaluation results show that the students have basically mastered the knowledge points of the financial management course and reached the present learning goals.

Through the statistics and collation of relevant data, this paper analyzes the effect of blended learning, and draws corresponding conclusions, in order to provide reference for college teachers to carry out hybrid learning based on cloud classroom environment. The analysis results of the questionnaire survey are shown in Table 2.

**Table 2.** Statistical analysis of blended learning effect

| Questionnaire title | Questionnaire analysis |
|---|---|
| Acceptance of the learning style | 88% of students said they could accept it; 10% of students said it didn't matter; only 2% of students said they could not accept it. This shows that the vast majority of students can accept blended learning |
| Can blended learning promote knowledge learning better | 59% of students think it is very good; 30% think it is good; 10% think it is fair; 1% think it is not good. This shows that the vast majority of students believe that blended learning can better promote knowledge learning |
| Satisfaction with blended learning | 75% of the students are very satisfied; 21% of the students are generally satisfied; 4% of the students are not satisfied. This shows that the vast majority of students approve of blended learning |
| A comparison between blended learning and traditional learning | 70% of students think blended learning is better; 20% of students think the two are equally good; 10% of students think that traditional learning methods are better. This shows that most students prefer blended learning |
| Satisfaction with financial management course platform | 80% of students are very satisfied with the MOOC platform; 10% are satisfied; 5% are generally satisfied; 5% are dissatisfied. This shows that the financial course management platform can provide good support for blended learning |
| Teacher's role in blended learning (multiple choice) | 80% of students think teachers are guides; 35% of students think teachers are managers; 20% of students think teachers are knowledge transmitters; 3% of students think teachers are dispensable |

It can be seen from Table 2 that the hybrid learning based on cloud classroom environment can better promote students' learning and mobilize their learning enthusiasm. Most students are satisfied with this learning mode. But there are still some students because of the inconvenient access to the Internet, unskilled computer operation and other factors, which makes them encounter some obstacles in blended learning, which requires teachers to provide appropriate help and guidance.

On this basis, in order to further verify the effectiveness of the blended learning mode of financial management courses in the cloud classroom environment, it is compared with the traditional learning mode. Under the condition of ensuring the same environment between the experimental group and the control group, 50 students and teachers were randomly selected to carry out evaluation on different learning modes, and the average score was calculated. The comparison results are shown in Fig. 3.

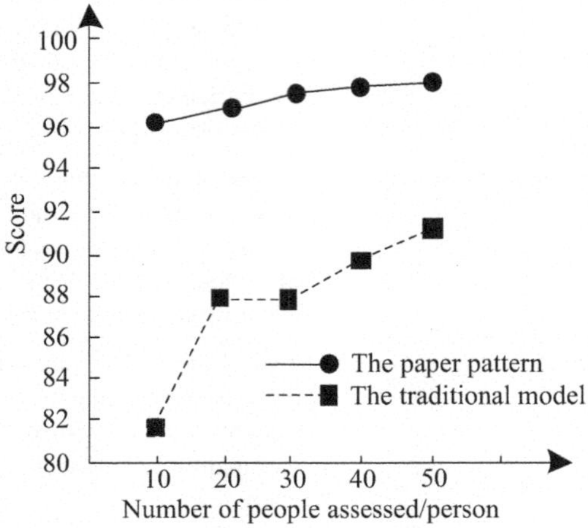


**Fig. 3.** Comparison of evaluation results of different learning modes

According to the results shown in Fig. 3, with the increase of the number of people assessed, the average test scores obtained by different learning modes also increased. However, in contrast, the average score curve of the learning model in this paper is always above that of the traditional model, which proves that the learning model in this paper has better evaluation effect. This result also explains the validity of the model in this paper to a certain extent.

## 5 Conclusion

The blended learning mode of financial course management based on cloud classroom environment designed in this study provides multiple evaluation methods and timely and effective feedback, which can help teachers to understand students' learning situation in time, so as to adjust the teaching schedule and methods timely.

In the following research, while further exploring the functions of the financial management course platform, the theoretical research of mixed learning will be deepened, and the best combination point of mixed learning and the platform will be explored, so as to continuously optimize the application effect of the mixed learning mode based on the cloud classroom environment.

## References

1. Song, Q., Chen, Q., Liu, Z., et al.: Exploration and practice of the engineering innovative talent's international cultivation for the emerging engineering education: based on the construction of "Dual Cross" team's experience and blended learning model. J. High. Educ. Manag. **12**(03), 102–108 (2018)
2. Feldman, E., Rawley, E., Figueiredo, R.J.P.D.: The costs of refocusing: evidence from hedge fund closures during the financial crisis. Strateg. Manag. J. **40**(08), 1268–1290 (2019)
3. Wei, Y., Xie, Y., Jiang, J.: Semi-supervised blending learning and teaching practice based on practical-style SPOC. Comput. Eng. Sci. **28**(01), 51–55 (2018)
4. Fu, W., Liu, S., Srivastava, G.: Optimization of big data scheduling in social networks. Entropy **21**(9), 902 (2019)
5. He, M., Liu, Y.: Teaching reform and practice of "web design and making" course based on the mode of "interactive and guidance learning" in colleges. Comput. Eng. Sci. **41**(01), 50–54 (2019)
6. Cai, R., Lu, X., Yi, X., et al.: Teaching reform of histology and embryology of placing the experiment class before the theoretical class. Chin. J. Anat. **41**(06), 102–104 (2018)
7. Wang, D., Zeng, P., Jin, X., et al.: Micro project driven cross teaching mode based on CDIO: taking daily chemical manufacturing technology as example. Chin. J. Chem. Educ. **39**(06), 49–54 (2018)
8. Zheng, D., Song, Y., Jiang, Y., et al.: Research status, evaluation and prospective of financial management and accounting in medical alliances. Chin. Health Econ. **37**(07), 75–79 (2018)
9. Liu, S., Li, Z., Zhang, Y., et al.: Introduction of key problems in long-distance learning and training. Mob. Netw. Appl. **24**(1), 1–4 (2019)
10. Liu, S., Glowatz, M., Zappatore, M., et al. (eds.): E-Learning, E-Education, and Online Training. Springer, Heidelberg, pp. 1–374 (2018). https://doi.org/10.1007/978-3-319-49625-2
11. Wen, Z.: Reflection on the development of blended learning in adult colleges and universities from the perspective of "cloud classroom". China Adult Educ. (12), 81–84 (2018)
12. Yan, T.: Exploration of mixed teaching model based on cloud classroom. China High. Educ. (17), 58–59 (2018)
13. Hu, E., Xie, B., Feng, L., et al.: NVIVO-based study on local undergraduate students' experience about blended learning. Heilongjiang Res. High. Educ. **38**(03), 139–143 (2020)
14. Jia, J., Huang, H.: Research on the construction of mixed teaching mode based on "rain classroom" under the new engineering background. Educ. Explor. (11), 38–42 (2020)
15. Zhu, Y., Wang, X.: A study on the bilingual mixed teaching mode of accounting from the perspective of SPOC – taking the bilingual course of "financial management" as an example. Commun. Financ. Account. (34), 32–35 (2019)

# Research on Pattern Recognition Method of Online English Education Based on Feature Self Learning

Xiao-xiao Duan[1](✉) and Ping Duan[2]

[1] International School, Chongqing Vocational Institute of Engineering, Jiangjin 402260, China
[2] Big Data and Internet of Things School, Chongqing Vocational Institute of Engineering, Jiangjin 402260, China

**Abstract.** Aiming at the problem of low accuracy of pattern recognition in online English education, a pattern recognition method based on feature self-learning is proposed. Using feature self-learning algorithm and convolution neural network, the feature extraction model of online English education is established, and the basic features and depth features of online English education are extracted. Z transform is introduced to standardize the feature data set of English online education, and Laplace gradient function is used to clean the wrong and missing data of English online education features. The fuzzy logic theory is used to infer the important parameters of English online education. According to the determined characteristics and parameter values of English online education, the difference between the characteristics and parameter values of English online education is calculated, and the mode of English online education is identified. The experimental results show that: This study of English online education pattern recognition method, can identify all the patterns of English online education, and English online education pattern recognition accuracy is high.

**Keywords:** Feature self-learning · English online education · Pattern recognition

## 1 Introduction

The deep integration of education and information technology has been the focus of our country for a long time, and the government has also issued many relevant policies to support online education. In this context, with the rapid development of online education, online learning has gradually become a common way of learning. Compared with traditional education, online education has the advantages of unlimited time, geographical location and resource sharing [1]. However, due to the late start of online education in China, there is a certain gap compared with developed countries. At the same time, there are also some problems such as the lack of monitoring and management of the platform, the same education mode, and many networks only stay at the level of resource sharing. Pattern recognition method, as a method to determine whether the element (the discriminated object) belongs to a certain set (a certain state), has been widely used


W. Fu et al. (Eds.): eLEOT 2021, LNICST 389, pp. 266–277, 2021.
https://doi.org/10.1007/978-3-030-84383-0_23

in various fields [2]. For pattern recognition methods at home and abroad, k-nearest distance discrimination method, various clustering analysis methods, artificial neural network and support vector machine methods have been developed [3–5]. However, the pattern recognition method of the above research does not consider the relationship between the classification features. In fact, there is a certain relationship between the extracted classification features. Therefore, the above research is not perfect, more or less has certain defects, which seriously restricts its further application in various fields. At present, many disciplines have adopted online education mode for teaching, among which English online education mode has the highest similarity, and it is difficult to judge which education mode is the most effective. Therefore, this paper introduces the feature self-learning algorithm, makes use of its excellent feature extraction ability for deep subspace and the advantages of running time to study the pattern recognition method of English online education, and puts forward the research topic of pattern recognition method of English online education based on feature self-learning.

## 2 Research on Pattern Recognition Method of English Online Education Based on Feature Self Learning

### 2.1 Establish Feature Extraction Model Based on Feature Self-learning

Based on the data collected by the mobile terminal, the basic features of English online education are obtained by simple calculation. Convolution neural network further processes the features of basic English online education and extracts the depth features of English online education. Based on the feature self-learning algorithm, the feature extraction model is established. The whole framework is generally composed of four parts as Fig. 1.

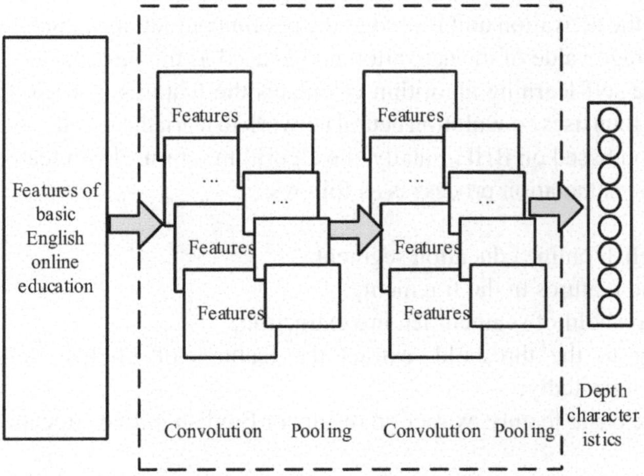


**Fig. 1.** Feature extraction model

In the feature extraction model of English online education shown in Fig. 1, the feature self-learning algorithm needs convolution in convolution neural network to get the features of English online education. In order to solve this problem, a basic artificial feature time series is composed of the sampling points of the English online education mode segment and the time sequence relationship. The convolution neural network is divided into two steps to pool the feature sequence. Firstly, the 2-D convolution network is used to map the sequence features, and the pooling layer is used to compress them. Then, the 1-D convolution is performed on the compressed sequence, and the 1-D depth features are obtained by pooling again. The convolution process is as Fig. 2.

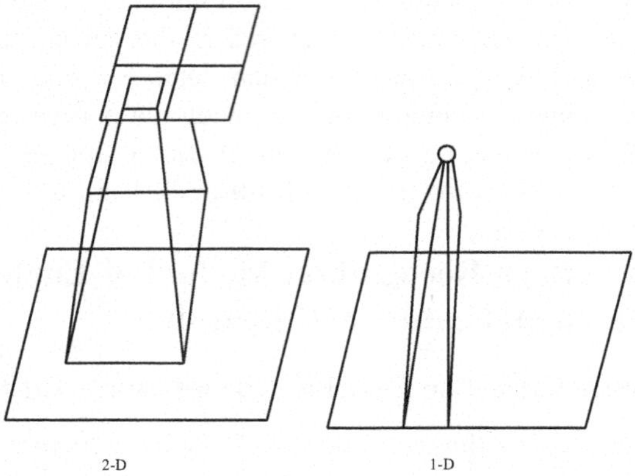


**Fig. 2.** 2-D and 1-D convolution processes

Pooling is another important operation in convolutional neural network processing. It can compress the feature maps generated after convolution. There are two common pooling strategies: maximum and average. Using the maximum pooling policy, the maximum value in the activation unit is used as the pooling output; using the average pooling policy, the average value of the activation unit is used as the output.

The feature self-learning algorithm calculates the features of basic English online education, and then uses convolution neural network to learn the features of basic English online education based on BHF. Finally, the algorithm returns depth features for further processing, The calculation process is as follows:

(1) Input English online education segment;
(2) Extract the features in the fragment;
(3) Set the threshold of segment feature extraction;
(4) According to the threshold, extract the features of English online education segments repeatedly;
(5) Output the basic feature extraction results of English online education segment.

Based on the above contents, the feature extraction of English online education is completed. According to the features of English online education extracted in Fig. 1, the feature database of English online education can be constructed, and the English online education mode can be identified according to the features of English online education.

### 2.2 Construction of English Online Education Feature Database

Based on the feature extraction model of English online education shown in Fig. 1, the extracted feature data of English online education is the original feature data set of English online education, including attributes and their corresponding attribute values. The data set contains duration data and accuracy data, both of which are continuous data. It will be inconvenient in the process of pattern recognition in English online education [6]. Therefore, it is necessary to transform and standardize the data to make all attribute values fall into the limited space, which is conducive to data mining and analysis. Therefore, Z-transform is introduced to standardize the feature data set of English online education, so that all the data fall into one range:

$$z = \frac{(x - \mu)}{\sigma} \tag{1}$$

In formula (1), $z$ represents the converted data; $x$ represents a certain data of the column of data to be converted; $\mu$ represents the average of this column of data; $\sigma$ represents the standard deviation [7].

Since the final data type of learning style is discrete value, the two types of data need to be analyzed later, so the online learning behavior data set also needs to be discretized. Therefore, the transformed data set is equally divided into five intervals, and finally the discrete value data set of all online learning behaviors is obtained.

The standardized data obtained from the conversion of formula (1) needs to be converted and cleaned accordingly. Therefore, the data are processed as follows. For information processing dimensions, use $H$ for active type, $B$ for balanced type, and $C$ for contemplative type; for information perception dimension, use $G$ for sensory type and $B$ for balanced type; $Z$ for intuitive type; for information input dimension, $S$ represents the visual type, $B$ represents the balanced type, and $Y$ represents the verbal type; for the information understanding dimension, $X$ represents the sequence type, $B$ represents the balanced type, and $Z$ represents the comprehensive type.

At this time, Laplace gradient function is used to calculate the second derivative of the data, so as to measure the data missing and error. If the variance of Laplacian operator of English online education data is lower than a fixed value, it means that the change of English online education data is not obvious, and the English online education data can be considered as missing error data. According to the Laplacian operator, cleaning the sample data of English online education, there are errors, missing data, all stored in the database, that is to complete the construction of English online education feature database.

### 2.3 Infer the Important Parameters of English Online Education

Fuzzy logic theory is introduced to infer the important parameters of online English education. Membership function is defined to represent the relationship between input and output variables in the inferential process. Finally, simple and clear results are output through fuzzy inference. The reasoning process is as follows:

(1) Determine the membership function of input variables, so as to determine the rules in the rule base that the input variables can trigger. Because there are a large number of rules in the rule base, when each input variable is input, it is impossible to trigger all the rules, only some rules related to the corresponding input variables will be triggered;
(2) Judge the credibility of the rules triggered by each input variable. We already know some rules that may be triggered by the input variable. At this time, we need to calculate the credibility of each rule triggered according to the actual situation, find the most likely rule, and then carry out the next step of fuzzy reasoning to judge the possible results;
(3) To judge the final output of the fuzzy reasoning system, we need to comprehensively judge the credibility of the rules triggered by the previous input variables to calculate and determine the final fuzzy reasoning result.

Based on the above three steps, determine the membership function of the input variable. $u(x)$ will be used to represent the membership function of the input function relative to the fuzzy set. Then the value of $u(x)$ is closer to 0, indicating that the variable $x$ is related to any feature of English online education in the domain. The relationship of the set $A$, the lower the degree of implication, that is, the lower the degree that $x$ belongs to the feature set $A$ of English online education. Conversely, when the value of $u(x)$ tends to 1, the higher the degree of implication between the $x$ variable and the feature set $A$ of English online education, that is, the higher the degree of membership [8, 9].

On this basis, a fuzzy logic rule library rule is determined, and its inference composition rules are as follows: suppose $r$ represents a fuzzy relationship in $uv$, where $u$ represents an element in the feature set of English online education; $v$ represents the feature of English online education Fuzzy collection. And $x$ represents a fuzzy subset in the domain $U$. Then, with the help of $x$ inference, the fuzzy subset $y = xr$ in $v$ is derived. This inference method is called Sup-Star inference synthesis rule, where $xr$ is the Sup of $x$ and $r$-Star synthesis. The specific synthesis rules are as Table 1.

## 2.4 Identify English Online Education Mode

Suppose that the matrix of all the original online English education models is $\underline{\varphi}$ and $\varphi = [\varphi_1, \varphi_2, \ldots, \varphi_c] \in R^{mN}$, where $c$ is the number of categories of online English education models, $m$ is the number of training samples, and $N$ is the total number of samples. According to the hypothesis object, the model of English online education is identified. Using the above three contents, the characteristics and parameters of English online education are extracted, and the neutral approximate sample is obtained. The difference between the test sample and the neutral approximation sample is made to obtain the difference of the English online education characteristics of the test sample.

The neutral approximate sample is a linear approximate representation of the neutral feature set of English online education, and its vector is represented as $y_n$, then:

$$y_n = \varphi \hat{w}_q \tag{2}$$

**Table 1.** Rules of fuzzy logic theory rule base

| | | |
|---|---|---|
| GMP | Premise 1 | *X* is *A'* |
| | Premise 2 | If *X* is *A*, then *y* is *B* |
| | Conclusion | *Y* is *B'* |
| | Fuzzy inference | $B' = A'(A \rightarrow B) = A'r$ |
| GMT | Premise 1 | *Y* is *B'* |
| | Premise 2 | If *X* is *A*, then *y* is *B* |
| | Conclusion | *X* is *A'* |
| | Fuzzy inference | $A' = (A \rightarrow B)B' = rB'$ |

Note: *r* represents the parameters containing fuzzy implication relations. The widely used fuzzy operations include fuzzy implication product operation and fuzzy implication minimum operation. Any form of fuzzy operation reasoning can be realized with the help of *r*; other letters do not have practical meaning, only indicate the reasoning process of fuzzy logic theory rule base

In formula (2), $\varphi$ represents the neutral feature set of English online education, $w_{q1}$ represents the weighted vector, the lower corner represents the *q* feature of English online education, which is obtained by the normalized least square optimization formula, then:

$$w_{q1} = \arg\min\left\{\left\|y_q - \varphi w_q\right\|_2^2 + \lambda\left\|w_q\right\|_2^2\right\} \tag{3}$$

In formula (3), $\lambda$ represents the normalization parameter, $y_q$ represents the test sample vector, $\|\cdot\|_2$ represents the norm vector, $w_q$ represents the *q* feature vector of English online education, which can be obtained by the following formula:

$$w_q = \left(\varphi^T\varphi + \lambda I\right)^{-1}\varphi^T y_q \tag{4}$$

In formula (4), *I* represents the identity matrix, *T* represents the matrix conversion.

At this time, the $\lambda$ in Eq. (5) is set to 0.1, and the differential test sample *y* can be expressed as:

$$y = \lambda\left(y_q - y_n\right) \tag{5}$$

English online education feature difference set *D* contains *N* difference training sample vectors, namely $D = [v_1, v_2, \ldots, v_c]$, which also contains *C* English online education feature categories. Each difference training sample vector can be expressed as $v_i$, where *i* represents differential training sample [10]. Assuming that $v_s \in R$ is a random training sample in the original English online education, the differential training sample $v_i$ is also obtained by calculating the difference between the training sample $v_s$ and its corresponding neutral approximate sample $v_n$. The solution method is the same as the differential test sample *y*.

Assume that the English online education mode corresponding to any difference vector $v_i$ is $I$, where $I_j = (1, 2, ..., n)$ represents the $I$ column of $j$. If $I$ is an even number, then the English online education feature vectors $s_1$ and $s_2$ of the English online education model $I$ can be expressed as:

$$s_1 = \begin{bmatrix} I_1 \\ I_2 \\ \vdots \\ I_{\frac{j}{2}} \end{bmatrix}$$
$$s_2 = \begin{bmatrix} I_j \\ I_{j-1} \\ \vdots \\ I_{\frac{j}{2}+1} \end{bmatrix} \tag{6}$$

In formula (6), $s_1$ is obtained by concatenating the parameter values from the first column to the $j/2$ column of the English online education model $I$. Similarly, $s_2$ is obtained by concatenating the parameter values from the last column to the $j/2 + 1$ column of the English online education model $I$ [11].

According to the difference value obtained above, the number of English online education features and parameter values is determined to be $p$. At this time, $X$ is used to represent English online education features and parameter values, then $X = [X_1, X_2, ..., X_p]$, for any one of the English online education features and parameter values English online education uses eigenvalues to predict $X_i$, where $j \neq i$ is:

$$X_i = f\left(X_j, b_0, b_j, b_{jj}, b_{jk}\right) + e \tag{7}$$

In formula (7), $X_i$ represents the predicted variable; $X_j$ represents the predictor variable; $e$ represents the prediction error; $b_0$, $b_j$, $b_{jj}$, $b_{jk}$, represents the English online education parameter [12].

According to formula (7), using the RBF network model with a three-layer network of input layer, hidden layer and output layer to identify the English online education mode, there are:

$$X_j = \sum_{r=1}^{h} \omega_r \cdot \phi_r(X_i) \tag{8}$$

In formula (8), $r$ represents the Gaussian node; $h$ represents the number of Gaussian nodes; $\omega_r$ represents the center vector of the $r$ Gaussian node in the hidden layer of the function; $\varphi_r$ represents the actual value of the $r$ Gaussian node in the hidden layer of the function output [13]. Through the above steps, the recognition result of English online education mode can be obtained. The pattern recognition process of online English education based on feature self-learning is shown in Fig. 3.

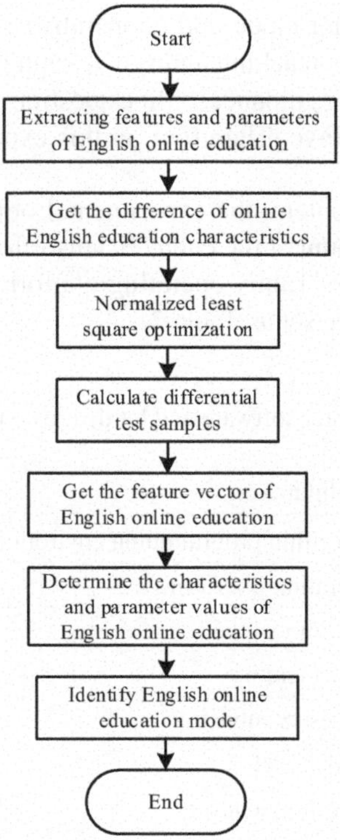


**Fig. 3.** Flow chart of online English education pattern recognition based on feature self-learning

# 3 Experiment and Analysis

In order to verify the pattern recognition method of English online education in this study, a comparative experiment is used to verify the pattern recognition method of English online education in the environment of Ubunt14.04, cuda7.5 and tensorflow. The pattern recognition method of English online education in this study is recorded as experimental group A, and the traditional pattern recognition method of English online education is recorded as experimental group B. This paper determines the formula for calculating the correct rate of pattern recognition type in English online education, and compares two groups of pattern recognition methods from subjective and objective perspectives to identify the effect and correct rate of English online education mode.

## 3.1 Experimental Preparation

Based on this experiment, the online English education courses of a certain platform are divided into four modes: teaching mode based on collective learning, teaching mode based on individual learning, teaching mode based on group learning, and improvement mode based on asynchronous teaching and self-study guidance. Among them, the teaching mode based on collective learning can also be divided into synchronous teaching and asynchronous teaching. The teaching mode based on group learning can also be divided into discussion learning mode and cooperative learning mode. The improved mode combining asynchronous teaching and self-learning guidance can also be divided into courseware learning, online guidance, online question answering, self-learning guidance and learning evaluation Five. Therefore, in this experiment, the above 13 modes were used as the test objects.

According to the above content, the experimental objects, the determined English online education mode, the Ubunt14.04, cuda7.5, tensorflow experimental environment, the Ubuntu 14.04 lts version of Linux operating platform, and the computer software and hardware specifications are set as Table 2.

**Table 2.** Computer software and hardware configuration table

| Experimental environment | Configuration | Configuration instructions |
|---|---|---|
| Software environment | Algorithm programming environment | Method framework |
| | Operating platform | Linux |
| Hardware environment | GPU model | Nvidia GTX 750 |
| | GPU memory | 2 GB |
| | Processor model | Intel(R)Core(TM) |
| | CPU model | i3-2130 |
| | Main frequency | 3.40 GHz |
| | RAM | 64 GB |

Based on this experiment, choose the type of English online education mode, respectively use this experiment, choose three groups of comparison method, verify the research of English online education pattern recognition method.

## 3.2 Experimental Results of the First Group

Based on this experiment, the first group of experiments are carried out to verify the pattern recognition method of English online education and its effect on the pattern recognition of English online education. In order to record the results of the experiment, 13 groups of modes were selected and expressed in letters as follows: teaching mode a based on collective learning, teaching mode B based on individual learning, teaching mode C based on group learning, improved mode D Based on asynchronous teaching and self-study guidance, synchronous teaching A1, asynchronous teaching A2 and discussion learning C1. The experimental results are as Table 3.

It can be seen from Table 3 that the experiment B group only identified 9 English online education modes, and four English online education modes were not recognized; while the experiment A group recognized all 13 groups of English online modes correctly. It can be seen that the pattern recognition method of English online education in this study can identify all the patterns of English online education.

**Table 3.** Comparison of pattern recognition effect in English online education

| Method | Mode | Whether to recognize | Mode | Whether to recognize |
|---|---|---|---|---|
| Experiment group A | a | √ | a1 | √ |
| | b | √ | a2 | √ |
| | c | √ | c1 | √ |
| | d | √ | c2 | √ |
| | – | – | d1 | √ |
| | – | – | d2 | √ |
| | – | – | d3 | √ |
| | – | – | d4 | √ |
| | – | – | d5 | √ |
| Experiment group B | a | √ | a1 | √ |
| | b | √ | a2 | √ |
| | c | √ | c1 | × |
| | d | √ | c2 | × |
| | – | – | d1 | × |
| | – | – | d2 | √ |
| | – | – | d3 | √ |
| | – | – | d4 | × |
| | – | – | d5 | √ |

Note: "√" means to identify the correct English online education model; "×" means to identify the wrong English online education model

### 3.3 Experimental Results of the Second Group

On the basis of the first set of experiments, conduct the second set of experiments. In this group of experiments, the correct rate of pattern recognition in English online education is introduced. Assuming that the number of correct recognition of English online education patterns is $R$, and the total number of tested English online education is $T$, the expression of the correct rate of recognition of English online education patterns is $P$:

$$P = \frac{R}{T} \tag{9}$$

According to the correct rate formula of image recognition shown in formula (9), the results of image recognition and image classification in the first group and the second group of experiments are counted, and three groups of image recognition methods are compared. For the correct rate of image classification recognition results in the test video, the comparison results are as Table 4.

**Table 4.** Image recognition accuracy

| Number of tests | Experimental group A | Experimental group B |
|---|---|---|
| 186 | 98.12% | 96% |
| 168 | 98.92% | 96.84% |
| 114 | 99.8% | 97.39% |
| 117 | 99.8% | 97.62% |
| 138 | 99.95% | 97.69% |
| 117 | 99.86% | 97.63% |
| 120 | 99.7% | 97.68% |
| 183 | 98.6% | 96.52% |
| 189 | 98.1% | 95.01% |

It can be seen from Table 4 that group B is obviously affected by the number of tests. With the increase of the number of tests, the accuracy of pattern recognition in English online education is decreasing. When the number of online English education pattern recognition reaches the maximum, the correct rate of online English education pattern recognition also drops to 95.01%. Experimental group A is less affected by the number of detection, and the accuracy of image classification and recognition is significantly higher than experimental group B. It can be seen that the pattern recognition method of English online education in this study will not be affected by the number of English online education pattern recognition, and the accuracy of English online education pattern recognition is high.

## 4 Conclusion

To sum up, considering the characteristics of e-learning, the research on the pattern recognition method of English online education. Based on the feature self-learning algorithm and convolution neural network, the feature extraction model of online English education is constructed, and the basic features and depth features are extracted. Z-transform is introduced to standardize the feature data set of English online education, and Laplace gradient function is used to eliminate the feature errors and missing data of English online education. so as to improve the stability, universality and accuracy of pattern recognition. The paper infers the important parameters of online English education by using fuzzy logic theory. According to the characteristics and parameters of online English education, the differences of online English education are calculated, and all the modes of online English education can be effectively identified. However, the pattern recognition method of English online education in this study only starts from the characteristics and parameters of English online education, and does not consider the inference error of fuzzy logic theory to determine the optimal convolution times of convolution neural network. Therefore, in the future research, we need to further study the pattern recognition method of English online education, determine the inference error of fuzzy logic theory, and reduce it to the minimum, find the optimal convolution times of convolution neural network, and further improve the accuracy of pattern recognition of English online education. With the rapid development of network technology, the application of online platform in English education and teaching has become an inevitable trend in the future. Online learning has been widely used. Online teaching platform provides English online learning, online testing and other functions. The intelligent test paper generation technology involved in online testing is becoming more and more mature. The method of pattern recognition of English online education in this study can identify all the patterns of English online education, and the accuracy of pattern recognition of English online education is high.

## References


1. Cai, Y., Wang, Z.: The research method of pattern recognition framework based on the distribution. J. Shandong Agric. Univ. (Nat. Sci. Ed.) **51**(2), 266–268 (2020)
2. Chen, L.: Application of artificial intelligence in pattern recognition. Sci. Technol. Innov. Herald **17**(19), 125–127 (2020)
3. Lu, H.: Machine vision pattern recognition method research. Mod. Inf. Technol. **4**(11), 83–85 (2020)
4. Mou, Z., Zhang, Q., Chen, S.: Learning behavior pattern recognition and teaching intervention based on behavior sequence. Mod. Educ. Technol. **30**(5), 74–80 (2020)
5. Guo, H., Zhao, J., Liu, X., et al.: Comprehensive design experiment for pattern recognition based on Python. Exp. Technol. Manage. **36**(8), 178–181 (2019)
6. Xu, X.: Trajectory distribution pattern adaptive recognition simulation based on matching algorithm. Comput. Simul. **36**(11), 410–413,440 (2019)
7. Zhou, B., Xie, G.: Research on key technologies of artificial intelligence in pattern recognition. Mod. Inf. Technol. **3**(22), 110–111 (2019)
8. Liu, H., Hou, S.: Research and practice on bilingual teaching of postgraduate pattern recognition course. J. Anhui Univ. Technol. (Soc. Sci. Ed.) **36**(1), 67–68 (2019)
9. Zhang, Z., Yang, C.: Identifying two refactoring patterns based on hunk and abstract syntax tree. Intell. Comput. Appl. **9**(3), 146–150 (2019)
10. Wang, H., Liu, G., Duan, J., et al.: Transportation mode detection based on self-learning of features. J. Harbin Eng. Univ. **40**(2), 354–358 (2019)
11. Liu, S., Li, Z., Zhang, Y., et al.: Introduction of key problems in long-distance learning and training. Mob. Netw. Appl. **24**(1), 1–4 (2019)
12. Fu, W., Liu, S., Srivastava, G.: Optimization of big data scheduling in social networks. Entropy **21**(9), 902 (2019)
13. Liu, S., Lu, M., Li, H., et al.: Prediction of gene expression patterns with generalized linear regression model. Front. Genet. **10**, 120 (2019)

# Pattern Recognition Method of English Distance Online Education Based on Big Data Algorithm

Xiao-xiao Duan[1](✉) and Ping Duan[2]

[1] International School, Chongqing Vocational Institute of Engineering, Jiangjin 402260, China
[2] Big Data and Internet of Things School, Chongqing Vocational Institute of Engineering, Jiangjin 402260, China

**Abstract.** In order to extract the features of English distance network education pattern, traditional pattern recognition methods of English distance network education result in low accuracy and large standard deviation of education pattern recognition. This paper proposes a pattern recognition method of English distance network education based on big data algorithm. Using big data technology, the digital English distance teaching resource database is established to avoid the duplication of acquired resources, the random forest algorithm of pattern big data is introduced, the single classifier of decision tree is used to distinguish characteristic data, the number of decision trees in the forest is adjusted, and the self construction process of random forest algorithm is optimized. In the process of pattern recognition, feature level state fusion and support vector machine are used to complete pattern recognition of English distance online education. The experimental results show that compared with the traditional algorithm, the standard deviation of the proposed algorithm is smaller, which can effectively improve the recognition accuracy.

**Keywords:** Big data algorithm · English distance online education · Pattern recognition · Random forest algorithm

## 1 Introduction

With the development of network technology, distance education system has gradually become a research hotspot. The purpose of distance education system is to achieve personalized, individualized and efficient teaching mode, which is a kind of broadening and extension of traditional teaching mode. The distance education system breaks through the limitation of time, region and resource sharing for knowledge seekers [1, 2]. However, most researchers focus on how to design personalized learning resources, provide navigation mechanism, diagnose learners' knowledge and skills, and develop effective learning programs. All education models are based on the interaction between learners and distance education system and the data reflected in the system for reasoning and judgment. If learners have correct learning attitude and pay attention in the learning process, then these data can fully reflect the education model of distance network, and


W. Fu et al. (Eds.): eLEOT 2021, LNICST 389, pp. 278–288, 2021.
https://doi.org/10.1007/978-3-030-84383-0_24

the education model recognition results obtained by the learning system based on these data the results are also true and reliable. If the attention is not focused, the result will have a certain deviation. However, the traditional pattern recognition method of English distance online education ignores the judgment of attention, which leads to low recognition accuracy. Therefore, this paper proposes a pattern recognition method of English distance online education based on big data algorithm. Using big data technology, the paper constructs the digital English distance teaching resource base, introduces the random forest algorithm of big data model, uses the single classifier of decision tree to distinguish the characteristic data, adjusts the number of decision trees in the forest, and optimizes the self-construction process of the random forest algorithm. In the process of pattern recognition, the feature level state fusion and support vector machine are used to realize the pattern recognition of English distance online education.

## 2 Pattern Recognition Method of English Distance Online Education Based on Big Data Algorithm

### 2.1 Establish Digital English Distance Teaching Resource Database

Big data technology can accurately capture business English reading resources on the Internet, and provide more diverse and comprehensive teaching resources for digital business English reading teaching. Therefore, this paper will use big data technology to establish digital English reading teaching resource database. Using web crawler technology, according to the key words of business English teaching, using breadth first traversal strategy to crawl resources from the Internet. After crawling, there are many kinds of resources and a large number of resources, and most of them will spread in multiple channels, resulting in the duplication of resources. Therefore, the collected teaching resources need to be processed [3, 4].

Extract metadata from resources for processing. Input the metadata of resources in the storage database, and process the resources according to the metadata. Audit whether the collection resources meet the collection requirements, whether the collection resources are duplicated, and whether the collection resources are missing. Using web resource filtering technology, the resources that do not match the keywords in the collected data are filtered, and the resources that do not match will be deleted directly. For the initial judgment of duplicate teaching resources, identify the resource information in the metadata, and calculate the similarity according to the following formula.

$$p(x, y) = \frac{\sum x_i y_i - n\overline{xy}}{\sqrt{n\sum x_i^2 - \left(\sum x_i\right)^2}\sqrt{n\sum y_i^2 - \left(\sum y_i\right)^2}} \tag{1}$$

In formula (1), $n$ is expressed as a hash function, $\overline{xy}$ represents the average value of resource data, $x_i, y_i$ is the resource data that is preliminarily judged to be repeated, and the resources with high similarity are divided into the same cluster. Use the Bloom filter to sort the metadata of all crawled data, create a $m$ bit array according to the amount of data, and set all the position values in the array to 0. $k$ mutually independent hash functions are respectively mapped to the data in the metadata collection [5, 6]. For any element in the set, the function value of the mapping position corresponding to the hash function will be set to 1. If the hash function values of all positions of the data array in the metadata collection are 1, the data is not duplicated. After filtering the repeated resource data by Bloom algorithm, the text data is normalized according to formula (2) to make the data in the same dimension.

$$x' = \frac{x - \mu}{\sigma} \tag{2}$$

In formula (2), $x$ is the normalization function, $\mu$ is the mean value of all text data, and $\sigma$ is the standard deviation of all data. After the establishment of a digital English reading teaching resource database, according to the requirements of business English teaching, integrated digital teaching methods, and research business English teaching models.

### 2.2 Introduction of Random Forest Algorithm of Big Data Model

Random forest is a combination classifier of multiple decision trees, which can play a better performance and recognition effect in the resource classification of English distance online education. The classifier provides some features of the decision tree, which is the basis of the decision system. The decision tree algorithm mainly produces rules by training classifiers [7, 8]. It is expected that the algorithm can realize a simple data cleaning process in the actual working process of the system, and classify the data sets with different location categories to further realize data mining. Determining the split attributes is the key step of constructing decision tree. Information gain should be taken as the measure in the process of attribute selection. The algorithm selects the attribute with the largest information gain after splitting to complete the main tree splitting.

Random characteristic variables are selected, and some attributes are randomly selected according to a certain probability distribution to participate in the node splitting process. The process of selecting split feature of random forest subtree is as Fig. 1.

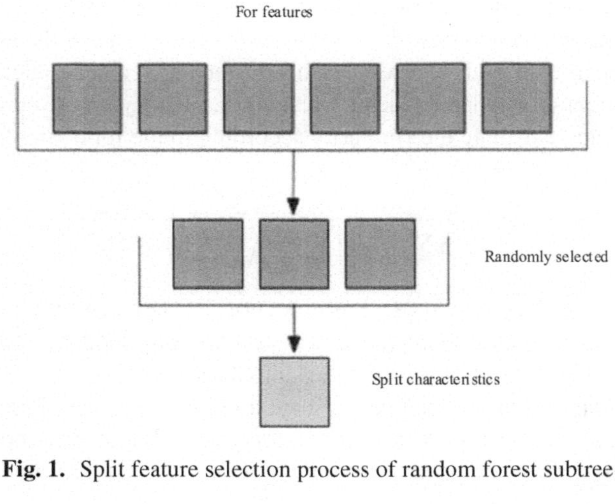


**Fig. 1.** Split feature selection process of random forest subtree

The change of information entropy mainly depends on the information gain to complete the appearance reflection [9], the definition formula of information entropy is:

$$E(X) = P(u_1)I(u_1) + P(u_1)I(u_2) + \ldots \\ + P(u_r)I(u_r) \tag{3}$$

In formula (3), information entropy represents the mathematical expectation of the amount of information contained in the message $u$ after it occurs. $I$ represents the self-information amount of message $u$, and $r$ represents the number of messages, $P$ is the probability of the amount of information. When using the above formula to define information entropy to generate decision tree, the decision tree with smaller depth will be generated, so there will be no bias due to quantity. Under the support of the above algorithm, we need to build a random forest and complete the sampling in the data set. In this process, the random tree generation algorithm can be used to generate different branches of the forest decision system. The pattern recognition classification algorithm and random forest algorithm are combined to adjust the number of decision trees in the forest. By analyzing the construction process of random forest algorithm, the optimization process is completed, the classification accuracy and execution efficiency of different algorithms are verified, and the optimal algorithm is selected.

## 2.3 Extract the Characteristics of English Distance Network Education Mode

In the process of pattern recognition, some big data information needs to be fused. Data level fusion is usually used for multi-source pattern composition, pattern analysis and understanding. In the process of pattern acquisition, multi-source pattern composition is the same period of education mode acquired by different sensors, which has the characteristics of registration, resampling and synthesis. After that, the technology of education pattern recognition results is obtained, simultaneous interpreting the limitations and differences of single sensor education mode in resources, modes and spatial resolution, and improving the recognition accuracy. In the aspect of pattern analysis and understanding, it mainly studies how to deduce the three-dimensional model of the observed scene by using the output of high-resolution scanning collector [10–13]. The fusion technology of data layer includes classical detection and estimation methods. Target state fusion is mainly used in the field of multi-sensor target tracking. Many methods in the field of target tracking can be modified to multi-sensor target tracking. The content of target state information fusion in feature layer is as Fig. 2.

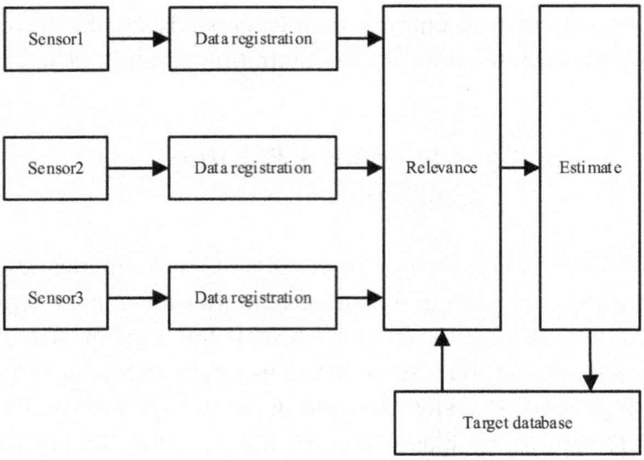


**Fig. 2.** Feature layer state fusion

Pattern recognition module is the core and the most important part of the system. The quality of this part directly affects whether the attention analysis module can be realized, and also directly affects the function of the system. This paper analyzes the characteristics and contents of English distance teaching mode, and under the guidance of Poa theory system, constructs digital English teaching mode by mixing flipped classroom teaching mode. The teaching mode of digital English course constructed in this paper is as Fig. 3.

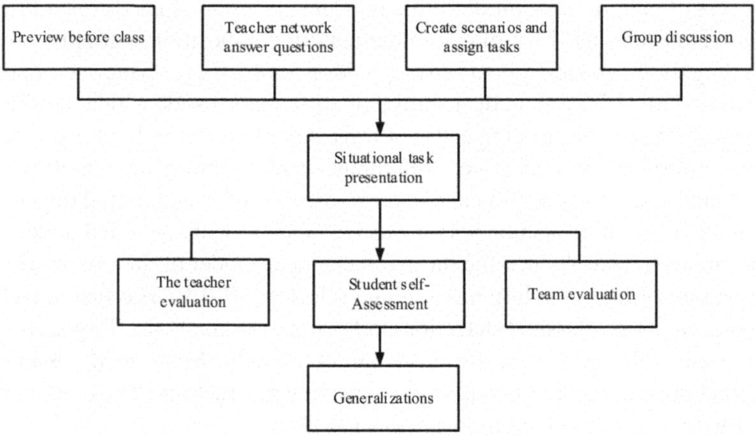


**Fig. 3.** English distance teaching mode

In terms of teaching content, we should flexibly select the real corpus, take the interest as the guidance, select new materials with certain gradients, pay attention to the explicit and implicit embodiment of western culture in English distance education, and update the content module of English.

In the pre class preparation stage, when teachers record English reading online courses, they should classify them reasonably according to the specific content of English reading courses, and each category is a unit. In each unit, it can be divided into 3–4 sections according to the theme, and each section records 8–10 min of relevant videos, text, questions and answers, etc.

In the stage of internalization and absorption of classroom knowledge, we need to adopt task driven teaching method to teach the classroom content, improve students' English reading comprehension ability and the ability to solve the problems they may encounter in their career. After the end of classroom teaching, the teacher counts the students' reading course summary and other information, summarizes the knowledge points and abilities that students should improve, and puts forward corresponding suggestions, so that students can review in time. In all teaching practice, it is advocated to take the student as the center, based on the big data platform of classroom teaching, teachers and students are not only the sender and receiver of information, but also the disseminator of information. Teachers can obtain the first-hand teaching data through the teaching platform, which is not only conducive to students' preview before class, review after class, and be familiar with the key and difficult points in each teaching link, but also conducive to teachers' overall grasp of teaching materials and students, so as to achieve targeted, individualized teaching, and enhance the interest and intelligence of classroom teaching.

## 2.4 Pattern Recognition of English Distance Online Education

For pattern recognition, this paper describes the basic idea of support vector machine. Support vector machine is essentially a non negative quadratic optimization problem, which can obtain the global optimal analytical solution in theory. Support vector machine is a machine learning method based on statistical learning theory. It adopts the principle of structural risk minimization, and has the advantages of small sample, non-linear and "avoiding digit disaster". Support vector machine can be used to solve linear and non-linear problems, and it has good performance in pattern recognition. Its main principle is to find the optimal classification surface to get the results of pattern recognition.

For nonlinear problems, we can also transform them into high-dimensional space by introducing kernel function. The linear support vector machine (LSVM) used in this paper is based on the maximum interval method. The maximum interval method transforms the problem of finding the optimal classification surface into the problem of finding the maximum classification interval. By Lagrange multiplication method and introducing dual function, the optimization problem is transformed into a quadratic linear programming problem, and the features of training samples are extracted. The extracted features are used as the feature vectors of training samples for SVM model training, so as to obtain the training model, namely classification the device. According to the statistical learning theory, if the training sample set is not wrongly separated by the hyperplane, and the distance between the nearest sample data and the hyperplane is the largest, then the hyperplane is the optimal classification hyperplane as Fig. 4.

First determine the number of classifiers, using the SVM algorithm, the goal is to divide the sample into 2 categories, this experiment only needs to train one classifier to determine the feature vector of the training sample. After the feature extraction of the above education mode, the training samples are obtained, and the feature $C_{i,j}$ and resource feature $T_{i,j}$ of the education mode are obtained, as the feature vector $F\left(C_{i,j}, T_{i,j}\right)$

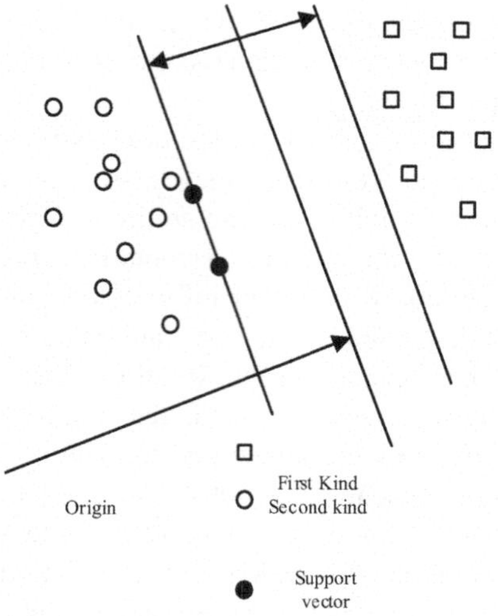


**Fig. 4.** The optimal classification hyperplane

of the training sample, $j$ represents the category, and $i$ represents the $j$ feature point in the $i$ category. The features of each feature point in R, G and B channels are extracted as follows:

$$C_{i,j} = \left(C_{i,j}^{R}, C_{i,j}^{G}, C_{i,j}^{B}\right) \tag{4}$$

The resource characteristics of pixels in energy $E(n)$, entropy $H(n)$, moment of inertia $I(n)$ and correlation $C(n)$ are:

$$T_{i,j} = \left(T_{i,j}^{E}, T_{i,j}^{H}, T_{i,j}^{I}, T_{i,j}^{C}\right) \tag{5}$$

In the training process, use the SVM toolkit that comes with Matlab, and use the following model model = svmtrain (TrainLabel, TrainData) to complete the training. Among them: TrainLabel is the category label, TrainData is the training sample data, and the extracted feature vector $F\left(C_{i,j}, T_{i,j}\right)$, import and perform model training, that is, build a classifier. The penalty parameter $C$ is introduced to implement the penalty for misclassification. In practical applications, some important samples have high requirements for correct classification, and some samples have low requirements for correct classification. Therefore, in the description of the optimization problem, a different penalty coefficient is used for each sampling point data to obtain a more accurate classification. This kind of support vector machine is called a weighted support vector machine, which can be expressed as:

$$\min \frac{1}{2}\|w\|^2 + C\sum_{i=1}^{i} S_i\xi_i \tag{6}$$

In formula (6), $w$ represents the weight, $\xi_i$ represents the number of samples, $S_i$ represents the weighting coefficient, and the weighted support vector machine needs to choose a reasonable $S_i$. The first sample in the sample set has the lowest importance, $S_i$ is set to a value less than 1, and the last sample has the highest importance, $S_i$ is set to 1, and linear interpolation is used to obtain the weighting coefficients of other sample points. $S_i$ has only 2 values, which is determined by the number of samples in each category in the second category. The obtained support vector machine avoids the problem that the classification result of the conventional weighted support vector machine will be biased towards the larger number when the number of categories is not balanced. The above is the recognition of education mode under the background of big data technology studied in this article.

## 3 Simulation Experiment

### 3.1 Design Simulation Experiment

Put the pattern recognition algorithm designed in this paper and the traditional recognition algorithm in the same experimental environment for simulation, and compare the results to verify the reliability of this algorithm. In the experimental platform of this article, the CPU is the Inter(R) Q4800 model, the frequency is 2.66 GHz, the computer memory is 512 GB, the simulation programming environment is Matlab 2016 under Windows10, the classifier uses LibSVM, and the grid search is used. Method for parameter optimization, where the kernel function used is Gaussian kernel:

$$k(x, y) = \exp\left(-\frac{\|x - y\|^2}{2\sigma^2}\right) \tag{7}$$

In formula (7), $\sigma^2$ represents the width of the function. According to the actual situation of this experiment, adjust the value of $\sigma^2$ to 0.64. Establishing distributed multi-sensor detection in the above simulation environment, the state of these sensors sent to the fusion center can be expressed as:

$$\hat{X}_j^i(i = 1, 2, ..., N; j = 1, 2, ..., n_j) \tag{8}$$

In the experimental simulation platform, set the initial parameters of the sensor: In sensor 1, its position coordinate is $(X, Y) = (120\text{ km}, 120\text{ km})$, the observation radius $r_1$ is 100 km, the ranging error $\sigma_{l_1}$ is 150 m, the angle measurement error $\sigma_{\theta_1}$ is 1°, and in sensor 2, its position coordinate is $(X, Y) = (140\text{ km}, 140\text{ km})$, the observation radius $r_2$ is 80 km, the ranging error $\sigma_{l_2}$ is 120 m, and the angle measurement error $\sigma_{\theta_1}$ is 1°. In the simulation experiment, five datasets of wine, forest, glass, iris and segmentation are used for recognition in UCI standard database. The basic information of datasets is as Table 1.

**Table 1.** Basic information of the data set

| Data set | Sample input dimension | Number of training samples | Number of test samples | Number of identifications |
|---|---|---|---|---|
| Wine | 24 | 133 | 133 | 4 |
| Forest | 47 | 247 | 317 | 7 |
| Glass | 18 | 159 | 114 | 2 |
| Iris | 11 | 121 | 84 | 3 |
| Segmentation | 37 | 331 | 3310 | 5 |

In the above five authoritative data sets, the algorithm designed in this paper and the traditional algorithm are respectively used to run 50 times, and the mean and standard deviation of the two algorithms are calculated.

### 3.2 Experimental Results and Comparison

In the above experimental process, the recognition accuracy of the two algorithms is counted as Table 2.

**Table 2.** Comparison of recognition accuracy of two algorithms

| Recognition pattern classification based on different algorithms | | Number of correct samples | Total samples | Recognition accuracy |
|---|---|---|---|---|
| Traditional algorithm | Wine | 107 | 133 | 80.4% |
| | Forest | 271 | 317 | 85.5% |
| | Glass | 87 | 114 | 76.3% |
| | Iris | 62 | 84 | 73.8% |
| | Segmentation | 2417 | 3310 | 73.0% |
| The algorithm in this paper | Wine | 128 | 133 | 96.2% |
| | Forest | 287 | 317 | 90.5% |
| | Glass | 107 | 114 | 93.9% |
| | Iris | 77 | 84 | 91.7% |
| | Segmentation | 3064 | 3310 | 92.6% |

The statistical results of the standard deviation of the five data sets of the two algorithms in the experiment are as Table 3.

**Table 3.** Comparison of standard deviation results of two algorithms

| Data set | Traditional algorithm | The algorithm in this paper |
|---|---|---|
| Wine | 0.084 | 0.051 |
| Forest | 0.087 | 0.071 |
| Glass | 0.109 | 0.066 |
| Iris | 0.036 | 0.067 |
| Segmentation | 0.071 | 0.059 |

From the experimental results in Table 2 and Table 3 above, it can be seen that for the recognition results of the same data set, the average accuracy of the traditional algorithm is 77.8%, and the average accuracy of this algorithm is 93.0%. The average standard deviation of the algorithm in this paper is 0.063 in the experiment, while the average standard deviation of traditional algorithm in the experiment is 0.077. The recognition standard deviation of this algorithm in the experiment is also smaller than that of the traditional algorithm, and it is relatively stable. Therefore, it can be concluded that the recognition accuracy of this algorithm is higher than that of the traditional algorithm high. In conclusion, the algorithm can effectively reduce the standard deviation of English distance education pattern recognition and improve the accuracy of the pattern recognition.

## 4 Conclusion

Pattern recognition technology has been developed rapidly in recent years. At the same time, pattern recognition technology is also a subject with scientific research and application prospects. With the efforts of researchers, pattern recognition technology has been applied in many industries. This paper analyzes the common problems of distance education system, and proposes a pattern recognition method of English distance education based on big data algorithm. That is to say, pattern recognition technology is applied to process the learner's head image captured by the camera to identify the degree of eye deviation in the learner's head image. Fuzzy set and probability theory are used to analyze the learner's attention and give necessary tips. To a certain extent, the system makes up for the shortcomings of the existing distance teaching system. The image processing technology such as Gaussian smoothing and binary is used to preprocess, which reduces the standard deviation of pattern recognition. The recognition of educational pattern is finished by using SUSAN operator algorithm and fuzzy set theory, so as to improve the recognition accuracy.

## References

1. Chen, X.C., Ding, P., Yan, N.Q., et al.: Study on discrete manufacturing quality control technology based on big data and pattern recognition. Math. Probl. Eng. **5**, 1–10 (2021)

2. Su, G.: Analysis of optimisation method for online education data mining based on big data assessment technology. Int. J. Contin. Eng. Educ. Life-Long Learn. **29**(4), 321–335 (2019)
3. Yang, H., Liu, J., Zhang, M.: Face recognition algorithm based on orthogonal gradient difference local directional pattern. Laser Optoelectron. Prog. **55**(4), 150–156 (2018)
4. Wang, S., Xue, J., Hu, H., et al.: Pattern recognition of partial discharge based on the feature parameter optimization selection and multi-algorithm combined methods. High Volt. Appar. **54**(10), 112–119 (2018)
5. Geng, C., Zhang, J., Guan, L.: A recommendation method of teaching resources based on similarity and ALS. J. Phys. Conf. Ser. **1865**(4), 042043 (8pp) (2021)
6. Xing, Z., Li, G.: Intelligent classification method of remote sensing image based on big data in spark environment. Int. J. Wirel. Inf. Netw. **26**(3), 183–192 (2019). https://doi.org/10.1007/s10776-019-00440-z
7. Yuan, S.: Research on pattern recognition of laser fluorescence spectrum data in big data background. Laser J. **39**(05), 124–127 (2018)
8. Zhao, J., Liu, Y.: Research on big data technology in computer network intrusion detection. J. Netw. New Media **7**(04), 45–49 (2018)
9. Song, M., Wang, D., Zhang, S., et al.: Flatness pattern recognition model based on recurrent neural network. Iron Steel **53**(11), 56–62 (2018)
10. Liang, Z., Lin, D., Huang, R.: New cloud security management model based on big data and cloud computing. Autom. Instrum. **2018**(07), 189–191+196
11. Fu, W., Liu, S., Srivastava, G.: Optimization of big data scheduling in social networks. Entropy **21**(9), 902 (2019)
12. Liu, S., Bai, W., Zeng, N., et al.: A fast fractal based compression for MRI images. IEEE Access **7**, 62412–62420 (2019)
13. Liu, S., Liu, D., Srivastava, G., et al.: Overview and methods of correlation filter algorithms in object tracking. Complex Intell. Syst. (3), 2580–2583 (2020). https://doi.org/10.1007/s40747-020-00161-4

# Big Data Based Human Resources Professional Distance Training Platform

Cai-ming Zhang(✉) and Li Liu

School of Labor Relations and Human Resource, China University of Labor Relations, Beijing 100048, China

**Abstract.** At present, the platform of human resources professional distance training and education, in the use of the process of training and education data, resulting in the platform response speed is slow, users wait for a long time, this paper proposed a big data-based platform of human resources professional distance training and education. Based on the functional characteristics of the big data platform, determine the functional modules of the platform and design the platform framework in consideration of the needs of the human resources profession for the distance training and education platform; deploy the network structure of the platform based on the intranet and extranet environment of the human resources profession; make full use of the big data platform to collect the data of the human resources professional training and education, and process the collected data; establish a platform database to store the information of the human resources professional training and education, and design the unified operation process of the database by considering the use needs of the database throughout the platform. The results show that the platform can automatically adjust the throughput of the platform, reduce the average request waiting time and improve the response speed of the platform according to the concurrency.

**Keywords:** Big data · Human resources specialty · Distance training · Education platform

## 1 Introduction

Human resources are the core resources of enterprises, the degree of human resources development and use determines the strength of enterprise competitiveness [1]. But the university, has the human resources specialized, provides the specialized human resources talented person for the enterprise. Therefore, human resources training and education is particularly important. A sound and scientific human resources training education can better capture the market dynamics and development trajectory, so that human resources training is strategic, forward-looking, effective and targeted. Therefore, providing excellent human resources talents for enterprises has become one of the core topics of human resources professional research [2, 3]. The theoretical research on professional training of human resources in foreign countries has entered a comprehensive


W. Fu et al. (Eds.): eLEOT 2021, LNICST 389, pp. 289–300, 2021.
https://doi.org/10.1007/978-3-030-84383-0_25

and systematic development stage. Some scholars put forward the development, application and evaluation of training and the theory of "learning organization" according to the risk of education and training, and completely updated the training concept. The training and education contents shall focus on improving the learning motivation, perseverance and ability of the students majoring in human resources, realize the transformation from "stage training" to life-long training, and realize the transformation from "imparting knowledge and skills" to "improving learning ability", so as to make the organization adapt to the market environment of development and change [4, 5]. In recent years, many human resources experts and scholars in China have made beneficial research and exploration on the theory of human resources training in Chinese enterprises by combining foreign training theories and practical experience with the actual situation of domestic enterprises. Some scholars point out that the training and education of human resources major should drive the formation and maintenance of core competencies of human resources major and accelerate the formation of core expertise and skills of human resources major students through the integration of human resources major [6, 7]. But in the above research, there are some problems, such as inconvenient use and high training cost. Therefore, a big data-based distance training platform for human resources is proposed. Based on the big data platform, the human resources professional distance training and education platform is divided into six modules, which are regulation management, human resources skill assessment management, online theory assessment management, training resource management, statistical analysis and training effect evaluation. The framework is client, application service, business service, application support, resource service, application support and training effect evaluation Data and support seven parts. The designed platform architecture enables the platform to connect users of different devices and locations through network communication protocol. It realizes that all users of the platform can be connected under any network, avoids space limitation, and solves the network problem when the number of network concurrent increases. Offline data collection and preprocessing, data cleaning, transmission to the database server, to achieve efficient human resources professional remote training.

## 2 Big Data Based Human Resources Professional Distance Training and Education Platform

### 2.1 Identify Platform Functional Modules

The design of professional distance training and education platform for human resources, in the overall framework of the platform design, taking into account big data platform features and timeliness [8]. Big data platform will be used as the technical support for the design of professional distance training and education platform for human resources professional distance training and education platform, provide good training environment and training resources.

Therefore, according to the needs of resources, management mode and training effect, the platform is divided into six modules: regulation management, human resource skill assessment management, online theory assessment management, training resource management, statistical analysis and training effect evaluation. Provide a good environment for human resources professional training and education, provide a good learning environment for human resources professional students, and form a good communication environment between lecturers and employees, improve the closeness of lecturers and employees, and enhance the learning effect of human resources professional students. Therefore, the identified professional training and education platform for human resources functional modules, as shown in Fig. 1.

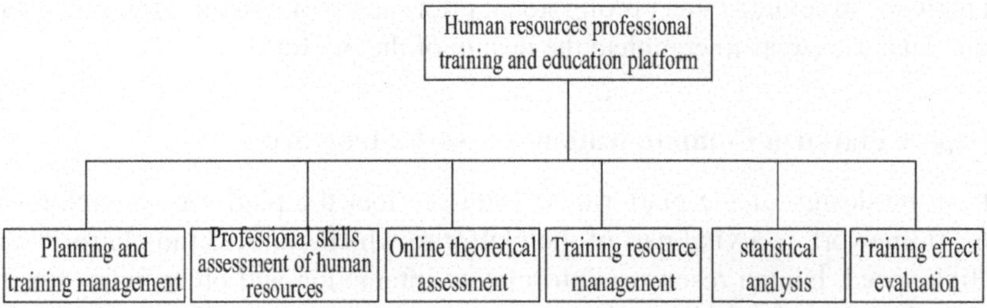


**Fig. 1.** Human resources professional training and education platform functional modules

From the function module of the platform, we can see that based on the six function modules, we can design the overall framework of the platform.

## 2.2 Design Platform Framework

The framework of the platform is divided into seven parts, namely, client, application service, business service, application support, resource service, data and support. The seven parts are independent of each other and support each other, and correspond to the functional modules determined in the platform.

The design of the client layer, that is, users use mobile phones, computers and other clients, to help users log in to confirm user identity. In the use of the process, by the training lecturer, choose the training content, determine the training method, through the training platform has the resources to complete the training of human resources students.

Specifically, the business online service providing layer, corresponding to the four functional modules of regulation management, human resources professional skills assessment management, online theoretical assessment management and statistical analysis, is the main management module of the platform; while the attendance information statistics included in the statistical analysis module needs to be counted through the application layer and identity identification function; the resource service layer corresponds to the training resource management functional module, management training lecturers and trainees, and all the professional training materials of human resources needed in the training process; the application support layer is the layer providing support for the business online service, such as examination practice and other examination contents, are stored in this layer; and the reflection evaluation at the application layer corresponds to the training effect evaluation, and is also the last step that the training lecturer needs to use in the use of the training distance training platform of human resources. Thus, the design of the human resources professional distance training platform, the design of the seven plates, each plate can be for human resources professional distance training and education work, provide good use of results.

However, the main frame of the platform is the support layer, which has the network communication protocol to maintain the operation of the platform. Once the network communication protocol collapses, it will directly cause the platform to stop running. Thus we can see the importance of the support layer in the distance training platform of human resources specialty.

Based on the design, as shown in Fig. 1, we need to deploy the platform communication network structure, collect professional information of human resources, establish platform database, so as to complete the design of the platform.

### 2.3 Deploy Platform Communication Network Structure

Based on the design of the platform, we can see that the platform's communication network framework is a vital part of the platform, which controls the platform's operation, link speed, human resources information interaction and other major functions. Therefore, based on the design of human resources professional distance training education platform framework, the network structure of the platform is divided into two parts: external network and internal network, and the platform content is received by the special router and processor of the university.

Because the platform framework designed in this paper enables the platform to connect users of different devices and locations through network communication protocols, the platform communication network structure deployed in this time can receive all network signals, and network communication network protocols edited by routers can convert network signals, and under any network, all users of the platform can be connected to avoid space restrictions. Moreover this kind of network deployment way, has avoided the platform user to increase effectively, creates the concurrent quantity to increase, produces the network carton question. Let the information on the platform to receive, transmission, more flexible, fast, stable and reliable.

Ethernet represents the Internet outside the human resources profession, through which the human resources professional distance training and education platform and the internal network need to be connected, and the signal is transmitted to the terminal, making full use of the high-speed, security, cost-effective advantages of the Internet itself. In the process of network use, it is also divided into three modules to meet the different levels of human resources training needs. Finally, the distributed network of professional distance training platform of human resources is formed, which makes the platform have certain expansibility, flexibility and compatibility.

The deployed platform communication network framework is divided into three layers: user access layer, functional application layer and data resource layer when it is applied to human resources professional distance training platform. Among them, the user access layer is the interface that connects with the outside world when the platform is running, such as the Internet, each client of the human resources profession, etc.; the function application layer is the main application layer of the platform, which needs to adopt the Web server, call the data in the database server, and pass the data through the server for processing, and finally pass the information to the users through the Web server. In addition, the user access layer can add new computers, increase the number of users' visits, improve the amount of bursts of the platform, increase the throughput of the application program, and avoid the Karton problem that may occur during the operation of the platform; in the data resource layer, all the training and education materials and information of the human resources profession are included, and it is necessary to collect and process the training and education data of the human resources profession, establish the database, meet the needs of the distance training and education platform of the human resources profession and the training materials.

## 2.4 Processing of Training and Education Data Based on Big Data

Based on the communication network application platform architecture shown in Fig. 4, consider the wide range of human resources specialties and complex data types [9]. Therefore, the big data platform, in the data resources layer, the collection and processing of human resources professional training education data, the data collection and processing process, as shown in Fig. 2.

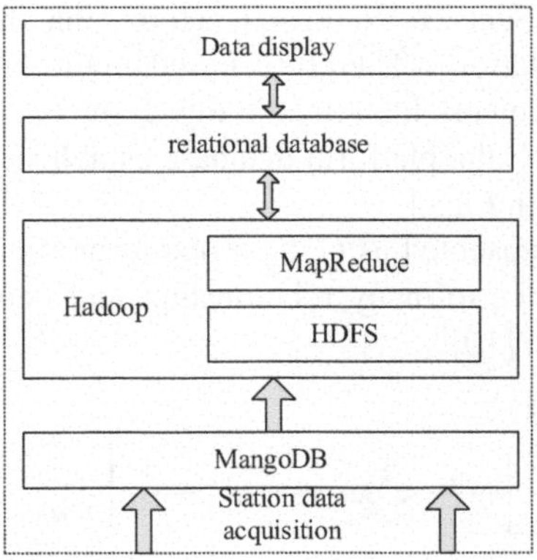


**Fig. 2.** Data acquisition and processing flow

As can be seen from Fig. 5, the big data platform used to collect human resources professional training and education data needs to collect from the human resources professional data side, and save the data to the big data platform of the Hadoop framework HDFS for subsequent processing and analysis. The big data processing framework carries on the preliminary statistical analysis operation to the collected data, and saves the operation result to the relational database to carry on the transaction operation and the statistical analysis.

In addition, there are some off-line data collection, data cleaning, data conversion will be saved to the big data platform Hadoop for subsequent processing and analysis.

We can find that there is a special data transmission structure in the data acquisition and processing process designed with big data platform, as shown in Fig. 3. Only when the collected and processed data are transferred according to the data transmission structure shown in Fig. 3, can the training and education data be transferred to the client for use by users.

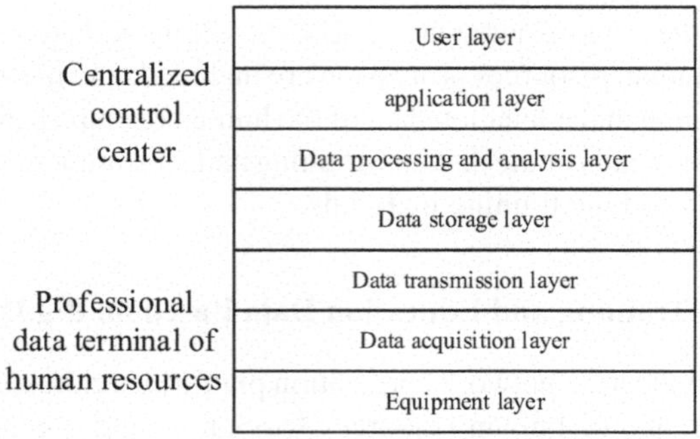


**Fig. 3.** Data transmission structure

## 2.5 Establishment of Platform Database

Combining the contents of Sects. 1.3 and 1.4, it is found that the database occupies a very important position in the platform. Therefore, based on the database functions identified in Fig. 1, the database framework identified in Fig. 2, the database network applications identified in Fig. 4, Layer 4, the platform database established for the primary purpose of database use, as shown in Fig. 4.

In Fig. 4, 1 can be represented as (1:1), a one-to-one relationship; 1 and $n$ can be represented as $(1 : n)$, a one-to-many relationship; and between $m$ and $n$, $(m : n)$, a many-to-many relationship [10].

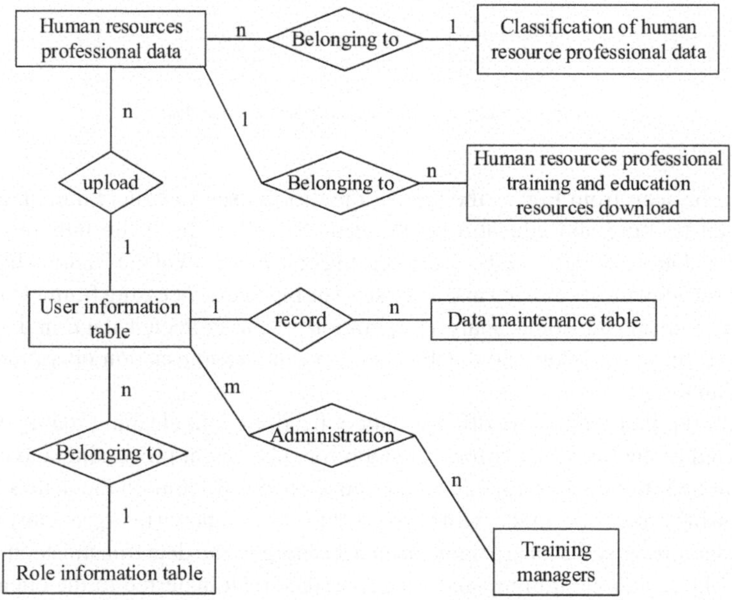


**Fig. 4.** Platform database E-R diagram

Based on the platform database E-R diagram shown in Fig. 4 and the database server identified as MySQL 5.7 server, the database will be managed using Microsoft SQL Server 2005 software. To this end, in the process of establishing the platform database, the size of the database is adjusted to an adjustable mode to facilitate the later addition of information and the expansion of the database; when the information in the database is used, it needs to be read out of the database and released immediately after it is used.

Therefore, the operation mode of the database is extracted separately, and the SQL-Help class structure is adopted to uniformly operate the database. The operation process is shown in Fig. 5.

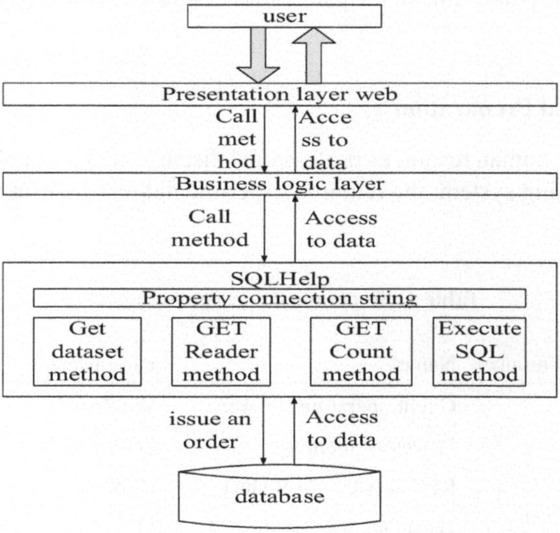


**Fig. 5.** Unified database operations

As can be seen from Fig. 5, the uniform operation procedure of the database designed this time is to, when a user performs certain operation, respond to the operation procedure of the user through the surface layer, judge whether the data manipulated by the user needs data processing, and if the data processing is needed, then call the method of the business logic layer, and pass in the data processing information, the sql operation parameters, the methods of SQLHelp classes such as Get DataSet, Get Reader, Get Count, SQL, etc., pass in the sql operation parameters, and determine the SQLHelp class operation methods needed by the user, process the data. After the data processing operation is finished, the data processing execution results will be returned to the logical structure layer, and then returned to the presentation layer by the logical structure layer, and finally returned to the user by the presentation layer, so as to complete the call of the data in the database.

## 3 Platform Testing

Verify the design of the human resources professional distance training education platform, using mobile client, using Windows 9 to operate the design of human resources professional distance training education platform. And the design of the human resources professional distance training and education platform, recorded as a platform, the two traditional human resources professional distance training and education platform, recorded as B platform and C platform. According to the operating characteristics of the platform, taking the operating effect of the platform as the experimental direction, the operating environment of the platform is determined, the concurrent volume of the system is changed, and the response time of the platform is compared with that of the three groups of platforms.

### 3.1 Experimental Preparation

The verification of human resources professional distance education platform, using the Windows 9 operating system, the required experimental test environment, as shown in Table 1.

**Table 1.** Experimental test environment

| Serial number | Name | Parameters |
|---|---|---|
| 1 | Client operating software | Windows9 |
| 2 | Processor memory | 8G |
| 3 | RPC service governance | Dubbo |
| 4 | Hard disk processor | IT |
| 5 | Client CPU | Intel Core i5-3230m |
| 6 | Registration centre | Z00Keeper |
| 7 | Client memory | 4G |
| 8 | Process CPU | Intel Core i5-5200u |
| 9 | Client hard disk | 500 GB |
| 10 | Processor operating software | Linux (centOS6.7) |
| 11 | Processor database | MySQL 5.7 |

Based on the experimental test environment of HR professional distance training and education platform shown in Table 1, professional platform testers will test the platform during the test. In the process of testing, the main functions of the platform are as follows: (1) Testing the login interface of the platform to test the login speed, identity recognition and other functions; (2) Testing the link of the webpage to test the connection speed between the various sections of the webpage; (3) Testing the webpage to test that the webpage is connected through the buttons, and the correctness, sensitivity and explanation of each button position affect the overall use effect of the platform. Therefore, the testing of the buttons occupies a major position in the use effect of the platform; (4) Checking the information entry interface, and the security and completeness of the information entry interface determines the training and inspection effect of the training system for human resources professional trainers. First, it avoids the information leakage of human resources professional trainers, and second, it avoids the evasion of training by human resources professional trainers. Therefore, when testing the human resources professional remote training and education platform, it is necessary to repeatedly check the information entry interface to determine the completeness of the information entry interface and the items that must be filled in; and (5) Checking interface of the webpage, which is the main embodiment of the platform for human resources professional remote training, therefore, it is necessary to carefully check the display effect of the interface, the effect of labeling, the typeface size, the.

From the aspects of training manual management, teaching activity management, evaluation management function, examination management function, examination paper management function, exercise management function, personnel information statistics function, achievement statistics, evaluation information statistics, attendance management statistics, teaching activity information statistics, etc., 5000 test cases of the platform for distance training and education of human resources specialty are designed, and the generated parallel quantities can be divided into five grades, such as 1, 50, 100, 500 and 1000, and can be used as the test objects of the experiment.

The human resources professional distance training platform test, choose Apache software AB test tools, test the three test platform, the test experiment, the use of testing tools, the instructions, as shown in Fig. 6.

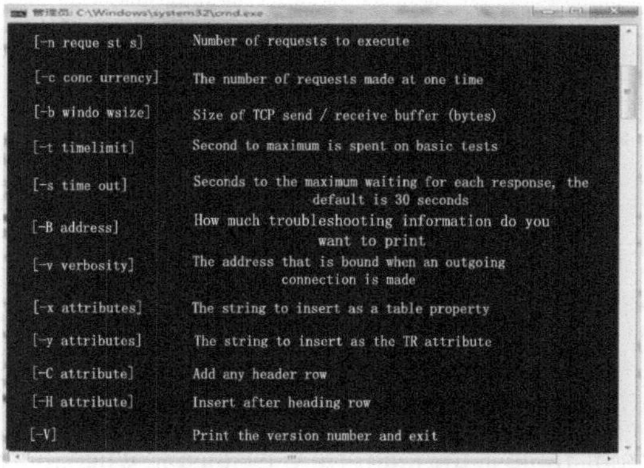


**Fig. 6.** Instructions for using the AB test tool

At this time, we can design three groups of platform contrast experiments to test the actual use of three groups of platform. In the test process, select a city university human resources professional teachers and students, as the test object of the platform.

### 3.2 Results of the First Set of Experiments

Based on this experiment, the designed experimental environment and method, using the AB test tool in Apache software, test three groups of platforms, in the experimental test environment as shown in Table 1, test the parallel quantities of five grades, such as 1, 50, 100, 500 and 1000, compare the throughput rate, average request waiting time of users, average request waiting time of servers and number of request errors on the distance training and education platform for human resources professionals, the test results are as shown in Table 2.

**Table 2.** Test case test platform comparison results

| Platform | Parallel quantities | Rate of throughput | Average user request waiting time | Average server request waiting time | Number of requests for errors |
|---|---|---|---|---|---|
| C Platform | 1 | 30 bps/s | 20 ms | 20 ms | 0 |
| | 50 | 756 bps/s | 69 ms | 6 ms | 0 |
| | 100 | 917 bps/s | 137 ms | 3.48 ms | 2 |
| | 500 | 198 bps/s | 1986 ms | 5.79 ms | 1 |
| | 1000 | 296 bps/s | 1978 ms | 3.96 ms | 1 |
| B Platform | 1 | 34.56 bps/s | 20 ms | 20 ms | 0 |
| | 50 | 857 bps/s | 87 ms | 8.11 ms | 1 |
| | 100 | 943 bps/s | 167 ms | 2.91 ms | 2 |
| | 500 | 195 bps/s | 1194 ms | 5.85 ms | 4 |
| | 1000 | 496 bps/s | 2018 ms | 4.87 ms | 7 |
| A Platform | 1 | 50 bps/s | 20 ms | 20 ms | 0 |
| | 50 | 1000 bps/s | 50 ms | 1 ms | 0 |
| | 100 | 1030 bps/s | 97 ms | 0.97 ms | 0 |
| | 500 | 488 bps/s | 1023 ms | 2.046 m/s | 0 |
| | 1000 | 545 bps/s | 1832 ms | 1.832 m/s | 0 |

As can be seen from Table 2, the platform C isism, and when there are age number of access users on the platform, the concurrent relatively large and the concurrency generated will small, and the average request waiting time of users, the average request waiting contrary; the platform B is only suitable for small parallelism, and when thereumber of access users, request errors will occur, which will affect the usnly the platform A, no matter how much the concurrency is increased, the number of request errors will always be 0, andoughput generated will be automatically adjusted according to the actual situation, so.

Therefore, the platform can support all the teachers and students to visit, and during the visit, it can automatically adjust the throughput, avoid the Karton phenomenon of the platform, improve the operating efficiency of the server, reduce the waiting time of the users, and improve the overall use effect of the platform.

## 4 Closing Remarks

To sum up, this design of human resources professional distance training education platform, make full use of big data platform, data processing ability, design a simple, efficient, comprehensive resources of human resources professional distance training education platform. However, the design of distance training platform for human resources professionals did not consider the training and education, the need for data evaluation model for training human resources professionals, the performance of evaluation, and in terms of the security performance of the platform, has not been studied and described. Therefore, in the future research, there is still a need for in-depth study, human resources professional distance training platform, human resources professional trainers performance evaluation, platform privacy protect the efficiency of the use and management of the platform and encryption protection of sensitive information.

**Fund Projects.** Funding of China National Social Science: Research on the knowledge-based evolution, organization pattern and its influence on decision innovation of Big data (No. 15BJY022), Funding of Researching Projects from China University of Labor Relations (No. 15YY006, No. JGZX1404, No. ZYTS201806).

## References

1. Gong, H.: How to implement enterprise human resources standardization management in the new era. Value Eng. **39**(3), 81–82 (2020)
2. Xiang, J.: Analysis of the professional development of human resource managers in universities. jiaoyu jiaoxue luntan (37), 7–8 (2020)
3. Chen, X.: A research on situational teaching in dual-innovation courses for human resource management majors in vocational colleges. J. Zhangzhou Tech. Inst. **22**(2), 17–21 (2020)
4. Li, Z.: Research on human resources training and incentive mechanism of civil aviation flight attendants. Value Eng. **39**(11), 58–60 (2020)
5. Shi, T.: Construction of human resources training management system for logistics enterprises in big data era. Logist. Technol. **39**(5), 38–40 (2020)
6. Yang, Y.: Current situation and the optimal path of human resource training and development in provincial agricultural scientific research institutes. J. Anhui Agric. Sci. **48**(17), 253–255 (2020)
7. Liu, S., Bai, W., Zeng, N., et al.: A fast fractal based compression for MRI images. IEEE Access **7**, 62412–62420 (2019)
8. Sun, Y.: A study of the application of the center for teaching and learning development in logistics human resource training system in colleges and universities. J. Zhejiang Bus. Technol. Inst. **18**(2), 74–76 (2019)
9. Li, Z.: Hierarchical storage simulation of public resources big data in cloud storage environment. Comput. Simul. **36**(10), 383–386,404 (2019)
10. Jiang, R.: Design and implementation of human resource system based on C#. Comput. Knowl. Technol. **16**(2), 51–53 (2020)

11. Liu, S., Li, Z., Zhang, Y., et al.: Introduction of key problems in long-distance learning and training. Mob. Netw. Appl. **24**(1), 1–4 (2019)
12. Vincenti, G., Bucciero, A., Helfert, M., Glowatz, M. (eds.): e-Learning, e-Education, and Online Training. LNICSSITE, vol. 180. Springer, Cham (2017). https://doi.org/10.1007/978-3-319-49625-2
13. Xiao, M.: Research on higher vocational teacher training system from the perspective of human resource management theory. J. Chang. Telecommun. Technol. Vocat. Coll. **19**(3), 62–65 (2020)

# Design of Personalized Employment Guidance System for College Students Based on Big Data

Mei-bin Qi[1] and Yu-juan Zhang[2](✉)

[1] Admission and Employment Office, Dongying Vocational Institute, Dongying 257090, China
[2] Xinyu University, Xinyu 338004, Jiangxi, China
hbdsfisdf545@sohu.com, zhangyujuan4546@sina.com

**Abstract.** In view of the traditional system using personality test for employment guidance, which leads to one-sided guidance results, outdated system design architecture and low operation efficiency, this paper designs a personalized employment guidance system for college students based on big data. After designing the system hardware to collect the information of students' employment environment, the system framework is designed based on B/S structure. Tptmf algorithm is used to recommend employment resources for users. After analyzing the system requirements, the database is designed to realize the system functions. The simulation results show that the response time of employment guidance system using big data is short, and the highest server occupation is only 11%, which is feasible.

**Keywords:** Big data · College students' employment · Personalized employment guidance · System design

## 1 Introduction

With the deepening of the popularization of higher education and the continuous optimization of the labor and personnel system in China, how to ensure the employment rate and employment quality of college students after graduation has become one of the common concerns of major universities. In addition to giving students high-quality professional education, comprehensive employment guidance is also essential. The difficulty of College Students' employment is one of the main contradictions in the domestic labor market at present. It is the common responsibility of students, schools and society to help college students achieve successful employment to the maximum extent. Compared with those who have work experience, college graduates are obviously weak in job hunting. First of all, fresh graduates lack professional quality, which is manifested in their lack of work experience, unclear career goals, and unclear what they will do and want to do. As a result, they are at a loss in front of many positions. Secondly, there are some problems in college students' values on employment. In terms of job-hunting attitude, they are either arrogant and rude, or pessimistic, passive and unwilling to bear hardships. Thirdly, college students lack the necessary skills of application and interview. It is not difficult to see from the interview occasions and job fairs that the effectiveness


W. Fu et al. (Eds.): eLEOT 2021, LNICST 389, pp. 301–310, 2021.
https://doi.org/10.1007/978-3-030-84383-0_26

of the interactive communication between them and employers is poor. The traditional employment guidance system has no scientific classification system because of its complicated employment information and lack of classification characteristics [1, 2]. But the current employment situation is grim, how to grasp the accurate information in an effective time, has become a major problem for graduates. In addition, the whole picture of employment situation is not enough in the guidance system, and the lack of statistical information leads to students' wrong judgment of their own employment expectations, and the employment situation is not ideal.

Colleges and universities have employment guidance centers to provide relevant services for students. With the rapid development of the Internet, a lot of education and guidance work has begun to be carried out on the Internet, serving students, teachers and schools [3]. In the Internet era, the rise and application of big data provides an opportunity to provide personalized guidance for college students' employment. The role of big data is to predict. At present, big data has been widely used in various fields of politics, commerce and society. As a frontier, colleges and universities can provide personalized employment guidance for college students by using the advanced technology of big data. After designing the system hardware to collect students' employment environment information, the system framework is designed based on the B/S structure. The Tptmf algorithm is used to recommend employment resources for users. After analyzing the system requirements, design the database to realize the system functions. In this paper, through the research on this topic, we hope to provide ideas for colleges and universities in using big data for personalized employment of college students, and make contributions to solve the problem of difficult employment of college students.

## 2 Hardware Design of Personalized Employment Guidance System for College Students Based on Big Data

The hardware design of student employment personalized guidance system mainly uses big data analysis module and student employment operation environment module for data collection, to get the information of student employment operation environment and network environment, and then carries out real-time information transmission control on the collected information of student employment operation environment. The structure of the hardware part of the guidance system is shown in Fig. 1 [4].

This paper uses the technology of student employment operation environment to collect the information collection module of student employment. At the information collection end, an electronic tag card is loaded on the interactive information terminal of each student employment guidance. In addition to the above collection part, in order to enhance the comprehensiveness of the collected information, radio frequency technology is used to identify the identity information of students, so as to obtain more detailed employment information of students. In order to reduce the energy consumption of the system, the mc9s08ac60 chip is selected as the data acquisition module. The chip has 8-bit hcs08 central processing unit (CPU), CPU clock is 40 MHz, internal bus frequency is 20 MHz, support HC08 instruction set and bgnd instruction; memory is equipped with 60kb on-chip flash memory, 2 KB on-chip RAM; optional clock source includes crystal oscillator, resonator, external clock or internally generated clock, through ICG module

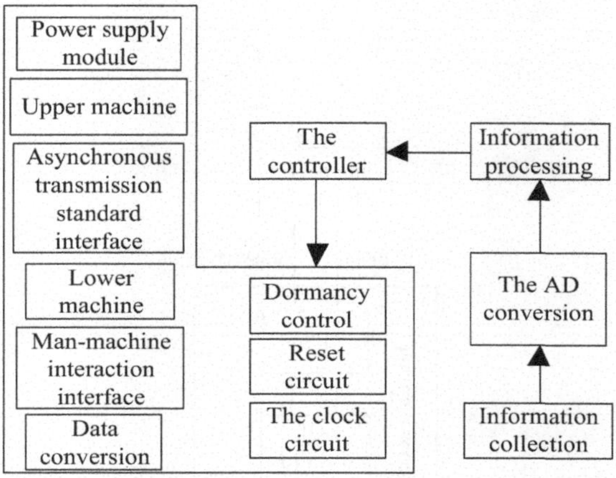


**Fig. 1.** Hardware architecture of personalized employment guidance system

for precision NVM adjustment [5]. The chip supports background debugging system, has breakpoint function, and allows single breakpoint setting in the process of online debugging (adding two breakpoints to the on-chip debugging module); the on-chip online simulation (ice) debugging module includes two comparators, nine trigger modes, eight depth FIFOs, and two control modes, Storage stream changes address and pure event data, supports label and forced breakpoint, and supports up to 32 interrupt/reset sources. The CRC unit supports fast cyclic redundancy check for memory. The main reset pin and power on reset (POR) · reset, IRQ and bkgd/MS pins of the chip have internal pull-up devices to reduce the system cost of customers. Fm1722 chip is used to read student identity information. The chip adopts 0.6 μm CMOS EEPROM process, supports type A/type B contactless communication protocol at 13.56 MHz frequency, iso15693 protocol, Mifare icode 1 and various encryption algorithms. Communication with other modules through serial port [6–8]. In the data processing module, the characteristics of students' employment status information are analyzed through the buffer, and the remote transmission control of personalized employment guidance information is carried out in the upper computer module.

Based on the hardware part of the system designed above, the software part of the system is designed by using big data technology to provide system function support.

# 3 Software Design of Personalized Employment Guidance System for College Students Based on Big Data

## 3.1 System Framework Design

The personalized employment guidance system for college students will use B/S structure to construct the system. Because B/S structure can operate in any place without installing specific software, the design of the system will adopt B/S structure, combine Internet and Intranet, take asenet as the platform, and realize data storage and call by connecting SQL Server database in the background. The system structure is shown in Fig. 2 [9].

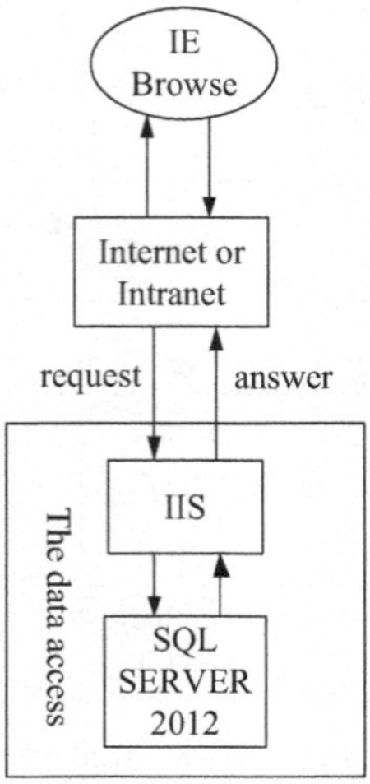


**Fig. 2.** System logic architecture

Personalized employment guidance system for college students is to manage and guide the employment information of college students. Through the demand analysis and detailed analysis and summary of user feedback, it is determined that the system mainly needs to achieve the following basic functions. They are the management of the basic information of the employer; employment policy and the latest trends; employment guidance function; data query.

### 3.2 Personalized Employment Information Recommendation

This paper uses ttlmf algorithm to recommend employment information according to the collected employment information and employment preference tag. The flow chart of ttlmf algorithm is shown in Fig. 3 [10–12].

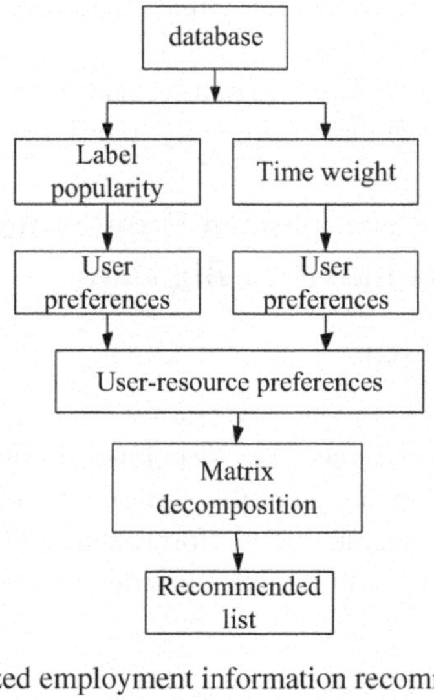


**Fig. 3.** Personalized employment information recommendation process

This section is divided into two parts: one is the user's preference for employment information resources based on tag popularity; the other is the user's preference for employment information resources based on time weight. According to the definition of tptmf algorithm: the more times a label is labeled by users, the more popular the label is to the users. This paper defines the popularity of tag $t_i$ for user $u$ as follows:

$$Popularity_{u,t_i} = \frac{\text{Freq}_{u,t_i}}{\sum\limits_{t_i \in T(u)} \text{Freq}_{u,t_i}} \tag{1}$$

Among them, the tag that user $u$ has operated is represented by $T(u)$, and the number of times user $u$ has used tag $t_i$ is represented by $\text{Freq}_{u,t_i}$.

User preference for tags can be used to represent user $u$ preference for employment information resource $r$. User preference for employment information resource based on tag popularity can be calculated by the following formula [13–15]:

$$\Pr e_{popu}(u, r) = \sum_{t \in T(u,r)} Populartity_{u,t} \tag{2}$$

Where, $T(u, r)$ represents the set of employment information resources $r$ labeled by user $u$. User's interest is often temporal. In short, user's interest will change with age, grade, education level, time and other factors. Traditional recommendation algorithm ignores the influence of time on user's interest. The essence of this part is that user's preference will change with time, compared with the user's past According to the time of tag $t_i$ on employment information resource $r$ marked by user $u$, the time weight is calculated as follows:

$$TimeWeight_{u,r,t} = \begin{cases} \exp\left\{-\left(1 + \tau \frac{t_0 - t_{u,r,t}}{l_{time\,u,r,t}}\right)\right\}, l_{time\,u,r,t} \neq 0 \\ \exp\left\{-\left(1 + \tau \frac{t_0 - t_{u,r,t}}{l_{\text{inter}\,u,r,t}}\right)\right\}, l_{time\,u,r,t} = 0 \end{cases} \tag{3}$$

In formula (3), $l_{\text{inter}\,u,r,t}$ is a constant, according to the relevant literature, the default value is 1000; $t_0$ represents the latest time for the user to label, $l_{time\,u,r,t}$ represents the time difference, that is, the time interval between the user's latest use of label $t_i$ and the initial use of label $t_i$. When the value of $l_{time\,u,r,t}$ is 0, formula (3) needs to use $l_{\text{inter}\,u,r,t}$ in the calculation Instead of the default value of, $t_{u,r,t}$ means the time when user $u$ labels the employment resource as $t_i$ [16–18].

Based on the above, we can use formula (4) to calculate the user's preference for resources which combines the factors of label and time.

$$\Pr e(u, r) = \delta \Pr e_{popu}(u, r) + (1 - \delta) \Pr e_{time}(u, r) \tag{4}$$

Through formula (4), we can get the preference matrix $R$, that is, the preference value of all users for all employment resources, where $\delta$ is the adjustment factor, and the value is between 0 and 1.

After obtaining the user's rating matrix $R_{m \times n}$ for employment resources, it can be decomposed into the product of two matrices through a specific vector dimension $K$. The matrix decomposition is as follows:

$$R_{m \times n} = P_{m \times K} \cdot Q_{K \times n} \tag{5}$$

The user characteristic matrix $P_{m \times K}$ and resource characteristic matrix $Q_{K \times n}$ can be obtained by formula (5), and the preference degree of user $u_i$ for employment resource $r_j$ can be predicted by the following formula (6).

$$\hat{r}_{i,j} = \sum_{f=1}^{K} P_{fi}^{T} \times Q_{fj} \tag{6}$$

The purpose of decomposing $R_{m \times n}$ is to find the optimal feature matrixes $P_{m \times K}$ and $Q_{K \times n}$. The essence of decomposing $P_{m \times K}$ is to minimize the error between the user's predicted preference value and the real preference value of related resources. If the feature matrix contains too large a value, there will be over fitting problem. Therefore, the over fitting term will be prevented to be added to the formula:

$$E = \left( r_{i,j} - \sum_{k=1}^{K} P_{i,k} Q_{k,j} \right)^2 + \frac{\beta}{2} \sum_{k=1}^{K} \left( P_{i,k}^2 + Q_{k,j}^2 \right) \tag{7}$$

According to the real value $r_{i,j}$ in the training set, the feature vectors $p_{i,f}$ and $q_{i,f}$ are updated and optimized according to the negative gradient direction of the error $e_{i,j}$ between it and the predicted value.

$$\begin{aligned} p_{if} &= p_{if} + \alpha \left( 2e_{i,j} q_{if} - \beta p_{if} \right) \\ q_{if} &= q_{if} + \alpha \left( 2e_{i,j} p_{if} - \beta q_{if} \right) \end{aligned} \tag{8}$$

Among them, $\alpha$ is the learning rate, $\beta$ is the regularization coefficient, repeated many times until the objective function $E$ is less than a certain threshold, so as to obtain the characteristic matrix $P$ and $Q$. Through formula (6) and the feature matrixes $P$ and $Q$, we can predict the user's preference for the resources that have not been operated. The preference values are sorted from high to low, and the resources represented by the top n values are recommended to the user to get the recommendation list topn1. According to the user's preference and other feature tags, personalized recommendation of employment information and employment guidance related resources is completed [19–23].

### 3.3 System Database Design

Database design is the first mock exam of database logic in a given application environment. Based on this model, database and its application system are built to enable them to store and manage data effectively, and satisfy users' needs, including data manipulation and information management. In front of the functional analysis and module design.

On this basis, this paper designs the database of employment guidance system, and some database tables are shown in Table 1.

**Table 1.** Employment guidance database for College Students

| Field name | Data type | Remarks |
|---|---|---|
| ID | int | Auto increment primary key number |
| title | nvarchar(50) | Title |
| leibie | nvarchar(20) | Category |
| createdate | datetime | Creation time |
| imgurl | nvarchar(50) | Written words |
| linkurl | nvarchar(50) | Picture |
| daleiid | int | Category number |
| jlid | Int | Auto increment primary key number |
| jlxm | nvarchar(10) | Full name |
| jlyx | nvarchar(50) | Mailbox |
| jlxx | nvarchar(50) | School |
| jlzy | nvarchar(20) | Major |

According to the above database table, complete the database design of the system. So far, the design of personalized employment guidance system for college students based on big data has been completed.

## 4 Test Experiment

In this section, we will test the reliability of the system through simulation experiments.

### 4.1 Experimental Content

This experiment is a comparative experiment. The traditional college students' employment guidance system is compared with the personalized college students' employment guidance system based on big data designed in this paper. The traditional college students' employment guidance system is the control group, and the personalized college students' employment guidance system based on big data is the experimental group. In the process of experimental test, the only experimental variable is controlled to avoid interference to the results of comparative experiment. The experimental environment is as follows: processor Intel g7250 3.65 GHz; hard disk 280G; operating system: Windows 8; 8 G memory.

The contrast index of the experiment is the response time of the college students' employment guidance system at run time and the CPU occupation of the system server at run time. The reliability of the system is verified.

### 4.2 Experimental Results

When testing the system, the response time of the system is shown in Fig. 4. The relationship between the curves in the figure is analyzed to judge the response performance of the system.

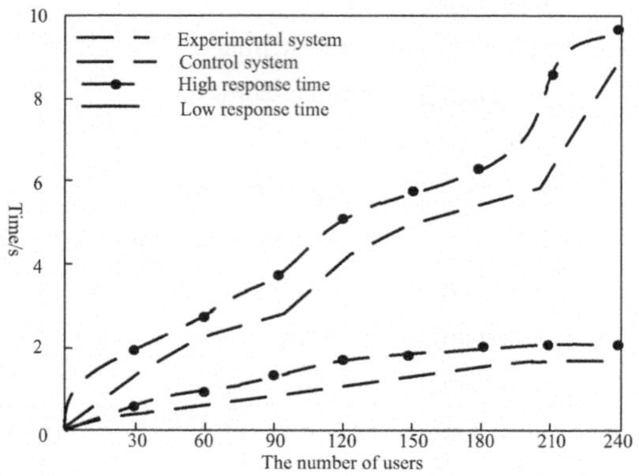


**Fig. 4.** System response time

According to the analysis of the curve in the figure above, compared with the highest system response time curve, the control group system is higher than the experimental group system; compared with the lowest system response time curve, the control group system is still higher than the experimental group system. It can be seen that the average response time of the experimental group is less than that of the control group. In addition, with the increase of the number of system users, the response time of the control group increased rapidly, while the response time of the experimental group remained relatively stable. It shows that the response performance of the experimental group is better.

When the system responds to different number of user service requests, the CPU usage of the server is shown in Fig. 5.

As can be seen from Fig. 5, with the increase of the number of users, the occupation of server CPU by the system in this paper keeps unchanged at first, then increases slowly, and no longer increases when it increases to 11%; while the occupation of server CPU by the traditional system has been growing, and the growth rate is faster and faster, up to 63.7%. It shows that the traditional system has poor server occupancy and limited system capacity.

To sum up, the personalized employment guidance system based on big data has the advantages of short response time and low system occupation.

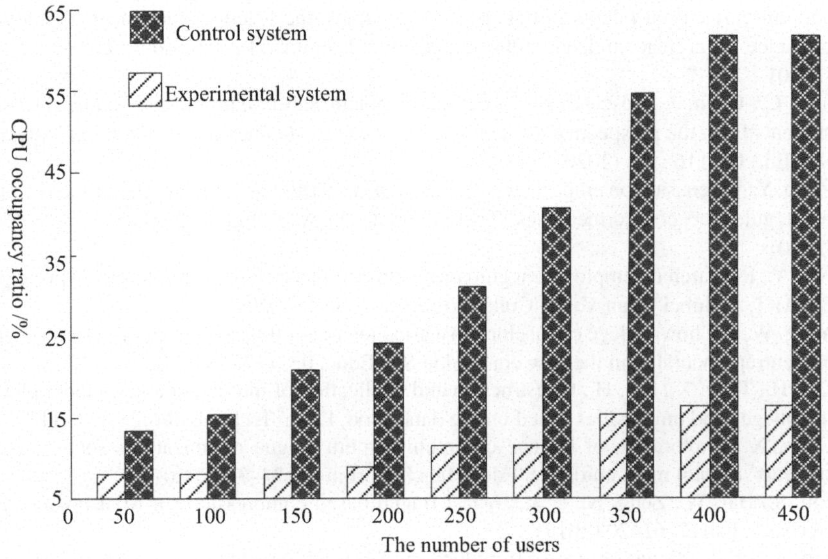


**Fig. 5.** CPU utilization ratio of server

## 5 Conclusion

With the development of economy and the progress of society, the demand for talents is increasing. It is an important task to improve the employment service for college students. In order to provide better employment guidance service, this paper designs a personalized employment guidance system for college students based on big data, and verifies the reliability of the system through comparative simulation experiments.

In this study, the system function development is not perfect, the system testing solution needs to be improved, and the communication function and information presentation form need to be enriched. I hope that the system research can have further development in depth and can provide a certain degree of help for college students' employment guidance.

## References

1. Wei, Y., Zhou, X.: Thinking about the employment guidance service for minority college students in inland with the method of the "smart employment" platform —take 91 smart employment platform for job in Jiangsu province as an example. China Univ. Stud. Career Guide **22**, 45–49 (2020)
2. Zhang, S.: Analysis of the employment ability structure of university students Based on SPSS. Comput. Knowl. Technol. **16**(32), 98–100 (2020)
3. Lin, Y.: Transform and innovation of the course of career planning and employment guidance in universities in the new era. J. Jilin Teach. Inst. Eng. Technol. **36**(10), 5–7 (2020)
4. Yan, Y.: The training mechanism of innovative and entrepreneurial talents in colleges: a case study the teaching reform of "employment guidance for the training mechanism of innovative

and entrepreneurial talents in colleges: a case study the teaching reform of 'employment guidance for college students' college students." J. Innova. Enterp. Educ. **11**(03), 163–166 (2020)
5. Yue, C., Chen, J.: Research on career development and employment guidance of college students from the perspective of ideological and political education. J. Chengdu Univ. (Soc. Sci. Ed.) **03**, 116–121 (2020)
6. Zhao, Y.: Discussion on employment situation of contemporary college students and employment guidance countermeasures. Theory Pract. Innov. Entrepreneurship **3**(12), 186–187 (2020)
7. Xie, Y.: Research on employment guidance path of college students based on the principle of SMART. J. Hubei Open Vocat. Coll. **33**(08), 62–63+68 (2020)
8. Yang, W.: On how college counselors do a good job in guiding college students' employment and entrepreneurship in the new era. Guide Sci. Educ. **03**, 187–188 (2020)
9. Liu, H., Teng, X., Bai, H.: Construction and application of intelligent employment platform in colleges and universities based on big data. Mod. Educ. Technol. **30**(02), 111–117 (2020)
10. Chen, X.: Exploration of college communist youth league organizations serving college students' employment guidance. Educ. Teach. Forum **05**, 34–35 (2020)
11. Liu, S., Bai, W., Zeng, N., et al.: A fast fractal based compression for MRI images. IEEE Access **7**, 62412–62420 (2019)
12. Liu, S., Li, Z., Zhang, Y., et al.: Introduction of key problems in long-distance learning and training. Mob. Netw. Appl. **24**(1), 1–4 (2019)
13. Vincenti, G., Bucciero, A., Helfert, M., Glowatz, M. (eds.): e-Learning, e-Education, and Online Training. LNICSSITE, vol. 180. Springer, Cham (2017). https://doi.org/10.1007/978-3-319-49625-2
14. Li, Y.: Visual education of music course for college students based on human-computer interaction. Int. J. Emerging Technol. Learn. (iJET) **15**(2), 175 (2020)
15. Yu, H., Zhang, G., Liu, J., et al.: Intelligent knowledge service system based on depression monitoring of college students. Int. J. Emerging Technol. Learn. (iJET) **14**(12), 71 (2019)
16. Jiang, S., Tian, F., Sun, S.: Integrated guidance and control design of rolling-guided projectile based on adaptive fuzzy control with multiple constraints. Math. Probl. Eng. **2019**(2), 1–17 (2019)
17. Zhang, F., Xi, L.: An evaluation model for the innovation and entrepreneurship thinking ability of college students based on neural network. Int. J. Emerging Technol. Learn. (iJET) **16**(2), 188 (2021)
18. Yi, M., Wang, Y., Tian, X., et al.: User experience of the mobile terminal customization system: the influence of interface design and educational background on personalized customization. Sensors **21**(7), 2428 (2021)
19. Han, Z.: Research on sports balanced development evaluation system based on edge computing and balanced game. Secur. Commun. Netw. **2021**(5), 1–8 (2021)
20. Huyan, W., Li, J.: Research on rural tourism service intellectualization based on neural network algorithm and optimal classification decision function. J. Ambient Intell. Hum. Comput. 1–21 (2021). https://doi.org/10.1007/s12652-021-03039-6
21. Yang, C., Huan, S., Yang, Y.: Application of big data technology in blended teaching of college students: a case study on rain classroom. Int. J. Emerging Technol. Learn. (iJET) **15**(11), 4 (2020)
22. Shi, Y., Yang, X.: A personalized matching system for management teaching resources based on collaborative filtering algorithm. Int. J. Emerging Technol. Learn. (iJET) **15**(13), 207 (2020)
23. Omisore, M.O., Ojokoh, B.A., Babalola, A.E., et al.: An affective learning-based system for diagnosis and personalized management of diabetes mellitus. Futur. Gener. Comput. Syst. **117**, 273–290 (2020)

# Design of Mixed Learning System of Tourism Planning Course Based on Mobile Terminal

Yu-xiang Liu[1(✉)] and Zhi-li Sha[2]

[1] College of Tourism and Urban-Rural Planning, Xichang University, Xichang 615000, China
[2] School of Foreign Languages, Xichang University, Xichang 615000, China

**Abstract.** There are defects in the processing and allocation of teaching resources in the current learning system, which leads to the phenomenon that the teaching information display is stuck and collapsed when the number of concurrent users is high. Therefore, a hybrid learning system of tourism planning course based on mobile terminal is designed. The overall framework of the system is designed from hardware and software. In hardware, the circuit board of single-chip microcomputer is designed. The power supply between modules is realized and the communication network architecture is optimized by changing the starting mode by setting different step sizes. In software design, database, system encryption technology and file data allocation mechanism are designed and optimized respectively. This completes the system design. In the system test performance experiment, the system test environment is built in the laboratory to simulate the multi-user login system at the same time to test the system performance. Experimental results show that the designed system can effectively improve the number of concurrent users and reduce the stuck situation.

**Keywords:** Mobile terminal · Tourism planning course · Learning system design

## 1 Introduction

The application of network technology in the field of teaching has received increasing attention from the education community. The Internet provides a good application platform for it. Computer-assisted teaching, computer-assisted learning and information technology education have been universally recognized today [1, 2]. The same is true for the concept of E-learning (digital learning). It is a way to promote teaching by applying the concept of digital learning to the teaching design process. This has attracted the favor of the education community and set off a climax of application in the education field. However, any teaching method must undergo the test of time. In practice, instructional designers gradually find out the disadvantages of e-learning teaching mode. Therefore, instructional designers have been trying to combine the advantages of E-learning with the advantages of traditional teaching, to extract the essence and discard the dross and form blended learning. This learning approach includes the rational use of a variety of information technology combinations, including video and audio conferencing, networks, CD boxes and other media, as well as the rational use of knowledge technology,


W. Fu et al. (Eds.): eLEOT 2021, LNICST 389, pp. 311–321, 2021.
https://doi.org/10.1007/978-3-030-84383-0_27

online activities and learner support systems. However, the current learning system is only a single learning system, and there are some defects in the internal processing of teaching resources, which leads to the problems of teaching information display stuck and collapse when the number of concurrent users is high. Therefore, a hybrid learning system of tourism planning course based on mobile terminal is designed. Through a general LCD module interface lcd1 of M32 MCU and another OLED interface, the connection between OLED and MCU is completed, and the hardware design of the system is realized; Design the resource management module of the database, obtain the file information on the web server, optimize the file data allocation mechanism by using the system encryption technology, so as to complete the software design of the system. Through the design of hardware and software, realize the design of mixed learning system of tourism planning course based on Mobile terminal. Finally, the simulation results verify the effectiveness of the design system, improve the number of concurrent users, and reduce the situation of stuck.

## 2 Design of Mixed Learning System of Tourism Planning Course Based on Mobile Terminal

The use of hybrid learning system for mobile terminal network teaching does not mean that teachers give up the traditional face-to-face teaching method. The traditional face-to-face teaching method has many advantages, such as conducive to the play of teachers' leading role, conducive to the teaching of system scientific knowledge and the completion of teaching objectives, which are incomparable with network teaching. We should organically combine the traditional classroom teaching and students' after-school online learning, formulate corresponding teaching plans and programs for different courses, give full play to the advantages of blended learning, and achieve the optimal teaching effect [3, 4]. Further study the blended learning mode, try to integrate the idea of blended learning into the network teaching system, build the network learning platform of tourism planning course learning, and help teachers to carry out more effective teaching management and teaching. The overall design framework of the system is shown in the figure below (Fig. 1):

The mobile terminal learning function module designed in this research is a supplement and optimization to the existing teaching platform. The mobile phone mobile learning module is embedded into the existing teaching platform through related technologies to achieve the purpose of assisting teaching. In the application process, student information and course resources are managed uniformly through the background. Learners can access complete course learning resources through computers, and develop contextualized and personalized independent learning support through the mobile phone assisted teaching system.

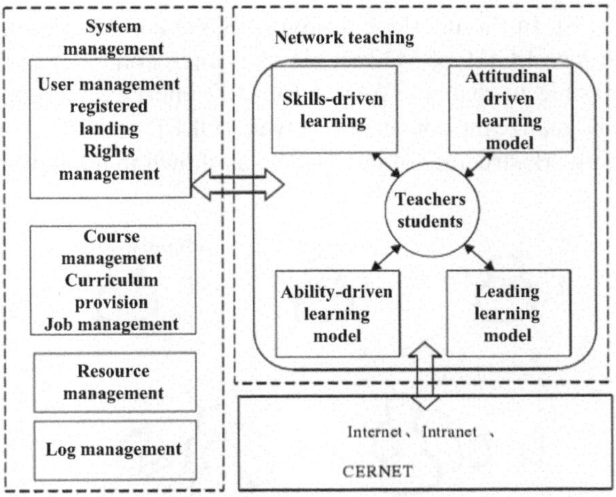


**Fig. 1.** Overall design of the system

### 2.1 Hardware Design

In the hardware design of the system, the microcontroller is mainly used as the core of system control. Since the display part of the system designed in this paper mainly uses a metal capacitive screen, the system includes four major components: website, server controller, client controller, and playback program. In the hardware part of the system, it is mainly composed of the main circuit board, control module, interface module and wireless transmission module of the ALIENTEK MiniSTM32 microcontroller. The main circuit board of single chip microcomputer mainly includes micro control unit (MCU). In the process of setting the control unit, M32 single chip microcomputer constitutes the core component of the control system. Under the expansion, the control circuit needs to be expanded and set before the main circuit module can be configured through $BOOT_0$ and $BOOT_1$ [5, 6]. The configuration mode is shown in the table below (Table 1):

**Table 1.** System boot mode configuration settings

| $BOOT_0$ | $BOOT_1$ | Startup mode |
|---|---|---|
| 1 | 1 | SRAM start |
| 0 | X | User flash mode |
| 1 | 0 | System storage mode |

In SRAM boot mode, it is mainly used in debugging code in SRAM. In system storage mode, after the system's built-in memory is started, hardware will download the source program code by serial port, and can be used for downloading serial port. When $BOOT_0$ is 0 and $BOOT_1$ is any value, pressing reset key can start the system's program and start user's flash mode, mainly depending on user flash memory. To complete the startup of flash [7, 8]. In the interface design of SWD and OLED, through a general LCD module interface LCD1 of M32 single-chip microcomputer and another OLED interface, it is possible to realize SWD and OLED interface to supply power to the display module, and realize the connection between OLED and MCU. And designed the communication network structure of the system, as shown in the figure below (Fig. 2):

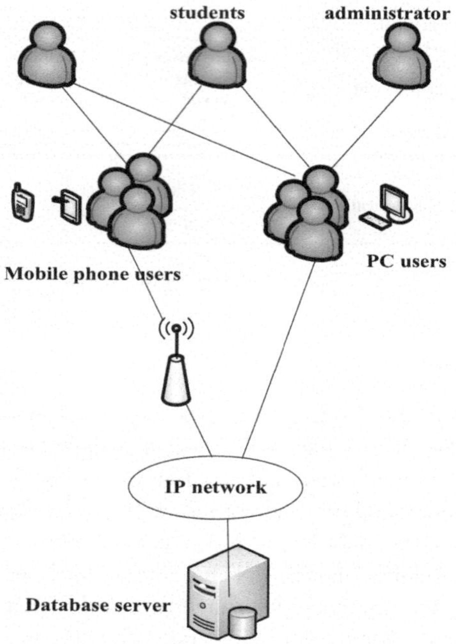


**Fig. 2.** Communication network design

So far, the hardware design of the system is completed.

## 2.2 Software Design

### Database Design

The user management function is the most basic function in each online learning system. Its main purpose is to manage all registered personnel who use this website, confirm user roles, assign corresponding permissions, and effectively manage the entire online teaching process from all aspects. The registered personnel include administrators, teachers and students. The administrators can use all the functions of this website. The identities of teachers and students are assigned by the course administrator. Teachers have the authority to manage course content, monitor student learning, and judge student performance. Students can use any learning resources provided on the website for online learning activities. In the system of this article, the user data table format in the database is as follows (Table 2):

**Table 2.** User data sheet

| Field name | Data type | Is it empty | Length |
|---|---|---|---|
| Number | Int | N | 10 |
| User name | Varchar | N | 100 |
| Use password | Varchar | N | 32 |
| Personal email | Varchar | N | 100 |
| Name | Varchar | N | 100 |
| Surname | Varchar | N | 100 |
| City | Varchar | N | 20 |
| Country | Char | N | 2 |
| First login time | Int | N | 10 |
| Last login time | Int | N | 10 |
| Login IP address | Varchar | N | 15 |
| Modification time | Int | N | 10 |

Visitors must register as a user before performing various operations. Each visitor can create his own account in the educational technology learning community and participate in online courses. If the registered user does not participate in activities for a period of time, the administrator will have a record. The system supports arbitrary electronic documents, PPT, Flash animation, video and sound files, and the system administrator can upload and manage files. The list of files uploaded by users and the operation of existing files are realized through directory functions and file system functions.

In the resource management module of the database, we can not only view and obtain the information related to the directory, but also obtain the information of the files on the web server and interact with these files.

**System Encryption Technology**

In this system, the encryption technology is MD5 technology. The full name of MD5 is message digest algorithm 5 (message digest algorithm). Its function is to "compress" a large amount of information into a secret format before signing private key with digital signature software (that is, transforming a byte string of any length into a large integer number of a certain length). The implementation process of one-way MD5 encryption algorithm is to add the security. CS class to the system card project, and define the security. Encrypt () method in the class. When we register users, we call the Security. Encrypt (passtex. Text) method in the Regist Click event to encrypt the cipher, and finally form a fixed length string stored in the database. The user registration information is shown in the following figure (Fig. 3):

The verification code is generated to prevent attackers from using harmful programs to register a large number of Web service accounts in vain, and then use these accounts to cause trouble for other users, such as sending spam or repeatedly logging in to multiple accounts at the same time to slow down the service [9, 10]. The verification code

| ResIssuerID | UserID | Pwd | SchoolID |
|---|---|---|---|
| 13 | 0506410136 | 9CE853EB7EE8E362E1D121EB4DF2DC91 | 2 |
| 16 | 123456 | E10ADC3949BA59ABBE56E057F20F883E | 1 |
| 18 | 0506410137 | 1BAE47CA9A88FCEB827E926DFEBFF70B | 1 |
| 19 | 51aspx | E10ADC3949BA59ABBE56E057F20F883E | 2 |
| 20 | 111 | 698D51A19D8A121CE581499D7B701668 | 1 |
| 21 | 1001 | 202CB962AC59075B964B07152D234B70 | 1 |

**Fig. 3.** User registration information

technology is used to prevent users from using robots to register, log in, and fill water in vain. The so-called verification code is to generate a picture from a string of randomly generated numbers or symbols. Add some interfering pixels to the picture (to prevent OCR). The user can visually recognize the verification code information, enter the form and submit it to the website for verification. After the validation is successful, you can use the function [11, 12].

**Optimize File Data Allocation Mechanism**

In the research and development of tourism planning course learning system, we found that with the growth of the number of users, the amount of data in the system will increase greatly. In order to meet the requirements of high concurrent read-write, high-efficiency storage, high scalability and high availability, the file system of this system adopts mongodb file processing mechanism. Mongodb is a kind of relational database in theory, but it contains some characteristics of non relational database, but its function is more powerful than non relational database. The data structure stored in mongodb database is relatively loose, and the data is stored in bjson format. Therefore, mongodb can easily face complex data types. Mongodb adopts sharding mechanism, which is a method of mongodb to extend load. Sharding can add more hardware devices to meet the data requirements without affecting the program running. The basic concept of mongodb sharding is to divide the collection into smaller chunks. These chunks are distributed on sharding. We don't need to know which sharding the data is stored on, we just need to run mongos, which knows where all the data is, so the application can normally connect to the database and make a request. When there is a request, you only need to know the storage location of chunks through mongos, which collects data and sends it to the application. As shown in the figure below (Fig. 4):

Separate sharding from application programs. Under this mechanism, users can expand the system without changing programs. When the amount of data and load change, fragmentation mechanism can automatically balance the changes of load and data distribution, and flexibly add new hardware devices. And its scalability is strong, and the fragmentation mechanism can be extended to one thousand nodes. The sharding mechanism can achieve no single point of failure, even if there is a failure, sharding can realize automatic failover.

Mongodb's data storage function is extremely powerful. It combines capability extension with many of the most useful features of relational databases, such as sub index range queries and sorting. Mongodb also has powerful fragmentation functions, such as built-in support of style aggregation and spatial index. However, mongodb still belongs

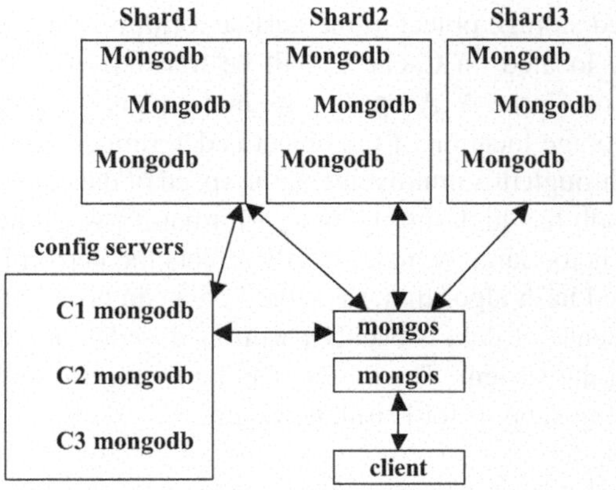


**Fig. 4.** Auto-sharding architecture diagram

to NoSQL in mechanism, but NoSQL's lack of experience and excessive CPU share also restrict the development of mongodb.

The hash algorithm is generally carried out in two steps. First, find the hash value of the cache. Then calculate the hash value of the object. If the hash value of the object matches the hash value of a certain cache, it is mapped to the cache.

The storage objects on Cache A are object 1; the storage objects on Cache B are object 2, object 3; the storage objects on Cache C are object 4, objects, and object6; the storage objects on Cache D are There are object 7, object8, object9, and objectl0; when Cache C is deleted, the object originally stored on Cache C will be transferred to Cache D, causing the load of Cache D to be too high. Similarly, when Cache E is added, because the hash value of the newly added Cache E is uncertain, the newly added Cache E may fall between Cache A and Cache D with less load, making the load of Cache A zero, resulting in resources Waste.

In view of the shortcomings of mongodb, the system uses hash algorithm to allocate data, so as to avoid the problem that mongodb takes up too much space. Therefore, in the process of optimization, we need to sort the cache according to the number of objects on the cache and the size of its object access. When a cache is deleted, the object located on the deleted cache is transferred to the smallest cache. When a cache is added, the cache is added to the largest cache to balance the load. When cache C is deleted, the objects originally located on cache C are transferred to cache a according to the cache sorting size to avoid excessive load pressure.

When a cache is added or deleted, the hash value of the rest of the cache will change due to the change in the number of caches, and the hash value of the storage object will also change. Object a is transferred from cacehA to cacheB due to the change in the hash value. Object b may be transferred from cacehC to cacheB for the same reason. Since there is no query priority judgment between a and b, the storage of objects a and b in cacheB is random, which is detrimental to the query performance of the system.

The optimization scheme proposes sorting the query probability of storage objects. When the cache changes, the conflicting objects determine the storage location according to the query probability. Through this measure, the query speed of the system is improved.

Add the improved storage object to the hash algorithm. When Cache C is deleted, the object originally located on Cache C will be transferred to Cache A. There are four objects located on Cache A. According to the frequency key carried by the object element itself, the storage location of the object is determined according to the size of the frequency key. Through this improvement, the speed of data query can be optimized.

Although mongodb has high throughput performance, when massive data is read, the CPU occupancy is too large, which directly affects the performance of the system. Through the improved hash algorithm, the stored data can be evenly distributed on the nodes, and the real sense of data is evenly partitioned, reducing the system's share of CPU and optimizing the system. The system can better realize the storage of massive data and provide strong support for learning system.

# 3 System Test

## 3.1 Build a System Test Environment

After the system design in this article is completed, the performance of the system needs to be tested, and the system's test environment is set up in a laboratory environment. The configuration of the test host is shown in the following table (Table 3):

**Table 3.** Test host environment configuration

| Classification | To configure | DESCRIPTION |
|---|---|---|
| Hardware | CPU | Pentium4, 4G memory, |
| | Monitor | Resolution 1024*768, color recognition 36 bits |
| | Sound card | The number of quantization bits is 32 bits |
| | Optical drive | 40 times faster transmission rate |
| Software | Windows 7 | Microsoft Corporation |

In the above-mentioned system test environment, the system designed in this paper and the original system were tested separately, and certain teaching information was randomly selected for viewing and access. In order to meet the requirements of the number of concurrent users in the experiment, this article constructed the following experimental network in a laboratory environment (Fig. 5):

The simulation and attack of multi-user concurrency is realized by using the structure of the above figure, and the same test is carried out with the original system under the same experimental environment. Record and analyze the test results.

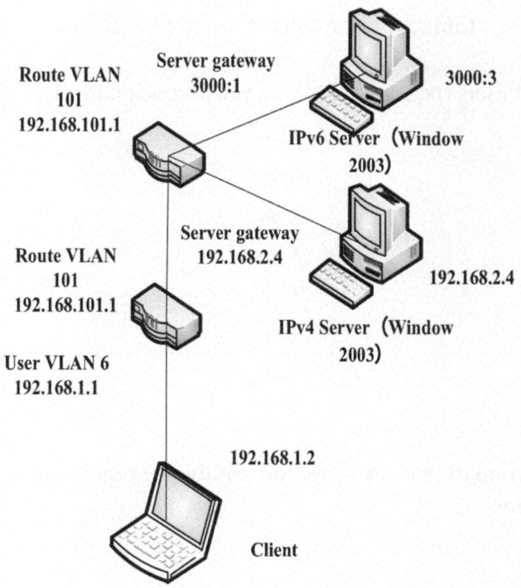


**Fig. 5.** Experimental network topology

## 3.2 Test Results

Under the above experimental environment, the test results obtained are shown in the following table (Tables 4 and 5):

**Table 4.** Test results of the original system

| Number of concurrent users (persons) | Can you access normally | Is it stuck? |
|---|---|---|
| 100 | Yes | No |
| 500 | Yes | No |
| 1000 | Yes | Have |
| 5000 | Yes | Have |
| 10000 | No | – |
| 20000 | No | – |
| 50000 | No | – |

According to the data test results in the above table, it can be seen that the original system is stuck when the number of concurrent users is 1,000. When the number of concurrent users is 10,000, the system crashes and cannot be accessed normally. The system designed in this paper can still work normally when the number of concurrent users is 50,000, but when the number of concurrent users is 20,000, the teaching information display is stuck. In summary, the system designed in this paper can improve system

**Table 5.** Test results of the original system

| Number of concurrent users (person) | Can you access it normally | Is it stuck? |
|---|---|---|
| 100 | Can | No |
| 500 | Can | No |
| 1000 | Can | No |
| 5000 | Can | No |
| 10000 | Can | No |
| 20000 | Can | Have |
| 50000 | Can | Have |

performance to a certain extent, increase the number of concurrent systems, and reduce the occurrence of jams.

## 4 Conclusion

The advantage of this system is that it can be directly operated and used, the interface is simple, easy to use, and does not require installation or debugging; it realizes a flipped classroom with the help of public platforms for learning; it provides convenience for students to study after class; and enhances students' travel planning The learning interest of the course.

The disadvantage of this system is that the mobile learning resources mentioned in this paper are only relatively simple and scattered learning materials compiled to meet the needs of students, which should be more purposeful, systematic, structured and integrated in the later stage; the answering function can only realize the fixed test questions, but can not realize the function of uploading the test questions from the background randomly; the system can only interact through the establishment of a group, but cannot realize the function of an interactive community through the system; although the mobile terminal learning is realized, learning in the classroom can not be completely idealized and face-to-face communication can not be avoided. With the development of mobile terminal equipment and the corresponding supporting environment, we believe that mobile terminals will be further popularized, and its application in education will be further deepened. I believe that in the near future, we can be more widely used in the teaching process. To conduct learning and teaching activities through mobile terminals, the mobile terminal-based learning and teaching model we advocate will also be practiced and promoted.

## References

1. Li, H., Hu, X., Men, X.: Designing mixed-mode teaching for management information system course——based on internet environment. J. Anshun Univ. **20**(02), 128–131 (2018)
2. Bai, L., Hu, Y., Zheng, L.: A blended teaching model based on learning behavior analysis. Comput. Eng. Sci. **40**(S1), 42–46 (2018)

3. Xie, X., Zhu, L., Zheng, Y., et al.: Research on personalized recommendation system for online learning based on collaborative filtering technology. Comput. Knowl. Technol. **14**(03), 173–174+176 (2018)
4. Zhang, X., Ma, W., Wang, L., et al.: Research on blended learning reform of Linux and embedded system in the Internet of Things engineering. Educ. Teach. Forum **30**, 99–100 (2018)
5. Lu, H., Lu, D., Zhao, Z., et al.: Exploration and practice of the blended teaching reform in the course of systematic anatomy under Internet+ background. J. Nongken Med. **40**(04), 376–378 (2018)
6. Xiong, J., Rong, W., Zhu, Y.: Introduction and assessment of a blended-learning model in neurologic trainee program. Med. Educ. Manage. **4**(06), 506–511 (2018)
7. Mou, Z., Li, Y., Yan, D.: The design and implementation of learning warning system based on learning behavior data in blended learning environment. J. Dist. Educ. **36**(03), 55–63 (2018)
8. Liu, S., Bai, W., Zeng, N., et al.: A fast fractal based compression for MRI images. IEEE Access **7**, 62412–62420 (2019)
9. Liu, S., Li, Z., Zhang, Y., et al.: Introduction of key problems in long-distance learning and training. Mob. Netw. Appl. **24**(1), 1–4 (2019)
10. Vincenti, G., Bucciero, A., Helfert, M., Glowatz, M. (eds.): e-Learning, e-Education, and Online Training. LNICSSITE, vol. 180. Springer, Cham (2017). https://doi.org/10.1007/978-3-319-49625-2
11. Chou, J.S., Hsu, S.C., Ngo, N.T., et al.: Hybrid machine learning system to forecast electricity consumption of smart grid-based air conditioners. IEEE Syst. J. **13**, 3120–3128 (2019)
12. Mishra, M., Rout, P.K.: Loss of main detection in distribution generation system based on hybrid signal processing and machine learning technique. Int. Trans. Electr. Energy Syst. **29**(1), e2676.1–e2676.26 (2019)

# Design of Digital Repair System for Damaged Cultural Relic Image in the Professional Training of Restoration

Shu-tao Shen[1](✉) and Yong-ming Chen[2]

[1] Tibet University School of Information Science and Technology, Lhasa 850000, China
[2] Huali College Guangdong University of Technology, Guangzhou 511325, China

**Abstract.** In the traditional cultural relic image digital repair system, there are obvious color aberrations and structural deviations between the restored part and the surrounding part, which weakens the visual connectivity of the restored result. In view of this, this research designs a digital repair system of damaged cultural relics image in professional training of restoration. In the hardware of the system, an integrated fast spherical camera is designed, and the transformation between image and pixel coordinate system is expressed by homogeneous coordinate system according to its parameters. In the system software, the damaged areas of cultural relics images are segmented and marked first, and the optimization algorithm of texture synthesis and restoration based on samples is designed. The experimental test results show that the system in this paper can ensure the use of the known information of the original image to the greatest extent, and make the repair result more reasonable on the basis of the minimum modification of the original image, so as to achieve the effect of professional practical training of repair.

**Keywords:** Restoration professional training · Cultural relic restoration · Image digital inpainting · Image region segmentation

## 1 Introduction

With the rapid development of science and technology and the continuous improvement of social system, people's quality of life is also improving. It is accompanied by people's demand for high-quality spiritual life, of which cultural life is a very important part [1, 2]. People are more and more interested in understanding the cultural history of their own country and the world, which leads to the emergence of various types of museums.

As there are currently a large number of unearthed cultural relics in a severely damaged state, the number of cultural relics restoration workers is far from enough to cope with the large number of damaged cultural relics restoration work. There are many problems in the artificial restoration of damaged ancient cultural relics, including slow restoration, consuming a lot of manpower and material resources, and easy to cause secondary damage to ancient cultural relics. Therefore, people eagerly hope that there


W. Fu et al. (Eds.): eLEOT 2021, LNICST 389, pp. 322–331, 2021.
https://doi.org/10.1007/978-3-030-84383-0_28

will be a system that can automatically complete the restoration of damaged images, so that the restoration workers can be freed from the processing of a large number of digital images, and at the same time, it can also ensure that the damaged ancient cultural relics can be repaired as soon as possible. And show it in front of the world [3, 4].

For this reason, cultural relic image digital repair system is applied in related cultural relic restoration profession. However, due to the operational deficiencies in the process of algorithm optimization in the traditional system, there will be obvious color difference and structural deviation between the repaired part and the surrounding part, which will weaken the visual connectivity of the repaired result. In order to solve this problem, this paper designs a new digital repair system of damaged cultural relics image in professional training of restoration. In this paper, an integrated fast spherical camera is designed in the hardware environment of the system. According to its parameters, the transformation between image and pixel coordinate system is expressed by using homogeneous coordinate system, and the camera is calibrated. In the software environment, an optimization algorithm of texture synthesis and restoration based on samples was designed on the basis of segmenting and marking the damaged areas of cultural relics images.

## 2 Design of Digital Repair System for Damaged Cultural Relic Images in Repair Professional Training

### 2.1 Hardware Design

In the hardware design, the main function is to identify the cultural relic image, complete the image information collection and transmission. The collection of cultural relic information image mainly depends on the camera. In this paper, the e588/G3 integrated fast spherical camera is selected. 128 preset positions are built in the camera. According to the above preset positions, the automatic timing activation function can be used to complete the omni-directional detection and automatic scanning of cultural relics [5, 6]. In addition, the camera needs to be calibrated to ensure that the image obtained by the camera is true and accurate. Firstly, the coordinate system of the vision system is established. The representation of several collected digital images in PC is an array of $P(M \times N)$. There are single pixels in the array. After the image is collected, the pixel coordinate system $(U, V)$ can be obtained. On the actual CCD sensitive surface, the transformation between image coordinate system and pixel coordinate system can be expressed by homogeneous coordinates:

$$\begin{bmatrix} u \\ v \\ l \end{bmatrix} = \begin{bmatrix} \frac{1}{d_u} & s & u_0 \\ 0 & \frac{1}{d_v} & v_0 \\ 0 & 0 & 1 \end{bmatrix} \times \begin{bmatrix} x' \\ y' \\ l \end{bmatrix} \tag{1}$$

In the formula, $d_u$ represents the pixel pitch in the U direction, and $s$ represents the tilt factor, which is mainly caused by the fact that the plane coordinate axes are not orthogonal to each other during the imaging process of the camera. $\begin{bmatrix} u \\ v \\ l \end{bmatrix}$ represents the coordinates of the pixel coordinate system, and $\begin{bmatrix} x' \\ y' \\ l \end{bmatrix}$ represents the coordinates of the image coordinate system. $d_v$ represents the pixel pitch in the $V$ direction. The schematic diagram of the conversion between the pixel coordinate system and the image coordinate system is shown in Fig. 1.

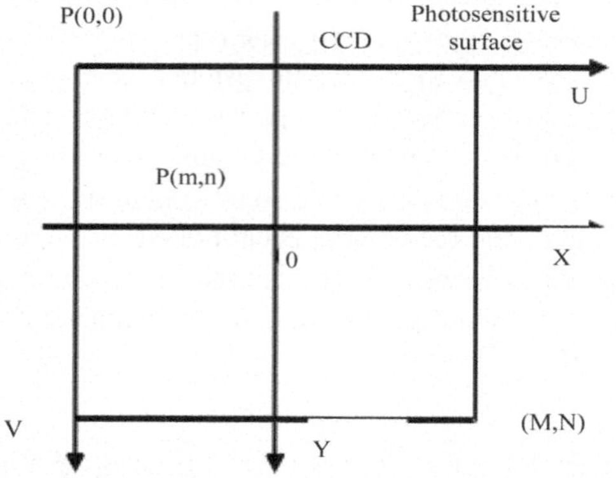


**Fig. 1.** Schematic diagram of pixel coordinate system and image coordinate system

In Fig. 1, the camera optical axis of image coordinate system $(x, y)$ is perpendicular to the coordinate plane, the coordinate origin is the intersection point of the optical axis and the coordinate plane, and the coordinate axis direction is the row and column direction of the image. In the process of imaging, the camera uses the pinhole perspective model. The imaging is linear, also known as perspective projection. The related scale relationship is as follows:

$$\begin{cases} x' = \dfrac{fx}{z} \\ y' = \dfrac{fy}{z} \end{cases} \tag{2}$$

Written in the form of formula (1) as a homogeneous coordinate relationship, it can be expressed as:

$$z * \begin{bmatrix} x' \\ y' \\ l \end{bmatrix} = \begin{bmatrix} f\,0\,0\,0 \\ 0\,f\,0\,0 \\ 0\,0\,f\,0 \end{bmatrix} \times \begin{bmatrix} x \\ y \\ z \\ l \end{bmatrix} \tag{3}$$

The above formula can describe the equation in the process of projecting the camera coordinate system onto the image plane. Based on the above calculations, the internal and external parameter models of the camera can be calculated, and the actual situation of the cultural relics corresponding to each pixel in the image coordinate system can be easily estimated through linear mapping. So far, the hardware design of the system is completed.

## 2.2 Segmentation and Marking of Damaged Area in Cultural Relic Image

In 1981, Bezdek and others first proposed the traditional fuzzy C-means (FCM) algorithm, that is, clustering method based on objective function. Taking $X = \{x_1, x_2, ...x_n\}$ as the sample set, $c$ as the number of cluster centers, $V = \{v_1, v_2, ...v_n\}$ as the cluster center. Euclidean distance as the similarity measure of clustering, and adding membership function $u_{ik}$ to the objective function, the objective function of clustering can be expressed as follows:

$$J_1 = \sum_{i=1}^{c}\sum_{k=1}^{n} u_{ik}\|x_k - v_i\|^2 \tag{4}$$

In the formula, when the value of $J_1$ is the smallest, the data set can be divided, $x_k$ represents the k-th sample in the sample set, $v_i$ represents the $i$th cluster center, and $n$ represents the weighting function to control the degree of blur. $u_{ik}$ represents the membership degree of the i th sample to the k th cluster center, and satisfies the following constraints:

$$\sum_{k=1}^{c} u_{ik} = 1 \tag{5}$$

In the formula, $u_{ik}$ is a number between 0 and 1. The clustering criterion based on the fuzzy c clustering algorithm is to make the objective function the smallest value under the condition of meeting the constraints [7–9]. At present, iterative methods are commonly used to find the approximate minimum value of $J_1(U, V)$ to solve this type of optimization problem.

Taking the damaged area of the cultural relic image as the foreground and the non damaged area as the background, the FCM algorithm is used to segment the mural, and the spatial feature information of pixels is introduced to avoid the influence of noise on the segmentation effect. Since a color image can be represented by a three-dimensional vector on a two-dimensional grid point, each grid point represents a pixel [10–12]. The coordinates of grid points, that is, pixel coordinates, can represent the spatial distribution of the image. In the segmentation process, R, G, B and three color components in RGB space model are used to represent the color feature vector $x_i^o = (r_i, g_i, b_i)$ of the mural, and the pair $x_i^s = (x_{i1}, x_{i2})$ $i = 1, 2, ..., N$ is used to represent the pixel coordinates. Therefore, a five dimensional vector is used to represent the mural image as the input feature vector based on FCM algorithm. Then the mural image is shown as follows:

$$X = \left(x_i^o, x_i^s\right)\ i = 1, 2, ..., N \tag{6}$$

In the formula, $N$ represents the number of pixels. The color features of cultural relic images include the brightness and chromaticity information of cultural relic images, which can be obtained by color histogram. The steps for segmenting and labeling the damaged areas in the image are as follows:

Step (1): determine the number of clusters $c$, $(2 \le c \le n)$ and set the iteration threshold value $\varepsilon > 0$;

Step (2): initialize membership matrix $U = [u_k(i,j)]$ and cluster center $V = [v_1, v_2, ..., v_c]$ with random numbers between [0,1];

Step (3): Input the feature vector and calculate $c$ cluster centers;

Step (4): Calculate the objective function and then calculate the difference with the last value function. If the difference is less than the preset threshold $\varepsilon$, the algorithm is completed, the membership matrix and cluster center are obtained, and the membership matrix is updated:

$$u_{ik} = \frac{1}{\sum_{k=1}^{c} \left(\frac{d_{ij}}{d_{kj}}\right)^{\frac{2}{m-1}}} \tag{7}$$

The image is segmented according to the classification matrix and clustering center. Mark the broken area in the original image as white.

## 2.3 Sample Based Texture Synthesis and Repair Optimization Algorithm

The sample-based texture synthesis image restoration algorithm has a better effect when repairing an image with a relatively large area to be repaired. The algorithm is mainly to randomly select a pixel on the boundary of the repair area of the image to be repaired in the repair process, and take a fixed pixel block at the center of the pixel as a matching sample block. The size of the sample block can be selected arbitrarily, such as 9 × 9. Then search and match the entire image area from the area to be repaired, find the texture block most similar to the sample block as the optimal matching block, and finally fill the center pixel of the optimal matching block into the sample block area. The repair diagram is shown in Fig. 2.

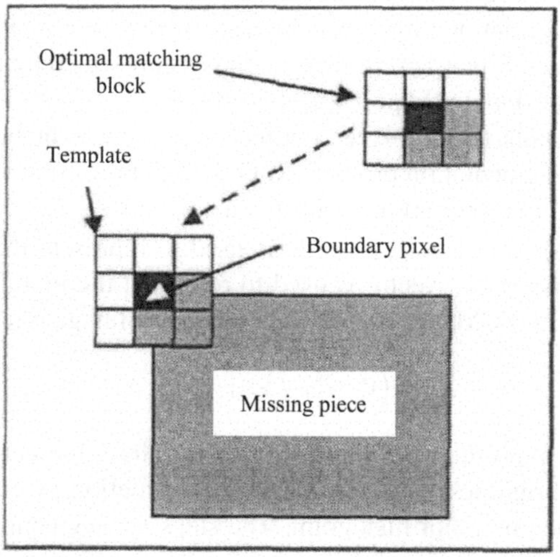


**Fig. 2.** Schematic diagram of sample-based texture synthesis image restoration

As shown in Fig. 2, the template sample block is a texture block with the same size centered on a pixel on the boundary of the region to be repaired. When matching the template sample block, search and match the white area in the image to find the optimal matching block. After matching, the center pixel value of the optimal matching block is updated to the center pixel of the template [12–14]. This algorithm is mainly through the calculation of the priority of the pixel to be repaired and the matching texture block and pixel value update three steps for texture synthesis to complete the region to be repaired in the repaired image.

# 3 System Performance Test

## 3.1 Build a Test Platform

In order to verify the system performance designed in this paper, a test platform is built in the process of system performance test. According to the number of cameras selected according to different cultural relic models, several cameras, image acquisition card, computer, auxiliary light source, experimental bench and other corresponding parts are selected. The final restoration results are output by the computer display screen. The core structure of the hardware part is 15 fourth-generation processor, 1050T1 graphics computer and Daheng DH-SV1421FC camera. The hardware components of the system are shown in Fig. 3.

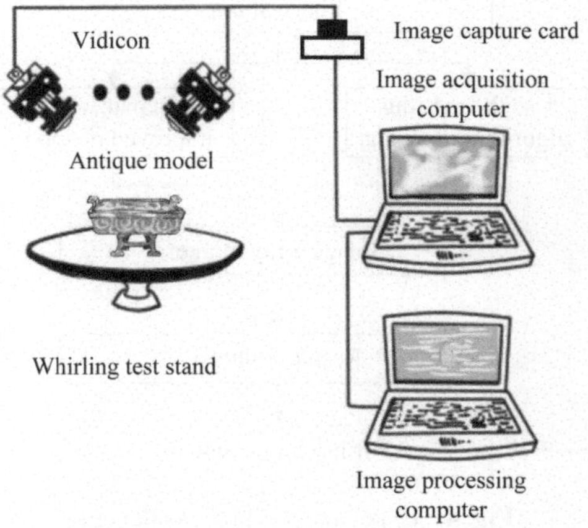


**Fig. 3.** Structure diagram of experimental system design

In the image acquisition process, the camera is used to shoot the damaged cultural relic model, and the image information of the real model is saved to the computer through the camera's dedicated image acquisition card to form digital information. Then judge the damaged area of the image or the missing area of the image information according to the requirements, and prepare for the later image repair and reproduction. The specific steps of the experiment are as follows:

Step (1): through multiple cameras (the number of cameras selected according to different cultural relic models), image acquisition card, computer, auxiliary light source, experimental bench and other corresponding parts, the final repair results are output by the computer display screen. The damaged cultural relic model is photographed by the camera, and the image information of the real model is saved to the computer by the special image acquisition card of the camera to form digital information. After the restoration of the damaged area, the image is ready for restoration according to the requirements of the image.

Step (2): use the existing digital image restoration algorithm program to achieve the restoration of the texture and structure information of ancient objects.

Step (3): analyze the repair results, find the shortcomings, and improve the algorithm.

The experimental flow chart is shown in Fig. 4.

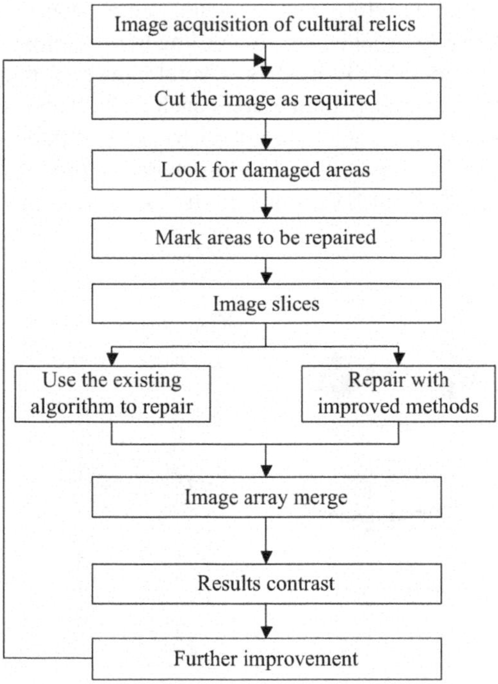


**Fig. 4.** Experimental process design

For the first part of the image acquisition process of the overall experimental process, the current plan is to use a monocular camera multi-angle shooting method, that is, to fix the camera position unchanged, and operate the experimental platform on which the cultural relic model is placed to make it rotate at a uniform speed. After the camera is fixed, the camera must be calibrated before proceeding with the operation of the experimental platform. Use linear transformation method to calibrate the camera: establish a set of basic linear constraint equations to express the relationship between the camera and the coordinate system of the space where the three-dimensional model is located, and use the least square method to solve the linear equation. In the process of image acquisition and preprocessing of the 3D cultural relic model, the surface texture and structure information of the 3D cultural relic model is stored by replacing the three-dimensional image with a two-dimensional image, realizing the process of "from 3D to 2D". After the overall restoration process is over, image stitching technology is used to "paste" the two-dimensional texture image on the surface of the three-dimensional cultural relic. The key steps of image stitching include two aspects of technology, namely image registration and image fusion. Figure 5 was repaired according to the above experimental method.

**Fig. 5.** Picture to be repaired

The original two systems and the system in this paper are used to repair the above figure, and the repair results are analyzed and compared.

## 3.2 Performance Test Results and Analysis

The test result is shown in Fig. 6.

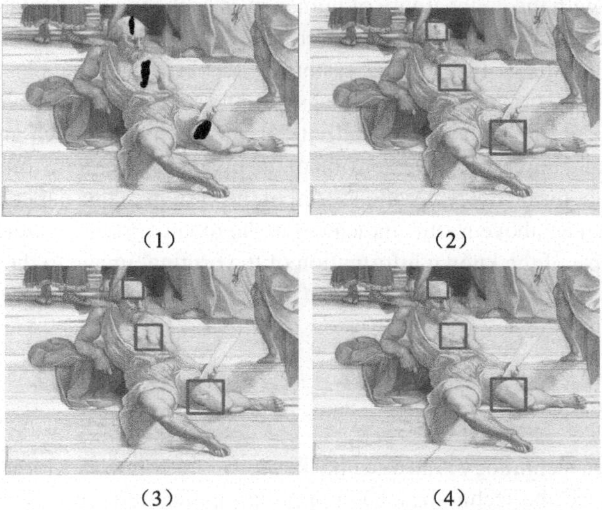


**Fig. 6.** Comparison of repair results

In Fig. 6, Fig. 6 (1) represents the cracked part of the marked human body; Fig. 6 (2) represents the repair result when the repair factor of the original system is 0.5; Fig. 6 (3) represents the repair result when the repair factor of the original system is 0.7; and Fig. 6 (4) represents the repair result of the present system.

In the experiment, the marked parts are respectively the head, chest and legs of the characters. These areas are the more seriously damaged parts, and there are great differences in the repair results after various methods. In the experimental results of the original system, we can see that the head, chest and legs of the characters have different degrees of unreasonable extension, resulting in obvious visual irrationality in the local part. There will be obvious color difference and structural deviation between the repaired part and the surrounding part. The visual connectivity of the repaired results in this paper is significantly enhanced.

The images repaired by different methods were compared with the original image for structural similarity detection, and at the same time, local structural similarity detection was performed on the repaired key area, namely the marked area. The repair results of each method and the original image structure similarity detection results are shown in the Table 1 shown.

**Table 1.** Experimental results SSIM value comparison

| System approach | R channel | G channel | B channel | Grayscale |
|---|---|---|---|---|
| Original image | 99.29% | 99.29% | 99.19% | 99.26% |
| The original system repair factor is 0.5 | 99.35% | 99.37% | 99.27% | 99.33% |
| The original system repair factor is 0.7 | 99.35% | 99.37% | 99.25% | 99.32% |
| Text system | 99.51% | 99.55% | 99.46% | 99.51% |

At present, the result evaluation of image restoration is usually based on the judgment of human eyes, with the connectivity of human eyes as the main judgment principle. By comparing the experimental results of different systems, it can be seen that: Compared with the repair results of the original system under different repair factors, the repair results of the cracks on the head, chest, legs, ground and steps of the characters in this system are more in line with the connectivity of human vision, which greatly improves the seam effect and unreasonable extension of the image. At the same time, the structural similarity value between the restoration result of the system in this paper and the original image is higher. The above results indicate that the repair system designed in this paper can ensure the use of the known information of the original image to the greatest extent and make the repair results more reasonable on the basis of the minimum changes to the original image.

## 4 Conclusion

Image restoration technology is an essential key technology in the restoration of damaged cultural relics, and the technology has important applications in many fields, such as photo restoration, film and game special effects production, the underlying application of mobile phone image software, etc. Due to the unreasonable algorithm optimization process in the traditional cultural relic image digital repair system, there will be obvious color difference and structure deviation between the repaired part and the surrounding part, which weakens the visual connectivity of the restored result. In order to solve this problem, this paper designs a digital repair system for damaged cultural relics image in professional training of restoration. This system has advantages in many aspects, which can make the restoration result more reasonable with the least modification to the original image. But at the same time, the system also has some shortcomings, such as long computing time, low timeliness, in the future research process, it needs to be improved and strengthened.

**Fund Projects.** 1. 2018 Tibet University Scientific Research and Cultivation Fund Project (Growth Plan) Project Number: ZDCZJH18–15.

2. "The Education Department of Tibet Autonomous Region'Building a National Team and Key Laboratory of Computer and Tibetan Information Technology' (Zang Jiao Cai Zhi [2018] No. 81)".

## References

1. Jiang, C., Wang, J., Yu, L.: Research on a digital restoration method for textile cultural relics. Silk **56**(11), 21–25 (2019)
2. Yao, Y., Hu, W., Ren, Y., et al.: Detection and localization of digital video regional tampering. J. Image Graph. **23**(06), 779–791 (2018)
3. Cui, T., Xu, K., Yan, S.: Improved criminisi algorithm based on sobel operator. Comput. Digit. Eng. **46**(10), 2111–2116 (2018)
4. Sun, J., Cao, F., Tang, Z., et al.: Trustable image inpainting method based on image mosaics. J. Univ. Shanghai Sci. Technol. **40**(02), 150–157 (2018)
5. Xiang, P., Wuzhen, J., Herong, Z., et al.: Combining interpolated subdivision and radial basis function for filling 3D scanning data. J. Image Graph. **23**(04), 564–571 (2018)
6. Lulu, Z., Shaoyan, G., Feipeng, D., et al.: Hole filling algorithm of three-dimensional point cloud based on structure from motion. Acta Optica Sinica **38**(06), 131–137 (2018)
7. Qi, Z., Suzhen, L., Jialu, B., et al.: Opening-hole repairing in point cloud based on improved curve contraction flows. Laser Optoelectron. Prog. **55**(09), 125–131 (2018)
8. Vincenti, G., Bucciero, A., Helfert, M., Glowatz, M. (eds.): E-Learning, E-Education, and Online Training. LNICSSITE, vol. 180. Springer, Cham (2017). https://doi.org/10.1007/978-3-319-49625-2
9. Fu, W., Liu, S., Srivastava, G.: Optimization of big data scheduling in social networks. Entropy **21**(9), 902 (2019)
10. Liu, S., Li, Z., Zhang, Y., et al.: Introduction of key problems in long-distance learning and training. Mob. Netw. Appl. **24**(1), 1–4 (2019)
11. Fan, C.Q., Ren, K., Meng, L.S., et al.: Advances in digital image inpainting algorithms based on deep learning. J. Sign. Process. **36**(01), 102–109 (2020)
12. Chen, Q., Zhang, L.H.: Design of simulation system for authenticity reproduction of cultural relics in digital museum. Sci. Technol. Eng. **19**(11), 195–200 (2019)
13. Zhang, Y., Geng, G. H.: Matching method of damaged cultural relic images based on scale invariant feature transform and bounded distortion mapping. J. Xiamen Univ. (Nat. Sci.) **58**(03), 449–454 (2019)
14. Tu, D.W., Lan, H., Zhang, X.: Digital three-dimensional reconstruction technology of cultural relics. Laser Optoelectron. Prog. **56**(19), 196–202 (2019)

# The Design of College Ideological and Political Teaching System Based on Online and Offline Mixed Mode

Fang Liu(✉)

Department of Foundational Courses,
Shenyang Institute of Science and Technology, Shenyang 110167, China

**Abstract.** The current design of the college ideological and political teaching system has a low amount of stored data, resulting in a small teaching range. In order to solve the above problems, a new college ideological and political teaching system based on the online and offline hybrid mode was designed. Using TS-6 flash data memory, the data memory is mainly composed of bus, data interface, single-chip microcomputer, and signal receiving module. The single-chip microcomputer uses a 64 G memory model with an area of 5 mm * 5 mm, which occupies a small area inside the system. It also provides a larger storage space for the data memory to ensure the smoothness of the system. The collector is mainly composed of DSZ6852 chip, clock, data interface and other small parts. DSZ6852 chip adopts 8-channel 16-channel mode to complete data transmission. It has resource video channels, audio channels, text channels, etc. to meet different resource types and improve data. The speed of collection. Realize software workflow through resource transcoding, resource push, online learning, and push information. The experimental results show that the college ideological and political teaching system based on the online and offline hybrid mode has a higher storage capacity and a wider teaching range.

**Keywords:** Online and offline · Mixed mode · College ideology · Political teaching · Teaching system

## 1 Introduction

The Internet has become the main tool of the 21st century and is omnipresent in people's daily lives. As the future successors of the motherland, college students have a deeper understanding of the Internet and use it more frequently. At present, colleges and universities are an important area for the development of network technology. Online learning of knowledge, communication of emotions, entertainment and relaxation, the Internet is subtly changing the efficient way of education, affecting the values of college students [1, 2]. In the network environment, how to improve the ideological and political education ability of college counselors has become an urgent problem in the development of college education. The development of network technology has brought


W. Fu et al. (Eds.): eLEOT 2021, LNICST 389, pp. 332–343, 2021.
https://doi.org/10.1007/978-3-030-84383-0_29

positive help to the ideological and political education of colleges and universities, but also brought a negative impact. College counselors are a key part of the ideological and political education of colleges and universities. After the advantages of traditional education, expand the ideological and political education environment, provide students with correct college counseling education programs, and open up a new situation in college ideological and political education.

At present, relevant scholars have proposed the design of college ideological and political teaching system, and the literature [3] proposed to combine virtual reality technology with college ideological and political theory courses. The virtual reality teaching group lasts for one month, virtual reality ideological and political theory class teaching, general teaching group or traditional teaching. The comparison shows that the teaching effect of virtual reality teaching is higher than that of traditional teaching. Literature [4] proposes an intelligent campus management system based on the Internet of Things technology. This research uses the unified data collection source of face recognition terminal hardware products based on the Internet of Things technology to perform unified management in the background of the system, and calculate and analyze the data to obtain valuable campus big data.

The new thinking of education and teaching theory points out that learning should be centered on learning, play the initiative of learning, have a desire for active exploration of knowledge, and let learners become active builders of learning knowledge. In order to realize this new educational thought in depth, a hybrid education method of online and offline modes has been introduced in various fields of learning to improve the efficiency of educational learning [5].

Therefore, this article uses the advantages of the online and offline hybrid education system of ideological and political teaching in colleges and universities to further study the education system and promote the development of ideological and political education resources. Optimize the functions of the system hardware area and software area. The hardware part is designed with data storage, collector, and DSZ6852 chip; the software realizes the software workflow through resource transcoding, resource push, online learning, and information push. The online and offline mixed education system of ideological and political teaching in colleges and universities is highly efficient and shared.

## 2 Hardware Design of College Ideological and Political Teaching System Based on Online and Offline Hybrid Mode

The hardware structure of the Japanese online + offline hybrid educational resource automation selective sharing system designed in this paper is mainly composed of collector and memory. The system hardware structure is shown in Fig. 1 below:

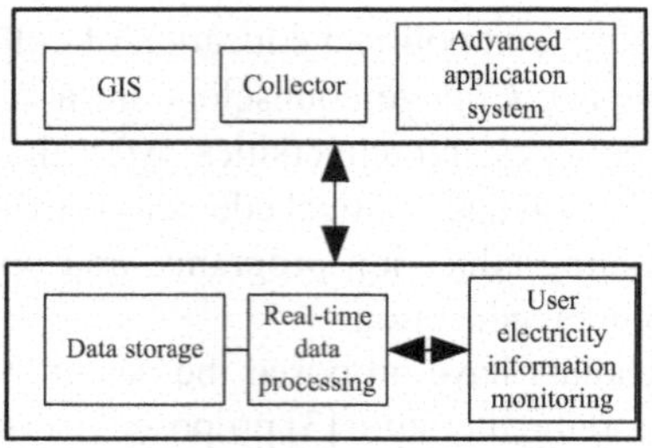


**Fig. 1.** The hardware structure of college ideological and political teaching system based on online and offline hybrid mode

## 2.1 Data Memory Design

Data storage is the key to the ideological and political teaching system of colleges and universities based on the online and offline hybrid mode. The work of data storage is to ensure the permanence of resources in the system, because some resources will automatically disappear at a stage, so the data storage must ensure that after the data disappears, Re-upload to the system through the backup information storage.

The data memory structure is shown in Fig. 2:

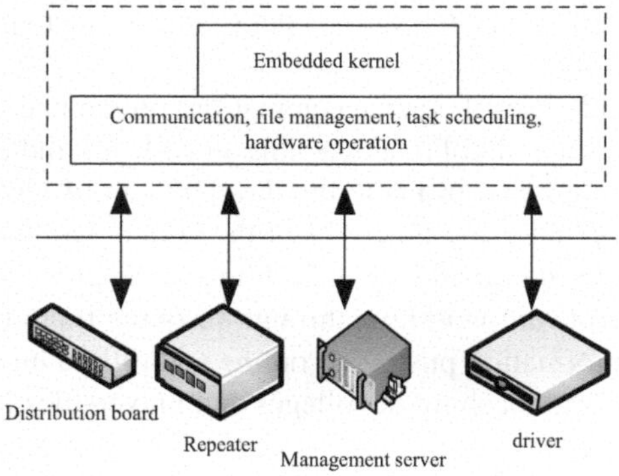


**Fig. 2.** Data memory structure

In order to realize the functions of the above system, TS-6 flash data memory is adopted. This series of memory is a device with low cost but the most functions in the field at present, and it has a higher cost performance. The advantage of the data memory is that 6 buses are used internally to work simultaneously, and each bus is connected to a different FPGA interface to receive data transmitted in different signal formats. The internal circuit diagram of the memory is shown in Fig. 3:

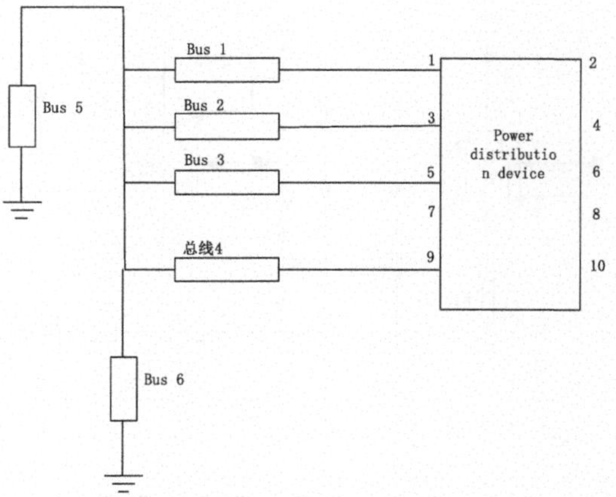


**Fig. 3.** Memory internal circuit diagram

According to Fig. 3, the interface of bus 1 adopts I/O mode to connect signals, and the link bit width is 52, which can be input and output in a two-way manner to realize the two-way exchange of data; Bus 2 is the OUT connection signal interface, and the link bit width is 84, Output the signal in a one-way manner, and the control signal enters. Bus 3 connects the signal interface with BSC, the link bit width is 16, and the chip select signal is output in a unidirectional manner. Bus 4 is the CLAS connection signal interface, the link bit width is 6, and the signal is input in a one-way manner to realize the signal board selection. Different types of signal input methods are different. Bus 5 is a BUSY interface, the link bit width is 81, and the input mode is busy signal input [6–8]. The data interface of bus 6 is ADD, the link bit width is 27, and the address signal [9] is output in a unidirectional manner.

## 2.2 Collector Design

The task completed by the data collector in the system is mainly to collect the resources transmitted by the uploader to the system, and then compress the collected resources and transmit them to the server to complete the authenticity identification of educational resources. According to the task of the data collector, it is necessary to ensure the collection speed of data collection and ensure the integrity of the data resources. Therefore, this article uses the HKS-920 data collector, which uses a large capacity battery of 5000 mA and can work in standby mode. 7 days, and the lowest power consumption during work. The internal structure of the collector is shown in Fig. 4:

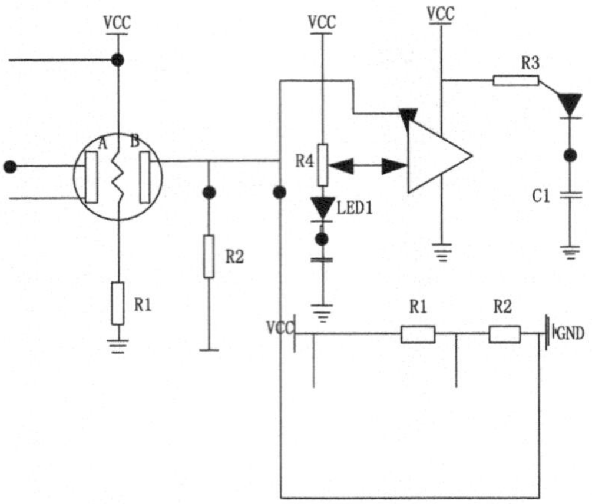


**Fig. 4.** Collector circuit diagram

The data interface of the data collector is PCI, HPI and Ethernet interface. Each interface is connected to the wireless network of the system and has the function of automatic backup. Once the data is lost during transmission, the backup can be called out. The uplink rate of the interface for data collection is 3.5 Mbit/s, and the downlink rate is 6.7 Mbit/s [10–12].

According to the combination of the operator and the design requirements of the virtual simulation experiment teaching environment, this paper draws a design plan. The ideological and political education system is mainly composed of five distributions of the graph. The ideological and political education system needs to sort out the arrangement of experiment courses and the arrangement of students' course selection. At this time, it will need some distinguishing information such as the operator's class and student number. The amount of data is large and difficult to store. This article uses database processing for storage, which reduces the memory of the experimental teaching multi-dimensional data visualization system. The design of the database concept is the basis for the design of the multi-dimensional data visualization system for experimental teaching. Only a certain operator and certain experimental teaching can make this virtual simulation experiment work. This article uses the database conceptual model ER for these basic information storage and screening operations. The model is completed [13–15].

## 3 Software Design of College Ideological and Political Teaching System Based on Online and Offline Hybrid Mode

College students' outlook on life, world outlook, and values have been initially formed, but due to lack of social experience and insufficient knowledge of things, it is easy to make wrong judgments. The network environment is complex, and the content involved is rich and diverse. This includes not only positive information, but also negative information. If students browse too much negative information while surfing the Internet, they may be affected by it and cause distortion of the world view. Therefore, it must be Optimize the ideological and political education in online colleges and universities, use online content to cultivate the moral quality of college students, enhance the professional skills of college students, and improve the practical ability of college students [16–18].

Enrich the content of online moral education, and use the content of education to subtly improve the moral level of students. The Internet is open, unconstrained, and secretive. Users will not be restricted by time and space in the process of communication. This poses a severe challenge to the current ideological and political education of college students. College students are easily affected by the Internet. Affected by all kinds of information on the Internet, counselors have an inescapable responsibility in guiding college students to establish a correct view of social cognition. Counselors must face such problems with a proactive attitude, develop various thematic columns, introduce different cases, and educate students. First of all, we must start with the Internet environment, optimize the students' online environment, strengthen the promotion of Internet morality, and use reward and punishment strategies to strengthen students' self-restraint ability; secondly, set up an online education APP or education website to help through the various modules in the website Students develop a better sense of self-discipline, improve their moral judgment level, so that students can better distinguish external things; finally, optimize the ideological, political and moral education chain, network education and campus education cannot be separated, counselors can use network technology to carry out Campus cultural activities stimulate students' innovative spirit, strengthen students' moral experience, and form a complete chain of ethical cultivating through the combination of online and offline, so that contemporary college students have a stronger sense of responsibility and more self-motivated. Higher creativity, which also has certain advancing significance for shaping a positive, healthy and positive network moral education environment [19–21].

Based on the above analysis of the hardware device design of the ideological and political teaching system based on the online and offline hybrid mode, and the analysis of the concept and significance of the ideological and political online and offline hybrid education methods, this article rationally calls each device to make the online and offline hybrid mode [22, 23]. The ideological and political teaching system of colleges and universities operates stably, and the specific working process of the system is shown in Fig. 5:

(1) First, clarify the hypertext protocol of the computer system to which the system belongs, because different hypertext protocols will transcode the resources in the system, making the resource text format chaotic. After preprocessing the system operating environment, start the operating environment, Make the education resource sharing system in a standby state;
(2) When a learner enters any homepage of the resource sharing platform, the system background will receive a service instruction and the system is in a service state. For beginners, the system will enter the learner's learning interests, identity information and other key information, To facilitate the system to complete selective resource push to learners;
(3) After the learner has registered and completed the system login account, he can enter the system to query the Japanese course he wants to learn according to the learning page. On the system designed in this article, any resource course is two modules online and offline. When the learner clicks on any learning course, the

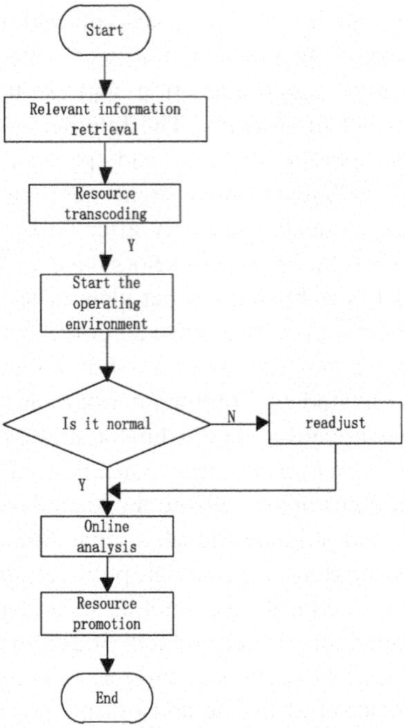


**Fig. 5.** Work flow of college ideological and political teaching system based on online and offline hybrid mode

system will call up the data of this resource in the data storage and present it to the learner, and then push the same type of course to the learner after the class to complete the teaching task. After learning online, the system will leave learners with offline learning tasks to deepen the learning of Japanese courses;

(4) During the operation of the system, internal resources will be updated in real time to ensure the real-time nature of system resources. Once new educational resources are uploaded to the system, the system's data collector will first check the authenticity of the resources After all qualifications, the resource information is encoded according to the existing types in the system, and stored in the system space by calling the memory, and then selecting a different path to push to each user recorded by the learning, and then converting the resource into a document format. The data is displayed with the correct encoding to complete the information resource sharing work.

The education system should set up a corresponding network ideological education assessment mechanism, take the network ideological and political education assessment mechanism as the assessment goal of college counselors, and construct corresponding commendations and rewards. The assessment content in the assessment mechanism must be updated regularly. The assessment content of ideological and political education in colleges and universities should be carried out from four aspects: the level of the counselor, the content of the ideological and political education carried out by the counselor, the investment in the ideological and political education of the counselor, and the level of students after the counselor's education. Comprehensive consideration, judge the ideological and political education ability of counselors. Affected by the external environment, the focus of ideological and political education is different, so the content of the network ideological education assessment mechanism should also be updated regularly to keep up with the times to ensure the effectiveness of ideological and political education for college students.

## 4 Experimental Analysis

In order to verify whether the system studied in this article is meaningful, this article is going to conduct a comparative experiment for verification. In order to achieve the experimental purpose, the control system used in this article is based on the online and offline hybrid mode of college ideological and political teaching system, and jointly complete the experimental analysis of this article. Set the experimental parameters as shown in Table 1:

**Table 1.** Experimental parameters

| Project | Parameter |
|---|---|
| Hard disk | 120 GB |
| Operating voltage | 100 V |
| Working current | 50 A |
| Operating system | Windows10 |
| Operating time | 10 min |

In order to ensure the fairness and scientificity of the experiment, this article randomly selects 20 young people with learning ability to complete the experiment. The 20 young people are randomly divided into two groups to learn the same knowledge on different educational resource systems. It is knowledge that the learner has never touched), and finally an exam is conducted according to the learning content, and the average score of each group member is used as the final test data result. The specific test process is to divide the learners into groups and carry out a three-day study, and the study time on different systems is controlled at 3 h a day, and the study is carried out at the same time period to avoid interference from other factors. After days, two exams were conducted, and the test scores of each youth were finally fitted, the data was settled, and the final result of this experiment was obtained.

The experimental results of the amount of data stored in the education system are shown in Fig. 6 below:

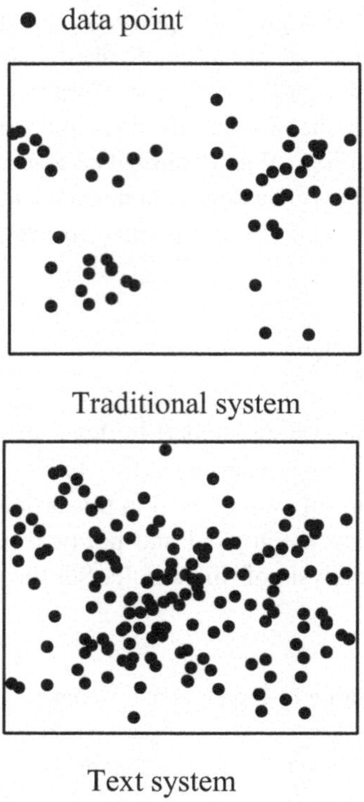


**Fig. 6.** Experimental results of system storage data volume

The experimental results of the improvement of student performance are shown in Fig. 7 below:

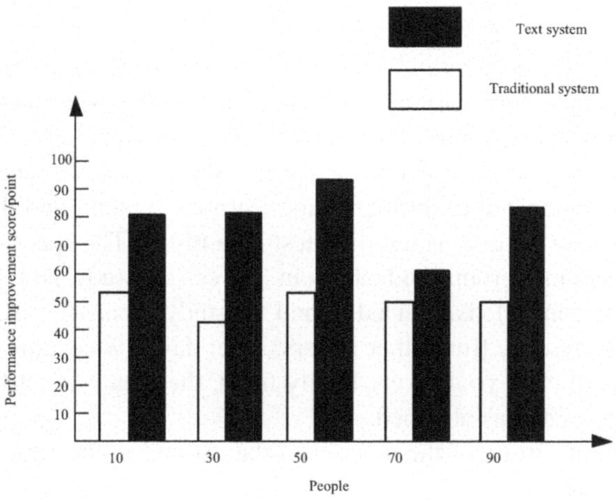


**Fig. 7.** Experimental results of student performance improvement effects

Through the experiment, the result is that the average performance of the ideological and political teaching system based on the online and offline hybrid mode is higher than the average performance of the ideological and political education resource automation selective sharing system.

Before this experiment was carried out, all possible interference problems from the outside world have been solved, so the authenticity of the experiment results can be guaranteed. On the one hand, this result is because the ideological and political teaching system designed in this paper is based on the online and offline hybrid mode. Sharing function. Before the learners learn the resources, the system will classify the educational resources according to different needs, and gradually teach the learners from simple to difficult, and the system will treat a whole educational resource when entering the resources. For detection, once there is redundant educational resource information or conceptual error or unclear information, the resource uploader will be contacted in time to ensure the sharing, accuracy and selectivity of educational resources in the system. Compared with the traditional educational resource teaching system, the data in the system has a certain degree of redundancy, which will cause a certain amount of knowledge confusion for beginners and affect the learning experience on the educational resource system. On the other hand, the hardware area data memory of the system designed in this paper is assembled by using six types of different buses, and the system adopts online and offline hybrid education to ensure the permanence of the internal resources of the system, online learning, and offline review after class. Form a good learning method and improve learning efficiency. The traditional education sharing system only completes learning on the system, and does not adopt online and offline hybrid education learning methods, and does not have a process to deepen learning resources, which leads to unreliable knowledge of learners and reduces learning efficiency.

## 5 Conclusion

This article first designs and analyzes the functions of data storage and collectors in the hardware area of the online + offline hybrid education resource automation selective sharing system. Each device has super-powered functions, and then analyzes the online + offline hybrid high-efficiency ideological and political education resources Exploring the essence and significance of the system, and finally based on the above research, summed up the workflow of a highly efficient ideological and political education resource automation selective sharing system based on online + offline hybrid, to achieve the efficiency and sharing of the system, and achieve the design of this article The purpose is to promote the development of efficient ideological and political education resources.

Colleges and universities must set up a guarantee mechanism, use the guarantee mechanism to protect the funds, personnel, venues, and online education of the colleges and universities, so that the resource allocation of colleges and universities can be better optimized, and regular planning and management are required to facilitate college counselors to use existing resources to learn knowledge and improve Self-education ability. In view of the openness of the network environment, it is difficult for network ideological education to divide school education and off-campus education. Therefore, relevant education authorities need to actively promote network ideological and political education organizations, establish organizational alliances, and optimize the network education environment. Corresponding support will be given so that the ideological and political education promotion system for counselors can be better established, and related ideological and political education projects can be better carried out.

## References


1. Rongfan, M.A., Yang, J.: Research on the identification mechanism of university young teachers' political institutional based on binary logistic regression analysis. Revista de Cercetare si Interventie Sociala **65**, 248–259 (2019)
2. Wang, H.: The mechanism of ideological-political education exchange and sharing platform in colleges under the new media era based on Internet web technology. Revista de Cercetare si Interventie Sociala **63**, 85–104 (2018)
3. Zhang, N., Chen, X., Yin, H.: Significance and possibility of VR technology embedded in the teaching of ideological and political theory course in colleges and universities. IEEE Access **8**, 2035–2043 (2020)
4. Li, W.: Design of smart campus management system based on Internet of Things technology. J. Intell. Fuzzy Syst. **40**(2), 3159–3168 (2021)
5. Gowda, V.D., Ramesha, M., Sridhara, S.B., et al.: Design of antilock braking system based on wheel slip estimation. J. Phys.: Conf. Ser. **1706**(1), 012216 (2020). 18 p.
6. Zhang, Y.: Design and curriculum optimization of college english teaching model based on esp. Int. J. Eng. Model. **31**(1), 359–364 (2018)
7. Huang, H.: Design and implementation of a college english listening learning system based on android platform. Int. J. Emerg. Technol. Learn. **13**(7), 43 (2018)
8. Dhanraj, J.A., Sivakumar, A., Krishnamurthy, B., et al.: Design of IoT based object tracking system for identifying the RSS value access point to trilaterate the location. In: IOP Conference Series: Materials Science and Engineering, vol. 988, no. 1, p. 012077 (2020). 8 p.
9. Ravikumar, L., Yashwant, K., Aravindan, B., et al.: Analytical and numerical approach on design of cageless open differential unit. In: IOP Conference Series: Materials Science and Engineering, vol. 988, no. 1, p. 012043 (2020). 14 p.
10. Zhang, S., Li, J., Jodylf, M.: The related factors analysis of ideological and political effectiveness in self-media based on data mining. J. Intell. Fuzzy Syst. **37**(1), 1–9 (2019)
11. Liu, S., Liu, D., Srivastava, G., et al.: Overview and methods of correlation filter algorithms in object tracking. Complex Intelligent Systems (2020). https://doi.org/10.1007/s40747-020-00161-4
12. Liu, S., Lu, M., Li, H., et al.: Prediction of gene expression patterns with generalized linear regression model. Front. Genet. **10**, 120 (2019)
13. Fu, W., Liu, S., Srivastava, G.: Optimization of big data scheduling in social networks. Entropy **21**(9), 902 (2019)
14. Darius, P.S.H., Gundabattini, E., Solomon, D.G.: A survey on the effectiveness of online teaching–learning methods for university and college students. J. Inst. Eng. (India) Ser. B (2), 1–10 (2021)
15. Bingzhuan, P.: Intercultural communicative competence teaching and assessment based on modern information technology. Int. J. Emerg. Technol. Learn. (iJET) **16**(7), 175 (2021)
16. Yu, Y.: Design and implementation of a teaching assistance platform for college students based on ASP.NET. Int. J. Emerg. Technol. Learn. (iJET) **14**(12), 97 (2019)
17. Li, Z.H., Yang, J.J., Qin, H.Q., et al.: A study of efficiency evaluation of national quality online courses during the epidemic: based on fuzzy logic calculation and bootstrap-DEA. Math. Probl. Eng. **2021**(30), 1–7 (2021)

18. Shi, X., Li, X., Wu, Y.: The Application of computer-aided teaching and mobile Internet terminal in college physical education. Comput.-Aided Des. Appl. **18**(S4), 163–174 (2021)
19. Zhang, E., Yang, Y.: Music dance distance teaching system based on Ologit model and machine learning. J. Ambient Intell. Humaniz. Comput. 1–17 (2021)
20. Han, Z.: Research on sports balanced development evaluation system based on edge computing and balanced game. Secur. Commun. Netw. **2021**(5), 1–8 (2021)
21. Zhou, J., Bai, J., Jiang, M.S.: White-box implementation of ECDSA based on the cloud plus side mode. Secur. Commun. Netw. **2020**(2), 1–10 (2020)
22. Wang, Y.: Analysis on the construction of ideological and political education system for college students based on mobile artificial intelligence terminal. Soft. Comput. **24**(11), 8365–8375 (2020). https://doi.org/10.1007/s00500-020-04932-6
23. Ding, M., Liu, S., Deng, W.: Exploration on the teaching mode of ideological and political course in MOOC environment. In: MATEC Web of Conferences, vol. 267 (2019)

# Design of Innovation and Entrepreneurship Teaching System for Ideological and Political Courses in Universities Based on Online and Offline Integration

Fang Liu(✉)

Department of Foundational Courses,
Shenyang Institute of Science and Technology, Shenyang 110167, China

**Abstract.** In current university teaching systems, single-threaded databases are often used as system databases, but such databases tend to occupy a high percentage of system servers during operation. Therefore, the design of innovation and entrepreneurship teaching system for college ideological and political courses based on online and offline integration is proposed. Use Mysq1 multi-threaded database as the system database, and use collaborative filtering to calculate the allocation of teaching resources. Design the network topology and data structure of the system. According to the requirements of online and offline integration, formulate functional modules and build a mixed teaching mode. The experimental results prove that the system meets the design function requirements, the server occupancy rate is low, and it has certain feasibility.

**Keywords:** Database · System design · Online and offline integration · Collaborative filtering algorithm

## 1 Introduction

Today with the development of computer network technology, online mobile education has developed into an extremely important part of the education field [1–3]. Mobile teaching is a way to make teaching methods and teaching resources quickly accepted by students through smart devices and wireless networks. In my country, mobile learning refers to the process in which teachers use smart devices for Internet teaching and students who listen to classes use smart devices to learn. At present, mobile terminals are widely used by major colleges and universities, currently using: blackboards, whiteboards, and projectors, as well as the use of advanced intelligent equipment, supporting intelligent teaching systems for new teaching [4–6].

Domestic researchers conducted detailed studies on traditional teaching methods, summarized the problems existing in traditional education methods, and proposed solutions to traditional education problems including: the design of cloud architecture requires the use of new cloud, network, and terminal technologies. And it requires a


W. Fu et al. (Eds.): eLEOT 2021, LNICST 389, pp. 344–354, 2021.
https://doi.org/10.1007/978-3-030-84383-0_30

wide range of application-side technologies and cannot be ignored. However, in order to reduce the complexity of the system, single-threaded databases are often used as mobile teaching databases, but such databases often require a lot of resources to query when extracting user data., The system occupies a lot and is not suitable for teaching systems under multiple users [7, 8].

## 2 The Software Design of Innovation and Entrepreneurship Teaching System for College Ideological and Political Courses

### 2.1 System Database Selection and Establishment

A database refers to a collection of data that is stored on a computer's storage device for a long time and organized according to a certain model, which can be shared by various users or applications [9, 10]. Including databases, database management systems, and database systems. A database is a warehouse for storing data. A collection of organized and shareable large amounts of data stored in the computer for a long time [11–13]. The data in the database is described and stored according to a certain model organization, while maintaining small redundancy, high independence and easy scalability, and the data can be shared [14–16]. This article chooses the Mysql database, which supports multi-threading and multi-processor. The database implements SQL function library through a highly optimized class library, without any memory allocation after query initialization. The main data types are: 1, 2, 3, 4 and 8 byte length unsigned/signed integers, DATETIME, DOUBLE, CHAR, VARCHAR, TEXT, BLOB, DATE, TIME, FLOAT, TIMESTAMP, YEAR and ENUM types. The system supports aggregate functions (COUNT, COUNT(DISTINCT), AVG, STD, SUM, MAX) and MIN, and fully supports the GROUP BY and ORDER BY clauses of SQL. The system supports LEFT 0UTER JOIN and ODBC of ANSI SQL, and all columns have default values. The system can mix tables from different databases in the same query. The system can use INSERT to insert a subset of the table columns, and those columns without clear values are set as default values.

### 2.2 System Collaborative Filtering Operation

The collaborative filtering algorithm is used to calculate the resource recommendation module. When a registered user of the system accesses the resource recommendation page, the recommendation system will calculate the teaching resources that the user may like based on the collaborative filtering algorithm, and then recommend it to the user. The recommended resources are calculated by the user's evaluation of the teaching resources. This system uses a combination of user-based collaborative filtering recommendation and item-based collaborative filtering recommendation for recommendation. The calculation process is shown in Fig. 1:

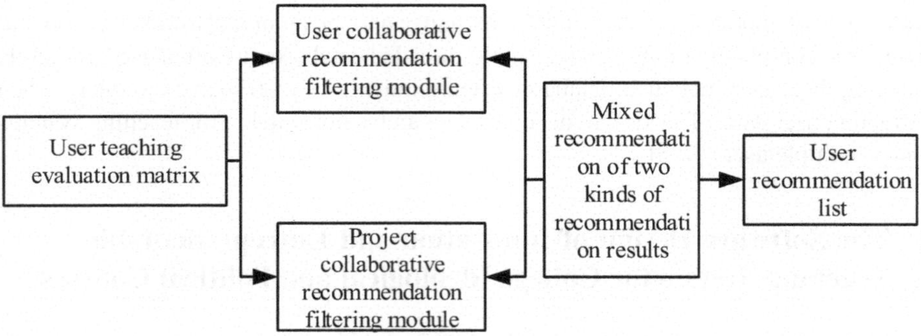


**Fig. 1.** Collaborative filtering operation process

In addition to recommendations, collaborative filtering operations can also indicate the user's teaching resource score. Take the matrix $R$ as an $m \times n$ matrix, $m$ represents the number of users, $n$ represents the number of corresponding teaching resources, $R_{i_j}$ represents the rating of the $i$ user on the $j$ teaching resource. The user's teaching resource scoring matrix is shown in Table 1:

**Table 1.** User-teaching resource rating table

| User/Item | 1 | … | i | … | N |
|---|---|---|---|---|---|
| U1 | $R_{1_1}$ | … | $R_{1_i}$ | … | $R_{1_n}$ |
| … | … | … | … | … | … |
| Ui | $R_{i_1}$ | … | $R_{i_i}$ | … | $R_{i_n}$ |
| … | … | … | … | … | … |
| Um | $R_{m_1}$ | … | $R_{m_i}$ | … | $R_{m_n}$ |

According to the user-teaching material scoring matrix, the adjusted cosine similarity formula is adopted to find the neighbors of the target user, and the neighbors are in descending order. For the target user $a$, the corresponding adjacent set is $M$, $M = \{M_1, M_2, ..., M_k\}$, and $a$ does not belong to $M$, and the similarity between $M_1$ and $M_k$ is $sim(a, M_k)$, and the similarity is arranged from small to large, then it shows that $M_1$ and user $a$ are the most similar, their interests are the closest, and $M_1$ and $M_k$ are the least similar. Then the similarity $sim(a, M_k)$ between user $a$ and user $k$ is shown in formula (1):

$$sim(a, k) = \frac{\sum_{p \in I} \left(R_{a,p} - \overline{R_a}\right)\left(R_{k,p} - \overline{R_k}\right)}{\sqrt{\sum_{p \in I} \left(R_{a,p} - \overline{R_a}\right)^2} \times \sqrt{\sum_{p \in I} \left(R_{k,p} - \overline{R_k}\right)^2}} \tag{1}$$

In formula (1), set $I$ represents the set of teaching resources required by user $a$ and user $k$, $R_{a,p}$ represents user $a$'s rating of teaching resource $p$, $R_{k,p}$ represents user $k$'s rating of teaching resource $p$, and $\overline{R_a}$ represents user $a$'s rating of teaching resource Average score, $\overline{R_k}$ represents the average score of user $k$'s rating of teaching resources. Among the users closest to the target user, predict the score, calculate the recommendation degree based on the similarity, and recommend the teaching resources with the top $n$ scores among all the teaching resources to the target user, and the template user $a$'s teaching of the score The score $P_{a,i}$ of resource $i$ is shown in formula (2):

$$P_{a,i} = \overline{R_a} + \frac{\sum_{k \in M_a} sim(a, k) \times \left(R_{k,i} - \overline{R_k}\right)}{\sum_{k \in M_a} (|sim(a, k)|)} \tag{2}$$

In the formula (2), $M_a$ represents the set of nearest neighbors of user $a$, $sim(a, k)$ represents the similarity between user $a$ and user $k$ calculated in the previous step, and $\overline{R_k}$ represents the average score of user $k$ for teaching resources, $\overline{R_a}$ represents user $a$ for the average score of the teaching resource score, $R_{k,i}$ represents user $k$'s score for teaching resource $i$.

## 2.3 System Network Topology

This paper divides the system's network structure into internal local area network and external network, and protects data users through security devices. The system protects internal data security and access security through a firewall. The various servers and developers of the system are protected in the firewall, while external users pass through the firewall through the Internet to access the system and corresponding resources deployed on the application server. This process is protected and restricted by the firewall. If malicious attacks and pressures are found, there will be corresponding security policies to ensure. The topological structure of the system is shown in Fig. 2:

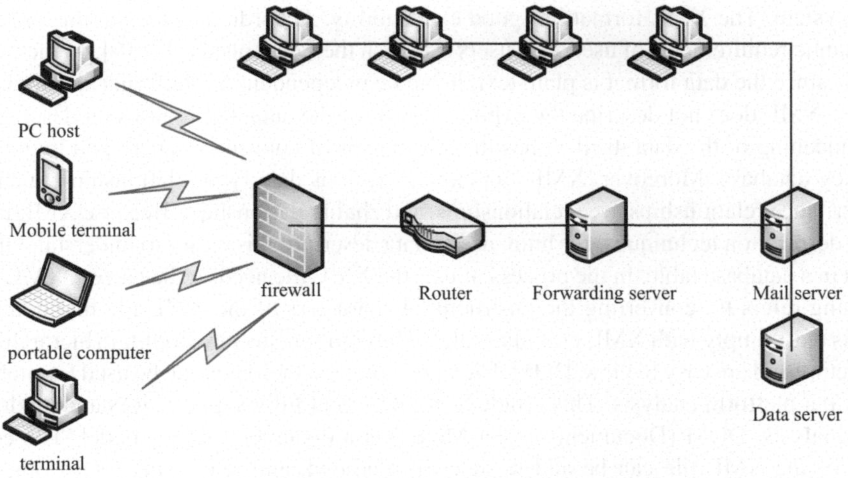


**Fig. 2.** System network topology

This system runs on the network inside the firewall to provide online teaching services for students and teachers. Because of the large number of people, there may be a large number of visits during use. In order to ensure that teachers and students are not hindered when using the system and ensure the speed of data processing, the data buffer pool technology is used to solve the problem of concurrent access by a large number of users on the Internet, allowing users to queue for access to prevent system instability or inability Respond to the access phenomenon in time to ensure system performance. Since the operating platform of the system is a campus network, the impact will be very large, and the system security requirements are relatively high, considering the three aspects of data security, network security and system security. For network security, the first step to ensure network security is to ensure the security of network equipment, so that unauthorized users cannot access related network equipment. Regarding ensuring the security of network equipment, the network center has configured related firewalls and intrusion detection systems in order to ensure the security of the server and prevent unauthorized intrusion by intentions. The second is system security. The system can be configured to use identity authentication for general users to restrict users from accessing certain information. It is stipulated that users can only enter the system and browse related information if they have a qualified user name and password. Special users not only need a username and password, but also an IP address in the whitelist set by the system to ensure that their information is not leaked during the operation of the system. The data security of the system uses RAIDS disk arrays as database server storage to ensure the normal operation of the system to prevent data loss and provide the system with complete and incremental backup methods such as off-site storage and CD burning. It can back up the past data to solve the problem of data and information loss caused by improper operation.

### 2.4 System Data Structure

This article chooses XML format as the system data format on the data structure used by the system. The XML format has good extensibility. According to the parameters and semantic requirements of user data, users establish their own needs [17–19]. At the same time, since the data format is plain text, it can be independent of platforms and applications. XML does not describe the explicit format of the data, but focuses on describing the meaning of the data itself. It has the advantages of convenient query and high efficiency database. Moreover, XML can express various data type relationships, such as inheritance relationships, tree relationships, and chain relationships. Because XML uses text description techniques, for humans, its data description is easier to understand than data in a database table. In the process of use, the XML file needs to be parsed. XML file parsing refers to: converting the unstructured characters of the XML file into components that comply with XML grammar rules. The components have a certain hierarchical structure and are easy to view. DOM, SAX and other technologies can be used for mobile WeChat platform analysis. This article uses DOM that fully supports iOS and Android for analysis. DOM (Document Object Model) is a document object model. The content of the XML file can be added, deleted, modified, and read using DOM objects. The working principle of DOM: parse the file into independent attributes, elements and other nodes. The content of the XML file is expressed in the form of a node tree, and the content of the XML file can be accessed and modified through the nodes of the node tree. So as to realize all aspects of dynamic operation of XML files. Since DOM has nothing to do with programming languages, programs and scripting languages such as Python and Shell can access and modify the content and structure of XML files [20, 21].

### 2.5 System Function Module Design

In the teaching system of this article, the released teaching system includes questionnaires, teaching notices, feedback, examination information, exercises and file management. Questionnaire: The teacher will conduct a questionnaire survey on the taught courses, which helps to improve the quality of teaching. Use the statistics module to count the information after the questionnaire survey and display it in a more intuitive way; through the import module, select the EXCEL file to import on the PC side to update the content of the questionnaire survey menu item in the mobile client; through the export module, the questionnaire survey The results are exported as EXCEL files. Teaching notice: It helps students to understand the school consultation in time. Through the import module, select the EXCEL file to import on the PC side to update the content of the teaching notification item in the mobile client; through the export module, export the results of the questionnaire as an EXCEL file. Feedback: For the questionnaire survey organized by the teacher, students will give feedback through the feedback menu of the client. Export the results of the opinion survey as an EXCEL file through the export module. Exam information: Through the import module, select the EXCEL file to import on the PC side to update the content of the individual test information in the mobile client; through the export module, export the results of the exam information as an EXCEL file. Exercises: through the import module, select the EXCEL file on the PC to import, update the content of the exercises in the mobile client; through the export module, export the results of the exercises as an EXCEL file. Document management: It is the database management of learning materials and learning consultation. It can add, delete, and modify the content of the mobile client's micro-classes, work display, and news reports.

### 2.6 Integrated Online and Offline Hybrid Teaching Construction

Blended teaching is a teaching mode constructed together with the online teaching of the design system and the offline teaching mode of normal teaching. With "interaction" as the core, online education, face-to-face learning, and group collaboration are integrated to achieve a new educational model of meaning construction, which makes networked learning and traditional education shift from dual opposition to dual integration. Integration refers to the real combination of the Internet and education, making the teaching process more intelligent and comfortable. In this system, in addition to helping students learn online, the teaching resources in the database can also be developed for teachers and provide corresponding teaching information to ensure openness. At the same time, the use of the system's collaborative filtering operation method of the system in this article can help teachers in offline teaching to conduct statistics on teaching conditions.

At the same time, teachers can view the results of students' online system exams in the system, thereby helping teachers understand the deficiencies of current teaching courses. Improve teaching efficiency.

## 3 Experimental Analysis

In order to verify the feasibility of the design system, this paper conducts system test experiments, using a university's ideological and political course innovation and entrepreneurship teaching resources as the experimental system database data.

### 3.1 System Test Environment

The system test environment in the system experiment of this article is shown in Table 2:

**Table 2.** The system test environment

| Equipment type | Name | Number |
|---|---|---|
| Hardware environment | PC (medium configuration) | 1 |
| | Web server | 1 |
| | Wifi device | 1 |
| | IOS smart mobile device | 1 |
| | Android Smart mobile device | 1 |
| | Windows smart mobile devices | 1 |
| Software environment | PC equipped with Windows 7 operating system | 1 |
| | IE browser | 1 |
| | Firefox browser | 1 |
| | Chrome browser | 1 |

### 3.2 Login Test Results

The purpose of this test is to test whether the system can correctly verify user login information, and to check the validity of the entered user name and password. The test results are shown in Table 3:

The results in Table 3 show that the design system can meet the expected normal login.

**Table 3.** System login test

| Experimental case | Experiment procedure | Expected result | Does it meet expectations |
|---|---|---|---|
| Do not enter information | Login directly without entering username and password | Login failed | Yes |
| Enter the username and password correctly | Enter the correct user name and corresponding password, and log in | login successful | Yes |
| Enter wrong username | Enter an available password, but enter a username that does not exist | Login failed | Yes |
| Wrong password | Output the existing user name, but input the wrong page | Login failed | Yes |

**Table 4.** Course creation test case

| Experimental case | Experiment process | Expected result | Does it meet expectations |
|---|---|---|---|
| Do not enter course information | Input is empty, preset conditions | Unable to create course | Yes |
| Enter only the course ID | Enter teacher username, preset conditions | Unable to create course | Yes |
| Enter only the course name | Add course name, preset conditions | Unable to create course | Yes |
| Enter the course ID and course name | Add course name and teacher user name, preset conditions | Create courses normally | Yes |

### 3.3 Teacher Course Test

The follow-up experiment is carried out based on the actual use of the system when the teacher creates the course, to test whether the system can achieve normal course creation, the test results are shown in Table 4:

The test results in Table 4 prove that the design system can realize normal course creation functions.

### 3.4 Student Learning Test

When the system tests the learning function of students, it is necessary to consider whether students can receive system courses normally on mobile devices. The test results are shown in Table 5:

**Table 5.** Student learning function test

| Experimental case | Experiment process | Expected result | Does it meet expectations |
|---|---|---|---|
| Use IOS phone to connect to Wifi | Use IOS mobile device to connect system Wifi | Automatically push out the course interface | Yes |
| Use mobile phones below Android 4.0 to connect to Wifi | Use mobile devices below Android 4.0 to connect to the system Wifi | No prompt | Yes |
| Use Android 4.0 or above to connect to Wifi | Prompt to open the browser to log in to the Wifi network | Automatically prompt to open the browser to push the course page | Yes |

Experimental tests have proved that after connecting with the design system Wifi, the system can push out related system connection courses, and the external connection of the system is not yet suitable for mobile phone connections below Android 4.0.

### 3.5 System Load Bearing Experiment

In actual use, the teaching system often carries a large number of users at the same time, so it is necessary to test the load bearing capacity of the system under the condition of a large number of users. 150, 250, 350, 450, 550 users were used to jointly use the system for login and simulation learning, and to detect the load of the system server when the number of users increased. The test results are shown in Table 6:

**Table 6.** System load test

| Number of experiments | Server memory load (%) | Server CPU load (%) | Number of participating classes in the experiment |
|---|---|---|---|
| 150 | 11.27 | 15.45 | 3 |
| 250 | 13.75 | 16.55 | 5 |
| 350 | 14.92 | 17.15 | 7 |
| 450 | 16.17 | 18.24 | 9 |
| 550 | 17.46 | 19.89 | 11 |

The results in Table 6 show that when the system is carrying multiple users at the same time, the system can still maintain the load within the normal range, which proves that the server occupancy of the system is good. The load bearing capacity of the system in this paper is good, the effectiveness of the course is good, and it can be used in practical learning.

## 4 Concluding

Based on the teaching principles of online and offline integration, this paper draws up a teaching system with corresponding functions. At the same time, it uses a multi-threaded database to improve the load capacity of the system. The feasibility of the system is proved through tests. The follow-up research will detect the loopholes in the main body of the system to ensure the perfect function of the system and facilitate subsequent development.

## References

1. Li, H.: Design and development of university teaching management system based on big data analysis. Mod. Inform. Technol. **3**(4), 22–24 (2019)
2. Huang, L., Zou, W., Wu, F.: Design of university teaching practice information resource integration system based on HDFS. Mod. Electron. Tech. **42**(19), 18–22 (2019)
3. Yang, D.: Design of bilingual teaching system for currency banking course. Jiaoyu Jiaoxue Luntan **41**, 148–149 (2019)
4. Luo, L.: Design of online and offline hybrid intelligent assistant teaching system. Microcomput. Appl. **35**(8), 105–108 (2019)
5. Huang, Z., Yang, Z., Wang, Y., Shao, P.: Design and implementation of flipped classroom teaching support service system. Softw. Guide **18**(1), 119–123 (2019)
6. Zhang, R.: Design and implementation of computer teaching integrated management system in colleges and universities. Chin. Comput. Commun. **2**, 118–119,126 (2019)
7. Yan, Y., Chen, M., Liu, T.: Design and implementation of virtual maintenance teaching system based on unity3D. Comput. Eng. Softw. **40**(11), 128–130 (2019)
8. Yang, Z.: Research on the design of multimedia auxiliary teaching system of ideological and political education in colleges and universities based on author-ware software. Tech. Autom. Appl. **38**(11), 54–57 (2019)
9. Guowei, L.J., et al.: Design and implementation of equipment and teaching management system of medical metrology laboratory. Chin. Med. Equipment **16**(5), 116–120 (2019)
10. Lü, P., Zhang, Q.: Design of socket-based information teaching system using C#. Mod. Electron. Tech. **42**(2), 80–84 (2019)
11. Liu, S., Glowatz, M., Zappatore, M., et al. (Eds.) e-Learning, e-Education, and Online Training. Springer International Publishing, Cham, pp. 1–374 (2018). https://doi.org/10.1007/978-3-319-49625-2
12. Liu, S., Li, Z., Zhang, Y., et al.: Introduction of key problems in long-distance learning and training. Mob. Netw. Appl. **24**(1), 1–4 (2019)
13. Fu, W., Liu, S., Srivastava, G.: Optimization of big data scheduling in social networks. Entropy **21**(9), 902 (2019)
14. Scheibenzuber, C., Hofer, S., Nistor, N.: Designing for fake news literacy training: a problem-based undergraduate online-course --- link to full article: https://authors.elsevier.com/c/1cx8D2f~UWF2Fl. Comput. Hum. Behav. **121**(2), 106–112 (2021)

15. Zhu, T.: Empirical research of novel coronavirus pneumonia prevention and control. Int. J. Emerg. Technol. Learn. (iJET) **15**(11), 119 (2020)
16. Hashemi, M.: A data-driven framework for coding the intent and extent of political tweeting, disinformation, and extremism. Inform. (Switzerland) **12**(4), 148 (2021)
17. Han, Z.: Research on sports balanced development evaluation system based on edge computing and balanced game. Secur. Commun. Netw. **2021**(5), 1–8 (2021)
18. Zhang, E., Yang, Y.: Music dance distance teaching system based on Ologit model and machine learning. Journal of Ambient Intelligence and Humanized Computing, pp. 1–17 (2021)
19. Li, Z.H., Yang, J.J., Qin, H.Q., et al.: A study of efficiency evaluation of national quality online courses during the epidemic: based on fuzzy logic calculation and bootstrap-DEA. Math. Probl. Eng. **2021**(30), 1–7 (2021)
20. Zhang, F., Xi, L.: An evaluation model for the innovation and entrepreneurship thinking ability of college students based on neural network. Int. J. Emerg. Technol. Learn. (iJET) **16**(2), 188 (2021)
21. Li, W.: Design of smart campus management system based on internet of things technology. J. Intell. Fuzzy Syst. **40**(2), 3159–3168 (2021)

# Design of English Listening Simulation Teaching System Based on Cloud Computing

Fa-li Mi[1](✉) and Jia-wei Yuan[2]

[1] Division of Humanities and Social Sciences, Shanghai Aurora College, Shanghai 201908, China
mifali12112@21cn.com

[2] College of Education, Hanghai Aurora College, Shanghai 201908, China

**Abstract.** In the design of traditional analog teaching system, the design is usually based on the Moodle framework, which requires a lot of calculations, which makes the host computer occupancy rate of the teaching system higher. Therefore, this research designed a new English listening simulation teaching system based on cloud computing. In the hardware, the PC host is removed and the RS484 converter is added to perform serial port control conversion. In the software program, first use the cloud computing service framework to construct the system framework, and draw up the connection process of the system server. Set up ordinary nodes and super nodes with different functions on the system nodes, and then establish the user's collaborative filtering operation and the collaborative filtering operation of the teaching item, and thus complete the design of the teaching system. In order to verify the effectiveness of the above-mentioned teaching system, a simulation test experiment is designed. The English listening course resources of a school are imported into the system, and the performance of the teaching system is tested. The test results show that the host occupancy rate of the teaching system is low, which meets the original intention of the design.

**Keywords:** Teaching system · Moodle framework · System design · Cloud computing

## 1 Introduction

The development and application of Internet are changing the way people work, live, learn and interact with each other. In the field of education, the application of the Internet has greatly expanded the spatial and temporal boundaries of education, changed the relationship between "teaching" and "learning" in English teaching, and also greatly improved people's interest, efficiency and initiative in learning [1, 2]. Based on this, relevant scholars use information technology to design a variety of information teaching systems, such as Moodle, big data, ZigBee and other technologies into the education system, and the combination of Grewptool and information technology, the integration of teaching resources and courses, so as to build a teaching system [3–5]. However, the computing process of the current teaching system is all realized in the host server. When


W. Fu et al. (Eds.): eLEOT 2021, LNICST 389, pp. 355–366, 2021.
https://doi.org/10.1007/978-3-030-84383-0_31

there are too many users, the pressure of the host server will be too large, resulting in a high occupancy rate of the host.

The cloud computing service technology can complete part of the operation in the cloud computing layer, and the use of this technology can reduce the computing load of the host, which has research value. Therefore, this study designed an English listening simulation teaching system based on cloud computing to reduce the host occupancy rate of the system.

## 2 System Hardware Design

The teaching system designed in this paper takes the PC as the main control computer, the single chip microcomputer of each subsystem as the slave machine, the serial ports of the master and slave computers are connected with each other through the bus, and the RS485 communication standard is adopted. PC communicates with MCU and transmits data by turn.

Among them, RS485 communication standard has the characteristics of simple interface, easy control and flexible use. RS485 is a half duplex mode with high sensitivity, and the transmission distance can reach 1200 m. When multi-point interconnection, it can save signal lines and facilitate long-distance transmission [6–8]. RS485 transceiver adopts balanced transmission and differential reception, which can effectively suppress common mode interference. The serial port of IBM-PC is RS232 standard, and the serial port of AT89C52 is TTL level. Therefore, with simple circuit, RS232-RS485 conversion and ttl-rs485 conversion can be realized [9, 10]. The RS232-RS485 converter is shown in Fig. 1.

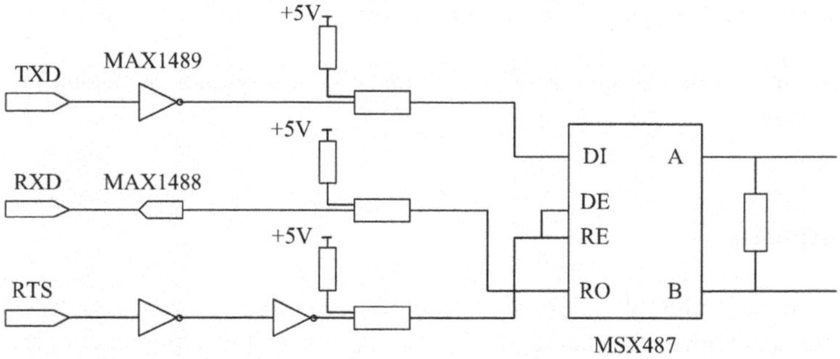


**Fig. 1.** Structure diagram of RS232-RS485 converter

In Fig. 1, MAX487 is the RS485 interface chip of Maxim company. With single + 5V power supply, it can complete the conversion from TTL to RS232. RS232 adopts negative logic, and the output level is ±12V. Therefore, no matter the output or input of PC serial port, the level conversion should be carried out. MAX1488 and MAX1489 to complete the corresponding conversion function. The RTS signal line of PC serial port is used to control the receiving and sending state of MAX487.

# 3 System Software Design

## 3.1 Cloud Computing Service Architecture Establishment

Cloud computing refers to the super computing mode based on the Internet, that is, the massive information and processor resources stored on personal computers, mobile phones and other devices are gathered together to work together [11, 12]. In order to improve the information processing ability and equipment collaboration ability of the teaching system, this system uses cloud computing as the service architecture of the system. The architecture design can be divided into three levels, as shown in Fig. 2.

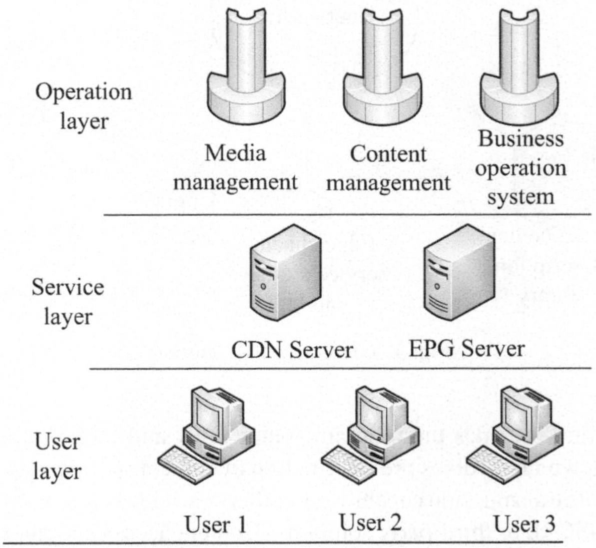


**Fig. 2.** Cloud computing service framework

In the cloud computing service framework of this article, it is divided into three levels. The top level is the content management layer, which is the operation layer, responsible for content arrangement and related calculations. The second layer is the service layer, responsible for content storage, transmission, user authentication, etc., and the last layer is the user layer, which implements services through the docking with the service layer. In the cloud computing architecture, CDN is used for deployment. Data resources and collaborative computing are concentrated at the core of the cloud platform. The terminal does not retain data, and media materials are played in a streaming manner, and interactive evaluation is accepted. The CDN structure is shown in Fig. 3.

CDN network is usually composed of media resource description library, media storage source and distribution control center. Content management for CDN, routing, and organization. All program resources are stored in the central media center, and copies of popular currently available program resources are stored in each edge cache (video server). In the pre-distribution and distribution of the backbone network, the usual CDN is used, and the P2P method is used to evenly store the load among the regional node groups.

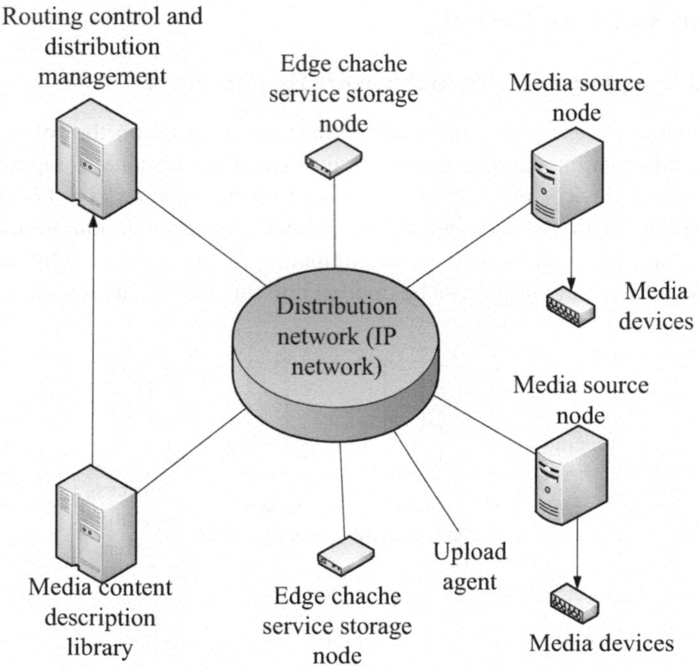


**Fig. 3.** CDN structure diagram

The CDN structure provides the program source copy and migration strategy for the teaching system, which involves pre-distribution of content (pre-distribution bandwidth control, resumable transmission capability, parallel distribution function), instant remote access (GFS + iSCSI, or third-party solutions) Content access and migration strategies such as real-time distribution (downstream limiting direct transmission, regional P2P distribution ---controlling P2P interference to the backbone network, etc.) also involve the space scheduling management of edge caches and program caching strategies.

## 3.2 System Server Connection Process

The implementation of the server is mainly composed of core services and processing modules. The core service is the interface between the user terminal and the processing module. The client sends or receives data information through RTP and RTSP, and the processing module is responsible for processing requests and sending packets to the client.

The implementation process of the streaming media server is described as follows: the main thread is responsible for checking the running status of the server and can control input and output; the idle task thread manages the periodic task queue, including timeout tasks and socket tasks, and sends the task queue to the processing module Idle task) module for processing; the event thread is responsible for receiving RTSP requests and RTP data packets, and transmits them to the corresponding task thread.

There are usually multiple task processes in task thread. RTSP request and RTP packet are received from event thread and placed in task queue. The task queue is sent to the process of processing module to request task module for processing. The send packet task module of the processing module sends the process request packet to the client. The task object mainly uses two methods. Signal is responsible for sending an event to the task object, and can send short messages to a process or a group of processes. If the same event is sent multiple times, only one will be put into the suspended queue of the receiving process. Run is responsible for specifying the processing time for the task object, and it will be called when there is an event to be processed. It can call the get events function to receive the current and previous events that have been signaled, and make the event automatically exit the queue.

### 3.3 System Node Settings

The ordinary node is the most basic operating entity of the system, and it can perform all operations in the system. In the design of this system, the common node mainly realizes the following 5 functional modules: user management, discussion group, electronic whiteboard, courseware management, homework management and online examination subsystem. The node settings are shown in Fig. 4.

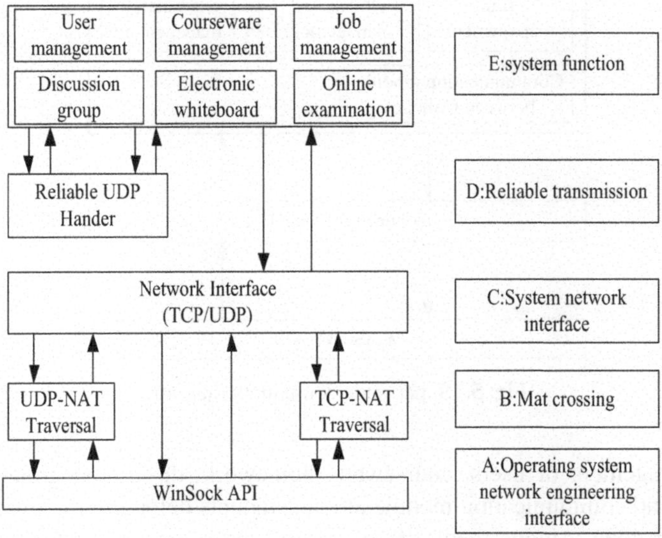


**Fig. 4.** Common node component diagram

In Fig. 4, the system section is divided into five layers. Layer a represents the network programming interface layer of the operating system, that is, the bottom layer of the system. This layer directly calls the network programming interface of the operating system. Layer B (NAT penetration layer) is used to penetrate the NAT devices of intranet users, so as to achieve the purpose of establishing a direct connection between any two hosts. Layer C (system network interface layer) is the network interface layer of teaching system. It is responsible for distributing the network requests of the system, and judging whether it is necessary to call NAT penetration module. If not, it directly calls the function module of layer a. Layer D (reliability transport layer) is mainly used to ensure the reliability of transmission.

Among them, the TCP protocol is connection-oriented, and the reliability is guaranteed by the protocol itself; while the UDP protocol is non-connection-oriented, and data packets are easily lost. Therefore, the reliability of the UDP protocol transmission is guaranteed at the application layer through the Reliable UDPHandler interface. The E layer (system function layer) mainly implements five auxiliary teaching function modules: user management, discussion group, electronic whiteboard, courseware management and homework management. And add a super node in it, the role of the super node is to process user requests and give responses, and set up a series of management interfaces for the administrator. The design of the super node is divided into three layers, as shown in Fig. 5.

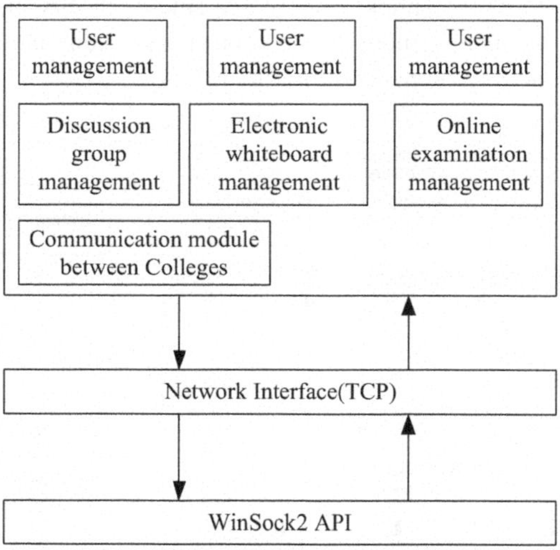


**Fig. 5.** Super node component diagram

The management of users, courseware, homework, discussion group, electronic whiteboard and communication module among students belong to the functional category of super node. Among them, the purpose of the latter is to find the school level courseware.

### 3.4 User's Collaborative Filtering Recommendation Calculation

In this paper, the system calculates the user's nearest neighbors and the recommendation degree of teaching resources based on the user's teaching resource rating matrix. Offline calculation is used for calculation. Due to the large amount of calculation, the user's neighbor and teaching resource recommendation matrix are updated regularly and the data is stored In the database. The user's rating of teaching resources can be represented by a matrix. For example, matrix $R$ is a matrix of $m \times n$, $u$ represents the number of users in the matrix, $v$ represents the number of teaching resources, and $R_i$, $R_j$ represents the score of the $i$th user for the $j$th teaching resource. The user-teaching resource scoring matrix is shown in Table 1.

**Table 1.** User-Teaching resources score sheet

| User/Item | I1 | … | Ij | … | In |
|---|---|---|---|---|---|
| U1 | R1,1 | … | R1,i | … | R1n |
| … | … | … | … | … | … |
| Ui | Ri,1 | … | Ri,j | … | Ri,n |
| … | … | … | … | … | … |
| Um | Rm,1 | … | Rm,j | … | Rm,n |

According to the user-teaching material scoring matrix, the adjusted cosine similarity formula is adopted to find the neighbors of the target user, and the neighbor set is arranged in similar order. For target user $a$, his neighbor set is $M$ , $M = \{M_1, M_2, ..., M_k\}$, where $a$ does not belong to $M$ . The similarity from $M_1$ to $M_k$ is $sim(a, M_k)$, and the similarity is arranged from small to large, that is, $M_1$ is the most similar to user $a$, and their interests are the most similar, while $M_k$ is the least similar. Then the similarity $sim(a, k)$ between user $a$ and user $k$ is as follows:

$$sim(a,k) = \frac{\sum\limits_{p\in I}\left(R_{a,p} - \overline{R_a}\right)\left(R_{k,p} - \overline{R_k}\right)}{\sqrt{\sum\limits_{p\in I}\left(R_{a,p} - \overline{R_a}\right)^2} \times \sqrt{\sum\limits_{p\in I}\left(R_{k,p} - \overline{R_k}\right)^2}} \tag{1}$$

In formula (1), set $I$ represents the set of teaching resources scored by user $a$ and user $k$, $R_{a,p}$ represents user $a$ is score for teaching resource $p$, $R_{k,p}$ represents user $k$ is score for teaching resource $p$, and $\overline{R_a}$ represents user $a$ is teaching resource The average score of resource rating, $\overline{R_k}$ represents the average score of user $k$ is rating of teaching resources. In the neighbors closest to the target user, predict the score, calculate the recommendation degree according to the similarity, and recommend the teaching resources with the top $N$ scores among all the teaching resources to the target user. It is estimated that the target user $a$ is score $P_{a,i}$ for the unrated teaching resource $i$ is as follows:

$$P_{a,i} = \overline{R_a} + \frac{\sum\limits_{k\in M_a} sim(a,k) \times \left(R_{k,i} - \overline{R_k}\right)}{\sum\limits_{k\in M_a} (|sim(a,k)|)} \tag{2}$$

In formula (2), $M_a$ represents the closest neighbor set with target user $a$, and $sim(a, k)$ is the similarity between user $a$ and user $k$ calculated in the previous step. $R_{k,i}$ represents the score of user $k$ on teaching resources $i$, and $\overline{R_k}$ represents the average score of user $k$ on teaching resources. $\overline{R_a}$ represents the average score of user $a$ on teaching resources.

### 3.5 Collaborative Filtering Recommendation Module for Teaching Projects

This module calculates the similarity and recommendation degree of teaching resources according to the user's rating matrix of teaching resources. It also uses offline calculation to avoid the system being too slow due to the large amount of calculation. Update the information in the library at a certain time. However, the similarity of teaching resources is similar to that of collaborative filtering. Firstly, the similarity of teaching resources is calculated, and the similarity between two teaching resources $i$ and $j$ is calculated as follows:

$$sim(i,j) = \frac{\sum_{a \in U_{i,j}} \left(R_{a,i} - \overline{R_a}\right)\left(R_{a,j} - \overline{R_a}\right)}{\sqrt{\sum_{a \in U_{ij}} \left(R_{a,i} - \overline{R_a}\right)^2} \times \sqrt{\sum_{a \in U_{ij}} \left(R_{a,j} - \overline{R_a}\right)^2}} \tag{3}$$

In Formula (3), $R_{a,i}$ represents user $a$'s rating of teaching resource $i$, $R_{a,i}$ represents user $a$'s rating of teaching resource $j$, $\overline{R_a}$ represents the average score of user $a$'s rating of teaching resource, and $U_{ij}$ represents the user set of rating of teaching resource $i$ and $j$. Then, the results are stored in the similarity table of teaching resources, and the results are arranged in descending order according to the similarity of teaching resources to predict the user's rating of teaching resources, and finally, the top $N$ rated ones are recommended to the user. The calculation formula of User $a$'s estimated score $P_{a,k}$ for teaching content $k$ is as follows:

$$P_{a,k} = \frac{\sum_{n \in N_k} sim_{k,n} \times R_{a,n}}{\sum_{n \in N_k} \left|sim_{k,n}\right|} \tag{4}$$

In formula (4), $sim_{k,n}$ represents the previously calculated similarity between teaching resource $k$ and teaching resource $n$, $R_{a,n}$ represents the score of user $a$ on teaching resource $n$, and $N_k$ represents the neighbor set of teaching resource $k$, and the results are saved in the database.

## 4 Experimental Test Analysis

In order to verify the practical application effect of the above-mentioned design of English listening simulation teaching system based on cloud computing, a junior high school English listening teaching resource is added to the cloud computing library of the teaching system, and the simulation test experiment is carried out.

### 4.1 System Test Environment Configuration

The experiment site selected the room No. 2, No. 6 and No. 7 of the students in a middle school, with a total of 158 student machines. The test participants included two computer teachers from the school and 147 students from class 3, Class 2 and Class 3. The configuration of the system server is: Intel dual-core E2140, DDR2 2G memory, 250G SATA hard disk. Student computer configuration: Intel P4, 2.66ghz,DDR 2GB RAM,160G hard disk, 10/100m adaptive network card, 100 MB campus network. The network connection is LAN and the network is unblocked.

### 4.2 System Function Test

Unit testing is also called functional module testing. Module testing is to test one module in the system design. Its focus is to test the relationship between module and module. Its purpose is to ensure that each module in the system can run correctly as a unit, so module testing is usually called unit testing. The test results of the system functional unit of the experiment in this paper are shown in Table 2.

**Table 2.** System function test results

| Test serial number | Test child | Test steps | Test expectations | Test Results |
|---|---|---|---|---|
| 1 | Correct login verification | Enter the correct user name and password | Realize normal login | Meet expectations |
| 2 | Wrong login verification | Input wrong username and password | Unable to log in, return error message | Meet expectations |
| | | Do not enter username or password | Warning user information cannot be empty | Meet expectations |
| 3 | Add courses correctly | Enter the course number and course name | Able to add courses correctly | Meet expectations |
| 4 | Verify courseware upload and assignment submission | Enter different types of assignments | Show that the job was successfully submitted and saved | Meet expectations |

Due to the limitation of space, the system function test is not listed completely. In the experiment, most of the system function tests meet the expected requirements. However, the following defects still exist (Table 3).

**Table 3.** System function problems

| Function name | Software error | Software defect | System limitations | Remarks |
|---|---|---|---|---|
| Upload courseware | Some webpage crashes | No | File size limit | Types are ppt and doc |
| Leave a message | No | Teachers cannot leave messages for teacher users | No | |
| User login | Possible SQL injection | No verification code input and verification | No | Registered user |
| Teaching video playback | No | Unable to control playback progress | No video download | Easy to download |

### 4.3 System Performance Comparison Test

In order to further verify the application performance of this system, it compares with the traditional English listening simulation teaching system based on Moodle. After the functional test, all the students and teachers participating in the experiment were organized to conduct online learning together. The hard disk configuration of the computer room in the middle school is 160G, the CPU is running at 1.5GHz, and the network bandwidth is about 200M. The experiment was carried out under the condition of 147 people using the system.

Firstly, the response time of different systems was tested, and the average response time of 100 records, 500 records, 1000 records, 5000 records and 10000 records were respectively queried. The results are shown in Table 4.

**Table 4.** Comparison of the average response times of different systems

| Test serial number | System of this paper | | | Traditional system | | |
|---|---|---|---|---|---|---|
| | Number of records (items) | Recorded data volume (MB) | Average response time (ms) | Number of records (items) | Recorded data volume (MB) | Average response time (ms) |
| 1 | 100 | 0.97 | 12 | 100 | 0.47 | 26 |
| 2 | 500 | 5.4 | 13 | 500 | 3.8 | 45 |
| 3 | 1000 | 12.7 | 18 | 1000 | 9.6 | 66 |
| 4 | 5000 | 44.5 | 415 | 5000 | 33.5 | 562 |
| 5 | 10000 | 102.6 | 655 | 10000 | 67.4 | 791 |

As can be seen from the test results in Table 4, in the response process of 100, 500 and 1000 records, the response time of the system in this paper has little difference. When the data is increased to 5000, the response time of the system in this paper increases significantly. However, in this test, the response time of the system in this paper is all within 1s, which is significantly less than that of the traditional system. It also records more data than traditional systems.

On this basis, the CPU utilization of different systems is tested. 300 users were simulated to input form data and save it. The experiment was divided into 50, 100, 150, 200, 250 and 300 hires for testing. The experimental results are shown in Table 5.

**Table 5.** Comparison of CPU occupancy of different systems

| Test serial number | Number of simulated users | System of this paper | | Traditional system | |
|---|---|---|---|---|---|
| | | Memory usage | CPU usage | Memory usage | CPU usage |
| 1 | 50 | 12% | 17% | 18% | 20% |
| 2 | 100 | 18% | 17% | 23% | 21% |
| 3 | 150 | 20% | 21% | 29% | 29% |
| 4 | 200 | 31% | 25% | 37% | 36% |
| 5 | 250 | 38% | 29% | 46% | 53% |
| 6 | 300 | 42% | 31% | 55% | 71% |

As can be seen from the test results in Table 5, the Memory and CPU usage of the system in this paper are both lower than 50%, which proves that the CPU and memory occupancy of the system is relatively ideal. However, when the number of simulated users reaches 300, the memory occupancy of the system in this paper reaches 42%, which meets the expectation but is too high. However, the memory and CPU occupancy of the system in this paper are lower than the traditional system.

## 5 Conclusion

The traditional simulation teaching system has a high host occupancy rate. To solve this problem, this study designed a new English listening simulation teaching system based on cloud computing. In the system hardware, remove the PC host, add RS484 converter to carry out the serial port control conversion. In the software program, ordinary nodes and super nodes with different functions are set up on the system nodes respectively, and then through collaborative filtering operation, the computation amount of the host is reduced and the pressure of the host is reduced. However, the compatibility of the system is low, and it is not suitable for more forms of teaching mode. The system compatibility needs to be further improved in the future.

## References

1. Li, H.: Design and development of university teaching management system based on big data analysis. Mod. Inform. Technol. **3**(4), 22–24 (2019)
2. Huang, L., Zou, W., Wu, F.: Design of university teaching practice information resource integration system based on HDFS. Mod. Electron. Tech. **42**(19), 18–22 (2019)
3. Yang, D.: Design of bilingual teaching system for currency banking course. Jiaoyu Jiaoxue Luntan **4**(1), 148–149 (2019)
4. Huang, Z., Yang, Z., Wang, Y.: Design and implementation of flipped classroom teaching support service system. Softw. Guide **18**(1), 119–123 (2019)
5. Zhang, R.: Design and implementation of computer teaching integrated management system in colleges and universities. China Comput. Commun. **2**, 118–119,126 (2019)
6. Yan, Y., Chen, M., Liu, T.: Design and implementation of virtual maintenance teaching system based on unity3D. Comput. Eng. Softw. **40**(11), 128–130 (2019)
7. Luo, L.: Design of online and offline hybrid intelligent assistant teaching system. Microcomput. Appl. **38**(8), 105–108 (2019)
8. Liu, S., Glowatz, M., Zappatore, M., et al. (Eds.) E-Learning, E-Education, and Online Training. Springer International Publishing, Cham, pp. 1–374 (2018). https://doi.org/10.1007/978-3-319-49625-2
9. Liu, S., Li, Z., Zhang, Y., et al.: Introduction of key problems in long-distance learning and training. Mob. Netw. Appl. **24**(1), 1–4 (2019)
10. Fu, W., Liu, S., Srivastava, G.: Optimization of big data scheduling in social networks. Entropy **21**(9), 902 (2019)
11. Kou, X.Y.: Analysis on the study and application of micro-lecture based "flipped classroom" mode in the independent college english listening teaching. Educ. Teach. Forum **26**, 165–166 (2017)
12. Wang, Y.: To construct a new mode of foreign language listening teaching with language ability, critical thinking ability and intercultural ability as the targets. Foreign Language Educ. **39**(6), 69–73 (2018)

# Design of Ideological and Political Intelligence Teaching System for Sino-German Dual System Course Based on MVC Architecture

Jiang-lin Lu(✉)

College of Intelligent Manufacturing and Automobilee,
Chongqing Vocational College of Transportation, Chongqing 402247, China

**Abstract.** In order to improve the accuracy and efficiency of Ideological and political intelligent teaching of dual system courses in China and Germany, and ensure the teaching effect, this paper designs an ideological and political intelligent teaching system of dual system courses in China and Germany based on MVC architecture. The WebKit engine is used as the core module of the browser client, and the information transmission results are passed to the client, and the Sino-German dual course is controlled through the operation buttons of the optical fiber Ethernet controller. Use multiple pins to complete a large number of signal transmissions, design virtual classroom modules to meet students' visual and auditory needs, design MVC function modules, and display the saved user list in the interface. The division of MVC can divide the ideological and political intelligence teaching system of Sino-German dual system courses and determine the teaching goals. The experimental results show that the teaching efficiency of the system is as high as 96%, and the teaching accuracy is as high as 93.2%.

**Keywords:** MVC architecture · Sino-German dual system · Ideological and political teaching · Virtual classroom

## 1 Introduction

As a subject with strong ideas and advanced scientific ideas, ideological and political course not only transfers important knowledge to students, but also promotes the reform of dual system education in China and Germany, deepens the integration of production and education, and plays an important role in the growth of students [1]. In the conventional teaching, the information source is very limited, influenced by the traditional teaching ideas, many teachers' teaching methods are often a blackboard, a piece of chalk, a book, which is difficult to stimulate students' learning enthusiasm [2]. The traditional teaching model with teachers as the center and students as the object, although it maintains the authority of teachers to a certain extent, cannot reflect the status of students' cognitive subjects. To a certain extent, the teaching effect is too dependent on the teacher's personal knowledge reserve and skill level, ignoring the interaction between


W. Fu et al. (Eds.): eLEOT 2021, LNICST 389, pp. 367–380, 2021.
https://doi.org/10.1007/978-3-030-84383-0_32

the two parties in the teaching activities, which has a certain negative impact on the teaching efficiency [3].

In order to better serve the adjustment of regional industrial structure layout, meet the actual employment needs of German funded enterprises, and carry out the reform of dual system vocational education, it is necessary to work closely with German funded enterprises in curriculum construction, teacher team construction and other aspects, and promote the rapid development of teaching system by deepening dual system teaching [4]. In the past, the ideological and political intelligent teaching system based on artificial intelligence network design was used to fully mine the space resources existing in the network by using the whole network node calculation. Although the resource utilization rate of this method is high, the information retrieval function is poor, which leads to the unsatisfactory teaching effect. To solve this problem, this paper proposes a design of Ideological and political intelligent teaching system based on MVC architecture. Compared with the traditional teaching methods, the ideological and political course teaching under the MVC framework has the characteristics of vivid, vivid, rich and interactive, which can better provide ideological and political course teaching practice service for both Chinese and German students.

## 2 System Overall Framework Design

MVC is a software design method, which is usually used for websites or web systems. In the dual system teaching of China and Germany, professional teachers can use multimedia technology, combined with scientific and technological elements, and use words, pictures, videos and other methods to explain the strict ideological and political knowledge and logical thinking of Chinese and German students vividly [5]. Give full play to the functional effects of hearing and vision, and change the interactive learning mode between subjects [6]. The teaching method based on MVC technology provides a convenient and efficient information exchange channel for the dual system teaching in China and Germany. For example, through cloud service, teaching resources can be shared everywhere, and teachers can participate in the whole process of students' learning, so as to improve students' thinking ability and think in class. The framework of teaching system based on MVC architecture is as Fig. 1.

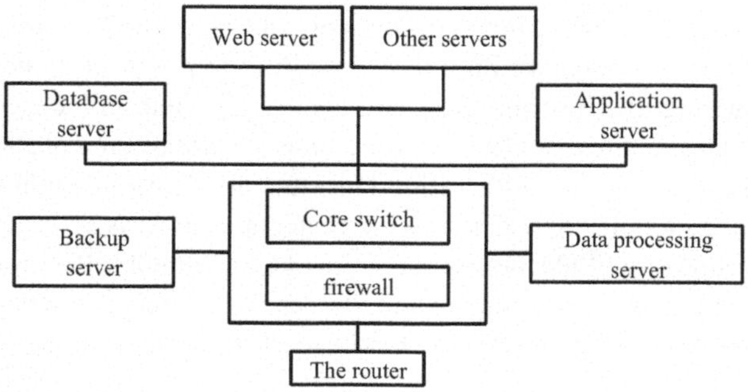


**Fig. 1.** Architecture of automatic assistance platform for ideological and political classrooms based on multimedia technology

As can be seen from Fig. 1, the framework can be independent of the network teaching resources, effectively integrate the scattered resources, and provide convenience for the acquisition and full utilization of teaching resources. Under the MVC framework, cloud storage has strong security storage capacity, teachers and students can save a lot of cloud storage resources, and provide stable and secure services for Chinese and German students [7]. Using the network teaching environment provided by MVC technology, teachers can access public teaching tools and use existing teaching resources. Teachers can carry out the ideological and political intelligent teaching of dual system courses online, which is convenient for both Chinese and German students to learn.

## 3 System Hardware Structure Design

The main idea of MVC is to separate business logic from data display, so that the three core modules of model, view, and control can operate concurrently [8]. The hardware structure diagram of MVC is as Fig. 2.

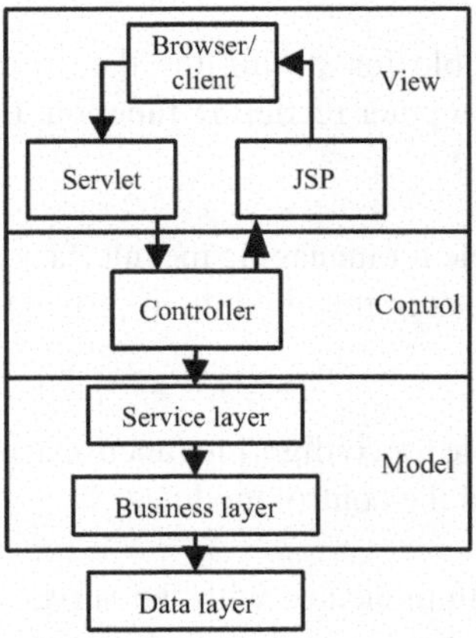


**Fig. 2.** MVC hardware structure

It can be seen from Fig. 2 that the model is used to store all the data objects of the application. For example, there may be a user model to store the user list, attributes and all logic related to the model. The model does not need to clearly understand the relevant details of the view and the controller. For other layers, it is a black box operation, that is, the model only receives data requests and returns the final processing results [9]. Views represent user interaction interfaces. For web applications, most of them consist of HTML, CSS, and JavaScript templates. As the link between the model and the view, control is obtained from the view to receive requests from users, process them, and update the view accordingly [10]. When the page is loaded, the controller will add some monitors to the view. When the user makes a request, the model can be effectively matched with the view immediately to complete the user's request.

The system is mainly based on MVC structure. By using the web distributed application, different users can access the remote learning teaching assistant system in different places by different access methods, which is convenient and flexible. At the same time, it can effectively protect the database platform and manage the access rights.

## 3.1 Browser

Because the browser client does not have high standards for the application platform, most of the processing and display work is achieved through the server. All data is transmitted to the client through the information transmission module, and the client's secure browser display module displays the transmission result. The WebKit engine is designed as follows:

(1) UI module
This module is responsible for managing and calling the browser core module, connecting to the network through the plug-in interface, and realizing data management and transmission under the UI control operation module.
(2) Browse module
This module is responsible for storing the data transmitted by the UI module, and through the main computer rendering function, the data transmission result is displayed on the interface.
(3) Control module
This module is responsible for managing the interface data of the browsing module. The plug-in interface is set in this module to provide channels for other extended functions.
(4) Configuration module
This module is responsible for configuring functional parameters for the UI module, the browsing module and the control module.
(5) Network module
The module directly communicates with the server. The communication can be divided into Http and Socket. According to the transmission protocol, it completes the integration with the background management agreed data, and uses the network module to update the database at any time.
(6) Management module
This module is responsible for managing the local data in the network module, which includes business data, historical data and cache data.

## 3.2 Controller

The optical fiber Ethernet controller is composed of an integrated media access physical interface and a media controller. When the network is controlled, it must follow the IEEE802.3 rules, and support the 100BASE-TX standard, and the media access control layer (MAC) and the physical layer (PHY) respectively correspond to the third and second layers in the ISO protocol model. The basic interface of the coordination controller is a simple bus interface at the media access control layer (MAC), which provides a way for network information transmission and reception, and provides a data transmission interface to the physical layer (PHY) through an internal media independent interface [11]. The layer (PHY) is mainly responsible for data transmission with optical fiber Ethernet, and its basic structure is as Fig. 3.

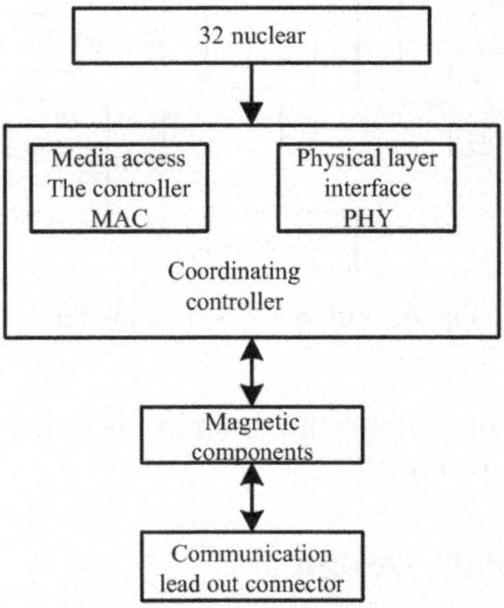


**Fig. 3.** Optical fiber Ethernet coordination controller structure

It can be seen from Fig. 3: When the coordination controller is designed, no matter whether the physical interface is serial or parallel, the work can be completed correctly. The physical interface uses IEEE1596.3 low-voltage signals and uses 8/16-bit links as protocol endpoints. The specification specifies in detail that when 8/16-bit link data is used for clock and frame signal transmission, it cannot deviate from the transmission path and cannot be repeatedly transmitted. When using low-voltage differential technology to transmit signals, short-distance, low-swing, constant-current differential signals can be used and implemented on complementary metal oxide semiconductors.

### 3.3 Virtual Classroom Module

Applying the Sino-German dual system based on the MVC framework to ideological and political education can make ideological and political education more quickly and better integrated into students' thinking [12]. Use the MVC framework to change the traditional blackboard writing teaching mode, so that the blackboard teaching content is single and the teaching process is not vivid. Video playback, screen switching, and sound matching are used to meet the needs of students for vision and hearing. Using three-dimensional space technology, the content of ideological and political education can be expressed more vividly and concretely. The virtual classroom module is as Fig. 4.

As can be seen from Fig. 4, colleges and universities, as the main place for cultivating high-quality talents, have become the primary goal of running schools and daily teaching to provide the society with excellent innovative talents of various specialties [13]. With the development of network technology, students' thinking activities are increasingly active. It is of great practical significance for higher education to correctly guide and

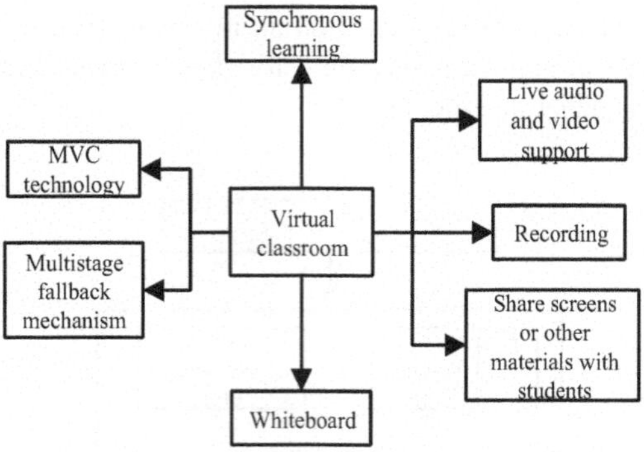


**Fig. 4.** Virtual classroom module

shape students' world outlook, outlook on life and values, and cultivate college students' patriotism and social responsibility.

# 4 System Software Part Design

The system adopts MVC structure and three-layer system function modules. Under the function module of the three-layer system of the MVC structure, design the order of adding users. After confirming that it is correct, submit the saved result, and display the saved user list in the interface. The three-layer system function module of MVC structure is as Fig. 5.

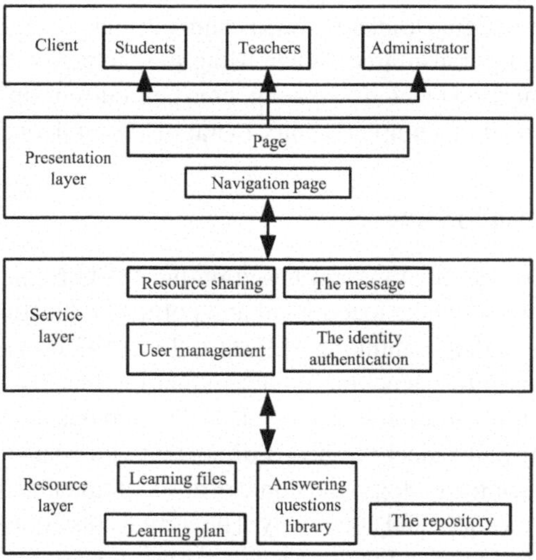


**Fig. 5.** Three-layer system function module of MVC structure

It can be seen from Fig. 5 that the detailed content of the three-layer system function module of the MVC structure is as follows:

Presentation layer: Provide a personalized interactive interface. After the user enters the system navigation page, after identity authentication, he can enter other functional modules through the home page navigation. Each user's navigation page has certain differences.

Application service layer: The teaching function module provided by the application service layer is the core module of the system. Students use the learning module to carry out learning activities, use the module to share learning resources, order interactive courseware, complete interactive homework, and implement self-test evaluation. In the teaching system based on the MVC multi-layer structure, the Chinese and German students use the communication module to achieve communication, complete collaborative learning and group study discussions, news releases, and online question answering.

Public service layer: it mainly provides public services which have no direct relationship with teaching. The function modules include user management, resource management, log management and so on. The public service layer provides information filtering function, which can provide users with personalized resources according to their learning status. The system uses the intelligent function to provide personalized guidance to users to help learners successfully complete the learning task and play the intelligent function of the system; the resource management function can realize the management of teaching resources such as teaching video, courseware and test questions; the user management function can realize the user's identity authentication; the log management module can realize the daily learning management of students.

Resource layer: The resource layer realizes data storage. It mainly stores user information, log information, teaching resource library information, learning process information, and learning results.

The intelligent teaching system based on the MVC multi-layer structure clearly plans the functions of each structure through a three-layer structure, which is conducive to the expansion of the system function and business. If you need to add new business functions, you only need to add functional modules in the application service layer, which greatly facilitates business expansion. By introducing the public service layer, a common structure is built for other business systems. The public service layer is responsible for managing logs and permissions. To add new business systems requires the development of corresponding functional modules at the application layer, which greatly improves the repeatability of the software.

### 4.1 Chinese-German Dual System Curriculum Ideological and Political MVC Division Design

The teaching knowledge base in the teaching system based on the MVC architecture is set to $D$; the content of the learned ideological and political knowledge is set to $S$, the content of the ideological and political knowledge that has not been learned is set to $SN$; the knowledge of the practical ideological and political teaching for students is $G$, and no The knowledge of practicing ideological and political teaching is $GN$. Then there are the following two formulas:

$$\begin{aligned} \{SN\} &= \{D\} - \{S\} \\ \{GN\} &= \{S\} - \{G\} \end{aligned} \tag{1}$$

If $\begin{matrix} \{SN\} = \{D\} - \{S\} \in (0,0) \\ \{GN\} = \{S\} - \{G\} \in (0,0) \end{matrix}$, it means that the student has learned all the knowledge of ideological and political intelligence teaching in the Sino-German dual system course;

If $\begin{matrix} \{SN\} = \{D\} - \{S\} \in (0,0) \\ \{GN\} = \{S\} - \{G\} \notin (0,0) \end{matrix}$, it means that the student cannot enter the next stage of Sino-German dual system curriculum ideological and political intelligence teaching. Students can only review the ideological and political knowledge that they have not learned in Unit $GN$, and practice continuously until all the ideological and political teaching knowledge that they have not mastered is $\{GN\} = \{S\} - \{G\} \in (0,0)$, before they can enter the next stage of teaching.

## 4.2 Teaching Function Design

**Knowledge Point Modeling**

The arrangement of curriculum knowledge points plays a leading role in the course. Integrating intelligent teaching system, combing teaching resources and guiding students to carry out personalized learning can help teachers push resources and complete students' personalized correction. By setting the course knowledge points, teachers can use the knowledge point system modeling tool to match and push the course resources and the related knowledge points in the question database resources according to the specific learning progress of the Chinese and German students before class, forming a set of resources closely connected with the knowledge points, and realizing the filtering and reconstruction of knowledge points.

**Permission Control Service**

In the Sino German dual system ideological and political intelligent teaching system, the user rights control mode based on the roles of students and teachers in China and Germany is as Fig. 6.

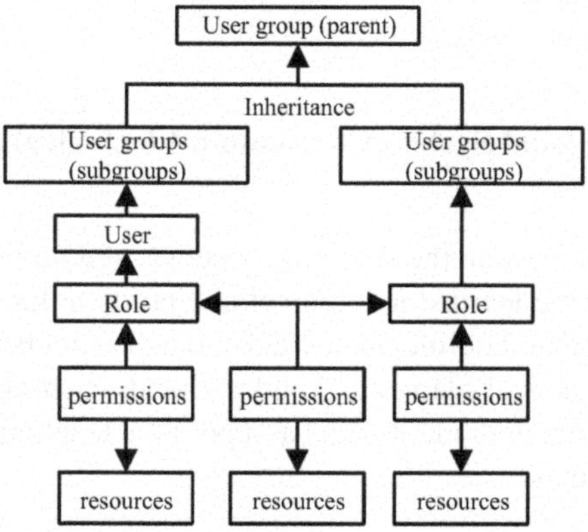


**Fig. 6.** Service flow of authority control

The main body of the teaching aid system authority system: teachers, Chinese and German students and system administrators. Since the school is divided into colleges as the teaching unit, the courses and teachers of each college are different. Therefore, the designed authority system includes student management, teacher management, course management, college management, maintenance management, role management, and authority management in both China and Germany. The logical structure of the permission system framework includes function points, users, and roles:

Function points: Function points are designed according to permissions, and each function point corresponds to a permission. When a user obtains a permission, the user obtains a certain system function.

Users: Students, teachers, administrators who use the system.

Role: A set of permissions for a role. The role is created by the system administrator. The role name and permissions are set when it is created. Each role can have multiple permissions, and the user can also have multiple roles.

Therefore, the specific process of designing the authority of teaching system is as follows:

(1) Establishing teaching assistant user information
Establish student information database, including student number, name, gender, college and other basic information, as well as login password; establish teacher information database, including teacher's job number, name, gender, college and other basic information, as well as its login password; at the same time, design an administrator user.
(2) Establishing teaching assistant college information and course information
Establish college information, including college code, college name, college basic information; establish course information, including course code, course name, etc.
(3) Establish role information for teaching assistant system
Establish all roles of distance learning teaching assistant system, including administrator, student, teacher, etc.
(4) Establish teaching auxiliary authority information
Establish system operation function points, including multiple usage rights and functions such as login, connection, query, modification, and deletion.
(5) Establish the corresponding relationship between roles and permissions
Different roles are given different permissions to form functional entities, and multi-level relationships are constructed to form a composite framework. It is associated with a permission ID and a role ID.
(6) Establish the correspondence between users and administrators of the teaching system
Establish the association relationship between user ID and administrator ID, so that each user has its own management organization, and establish different user rights for users.
(7) Grant roles to users of the distance learning system
After the role is assigned to the user, the role possessing the authority is also assigned to the user. After the user logs in, the corresponding authority system operation can be performed.

**Teacher Terminal Service**

Teacher terminal services are applied to mobile terminals such as mainframes, tablets, and mobile phones to provide statistical analysis tools for classroom interaction. In the process of preparing videos, resources and materials for the micro-class, teachers can select existing resources from the system "course resources" and push the targets that can be selected. The editing and processing of teaching resources requires the help of knowledge point modeling tools to accurately push teaching resources. In the classroom, the student intelligent terminal system provides interactive tools to satisfy the interaction between teachers and students in the classroom.

**Classroom Interactive Services Between Students and Teachers in China and Germany**

In the process of classroom interaction service between students and teachers in China and Germany, we mainly focus on the deep interaction of data analysis, timely analyze the classroom data, and focus the interactive system functions on the most commonly used functions in classroom teaching, and discard fragmentary functions, so as to make the communication between teachers and students more convenient.

## 5 Experimental Analysis

### 5.1 Experimental Environment and Parameter Settings

The experiment is carried out on the MATLAB platform, using a desktop computer, and installing a dual port 10 Gigabit fiber Ethernet controller, supporting peripheral components interconnection standard bus. The hardware optimization features of virtualization support the unified network pattern, allowing LAN, storage network and other network sharing. In addition, it uses the adapter of integrated physical layer (PHY) and blade server mezzanine card. The parameter settings are as Table 1.

**Table 1.** Communication network parameter setting

| Parametric variable | Set value |
|---|---|
| Network coverage area | 1500 m × 1500 m |
| Number of nodes | 200 pcs |
| Data transmission consumes energy | 15/KJ |
| Shortest data transmission path | 8 lines |

### 5.2 Experimental Results and Analysis

**System Functional Test**

In order to have an objective evaluation of the system function, a comprehensive test is carried out. The test example is as Table 2.

**Table 2.** System function test cases

| Test instructions | System operation correctness |
|---|---|
| Login problem | Can students log in Q1 normally |
| | Can teachers log in Q2 normally |
| Class recommendation question | Click to view teacher recommendation, can you enter the recommendation view normally Q3 |
| | Normally display the personalized recommendation results, can you directly enter the recommendation view Q4 |
| | Click the recommended letter, can it display the main activity Q5 |
| Class discussion questions | Click the discussion button, can you directly enter the topic discussion interface Q6 |
| | Click to view the view, can you receive the reply topic Q7 |

The artificial intelligence-based network system and the MVC-based system were used to analyze the safe use of various test cases of the ideological and political classroom system. The comparison results are as Table 3.

**Table 3.** Comparative analysis of the security usage of test cases on the two technology platforms

| System operation correctness | Based on artificial intelligence network system | Based on MVC system |
|---|---|---|
| Q1 | Correct | Correct |
| Q2 | Correct | Correct |
| Q3 | Correct | Correct |
| Q4 | Incorrect | Correct |
| Q5 | Incorrect | Correct |
| Q6 | Incorrect | Correct |
| Q7 | Correct | Correct |

It can be seen from Table 3 that the artificial intelligence based network system can not directly access the recommendation view, display the main activities by clicking, and can not directly enter the topic discussion interface, display the recommendation results, and click the recommendation letters and discussion buttons, resulting in incomplete system functions. The MVC based system can complete the system operation normally and has complete system functionality.

**Teaching Effect Test**

In order to improve the persuasion of the experimental results, students of different levels were selected to participate in the experiment, and 10 experiments were added, and the average value of 10 experiments was taken. The teaching effect based on artificial intelligence network system and MVC system is compared and analyzed. Based on the full score of 100 for each student, the teaching results of the two systems are compared as Table 4.

**Table 4.** Comparative analysis of scores obtained in two systems of ideological and political teaching

| Number of students/person | Based on artificial intelligence network system/points | Based on MVC system/points |
|---|---|---|
| 100 | 800 | 1000 |
| 200 | 1800 | 1998 |
| 300 | 2500 | 3000 |
| 400 | 3200 | 3995 |
| 500 | 4500 | 5000 |

It can be seen from Table 4 that when the number of students is 200, the maximum score obtained using the artificial intelligence network system is 1800 points, which is 200 points away from the full score. When the number of students is 500, the score obtained using the artificial intelligence network system is 4,500 points, which is 500 points away from the full mark; When the number of students is 200, the score obtained using the MVC-based system is 1998 points, which is 2 points away from the full mark. When the number of students is 400, the score obtained using the MVC-based system is 3995 points, which is 5 points away from the full score. From the above content, we can see that using the MVC-based system can more stimulate students' interest in learning, the teaching effect is good.

**Teaching Efficiency Test**

Based on the above contents, the two systems are used to compare and analyze the teaching efficiency, and the results are as Fig. 7.

It can be seen from Fig. 7 that when the number of students is 50, the teaching efficiency of the artificial intelligence network system is 68%, and the teaching efficiency of the MVC-based system is 96%; When the number of students is 200, the teaching efficiency of the artificial intelligence network system is 60%, the teaching efficiency of the MVC-based system is 94%; When the number of students is 400, the teaching efficiency of the artificial intelligence network system is 50%, and the teaching efficiency of the MVC-based system is 91%.

**Teaching Accuracy Test**

The teaching accuracy based on artificial intelligence network system and MVC system is compared and analyzed, and the teaching accuracy of the two systems is compared, as shown in Table 5.

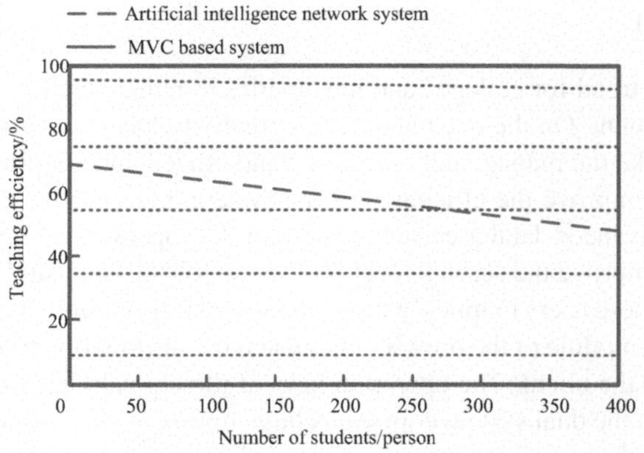


**Fig. 7.** Comparative analysis of teaching effectiveness of the two systems

**Table 5.** Comparative analysis of Ideological and political teaching accuracy of two systems

| Number of students/person | Based on artificial intelligence network system/% | Based on MVC system/% |
|---|---|---|
| 100 | 83 | 92 |
| 200 | 85 | 95 |
| 300 | 86 | 93 |
| 400 | 82 | 94 |
| 500 | 87 | 92 |

From Table 5, it can be seen that when the number of students is 500, the average ideological and political teaching accuracy of using artificial intelligence network system is 84.6%, while that of MVC system is 93.2%. Therefore, the ideological and political teaching accuracy based on MVC system is relatively high.

To sum up, the teaching effect based on MVC system is better, which can effectively improve the teaching efficiency and accuracy. Because the system uses the operation button of the optical fiber Ethernet controller to control the Sino German dual system course, and uses multiple pins to complete a large number of signal transmission, so as to improve the teaching efficiency. The MVC function module is designed to display the saved user list in the interface. Through the MVC division, the ideological and political intelligent teaching system of the dual system course in China and Germany can be divided, so as to improve the teaching accuracy and ensure the teaching effect. However, the teaching goal of using artificial intelligence network system is not clear, which leads to the problems of low teaching efficiency and accuracy, and poor effect.

## 6 Conclusion

It is an inevitable trend for colleges and universities to realize the intellectualization of teaching management. On the one hand, it can greatly reduce the workload of teaching managers and make the management process standardized and simplified. On the other hand, it can also improve the efficiency of the system and improve the teaching level with the help of advanced database teaching system. The operation of intelligent teaching system can also improve the service level for the school staff and students, and provide convenience for these users to quickly input and query information. The WebKit engine is used as the core module of the browser client, and the information transmission results are transmitted to the client. The operation keys of the optical fiber Ethernet controller are used to control the dual system courses. A large number of signals are transmitted by multiple pins, and the virtual classroom module is designed, improve teaching efficiency and accuracy. The MVC function module is designed to display the saved user list in the interface. Through the MVC division, we can divide the ideological and political intelligent teaching system of the dual system curriculum between China and Germany, determine the teaching objectives, and ensure the teaching effect.

## References

1. Chen, J., Wang. Z., Chen, J., et al.: Design and research on intelligent teaching system based on deep learning. Comput. Sci. **46**(S1), 550–554+576 (2019)
2. Yi, P., Liu, Y., Shi, Y., et al.: Design and development of engineering graphics teaching system on mobile devices based on the augmented reality technology. J. Graph. **39**(06), 1207–1213 (2018)
3. Sun, Q., Li, X.: Research on self-education system design of resource intelligent agent curriculum. E-educ. Res. **40**(06), 98–104 (2019)
4. Zhu, Q.: Development and design of curriculum network teaching system based on MVC structure. Electron. Des. Eng. **26**(23), 85–88+93 (2018)
5. Yu, L.: Design and implementation of english teaching system based on MVC architecture. Tech. Autom. Appl. **38**(10), 149–151+158 (2019)
6. Liu, Q.: Design and application of english teaching system based on MVC architecture. Microcomput. Appl. **34**(11), 107–109 (2018)
7. Chen, Y., Wang, X., Zhou, X.: Research on "five docking" in vocational education —— enlightenment from vocational education and training regulations in german dual system. Adult Educ. **38**(08), 56–60 (2018)
8. Liu, T., Zeng, Z.: Design and implementation of website under MVC architecture. Comput. Technol. Dev. **30**(02), 188–191 (2020)
9. Xiang, J.: The role taking of german firms in vocational education. Adult Educ. **02**, 88–93 (2019)
10. Chen, Y.: An analysis of critical success factors of german dual-system vocational education. Adult Educ. **39**(10), 79–84 (2019)
11. Vincenti, G., Bucciero, A., Helfert, M., Glowatz, M. (eds.): e-Learning, e-Education, and Online Training. LNICSSITE, vol. 180. Springer, Cham (2017). https://doi.org/10.1007/978-3-319-49625-2
12. Liu, S., Li, Z., Zhang, Y., et al.: Introduction of key problems in long-distance learning and training. Mob. Netw. Appl. **24**(1), 1–4 (2019)
13. Fu, W., Liu, S., Srivastava, G.: Optimization of big data scheduling in social networks. Entropy **21**(9), 902 (2019)

# Design of Virtual Simulation Experiment Teaching System for Electrical Engineering and Automation Specialty

Quan -wen Chen[1](✉) and Ping Gong[2]

[1] School of Information and Control, Shenyang Institute of Technology, Shenyang 113112, China
[2] Shengyang Tristar Hardware Manufacturing Co. Ltd., Shenyang 110000, China

**Abstract.** In order to improve the real-time interaction of virtual simulation experiment teaching system for electrical engineering and automation specialty, an experiment teaching system is designed. Through the selection of arm devices, USB interface design, hardware design of oscilloscope module and controller design, the hardware design of the system is realized. In the software part of the system, the virtual simulation transformation is designed, so as to complete the research on the virtual simulation experiment teaching system of electrical engineering and automation specialty. The experimental results show that the teaching system in this study has better real-time interaction, lower packet loss rate and strong practical significance than the traditional system.

**Keywords:** Electrical engineering · Virtual simulation · Oscilloscope

## 1 Introduction

Electrical engineering and automation are undergraduate majors in general colleges and universities, and belong to electrical majors. Electrical engineering is mainly a discipline that studies the generation, transmission, conversion, control, storage and utilization of electrical energy. This major belongs to the electrical category. It cultivates the basic theory, professional skills and practical ability related to the field of electrical engineering. It can be engaged in the design, research and development and operation of equipment manufacturing, system operation, and technology development.

With the continuous development of China's economy and the continuous development of modern industries, the electric automation technology talent market has huge potential. Especially in Guangdong, the continuous improvement of automated production technology, the continuous popularization of automation products, the application of smart buildings and smart homes, and the continuous development of smart transportation provide broad development prospects for electrical automation technology. In the professional learning process, theoretical knowledge alone is not enough. Therefore, a virtual simulation experiment teaching system of electrical engineering and its automation is designed to improve the learning effect of students.


W. Fu et al. (Eds.): eLEOT 2021, LNICST 389, pp. 381–394, 2021.
https://doi.org/10.1007/978-3-030-84383-0_33

In order to vividly reproduce the operation process and operating status of various links in the electric power industry, let students understand the operation of electric power engineering, virtual simulation has become an important means of experimental teaching of electrical engineering, and it is the development direction of experimental teaching of electrical engineering in various colleges and universities today. The construction of the domestic electrical engineering virtual laboratory started late, but it has developed very rapidly. Tianjin University has established an electrical automation virtual simulation experiment teaching center, introducing simulation and semi-physical real-time simulation technology, and has the design and simulation capabilities of multi-source distributed power generation, energy storage, intelligent power distribution and energy management such as wind, light, and ocean energy. Northeast Dianli University has established a virtual simulation experiment teaching center for the production process of the electric power industry, which can simulate subcritical to ultra-supercritical domestic units, can simulate the power production process of nuclear power plants, and the power transmission and distribution process of 35–500 kV substations. In addition, other colleges and universities have also established electrical engineering virtual simulation laboratories. For example, Xi'an Jiaotong University has established a nuclear power plant and thermal power plant system virtual simulation experiment teaching center, the electrical engineering and automation virtual simulation experiment teaching center of Nanjing University of Science and Technology, and the transmission line engineering experiment teaching center of the Three Gorges University.

## 2 Teaching System Hardware Design

### 2.1 ARM Device Selection

The ARM workflow is as follows: After the data acquisition card is powered on, the program in the Flash is first loaded into the SDRAM designated program running space to run. The first operations to be completed after the ARM program runs are:

Reset Stop Counter:
Reset the chip ax88180 and 88e1111; set the IP address of the lower computer according to the position of the dial switch; initialize the network interface, and then wait to receive the ARP data packet from the upper computer, according to the received ARP data packet with the MAC address and IP address of the new lower computer, and then send the ARP packet to the upper computer, and inform the lower computer of the MAC address, so as to establish contact with the upper computer Communication; configure the I/O status of the board (8-way input and 10-way output), configure the pin function [1, 2]; set the corresponding memory interval configuration of FPGA and corresponding I/O port configuration; configure interrupt, f'pga output interrupt signal uses external interrupt 1. After initialization and configuration, arm enters the user mode, executes the program main cycle, and enters the working state. The work flow chart is shown in figure below (Fig. 1).

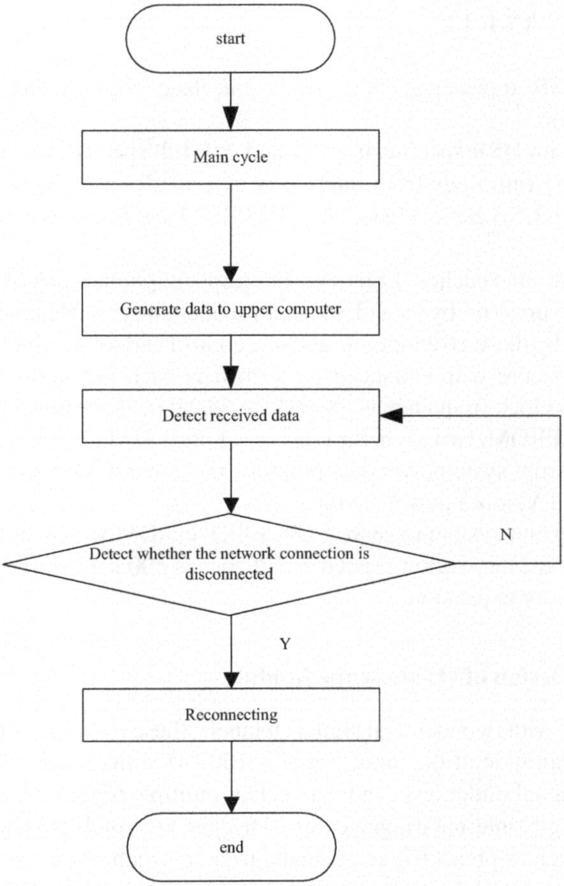


**Fig. 1.** Arm work flow chart

## 2.2 Design of USB Interface

Considering factors such as development cost, development cycle and chip purchase, we chose Cypress's CY7C64613. This chip is the second-generation product of Cypress, which supports full-speed transmission and is compatible with USBl. Version 1 and USB2.0 version (full-speed device). This chip integrates considerable resources [3], which is conducive to hardware expansion and development of various target devices. CY7C64613 is the second-generation product of Cypress, which supports USB full-speed transmission. Compared with the first-generation products, CY7C64613 has stronger performance and higher integration. It inherits the advantages of the first generation, integrating smart USB core, enhanced 8051 core, 8-Kbyte RAM and high-performance I/O on the chip, and at the same time further improves the execution speed and provides more expansion resources on this basis.

Features of CY7C64613:

1. Integrated USB transceiver, Sie (serial interface engine) and enhanced 8051 microprocessor;
2. Compatible with USB specification 1.1 and 2.0 (full speed device);
3. Software: 8051 runs code from internal or external RAM. The code can be downloaded through USB cable, loaded from EEPROM and run in external memory, such as flash;
4. Many endpoints and caches: 14 blocks, interrupt endpoints, each of which can transmit a frame of up to 64 bytes and 16 isochronal endpoints. Meanwhile, 2 KB cache can be shared by these 16 endpoints and one control endpoint, which is bidirectional;
5. Standard 8051 core with enhanced performance: each instruction cycle is 4 clock cycles [4], the clock frequency is 48 MHz or 24 MHz, determined by the configuration in the EEPROM, two asynchronous serial ports UARTS, three counters/timers, extended interrupt system, two data pointers, the general 8051 has only one DPTR;
6. Working at 3.3 V, more power saving;
7. Extended interrupt system to serve USB, FIFO and DMA interrupt events;
8. Support 12C bus; the working speed of 12C bus is 400 kHz or 100 kHz;
9. External memory expansion.

### 2.3 Hardware Design of Oscilloscope Module

Demand analysis, with two identical signal channels, these two channels can work independently; the amplitude of the input signal is 100–40 V, the bandwidth is 1 MHz; the DC level of the signal under test can be adjusted; multiple trigger sources are required, such as Clock trigger, internal trigger, external trigger, etc.; multiple trigger methods are required [5, 6], such as preset trigger, delayed trigger, synchronous trigger.

The oscilloscope module has two independent signal channels. When the measured signal is sent to the signal channel, the MCU writes the appropriate channel parameters, so as to adjust the measured signal to the level range suitable for ADC acquisition and send it to ADC for acquisition [7, 8]. At this time, MCU writes initialization parameters to the acquisition control logic, and then starts an acquisition. The next acquisition process is managed by the acquisition control logic. After a/D conversion, the measured signal becomes digital information and is stored in RAM. When the acquisition is finished, the control logic informs MCU that the acquisition is finished. At this time, the computer can read these digital information through the USB interface and process and display them. The function of MCU is to respond to the USB interrupt, move the data in RAM to the predetermined endpoint register, and then put the acquisition control logic in the initial state again, and start the next acquisition.

On this basis, for the signal channel design, this oscilloscope contains two signal channels CHI and CH2, these two signal channels are exactly the same, so this section only introduces channel CH1. The signal channel CH1 is composed of high-impedance attenuator, three-stage amplifying circuit and DC level generating circuit. Below we will introduce each part of the signal channel in detail.

High-impedance attenuator, the measuring range of the oscilloscope is limited, especially the digital oscilloscope, it uses the AD converter [9, 10], the input signal requirement of the AD converter that we choose is Vpp is 1 V. Therefore, the input of the first stage amplifier and the amplification factor of the amplifier must be limited. The maximum input amplitude of the oscilloscope designed this time is 40 V, and the minimum amplitude is 100 my, so the signal must be amplified or attenuated during the signal conditioning process. Two sets of attenuators are designed in the circuit to attenuate when the signal is too large, and when the signal is small, the signal passes through.

In the circuit of digital oscilloscope, the three processes of digitizing analog quantity, sampling, quantization and coding, are completed by a/D converter. An analog-to-digital converter converts an unknown continuous analog signal [11–13] (usually voltage) into a discrete digital signal for further processing, display, recording and transmission. It is the core of digital oscilloscope, which determines the storage bandwidth and resolution of oscilloscope. In digital oscilloscope, data acquisition and storage of broadband signal are involved. High speed data acquisition technology is the key technology of broadband analog signal data acquisition.

A/D converters, with the rapid development of VLSI technology and the widespread use of computer technology in the industrial field, new design ideas and manufacturing technologies for A/D converters emerge in endlessly. In order to meet the needs of various detection and control tasks, a large number of A/D conversion circuits with different structures and performances have emerged. The ADC used in this design is a chip of Analog Devices-AD9288. AD9288 is an 8-bit dual-channel monolithic integrated analog-to-digital converter with sample-and-hold circuits. It has the characteristics of low power consumption, small size, good dynamic characteristics and easy to use.

## 2.4 Controller Design

In addition to the interrupt signal, the interface of the SPI controller is mainly composed of the APB signal and the SPI signal. The two sets of signals are introduced below. The SPI controller provides an SPI bus to connect to the SPI device, and on the module [14–16], it is necessary to design more interface signals than the SPI bus protocol requires to meet the needs of the SPI controller configurable to work in different modes. The description of each interface signal is shown in the following table (Table 1):

**Table 1.** Signal description of SPI controller

| Pin name | Direction | Function description |
|---|---|---|
| pclk | Input | Bus clock |
| present | Input | Global reset signal |
| penable | Input | The transmission enable signal can represent the second cycle of an APB transmission, and its rising edge appears in the middle of the APB transmission |

*(continued)*

**Table 1.** (*continued*)

| Pin name | Direction | Function description |
|---|---|---|
| psel | Input | Select the signal from the device. When the signal is high, it indicates that the current transmission is aimed at the SPI controller, and the controller needs to make the correct response |
| paddr | Input | Address bus signal to locate the register of the current operation |
| pwrite | Input | For the signal of transmission read-write type, when the level is high, it means~times of APB write access, and when the level is low, it means one time of APB read access |
| pwdata | Input | Write data bus signal received by SPI controller |
| prdata | Output | Read data bus signal of SPI controller response |
| spijxejntr | Output | Send FIFO air break request, when the data to be sent in transmit FIFO is equal to |
| spijxojntr | Output | Or less than the set threshold |
| spi—rxLintr | Output | The transmit flf0 overflow interrupt is generated when data is written to the full transmit FIFO |
| spLrxu—Intr | Output | The receive FIFO full interrupt is generated when the data received in the receive FIFO is greater than or equal to the set threshold |
| SS-l | Input | Receive fjfo underflow interrupt is generated when receive FIFO is empty and the FIFO is read |

The specific design description of each sub-module in the module is introduced as follows:

APB slaves, according to the AMBA standard, are slave devices on the APB bus except the APB bridge [17, 18]. All hosts in the system can access the slave devices connected to the APB bus through the APB bridge. Since APB is designed for modules that do not require high bandwidth, compared with the interface of the AHB bus slave device, the interface of the slave device is much simplified, as shown in the following figure (Fig. 2):

The slave of APB is mainly responsible for address decoding, and realizes the connection between SPI controller module and APB bus. Through this module, ARM processor can read and write the corresponding registers in SPL controller in strict accordance with APB bus protocol, so that it can control the module and peripherals. When writing to the controller, the write data can be locked at the following two time points: when the PSEL is high, at the rising edge of any PCLK; when the PSEL is high, at the rising edge of the pen able. Select signal PSEL to select SPI controller, pwrite to indicate write operation, and address paddr to determine which register is updated by write operation.

The clock divider and frequency dividing logic are used to divide the PCLK clock signal in the host mode. In this design, according to the need, we only use even frequency division and use a frequency division variable bauq step to achieve frequency division control. The frequency division variable is valid when the count value of the internal subtraction counter is zero and the SPI controller is working_ Only. Included in the main

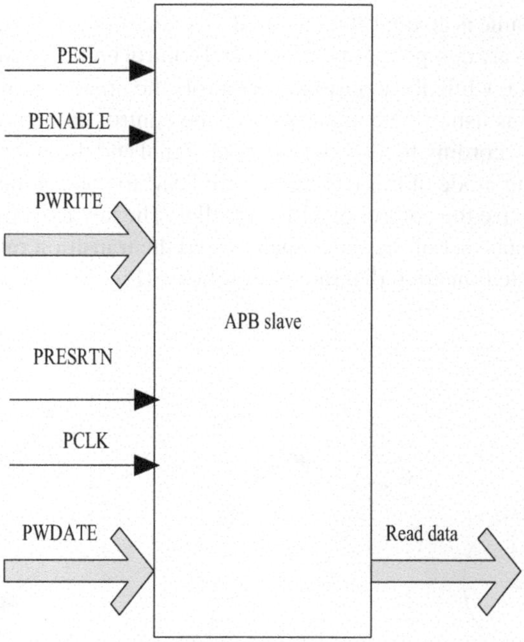


**Fig. 2.** APB end interface

mode state machine control logic and port control logic. When baud_ When step is high, the state machine will jump.

In the data buffer module, in the SPI controller, the data FIFO is used to buffer data, and it is divided into receiving FIFO and sending FIFO. FIFO is a first-in, first-out data buffer different from general memory. It does not have a read-write address line, and it cannot address a unit that needs to be read or written by an address line like a general memory, and data can only be written in and read out sequentially, so it is very simple to use. When designing the FIFO, the first-in-first-out data is realized by controlling the movement of the reading and writing pointer. Therefore, the key to the design is to control the movement of the read and write pointers, and the relationship between the read and write pointers to determine whether the FIFO is empty or full. The specific implementation process is: after reset, the read pointer and the write pointer are both 0 and point to the same storage unit. Each write operation to the FIFO is to write data to the storage unit corresponding to the current write pointer, and then the write pointer executes the addition. 1 operation, pointing to the next storage unit of data to be written; every time the FIFO is read, the data pointed to by the current read pointer is read, and then the read pointer performs an operation to increase by 1, thereby pointing to the next data to be read Storage unit. In this way, the requirement that data is written first and read first can be realized, which is completely consistent with the timing before and after the data cache. A valid empty signal means that the current FIFO has no data dimensions, and a valid full signal means that the current FIFO is full and data cannot be written. According to needs, our FIFO depth and width are both 32 bit.

Finite state machine is an important method to realize control logic in digital system. Most digital systems are composed of data unit and control unit. The data unit can process and transmit the data, while the control unit controls the operation of the data unit. The finite state machine is usually the main body of the control unit, and its output control signal is generated according to the external input signal and the state information of the data unit. In the main mode of this design, we use FSM to control the data transmission process, so as to realize the control of SPI controller. The key to design a state machine is to determine the state set of the state machine and the transition relationship between these states. The state transition diagram is as follows (Fig. 3):

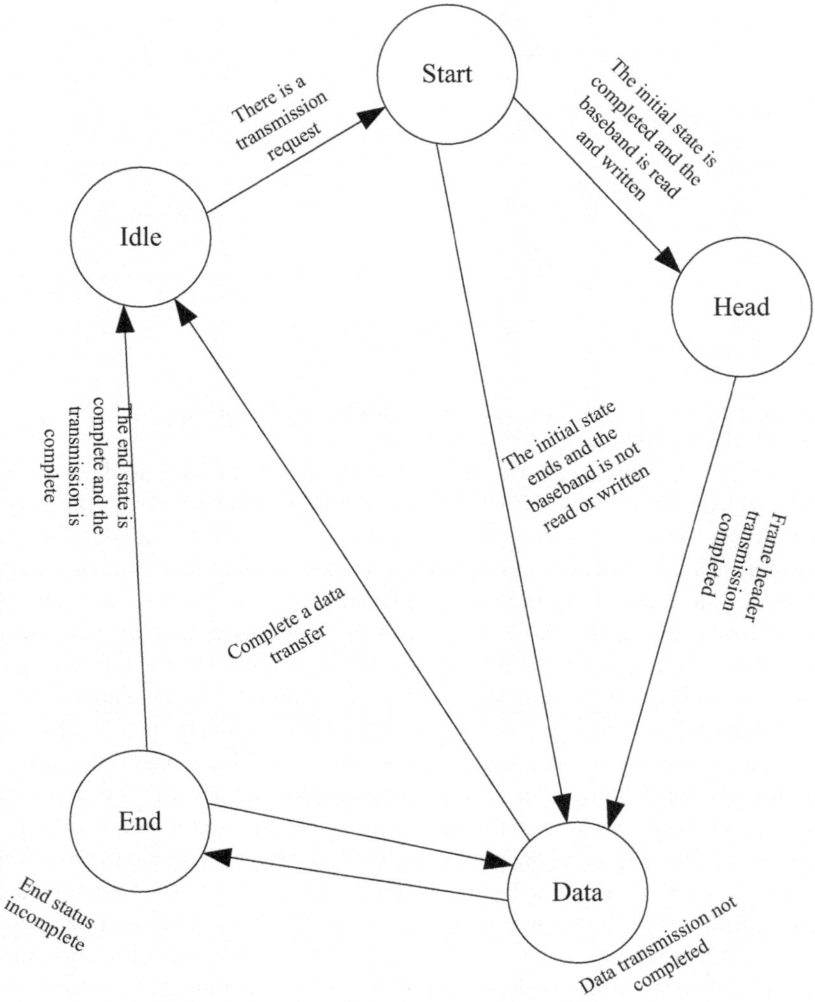


**Fig. 3.** State transition diagram

The register module includes control register, data register and status register. First, define the type, word length and address of all registers in SPI controller, as shown in the following table (Table 2):

**Table 2.** Register summary of SPI controller

| Register name | Type | Width | Describe |
|---|---|---|---|
| SPCR0 | R/W | 16 | SPI control register |
| SPCRl | R/W | 32 | Transmit control register |
| SPCR2 | R/W | 32 | Receive control register |
| SPCR3 | R | 16 | Baseband data register |
| SPDR0 | W | 32 | Transmit FIFO data register |
| SPDRl | R | 32 | Receive FIFO data register |
| SPSR | R | 16 | Status register |
| SPBRR | R/W | 16 | Baud rate configuration register |
| TXFTLR | R/W | 8 | Transmit fif0 threshold register |
| RXFTLR | R/W | 8 | Receive fif0 threshold register |
| SPRISR | R | 8 | Interrupt original status register |
| SPIMR | R/W | 8 | Interrupt final status register |
| SPISR | R | 8 | Interrupt clear status register |

## 3 System Software Design

In the virtual scene, the attribute transformation of 3D model, such as position, size and rotation, is based on the corresponding mathematical model. The transformation of 3D model can be regarded as the transformation of model with the coordinate system unchanged or the transformation of model with the coordinate system unchanged. The essence of three-dimensional model transformation is the calculation of linear equation by computer. The basic formula of the calculation is as follows:

$$M_v = \begin{bmatrix} m_{00}m_{01}m_{02}m_{03} \\ m_{10}m_{11}m_{12}m_{13} \\ m_{20}m_{21}m_{22}m_{23} \\ m_{30}m_{31}m_{32}m_{33} \end{bmatrix} \begin{bmatrix} v_0 \\ v_1 \\ v_2 \\ v_3 \end{bmatrix} \tag{1}$$

By performing matrix operations on the data of the three-dimensional model, the computer obtains the new data of the three-dimensional model after the specified action is completed, and realizes the translation, rotation, and scaling transformation of the three-dimensional graphics.

Graphic translation transformation. Translation refers to moving every vertex of an object by the same displacement without changing its face and face normal. The translation matrix is expressed in the following formula:

$$T\left(t_x, t_y, t_z\right) = \begin{bmatrix} 100t_x \\ 010t_y \\ 001t_z \\ 0001 \end{bmatrix} \tag{2}$$

In formula (2), $\left(t_x, t_y, t_z\right)$ represents the displacement vector of translation.

Graphics rotation transformation, rotation matrix is through the origin of the line as the axis of rotation, each vertex of the object is rotated by a certain angle. Rotation changes the direction of the vertex and face normals of an object, but does not change its face information. The three-dimensional graphics rotate around the $x$, $y$, $z$ axis, and the rotation matrices are shown in the following formulas:

$$R_x(\theta) = \begin{bmatrix} 1 & 0 & 0 & 0 \\ 0 & \cos\theta & -\sin\theta & 0 \\ 0 & \sin\theta & \cos\theta & 0 \\ 0 & 0 & 0 & 1 \end{bmatrix} \tag{3}$$

$$R_y(\theta) = \begin{bmatrix} \cos\theta & 0 & \sin\theta & 0 \\ 0 & 1 & 0 & 0 \\ -\sin\theta & 0 & \cos\theta & 0 \\ 0 & 0 & 0 & 1 \end{bmatrix} \tag{4}$$

$$R_z(\theta) = \begin{bmatrix} \cos\theta & -\sin\theta & 0 & 0 \\ \sin\theta & \cos\theta & 0 & 0 \\ 0 & 0 & 1 & 0 \\ 0 & 0 & 0 & 1 \end{bmatrix} \tag{5}$$

Based on the above formulas (3)–(5), the transformation matrix rotating around any axis can be obtained.

Graphic scaling transformation, scaling refers to reducing or enlarging an object in a certain proportion. Scaling transformation changes the shape of the object. Usually the scaling matrix is also expressed as a matrix of three scaling factors relative to the three coordinate axes as shown below:

$$S\left(s_x, s_y, s_z\right) = \begin{bmatrix} s_x & 0 & 0 & 0 \\ 0 & s_y & 0 & 0 \\ 0 & 0 & s_z & 0 \\ 0 & 0 & 0 & 1 \end{bmatrix} \tag{6}$$

In formula (6), $s_x$, $s_y$ and $s_z$ represent the object's scaling factor in $X$, $Y$ and $Z$ axes respectively.

According to the above process to complete the virtual scene processing, in order to complete the design of electrical engineering and automation professional virtual simulation experiment teaching system.

# 4 Experimental Comparison

In order to verify the effectiveness of the virtual simulation experiment teaching system of electrical engineering and automation specialty, the experimental comparison is carried out, and the traditional system is compared with the system of this study, and the effectiveness of the two systems is compared.

## 4.1 Real-Time Comparison of System Interaction

The system of this study and the traditional system are used for learning, and the real-time interaction of the two systems during learning is compared (Fig. 4).

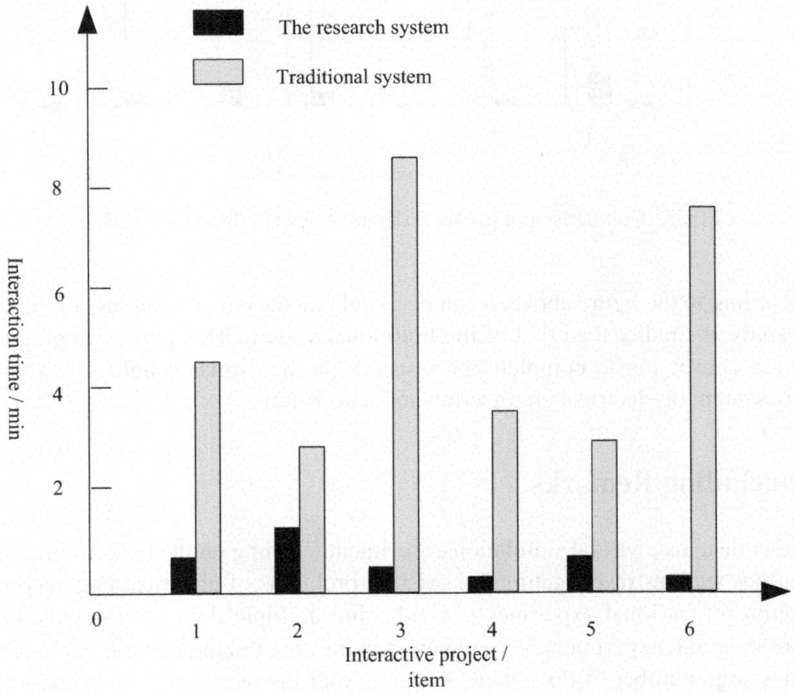


**Fig. 4.** Real-time comparison of system interaction

From the above figure, it can be found that the real-time interaction of the system in this study is better than the traditional system.

### 4.2 Comparison of System Data Transmission Packet Loss Rate

For the two systems during data transmission, the loss rate of data transmission in the system, the comparison results are shown in the following figure (Fig. 5):

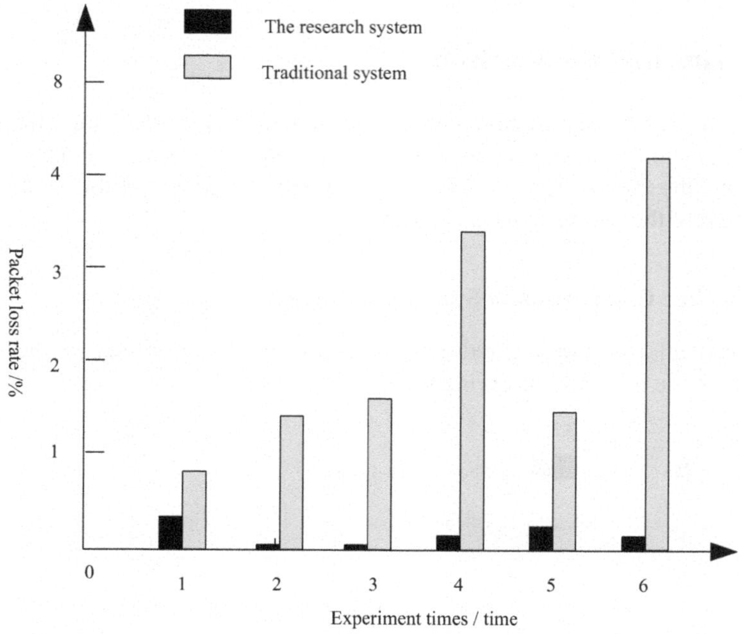


**Fig. 5.** Comparison of packet loss rate of system data transmission

According to the figure above, it can be found that the data packet loss of the system in this study is smaller than that of the traditional system. This paper design a virtual simulation conversion to complete the research on the virtual simulation experiment teaching system of electrical engineering and automation.

## 5 Concluding Remarks

This paper designs a virtual simulation experiment teaching on the basis of preliminary preparations such as investigating the existing problems of electrical engineering and automation professional experiments, conducting multiple field experiments, collecting laboratory and experimental equipment pictures, organizing experimental data, and reading a large number of documents system. After the user enters the virtual experimental system, according to the operating prompts, with the help of a computer mouse and keyboard, etc., they can learn about the punching equipment, the operation of the experiment, and the learning of the experimental principle.

In the follow-up research, the system logic design and script design should be improved to enhance the real-time nature of interaction and the fluency of operation. This is the difficulty that needs to be overcome in future research. At the same time, in the system, the user interacts with the objects in the virtual experiment scene through the computer mouse and keyboard, and the operation is not convenient enough. In the future, the experiment operation can be carried out through the helmet display, the data glove or the handle, and the immersion is stronger. This system does not involve multi-person collaboration. In the future, the virtual experiment system will develop in the direction of multi-person collaborative experiment operation. Northeast Dianli University has established a virtual simulation experiment teaching center for the production process of the electric power industry, which can simulate subcritical to ultra-supercritical domestic units, can simulate the power production process of nuclear power plants, and the power transmission and distribution process of 35–500 kV substations.

## References


1. Manero, A., et al.: Utilizing additive manufacturing and gamified virtual simulation in the design of neuroprosthetics to improve pediatric outcomes. MRS Commun. **9**(3), 941–947 (2019)
2. Li, Y., Zhang, D., Guo, H., Shen, J.: A novel virtual simulation teaching system for numerically controlled machining. Int. J. Mech. Eng. Educ. **46**(1), 64–82 (2018)
3. Sun, X., Liu, H., et al.: Training effectiveness evaluation of helicopter emergency relief based on virtual simulation. Chin. J. Aeronaut. **151**(10), 75–87 (2018)
4. Coelho, R.C.: A mobile device tool to assist the ECG interpretation based on a realistic 3D virtual heart simulation. SIMULATION **94**(6), 465–476 (2018)
5. Zhao, H., Zhao, X., Zhang, L., Jia, L., Jiang, J., Wang, L., et al.: A mineral feature extraction method based on virtual band simulation. Remote Sens. Lett. **8**(4), 547–556 (2017)
6. Sommer, A.F., Rao, A., Koh, C.: Leveraging virtual experimentation and simulation to improve R&D performance. Res. Technol. Manag. **60**(5), 31–41 (2017)
7. Marques, L., Magalhes, R.R., Lima, D.A.D., Tsuchida, J.E., Fuzatto, D.C.: Virtual environment for smart wheelchair simulation. IEEE Lat. Am. Trans. **18**(12), 1–10 (2020)
8. Li, Z., Wang, Z., Deng, Z., Wu, W., Sun, Y.: Experimental study on three-dimension simulation design and virtual shear test of asphalt mixture. Tongji Daxue Xuebao/J. Tongji Univ. **46**(8), 1049–1056 (2018)
9. Yuanxiang, C., Haiyan, J., Jianqiang, F.: Research on sports dance teaching and training practice simulation based on virtual environment. Tech. Bull. **55**(20), 283–288 (2017)
10. Yubao, Q., Weifeng, Q., Jiayi, L., Feng, G., Qiang, Z.: Application of virtual simulation and computer technology in experiment and practical teaching. Rev. Facul. Ingen. **32**(2), 450–459 (2017)
11. Forcan, M., Banjanin, M., Vukovic, G.: Advanced teaching method for balanced operations of overhead transmission lines based on simulations and experiment. Int. J. Electr. Eng. Educ. **55**(1), 14–30 (2018)
12. Sari, U., Kirindi, T.: Using arduino in physics teaching: arduino-based physics experiment to study temperature dependence of electrical resistance. J. Comput. Educ. Res. **7**(14), 698–710 (2019)
13. Tao, S., Jiajun, W., Xiuzhi, L., et al.: Application of packet tracer in the industrial computer network and communication experiment teaching. Q. J. Ind. Pulp Pap. Tech. Assoc. **30**(4), 521–526 (2018)

14. Jianhua, Y., Shoujin, Z., Weidong, H.: Construction of a virtual simulation experimental teaching system of equipment manufacturing and automation. J. Fujian Univ. Technol. **17**(4), 403–408 (2019)
15. Tomlinson, B., Silberman, M.S., Torrance, A.W., et al.: Environment-selected directors: an interactive simulation experiment of environmental representation on corporate boards. Ecol. Econ. **178**, 106795 (2020)
16. Everett-Thomas, R., Joseph, L., Trujillo, G.: Using virtual simulation and electronic health records to assess student nurses' documentation and critical thinking skills. Nurse Educ. Today **99**, 104770 (2021)
17. Sultana, N., Betran, A.P., Khan, K.S., et al.: Simulation-based teaching and models for caesarean sections: a systematic review to evaluate the tools for the see one, practice many, do one slogan. Curr. Opin. Obstet. Gynecol. **32**(5), 305–315 (2020)
18. Dai, F., Fei, G., Lei, L.I., et al.: Construction and practice of virtual simulation experimental teaching center of chemical engineering majors. Exp. Technol. Manag. (2019)

# Design of Simulation Teaching System of Automatic Control System Course Based on MATLAB

Ru Yan[1(✉)] and Chun-ni Zheng[2]

[1] Inner Mongolia Vocational College of Chemical Engineering, Huhhot 010010, China
[2] Chongqing Chemical Industry Vocational College, Chongqing 401228, China

**Abstract.** In the simulation teaching of automatic control system courses, the traditional teaching system is limited by experimental equipment and resources, and the teaching effect is relatively poor. For this reason, the design of the simulation teaching system of the automatic control system based on MATLAB is proposed. Optimize the original teaching simulation system of the automatic control system course, based on this, establish the mathematical model of the automatic control system, describe the dynamic characteristics of the automatic control system operation process, determine the construction rules of the simulation teaching system, and use the virtual simulation laboratory Repeated training to train the simulation operation of automation equipment, combined with the dynamic characteristics of the operation of the automatic control system, construct a simulation teaching system of the automatic control system course. The experimental results show that the proposed MATLAB-based automatic control system course simulation teaching system has high teaching quality and high consistency and reliability, enabling students to understand the working principle of the automatic control system and master the design method of the automatic control system.

**Keywords:** MATLAB · Automatic control system course · Simulation design · Teaching system

## 1 Introduction

Simulation experiment teaching is one of the main experimental links in higher science and engineering schools. It plays an extremely important role in cultivating students' practical operation ability, problem analysis and problem solving ability; professional comprehensive experiment courses also shoulder comprehensive application. The basic knowledge and professional knowledge learned are the task of cultivating students' creativity [1]. At present, there are still some problems and shortcomings in the experimental teaching of automatic control system courses in various universities: First, the experimental device is composed of discrete devices such as transistors, resistors, and capacitors, and uses a proportional control method. The experiments done on this device are mainly confirmatory experiments, which have played an active role in cultivating


W. Fu et al. (Eds.): eLEOT 2021, LNICST 389, pp. 395–404, 2021.
https://doi.org/10.1007/978-3-030-84383-0_34

students' basic circuit analysis and practical ability [2]. However, the control method is single, the adjustable parameters are limited, and the experiment is not flexible enough to fully mobilize the subjective initiative of students. Second, it is very difficult to conduct experiments on the device to observe the dynamic process. Third, with the reform of education Advance, the enrolment scale continues to expand, resulting in insufficient experimental equipment and shortage of experimental resources [3]. New experimental methods and methods must be used to make up for these deficiencies and solve existing problems.

The popularization and promotion of computers have provided a good foundation for multimedia teaching and simulation. It is very beneficial to introduce simulation in experimental teaching. First of all, under the provided simulation platform, design experiments can be carried out. Students can flexibly change parameters, increase or decrease some links, and adopt different control methods. This will not only allow a deeper understanding of the experiment content, but also mobilize the creativity of students. Secondly, the simulation method can be used to relatively easily realize the observation of some dynamic characteristics and dynamic processes of the control system [4]. Third, through the combination of simulation and experiment, the efficiency of the experiment can be improved and equipment damage can be reduced. Students can simulate the experiment to be done first, and after fully understand the principle, then carry out the experiment and debugging of the actual device, so that the experimental hours can be compressed to solve the problem of insufficient experimental resources. By analyzing and comparing simulation results and experimental results, students can improve their ability to analyze and solve problems [5].

Aiming at the problem of poor teaching effect gain in the traditional teaching system, a MATLAB-based automatic control system course simulation teaching system design is proposed to solve the above-mentioned problems in the traditional teaching system. Drawing lessons from the overall concept of CDIO and the design ideas of integrated teaching system, construct a simulation teaching system of automatic control system courses. Enable students to choose related courses according to their own interests and hobbies, and promote the cultivation of students' personality and innovation ability.

## 2 Design of the Simulation Teaching System of the Automatic Control System Course Based on MATLAB

### 2.1 Design MATLAB Teaching Simulation

In order to achieve the real simulation of the object in MATLAB teaching simulation, MATLAB hardware and software systems should be used as much as possible. In addition to the control station and operating station, the actual MATLAB system also includes Field Bus Module (Field Bus Module) that provides interfaces for field sensors and actuators., Bus isolator, cabinet and power supply, etc. [6]. For simulation, field devices are replaced by mathematical models. MATLAB's control strategy, information management, and operation display functions are all completed in CP and WP. Other devices are only responsible for information exchange. Therefore, MATLAB teaching machine only needs CP and WP hardware and corresponding software system [7].

In the hardware structure of MATLAB teaching simulation designed, the trainer station plays the role of process model machine and network server at the same time, and the engineer station is mainly used for configuration and monitoring, so it can also be used as a control model machine [8]. In this way, the hardware structure is mainly composed of trainer station, engineer station, and operator station.

In the actual teaching site, the hardware connection between the MATLAB system and the power generation equipment is adopted, and each control target and sampling point corresponds to the field bus component FBM [9]. In order to ensure the teaching function of the system, the control system configuration software and screen configuration software are protected in the application software. When the operator configures the flow chart and control logic, the information applied is simulated from the appearance and configuration results. The influence of the model is consistent with the field configuration.

## 2.2 Establish a Mathematical Model of the Automatic Control System

In the course of automatic control system, it is mainly to analyze and understand the automatic control system. One of the first tasks of analyzing the automatic control system is to establish the mathematical model of the system, because it is necessary to understand the performance of simple systems or the performance of complex systems. Grasp the relationship between variables in the system. These relationships are described by mathematical equations, which are called mathematical models of the system.

The mathematical model of the system can be described from two aspects. The first is to study the steady-state operating conditions of the system. Under steady-state conditions, the parameters of the system are independent of time, and the mathematical equations that determine the relationship between the parameters of the system are algebraic equations. However, it is more important to study the dynamic equations of the system, because the control system itself is not static, its output always changes with changes in the input, and the system will also be subject to various disturbances that change over time. Therefore, the various variables of the system are not constants, but change with time. It can be seen that the mathematical equation describing the dynamic characteristics of the system includes not only the variables themselves, but also the rate of change or derivatives of these variables. Such mathematical equations are differential equations. Differential equations are one of the most basic characterizing the dynamic characteristics of the system. Mathematical equation.

When studying system characteristics, the concept of linearity is very important. When there is a linear relationship between the input variables and output variables of several devices, after connecting them in series, parallel or feedback mode, the relationship between the total input and output is also linear [10]. The linear system satisfies the principle of superposition, that is, when the linear system has more than two input variables, the output variable of the system is equal to the sum of the output variable changes caused by the independent action of each input variable [11].

However, the actual teaching process is often very complicated, and most parameters exhibit nonlinear characteristics. If this nonlinear relationship is accurately represented by nonlinear equations, it is extremely difficult to solve these differential equations. In order to simplify the analysis of the regulation system, in the teaching process, the nonlinear system is usually approximated to linearization [12]. Under certain working conditions, when the system parameters change in a small range, the "small deviation method" is used to linearize some nonlinear systems. The so-called "small deviation method" is to use Taylor formula to expand the nonlinear function of variables into incremental expressions of these variables near the equilibrium point. Then omit the items higher than one increment to obtain an approximate linear function [13].

Assuming that the output $y$ is a nonlinear function of the input $x$, $y = F(x)$, at the equilibrium point $(x_0, y_0)$, expand $F(x)$ into a Taylor series:

$$F(x) = F(x_0) + F'(x_0)(x - x_0) + \frac{F''(x_0)}{2!}(x - x_0)^2 + \dots \quad (1)$$

make:

$$\Delta y = y - y_0 = F(x) - F(x_0) \quad (2)$$

$$\Delta x = x - x_0 \quad (3)$$

then:

$$\Delta y = F'(x_0)\Delta x + \frac{F''(x_0)}{2!}\Delta x^2 + \dots \quad (4)$$

Since $\Delta x$ is a small increment, the high-order infinitesimal term and remainder can be omitted to obtain an approximate formula:

$$\Delta y = F'(x_0)\Delta x \quad (5)$$

The above-mentioned linearization is performed under the assumption that the input and output variables change in a small range around the equilibrium point, and this precondition is in line with the actual situation in many control systems. If the actual variation of the system is large, the linear model with small deviation will have a large calculation error. For non-linear characteristics such as relays and gaps, it is not suitable to use the deviation method for linearization due to the inability to perform derivative calculations.

The application of digital computers has opened up a new way to establish precise mathematical models. The calculation speed of digital computer is fast and the precision is high. If necessary, hundreds of equations can be used to describe a complete system, but in most cases, people often use a low-order linear mathematical model to describe the operation of automatic control system. The dynamic characteristics of the process, because the low-order approximate model has sufficient accuracy when analyzing the control system, and the calculation workload is significantly reduced.

### 2.3 Determine the Principles of Constructing a Course Simulation Teaching System

In order to ensure the realization of the content and training objectives of the originally determined curriculum plan, the key is to determine an appropriate and reasonable organizational form for the curriculum plan. Adopting the CDIO concept, emphasizing the real background environment of engineering practice, and emphasizing the life cycle activities under the engineering chain, this makes the design of the curriculum simulation teaching system not only to achieve the integration of knowledge, ability and quality training, but also the training of technical elements and non-technical elements Integration and mutual support between theoretical knowledge must be realized. In view of this, the construction principles of the simulation teaching system of the automation control system course are mainly reflected in the following two aspects:

First, the organizational principles of the overall design. The overall design of the teaching system is mainly to solve the problem of how to integrate training objectives, theoretical knowledge content and practical links into the curriculum plan. According to the target value orientation determined by the teaching vision and syllabus, the curriculum plan under the CDIO concept chooses the most integrated curriculum simulation teaching model. This model is based on mutually supporting theoretical knowledge and a series of abilities or project links. Weft, warp and weft weave the two organically, realizing the combination of theory and practice, and the organic integration of knowledge, ability and attitude training.

Second, the organization principle of the content order of the teaching system. The content order of the teaching plan is the schedule arrangement of the students' learning, which mainly involves the order arrangement of the subject curriculum content and the ability teaching content. The schedule of subject teaching content can be established on the basis of the perfect subject content sequence in the past, while the ability teaching content sequence is difficult to be clear and can be formed in the specific design process of the teaching system.

## 2.4 Constructing a Course Simulation Teaching System

After determining the principles of constructing the course simulation teaching system, drawing on the overall concept of CDIO and the design ideas of the integrated teaching system, the construction of the automatic control system course simulation teaching system is shown in Fig. 1.

Based on the current problems in the teaching of automatic control system courses, too much emphasis is placed on the learning of professional courses, the training of students' hands-on ability is ignored, and the proportion of practical courses is low. Under the guidance of the CDIO concept, the automatic control system course simulation teaching structural elements. The following principles should be adhered to when setting:

The principle of combining theoretical teaching with engineering practice training. The design of the teaching system emphasizes engineering practice and increases the proportion of practical links. It does not mean that scientific theories are not important, but to return to the practical nature of engineering on the basis of theoretical knowledge. Students must have both solid scientific theoretical knowledge and Have the ability to solve practical engineering problems in a real environment.

Pay attention to the principle of profound professional basic theoretical knowledge. The CDIO model focuses on the learning of profound engineering technology basic knowledge. The design of the teaching system should focus on basic science and engineering science courses, set appropriate proportions, and provide necessary and systematic basic knowledge for professional courses, but at the same time ensure that it provides

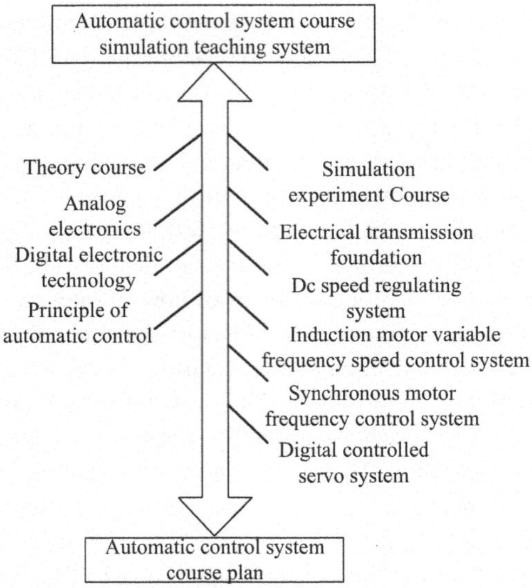


**Fig. 1.** Course simulation teaching system

engineering talent training. The necessary professional knowledge and professional skills training.

The principle of combining technical and non-technical elements. The teaching system should not only provide necessary technical education for the training of engineering talents, but also pay attention to non-technical education such as society, politics, economy, culture, and art, so as to improve students' humanistic and professional qualities, and cultivate their international vision and sustainable development. Philosophy makes it a modern engineer with both ability and political integrity.

Strengthen the principle of innovation and focus on the cultivation of students' personality. An appropriate proportion of elective courses should be maintained in the teaching system, so that students can choose relevant courses according to their own interests and hobbies, and promote the cultivation of students' personality and innovative ability.

Use the virtual simulation laboratory to repeatedly train the simulation operation of the automation equipment, and combine the dynamic characteristics of the automatic control system to construct the automatic control system course simulation teaching system. So far, the design of the simulation teaching system of the automatic control system based on MATLAB is completed.

# 3 Experimental Research on Simulation Teaching System of Automatic Control System Course

## 3.1 Experiment Preparation

In the experimental research of the simulation teaching system of the automatic control system course, various factors in the experimental process of the experimental variables are clarified. In the experiment, the proposed MATLAB-based automatic control system curriculum simulation teaching system, the traditional DCS-based simulation teaching system and the fuzzy control-based simulation teaching system are used as independent variables to unify the experimental goals. The above three teaching systems are used for teaching. After the teaching course is over, the consistency reliability and teaching quality scores are calculated, and the pros and cons of the three teaching methods are compared based on the results. The dependent variables in the experiment are consistency reliability and teaching quality score.

The goal of the experiment is a freshman in a key university. In order to more objectively reflect the students' learning situation and effects, in addition to processing the data analysis of the students' pre-test and post-test, it is also necessary to analyze the students' learning data in the course to ensure the data consistency. The consistency reliability in the experiment is only for the performance of the students in the teaching process and the implementation process of the teaching system; the teaching quality score is for the comprehensive results of the students after teaching, which is the effect of the teaching system. In the comprehensive evaluation of teaching quality, the fuzzy evaluation method is used to obtain the comprehensive evaluation of teaching quality.

### 3.2 Determine the Evaluation Level of Teaching Quality

Suppose $U = \{u_1, u_2, u_3, u_4, u_5\}$ represents the scoring factor, and $V = \{v_1, v_2, v_3, v_4, v_5\}$ represents the $n$ levels of the state of each scoring factor. In the experimental research of the simulation teaching system of the automatic control system course, 5 grades are set, as shown in Table 1.

**Table 1.** Interval table of different scoring levels

| Rating level | Score interval | Description |
|---|---|---|
| I | 100~90 | Excellent |
| II | 89~80 | Good |
| III | 79~70 | General |
| IV | 69~60 | Pass |
| V | 59~0 | Failed |

According to the score interval of different grades, after the evaluation, the fuzzy evaluation matrix $G$ is established, and the obtained scores are normalized. Use $g$ to represent the degree of membership to determine the fuzzy relationship $G$. The relationship between matrices $G$ and $g$ is as follows:

$$G = (g_{ij})_{4\times 4} = \begin{pmatrix} g_{11}, g_{12}, g_{13}, g_{14} \\ g_{21}, g_{22}, g_{23}, g_{24} \\ g_{31}, g_{32}, g_{33}, g_{34} \\ g_{41}, g_{42}, g_{43}, g_{44} \end{pmatrix} \quad (6)$$

Use the synthetic factor of the fuzzy matrix to obtain a comprehensive evaluation matrix of all scoring factors:

$$W = U \times G = U(G_1, G_2, G_3, G_4) \tag{7}$$

The comprehensive evaluation value of teaching quality is calculated through the comprehensive evaluation matrix, and different teaching methods are compared and analyzed in combination with consistency reliability.

### 3.3 Consistency Reliability Experiment Results and Analysis

Consistency reliability refers to the measurement of whether there is the same result every time the same teaching system is used to teach the same object under the same conditions. Under normal circumstances, a consistency reliability of more than 75% is considered reliable and meets teaching needs. The calculation formula is:

$$\eta = \left[\frac{1-(X-Y)}{(X+Y)}\right] \times 100\% \tag{8}$$

In the formula, $X$ and $Y$ respectively represent the test records of different teaching observers. The default condition is $X > Y$. Through the observation of the actual teaching process of different teaching modes by different observers, the observation results are recorded, and the agreement between the observers is calculated degree. The result is shown in Fig. 2:

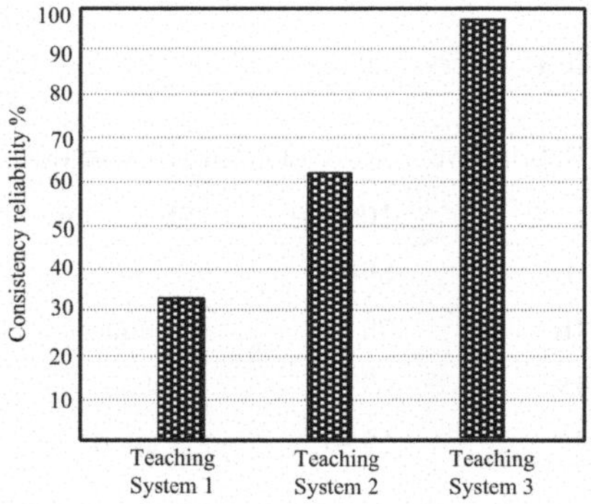


**Fig. 2.** Experimental results of consistency reliability of different teaching systems

The teaching system 1 shown in the figure is a simulation teaching system based on MATLAB, teaching system 2 is a simulation teaching system based on fuzzy control, and teaching system 3 is a simulation teaching system based on DCS. Comparing the results in the observation graph, it can be seen that the consistency reliability of teaching system 1 is 34.6%, the consistency reliability of teaching system 2 is 62.4%, and the consistency reliability of teaching system 3 is 97.6%. It can be seen from this the consistency reliability of System 3 exceeds the 75% limit, far exceeding the values of the other two teaching systems. Therefore, it can be considered that in the consistency reliability experiment, the application of the MATLAB-based automatic control system curriculum simulation teaching system can better ensure the quality of curriculum teaching.

### 3.4 Teaching Quality Evaluation Results and Analysis

Considering that some teaching factors are affected by time, the teaching quality score is calculated in three stages. The scoring results obtained by three different teaching methods are shown in Table 2.

**Table 2.** Teaching quality evaluation results of different teaching systems

| | Project | The first stage | Second stage | The third phase |
|---|---|---|---|---|
| Simulation teaching system based on DCS | Rating level | General | Pass | Pass |
| | Fraction | 71 | 62 | 61 |
| Simulation teaching system based on fuzzy control | Rating level | Pass | Pass | Good |
| | Fraction | 64 | 69 | 80 |
| Simulation teaching system based on MATLAB | Rating level | Excellent | Excellent | Excellent |
| | Fraction | 97 | 98 | 98 |

Observe the results in the table. Among them, the teaching quality score of the DCS-based simulation teaching system in the three stages is between pass and general; the simulation teaching system based on fuzzy control has the teaching quality score of the three stages between pass and good; The simulation teaching system based on MATLAB has excellent teaching quality in the three stages. Because the MATLAB-based simulation teaching system uses MATLAB to establish the mathematical model of the automatic control system, describe the dynamic characteristics of the automatic control system's operation process, and construct the automatic control system curriculum simulation teaching system, which improves the stability of the teaching system. Combined with the results of the consistency reliability experiment, it can be seen that the proposed MATLAB-based automatic control system course simulation teaching system has high teaching quality and high consistency reliability. In the actual automatic control system course teaching, the teaching effect is better.

## 4 Concluding Remarks

This paper focuses on the research and analysis of the automatic control system course teaching. With the support of the original teaching system materials and literature, a MATLAB-based simulation teaching system design for the automatic control system course is proposed. After the design is completed, it is verified by multiple sets of comparative experiments. The practical performance of the proposed MATLAB-based simulation teaching system solves the problems faced by the simulation teaching of the automatic control system course at this stage to a certain extent. However, due to the limitation of one's own ability and knowledge, coupled with the fact that the automatic control system course teaching system is a research field involving a wide range and high requirements, there will inevitably be some shortcomings in the research, which will be carried out in the follow-up research. In-depth research and discussion.

## References

1. Xie, H., Chen, X., Chen, D., et al.: Research on quaternity and connotative form of Microbiology and Immunology based on "characteristic textbook + cloud platform + mobile terminal + virtual system" through blended teaching. Chin. J. Immunol. **35**(17), 2141–2146 (2019)
2. Zheng, S., Cao, B., Yang, S., et al.: Design scheme of route plan's teaching and evaluation system based on simulation chart room. Navig. China **43**(02), 41–45 (2020)
3. Liu, J., Liu, Y.: The construction of practical teaching system of professional courses of industrial design under the concept of OBE-CDIO. J. Graph. **40**(02), 416–421 (2019)
4. Zhong, J., Shao, J., Wang, H.: Optimization design of curriculum system for information management and information system specialty based on QFD. Inf. Sci. **36**(10), 105–109 (2018)
5. Sha, Y., Li, Q., Li, Y.: Development and design in computer simulation experiment teaching of fluid mechanics. J. Exp. Mech. **33**(04), 655–664 (2018)
6. Ge, L., Shi, M., Yu, G.: Instructional unit design based on UbD theory: using analytic geometry as an example. J. Math. Educ. **29**(05), 25–31 (2020)
7. Yang, L., Wang, G., Qin, S., et al.: A study on reconstruction algorithm of multi-bearing vibration signal based on DCS. Comput. Simul. **36**(05), 316–319+324 (2019)
8. Sun, Z., Wang, Q., Hu, S., et al.: DCS access modification for coal transportation subsystem of field bus control system. Mod. Electron. Tech. **42**(08), 6–10+15 (2019)
9. Wang, F., Sun, Q., Jiang, G., et al.: Nuclear energy 5.0: new formation and system architecture of nuclear power industry in the new IT era. Acta Automatica Sinica **44**(05), 922–934 (2018)
10. Zhang, X.: Construction of the curriculum system of adult higher education in the hybrid teaching mode. Adult Educ. **38**(07), 25–28 (2018)
11. Liu, S., Liu, D., Srivastava, G., et al.: Overview and methods of correlation filter algorithms in object tracking. Complex Intell. Syst. (2020). https://doi.org/10.1007/s40747-020-00161-4
12. Liu, S., Lu, M., Li, H., et al.: Prediction of gene expression patterns with generalized linear regression model. Front. Genet. **10**, 120 (2019)
13. Fu, W., Liu, S., Srivastava, G.: Optimization of big data scheduling in social networks. Entropy **21**(9), 902 (2019)

# Design and Practice of Online and Offline Mixed Education System

Ying-jian Kang[1](✉), Xin-yu Lv[2], Mei Chen[1], and Lei Ma[1]

[1] Beijing Polytechnic, Beijing 100016, China
[2] School of Mathematics and Statistics, Wuhan University, Wuhan 430070, China

**Abstract.** With the widespread application of information technology in Colleges and universities, modern information technology provides effective support for the optimization of traditional teaching mode. In this study, computer network as the main technical support, on-line and offline hybrid intelligent assistant teaching system research. The system effectively integrates the two modes of network teaching and traditional teaching, and completes the design of the overall architecture of the system from the perspective of taking students as the main body and improving the effect of communication between teachers and students. Then, the functions of the key modules of the system are described, and the specific functions of the education system are realized by combining with the database. On this basis, this study also verified the effectiveness of the system through practical teaching application.

**Keywords:** Online and offline mixed education · Education system · Practice analysis · Communication effect between teachers and students

## 1 Introduction

With the popularity of computers and mobile devices, the form of learning is no longer confined to the traditional classroom teaching mode, but gradually to the media, network development. In this context, online education has become the general trend. As a kind of network course, excellent resource sharing course serves college teachers and students as well as social learners. Its purpose is to promote the co construction and sharing of high-quality course teaching resources. Its curriculum resource system is more suitable for network communication and can promote the improvement of professional course teaching quality. Therefore, it is of great practical value to study the online and offline hybrid curriculum construction based on the network platform. The network assisted teaching system has changed the traditional teaching mode and plays an important role in improving the teaching quality.


W. Fu et al. (Eds.): eLEOT 2021, LNICST 389, pp. 405–417, 2021.
https://doi.org/10.1007/978-3-030-84383-0_35

## 2 Analysis of Educational Concept of Mixed Teaching Mode

Teachers play a leading role in teaching knowledge in traditional classroom teaching and network teaching, and guide students to learn through a variety of teaching methods (including cramming, heuristic, guiding and so on). Teachers will be limited by limited class hours and other factors in the classroom. Online classroom is an effective extension and supplement of classroom. It has the advantages of rich teaching resources and unlimited time and space. Students can realize the process of autonomous learning through the use of online classroom teaching resources [1].

The blended learning process integrates a variety of teaching methods. In addition to the integration of face-to-face teaching and network teaching, it also includes the integration of a variety of modern educational technologies (including multimedia, computer, network and communication technologies), giving consideration to the leading role of teachers and the dominant position of students. At the same time, relying on the online auxiliary teaching system, the initiative and enthusiasm of students can be effectively improved, so as to form a teaching system that organically combines theory and practice teaching [2, 3].

## 3 Design of Hybrid Assistant Teaching System

### 3.1 System Architecture Design

At present, we can use a variety of languages and technologies (such as net, ASP, PHP, Java, C#) to complete the development of the website. The design pattern should take rationality as the basic principle to complete the compilation, classification and summary of the system. The system should include code, design module, upgrade system functions, etc. the code compilation should meet the system functions and complete the establishment of the effective structure of the software project. In order to solve the problem of easy to be attacked when revising or upgrading the system, the business relationship in this paper is based on J2EE and three-tier B/S system. The three levels need to complete data analysis according to the logical relationship in the program, which improves the intelligence of the system and effectively improves the stability and security of the teaching aid system on the basis of reducing the maintenance or upgrading cost. The overall architecture of the system is shown in Fig. 1.

(1) Presentation layer. After the user interaction instructions are executed in the presentation layer, the system service requirements can be completed by inputting the relevant requirements information in the client. After the web server displays the page, the browser is used for the same transmission. J2EE platform can meet the needs of diversified clients, and can realize the functions of most software (such as HTMLClient.Java The examination system is mainly realized by applying JSP, JS,

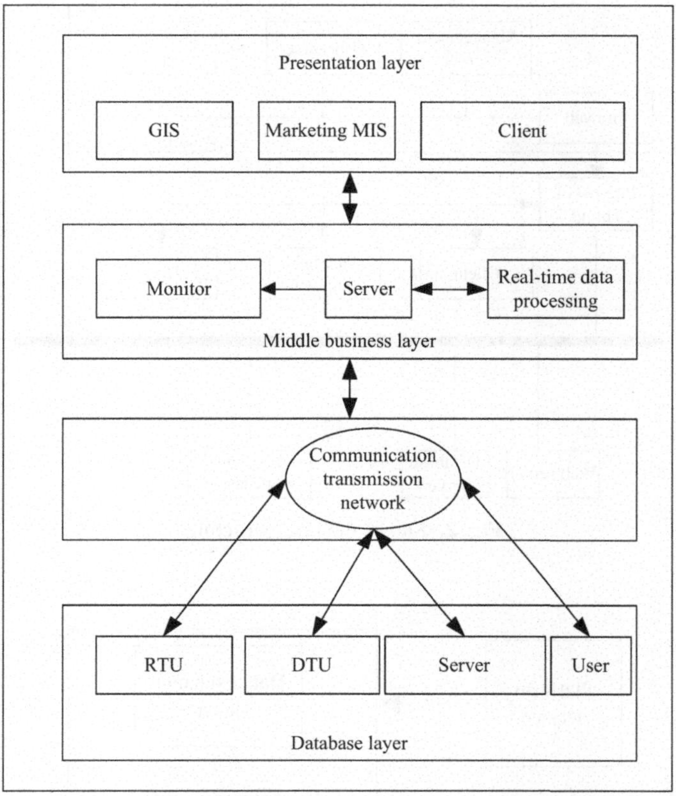


**Fig. 1.** Overall architecture of the system

HTML and other technologies, which helps the system to realize the examination management, intelligent test paper generation and analyze the common problems in the answering process. The structure of presentation layer is shown in Fig. 2.

(2) Intermediate business layer, including Web and J2EE server types. By connecting the two servers in parallel, the processing results can be transmitted from Web to J2EE, thus ensuring that multiple requests (such as adding and deleting database information, forwarding server information, etc.) can be processed simultaneously. In addition, the design pattern of the intermediate business layer of the system in this paper adopts Spring MVC pattern, which can further improve the flexibility of the system. Through the use of logical DAO layer and database connection (application server management), the interactive interface of data layer can not only meet the functional requirements, but also take into account the irrelevance and system scalability [4, 5]. The intermediate business layer structure is shown in Fig. 3.

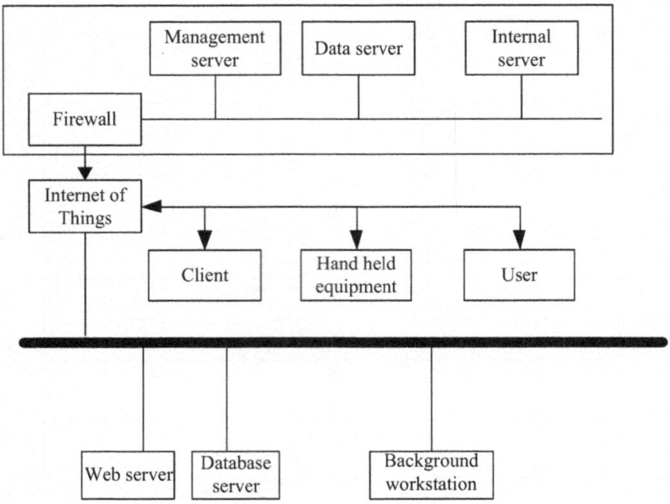


**Fig. 2.** Shows the layer structure

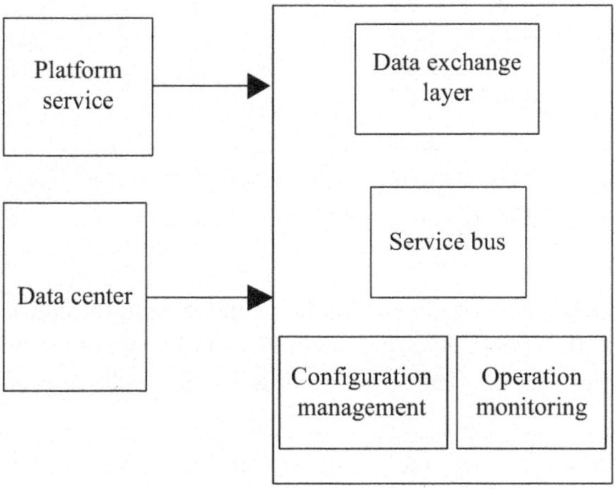


**Fig. 3.** Structure of middle business layer

(3) In order to improve the security of the system, this paper makes the database server independent, and provides great convenience for system maintenance and security management. The database layer is shown in Fig. 4.

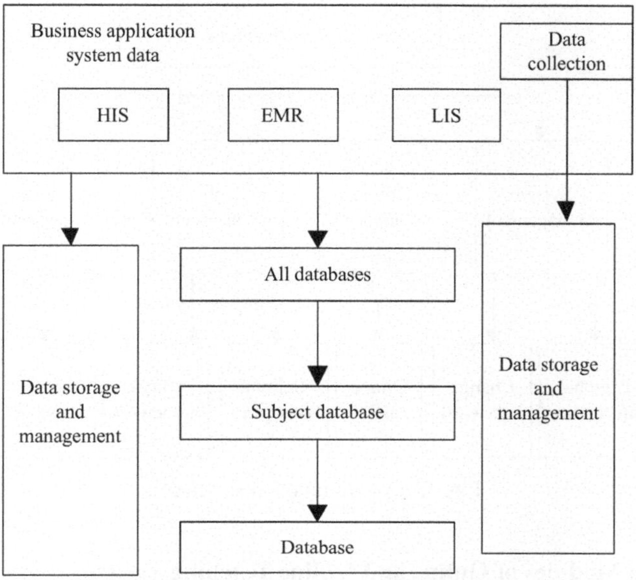


**Fig. 4.** Database layer structure

## 3.2 System Function Design

### Functional Structure

According to the different needs of users, the system users are divided into different user roles, and on this basis, the user rights are limited. The system administrator is responsible for setting the basic information of the system; The authority of teachers lies in the management of information, homework, question bank, work sharing, forum, etc., the setting of examination parameters and the realization of online examination view; the core functions of the system can be used by students, including online learning, submitting homework, sharing work, examination and mutual exchange, etc., and the system can realize online teaching, test training and online examination through the knowledge map constructed in the background The main function modules of learning feedback are flexibly linked together to provide teachers with more intelligent guidance function. The test question training environment not only provides students with the functions of automatic test paper generation exercises and special exercises, but also provides teachers with convenient test question bank management tools, reducing the burden of test question bank management [6]. The functional structure of the system is shown in Fig. 5.

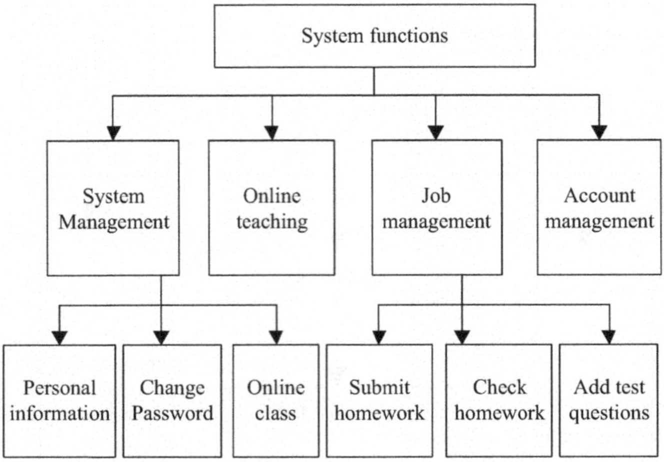


**Fig. 5.** System function structure

**Key Function Modules of Online and Offline Teaching System**
The workflow of online and offline teaching system is shown in Fig. 6.

(1) The new classroom (Data Management) is convenient for teachers to open many different classes. The contents mainly include: modifying or adding the name of the class according to the actual needs (changing the format for grade, major and course); setting the start and end time of the class; setting the user's permission to join and use (if allowed or not allowed); in order to facilitate students to understand the course, the new classroom can be added Set up the relevant introduction of the class, list the content to preview in advance, add new preview content, students preview in advance according to the preview list, and teachers view the preview results [7–9].
(2) In online teaching, the teaching materials are divided into knowledge point database (Chapter one knowledge point test questions) and homework question database (secondary structure: Chapter one homework) for management. Test questions can be directly converted into assignments under this chapter, which is convenient for teachers to answer students' difficult questions in time, and is helpful for students to interact with teachers in real time. The online teaching module mainly includes switching knowledge points, switching demonstration and practice, and manages the coding area of teachers and students, and online student list.
(3) Through the intelligent auxiliary teaching system, teachers can complete the layout and management of the corresponding classroom assignments; through clicking to publish the assignment questions and examination questions, mainly including the name and type of the examination questions, purpose, description of the examination questions, etc.; The default start time and end time are the current time and seven days later respectively. If the time limit is exceeded, the homework cannot be submitted and students are not allowed to view it. To correct the homework,

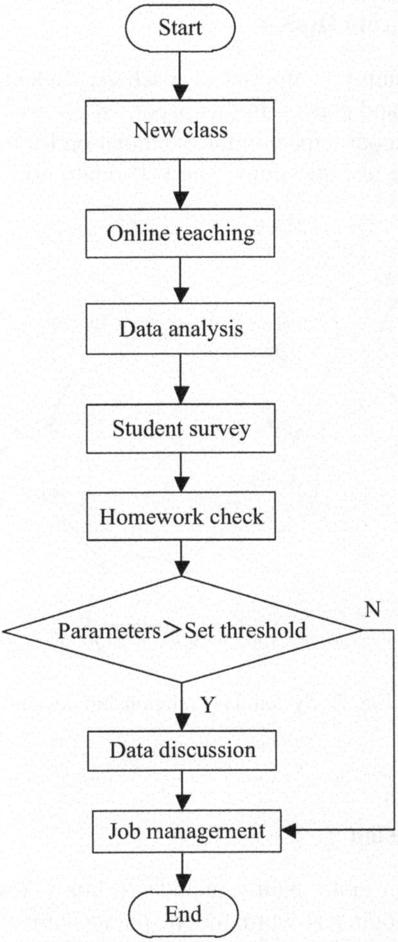


**Fig. 6.** Work flow of online and offline teaching system

complete the correction of the corresponding batch of homework on the homework list page (manual correction by default) [10].

# 4 Implementation of Online and Offline Teaching System

The key to the realization of the system lies in the data input, storage, modification and management, which are based on the design of the database, and the database is the core part of the system. This paper mainly starts from the E-R conceptual model to complete the design of the logical structure of the data table and the database relational model, and then completes the design of the database.

### 4.1 Database E-R Diagram Design

The database entity is mainly composed of teachers, students, assignments, teaching materials, test questions and papers. In this paper, "n" is used to represent multi-layer relationship. Students can participate in the examination for many times. For example, teachers can add multiple test questions. The E-R relationship design of the system is shown in Fig. 7.

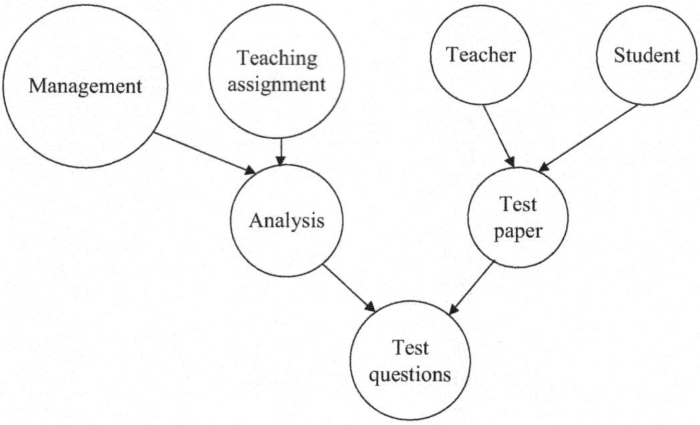


**Fig. 7.** System E-R relationship design

### 4.2 Table Structure Design

(1) The user information table mainly includes primary key, user account number, type and nickname, login password, mobile phone number and e-mail, as shown in Table 1.

**Table 1.** User information table

| Name | Field type | Length | Meaning |
|---|---|---|---|
| ID | VAR CHAR | 255 | Primary key |
| User account | VAR CHAR | 255 | User account number |
| User name | VAR CHAR | 255 | User nickname |
| PWD | VAR CHAR | 255 | Login password |
| Mobile | VAR CHAR | 255 | Cell-phone number |
| Email | VAR CHAR | 255 | Mail box |
| User type | INT | 19 | Customer type |

**Table 2.** Teaching materials

| Name | Field type | Length | Meaning |
|---|---|---|---|
| ID | VAR CHAR | 255 | Primary key |
| Sys account id | VAR CHAR | 255 | User account number |
| User name | VAR CHAR | 255 | User nickname |
| Title | VAR CHAR | 255 | Subject |
| Upload data | VAR CHAR | 255 | Upload date |
| Remark | VAR CHAR | 255 | Detailed description |
| Status | INT | 19 | State |

(2) The teaching data table is mainly composed of primary key (ID), user name, foreign key (user ID), title, update date, detailed description, etc., as shown in Table 2.
(3) The job list mainly includes ID, user ID, user name, job number, name, date and status, online preview path, name of the correcting person and correcting information and date. Detailed description is shown in Table 3.

**Table 3.** Operation table

| Name | Field type | Length | Meaning |
|---|---|---|---|
| ID | VAR CHAR | 255 | Primary key |
| Sys account id | VAR CHAR | 255 | User account number |
| User name | VAR CHAR | 255 | User nickname |
| Work name | VAR CHAR | 255 | Assignment topic |
| Work data | VAR CHAR | 255 | Operation date |
| Remark | VAR CHAR | 255 | Detailed description |
| Status | INT | 19 | State |

User data is the core of data design, and data tables representing system functions are directly or indirectly associated with user tables. General system functions (such as attachments, system settings, etc.) have no direct relationship with business function tables, and are set as independent tables. The specific data table association model is shown in Fig. 8.

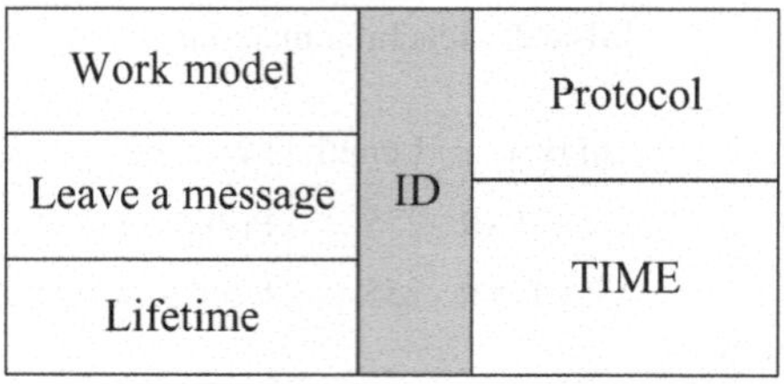


**Fig. 8.** Data table association model

## 5 Practice Analysis of Online and Offline Mixed Education System

The education system proposed in this paper can improve the training effect from many aspects. In-service training is different from ordinary diploma education. The trainees have a strong learning purpose, which may be due to the need of career development or the improvement of their own economic capacity. This requires that they should respect their right of choice when implementing distance education, that is, they should be able to learn selectively according to their own needs. After the introduction of online and offline interactive teaching, with the overlapping of online and offline learning in time and space dimensions, it can help students complete online learning according to their own needs, while offline can ask teachers or students for advice under the guidance of specific problems.

A good learning atmosphere can not only improve the learning efficiency of the students, but also promote the students to realize the learning sustainability. Establish online and offline interactive distance education mode, students mainly use online discussion group and offline class learning activities to obtain this learning atmosphere. It needs to be pointed out that in order to improve the effect of distance education, it is necessary to be clear about their learning preferences before providing education services. Therefore, it's very important to create a learning atmosphere for them.

The traditional distance education is influenced by the internal teaching technology and plan, which has rigid characteristics in teaching, which weakens the students' interest in learning. However, it is impractical to focus on optimizing the form of online education to solve the problem of rigidity of online education. First of all, online education has its own educational technology constraints, as well as the cost control requirements of educational service institutions in providing products. Therefore, while optimizing the online teaching form, we should also focus on finding strategies from the way of offline teaching as a supplement.

On the job training should be strictly in accordance with the syllabus and examination syllabus to organize teaching, although sometimes the teaching content is recorded in advance, the disadvantages of this kind of programmed teaching have been described above. In the mode positioning, it can not only be limited to the optimization of online teaching mode, but also can not be separated from the functionality of online teaching. Therefore, the mode can be positioned as follows:

(1) Optimize the interactive interface of online teaching, and pay attention to students' autonomous learning requirements;

(2) Expand the form and content of offline learning, and help students establish an informal organization for learning and mutual assistance. It is not difficult to see that from these two ways, we can effectively solve the problems brought about by programmed teaching.

No matter how to improve and transform the distance education, the education service content is still mainly from online teaching. This shows that offline teaching always plays an auxiliary function, so we should strengthen this auxiliary function at present.

(1) Strengthen the understanding of the importance of offline teaching. Educational service institutions need to recognize the important role of offline teaching in supporting online teaching when carrying out distance education projects. This effect comes from the social attributes of on-the-job staff, and also from the mutual motivation factors in teamwork learning.
(2) Pay attention to the role of offline teaching for on-the-job staff. Employees should participate in training programs with a strong sense of purpose. Therefore, educational service institutions should attach importance to the role of interpersonal interaction platform built by offline teaching.

In addition, to carry out online and offline interactive distance education activities, it is necessary to improve the organization and management of the offline teaching process. First of all, we should improve the teacher in charge system, through the selection of teacher in charge to promote the class management under the leadership of the class committee more reasonable, and can help to improve the learning efficiency. Moreover, it is still necessary to emphasize the regulatory role of class rules for students, so as to provide institutional guarantee for creating a good class learning atmosphere and cultivating their learning mentality.

## 6 Experiment and Analysis

In order to verify the practical application performance of the online and offline mixed education system designed above, the following experiments are designed.

In view of the two parts of the same degree of difficulty of teaching content, the paper system and the traditional system are respectively used to teach 10 students, students are required to fully master the content to be learned. Then the time for students to fully accept the teaching content after applying different systems was tested. The comparative results are shown in Table 4.

By analyzing the experimental data in Table 4, it can be seen that due to the different teaching methods adopted by the two teaching systems, the time for students to receive the teaching content is quite different. After using the traditional system, the time for students to accept the teaching content is more than 36 min. However, after the application of the system in this paper, the time for students to accept the teaching content is significantly shortened, and the minimum time is only 20.96 min. Therefore, the application effect of the system in this paper is better.

**Table 4.** Students receive the statistical results of teaching content time

| No. | The time required for students to receive the content/min | |
|---|---|---|
| | System of this paper | Traditional system |
| 01 | 22.32 | 36.21 |
| 02 | 23.14 | 36.40 |
| 03 | 21.01 | 36.37 |
| 08 | 22.53 | 36.75 |
| 04 | 21.70 | 36.27 |
| 05 | 22.14 | 35.14 |
| 06 | 22.85 | 35.86 |
| 07 | 20.96 | 37.02 |
| 08 | 22.53 | 38.58 |
| 09 | 21.47 | 38.56 |
| 10 | 22.52 | 38.75 |

## 7 Conclusion

With the popularization of information application in Colleges and universities, modern information technology provides support for the optimization of traditional teaching mode. Taking computer network as the main means, this paper studies the design of online and offline hybrid intelligent auxiliary teaching system, which takes students as the main body, enhances the communication between teachers and students, effectively integrates network teaching and traditional teaching mode, and completes the design of system architecture This paper describes the function of the key modules, combined with the design of the database to achieve the function of the auxiliary teaching system, and through the actual teaching application to verify the function of the system, the hybrid auxiliary teaching system through the integration of all aspects of teaching resources, can provide multi angle guidance for students' learning, can effectively meet the teaching needs, and has great practical application value.

## References

1. Ross, G.: Airlines, mayonnaise, and justice: reflections on the theory and practice of legal design and technology. Des. Issues **36**(3), 31–44 (2020)
2. Khinikadze, T., Pershin, V., Karagodskaya, Y.: Simulation of the hydraulic system of a device with self-adaptation by power and kinematic parameters on the working body. In: IOP Conference Series: Materials Science and Engineering, vol. 10, no. 1, pp. 61–66 (2020)
3. Joo, S., Lu, K., Lee, T.: Analysis of content topics, user engagement and library factors in public library social media based on text mining. Online Inf. Rev. **44**(1), 258–277 (2020)

4. Van Kuijk, J., Daalhuizen, J., Christiaans, H.: Drivers of usability in product design-practice: induction of a framework through a case study of three product development projects. Des. Stud. **60**(1), 139–179 (2019)
5. Liu, H., Liu, Y., Wang, H., et al.: Research on the coordinated development of greenization and urbanization based on system dynamics and data envelopment analysis: aA case study of Tianjin. J. Clean. Prod. **214**(20), 195–208 (2019)
6. Yao, K.C., Wu, T.C., Hsu, L.C., et al.: Evaluating thematic-approach teaching of robot design and practice course through psychomotor and affective domains. ICIC Express Lett. **13**(1), 41–49 (2019)
7. Majid, A.Z.A.: Evaluation on students' service design concepts using the principles of service innovation and design process. Test Eng. Manag. **82**(2), 9638–9646 (2020)
8. Fu, W., Liu, S., Srivastava, G.: Optimization of big data scheduling in social networks. Entropy **21**(9), 902 (2019)
9. Liu, S., Glowatz, M., Zappatore, M., et al. (eds.): E-Learning, E-Education, and Online Training. Springer, Heidelberg, pp. 1–374 (2018). https://doi.org/10.1007/978-3-319-49625-2
10. Liu, S., Li, Z., Zhang, Y., et al.: Introduction of key problems in long-distance learning and training. Mob. Netw. Appl. **24**(1), 1–4 (2019)

# Design of Auxiliary Teaching System for Oral English Training Based on Cloud Computing

Ying Lin[1](✉), Ying-di Xi[1], and Yang-bo Wu[2]

[1] College of Foreign Languages, Xinyu University, Xinyu 338000, China
[2] College of Mathematics and Computer, Xinyu University, Xinyu 338000, China

**Abstract.** In order to further improve the effect of college students' oral English training, a cloud computing-based English oral training auxiliary teaching system design is proposed. Based on the existing oral English teaching methods and equipment, a network-based college oral English teaching system is developed and the hardware is optimized. Configuration and functions, design auxiliary teaching data processing equipment, system operation management framework, improve system software operation process, design the functional structure of the auxiliary teaching system for oral English training through cloud computing, optimize the auxiliary method of system oral training, and realize oral English training based on cloud computing Auxiliary teaching system design. The experimental results show that the designed system effectively enhances the interest of college students in English learning, and the effect of classroom application is better. The application of this system can allow more college students to participate in oral English teaching, improve the efficiency of oral English teaching, and improve the oral English level and English application ability of college students.

**Keywords:** Cloud computing · Spoken English · Training aid

## 1 Introduction

College oral English is a very practical course. Teachers need to organize various activities so that college students can use the language they learn and communicate according to the situation. However, according to the survey, many schools can use communicative methods to teach, create a real English environment, and carry out immersion teaching [1]. Some schools have very little time for oral teaching, and even some schools do not have special oral classes. In addition, in such schools, few foreign teachers come to teach spoken English, and college students rarely have the opportunity to get in touch with teachers whose mother tongue is English.

As far as speaking classes are concerned, the specific issues are as follows: First of all, most of the university courses in our country are very large. Due to the large number of classes, it is difficult to organize effective oral training activities. As a result, college students have fewer opportunities to practice, and it is naturally difficult to improve their oral expression skills. Secondly, large-class teaching makes the oral class mainly focus


W. Fu et al. (Eds.): eLEOT 2021, LNICST 389, pp. 418–429, 2021.
https://doi.org/10.1007/978-3-030-84383-0_36

on the teacher's language knowledge, and college students rarely have the opportunity to speak. This teacher-led classroom has led to a lack of subjectivity or motivation for communication among college students [2]. Third, among the very few college students' practice time, the time and opportunities for college students to practice oral English are unevenly distributed. Teachers cannot accurately control the speaking time of college students in the classroom, which may lead to a decrease in the effective oral practice time of some college students. In addition, due to the limitation of classroom teaching time, teachers cannot participate in every group discussion, cannot pay attention to every college student, nor can they guide every college student. Finally, the traditional oral teaching evaluation method is single and cannot save the oral data of college students, which is not conducive to the formative evaluation of college students, and it is not conducive to the development evaluation of college students' self-evaluation and mutual evaluation [3].

In order to solve the above problems, a cloud computing-based English oral training auxiliary teaching system design method is proposed to better improve the oral learning and application ability of college students.

## 2 Auxiliary Teaching System for Oral English Training

### 2.1 Hardware Configuration of the Auxiliary Teaching System for Oral English Training

The cloud computing-based oral English teaching system includes: digital integrated language laboratory and network virtual oral equipment. In order to meet the requirements of new oral teaching, the oral English training auxiliary teaching system integrates multimedia equipment, network technology, examination center, and open learning Center, etc. to optimize. The integrated voice equipment will use 48 kHz voice sampling rate, supplemented by a new digital voice processing algorithm, to ensure the pure and true voice [4]. In addition, the system can support two-way discussions with a group of 64 people to meet the requirements of teacher-student, student-student interaction in the oral class, and record the audio files of college students' oral practice through recording software, and save these audio software in the college students' electronic files.

The oral English training auxiliary teaching system uses online teaching technology and teaching resource research and development technology to create a virtual oral learning environment for college students, which greatly fills up the gaps in extracurricular oral teaching and allows college students to get more exercise opportunities [5]. The network virtual oral classroom includes the main function area, teaching auxiliary area and related information area. These three parts are subdivided into teaching content introduction, learning and teaching blanks, so that college students can get more oral training opportunities. In the design of the English teaching system based on the cloud computing platform, three modules of teachers, college students, and administrators must be ensured to ensure that the system design meets the design requirements. The overall design structure of this system is shown in Fig. 1.

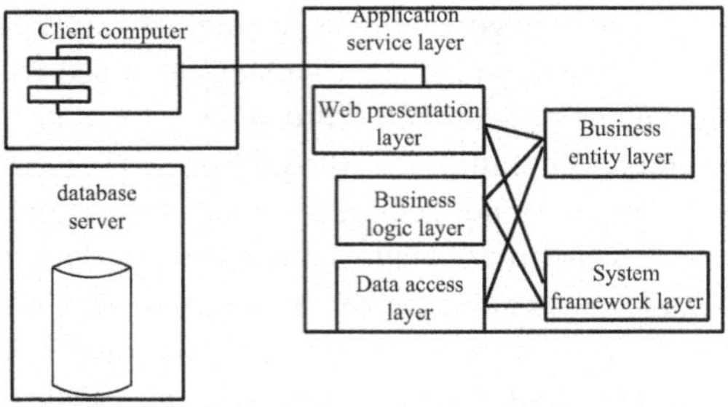


**Fig. 1.** The hardware structure framework of the auxiliary teaching system for oral English training

The system is developed based on the cloud computing platform technology system, and is supported by the Strust1.2 + Hibernate3.0 technical framework to build the system environment. Create a web project in the Myeclipse6.5 integrated development environment and name it wangljx; import all relevant jar packages of Strust1.2 and Hibernate3.0, and import the strust-config.xml file under WEB-INF and hibernate under the src directory. cfg.xml and log4j.properties configuration files; import the bin and jre/bin of the local JDK installation directory where Jsp Smart Upload and JACOB are located, and place the JACOB dynamic link library file jacob-1.15-M3-x86.dll; Configure the application server Jboss5.0, and set the jdk of Jboss to the jdk configured above, import the database connection jar package: mysql-connector-java-5.0.8-bin.jar, to provide the necessary environmental support for the development of the project [6]. In the system design, it should be ensured that a good system interface can be provided to users to improve the usability of the system design and meet the overall design requirements of the system.

In the design process of the auxiliary teaching system for oral English training, the relationship between the object categories of the system is complicated. In order to refine the different categories, the MVC design pattern, namely model-view control, is introduced. System operation objects are divided into category operation objects, data operation objects, image operation objects and query objects. The MVC model is composed of data layer, business layer and query object layer [7]. This system combines the MVC design model with the B/s network model to design the level of the college English auxiliary teaching system. In the application of teaching practice, the control of view technology is mainly controlled by JSP, because JSP can establish a direct interaction process between the teaching system and the user [8]. In the development and design process of the actual teaching system, designers mainly design the page, and JSP can use the program group in the view to process the data. Servlet controller plays a control role between EJB and JSP. It transforms user requests and model data. The results showed that EJB played a role in data encapsulation and logic processing. Its application objects are models and servlet controllers [9]. The data request generated by the EJB processing controller and the related results after data processing are stored in the database. In order to meet the processing effect of massive data, the auxiliary teaching data processing equipment is optimized, as shown in Fig. 2.

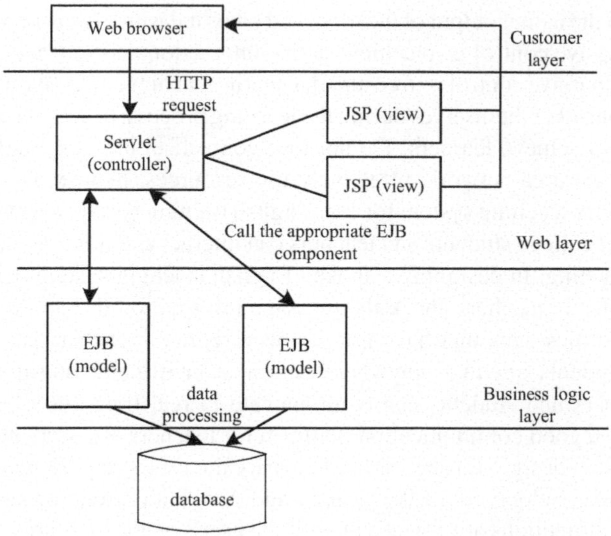


**Fig. 2.** Auxiliary teaching data processing equipment

From the application processing framework in the figure, it can be seen that the system is based on the B/S network mode and the combined structure is composed of browser, controller, view and model. Each part completes its own function and does not affect each other and is easy to proceed. Failure recovery and maintenance. In order to ensure the operation effect of the above steps, the operation management framework of the auxiliary teaching system for oral English training is further demonstrated, as shown in Fig. 3.

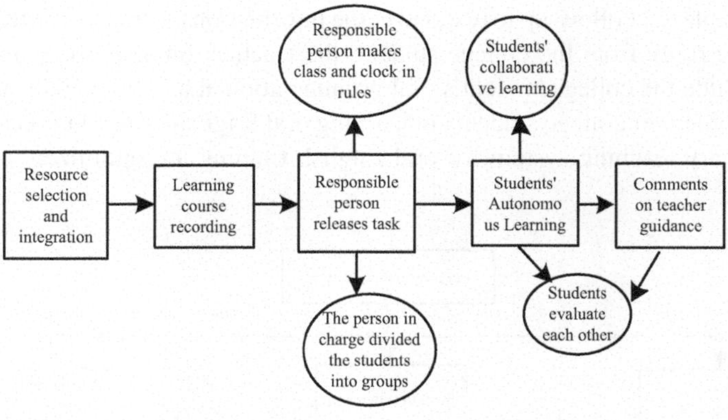


**Fig. 3.** System operation management framework

Active control in the system is to analyze the possibility of deviation from teaching objectives in advance, and to formulate and take various preventive measures to achieve the planned objectives. Passive control is a control method in which the controller finds deviations from the actual output of the plan, and takes measures to correct the deviations in time [10]. Passive control is to achieve active interaction and self-active control. The ultimate goal of passive control is to ensure that learners achieve effective use of resources and effective control of themselves during the learning process, to achieve teaching goals, and ultimately to achieve learners' Do not lose yourself in the oral English classroom based on the local area network, effectively use resources, realize active control, and design an auxiliary teaching system for oral English training based on a cloud computing platform, so that college students and teachers can interact and improve the efficiency of oral English teaching. In designing a spoken English teaching system based on a cloud computing platform, teachers check the message information through the message list and reply to the messages that have not yet been replied. Teachers can communicate with college students anytime, anywhere, and answer difficult questions for college students. Teachers and students can communicate in real time online and interact in time, providing a good communication platform for teachers and students. At the same time, in the system design, it is necessary to clarify the user's requirements, confirm the feasibility of the development of the system, and design a reasonable system to ensure that the system's functions are consistent with the user's needs to improve the efficiency of English teaching.

## 2.2 Optimization of the Software Function of the Auxiliary Teaching System for Oral English Training

Based on the oral English training auxiliary teaching system, it is not restricted by the traditional teaching on time, place, and personnel, and it also releases the learners' all kinds of distress and rejection of the classroom. Teachers can purposefully and periodically publish some oral English learning skills and examples through the cloud computing platform. These skills and examples will be transmitted to learners' mobile phones based on the Internet in real time. College students can use a small amount of time to imitate at any time and place., Follow-up to respond to the information pushed by the teacher. After receiving the reply from the college student, the teacher can also use a small amount of time to guide the college student's oral pronunciation at any time and place, so as to solve the problem of college students in learning oral English. The equipment functions of the auxiliary teaching system for oral English training are optimized, as shown in Fig. 4.

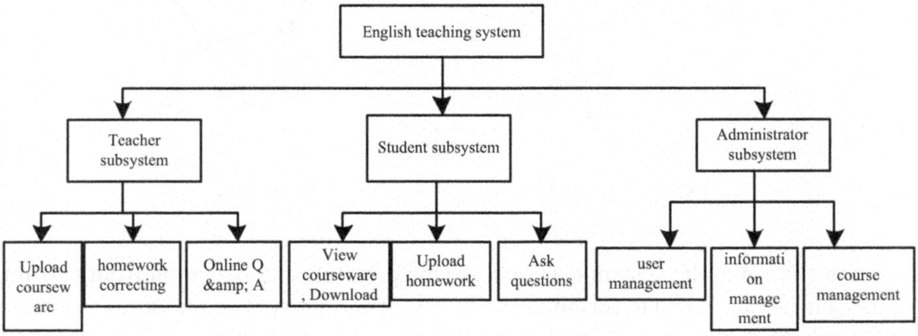


**Fig. 4.** The functional structure of the auxiliary teaching system for oral English training

The cloud computing platform-based English oral training supplementary teaching system consists of teachers forming learning groups, selecting appropriate teaching resources and integrating them. Starting from the teacher's release of learning tasks, college students study the day's course on their own within the specified time and complete the teacher's assignment task. The task form is generally based on reading short sentences or uploading notes and photos. This can make good use of the voice and picture publishing functions of the cloud computing platform for learning feedback. Teachers will evaluate and guide the completion of tasks for college students on the day. Provide information and study guidance during the process. The workflow of the system is as follows: the web browser client page requests data from the server, the servlet receives and processes it, and the processing result is returned to the web browser client; the servlet (controller) processes different data requests and then sends them to the logical processor Corresponding numbers, to achieve non-business invocation of different databases [11]; after the data logic processor completes the data logic operation, it returns different types of data results to the JSP (view), and the result after the view completes the operation is transmitted back to the web in HTML format Browser client. The use of clear data structure and data flow mode in the English teaching system can greatly improve the performance of the system. The three-tier structure of browser + JSP (servlet) + sqlserver is adopted in the design of the system. In database design, courseware resources can be stored and updated, involving multiple pages and multiple functions [12]. For system design, for users, systems, and databases, the data flow performance is shown in Fig. 5.

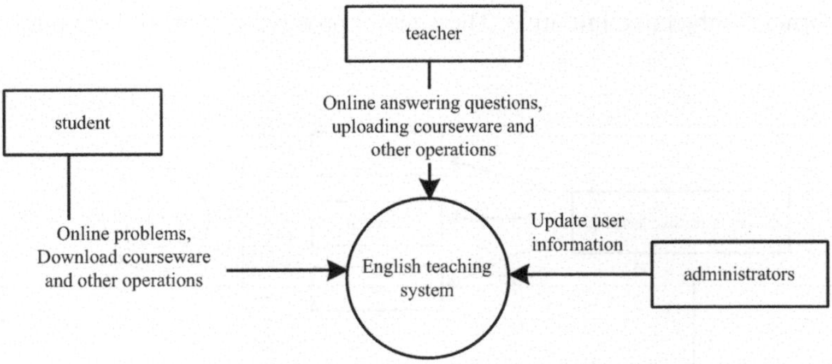


**Fig. 5.** Optimization of system oral training auxiliary method

In the system database, system information can be dynamically stored. The main database tables include: personnel table, courseware table, homework table, administrator, etc. Electronic learning files refer to the information technology environment where learners use information to perform and demonstrate learning In the learning process, the learner is a collection of related learning about learning goals, learning activities, learning results, learning performance, learning efforts, academic progress, and reflections on the learning process and learning results. With the help of electronic learning files, teachers can not only guide college students' oral practice in class, but also analyze the spoken language of each college student through recording data after class, and give feedback on the problems of university survival [13].

### 2.3 The Realization of Auxiliary Teaching for Oral English Training

Through real-time interaction, teachers can provide immediate answers to the problems in college students' spoken language and their questions. Real-time interactive systems can arouse learners' resonance, but it is easy to destroy the continuity of teaching, deviate from the theme of teaching, and it is not easy to think deeply. Non-real-time interaction can make up for this defect. In the case of non-real-time interaction, learners will think deeply about problems and have more time to practice and prepare for the questions raised by the teacher. At the same time, the non-real-time interactive system also provides sufficient time for teachers to analyze the problems in the university and find relevant ones. In addition, in the past oral English teaching, there was mostly real-time interaction between teachers and students. Teachers could not or seldom retain the voice data of college students and could not make formative evaluations of college students. College students are also unable to understand their own mistakes and practice repeatedly to improve their oral English. In the new spoken language teaching system, real-time interaction and non-real-time interaction are combined with each other and complement each other.

Oral English learning has always been a relatively difficult problem to solve uniformly. The general English learning process is mainly based on classroom teaching, and classroom teaching emphasizes vocabulary, grammatical structure and reading comprehension training. There is very little time for oral learning and communication. College students passively accept knowledge, and teachers assign tasks after class to college students. Teachers are more dominant, and oral learning itself is training that requires higher learners' subjective initiative. The general process of English learning is shown in Fig. 6.

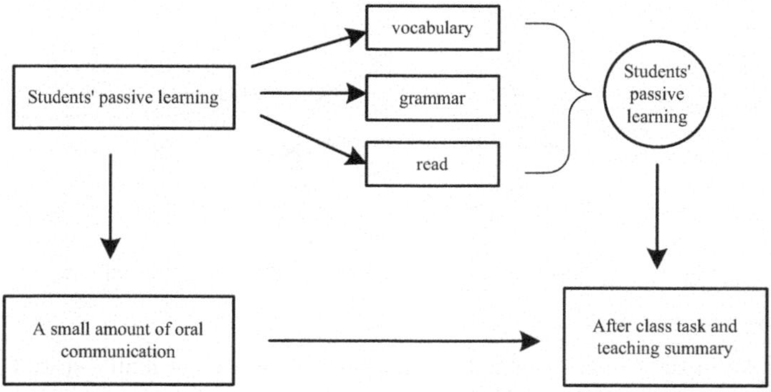


**Fig. 6.** The general process of oral English learning

The interface architecture model of the college oral English teaching system installs the technical system on the database equipment to facilitate centralized management of components. The software program, database and information release for task processing are all completed by the server, reducing the workload on the user side. Based on the network structure, the auxiliary teaching system with the background database as the core will serve users as the goal, and reasonably arrange the course resources, such as uploading of course videos, processing and maintenance of examination questions, and providing assistance and support for English teaching. The functions of this system include user registration, teacher teaching, college student learning and teaching management. The auxiliary teaching steps of oral training are further optimized, as shown in Fig. 7.

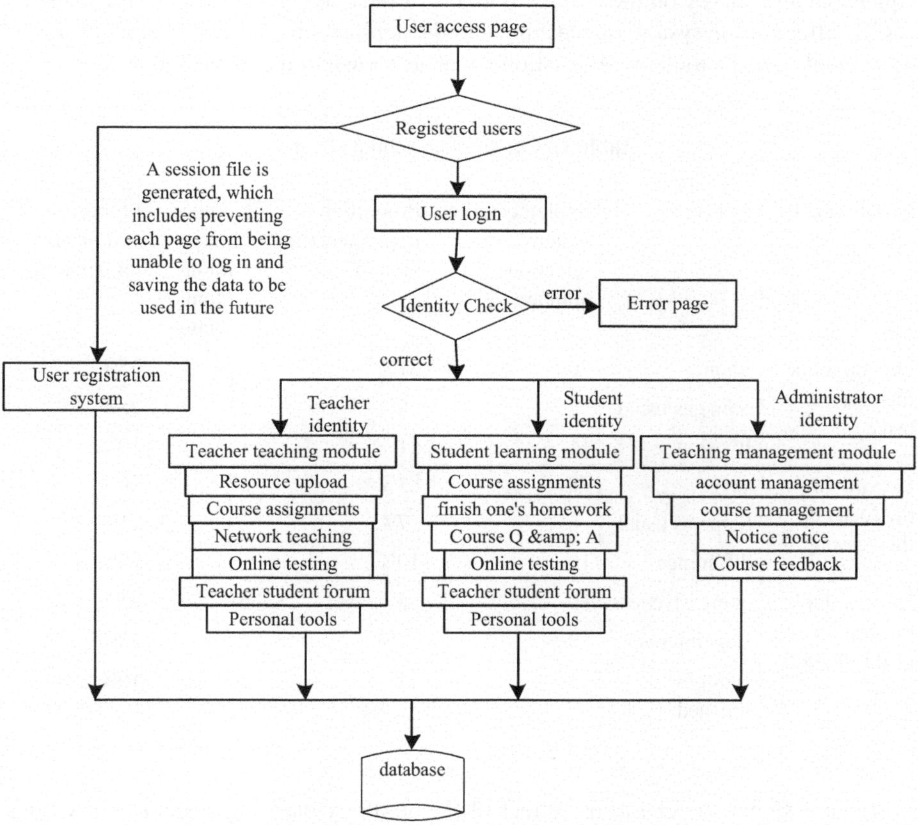


**Fig. 7.** Auxiliary teaching steps for oral training

Oral English teaching training based on Fig. 7 can better improve the teaching effect, help college students use English to communicate with others fluently, and promote the improvement of college students' oral English expression ability. This is a problem faced by the majority of English teaching workers. The application of the latest information technology to assist oral English teaching can make up for the shortcomings in the original oral teaching, truly implement the oral teaching, and transform the traditional oral evaluation model.

## 3 Analysis of Experimental Results

In order to verify the effect of the system, the experiment selected a certain English class of a certain university English major using the system to conduct a questionnaire, mainly to analyze the classroom effect of the system in English teaching and the effectiveness of teaching strategies. Before and after adopting this system, the experiment conducted a questionnaire survey on the college students of the class. The setting of the question was the effect of the system on teaching and the application of teaching strategies. The experiment issued a total of 94 questionnaires, as shown in the Table 1 shows.

**Table 1.** Classroom teaching effect

| Questionnaire title | Option | Implementation system selection number | Proportion of implementation system | Number of people without system selection | Proportion of systems not implemented |
|---|---|---|---|---|---|
| Do you think this class is fast? | Soon | 76 | 81% | 61 | 65% |
| | Same as usual | 7 | 8% | 23 | 25% |
| | It's slow | 11 | 11% | 10 | 10% |
| Do you think the focus of this lesson? | very | 78 | 83% | 62 | 66% |
| | Same as usual | 6 | 7% | 20 | 21% |
| | difference | 10 | 10% | 12 | 7% |
| Do you think the completion of this class is good | aggressiveness | 80 | 85% | 61 | 65% |
| | Low interest | 3 | 4% | 23 | 25% |
| | Barely finished | 11 | 11% | 10 | 10% |

Table 1 shows the classroom effect of the auxiliary teaching system on teaching. According to the experimental data in the table, the students who use this assisted teaching system are greatly satisfied with the classroom effect. Most students think that the classroom rhythm using multimedia teaching is more compact, which is 16% higher than before using this system. % Percentage points, indicating that the college students under this teaching system are very interested in English classes, feel that time passes quickly, and the number of students who feel bored in English classes is decreasing, indicating that the classroom effects are better. In order to obtain the application of teachers' teaching strategies to college students, the following questionnaire questions are set up, and the results of the questionnaire are analyzed, and the application of classroom teaching strategies of this system is obtained, as shown in Table 2.

**Table 2.** Classroom teaching application situation

| Questionnaire title | Option | Number of people | Proportion |
|---|---|---|---|
| Adopt group discussion attitude? | Like | 86 | 91% |
| | Have no feelings | 3 | 4% |
| | Dislike | 5 | 5% |
| What's your attitude towards this lesson? | Like | 88 | 93% |
| | Have no feelings | 2 | 3% |
| | Dislike | 4 | 4% |
| Hope for the way the clock teaches | Keep going | 90 | 95% |
| | casual | 4 | 5% |
| | Give up | 0 | 0% |

From the questionnaire data in the table, it can be seen that college students like this auxiliary teaching system that can combine multiple elements. Simple text teaching can no longer satisfy college students' desire for knowledge exploration. Adding multimedia animation to the classroom can bring college students into the ocean of animation has a strong interest in English learning. The use of grouping has made students have a sense of cooperation and competition, and greatly improved the self-confidence and satisfaction of college students. From the data in the table, it can also be seen that In English classrooms, the advantages of computer multimedia are applied to teaching through animation, which is generally recognized by college students. Most students are very satisfied with the teacher's courseware design. English teaching strategies have achieved effective results. More than 90% of the students are the system is very satisfied with the teaching strategy of introducing multimedia teaching into the English classroom. I hope to continue to learn through this teaching strategy, which affirms the feasibility of this system in English teaching.

Two months after applying this system for teaching, the experiment conducted a new questionnaire on college students' attitudes towards oral English learning, and compared them with the situation of learning attitudes that did not use this system for teaching two months ago. The results are shown in Table 3.

Analyzing Table 3, it can be concluded that after using this teaching system for two months of study, the percentage of college students who like English has increased significantly, indicating that the application of the system to English teaching has increased the enthusiasm of college students to learn English and is beneficial to the development of classroom teaching.. It shows that this teaching system has internally improved the attitude of college students to learn English, and the reason why college students learn English has changed from being dominated by parental requirements in the past to being interested in English. Through the above experimental results, we can see that the use of this system can effectively enhance college students' interest in English learning.

**Table 3.** Comparison of test results before and after using the system

| Investigation questions | Option | This system is not used | This system is adopted |
|---|---|---|---|
| How much do you like English | like it very much | 11% | 88% |
| | I like it better | 36% | 8% |
| | Indifferent | 53% | 4% |
| On the value of learning English | Very useful | 55% | 72% |
| | It's useful | 36% | 25% |
| | It's totally useless | 9% | 3% |
| | Key skills | 54% | 45% |
| | Enrich knowledge | 22% | 48% |
| | Further education | 20% | 5% |
| | It's useless | 2% | 1% |
| | Other | 2% | 1% |
| To investigate the motivation of learning English | Like English | 11% | 85% |
| | Study abroad | 22% | 10% |
| | Parents request | 67% | 5% |

## 4 Concluding Remarks

Using English to communicate and communicate with others fluently is an important purpose of English teaching and an inevitable requirement of social development. How to improve the efficiency of oral English teaching and promote the improvement of college students' oral expression ability is a problem faced by the majority of English teaching workers. Based on this, the design of an auxiliary teaching system for oral English training is proposed. The application of the latest information technology to assist oral English teaching can make up for the shortcomings of the original oral teaching, truly implement the oral teaching, and change the traditional oral evaluation mode.

## References

1. Malinee, V.V., Senthamarai, T.: The use of web 2.0 tools in English for specific purpose: a blended learning approach in English language teaching. J. Shanghai Jiaotong Univ. (Sci.) **16**(8), 703–716 (2020)
2. Yuan, F.: An English language multimedia teaching model. Int. J. Emerg. Technol. Learn. **13**(8), 198 (2018)
3. Santikarn, B., Wichadee, S.: Flipping the classroom for English language learners: a study of learning performance and perceptions. Int. J. Emerg. Technol. Learn. **13**(9), 123 (2018)
4. Herath, B., Dewmin, G.H.S., et al.: Design and development of a novel oral care simulator for the training of nurses. IEEE Trans. Biomed. Eng. **67**(5), 1314–1320 (2019)
5. Mitani, A., Muramatsu, M.: Development of human tongue model for mealtime assistant training using oral care simulation model. Int. J. Autom. Technol. **13**(4), 499–505 (2019)

6. Wickens, J.D.J., Norris, D.H.: The imperative of soft skill development in preventive conservation practice and training. Stud. Conserv. **63**(9), 301–306 (2018)
7. Guil, F.: Associative classification based on the transferable belief model. Knowl. Based Syst. **182**(8), 1048–1059 (2019)
8. Hou, W., Hou, X.: Spatial–temporal changes in vegetation coverage in the global coastal zone based on GIMMS NDVI3g data. Int. J. Remote Sens. **41**(21), 1–21 (2019)
9. Korepin, V.N., Dorozhkin, E.M., Mikhaylova, A.V., et al.: Digital economy and digital logistics as new area of study in higher education. Int. J. Emerg. Technol. Learn. **15**(13), 137 (2020)
10. Huang, Y.Y., Wang, Z.H., Deng, L.H., et al.: Oral administration of quercetin or its derivatives inhibit bone loss in animal model of osteoporosis. Oxid. Med. Cell. Longev. **20**(3), 1–21 (2020)
11. Yang, T., Cappelle, C., Ruichek, Y., et al.: Multi-object tracking with discriminant correlation filter based deep learning tracker. Integr. Comput. Aided Eng. **26**(3), 273–284 (2019)
12. Pan, G., Chen, G., Kang, W., et al.: Correlation filter tracker with siamese: a robust and real-time object tracking framework. Neurocomputing **358**(9), 33–43 (2019)
13. Fu, W., Liu, S., Srivastava, G.: Optimization of big data scheduling in social networks. Entropy **21**(9), 902 (2019)

# Design of Computer Professional Training Teaching System Based on Big Data Under the Background of "Three Integration"

Jie-lan Zhang(✉)

Jiangxi Teachers College, Yingtan 335000, China

**Abstract.** In order to meet the needs of the society for the application-oriented computer talents, define the professional orientation and training goal of the application-oriented computer talents, according to the requirements of companies and enterprises for the computer talents, and based on the current big data information, a computer professional training and teaching system is designed. The hardware unit includes controller configuration unit, audio control chip selection unit and wireless communication unit, and the software module includes training teaching content module, wireless node configuration module and database building module. Through the design of the hardware unit and software module, the operation of the computer professional training teaching system is realized. Set up computer professional training teaching environment, set up the software module configuration program, carry out simulation experiments. Experimental results show that the server utilization rate of the design system is lower than 70% compared with the existing system, which indicates that the design system is effective and feasible.

**Keywords:** Three financing background · Big data · Computer specialty · Practice teaching

## 1 Introduction

The computer speciality is a key construction speciality of the state. In the course of demonstration construction, this speciality actively adapts to the needs of regional economic and social development, adheres to the principle of service-oriented and employment- oriented, and takes the road of industry-university-research-integrated development; and in the demand of social electronic enterprises for highly-skilled talents, actively probes into the talent cultivation mode of "combination of three types of talents and integration of three aspects of work and study", obtains obvious achievements in reconstructing the curriculum system of the speciality, creating excellent teaching teams, and jointly constructing practical training bases inside and outside the school, etc., and the quality of talent cultivation keeps improving. The "three combinations" refers to the combination of industry, enterprise and school, and the "three financing" means the accommodation of courses, posts and vocational qualification certificates.


W. Fu et al. (Eds.): eLEOT 2021, LNICST 389, pp. 430–441, 2021.
https://doi.org/10.1007/978-3-030-84383-0_37

Through the establishment of electronic information "School-enterprise" cooperative education work committee, to achieve "School-enterprise" close combination, trinity common development. Through the "three combinations", highlight the guiding role of electronic associations, electrotechnical associations and other industrial institutions in talent training, new technology training and other aspects; highlight the guidance and enthusiasm of enterprises in the process of deep cooperation in talent training [1].

Under the background of "three integrations", the computer specialty is a highly practical engineering specialty, and the practical teaching is an important part of the talent training program and teaching plan. With the rapid development of informationization in our country, the information technology with computer technology as the core will play a key role in promoting the rapid development of national informationization and economy. At present, the country's information and economic development of computer professionals in growing demand. However, in the supply and demand of computer talents, there are two contradictory situations. On the one hand, companies and enterprises cannot recruit the computer talent they need; on the other hand, there are difficulties in finding jobs for graduates majoring in computer science [2]. The reason is that the school does not understand the requirements of computer talents' knowledge structure, professional ability and professional quality in the corresponding positions of companies and enterprises. In the formulation and implementation of the talent training program, the emphasis is laid on theory rather than practice, and students' practical and hands-on abilities are generally not high. Therefore, we have carried on the reform to the university applied undergraduate computer specialized personnel training plan, and made clear the specialized localization and the training goal of training computer applied talents.

## 2 Design of Hardware Unit of Training and Teaching System for Computer Specialty

Hardware unit is the precondition and foundation of system operation and application. The hardware unit of the system, including controller configuration unit, audio control chip selection unit and wireless communication unit, shall be designed based on the needs of practical training and teaching of computer specialty. The specific design process is as follows:

### 2.1 Controller Hive

The controller is also called sandbox in the design system. The controller is an important condition to ensure that the students can be trained. In the process of configuring the controller, there are two methods:

(1) Configuration using the Console port of the controller (sandbox)
On each controller of the system, there is a Console interface that configures the system. Once properly connected to the human console, the controller's associated communication interface can be configured on the command line, with basic configuration such as the IP address of the CFG interface to complete the associated configuration [3]. The specific configuration method is as follows:

Set smc 192.168.1.253:9600.
Set intcfg eth0 192.168.1.1
Set DNS 255.255.255.0
Such configuration is a necessary configuration, and then set up the communication configuration of the design system, you can carry out normal communication. After configuration, the controller (sandbox) device uses the eth0 interface to register the data of the system with the system server. After configuration is completed, the configuration of the system server SMC can be viewed through the show efg command, or the ethnic 0 command can be used to view the interface configuration area of the system and other relevant situations.

(2) Configure by using the controller's configuration network port (CFG)
Typically, there is a CFG interface in the controller's device that has a default configuration address of 1.1.1.1, which is built-in to the system and is not allowed to be changed. However, in the system, port 212 can adopt 1.1.1.2 address for remote connection, which means that the IP address of the student or teacher machine is set to 1.1.1.2 for data communication, and the communication within the system can be realized by connecting the CFG interface of the controller device with cross wires [4].

## 2.2 Audio Control Chip Selection Unit

Computer professional training teaching system needs teachers to carry out certain teaching through audio, so we need to choose the appropriate audio control chip [5].

At present, multimedia equipment is favored by people because of its intuitive sense of vision and the enjoyment of hearing. In audio, many audio systems to CD, digital TV audio, digital audio processors and digital audio tapes, in the market deeply attracted a large number of consumers. S3C2440 core microprocessor internal integrated with IIS bus interface, can be external 8/16 bit stereo audio decoder integrated chip connected to the development of audio applications. S3C2440's IIS bus interface supports two data formats: MSB-aligned data formats and IIS bus data formats. Its interface uses DMA mode instead of interrupt mode to access FIFO, so that the core processor can receive and send data simultaneously at the same time. With the core processor interface support, in order to achieve the overall design goal of the audio module design, but also need to add audio control processor to assist. Here, the type of audio processing chip for the UDA1341TS is selected.

UDA1341TS is a DAC signal processing chip based on Bit Stream Converter. Its fully integrated analog front-end includes digital AGC and programmable gain amplifier. The UDA1341TS audio processing chip can support a variety of data formats, including 20-bit IIS bus data format, 20-bit highest significant bit alignment format, 16–18/20-bit lowest significant bit alignment serial data format, and complex data format combining the highest significant bit output with 16-or 18-or 20-bit lowest significant bit alignment data input. In playback mode, the UDA1341TS has digital sound processing features such as volume, treble, bass, stress removal, and soft mute, all of which can be controlled through the L3 - interface of the microcontroller. The UDA1341TS has digital sound processing capabilities that make it a great choice for home stereo mini drives and other applications. It is also ideal for portable applications such as laptops, MD/CD stereos and digital video cameras because of its low power consumption and low voltage.

### 2.3 Wireless Communication Unit

Now the design system is developing towards the direction of network interconnection, so the training platform as a teaching device, Ethernet interface has become an indispensable module. In general, Ethernet communication is more complex, in addition to the core microprocessor to provide some necessary pins for use, usually need a more powerful, pin-complicated control chip to assist, so that it is easier to achieve the full function of Ethernet interface. At present, there are many kinds of Ethernet control chips on the market, and the quality of chips varies, and different types of chips can be used in different environments. Considering that the training platform needs to support the Linux 2.6 kernel operating system, that is, its network communication function should be the same as that of the PC used in our daily life. Therefore, the Ethernet control chip required to be selected has higher processing capacity and better functions. Based on these factors, the DM9000, which is widely used in the industry and developed by DAVICOM, is chosen as the control chip of the Ethernet module of the training platform [6].

The DM9000 control chip is a fast Ethernet control processor integrated with MAC, PHY and MMU. It is also known as the DM9000 network card. Its internal configuration has a 4 KB double-word SDRAM buffer space, as well as 10/100 Mbps adaptive transceivers. The DM9000 offers four general-purpose, versatile GP10 pins that allow the core microprocessor to read and write data and manipulation commands from its internal memory at a byte/byte/double Word length to support different processors. The DM9000 supports both half-duplex and full-duplex modes and provides a media-independent interface that can be effectively connected to all transceivers or network devices that support media-independent interface functionality. In addition, the DM9000 also has a power failure handling capacity, ultra- low power consumption, compatible 5 V and 3.3 V input and output voltage, easy to use, easy to port and so on.

The above process realizes the selection and design of the hardware unit of the design system, but it is still unable to carry out the training and teaching of computer specialty.

## 3 Design of Software Module of Training and Teaching System for Computer Specialty

The software module of the design system includes the training content module, wireless node configuration module and database building module. The specific design process is as follows:

### 3.1 Content Module of Practical Training

Starting with the analysis of professional demand, the professional post quality, ability and key post skills of computer major are decomposed and the core professional ability is cultivated. According to the quality and key professional ability requirements corresponding to the job positions, design the talent training program for the specialty according to the production process of typical electronic products, and really implement the work-study talent training mode with real (enterprise) work tasks as the carrier [7].

Computer professional training teaching is divided into three stages.

(I) Stage of cultural quality cultivation. Students first learn English, computers, advanced mathematics, two courses and other cultural quality courses at school. Then they choose a certain social work post to carry out social practice for one month during winter vacation to understand the quality requirements of society for highly skilled talents and accumulate certain social work experience. Teaching time is 1 semester.

(II) Stage of basic skills training. Students in the school to professional basic ability training as the center, as the carrier of the item to complete the multimeter, radio, television and other electronic products installation and commissioning and electronic measurement technology learning. During the second and third semesters of study, students shall take turns to take such posts as the assembly and debugging of electronic products and electronic measurement technology in the typical training bases within and outside the school, participate in the production training and labor for two months, and complete certain work tasks under the joint guidance of the training teachers and the enterprise masters. Through practical training, practice, learning by doing, learning by doing, integration of "teaching, learning, doing" in one, so that students master professional knowledge at the same time with the professional skills required for the post. Teaching time is 3 semesters.

(III) Stage of post comprehensive ability training. Students can complete the design, installation and debugging of SCM control system, innovative design, installation and debugging of multi-function digital clock, electronic display and other typical electronic products. In the sixth semester, students in the cooperative enterprise off-campus internship base selection and application of electronic technology professional related posts, post comprehensive ability training, complete the 6 months internship. Through innovative design and production, on-the-job practice and other practical teaching links to carry out comprehensive training of professional skills, cultivate students' knowledge application ability, independent learning ability and coordination and cooperation ability. Teaching time is 2 semesters [8].

Under the background of "three finances", the main characteristics of computer professional training teaching are: First, to achieve three years of uninterrupted integration of the whole process. In the process of learning, students alternate skills training and on-the-job practice in classroom, society and practice bases both at home and abroad for three years without interruption, which is conducive to the cultivation of professional quality and practical ability. In the training of basic professional skills and comprehensive abilities for posts, students shall be assessed in accordance with the standards for the assessment of abilities for posts and vocational standards, and the certification of professional qualifications such as "Assembly and Deployment of Electronic Instruments and Meters i}", "Certificate of Technician for Electronic Products" and "Certificate of Debugger for Electronic Products" shall be completed, so as to realize the integration of diploma and diploma and vocational qualification certificate; and thirdly, the training of professional qualities in the whole process. Attention shall be paid to the cultivation of students' professional ethics, technical knowledge, operational skills and basic professional quality, and the cultivation of professional quality shall run through the whole teaching process. At the same time, actively help students with career planning.

### 3.2 Wireless Node Configuration Module

The wireless node module in the design system includes fixed node and mobile node, and all modules are integrated with two parts: CC2530 controller and functional equipment. The functional equipment is all kinds of sensors, and the CC2530 controller is the core of the whole module. This design completes the design and implementation of the whole wireless node on CC2530 chip. This design uses the Z-Stack protocol stack issued by TI Company, which has been widely used as the specification of software in wireless networking industry [9].

The Z-Stack protocol stack hierarchy is shown in Table 1.

**Table 1.** Z-stack protocol stack hierarchy table

| Arrangement | Name | Describe |
|---|---|---|
| APP | Application layer | Functions created by developers based on requirements |
| HAL | Hardware layer | Contains hardware related driver configuration and functions |
| MAC | Mac layer | Contains configuration parameters and lib library |
| MT | Monitoring and debugging layer | Control other layers through serial port to realize interaction |
| NWK | Network layer | Contains network configuration and interface library |
| PROFILE | Af layer | Including af layer interface |
| SECURITY | Security layer | Include security processing interface |
| SERVICES | Address processing layer | Contains interfaces that define address patterns and processes |
| TOOLS | Engineering configuration layer | Including space partition and z-stack configuration |
| ZDO | ZigBee device layer | Contains service objects used by developers |
| ZMAC | ZMac layer | It includes the interface of mac layer and network layer in z-stack |

(*continued*)

**Table 1.** (*continued*)

| Arrangement | Name | Describe |
|---|---|---|
| ZMAIN | Main function layer | Contains related hardware configuration and entry function |
| OUTPUT | Output layer | Automatically generated information |

As shown in Table 1, the Z-Stack protocol stack is a semi-open source software, and part of the code is provided to the developers as a function library. In the actual application development process, the developers do not need to change the underlying function implementation, but only need to provide the function interface to achieve the function they need, which greatly reduces the difficulty of development. The Z-Stack protocol stack realizes each level of software function according to ZigBee standard, and the developer realizes his own function in this level of software. It can be said that the Z-Stack protocol stack is a complete small operating system. The system mainly completes the running and task execution of the system by the way of round robin and event-driven.

This design mainly completes the system design and realization in the wireless node module through the IAR project. The whole system starts from the main () function of ZMain.c file under ZMain layer. This function mainly realizes two tasks: initializing system configuration and running operating system. In the task of initializing system configuration, the main task is to initialize hardware devices and some modules needed in the protocol stack, such as interrupt configuration and timer configuration. When the initialization is completed, the system is a dead loop, which processes events by querying the current task list. The implementation can be polling or event-driven, depending on the configuration. Query and process tasks in the current system are processed according to the level, the priority of different levels is different, in which the MAC layer is the highest priority and the application layer is the lowest priority. Once the entire Z-Stack stack has been configured, the next thing to do is to implement the functionality for each wireless node. User function is implemented in the application layer, through the specific functional requirements to complete the corresponding system configuration, functional programming, so as to achieve the corresponding implementation.

It should be noted that the platform uses a multi-hop approach to complete the entire wireless node networking implementation, as shown in Fig. 1.

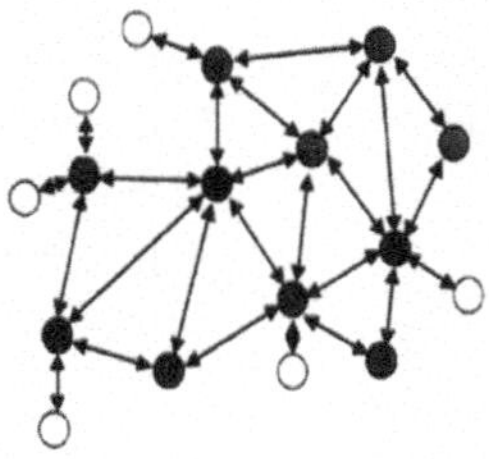

**Fig. 1.** Effect of wireless networking

After the whole system starts up, the functions of each layer will be handled automatically according to the configuration, and after the processing is completed, the functions of the current nodes in the whole network will be set up according to the configuration of the current application layer: the coordination node, the routing node and the terminal node, among which the coordination node is also the root node, which mainly completes the selection of the whole network channel and the creation of the network; the routing node is the transit node, which mainly assists other nodes to join the network; the terminal node is the sensor node, which is mainly used to collect data and forward data. When the network is started up, both the routing node and the terminal node will automatically find and join in the created network, and the routing node can be used as a transit node to connect to the wireless network indirectly.

### 3.3 Database Creation Module

There are many subsystems in the system, such as the content inquiry subsystem, the result management subsystem, the computer room management subsystem, the flow management subsystem, the consumption management subsystem and the reading room management subsystem. Eclipse can also meet the needs of different vendor tools in the same integrated development environment, so that the tools among vendors can achieve interoperability, and then optimize the project workflow. Eclipse extension point mainly refers to the use of conventional expression filter to complete a simple string description of the Java class, the process can be done with Eclipse extensibility, effectively reducing the complexity of the program. And extension points defined by Eclipse plug-ins can meet the needs of other plug-in applications, and can also work in extension points defined by other plug-ins. Apart from having prior knowledge of the interfaces defined by the extension point, there is no way at the plug-in port to know how the services it provides from the extension point will be utilized. When operating with Eclipse, the system designer fulfills complementary requirements by combining high-level design with low-level development tools that are connected by Eclipse extension points. When the system developer checks with the debugger, the UML dialog box feeds the actual operation of the device back into the hands of the system designer and developer. Because Eclipse does not know the development language, either the Java language debugger, the C 10 debugger, or the assembly debugger is valid and can target different processes or nodes simultaneously within the same framework [10].

The algorithm for brushing professionalism is as follows:

Step 1: the program starts, transfer income function initialization serial port;
Step 2: Use SndCmdQuery to check the status of the professional machine, if no professional is found to continue;
Step 3: Use the SndCmdldentifyCardType function to check the professional type, if there is no specific training professional content, then turn to step two; if you find the professional code, you need to return to the professional page. If it can not identify the professional, remind them of the relevant information after the second step;
Step 4: transfer the function to compare passwords, read and write professional processing;

Step 5: If the received message is wrong, it is necessary to send and retransmit the request message according to the degree, and wait for retransmission; If the professional machine does not appear due to noise after a certain time, it needs to reset the professional machine with the IcReset function;
Step 6: Operation process need to display, call can be mobilized when the corresponding function;
Step 7: When the professional reading and writing of the professional operations completed, ScdCardOver can be used to represent the end of the function;
Step 8: To continue processing, you need to go to Step 2.

Through the design of the hardware unit and software module, the operation of a computer professional training teaching system is realized, which provides some help for the education and training of computer majors.

## 4 Experiment and Result Analysis

The above process realizes the design of practical training and teaching system for computer specialty. In order to verify the performance difference between the design system and the existing system, a comparative simulation experiment is designed. The specific experimental process is as follows:

### 4.1 Construction of Practical Teaching Environment for Computer Specialty

In order to meet the requirements of large-scale student training, the cloud operating platform environment needs to set up 6 nodes. Specifically, by configuring 6 working virtual machines in the Vmware Workstation, the management of the system can be controlled in real time. Each virtual machine should be configured with 1 node and connected to the server. Among them, it is necessary to set up one node as the main node or name node (Nameno-deb) to connect with the main server of the system, and the remaining five nodes are the children of the system or data nodes (DateNode). In the specific configuration process, it is necessary to configure these nodes with corresponding IP address assignment and host, and the specific configuration is shown in Table 2.

**Table 2.** Configuration table of IP and host of design system node

| Node type | IP Address | Host name |
|---|---|---|
| NameNode | 192.168.1.110 | Master |
| DateNode | 192.168.1.111 | Slaver1 |
| DateNode | 192.168.1.112 | Slaver2 |

(*continued*)

**Table 2.** (*continued*)

| Node type | IP Address | Host name |
|---|---|---|
| DateNode | 192.168.1.113 | Slaver3 |
| DateNode | 192.168.1.114 | Slaver4 |
| DateNode | 192.168.1.115 | Slaver5 |

It is a complicated process to set up a big data-based computer professional training platform. In this process, it is necessary to set up the SSH password-less login password of the system, and generate the key pair on each node of the system to manage the system.

### 4.2 Implementation of Design System Software Module

Students can submit their own training tasks by entering the management page, selecting and clicking the corresponding training task submission list option after completing the training operation. As for the results, if the submission status is displayed as complete, it means that the user's training project has been submitted and completed 9. After the submission information is completed, students can, on the one hand, generate test papers according to their own needs and measure their learning effects; on the other hand, they can browse the content of the test papers after clicking. If the submission status displays incomplete, the student is not likely to complete subsequent related operations.

According to the corresponding specifications for software system testing, this system mainly adopts the mixed mode of B/S and C/S of the computer practical training platform based on cloud computing in the actual testing link, sends the source program to the evaluation server through the browser at the client end of the system, analyzes the stability, security, fault-tolerance and other related performance tests of the server during the working process, and analyzes the relevant test data. Through testing the function of the system, such as the function of training, the function of generating test paper, the function of evaluation, the function of students and teachers, the function of broadcasting, the function of virtual experiment, the function of program debugging, the function of courseware uploading and downloading and so on, it is found that the system runs stably and can meet the requirements of the system.

### 4.3 Analysis of Experimental Results

Server utilization is used to show system performance. Experimental server utilization data is shown in Table 3. Server utilization is a measure of data utilization within a specified time. The formula is as follows.

$$\gamma = \frac{\alpha}{\beta} \times 100\% \tag{1}$$

Where, $\gamma$ represents server utilization, $\alpha$ represents the amount of server data, and $\beta$ represents the amount of data that the server can hold.

**Table 3.** Server utilization data table

| Number of experiments | Existing systems | Design system |
|---|---|---|
| 1 | 70.15% | 56.42% |
| 2 | 86.12% | 60.12% |
| 3 | 85.56% | 60.00% |
| 4 | 80.12% | 58.75% |
| 5 | 84.75% | 54.45% |
| 6 | 89.45% | 54.12% |
| 7 | 87.12% | 50.13% |
| 8 | 81.24% | 54.78% |
| 9 | 87.50% | 59.58% |
| 10 | 81.01% | 50.14% |

As shown in Table 3, compared with the existing system, the server utilization rate of the design system is lower, which is less than 70%, indicating that the design system has good operation effect, which fully proves the effectiveness and feasibility of the design system.

## 5 Conclusion

Under the background of "three financing", this paper designs a new computer professional training teaching system based on big data, which greatly reduces the server utilization rate, ensures the stable operation of the system, and provides help for computer teaching.

## 6 Fund Projects

Source: General Project of Jiangxi Provincial Department of Education Science and Technology.

Research Title: Research and Practice on the Construction of Maker Service Base for College Students Based on Mobile Internet of things.

Project Number: 171223.

## References

1. Zhao, Y., Le, J., Zhu, L.F., et al.: Study on the effect of hypertensive treatment based on drug factor analysis model under the background of big data. J. Intell. Fuzzy Syst. **37**(11), 1–14 (2019)

2. Shim, J.P., et al.: Purchase-based analytics and big data for actionable insights. IT Prof. **21**(5), 48–56 (2019)
3. Song, W., Xu, M., Dolma, Y.: Design and implementation of beach sports big data analysis system based on computer technology. J. Coast. Res. **94**(1), 327 (2019)
4. Li, W., Zhu, J., Zhang, Y., et al.: Design and implementation of intelligent traffic and big data mining system based on internet of things. J. Intell. Fuzzy Syst. **38**(2), 1–9 (2020)
5. Tian, C., Tian, Z.: Optimization research of ship power system based on big data. J. Coast. Res. **94**(1), 137 (2019)
6. Hu, Z.M., Luo, L.L., Li, L., et al.: Indigenization of the median of markers for down syndrome screening based on statistical analysis of medical big data. Taiwan. J. Obstet. Gynecol. **59**(4), 556–564 (2020)
7. Wu, J., Jia, D., Wei, Z., et al.: Development trends and frontiers of ocean big data research based on citespace. Water **12**(6), 1560 (2020)
8. Liu, S., Bai, W., Zeng, N., et al.: A fast fractal based compression for MRI images. IEEE Access **7**, 62412–62420 (2019)
9. Breen, C., Zhu, T., Bond, R., et al.: The evaluation of an open source online training system for teaching 12 lead electrocardiographic interpretation. J. Electrocardiol. **02**(3), 454–461 (2016)
10. Jianqiu, L.: Construction of real-time interactive mode-based online course live broadcast teaching platform for physical training. Int. J. Emerg. Technol. Learn. **13**(06), 73 (2018)

# Design of Multimedia Intelligent Classroom Interactive Teaching System Based on Internet of Things Technology

Wei He[1](✉), Cheng-hui Zhang[2], and Yang-bo Wu[1]

[1] College of Mathematics and Computer, Xinyu University, Xinyu 338031, China
[2] Xinyu University, Xinyu 338004, China

**Abstract.** At present, smart teaching system has the problem of poor contact point tracking effect, so we design a multimedia smart classroom interactive teaching system based on Internet of things technology. According to the requirements of software module development, the system hardware optimization is divided into two parts: the core circuit design and the system memory expansion chip design. The optimized system hardware is used as the basis of software development, and classroom resource management module, classroom teaching action collection module and teaching gesture recognition module are designed. The system hardware and software are combined to complete the design process of multimedia intelligent classroom interactive teaching system based on Internet of things technology. According to the results of the system test, the auxiliary teaching effect of this system is better than that of the traditional system. In the future teaching process, this system can be used to complete the teaching process.

**Keywords:** Internet of things technology · Multimedia smart classroom · Interactive platform · Teaching system

## 1 Introduction

With the development and popularization of network technology, especially Internet technology, network teaching using the Internet has become an important and development direction of teaching. Network teaching is the product of the application of computer and network communication technology to the teaching field. This teaching mode is completely realized through the network, which can give full play to the advantages of network in teaching. It is a new educational mode to build people's lifelong learning in the era of knowledge economy and a trend of future education development [1, 2]. Since the 1960s, the application of information technology in teaching has roughly experienced three education modes: Cai, computer-aided learning, information technology and curriculum integration. Facing the new century, educational theories and methods have been deeply explored in colleges and universities and social education, and a modern teaching mode in multi-disciplinary fields has been formed. Combined with


W. Fu et al. (Eds.): eLEOT 2021, LNICST 389, pp. 442–452, 2021.
https://doi.org/10.1007/978-3-030-84383-0_38

the application of computer system and projection display system, the network teaching, which is based on the advanced technology of informatization, digitization and networking, has been widely used. Under the influence of the network teaching system, daily teaching from the traditional blackboard, projector and other conventional teaching methods. The development of multimedia teaching methods based on computers and networks has a great influence on the teaching method of knowledge.

Nowadays, the research and application of multimedia intelligent classroom interactive teaching system in China mainly focus on the application level of classroom teaching. Students carry out self-study through multimedia terminals, and get help from teachers through online communication and other methods when they encounter problems in learning [3, 4]. At the same time, a large number of multimedia intelligent classroom interactive teaching systems provide the functions of course selection, grade examination registration, score query, exchange forum, etc., which realize the communication between teachers and students.

On the basis of the actual teaching situation, according to the guidance of Internet of things technology, this research carried out the demand analysis of multimedia intelligent classroom interactive teaching system. According to the conclusion of the demand analysis, the overall design of the system and the design of database and table are planned reasonably. According to the functional characteristics of interactive teaching, the system modules are divided. And innovative design of classroom teaching action acquisition and teaching gesture recognition module, not only improves the interaction between teachers and students in teaching, but also use the image frame difference method to reduce the amount of calculation of the system, improve the quality of interactive teaching. Finally, through the research of the Internet of things technology, combined with its specification and architecture, the paper attempts to use the Internet of things technology to carry out the realization principle and method of data transmission, which has a certain reference value.

## 2 Hardware Design of Multimedia Intelligent Classroom Interactive Teaching System

### 2.1 Core Circuit Design

Through the analysis of the original system, the main control module needs to complete the network communication function with the server layer, the serial communication function of wireless sensor network and the display function of multimedia devices. In order to achieve these functional requirements, the processor chooses S3C2440 chip from SamSung company as the main control chip of the system [5]. The chip adopts 32-bit RISC instruction set, which has the advantages of low price, low power consumption and high performance. The chip has an arm core based on 32 KB instruction cache and 32 KB data cache, which reduces the cost of the system and the number of useless components. It is especially suitable for low-power applications. The data processing module is composed of processor, ram and ROM, which is set as the core controller of the system. In order to ensure the normal operation of the controller, the core circuit is set as 4 MB Nor Flash, 164 MB NandFlash on-board ROM, 32 MB SDRAM, 15 MHz crystal oscillator circuit and other circuits. The block diagram of hardware composition is shown in Fig. 1.

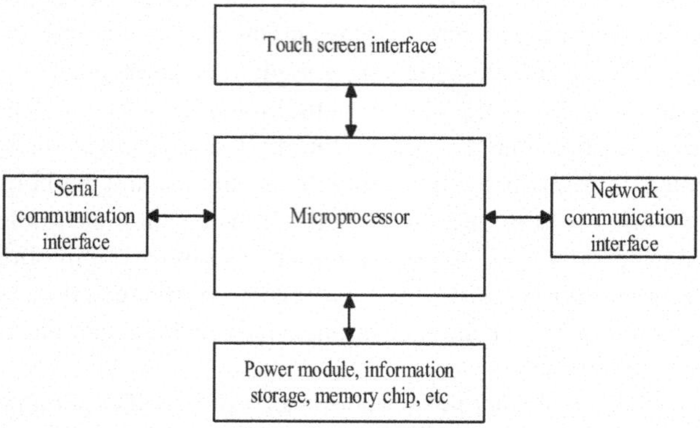


**Fig. 1.** Framework of gateway main control module

The power supply of system gateway is mainly responsible for the power supply of S3C2440, CC2530, MAX3232, DM9000 and network transformer. S3C2440 needs three kinds of voltage: 1.5 V, 1.8 V and 3.7 V. Among them, 1.5 V is replaced by a similar 1.3 V power supply, while other chips are 3.7 V.

## 2.2 Design of System Memory Expansion Chip

According to the design results of the central controller, the system expansion module is embedded in the controller to improve the use effect of the central controller. This module and the core module of the system constitute a super compact embedded PC system. These modules have the characteristics of rich functions, complete, standard size, and can face a variety of users. SysExpanModuleTM/CSD is designed according to PC/104 bus standard. Its core functions are CAN controller, serial communication port and digital IO. The main technical performances are summarized as follows.

Four independent can bus controllers which conform to CAN protocol 4.0B. Six independent serial communication ports, each of which can be set to RS232C, RS485, RS422 working mode. CAN communicates with host in memory mapping mode, and serial port communicates with host in I/O mode. The transmitting and receiving rate of CAN bus is programmable, and the rate range is 10 kb/S-500 kb/s, which is divided into 10 levels. The serial communication rate can be set by programming, and the rate range is 5 kb/s-50 kb/s, which is divided into 15 levels. With the functions of WATCHDOG and EEPROM, important field data can be saved automatically. Multiple software selectable interrupt request lines and port read/write base addresses (BA). PC/104 standard size (50 * 55 mm), directly connected with PC/104 TMCPU and expansion board. DC + 5 V operation voltage, low power CMOS circuit design. Working environment temperature range: 0C – 50C, humidity range: 0–90% RH. CSD is configured with four independent CAN controllers. The CAN controller (SJA1000) is accessed through memory mapping mode, and A2 connector is the two connecting terminals. The function definition of each pin of A2 connector is shown in Table 1.

**Table 1.** Function interface design of system memory expansion chip

| Function serial number | Chip pins | Function |
|---|---|---|
| 1 | 1 | CANL |
| 2 | 2 | CANH |
| 3 | 3 | Isolated place |
| 4 | 6 | Isolation + 3V |
| 5 | 7 | Isolated place |
| 6 | 8 | Isolation + 3V |
| 7 | 9 | CANL |
| 8 | 10 | CANH |
| 9 | 4, 5 | None |

In the long-distance communication, the common mode voltage of the isolated ground node of each CAN node is limited within 3 V to ensure the normal communication. The CAN bus transmits differential signal through twisted pair. The 110 Ω terminal matching resistance between the two twisted pair must be connected by wire. A1/A2 is the setting end of resistance jumper. The nodes at both ends of the bus shall be set with CAN 1/CAN2 terminal matching.

The above hardware part is combined with the original system hardware to complete the system hardware optimization design part. At the same time, this part is used as the system software development environment.

## 3 Software Design of Multimedia Intelligent Classroom Interactive Teaching System

In this design, the composition of the software module is optimized, and the optimized software module architecture is shown in Fig. 2.

According to the above setting results, the software optimization process of the design system is completed. In order to reflect the software optimization results more concretely, it is divided into three modules for analysis.

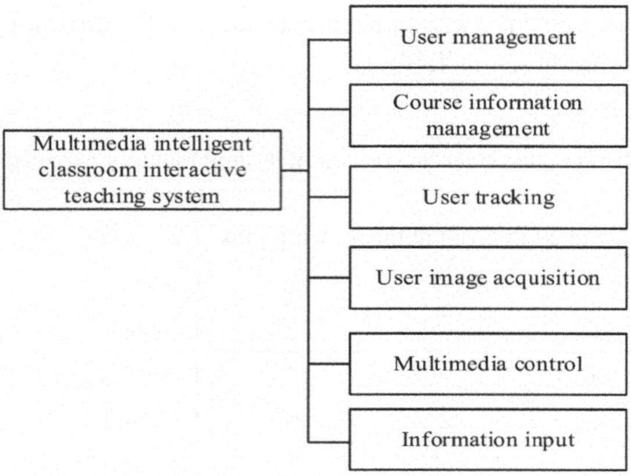


**Fig. 2.** Software module optimization results

### 3.1 Design of Classroom Resource Management Module

In this design, the content of curriculum management module is set as curriculum design, curriculum display, curriculum design, and other sub modules. Curriculum design mainly refers to curriculum design, curriculum arrangement, curriculum input and other operations [6]. The course display mainly uses 3D technology, animation effect and artistic way to show the course content more vividly. Curriculum design is mainly for the corresponding curriculum design. Course management module is the basis of teaching. A good and orderly management module can make students study and live well. Therefore, the module is very worthy of attention. The course management module is shown in Fig. 3.

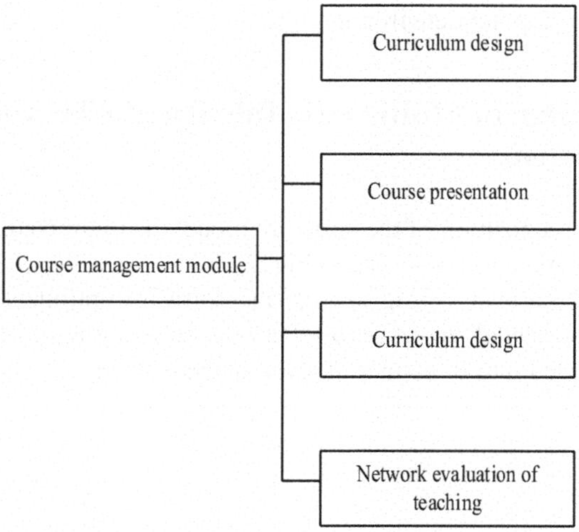


**Fig. 3.** Schematic diagram of course information management module

In addition to the basic course management, this module also includes three sub modules: course input, course modification and course query. Curriculum input refers to the administrative teacher according to the teaching plan arrangement to the students to input courses, so that students can choose. Curriculum modification is the teacher will not meet the course content to modify, as well as students' own classroom Q & A on the way to chooseing the wrong modification. Course query mainly refers to the statistical analysis of the selected courses by the academic affairs office or administrative teachers.

### 3.2 Design of Action Collection Module in Classroom Teaching

The first calculation step in the process of classroom teaching action collection is the feature extraction calculation process of digital image, that is to say, the first step of processing a frame of digital image is to extract the graphic feature points in the image. Each pixel value in the image is detected to determine whether the pixel has certain characteristics. If the detected image contains a lot of data information, the feature extraction method is used to extract the needed useful image information. As the original data of the follow-up research, the workload and difficulty of the research are greatly reduced, and the accuracy of the research results is improved.

The system designed in this study mainly uses infrared camera to collect user gesture information. According to the distance of the user's gesture, the brightness of the infrared reflection in the camera is also different. When the user's finger touches the screen, the contact will prevent a large number of infrared rays from penetrating the screen and will produce reflection. Thus, the brightness of the contact in the infrared camera is higher, and it can be distinguished from other objects obviously. According to the difference of contact brightness and background brightness, the system extracts the contact, and then through a series of image processing, so as to recognize the user's operation gestures and instructions on the display screen.

In the operation gesture video of this system, the main research object is the moving contact, and the contact object background separation is to extract these moving objects from the video frame sequence in real time [7, 8]. Background separation is the basis of image processing technology in this paper. Only after the contact target is detected and separated from the background, can the follow-up work such as target contact recognition, contact tracking and gesture analysis be carried out. Firstly, this paper studies the background separation technology, and the contact detection is mainly divided into two steps. The first step is to extract the contact area from the background image of the video frame sequence. Then the contact foreground image is processed to obtain the contact target. Then, the collected image is processed by background separation.

Background separation is the basis of contact tracking process, and the effect of separation determines the effect of contact tracking. Therefore, it is necessary to study the method of contact target background separation. In order to make the edge of the image more prominent, the image needs to show obvious black-and-white contrast effect. But at the same time, the characteristic region of the image should be preserved. The system performs binary processing on the sharpened image. The result of image binarization will further reduce the calculation of the system and the gray level of the image. At the same time, the edge information of the image is clearer, which provides technical support for the subsequent edge extraction and ensures the accuracy of the whole system.

### 3.3 Design of Teaching Gesture Recognition Module

The images collected by the system are continuous video images. When the user carries out a series of operations on the screen, the system needs to detect the target contact and recognize the target gesture for each frame image. According to the needs of the system, this paper needs to carry out contact detection for each frame image in the video, involving a large number of frame difference detection technology [9, 10].

According to the extracted contact $a$ edge, there are a total of pixels, which are respectively recorded as $S_1(x_1, y_1)$,$S_2(x_2, y_2)$,$S_i(x_i, y_i)$,...,$S_n(x_n, y_n)$ and the geometric center of the pixel $a$ is calculated. According to the coordinate average of geometric principle, the area center of the contact in the image is calculated. The calculation formula is shown in formula (1) and formula (2), and the coordinate $J(x, y)$ of the central point of the contact area is obtained.

$$x = \frac{x_1 + x_2 + x_3 + ... + x_n}{n} \tag{1}$$

$$y = \frac{y_1 + y_2 + y_3 + ... + y_n}{n} \tag{2}$$

According to formula (1)– (2), the coordinates of the central point of the contact area $J(x, y)$. At the same time, in order to facilitate the identification and ensure the accuracy of the system, take $J(x, y)$ as the center of the circle and 3 mm as the radius to mark the circular area, so as to facilitate the follow-up frame difference contact real-time tracking.

The contact area center of each frame image in the video has been identified. Combined with the image frame difference method, the real-time tracking of contact trajectory is carried out [11–13]. The basic principle of image frame difference method is to arrange the video frames in time order and extract three consecutive frames for corresponding processing. The three frames are represented as $B_{k-1}(x_{k-1}, y_{k-1})$, $B_{k-1}(x_{k-1}, y_{k-1})$ and $B_{k+1}(x_{k+1}, y_{k+1})$, and the difference between $B_{k-1}$, $B_k$ and $B_{k+1}$ is calculated, as shown in formula (3) – (4).

$$B_u(x, y) = B_k(x_k, y_k) - B_{k-1}(x_{k-1}, y_{k-1}) \tag{3}$$

$$B_v(x, y) = B_{k+1}(x_{k+1}, y_{k+1}) - B_k(x_k, y_k) \tag{4}$$

In formula (3)– (4), $B_v(x, y)$ and $B_u(x, y)$ are the difference between $B_{k-1}$, $B_k$ and $B_{k+1}$ respectively. The intersection of $B_v(x, y)$ and $B_u(x, y)$ is processed. Formula (5) is as follows, and the trajectory $R(x, y)$ of the target object can be obtained.

$$R(x, y) = B_u(x, y) \cap B_v(x, y) \tag{5}$$

According to the characteristics of the target object processed by the system, the above calculation method is improved to make it more suitable for the processing requirements of the system [14, 15]. Since the system has calculated the area center of the contact in each frame of the video so far, in order to improve the response speed of the system, we need to reduce the amount of calculation as much as possible. Only the center point $R(x, y)$ of the contact area is tracked. According to the position change of the center of the contact area, the movement track and gesture command of the contact can be judged to realize the interactive process in the teaching process.

By combining the above system hardware and software, the design of multimedia intelligent classroom interactive teaching system based on Internet of things technology is completed.

## 4 System Test Analysis

### 4.1 System Test Environment Design

In order to verify the performance difference between the designed system and the original system, the corresponding system test link is set to analyze its use effect. The specific system test platform parameters are as follows.

PAD client: using modern Play X900 Android Pad, operating system is Android 4.1, processor is Ruixin micro 3066 (dual core CortexA9, main frequency is 1.6 GHz), 1 GB DDR3 RAM, 16 GB Flash, screen resolution is 2048 * 1536, supporting front and rear 200 J7 pixel cameras.

Teacher's PC workstation: DELL 990M is used as the carrier of the workstation, the operating system is Windows 2010, the processor is I5–2400, and the memory is 4G DDR3.

Network environment: the wireless network supports IEEE 802.11n.11n, and the maximum network speed is 300 Mbps; the LAN is 802.3 Ethernet, and the network speed is 100 Mbps.

According to the parameters, the performance comparison between the designed system and the original system is completed.

### 4.2 System Test Plan

Through literature research, it can be seen that system testing is a necessary and very important testing process to comprehensively test the primary products of the system to the realization of system design ideas and script design requirements. After the development of the design system is completed, before it is put into use, it is necessary to conduct a reasonable and comprehensive test and evaluation. In the process of testing, the problems found should be modified in time to reproduce the design requirements of the script as much as possible, so as to achieve the goal of system design.

In this system test, we will mainly test the touch screen tracking of teachers in the design system and the traditional system. Therefore, the indicators are set to the touch screen tracking accuracy and the number of touch screen tracking points. In the preset test cycle, the above contents are taken as the basic performance analysis contents of the design system and the traditional system.

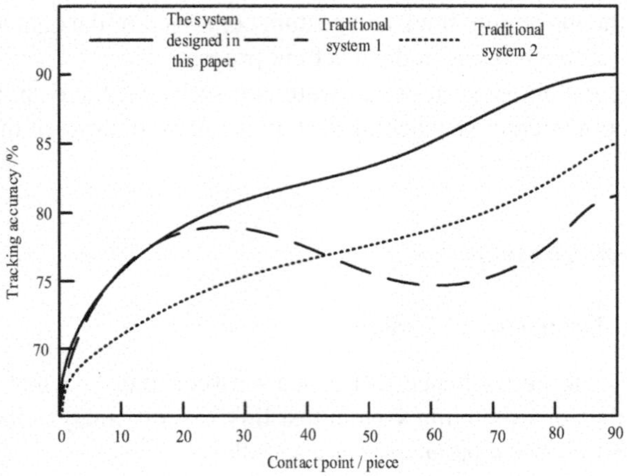


**Fig. 4.** Touch screen tracking accuracy test results

### 4.3 Analysis of System Test Results

The test results of touch screen tracking accuracy are shown in Fig. 4.

From the above test results, it can be seen that the touch screen tracking effect of the system designed in this paper is good, and the tracking accuracy is stable and the fluctuation is small in the process of multiple tests. Compared with the system designed in this paper, the tracking effect of the system in use is obviously poor. When the teacher's gesture moves too fast, the tracking effect decreases obviously, which shows that the performance stability of the system is poor. At the same time, through the analysis of the tracking reaction degree of the system, we can see that the tracking reaction effect of the system designed in this paper is better, because this method innovatively designs the classroom action collection module and teaching gesture recognition, which improves the accuracy of touch screen tracking (Fig. 5).

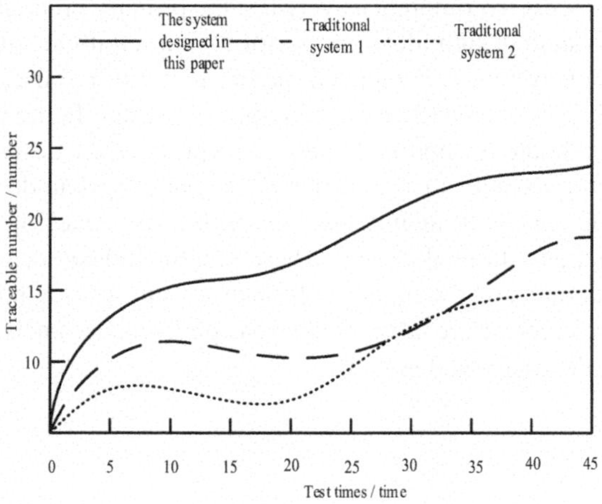


**Fig. 5.** Test results of the number of touch screen tracking points

From the above test results, we can see that the designed system can track a large number of contact points, realize the interaction between teachers and students in the process of classroom teaching, and increase the communication between teachers and students. In the process of traditional system testing, the test results are poor and the number of traceable contact points is small. In the process of daily use, it is limited for teachers' teaching activities, and can not achieve daily interaction between teachers and students. Because the method of this paper simplifies the calculation of action recognition by using the image frame difference method, the effect of the design system is better than that of the traditional system.

## 5 Conclusion

This system is supported by campus network. Firstly, the existing classroom interactive teaching system is deeply analyzed. Then from the basic theory of software development, software architecture research, development platform related technical characteristics, the design and development of classroom interactive teaching system are fully analyzed and discussed. According to the theory of software engineering, the project management is developed and tested. Through the system test, we can see that the design system in this paper is scientific and can be applied to daily teaching. Education has always been a great cause in human history. With the progress of science and the development of educational learning theory, the design system can make full use of modern information technology to integrate excellent educational resources. Due to the limitation of research time and experimental conditions, only the touch screen tracking accuracy and the number of tracking points were tested. Therefore, the next step will be to take more indicators for research.

## References

1. Huang, Z., Zhou, R., Wan, L.: Design and empirical research on interactive classroom ecosystem in blended learning environment. E-educ. Res. **41**(04), 78–85 (2020)
2. Wu, Y.: Design of data analysis and processing system for teaching quality evaluation of interactive electronic whiteboard classroom. Mod. Electron. Tech. **43**(10), 89–91+96 (2020)
3. Zhao, M., Fan, Z., Wang, R.: Design of synchronous teaching system for hydraulic component theory and experiment based on interconnection. Mach. Tool Hydraulics **48**(02), 106–109+113 (2020)
4. Yao, L., Zhang, L.: Design and implementation of Chinese architecture history teaching system based on mixed reality technology. J. Comput. Appl. **39**(09), 2689–2694 (2019)
5. Liu, S., Li, Z., Zhang, Y., et al.: Introduction of key problems in long-distance learning and training. Mobile Netw. Appl. **24**(1), 1–4 (2019)
6. Fu, W., Liu, S., Srivastava, G.: Optimization of big data scheduling in social networks. Entropy **21**(9), 902 (2019)
7. Liu, S., Glowatz, M., Zappatore, M., et al. (eds.): E-Learning, E-Education, and Online Training, pp. 1–374. Springer International Publishing, (2018)
8. Lv, B., Wang, D.: Multi path intelligent recognition algorithm of face identity in the environment of Internet of Things. Comput. Simul. **37**(07), 436–439+484 (2020)
9. Zhao, M., Chen, H., Zhang, G., et al.: Design and application of optical laboratory system based on Internet of Things. J. Daqing Normal Univ. **39**(06), 32–36 (2019)

10. Cao, S., Li, C., Li, X., et al.: Design of experimental curriculum evaluation system for educational technology specialty based on SSM framework. J. Hubei Normal Univ. (Nat. Sci.) **39**(01), 30–34 (2019)
11. Xu, Q., Xiong, X., Feng, G.L, et al.: Design of intelligent campus multimedia interactive system based on Internet of Things technology. In: 2019 International Conference on Virtual Reality and Intelligent Systems (ICVRIS), pp. 223–226. IEEE (2019)
12. Cai, J.Y., Zhang, P.P., Tan, X.: A novel physical education environment platform using Internet of Things and multimedia technology. Int. J. Electr. Eng. Educ. 0020720919879390 (2019)
13. Dong, H.J., Abdulla, R., Selvaperumal, S.K., et al.: Interactive on smart classroom system using beacon technology. Int. J. Electr. Comput. Eng. **9**(5), 2088–8708 (2019)
14. Liang, W.: Scene art design based on human-computer interaction and multimedia information system: an interactive perspective. Multimedia Tools Appl. **78**(4), 4767–4785 (2019)
15. Bai, H., Zhang, Q.: English smart classroom teaching system based on 5 network and Internet of Things. Microprocess. Microsyst. 103421 (2020)

# Design of Dance Action Simulation Teaching System Based on Cloud Computation

Yi-jia Shang(✉) and Dong-dong Suo

Zhengzhou Technical College, Zhengzhou 450121, China
shangjiayi1212@yeah.net

**Abstract.** In order to improve the performance of the dance movement simulation teaching system, cloud computing technology is used to realize the optimization design of the dance movement simulation teaching system from the three aspects of hardware, database and software. In terms of hardware, the system's network environment, processor and video capture module have been modified and optimized, and the internal connection network of the hardware system has been adjusted. Collect dance moves and related teaching resource data in the teaching system, install them in a certain format to form a database table, and obtain the design result of the system database through the logical relationship between the database tables. With the support of hardware equipment and database, a cloud computing framework is constructed to collect and process complete dance motion simulation video data as the basic content, and to realize the functional design of the system from both the classroom and the students. Through the system test experiment, it is concluded that compared with the traditional teaching system, there is no obvious difference in the function of the design system, but the operating performance of the system has been improved, which effectively improves the safety and stability of the system. The system has certain practicability and can be used in dance teaching to improve the accuracy of dance movements of students.

**Keywords:** Cloud computing · Dance action · Simulation teaching · Teaching system

## 1 Introduction

Dance is the most unique form of artistic expression in artistic aesthetics. It can not only express emotions, but also express beauty. It combines time and space to show a harmonious rhythm. It is not only an art that beautifies human movements, but also transcends the flesh. And the appreciation of the beauty of the soul [1]. Dance education is to display artistic images through aesthetic methods and to infect, inspire and educate people subtly. In order to improve people's dance appreciation ability, dance education is needed [2]. Popular dance education is mainly for non-dance major students and amateur dance enthusiasts, training them in dance aesthetics, dance training and basic performance. Dance teaching uses the body and cooperates with music, costumes, props, lighting and other artistic methods. Due to the influence of time and space, it is impossible


W. Fu et al. (Eds.): eLEOT 2021, LNICST 389, pp. 453–463, 2021.
https://doi.org/10.1007/978-3-030-84383-0_39

to develop on a large scale. Through mobile learning, the use of live video or rebroadcast provides new ideas for popular dance education [3]. Dance simulation teaching is online learning at any time and any place with the help of mobile terminals, breaking the boundaries of traditional teaching in practice and space, and is of great significance to improving the level of popular dance education.

The dance movement simulation teaching system takes dance movement as the teaching content, and is an activity system that involves the participation of teachers and students to achieve the teaching goals. It is composed of teaching staff, teaching information, teaching materials and equipment. It includes three subsystems: control, execution, and feedback. The control system determines the movement direction and work content of the entire system, and adjusts the work of other subsystems. The teacher plays the main role of control and implementation. At present, domestic and foreign distance teaching systems are mainly developed for traditional teaching subjects, including Web-based teaching systems, multimedia-based teaching systems, and project-based teaching systems. However, traditional teaching systems are applied to dance among the subjects, there will be problems such as poor processing of dance motion simulation video and video playback failure. For this purpose, a dance motion simulation teaching system based on cloud computing has been designed.

The dance movement simulation teaching system based on cloud computing introduces cloud computing technology on the basis of the traditional teaching system. Cloud computing is a super computing model based on the Internet. There are many calculation modes, which are executed on dedicated supercomputers. There are mainly parallel computing, distributed computing and grid computing, utility computing and network storage. It has the characteristics of virtualization and load balancing, and is the result of the integrated development of computer technology and network technology. Cloud computing can integrate computer resources to increase the computing power of devices horizontally, and has strong disaster tolerance and less inter-device dependence. Through the application of cloud computing technology, it will no longer need to spend a lot of financial resources to purchase dance equipment and dance environment, thereby greatly reducing the hardware cost of its teaching resources. At the same time, cloud computing can provide high security performance for data storage centers to ensure the security of all data. Teachers and students do not need to worry about data loss caused by viruses and hacker attacks, and can conduct interactive teaching on the network platform anytime and anywhere [4]. Finally, in the cloud computing environment, the resources of various schools can be shared, which is conducive to the balanced distribution of teaching resources, and greatly improves the utilization of teaching resources in various universities.

## 2 The Hardware System Design of Dance Action Simulation Teaching

Before starting the design of the dance movement simulation teaching system, first conduct a demand analysis. From the perspective of functional requirements, it can be divided into two aspects: student client function and teacher client function. The student client requires the system to download and play dance resources. Search and other functions, and the teacher client is required to be able to perform functions such as uploading teaching resources and setting dance courses. In addition, the analysis of non-functional requirements mainly analyzes the number of users and the speed of response time. The system is required to operate stably when 500 people access the platform at the same time. When users use dance resource uploading and other functions, the response time can be appropriately delayed, but not more than 10 s, the response time of other functions is within 3 s [5]. When the dance movement simulation system fails to run, the administrator needs to eliminate the fault in time and restore the system to run, but the troubleshooting time cannot exceed 6 h, otherwise it will seriously affect the dance students' learning.

Based on the results of system requirements analysis, following the design principles of economy, safety, scalability, advancement, reliability, practicability, simplicity, etc., specific optimization designs are carried out from the three parts of hardware, database and software. And get the final dance action simulation teaching system optimization design results. The basic hardware connection structure of the system is shown in Fig. 1.

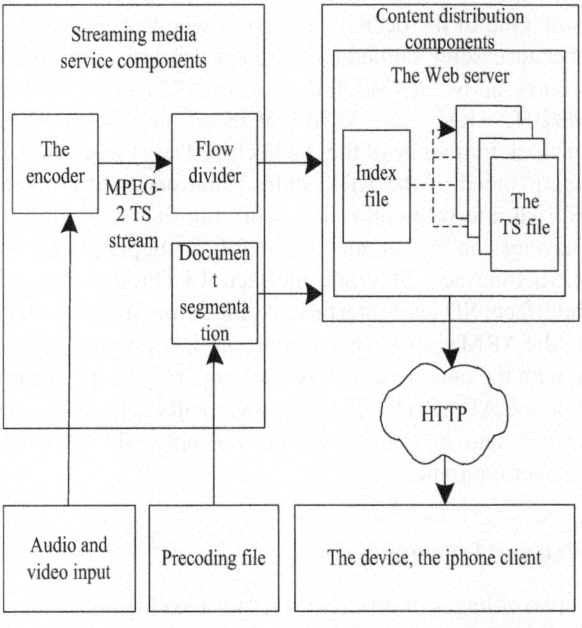


**Fig. 1.** Hardware system structure diagram of dance movement simulation teaching

## 2.1 Communication Network Design of Analog Control Board

The network structure design covers the interface type used by the user, the network protocol used, and the type of network wiring that may be used. The top layer contains the database server, application server and client; the first layer contains the firewall, numerous clients and network structures.

### 2.2 Dance Action Simulation Video Acquisition Module

Cameras are divided into two types: digital cameras and analog cameras. With digital camcorder video capture devices, analog video signals can be converted to digital, and then stored in a computer. The video signal captured by an analog camera must pass through a specific analog video capture card, first converted to digital mode and compressed before it can be converted to use on a computer. Digital video cameras can directly capture images, and then display them on the computer screen via serial, parallel or USB interfaces. Choose the latest USB camera. According to the USB standard, the longest transmission distance of a USB device is 5 m. This design can extend the transmission distance through the USBHUB (active hub can amplify or regenerate the signal), each additional HUB can be extended by 5 m, a total of 5 HUBs can be added, that is, the extension is 5 times, so the longest can be extended 25 m.

### 2.3 Embedded Processor

By choosing ARM chips to realize the modification of processor devices, first choose from the ARM core. One of the decisive factors is whether the ARM core has its own MMU function, because some embedded systems can only run on chips with MMU functions. ARM cores above ARM720T all have ARM chips with MMU function, ARM720T, ARM920T, ARM922T, ARM926EJS all have MMU function. Secondly, choose the system clock frequency of the ARM chip. The system clock frequency determines the processing speed of the ARM chip. What needs to be considered again is the number of external interface controllers built into the ARM chip [6]. The selected ARM chip must have or can be extended to the following peripheral interfaces: RS232 serial interface, USB interface, Ethernet interface, LCD/touch screen interface, audio interface, JTAG interface, SD card interface. At the same time, it is better to integrate a DMA controller in the ARM chip, so that a large amount of high-speed data transmission can be carried out with the outside world. After comparing the performance of all ARM chips on the market, the AT91SAM9263 chip was finally selected as the processor chip of this teaching system, and the traditional chip was replaced to realize the modification of embedded processor equipment.

### 2.4 Circuit Design and Debugging

The system needs two voltages of different sizes for the chip and each peripheral to use, 3V3 voltage and 1V2 voltage, respectively, for the system' s memory module and ARM chip. Because there is only one input voltage from the mother board to the daughter board, that is, the 3.3 V power supply voltage, a level conversion circuit should be designed in the hardware design to convert 3V3 to 1V2. In addition, the crystal oscillator circuit is an indispensable part of the embedded hardware circuit, and the ARM chip obtains the master clock by using an external crystal oscillator for frequency multiplication. According to the requirements of the ARM chip S3C2440, it is designed to provide two crystal oscillators of 16.9344 MHz and 32.768 MHz with different frequencies for the ARM chip, which are used in normal working mode and sleep mode respectively. The reset circuit is an essential part of the embedded hardware circuit. The reset circuit in the design can be used for power-on reset or reset by manual button. At the same time, because the network interface chip CS8900A requires a high-level reset, a 74HC14 inverter is added to invert the negative pulse of the system reset signal to obtain a positive pulse reset signal.

The audio interface of the system is realized by connecting the audio codec AD1981 through the AC97 interface provided by the ARM chip [7]. AC97 controller provides two serial data lines, clock lines and control lines to the external AD1981. AD1981 has expanded three interfaces, namely: headphone jack, microphone jack, and audio conversion interface.

## 3 Database Design of Dance Movement Simulation Teaching System

For the system, the design of the database structure largely affects the efficiency of system access and user experience. Therefore, the analysis and design of the database during the system development process should follow strict specifications. Under the premise of ensuring data consistency and integrity, the degree of data redundancy should be reduced as much as possible [8]. The dance movement simulation teaching system uses a database to store each entity object. It mainly includes courseware table, faculty table, professional table, system parameter table, class table, transcript table, forum topic table, forum discussion table, etc. The courseware and video release status of dance action simulation courses are shown in Table 1.

**Table 1.** Dance action simulation courseware and video release form

| Field name | Field type | Field constraint | Field description |
|---|---|---|---|
| Video slide id | Int | Primary key, automatic number, not empty | Numbering |
| Publisher | Varch (50) | Not empty | Publisher |
| Upload date | Datetime | Not empty | Upload time |
| Video slide url | Varch (50) | | File name |
| Download times | Mt | Not empty | Download times |
| Title | Varch (50) | – | Title |
| Description | Varch (50) | – | Description |
| Tag | Int | – | 0 Means teaching courseware, 1 Means instructional video |
| Course_id | Int | Foreign key, not empty | Course code |

In the same way, the storage structure and content of other system data can be obtained, and the link between the databases is formed according to the relationship between the data.

# 4 Software Function Design of Dance Movement Simulation Teaching System

The dance movement simulation teaching system is divided into 7 modules according to functions. They are user registration and login module, file management module, score management module, courseware release and download module, system maintenance module, teacher-student communication module, and distributed file management system module. Among them, the user registration module includes student registration and other user registration, and file management includes file upload, download, and modification [9]. The score management includes the entry, modification and query of scores. The release and download of courseware includes courseware upload, download, delete, etc. System maintenance includes setting up user role maintenance and system functions. The teacher-student communication module includes the management of teacher and student forum messages. The distributed file system module includes file system configuration and data node configuration, etc. With the dual support of hardware equipment and database, cloud computing technology is used to optimize the design and realization of system functions.

## 4.1 Build a Cloud Computing Framework

Services under the cloud computing framework are mainly composed of three roles: service provider, service consumer, and service registry. The service released by the service provider is based on the service under the cloud computing environment. This service consists of four levels: cloud computing service physical layer, cloud computing service virtual machine layer, cloud computing service management layer, and cloud computing service application layer [10]. In the cloud-based framework, the relationship between the three service roles is shown in Fig. 2.

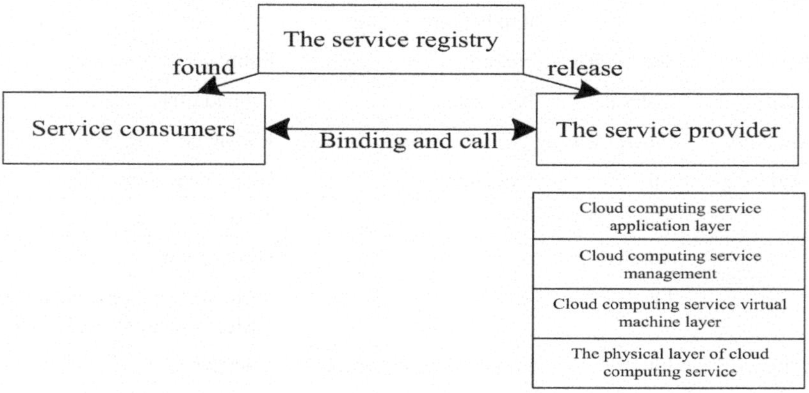


**Fig. 2.** Cloud computing framework

The service provider in Fig. 2 is a node on the network, which provides service access for software using the service interface. In cloud computing, service providers often have to provide services to multiple consumers at the same time, so service providers need to have strong computer processing capabilities. Using cloud computing structure to build service providers is a good choice in cloud environment. The cloud computing service application layer is user-oriented, and it provides a service interface on the Internet that can be accessed by all service consumers uniformly. These application layers publish services to the registry, and users can find specific services they need through the service registry. After selecting the service, directly bind and use the service with the service interface provided by the service application layer. The cloud computing service management layer mainly realizes the management of cloud service requests and cloud service responses [11]. It plays a decision-making role for services in the cloud computing system. Service consumers are also nodes on the network. Through the service registry, it can bind with service providers and use the services published by the providers. Usually, it can use multiple services, then integrate and integrate these services, and finally realize the specific business logic it needs. In the cloud computing environment, any user who uses the cloud service interface is a service consumer. The service registry is also a type of node on the network. It stores service interface description information, and providers can publish their own services on it. In the service use process, the service registry plays the role of an agent. Consumers find the specific location of the service they need on the service registry. After finding the location information of the service, the consumer can bind with the service provider and use the service provided by the provider.

### 4.2 Dancing Motion Simulation Audio and Video Processing

In the system environment, a cloud computing framework is used to build a 3D basic model. First, a new data project called algorthmicskeleton is created through the 3 DsMax system, and then the basic framework model spliced with the basic model is used to execute instructions in batches. After running, get the basic skeleton model needed. Disassemble the body parts that need to be converted in 3Ds Max, and then save them in separate files. The purpose is to consider that the number of loaded files is too large, so it needs to be disassembled into parts and used, which can simplify the later stage of the program. Call the procedure. A Skeleton class is defined in the ADD3ds.h file. Collect the disassembled parts of the body in need, and include the definition of the project' s drawing mode, the acquisition method and the setting method in this class [12]. Set the mobile conversion and rotation conversion programs respectively to realize the control of the virtual environment model. The actual video of the dance action is converted into an action track, imported into the environment, and a simulation video of the dance action is obtained through the control program.

### 4.3 Teacher's Function Design

The core functions of the teacher end include the production and release of teaching courseware, the production and release of teaching videos, the assignment of coursework, the evaluation of homework, the organization of teaching resources, the setting of classes, the addition of students, and the construction of courses.

Teacher-end users can select the semester they want to start on the main interface of the system, click "Apply to start", and enter the page of applying for starting a course and creating a new course. When creating a new course, you must first select the semester and type of course to start. You can create a new course and enter the course name. If there is no matching course in the background, a new course number will be generated in the background; you can also click "Associate Course", to choose from the existing courses, first select the department, and after selecting the starting department, search and associate the existing courses. After you find the associated result, click to select the course, and then click OK to complete the association.

When a user logs in with teacher authority, the teacher can upload teaching videos and related teaching courseware materials for students to watch and download online for learning. After logging in, users can choose to query and download courseware and related sports dance videos according to the type of video and the applicable people. Each user can upload his own recorded dance video, but, except for the administrator, after logging in, each user can only delete or modify the data uploaded by the current user. The materials uploaded by other users can only be browsed and watched online, and have no right to delete them.

### 4.4 Student-Side Functional Design

The main function of the student terminal is to realize the learning of dance courses, so you can search, download and play dance video information in the system environment, upload student homework and online questioning, and realize dance online exams after the phased learning is over And other functions. Among them, the search of dance resources is to use dance resource attributes to search for matching dance resource information. The student enters the resource name and other attributes in the main interface of the system, and the system uses the check method to check whether the keyword meets the requirements, and prompts the student if it does not. Use XML files to store search keyword information, and then use HTTP protocol to transfer XML information to the server [1, 13, 14]. The server needs to parse the content in the XML file and obtain search keywords. After obtaining the keyword, it is necessary to generate the select SQL statement, and use the statement object to execute the dance resource query SQL. Perform a matching query in the dance resource table. After the results are obtained, the XML files are assembled to store the search results, and then the XML files are returned through the HTTP protocol. The mobile terminal parses the XML file and displays the search results. In the same way, the functions in the system can be used to run the program to realize other functions and realize the students' dance movement learning needs in the system.

## 5 System Test

The current development environment is Microsoft Windows 7 Professional Edition + Microsoft Visual Studio 2018 + Micorosoft SQL Server 2000, and the system' s development and operating environment is adjusted according to the hardware design results. The principles of system testing specifically include the completion of testing of the software system and the search for various types of error repairs hidden in the software system. The software testing link requires that the software system fully meet the actual requirements of the requirements analysis specification. In this system design, the system test content is divided into two parts: function test and performance test. The function test is whether the system can output the expected result after inputting instructions from the teacher and the student. The performance test is the changes in the operating parameters of the system and the changes in response speed as the number of online users increases. In order to form an experimental comparison, the traditional dance movement virtual teaching system was also set up in the system test experiment as the experimental comparison system, and it was developed and operated in the same environment.

The video data and instruction data of the experiment are prepared in the experimental environment. The video data comes from on-site recordings of students and teachers in major dance departments of major universities, and the instruction data set integrates the high-frequency instructions used in the system over the years.

Import the same instruction data into the two system environments at the same time, and get the corresponding function execution results.

From this, the results corresponding to all the functional commands can be obtained. After statistics and comparison, it is found that the design system and the traditional system have no obvious difference in operating functions.

With the gradual increase in the number of users, the running performance of the test system, the performance test results are shown in Fig. 3.

The test results show that in terms of different requirements, the online system can meet the required design maximum concurrency of 1000. During this process, the server performs well. From the test data, the concurrency is around 800. The performance is the best in all aspects, and the data is also compared. Meet the current scale of system operation. After a vertical comparison of the two systems, it is found that when the number of users in the traditional system gradually increases, the CPU temperature, CPU package, CPU core, graphics card temperature, hard disk temperature and fan speed also gradually rise, which means the corresponding CPU share And the graphics card share began to rise. In Fig. 3(b), there is a repeated situation, which shows that the system has a self-protection mechanism. When the CPU or memory occupancy rate reaches a certain stage, the computer system automatically turns on the internal protection mechanism to prevent the hardware from being caused by excessive temperature. Irreversible damage to other institutions. Therefore, the designed dance movement simulation teaching system based on cloud computing has a certain degree of stability and security, and provides a foundation for the majority of universities to carry out similar teaching work.

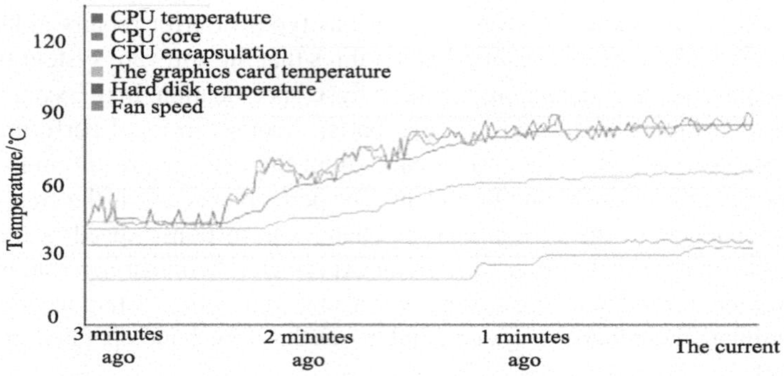


(a) Performance change curve of traditional system

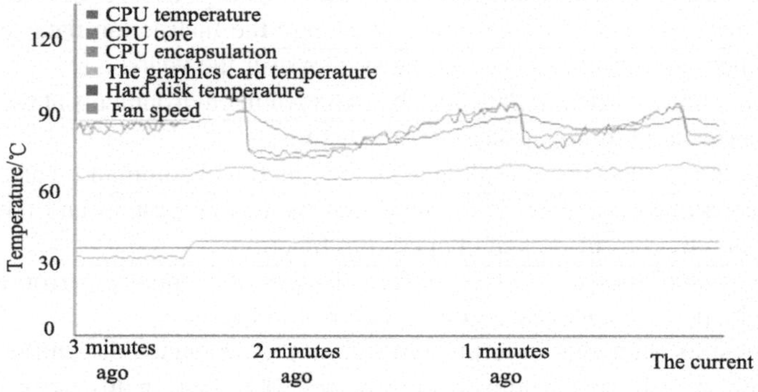


(b) Design system performance change curve

**Fig. 3.** Teaching system performance test results

# 6 Concluding

By testing the function and performance of the dance course online teaching system, and comparing it with the previous requirement analysis and design documents, you can see that the results show that the system is fully functional and well-performed, which meets the actual needs of users, and can be launched and officially invested Operation, but also foreshadowed the development of similar distance education courses.

# References

1. Hwang, S.Y.: Seeking rhythmic attunement: teaching to dance; dancing to teach. Curric. Inq. **49**(5), 1–19 (2019)
2. Yao, F.: Design and simulation of integrated education information teaching system based on fuzzy logic. J. Intell. Fuzz. Syst. **37**(4), 1–9 (2019)
3. Chi, Z.: University B: design and implementation on dance teaching live system for iOS platform. Comput. Technol. Develop. (2016)
4. Zhao, S.Z., Zhang, L.: Analysis of enterprise management information system based on cloud computing. J. Phys. Conf. Ser. **1533**, 022038 (2020)

5. Huang, L., Lin, M., Chen, X.: Research on teaching design based on BOPPPS mode: a case study of the course "Principles of Visual Communication Design." IOP Conf. Ser.: Mater. Sci. Eng. **573**, 012054 (2019)
6. Linlin, Y., Song, Z.: English teaching model and cultivation of students' speculative ability based on internet of things and typical case analysis. J. Intell. Fuzz. Syst. **37**(5), 1–9 (2019)
7. Cuellar-Moreno, M., Caballero-Julia, D.: Student perceptions regarding the command and problem solving teaching styles in the dance teaching and learning process. Res. Dance Educ. **2019**(8), 1–14 (2019)
8. Kim, M., Park, C.W., Baek, J.H., et al.: Teaching dance through Korean fan dance. J. Phys. Educ. Recreat. Dance **90**(6), 7–17 (2019)
9. An, S., Tillman, D., Kim, S.J., et al.: Teaching numbers through dance: developing a choreography-themed mathematics curriculum for early childhood students. J. Dance Educ. **19**, 148–157 (2019)
10. Wang, Y.: Development and application of 3d holographic technology in dance teaching. IPPTA: Q. J. Ind. Pulp Pap. Tech. Assoc. **30**(8), 488–492 (2018)
11. Levenberg, M.G., Armstrong, T., Johnson, I.L.: Teaching dance for understanding: reconceptualizing dance in physical education. J. Phys. Educ. Recreat. Dance **91**(6), 3–7 (2020)
12. Liu, S., Bai, W., Zeng, N., et al.: A fast fractal based compression for MRI images. IEEE Access **7**, 62412–62420 (2019)
13. Ls, A., Jing, Y.B., Xj, B., et al.: Based on Delphi method and analytic hierarchy process to construct the evaluation index system of nursing simulation teaching quality. Nurse Educ. Today **79**, 67–73 (2019)
14. Guo, J., Liu, J.: Optimal system design of language training strategy based on artificial intelligence. J. Intell. Fuzz. Syst. **4**, 1–11 (2020)

# Design of Enterprise Job Training Education Management System Based on J2EE

Yong-lan Yan[1(✉)] and Jun-mei Li[2]

[1] Guangzhou College of Technology and Business, Guangzhou 510850, China
yanyonglan120@163.com

[2] School of Computer Engineering, Jingchu University of Technology, Jingmen 448000, China

**Abstract.** Aiming at the impact of severe market competition on corporate job training and education management, the performance of the corporate job training education management system has deteriorated. In order to improve the performance of the corporate job training education management system, a J2EE-based corporate job training education management system design is proposed. J2EE is used to design the overall structure of the system. Through the design of personal information management module, training course management module, training information management module, statistical management module and database logic design, the design of enterprise job training education management system is realized. The test results show that the J2EE-based corporate job training and education management system has high performance, can realize the stable and efficient management of corporate job training and education, and can effectively meet the requirements of the company.

**Keywords:** J2EE · Enterprise job training · Education management · Module design

## 1 Introduction

With the rapid development of the domestic economy, domestic companies have begun to continuously expand foreign markets. There is not only fierce competition among companies in terms of product quality and sales channels, but also the pressure of strong talents from Western developed countries [1]. In the era of knowledge economy, if an enterprise wants to achieve sustainable development, it must strive to build a learning team, and strive to cultivate the learning attitude and sense of progress of employees and managers, so that the overall quality of the enterprise is continuously improved and progressed in the development. An important factor for measuring and investigating the management level of major domestic brands and multinational corporations is the overall quality of their employees. These companies have formulated a very complete staff training system, and use a complete technical training system to train their employees. With the fiercer competition in the economic market, the requirements for employees of various positions in the enterprise are no longer as good as basic operations [2, 3]. It is


W. Fu et al. (Eds.): eLEOT 2021, LNICST 389, pp. 464–475, 2021.
https://doi.org/10.1007/978-3-030-84383-0_40

necessary to have more professional technical skills, a better attitude and comprehensive work quality in order to effectively fulfill the ever-increasing customer requirements.

Literature [4] proposed the idea of using Windows Azure cloud computing platform to build and optimize enterprise management training system, and then analyzed the needs of enterprise management training system, believed that the system should include learning module, examination module and analysis report module, and then designed according to the demand The enterprise management training system based on the cloud computing platform, including the new test question process, the new test process, the employee training and the test process, is included. Finally, it introduces the building of integrated access control subsystem based on the Windows Azure cloud computing platform and exam management Subsystem, an online examination subsystem in an enterprise management training system. After testing, the system runs smoothly, with low cost, high safety and practicability. Literature [5] studies the design of a personnel training information management system based on a business rule engine And implementation, through the analysis of the main business process, the design of functional modules and the description of the business data relationship, examples of the main business rules are given, and the implementation of the key rules is described in detail. The online use of the system shows that the organization, management and analysis of personnel training have been significantly improved; however, under the new situation, the traditional training content and methods have shown more and more unsuitable states, and the training effects and methods are compared It is time-consuming and laborious and cannot meet the needs of corporate employee training.

This article closely follows the current trend of informatization, improves the training methods of small and medium-sized enterprises, introduces information technology into the entire process of enterprise employee training management, and helps enterprises establish an open network learning and knowledge sharing environment [6]. Help companies improve their staff's job competency, provide powerful data support for corporate human resource management departments to conduct fair evaluation and accurate analysis of employee quality, so as to provide various small and medium-sized enterprises with "Enterprise Training Network Courses" as the basic teaching unit Flexible training project management methods play an active role.

Based on the above research background, this article applies J2EE to the design of enterprise job training education management system, designing the overall system structure, personal information management module, training course management module, training information management module, statistical management module, database logic design, based on J2EE Realize the connection of various modules, build a J2EE-based corporate job training and education management system, thereby improving the efficiency of corporate job training and education management.

## 2 Enterprise Job Training Education Management System Design

### 2.1 System Overall Structure Design

The overall structure design of the system is an important process of the system development process. The overall structure design of the enterprise job training and education management system is based on the system analysis of the previous stage, according to the enterprise goals, weighing the pros and cons of various technologies and implementation methods, defining the external boundaries and interfaces of the system, and rationally using various resources. In the process of processing, coordinate the relationship between various departments according to the overall requirements of the system, and characterize the internal and various components of the system and their mutual relationships.

The main model structure of the enterprise job training education management system studied in this paper: The main users of this system include training teachers, system administrators, corporate administrators and corporate training employees. Different people have different needs for information. For corporate training teachers, the different content or courses of training lead to different needs for the content and form of training information. For teachers who have completed corporate culture or employee quality training, they may only a small amount of training materials, PPT and video information are needed. As a teacher of professional competence training for enterprise employees, the demand for training resources will be very huge, and rich and detailed professional training materials need to be provided [7]. Some trainers not only can use the system well, but also need to help system administrators update and maintain database resources. Based on the module design process, referring to the characteristics of different training resource types, a complete training process management module is constructed in turn, and each module corresponds to a different set of data resources, such as classification, retrieval, deletion, and modification. These operations need to be hierarchically controlled according to the user's authority. Therefore, it can be concluded that when designing a J2EE-based enterprise job training and education management system, on the one hand, it is necessary to clarify the relationship between the main modules of the system, and on the other hand, it is necessary to design the access control of the internal data of the system. The following is the design of the role-based data access control model established by the system, and the overall structure of the system is built with the relationship between users, roles, various functional modules and various training resource objects, as shown in Fig. 1.

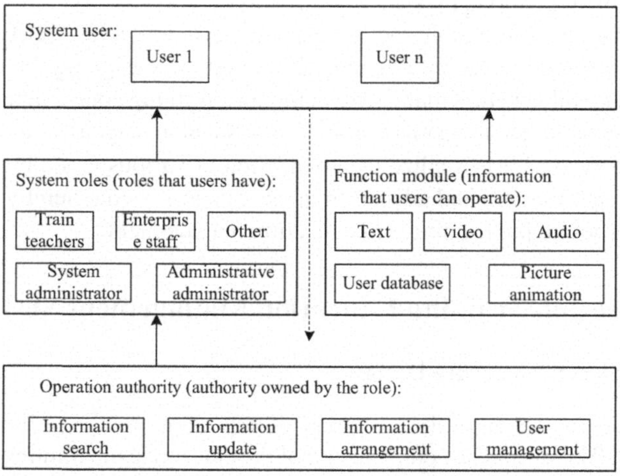


**Fig. 1.** System overall architecture diagram

The management of permissions in the system mainly uses role-based access control. The core of RBAC is that users are only associated with roles, and roles represent permissions. The advantage of this design is that for users, only roles are needed. Yes, and a role can have various permissions and can be inherited. RBAC logically separates users and access permissions, and this design idea facilitates permission management. Discuss with multimedia data information. For static authorization, during system design and demand analysis, the type of system role can often be determined. For example, in a multimedia system, there may be information publishers, information reviewers, and information Viewers, administrators and super administrators. These roles have also been bound to corresponding operations during design.

### 2.2 Personal Information Management Module Design

There are many users of the training system, which will generate a large amount of user personal information, which is very necessary for the management of system users' personal information. This module is mainly provided to the users of the system to manage their personal information. For example, corporate training students change their basic personal contact information, passwords, permissions, etc. The specific functions are shown in Fig. 2.

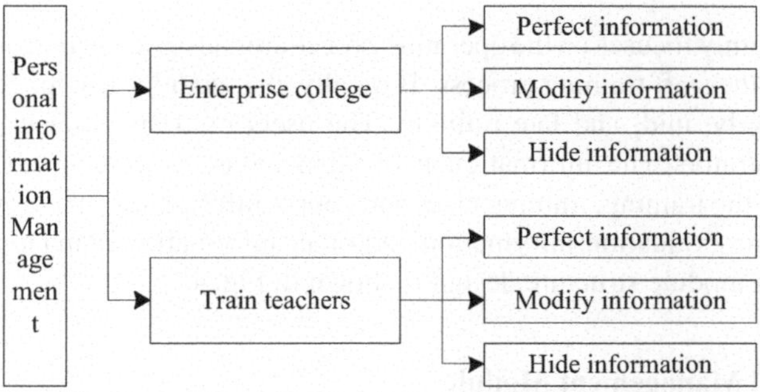


**Fig. 2.** Personal information management function diagram

The modification and improvement of personal information by users is only for individuals, and other users with the same level of access rights cannot view them. Only the system administrator can perform unified operations on it through the system user information management module.

### 2.3 Training Course Management Module

This module is mainly operated by enterprise training employees and training teachers. The human resources department of the enterprise arranges related training subjects according to the training plan and requirements, or the trainees determine their own training arrangements according to personal skill requirements and job positions [8–10]. Enterprise employees can query and browse the teaching content and requirements of each training course, and choose according to personal training needs. Training teachers can manage the teaching content of training courses and training resources online within the scope of authorization. The specific functional module structure design is shown in Fig. 3.

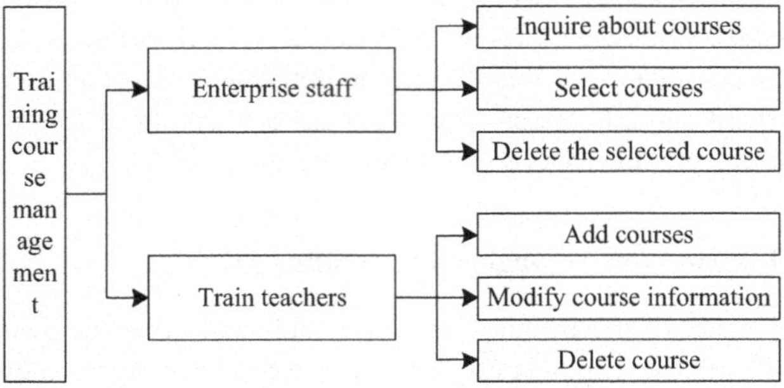


**Fig. 3.** Training course management function diagram

## 2.4 Training Information Management Module

This module mainly focuses on the operating procedures designed to manage the relevant information of the staff training process. Basically, the module structure is divided into three stages: early, mid, and late training. The users used are trainees, trainers, and system administrators. The information involved includes: information about employees participating in the training, training class and course information, Train students online learning, training evaluation information and other information management based on this, the system module structure design is shown in Fig. 4.

## 2.5 Statistical Management Module

This module is mainly provided to system managers (person in charge of corporate training) to perform statistics on various information in the training. The module structure can be divided into trainee information statistics, training resource statistics, trainee training results report statistics and system operation log statistics. The functional module structure is shown in Fig. 5.

The training information statistics of trainees mainly help the person in charge of corporate training to make statistics on the training that employees have participated in, so as to facilitate the annual training summary, view the training effect, and facilitate the formulation of the company's employee training plan for the next year. The statistical information includes statistics on the personnel participating in various departments of the enterprise, statistics on training participation in various regions, and statistics on employees participating in training subjects.

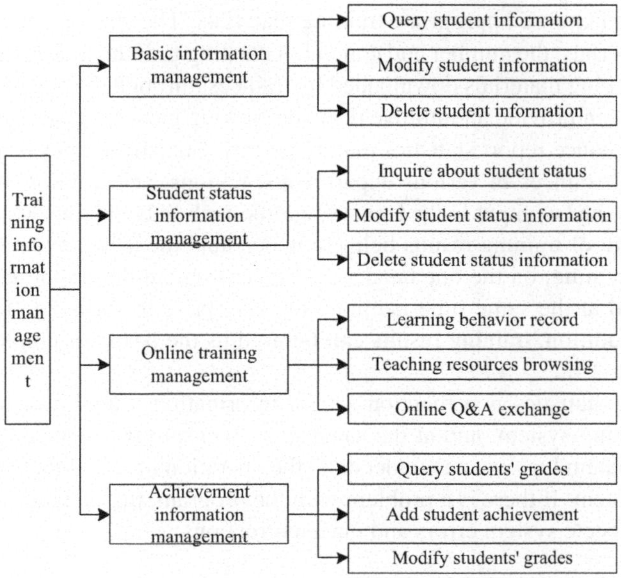


**Fig. 4.** Function diagram of student information management

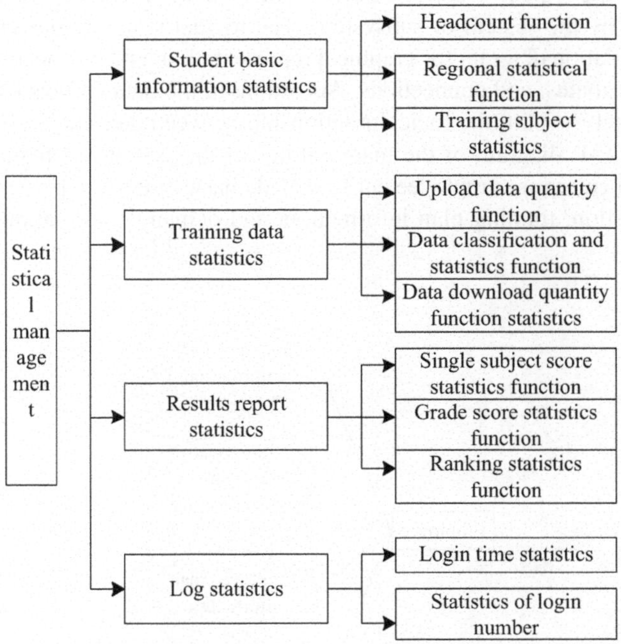


**Fig. 5.** Statistical management function diagram

Training data statistics are used to count the use of training materials in different training subjects during the training process, so that human resources management departments can choose appropriate training materials. The statistics include: the type of training materials, the number and content of existing training materials. The number and type of training materials downloaded by trainees, through the above three types of data statistics, can provide an intuitive decision-making basis for training materials.

The performance report statistics mainly perform statistical analysis on the assessment results of trainees in various departments, regions, and training subjects of the enterprise, and can be output in the form of reports, such as Excel files. On the one hand, the management of training results helps to understand the actual situation and results of employee training, on the one hand, it can also promote the importance of trainees to training, and at the same time facilitate the enterprise to formulate training teaching plans. In addition, training results can be used as the basis for employee year-end assessment [11–13].

System log statistics is a function set for information statistics on the use of the enterprise training system, and at the same time to ensure the security of the system. Through the system log, you can understand the operation of each functional module of the training system. If there is a problem with the program, the system log can help the administrator locate system errors and make corrections.

### 2.6 Database Logic Design

The content of the logical structure design of the database is to briefly explain the data structure used by the system or subsystem. The logical structure design mainly uses the entity association diagram for graphical representation, and its constituent elements are entities, attributes, and connections. According to the data entities obtained by the requirement analysis part, the logical relationship between them is established respectively, and the E-R diagram of the main entities of the system is obtained. The main attributes of an enterprise employee entity include basic employee information, performance information, training plan information, and demand information, as shown in Fig. 6.

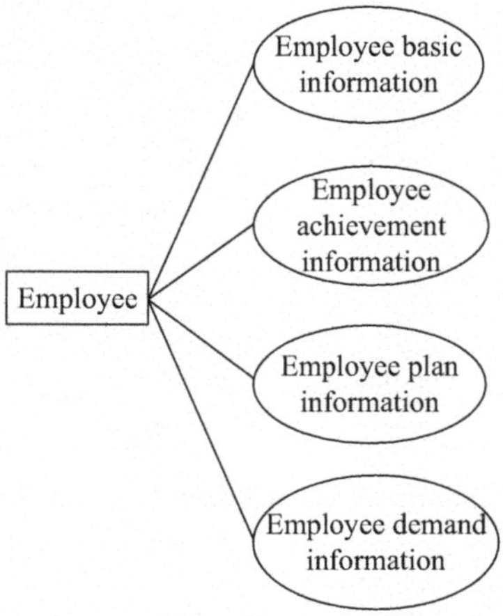


**Fig. 6.** Training employee entity attributes

Figure 7 shows the various entities in the employee training module, which are mainly used to represent the basic data information of different business departments of the enterprise. The entity attributes include department code, department name, department head, department office location and other attributes.

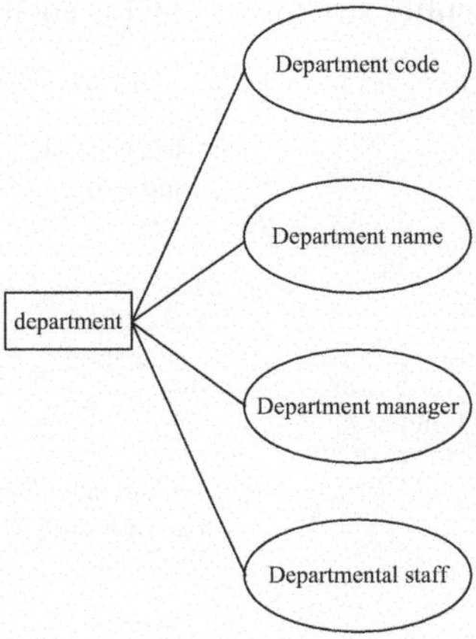


**Fig. 7.** Department entity attribute diagram

The training course entity is mainly used to indicate the main content information of employees participating in the training. Its entity attributes mainly include the following attribute information, such as course code, course name, training hours, training category to which the course belongs, relevant equivalent training, etc. [14–16], its ER The model design is shown in Fig. 8.

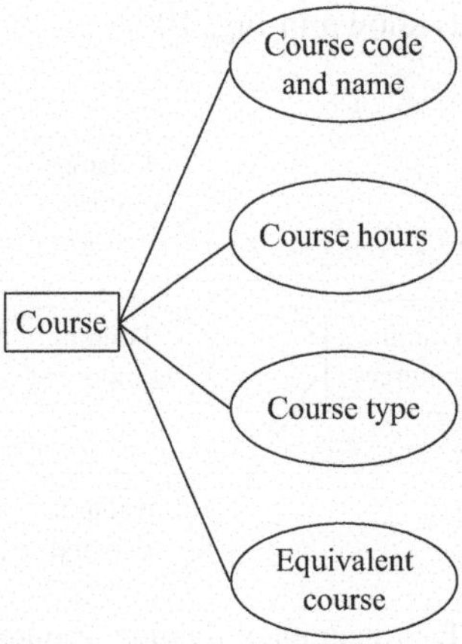


**Fig. 8.** Course entity E-R diagram

Instructors are training teachers who mainly undertake training courses and content teaching in the training system [17–19]. They can come from experienced employees or managers from different departments of the company, or they can hire staff from professional training institutions. Its entity attributes are mainly used to describe the relevant information of the teacher, such as the trainer's number, name, academic qualifications and other personal attributes. At the same time, it can include third-party data information such as the time, place and teacher evaluation of the teacher responsible for the training course [20]. The entity structure model is such as Shown in Fig. 9.

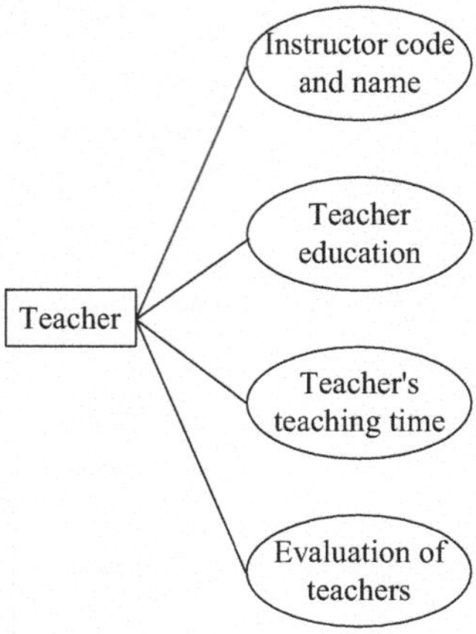


**Fig. 9.** E-R diagram of teacher entity

The entity content of the training resource includes the relevant description information of the educational resource, including the description of the existing resources in the enterprise knowledge management module, such as resource name, type, main content introduction, etc., and other attribute information such as training cost and training resource demand. The model is shown in Fig. 10.

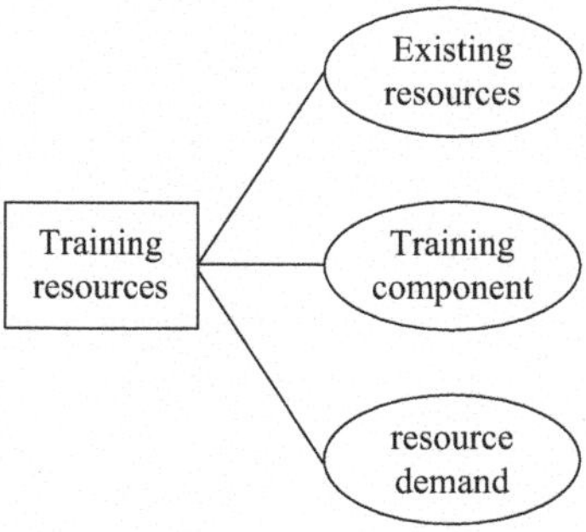


**Fig. 10.** E-R diagram of training resource entity

Integrating the above-mentioned independent system main entity attribute diagrams, and according to the enterprise training business management data flow diagram, the mutual management between different entities in the enterprise training management system can be established respectively, such as the relationship between trainers and training courses is a one-to-many relationship. That is, one trainee can be responsible for the teaching of multiple courses, and at the same training time, any company employee can only participate in the training of a certain course.

## 3 Test Analysis

### 3.1 System Test Type

The main task of software testing is to conduct preliminary acceptance third-party testing of the J2EE-based enterprise job training and education management system. The main content of the test is: interface test, system function test, safety test, fault tolerance test, usability test, regression test for problems found in supervisor test, and system performance test.

### 3.2 Analysis of Performance Test Results

The performance test is performed after the functional test is completed. The test environment should be as consistent with the user environment as possible. The performance test cases mainly involve the problem of the entire system architecture. Therefore, once the test cases are generated, the changes are generally not large, so the performance test is repeated. The utilization rate is generally relatively high. If the user does not propose performance indicators, design various test indicators according to user needs and the experience of test designers. Multi-user concurrent performance testing is the core content of performance testing, including all multi-user related tests. This article takes all users into consideration when performing performance testing, and uses the automated performance testing tool Load Runner to simulate the operation of the actual system to ensure the accuracy of the system performance testing.

In this system, a series of operations of trainee users, such as "student training courses and announcements viewing, online training course project selection, training resources and assignment submission" are tested as a set of combined services, and the test examples are within 500 whether users are online at the same time can be normal. Use Load Runner's recording tool to record the above three businesses, and each business is assigned a certain number of users. The specific test data and results are shown in Table 1.

As shown in Table 1, the average response time, data transmission rate, network utilization rate, CPU utilization rate and denial of service error rate of the J2EE-based enterprise job training education management system are all due to other systems, which reflect the superiority of the designed system. Applying it to enterprise on-the-job training can effectively improve the level of enterprise on-the-job training and education management.

**Table 1.** System performance test data and results

| Concurrent client | 10 | 50 | 100 | 150 | 200 |
|---|---|---|---|---|---|
| Average response time | 0.044 (s) | 1.253 (s) | 2.475 (s) | 4.238 (s) | 4.873 (s) |
| Data transfer rate | 5143 (KB/s) | 4753 (KB/s) | 4238 (KB/s) | 3826 (KB/s) | 3655 (KB/s) |
| Network utilization | 16% | 28% | 48% | 56% | 70% |
| Average memory usage | 28% | 35% | 44% | 51% | 54% |
| CPU usage | 9% | 15% | 42% | 48% | 56% |
| Denial of service error rate | 0% | 0% | 1.2% | 2.2% | 3.6% |

## 4 Concluding Remarks

This paper proposes a J2EE-based corporate job training education management system design, modular design of corporate job training education management, combined with database logic design, to achieve the corporate job training education management system design, test results show that the system has high performance.

## References

1. Samanta, R.K.: National Agricultural Research System (NARS) scientists and their management training needs. Clin. Rehabil. **27**(12), 1084–1096 (2013)
2. Kosendiak, J., Cieśliński, W.B.: Computer-aided training design as a factor in sports training process management. Int. J. Biol. Macromolecul. **62**(11), 341–347 (2014)
3. Yanxia, L., Lin, L., Qiang, W.: Research and development of the integrated management system of the college sports based on the network. IEEE **2013**, 440–443 (2013)
4. Zhang, X., Wang, R.: Optimization design of enterprise management training system based on cloud computing. Mod. Electron. Tech. **43**(18), 22–25 (2020)
5. Yu, J.-Y., Gu, Z.-Y.: Design and implementation of personnel training information MS based on business rule engine. Comput. Sci. **40**(2), 428–431 (2013)
6. Sherry, L., Fennell, K., Feary, M., et al.: Human-computer interaction analysis of flight management system messages. J. Aircr. **43**(5), 1372–1376 (2012)
7. Cho, S.H., Kim, K.W., Park, S.S.: An analysis on the cockpit crews' perception on airline's safety management system and their safety behavior. Alcohol **22**(2), 60–70 (2014)
8. Stenner, S.P., Johnson, K.B., Denny, J.C.: PASTE: patient-centered SMS text tagging in a medication management system. J. Am. Med. Inform. Assoc. **19**(3), 368–374 (2011)
9. Giyanto, S.P., Hakim, D.A.: Coral reef management information system: integrated data management on coral reef under coremap. J. Comput. Phys. **59**(2), 264–289 (2011)
10. Weiss, R.L., Hassell, L.A., Parks, E.R.: Progress toward improved leadership and management training in pathology. Arch. Pathol. Lab. Med. **138**(4), 492–497 (2014)
11. Liu, S., Bai, W., Zeng, N., et al.: A fast fractal based compression for MRI images. IEEE Access **7**, 62412–62420 (2019)
12. Liu, S., Li, Z., Zhang, Y., et al.: Introduction of key problems in long-distance learning and training. Mob. Netw. Appl. **24**(1), 1–4 (2019)

13. Peng, Y., Wu, I.C.: A cloud-based monitoring system for performance analysis in IoT industry. J. Supercomput. **77**, 9266–9289 (2021)
14. Vincenti, G., Bucciero, A., Helfert, M., Glowatz, M. (eds.): e-Learning, e-education, and online training. LNICSSITE, vol. 180. Springer, Cham (2017). https://doi.org/10.1007/978-3-319-49625-2
15. Gao, X.: The prototype of marine data integration system based on J2EE. J. Coast. Res. **112**, sp1 (2020)
16. Sun, W., Gao, Y.: The design of university physical education management framework based on edge computing and data analysis. Wirel. Commun. Mob. Comput. **2021**(2), 1–8 (2021)
17. Mao, K.: Research on key technology analysis and system design of enterprise patent management system. J. Intell. Fuzz. Syst. **38**(3), 1–10 (2019)
18. Li, H.: Optimization of the enterprise human resource management information system based on the internet of things. Complexity **2021**, 1–12 (2021)
19. Radzievskyi, R., Plisko, V., Bondarenko, V.: Professional training of security guards on the basis of system modular project of object protection. Sci. Educ. **20**(3), 109–117 (2020)
20. Kile, D., Eaton, M., Devalpine, M.: The effectiveness of education and cognitive rehearsal in managing nurse-to-nurse incivility: a pilot study. J. Nurs. Manag. **27**(3), 543–552 (2019)

# CAD Drawing Teaching Assistant System of Civil Engineering Based on Digital Technology

Yu Liu(✉)

School of Road Bridge and Architecture, Chongqing Vocational College of Transportation, Chongqing 402247, China

**Abstract.** The traditional civil and architectural CAD drawing teaching aid system, under the application of traditional technology, does not have accurate calibration and data switching functions, resulting in poor communication capabilities, classification capabilities and tracking capabilities of the system, affecting the overall teaching performance of the system, so Based on digital technology, design a new CAD drawing teaching aid system for civil engineering. In the system hardware design, the SDRAM circuit and RS323 bus circuit are redesigned. In the system software design, the system CAD drawing calibration mode is optimized, and the system switching algorithm is set based on digital technology. The experimental test results show that the MOS value, MAE value and RMSE value of the system designed this time are lower than that of the teaching aid system under traditional technology, indicating that the data switching of the system is smoother and the classification deviation is smaller. In general, this time. The design system has better tracking performance for CAD drawing data. It can be seen that digital technology is more suitable for drawing teaching aid systems.

**Keywords:** Digital technology · Civil architecture · CAD drawing · Teaching assistant system

## 1 Introduction

CAD drawing teaching assistant system solves practical problems of CAD drawing teaching by means of mechanization and automation, and provides real teaching means for students' drawing. However, due to the relatively backward technology used in the traditional teaching auxiliary system, the performance of the system is gradually difficult to meet the teaching requirements under the influence of external environment noise and massive heterogeneous data. Therefore, taking the digital technology as the innovation point, the CAD drawing teaching assistant system of the whole department is designed. The hardware of CAD drawing teaching assistant system is designed by SDRAM circuit and rs323 bus circuit; the calibration task is carried out according to the similarity of image features. Therefore, the calibration mode of CAD drawing is set through the similarity index. A large number of drawing data sets are divided and processed according to the time characteristics by using the sliding window to generate


W. Fu et al. (Eds.): eLEOT 2021, LNICST 389, pp. 476–486, 2021.
https://doi.org/10.1007/978-3-030-84383-0_41

data sequences in different time domains; then, the time information redundancy fusion method is used to extract the frequency domain features, and the attribute change rule is obtained through the optimal estimation. The data sequence is processed twice to get the fused data. Finally, in the state space, the vector with associated features is fused with the multi-sensor information fusion technology to fuse the drawing information in the space to calibrate the information, set up decision-making instructions, complete the design of CAD drawing teaching assistant system of civil engineering based on digital technology. The effectiveness of the system is verified by simulation experiments.

## 2 Hardware Design of CAD Drawing Teaching Assistant System

### 2.1 Design SDRAM Circuit

Digital signal processor is abbreviated as DSP, which is a microprocessor specially used for rapid signal processing. As the main processor of the maneuvering target tracking circuit board, it directly affects the library information tracking function of the resource integration system. Therefore, considering the system's calculation accuracy, calculation speed, hardware resources and power consumption and other factors, select the DSP chip according to the functional requirements of the auxiliary teaching system. The I/O working voltage of the processor is 3.3 V, and the core voltage is 1.6 V. Through non parallel energy-saving configuration, the automatic management of information is realized, which meets the requirements of power consumption of integrated system. Considering the factors such as hardware resources, speed level and development tool support, FPGA chip is selected to replace the field programmable gate array in the original CAD drawing teaching assistant system, and a high-performance programmable logic is set to complete the circuit function of complex sequence and combination logic [1, 2]. In the process of target tracking, the teaching system needs a large capacity of storage space to store a large amount of drawing information, and needs to use the space to filter the collected information resources. Although the selected DSP solves the problems of the system to a certain extent, due to the limited storage space of DSP itself, SDRAM chip is added on the basis of the above hardware selection. The SDRAM model selected in this study is mt48lc4m16a2tg, which provides 64 MB memory for the teaching assistant system. The chip has four memory blocks, each with a capacity of 16 MB and a total of 16 bit bus. According to the actual specifications of the chip, connect SDRAM address line a [0:9] with DSP address bus a [1:10], and connect A10 with sda10, a11 with A12, and then connect data bus d [0:15] with DSP data line D [0:15]. Let the block selection signals BA0 and BA1 of A12 and A13 be connected with A13 and A14 of DSP. Then the connection between SDRAM and FPGA chip is established through SDARS, SDCAS and sdwe signal lines. Using this circuit to store target information, it is convenient to integrate the image resources in the process of drawing teaching after the end of target tracking.

### 2.2 Design of rs323 Bus Circuit

When the system receives drawing information, there are synchronous transmission data and asynchronous transmission data. Therefore, it is necessary to design the RS323 bus circuit to ensure that the system can receive all different types of information. The RS323 interface has 9 pins or 25 pins. In this study, the RS323 with 25 pins was selected and tested at 50, 100, 600, 1200, 2400, 4800, and 9600 and 19200 baud rates respectively. Whether the selected RS323 allows a 2500pF capacitive load, and on the basis of expanding the communication distance, ensure that the hardware has the ability to suppress noise and other interference information. Figure 1 below is the RS323 transceiver circuit structure diagram designed this time [3].

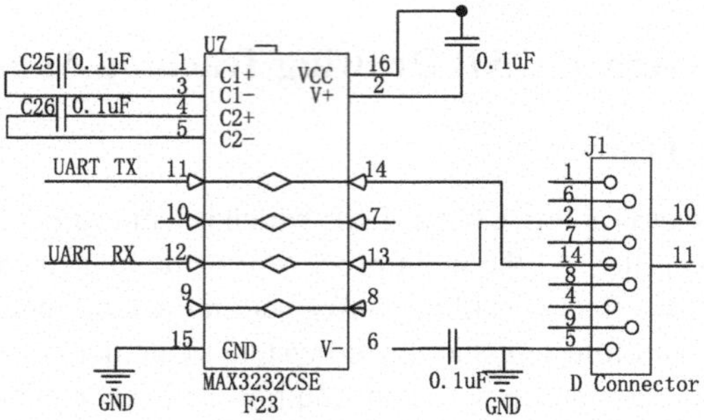


**Fig. 1.** RS323 transceiver circuit

Considering the connection between the system and the computer, in the RS323 bus circuit designed, the MAX3232 chip is used as the transceiver chip of the hardware. The selected chip has dual channels, and its proprietary low dropout transmitter output stage, through two receivers and two drivers, realizes data transmission and reception at a data rate of 240 kps, ensuring the working efficiency of the auxiliary teaching system. So far, the hardware design of the CAD drawing teaching auxiliary system for civil engineering is completed.

## 3 Software Design of CAD Drawing Teaching Aid System for Civil Engineering Based on Digital Technology

### 3.1 Set System CAD Drawing Calibration Mode

When assisting CAD drawing teaching, it is necessary to perform calibration tasks based on the similarity of image features, so the system CAD drawing calibration mode is set through the similarity index. This index can be represented by $sim(x, y)$, where $x$ and $y$ represent the basic parameters of student drawing and system calibration standards. In terms of calculation form, the following calculation requirements need to be met:

Let the similarity index be a real number between [0, 1], so $sim(x, y) \in [0, 1]$. When the two parameters are completely similar, then $sim(x, y) = 1$; when the two references are completely different, there is $sim(x, y) = 0$ [4]. At the same time, the similarity index has symmetry characteristics, so there is $sim(x, y) = sim(y, x)$. According to the above calculation requirements, combined with its decreasing function relationship, assuming that the change degree between the similarity index and the calibration gap is represented by $\lambda^{-dis(U,V)}$, the influence of students' CAD drawing parameters on the similarity index can be described by the following formula:

$$F(x, y) = \frac{f(x) + f(y)}{|f(x) - f(y)| + 1} \tag{1}$$

In the formula: $f(x)$ and $f(y)$ represent the standard level of $x$ and $y$ respectively. When $F(x, y) > 1$ is not in line with the similarity index value range, so divide $F$ by 2 times the layer depth $H$ to keep the influence of layer factors on the conceptual similarity within the range of [0, 1], and obtain a new calculation result:

$$F(U, V) = \frac{f(x) + f(y)}{2H \cdot (|f(x) - f(y)| + 1)} \tag{2}$$

According to the above calculation formula, the similarity between the two parameters increases with the increase of concept level, and the hierarchical difference between the two parameters is enlarged, which makes the similarity between calibration data gradually decrease. Therefore, the degree of change between the two elements is obtained:

$$dis(x, y) = f(x) + f(y) - 2\varphi(F(x, y)) \tag{3}$$

In the formula: $dis(x, y)$ represents the distance between two parameters; $\varphi(F(x, y))$ represents the minimum classification level of the two parameters [5]. Quantify the influence of calibration distance and level factors on the similarity index, so we get:

$$K_1(x, y) = \frac{\lambda^{-dis(x,y)} \cdot h_{x,y}}{2H \cdot (dis(x, y) + 1)} \tag{4}$$

The sum of $f(x) + f(y)$ is the level of $h_{x,y}$. At the same time, the logarithmic function is introduced and the nonlinear function is used to evaluate the similarity:

$$K_2(x, y) = \log_2\left(1 + \frac{|ud(x) \cap ud(y)|}{|ud(x) \cup ud(y)|}\right) \tag{5}$$

In order to avoid the infinite value of $x$ and $y$, 1 is added to the true number part of logarithmic function to make it take the value of 0. Therefore, through the above calculation process, the similarity calculation model is designed, and parameters $b_1$ and $b_2$ are added to adjust the similarity index:

$$sim(x, y) = \begin{cases} b_1K_1 + b_2K_2 \; x \neq y \\ 1 \; x \neq y \end{cases} \tag{6}$$

According to the above calculation formula, the design of the similarity calculation model is realized. Use the similarity model to calibrate the drawing, so the calibration algorithm is set to control the calibration of the model. Control the calibration of the similarity model according to the basic connotation of deep learning and the basic characteristics of drawing elements. Use the deep structure and learning ability of the deep learning network to track the effective features of the drawing data in a hierarchical manner, and use the recognition signal to determine whether the drawing data comes from the same target. In the process of deep learning network training, the label signal data is input into the self coding network to achieve the task of nonlinear depth feature extraction, and then these depth features are mapped to the recognition class by softmax function. The purpose of this design of teaching assistant system is to provide more accurate data for students' architectural drawing. Therefore, according to the characteristics of back propagation, in the process of data iteration, the weights of deep learning network are optimized to realize image calibration [6]. It is known that the verification signal makes the characteristics of the third hidden layer similar. Therefore, a loss function is used to set the model calibration algorithm based on deep learning, as follows:

$$P\left(sim_i, sim_j, s_{ij}, \alpha\right) = \begin{cases} \frac{1}{2}\left|sim_i - sim_j\right|^2 \; s_{ij} = 1 \\ \frac{1}{2}\max\left(0, \mu - \left|sim_i - sim_j\right|^2\right) \; s_{ij} = -1 \end{cases} \tag{7}$$

In the formula: $sim_i$ and $sim_j$ are the calculation results of the similarity index of the two elements of the model; $s_{ij} = 1$ means that the two data belong to the same image; $s_{ij} = -1$ means that the two data do not belong to the same image; $\mu$ means different architectural drawing requirements; $\alpha = \{\mu\}$ means deep learning After verifying the loss function, the parameters to be learned. The deep learning process is completed through pre-training and fine-tuning, and the back-propagation algorithm is used to control the similarity model. The following codes are some of the key codes when the algorithm performs retrieval tasks:

```
def cos(vector1,vector2):
dot_product=0.0
normU=0.0
normV=0.0
for U,V in zip(vector1,vector2):
dot_product+=U*V
normU+=U**2
normV+=V**2
if normU==0.0 or normV==0.0
return None
else
```

Use the above code to run the basic calibration procedure of the calibration algorithm to optimize the system's calibration capability [7].

### 3.2 Setting System Switching Algorithm Based on Digital Technology

According to the characteristics of digital technology, the data fusion process of auxiliary teaching system is designed. Firstly, a large number of drawing data sets are divided and processed by using sliding window according to the time characteristics; Secondly, time information redundancy fusion method is used to extract frequency domain features, and the attribute change law is obtained by optimal estimation. In this stage, the data sequence is processed twice, that is, the operation is carried out in the system measurement space.

In the attribute space, according to the feature vector of the data sequence, find out the external and internal relations between the data. Finally, in the state space, multi-sensor information fusion technology is used to fuse the drawing information calibration information in the state space with the vector with associated characteristics, and the decision instruction is set according to the fused data [8].

According to the process described above, it is assumed that sliding window a contains $N$ data, which is the basic drawing data of $\left[c_i, c_{i+1}\right]$ certain set among multiple drawing sets, and the data sequence composed of the data is described by $\{z_n|n = 0, 1, 2, \ldots, N-1\}$. The data at this time is divided into different data sequences according to the current sliding window, and these data sequences are defaulted as the basic unit of system processing to ensure the internal correlation of the data while also reflecting the characteristics of the drawing data under the current time window. When the system performs data collection and calibration tasks, mechanical and environmental noise interference has a great impact on the drawing data. Therefore, the default sensor data contains real data and noise data. The known noise $u_i(c)$ can not be predicted and unknown, so it is assumed that noise $u_i(c)$ satisfies Gaussian distribution, and its variance and mean value can be determined according to the actual working environment. It is known that there is a certain law for the change of attribute measurement in time and space. This study uses function $g(z)$ to express the law, but the law is complicated and objective, and the mathematical formula of function $g(z)$ is difficult to directly determine. Therefore, assuming that the environmental noise is additive noise, the real data is mixed with noise and sent to the receiving end in the form of data stream $\{\ldots, z_i, z_{i+1}, \ldots, z_n, \ldots\}$. The data received by the server also appears in the form of data stream. The physical environment at this time can be simplified as the model shown in Fig. 4 [9].

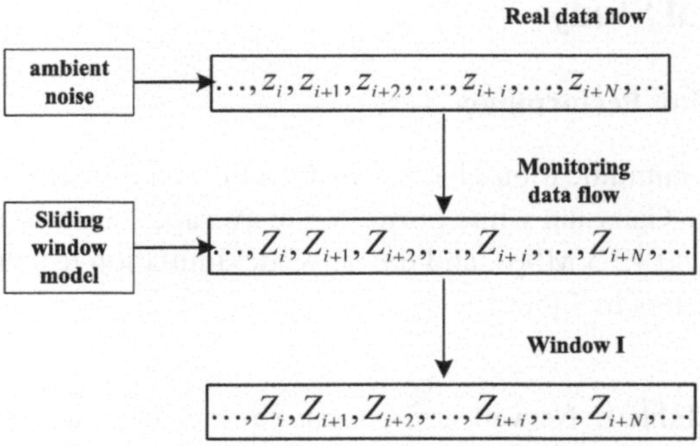


**Fig. 2.** Data flow and sliding window model

According to the model in Fig. 2, the system monitoring data with multiple sensors is abstracted into the following form. For the convenience of visual observation, the default number of architectural drawings that the system can calibrate at one time is three, then:

$$\begin{cases} A(c) = \beta(c) + u_\beta(c) \\ B(c) = \theta(c) + u_\theta(c) \\ C(c) = \gamma(c) + u_\gamma(c) \end{cases} \tag{8}$$

In the formula: $A(c)$, $B(c)$, and $C(c)$ respectively represent the calibration values of the three images; $\beta(c)$, $\theta(c)$, and $\gamma(c)$ represent the actual parameters of the image; $u_\beta(c)$, $u_\theta(c)$, and $u_\gamma(c)$ represent the image noise during the calibration process. The server divides the data according to the time window to get the function:

$$\begin{aligned} g(c) &= g_0(c - c_0) + g_1(c - c_1) + \cdots + g_i(c - c_i) \\ &+ \cdots = \sum_{i=0}^{\infty} g_i(c - c_i) \end{aligned} \tag{9}$$

In the formula: $g_i(c - c_i)$ represents the true value of the property when the window time is $\left[c_i, c_{i+1}\right]$. On the entire time axis, the data sequence is divided according to the sliding window, and each data sequence is represented by $g_i(c - c_i)$. However, because $g_i(c)$ is only a continuously changing physical property, a discrete sequence after sampling in time, the sampling frequency is taken as the frequency at which the sensor collects data, and $g_i(c)$ can be expressed according to the following formula:

$$g_i(c) = \sum_{n=0}^{N-1} g_i(z) \cdot \lambda(z - c_n) \tag{10}$$

Therefore, in order to obtain the real basic data of building image, $g_i(c)$ can be estimated. Since $g(c)$ is continuous in time, the frequency domain characteristic of analog value $g_i(c)$ can be used as the feature of time window [10–12]. So far, under the application of digital technology, the design of civil architecture CAD drawing teaching assistant system has been completed.

# 4 Experimental Study

## 4.1 Communication Performance Test

Suppose that the communication channel of CAD drawing teaching assistant system experiences additive Gaussian white noise, so the average transmission rate of network is set between 8.5 and 12.5 Mbps, and the network simulation test environment is built by using the parameters in Table 1.

**Table 1.** Network environment simulation parameters

| Parameter name | Value | Parameter name | Value |
|---|---|---|---|
| Path loss | 4.55 | Spreading factor | 5–255 |
| RTS | 20 μs | CTS | 15 μs |
| Distributed frame interval | 50 μs | Short frame interval | 10 μs |
| Discount factor | 0.96 | Learning parameters | 0.1 |
| Time to transmit ACK | 10 | – | – |

According to the data in Table 1, build a simulation test environment, respectively use the designed system and traditional teaching auxiliary system to switch the content of the same civil architecture CAD drawing teaching. Table 2 shows the comparison results of MOS values to measure the communication quality of the system.

**Table 2.** Comparison of MOS values

| Auxiliary users | System in text | Traditional system |
|---|---|---|
| 10 | 4.88 | 3.57 |
| 20 | 4.64 | 2.33 |
| 30 | 4.89 | 3.31 |
| 40 | 4.63 | 2.21 |
| 50 | 4.72 | 2.54 |
| 60 | 4.85 | 3.45 |
| 70 | 4.66 | 3.22 |
| 80 | 4.77 | 3.11 |

According to the test results in Table 2, the MOS value of the auxiliary system studied has always been above 4.5 when processing multiple drawing tasks. However, due to the poor concurrency effect of the communication module in the traditional system, the MOS value is greatly reduced when a large number of drawing data are switched. It can be seen that the teaching assistant system designed based on digital technology has better communication function, and drawing teaching can provide better auxiliary effect.

### 4.2 Classification Performance Test

The integrated quality evaluation index is used as the basis for analyzing the system performance, and the system classification performance test is carried out to analyze the integration ability of different systems for information resources. The mean absolute error between the predicted value of the system score and the actual score is reflected by the precision measurement method, and the root mean square error of the precision of the predicted result is calculated. The calculation results of the two parameters can be obtained directly by the following formula:

$$\begin{cases} MAE(\kappa) = \dfrac{1}{|\delta|} \sum\limits_{\tau_i \in R} |\tau_i - \tau_i'| \\ RMSE(\kappa) = \sqrt{\dfrac{1}{\delta} \sum\limits_{\tau_i \in R} (\tau_i - \tau_i')^2} \end{cases} \tag{11}$$

In the formula: $MAE(\kappa)$ represents the average absolute error of the error; $RMSE(\kappa)$ represents the root-mean-square error of the precision of the prediction result; $\delta$ represents the actual number of drawing teaching scoring items; $\tau_i$ represents the user's actual rating of the system; $\tau'$ represents the user's predicted rating of the system; *R* represents the score set. When the calculated $MAE(\mu)$ and $RMSE(\mu)$ values are smaller, the more it shows that the system's drawing data classification work is more compatible with the actual building frame. Based on the above calculations as the evaluation basis for the test results, select any 5 sets of data in the Movielens 100 k data set, and train and test the data set according to the ratio of 8:2. According to the above calculation formula, the performance evaluation results of different systems are obtained, as shown in Table 3 below.

**Table 3.** Comparison of classification performance of different systems

| Test group | The system designed in the article | | Traditional integration system | |
|---|---|---|---|---|
| | MAE | RMSE | MAE | RMSE |
| D1 | 0.6285 | 0.9007 | 0.9091 | 1.5542 |
| D2 | 0.5947 | 0.8826 | 0.9184 | 1.7384 |
| D3 | 0.5982 | 0.8849 | 0.9036 | 1.7109 |
| D4 | 0.6035 | 0.8787 | 0.9155 | 1.7488 |
| D5 | 0.6184 | 0.8912 | 0.8998 | 1.5666 |

According to the above calculation results, the MAE value and RMSE value of the designed system are lower, which indicates that the research system has more accurate division and matching effect for the classification of drawing data.

### 4.3 Tracking Effect Test

Use simulation testing software to simulate the basic structure of a building, let students draw a CAD image based on the structure, and then use the system designed in the article and the traditional system to track the data source of the image, and pay attention to adding noise in the process. The information fusion technology of different systems is compared, and the errors of the three test groups are estimated. Table 4 below shows the statistical results of the system's error sequence mean and variance.

**Table 4.** The statistical results of the mean and variance of the error series

| Test group | Mean value | Variance | Deviation |
|---|---|---|---|
| System in text | 0.0036 | 0.0223 | 0.1492 |
| Traditional system | 0.0067 | 0.1538 | 0.3965 |

The deviation in the table is the degree of deviation between the result obtained and the actual drawing data after the system's quantitative calculation. According to the data in the table, it can be seen intuitively that after the system designed this time uses digital technology, its data accuracy is higher than that of the traditional system, and its mean, variance and deviation are respectively 0.0031 and 0.1315 smaller than the traditional system. And 0.2473. It can be seen that digital technology can more accurately process the drawing data obtained by the system. At the same time, the tracking effect of the two systems on the drawing data is shown in Fig. 3 below.

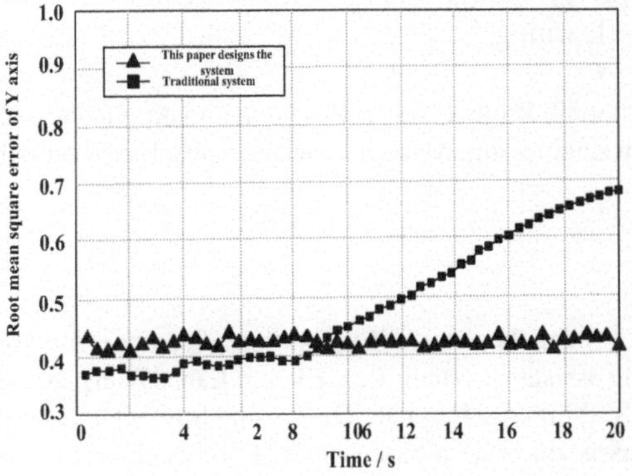


(a) Root mean square error of target X axis

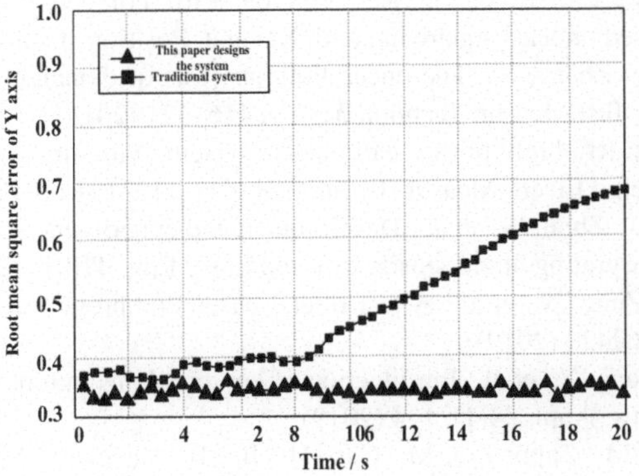


(b) Root mean square error of target Y axis

**Fig. 3.** Comparison Test of system target tracking effect

From the two groups of test results in Fig. 3, it can be seen that with the increase of time, the tracking error of the designed system on two coordinate axes is far less than that of the traditional system. It can be seen that the design of the system, with the help of digital technology, enhances the anti-interference performance of noise information.

## 5 Concluding Remarks

Through three groups of experimental demonstrations, it is found that the drawing teaching aid system designed based on digital technology has better performance and provides a more complete teaching method for civil engineering CAD drawing teaching. However, the system designed this time still has shortcomings. In the future research work, PLC technology and clustering algorithm can be applied to the system to further improve the effectiveness of the system and provide more reliable teaching methods for civil engineering work and learning.

**Fund Projects.** No. 203683, Project Name: Research and Application of Teaching System and Method of Construction Engineering Management Specialty Based on BIM Technology.

## References

1. Qin, Y., Zhang, J., Shen, H., et al.: Exploration of competency-oriented based medical experiment teaching assistant system. Res. Explor. Lab. **37**(08), 202-205+274 (2018)
2. Zhuang, Z., Peng, X., Shiliang, H., et al.: Design and implementation of data structure experiment instruction assistant system based on NAO robot. Electron. World **2018**(05), 14–16 (2018)
3. Fu, H., Lu, L.: Design and research of teaching assistance system based on wechat public platform. J. Jinhua Polytech. **19**(06), 68–72 (2019)
4. Liu, Y., Chen, Y., Lu, Y., et al.: Research on error compensation and calibration of magnetometer based on least square method. Navigat. Position. Timing **5**(01), 17–21 (2018)
5. Ma, Z., Zhang, Z., Zhang, R.: The uncertainty analysis of dynamic calibration system for pressure sensor. J. Test Measur. Technol. **32**(05), 416–421 (2018)
6. Yu, M., Lan, Y.: RF high power calibration system with high harmonic suppression performance. Foreign Electr. Measur. Technol. **38**(01), 116–121 (2019)
7. Zhang, W., Lao, D., Zhou, W., et al.: Development and experiment of online self-calibration system for circular grating angle sensor. Infrared Laser Eng. **47**(01), 224–229 (2018)
8. Liu, S., Bai, W., Zeng, N., et al.: A fast fractal based compression for MRI images. IEEE Access **7**, 62412–62420 (2019)
9. Liu, S., Li, Z., Zhang, Y., et al.: Introduction of key problems in long-distance learning and training. Mob. Netw. Appl. **24**(1), 1–4 (2019)
10. Liu, S., Glowatz, M., Zappatore, M., Gao, H., Jia, B., Bucciero, A. (eds.): eLEOT 2018. LNICSSITE, vol. 243. Springer, Cham (2018). https://doi.org/10.1007/978-3-319-93719-9
11. Syed, Z.A., Trabookis, Z., Bertrand, J.W., et al.: Evaluation of virtual reality based learning materials as a supplement to the undergraduate mechanical engineering laboratory experience. Int. J. Eng. Educ. **35**(3), 842–852 (2019)
12. Jago, R., Tibbitts, B., Porter, A., et al.: A revised teaching assistant-led extracurricular physical activity programme for 8- to 10-year-olds: the action 3:30R feasibility cluster RCT. Publ. Health Res. **7**(19), 1–128 (2019)

# Design and Development of Online Education System

# Construction of Online Open Distance Teaching Platform for Meridians and Acupoints of TCM

Yu-juan Zhang[1(✉)] and Mei-bin Qi[2]

[1] Xinyu University, Xinyu 338004, China
zhangyujuan4546@sina.com
[2] Admission and Employment Office, Dongying Vocational Institute, Dongying 257090, China

**Abstract.** In the traditional teaching platform, because the function of the platform is not perfect, the interaction of the platform is poor, and the response time of the platform is affected. Through setting up self-study function and micro-courseware teaching function, self-study course of the platform is completed, and through setting up videotape course, live broadcast course and online discussion mode, the teaching of meeting course is optimized to realize the optimization of SPOC network to the online teaching function of the Aike platform. Through adjusting the formula of error function and pixel resolution, the teaching environment is established, and the interaction between students and the platform is realized by transforming the human model of TCM meridians and acupoints. Experimental results: Compared with the three groups of traditional platforms, the platform is more interactive and has a faster response time when facing the same teaching content.

**Keywords:** TCM meridians and acupoints · Online remote · Open teaching platform · The human body model

## 1 Introduction

Online teaching, also known as distance education, realizes any learner's personalized learning task at his own pace at any time and at any place through the Internet, and the virtual learning community it provides also makes the communication and interaction between teachers and students, learners quick and convenient. It is a new type of education method that combines flexibility, initiative, creativity and interaction in one. It has the characteristics of individualized learning, information transmission of teaching information and popularization of educational objects. The science of meridians and acupoints is the basic theory and core content of acupuncture and moxibustion, which is composed of the science of meridians and collateral and the science of acupoints [1]. Meridian, which relates to the physiology, pathology, diagnosis and treatment of TCM, is of great significance to acupuncture and other clinical subjects of TCM. The science of acupoints is a subject which is guided by the meridian theory and expatiates on the distribution, function and clinical application of acupoints. As one of the classic disciplines


W. Fu et al. (Eds.): eLEOT 2021, LNICST 389, pp. 489–501, 2021.
https://doi.org/10.1007/978-3-030-84383-0_42

of TCM, the science of meridians and collaterals and acupoints has been concerned by people all over the world. With the progress of the times, traditional classroom teaching alone can not meet the demand of today's learning [2]. With the help of online education platforms, we can break traditional classroom teaching on time, space and personnel constraints, so that more people have the opportunity to understand account knowledge. At the same time, the online teaching of meridian and acupoint science also provides a good way for students to selectively learn independently before and after class and to communicate with teachers conveniently.

At present, many colleges and universities of TCM are organizing a large number of professional manpower and material resources to develop and build an online teaching platform of meridian and acupoint science. Although many schools have obtained or are applying for the construction of state-level, provincial level and school-level excellent courses in the study of meridians and acupoints, there are also teaching syllabuses, related courseware, video recordings of teachers' lectures and so on for this course on their excellent course websites in the study of meridians and acupoints. Some also include teaching notes and exercise questions, which are conducive to students' systematic and standardized knowledge learning, induction and consolidation [3]. However, the online teaching content is mainly based on the mode of "courseware teaching video", with a single and boring form, which is only open to teachers and students, lacks vitality and communication, and cannot show the advantages of open sharing of resources and convenient and free exchange between teachers and students.

Therefore, this paper studies the construction method of a new online open teaching platform for TCM meridians and acupoints.

## 2 Establishing an Online Open Teaching Platform for Meridians and Acupoints of Traditional Chinese Medicine

### 2.1 The Online Teaching Function of AIKE Platform is Set up Based on SPOC Network

The teaching plan of TCM meridian and acupoints is based on 4 meridians as a teaching unit, including 2 self-study courses online, 2 meetings offline and 1 practice of acupoint pointing. In order to realize the online distance open teaching task, the online teaching mode of the distance teaching platform is adjusted. Therefore, the SPOC network teaching of the teaching platform should adjust the online teaching content according to the students' self-study status in time to ensure the students can study "Acupoint Study of Meridians" at home.

First, set up a platform for self-study courses. Online autonomous learning is "student-centered", which includes four links: self-study, micro-teaching, cooperation and mutual study, and online test. The self-study course of SPOC teaching platform of "Acupoint Study of Meridians and Collaterals" is mainly online study. Teachers use the platform to upload videos and Scorm courseware to guide students to learn the contents of meridians and acupoints, and make video recordings and live broadcasts to assist students to learn, "self-learning" and "micro-learning". On the Aike Teaching Support Platform, set up a "Self-Study Question Area" to guide students to publish learning postings about difficulties and puzzles encountered in self-study or experience sharing, so that teachers and students can discuss with each other and realize "cooperation and mutual learning". In addition, the teacher will test questions embedded in the Scorm courseware, in each unit, after the setting of the relevant homework and tests, complete the "online test" link. Therefore, on the self-study function of the platform, teachers upload relevant learning materials on the Aike teaching support platform, including electronic version of textbooks, Scorn courseware and bilingual teaching. After downloading the electronic version of the textbook and syllabus, students will understand the original text of the textbook and the learning requirements of each chapter, and use the scorm courseware to learn the basic contents of the course, such as the understanding of the original text of the circulation of channels and the application of specific points. After mastering the basic knowledge of books, students can watch the video of acupoint pointing to deepen the memory of acupoint positioning. Students who have the ability to learn can use bilingual teaching materials to learn the English expressions of meridians and collaterals and acupoints, so as to conduct multi-way and all-round self-study. Secondly, the platform is designed to help the teaching function. Online teaching with prominent teaching theme. Because the course is usually presented by short video, and the topic is prominent, it has the characteristics of fragmentation of knowledge points, such as rehabilitation and health care methods about acupoints, acupoints selection methods and so on, it can let students learn new knowledge intuitively and strengthen the absorption of new knowledge.

In addition, the length of the video teaching can be looked at indefinitely, there is no time limit, and the time arrangement is relatively loose, which is convenient for students to make use of spare time to study independently according to the actual situation and their own needs, strengthen the flexibility of self-study, and construct the knowledge of meridians and acupoints preliminarily. Also in the cooperation mutual study aspect, the student who can not understand question may through "the self-study discussion question area" carries on the post question. Other students can answer the questions according to the book knowledge, or by consulting the literature, not only relieving others of the confusion encountered in self-study, but also enriching their own acupuncture knowledge [4]. In addition to the problems encountered in self-study, teachers can guide students to express their views on acupoints learning, such as "small tips on acupoints positioning memory", "personal views on the essence of meridians" and so on. In order to strengthen online mutual help and mutual learning.

Through the backstage data of Aike Teaching Support Platform, the teaching team counts the times each student speaks, and adds corresponding scores to the students according to the number of questions and answers. Online discussion can not only stimulate students' inner drive and promote them to reflect on their own self-study, but also deepen the knowledge structure of acupuncture, form a good class atmosphere and realize "cooperation and mutual learning". Finally, in order to let the students master and apply the knowledge of acupoints further, the teacher arranges the network homework and test on the Aike platform to carry on the "online test". Assignments and exams submitted by students will be graded accordingly. According to the students' grades, the teaching team understands the situation of students' mastering meridians and collaterals, and summarizes the problems existing in students' self-study. The teacher guides the students to think and discuss these questions in the online meeting class, and strengthens the students' self-study effect.

Second, set up a platform for meeting courses. Online teaching has synchronous, asynchronous, mixed and other forms, "Acupoint Science of Meridians and Collaterals" SPOC teaching adopts mixed online teaching mode. Students can finish the task of self-study by watching the video of micro class, recording and playing video and learning Scorm courseware. On this basis, teachers take the form of live teaching, online learning at the same time. The meeting class in the form of recording and live broadcast can deepen mutual understanding, facilitate face-to-face teaching in the future, achieve the best learning effect and promote teaching informationization. Therefore, the first set of recorded courses. The teacher collects and identifies the learning difficulties and common problems of the students during the course of self-study, and records the first round of tutoring videos in combination with the assessment of the students' in-class tests, so as to further guide the students to solve the problems, integrate the new and old knowledge and deepen their understanding of the new knowledge. For example, in the first video recording and broadcasting, the method of acupoint selection of some acupoints is explained to answer the doubts of students when they study on their own. After the live meeting, the class representative collected the students' problems, and the teacher recorded the second round of video and uploaded it to the Aike teaching support platform to answer questions and strengthen the teaching effect. Video recordings can be viewed repeatedly when students are confused, and can be paused and started at any time, through the flexibility of video viewing time, to meet the needs of personalized learning [5]. Second, set up live courses.

In the process of live teaching, the teacher first of all the focus of each meridian point and the need to master the content of crosstalk, and then systematize the knowledge. For example, the three meridians of the Foot Three-Yang Meridian should be told together to compare the following parts and indications of each meridian, so as to strengthen the horizontal comparison of students' and deepen the positioning memory of acupoints. In addition, the points will be classified by location, focusing on key areas, such as sternocleidomastoid muscle, elbow lines and other parts. Students memorize the points of each meridian in order, then memorize according to the position, and finally memorize according to the points with the same characters, such as the points with the word "Tian". Teachers through the live platform to talk about the difficult content, and the pre-operation for comments, summed up and evaluation of students self-study, and then answer questions. Teachers in the QQ group so that each group leader summed up the process of autonomous learning in each group before class problems encountered. Then the teacher in the process of live broadcast, the summary of the problems presented on the computer screen and share. Instead of answering questions directly, the teacher should encourage students to speak up, think, and discuss the questions together. Each student will attempt to answer questions from other groups.

The teacher will record the number of times the students answer the questions and make them part of their grades. After the students speak, the teacher makes comments and corresponding supplements. After the students have all spoken, if the problem has not been solved, the teacher will give the final unified answer. For example, the students have doubts about the corresponding relationship between three yin and three yang of the twelve meridians, because the Shaoyin Meridian corresponds to the Taiyin Meridian, the Taiyin Meridian and the Yangming Meridian, that is, the corresponding relationship between two yin (Shaoyin) and three yang (Taiyin) and two yang (Yangming) in the twelve meridian and the corresponding relationship between one yin (Jueyin) and one yang (Shaoyin) and two yang (Yangming) in the Neijing. Teachers can explain the origin of meridian naming by combining relevant materials and deducing the initial meridian theory through the theory of "correspondence between man and nature". Not only can answer the students' doubts, but also the corresponding knowledge expansion, expand the students' professional field of vision, and strengthen their interest in learning acupuncture. Finally, set the online discussion mode. Online discussion is a step for students to deepen their knowledge.

Compared with the self-study question area set up in the self-study course, the online discussion takes a relatively long time to learn, and can be discussed repeatedly in the online forum. In addition, the online discussion can get the teacher's answer immediately, and the teacher will expand and extend accordingly to enrich the students' acupuncture knowledge. The "online discussion" link of meeting class and the discussion link of "cooperation and mutual learning" of self-study class echo each other, promote the communication and interaction between teachers and students through the collision of thinking, and strengthen the learning effect of students' self-study points [6].

## 2.2 Building a Virtual Teaching Platform with Human-Computer Interaction

According to the functional characteristics of the online teaching platform of meridians and acupoints of traditional Chinese medicine, a virtual scene is built by using the remote multimedia teaching system, and a virtual teaching platform with human-computer interaction is built by using model-based technology and image-based drawing technology, both of which can be realized in 3DMAX software. Upload the entity data information of Chinese medicine meridian and acupoints online teaching to the computer, simulate the curved surface of Chinese medicine meridian and acupoints with different curves or figures, and create the basic models at different body positions. The selected model components can be triangles, rectangles or other polygons. Then, according to the trend of meridians, the error adjustment function is used to adjust the size of a single model, and three-dimensional meridian acupoint models with various shapes and types are made through model building and splicing [7]. The error function for adjusting the model size is:

$$s = \frac{\Delta q}{\gamma} = \frac{\alpha\omega_i - \gamma}{\gamma} \quad (1)$$

In the formula: $s$ represents the actual relative error, which is the ratio of absolute error to actual true value; $\Delta q$ represents absolute error, which not only indicates the size of data difference, but also indicates the positive and negative directions of the difference; $\alpha$ is a coefficient, which indicates the ratio between virtual model components; $\omega_i$ represents the drawn independent virtual model assembled by $i$ independent sub-models. Then, according to the functional requirements of the teaching platform of Chinese medicine meridians and acupoints, the parameters of the established model are adjusted to obtain virtual models with different resolutions, which meet the display requirements of the platform for the teaching content of Chinese medicine meridians and acupoints. It is assumed that there are $m_i$ pixels in the horizontal direction and $n_i$ pixels in the vertical direction of the designed model, and the total pixels of the model are $p = m_i n_i$ [8–10]. To adjust the pixel resolution of the module, the calculation expression is:

$$\begin{cases} \lambda_1 = x_1 \cos \beta tb \cdot s \\ \lambda_2 = x_2 \cos \beta tb \cdot s \end{cases} \tag{2}$$

In the formula, $\lambda_1$ represents the model pixel in the positive direction; $\lambda_2$ represents the model pixel in the reverse direction; $x_1$ is the model length in the positive direction; $x_2$ represents the model length in the reverse direction; $\beta$ indicates the connection angle between components [11, 12]; $t$ represents the trend control parameter of meridians in each stage; $b$ represents the number of model component surfaces in each direction.

All meridians and acupoints of traditional Chinese medicine are marked on the model, and students can communicate with the teaching content by rotating, zooming in and zooming out the manikin in the virtual platform. The core of the designed teaching platform lies in the design of interactive functions [13]. Therefore, VRML language is used to simulate the equipment function, and set the three-dimensional coordinates of the teaching equipment to meet the spatial transformation of the virtual human body model and ensure that the model can be arbitrarily adjusted, as shown below:

```
DEF Cylinder01-TIMER TimeSensor {loop TRUE enabled FALSE cycleInterval}
TimeSensor
DEF xiabie-POS-INTERP Position Interpolator
key{0,0.2,0.22,0.47……0.54,0.57,}
keyValue{36.54 3.766-3.345……16.87 3.766-35.45}
DEF xiabie-ROT-INTERP Orientation Interpolator
key{0,0.2,0.22,0.47……0.54,0.57,}
keyValue{1000,1000……0 -1 0 -1.134}
```

According to the instruction program compiled by the above code, set the dynamic demonstration rules in the teaching scene, and import the dynamic teaching scene with a certain duration into VRML to realize the set interactive function [14, 15]. The behavior interaction module is assigned to a virtual meridian, and the analysis of meridian trend is realized in the form of flow chart. According to the existing online teaching framework of meridians and acupoints of traditional Chinese medicine, the open operation mechanism of the platform is arranged, and the trigger [16], data transmission and model conversion of complex teaching programs are completed by using response functions. The calculation expression of the response function is [17–19]:

$$f(k) = \mu\varphi - \theta_i \tag{3}$$

In the formula: $f(k)$ represents the response function under the $k$ teaching program; $\mu$ represents the response conventional coefficient of the platform, $\varphi$ represents the online teaching level of Chinese medicine meridians and acupoints, and $\theta_i$ represents the comprehensive response coefficient of the teaching model to the problem under the selected $i$ operation objective. Using this function, the students can trigger the operation program when learning Chinese medicine meridians and acupoints, and then quickly enter the virtual scene according to a series of chain reactions [20–23]. After students enter the virtual teaching environment, they switch scenes through joysticks or data gloves, send instructions to the virtual platform, and obtain teaching information fed back by the platform. So far, the online remote open teaching platform of Chinese medicine meridians and acupoints has been completed.

## 3 Experimental Research

Platform function test is an important link in the task of platform construction, so as to analyze the performance of the designed teaching platform and whether it meets the design requirements. In order to make the test results more intuitive, three groups of traditional teaching platforms were taken as control group A, control group B and control group C, and the platform constructed this time was taken as experimental group. Compare the platform constructed by traditional methods with the designed platform, and find out the functional differences between them. Upload the designed platform and three groups of traditional platforms to four computers with the same configuration. The hardware environment selected in the experiment is: 4 pieces of 1024 MB memory constitute a communication dual channel, the CPU is dual-core 2.65 GHz, the GF9800GT graphics card supports 3D model, and the 64-bit operating system Windows XP is pre-installed.

### 3.1 Interactivity Test

Figure 1 shows the comparison test results of four groups of platform interaction performance.

In order to make the experimental results more convincing, four sets of test schemes are set up for the online teaching content of TCM meridians and acupoints. At the same time, the preset interaction index value is greater than or equal to 0.95, which proves that the online teaching platform has excellent interaction performance. According to the test results in Fig. 1, the interaction index of the experimental group is more than 0.95, and the interaction index test results of the three groups of traditional methods are less than the test results of the experimental group, and also less than the preset interaction performance test standard. The average value of interaction performance index of four groups of online teaching platform is counted, and the results are shown in Table 1.

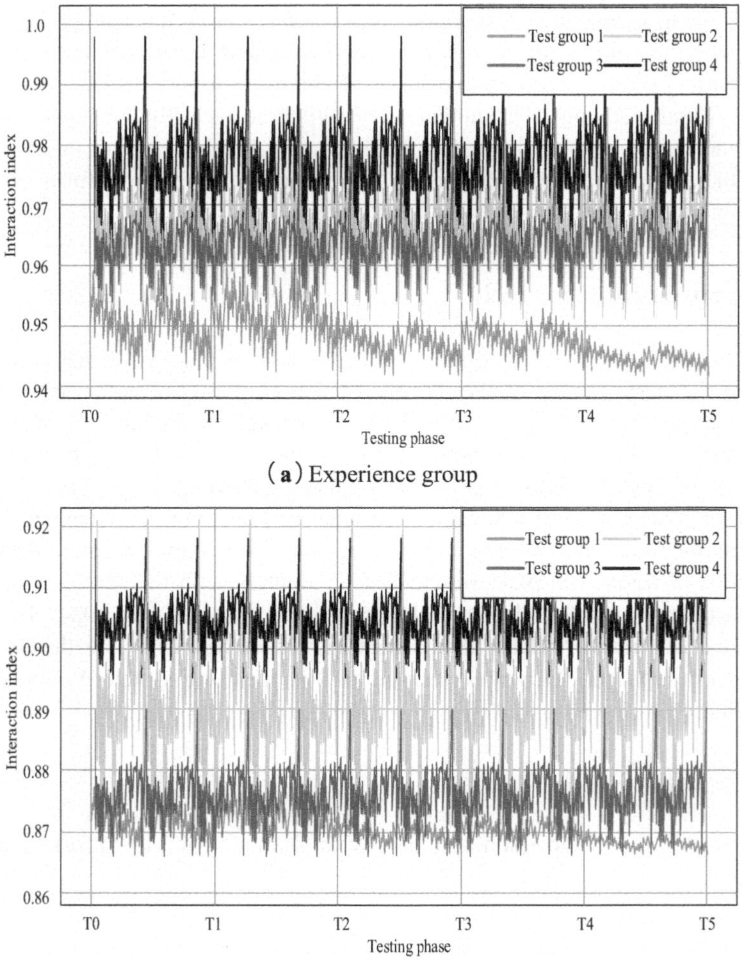


(b) Control group A

**Fig. 1.** Platform interactivity test results

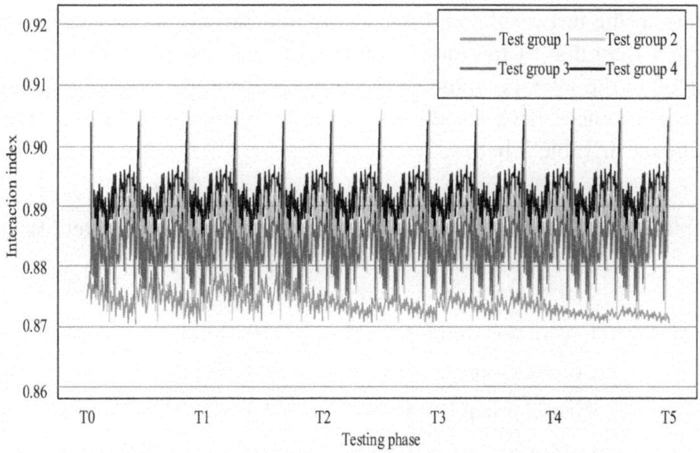


(c) Control group B

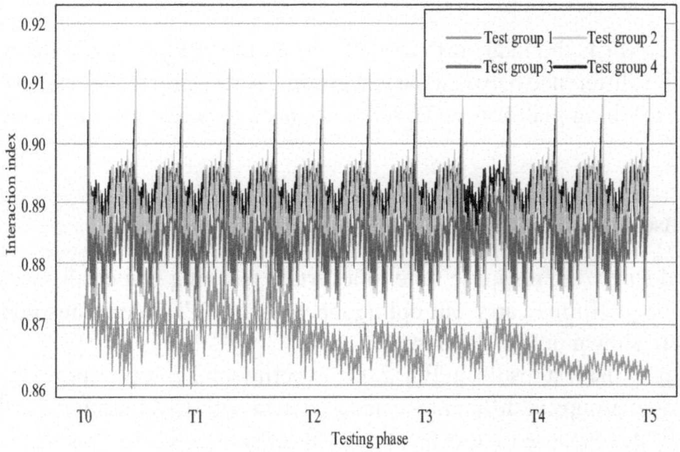


(d) Control group C

**Fig. 1.** *(continued)*

**Table 1.** Statistical table of average value of platform interactivity index

| Test plan | Experience group | Control group A | Control group B | Control group C |
|---|---|---|---|---|
| 1 | 0.9763 | 0.9024 | 0.8952 | 0.8947 |
| 2 | 0.9658 | 0.8986 | 0.8917 | 0.8894 |
| 3 | 0.9612 | 0.8922 | 0.8874 | 0.8851 |
| 4 | 0.9507 | 0.8745 | 0.8695 | 0.8628 |

According to the test results in Table 1, the interactivity index of the experimental group is higher than that of the three traditional platforms. In order to facilitate comparison, calculate the average value of the four test groups' interactivity indexes, and compare the differences between the four groups' results and the preset values. The results are shown in Table 2 below.

**Table 2.** Statistical results of platform interaction index differences

| Test group | Average value | W1 | W2 |
|---|---|---|---|
| Experience group | 0.9635 | 0.0135 | – |
| Control group A | 0.8919 | 0.0581 | 0.0716 |
| Control group B | 0.8860 | 0.064 | 0.0775 |
| Control group C | 0.8830 | 0.067 | 0.0805 |

In Table 2, W1 is the index difference between the test group and the preset value; W2 is the index difference between the test groups. According to the test results in Table 2, the online teaching platform of TCM meridians and acupoints has better interactive effect.

### 3.2 Response Time Test

In the second stage, the response time to a certain teaching content is tested when the four groups of platforms carry out online teaching of TCM meridians and acupoints. The results are shown in Fig. 2 below.

According to the test results in Fig. 2, the experimental group responded within 1.0 s when facing two groups of different teaching contents of TCM meridians and acupoints, while the average response time of the three control groups were 1.28 s, 1.37 s and 1.39 s respectively. According to the above test results, the open teaching platform has good response performance.

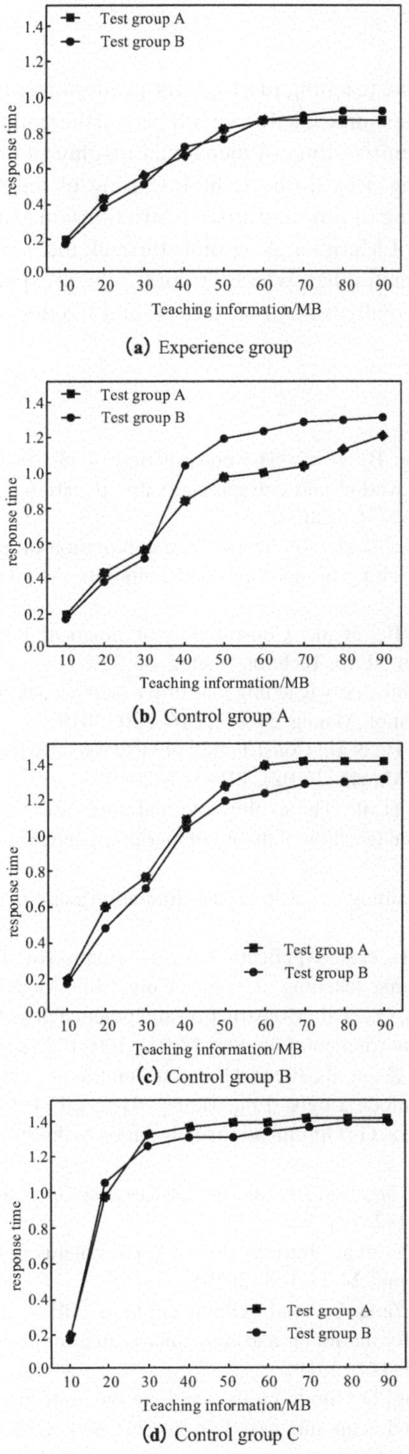


**Fig. 2.** Platform responsiveness test results

## 4 Conclusion

An ideal and mature online teaching platform for professional meridians and acupoints, with the help of network resources, will give full play to the standardization and vividness of basic teaching, the intuitive three-dimensional display of content, and the freedom and autonomy of learning. Based on the high sharing of online teaching of Meridian Acupoints and the breaking of time and space restrictions on learners, anyone can access professional knowledge of Meridian Acupoints through the network platform, and learn and communicate with each other, which promotes the prosperity and development of Meridian Acupoints and realizes the true fairness and freedom of learning.

## References

1. Sun, C., Qi, Y., Zhang, B., et al.: The construction of pharmaceutical virtual simulation platform based on innovation and entrepreneurship education. Chin. Med. Mod. Distance Educ. China **18**(05), 163–164 (2020)
2. Li, J., Yang, X., Luo, L., et al.: Application and exploration of game CARDS of meridians and acupoints in the teaching of meridians and acupoints. Asia-Pacific Tradit. Med. **15**(10), 213–215 (2019)
3. Li, T., Ren, H., Liu, B., et al.: Construction of practical teaching platform for urban underground engineering. Exp. Technol. Manag. **36**(03), 242–246 (2019)
4. Dong, X.: Optimizing university teaching platform to serve teaching and learning for teachers and students. Exp. Technol. Manag. **36**(06), 216–220 (2019)
5. Wang, P., Yan, W., Cai, H., et al.: Construction of virtual reality teaching platform for nursing science. Exp. Technol. Manag. **36**(02), 145–147 (2019)
6. He, L., Ji, F., Lin, D., et al.: The exploration and application of ideological and political education in the bilingual teaching of theory of meridians and acupoints. Educ. Teach. **18**(15), 9–10 (2020)
7. Gao, H.: Engineering training based on virtual simulation technology. Comput. Simul. **37**(07), 391–393+408 (2020)
8. Liu, A., Wang, J., Kan, L., et al.: Application effect evaluation of 3D Body software on subject of channel-acupoint course teaching . J. Gansu Univ. Chin. Med. **37**(01), 119–122 (2020)
9. Huang, J., Zhao, L., Du, G., et al.: Construction and practice of virtual simulation experiment teaching platform of environment. Lab. Sci. **22**(02), 169–172 (2019)
10. Yang, Y., Bai, Q., Liu, Z., et al.: Research on curriculum system platform based on virtual reality stereo teaching mode. Logist. Eng. Manag. **41**(03), 174–176 (2019)
11. Fu, W., Liu, S., Srivastava, G.: Optimization of big data scheduling in social networks. Entropy **21**(9), 902 (2019)
12. Liu, S., Bai, W., Zeng, N., et al.: A fast fractal based compression for MRI images. IEEE Access **7**, 62412–62420 (2019)
13. Liu, S., Li, Z., Zhang, Y., et al.: Introduction of key problems in long-distance learning and training. Mob. Netw. Appl. **24**(1), 1–4 (2019)
14. Zhang, Z., Huang, Y., Yang, L., et al.: Organization of offline study in blended learning—taking teaching design for meridians and acupoints as an example. Chin. Med. Mod. Distance Educ. China **45**(3), 125–124 (2019)
15. Chen, X., Ma, R., Liang, D.: Study on the teaching mode of flipped class for the course of science of meridians and acupoints based on internet plus. China High. Med. Educ. **12**(3), 77–89 (2019)

16. Wang, X.Y., Li, C.Y., Zhang, Y.C.: Exploration of new teaching mode of Science of Meridians and Acupoints based on three-dimensional practice platform. Zhongguo zhen jiu = Chin. Acupunct. Moxibustion **40**(1), 106–108 (2020)
17. Zhang, T., Liu, C., Hu, G., et al.: Synchronous vasomotion of skin microvessels at acupoints on the twelve main meridians of beagle dogs. Skin Res. Technol. **26**(6), 45–56 (2020)
18. Wang, L., Zhao, J.S.: Exploration on "moxibustion on a meridian" in Moxibustion Classic of Eleven Yin-Yang Meridians. Zhongguo zhen jiu = Chin. Acupunct. Moxibustion **40**(11), 1251–1254 (2020)
19. Wang, R.: Mastering specificity of acupoints based on clinical verses of acupuncture and moxibustion. Chin. J. Integr. Med. **9**, 456–468 (2019)
20. Yeh, H.Y., Chao, C.T., Lai, Y.P., et al.: Predicting the associations between meridians and Chinese traditional medicine using a cost-sensitive graph convolutional neural network. Int. J. Environ. Res. Public Health **17**(3), 49–58 (2020)
21. Li, H., Long, D., Li, B., et al.: A clinical study to assess the influence of acupuncture at "Wang's Jiaji" acupoints on limb spasticity in patients in convalescent stage of ischemic stroke: study protocol for a randomized controlled trial. Curr. Control. Trials Cardiovasc. Med. **8**, 75–86 (2019)
22. Yi-Jun, Y.E., Wang, B., Wen, M.A., et al.: Analysis on the difficulties in teaching the theory of meridians and acupoints. Guiding J. Tradit. Chin. Med. Pharm. **14**(2), 1235–1245 (2019)
23. Qu, N., Huang, H., Zhang, J.: Analysis of the regularity of acupuncture at meridians and acupoints on migraine based on data mining technology. J. Emerg. Tradit. Chin. Med. **44**(3), 126–137 (2019)

# Design of Spoken English Distance Teaching Training System Based on Virtual Reality Technology

Zhi-li Sha[1(✉)] and Yu-xiang Liu[2]

[1] School of Foreign Languages, Xichang University, Xichang 615000, China
[2] College of Tourism and Urban-Rural Planning, Xichang University, Xichang 615000, China

**Abstract.** At present, the spoken English long-distance teaching training system has not designed a dynamic dictionary for spoken English teaching training, which leads to a high occupancy rate of the system server hardware during the operation of the system. A virtual reality technology-based remote teaching training system for spoken English is designed. In terms of hardware design, adopt the cloud-based MVC architecture model, design the system architecture, consider the system design purpose, and system functions, individually design the system I/O module, and complete the system hardware design. In terms of software design, it sets up voice recognition function, simulates the remote teaching environment, sets up a dynamic oral English teaching training vocabulary, increases the system vocabulary, sets up remote oral English teaching training rules, and the transformation system has the function of remote teaching and training oral English. The experimental results show that: comparing the three groups of systems, operating performance and server hardware performance, the English spoken remote teaching training system designed this time has a faster operating speed and a usable server utilization rate.

**Keywords:** Virtual reality technology · Spoken English · Distance teaching · Teaching and training system

## 1 Introduction

The increasingly frequent exchanges between countries have made the role of English as the language of international communication increasingly prominent in foreign exchanges. More and more people pay attention to the learning of English, their investment in English is increasing day by day, and the effect of English teaching has also been continuously improved [1]. However, the students taught in English teaching in our country generally have poor oral expression skills and high scores. For this reason, our country has put forward new requirements for proficiency in spoken English for English teaching. After discovering the shortcomings of English teaching, some reforms have been made to language teaching at home and abroad. The combination of information


W. Fu et al. (Eds.): eLEOT 2021, LNICST 389, pp. 502–514, 2021.
https://doi.org/10.1007/978-3-030-84383-0_43

technology and foreign language discipline can make up for the shortcomings of traditional language teaching, make foreign language learning more vivid and vivid, and stimulate learners' learning motivation. At the same time, foreign language learning is endowed with situational, communicative and practical features. However, in terms of oral English learning software, multimedia technology and speech recognition technology are mainly used to design language learning systems, such as FLUENCY, EduSpeak, SPHINX, English phonetic pronunciation software, Big Mouth English, and English talk-speaking software [2, 3]. However, in the above design, the design focuses on simple pronunciation and reading exercises, accumulating all kinds of English materials together, allowing learners to learn in the environment they build, this pure use of technology to accumulate materials the method does not change the essence of oral teaching, let alone the integration of information technology in English courses, and most of the functions are similar to repeaters. Therefore, the design of oral English distance teaching and training system based on virtual reality technology, through the cloud design of oral English distance teaching and training system architecture, using audiorecord class method to record voice signals, complete the I/O module design; On this basis, the relevant speech signal processing methods are used to extract the acoustic features of the required speech. On this basis, the speech template required for speech recognition is established. According to a certain matching strategy, the similarity between the test speech template and the standard speech template is calculated. Finally, the recognition result is expressed in a certain form, Complete the software design of oral English distance teaching training system. Finally, the effectiveness of the system is verified by simulation experiments. It has certain significance and design value both in theory and practical application.

# 2 Hardware Design of Distance Teaching and Training System for Spoken English

## 2.1 System Architecture Design

In order to meet the needs of users for remote learning of spoken English, the design of a distance teaching training system for spoken English adopts the cloud-based MVC architecture model. The cloud is also called the server, which mainly provides various Chinese learning resources for the client; the client is the user interface of the system, which is mainly responsible for various interactions with the user, but the main business logic is executed on the server [4]. Therefore, the main functions of the system in the cloud are as follows: 1. To achieve various operations on the database; 2. To provide a variety of rich knowledge base for the client; 3. To provide voice recognition services; 4. To provide word recognition services; 5. To provide upgrade scripts for the client; 6. To process various business logic of the system. The main functions of the client are as follows: 1. Responsible for direct interaction with the user and provide a graphical interface for the user; 2. Implement the cloud service proxy module and provide a cloud service interface for the client. Based on the above-identified main functions of the system cloud and client, the designed system architecture is shown in Fig. 1.

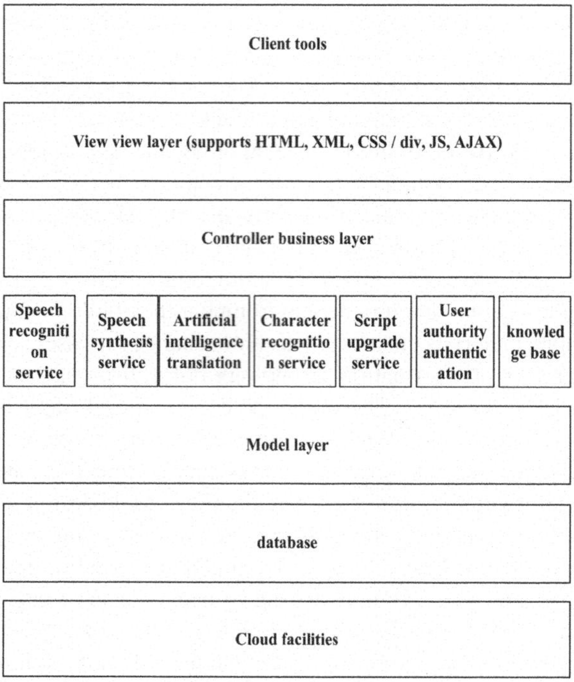


**Fig. 1.** System architecture

In Fig. 1, except for the client tool, everything else belongs to the server. It can be seen from Fig. 1 that the speech recognition service and text recognition service functions of the design system are placed on the system server side, simplifying the design of the client side, and achieving the cross-platform goal of the client side, thereby promoting the stability of the system client side. It runs locally on PC, android, ios and other platforms, so as to achieve the purpose of remote training of spoken English.

## 2.2 I/O Module Design

Based on the system architecture shown in Fig. 1, it can be found that the voice function of the English speaking distance teaching training system designed this time is an important part of the system. Therefore, the I/O module of the system is designed separately, that is, the system voice recognition and synthesis function.

The recording and playing of voice is the basis of realizing the system function [5]. As a long-distance oral English teaching and training system, voice recording and playing function is equivalent to the "ear" and "mouth" of the system, which is an indispensable part of human-computer interaction.

Since the system designed this time, its main purpose is to achieve remote training of spoken English, so the client chooses the mobile terminal that supports PC, android, ios and other systems, and the mobile terminal that runs on PC, android, ios, etc., comes with With a headset, it has achieved good results for general voice recording and playback. Therefore, the system uses the phone's built-in headset as the voice recording and playback device.

At present, the mobile client provides two implementation methods for recording, one is to use the relevant methods of mediarecorder class, the other is to use the method of audiorecord class [6]. In order to process speech signal in the future, it is necessary to determine the sampling rate, sampling bit and other parameters, and flexibly set the basic parameters of speech signal, such as the size of audio buffer, sampling rate, sampling bit, etc. Therefore, the system chooses the method of recording audio to the audiorecord class in the buffer to record the voice signal.

Consider that the AudioTrack class corresponds to the AudioRecord class and has the function of playing voice signals. Therefore, the method of the AudioTrack class is also used to play the corresponding voice signal. Based on the above analysis content, the final system audio format is determined as follows: 1. The sampling frequency is 8000 Hz; 2. The sampling channel is mono; 3. The sampling number is 16 bits.

In addition, the system has set the voice mouth demonstration function for all phonetic pronunciation, which is mainly realized by playing the built-in pronunciation animation video. The video playback uses the related methods of videoview class in Android SDK.

## 3 The Software Design of the Training System for Spoken English Remote Teaching Based on Virtual Reality Technology

Based on the hardware design of the spoken English distance teaching and training system, this paper designs the English speech recognition process, uses virtual reality technology to simulate the oral English teaching and training environment, sets up the dynamic vocabulary of oral English teaching and training, and formulates the training rules of oral English distance teaching, so as to make the system have the function of distance teaching and training spoken English, and complete the distance teaching of spoken English Training system software design.

### 3.1 Design an English Speech Recognition Process

Speech recognition includes input speech signal preprocessing and speech signal recognition. In the first stage, relevant speech signal processing methods are needed to extract the acoustic features of the required speech, and then the speech template for speech recognition is established. In the second stage, we need to extract the acoustic features of the speech signal from the processed input speech signal, and compare it with the existing speech template according to certain criteria. Then, according to certain search and matching strategies, we can find out a series of optimal templates that match the input speech, or calculate the test speech templates according to certain matching strategies Finally, the recognition results are expressed in a certain form. Its English speech recognition process is shown in Fig. 2.

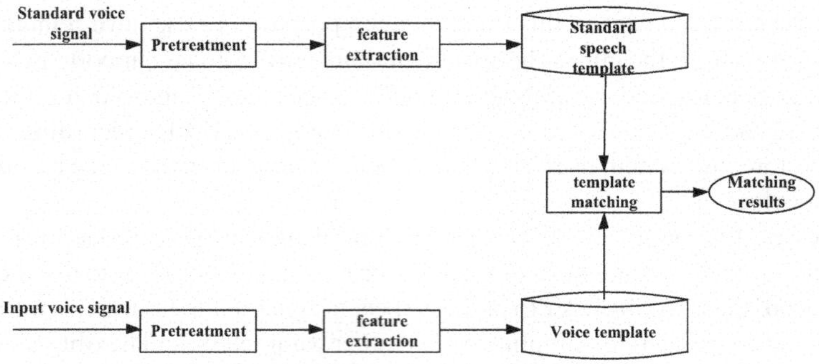


**Fig. 2.** English speech recognition process

Based on the English speech recognition process shown in Fig. 2, the speech signal preprocessing, feature extraction and recognition methods are designed. Considering that there will be problems such as unclear speech and dialectization in the process of English speech training, for this reason, the method of identifying speech sequence features in frames is used to recognize the speech sequence. Therefore, if the frequency domain of speech is z, the user's speech input sequence is $H$, $n$ is used to represent the number of frames, and $n$ value is taken as 20 ms. The overlapping part of the two frames is called frame shift, which is represented by $m$. in the process of processing the speech sequence, the generated transformation is represented by the symbol $T$, then the speech sequence $Q_{\mathrm{n}}$ at frame $n$ is:

$$Q_{\mathrm{n}} = T[H(m)n(z-m)] \tag{1}$$

At this time (2) in the formula $n(z-m)$ can represent the minute hand hour of the speech sequence, multiplied by the amplitude. Incorporating the formula (1) into the speech sequence, after the second pre-emphasis processing is performed on the speech sequence, the Hamming window is used as the window function for speech signal processing, then:

$$w(\mathrm{z}) = \begin{cases} 0.54 - 0.46\cos\left[\frac{2z\pi}{(L-1)}\right] & 0 \le z \le L-1 \\ 0 & \text{Other} \end{cases} \tag{2}$$

In formula (2), $L$ is the length of Hamming window function, and $w(z)$ is the $w$ speech sequence in z frequency domain, which is the processed $H(\mathrm{z})$ speech sequence [7]. At this time, the $w(z)$ speech sequence has become smooth, and closer to the spectrum of short-term speech, improve the spectrum leakage caused by truncation effect, shield the interference information in the process of speech sequence input, and the mutual interference between speech frequency domains.

The extraction of speech features is to obtain an estimated value of a speech input sequence in the limited frequency domain of the speech recognition model. The estimated value and the actual value are analyzed for error, and the minimum square sum of the analysis result is taken. The calculation process is (2) The speech input sequence processed by the formula is input to the speech recognition model, and the characteristics of the speech sequence are output.

$$\sum_{z} w(z)w(z-P) = \sum_{i=1}^{P} a_i \sum_{z} [w(z-P)w(z-i)]^2 \tag{3}$$

In formula (3), $P$ indicates that there are $P$ sample values in speech sequence $w$, i.e. $P = 1, 2, 3, \cdots, P$. the predicted value of speech recognition model is a, the coefficient is $i$, and $i = 1, 2, 3 \cdots, i$. By solving equation (3), the speech feature parameters can be obtained, which reflect the characteristics of speech sequence.

Based on the formula (3), the language sequence recognition parameters are obtained, and the system speech recognition result $B$ is obtained:

$$B_{Hw}(O) = P(O|H, w) = \frac{1}{(2H)^{P/2}|E_{Hw}|^{1/2}} \exp\left\{-\frac{1}{2}(O - e_{Hw})E_{Hw}^{-1}(O - e_{Hw})\right\} \tag{4}$$

Equation (4) is the result of system speech recognition, $O$ is the language sequence output by navigation, $e_{Hw}$ represents the error value between the input speech sequence and the output speech sequence, and $E_{Hw}$ represents the mean square error between the input speech sequence and the output speech sequence Value [8].

At this time, the speech sequence input into the system is smooth and clear with obvious features, which can quickly identify the voice sequence input by users.

### 3.2 Simulation of Teaching Environment Based on Virtual Reality Technology

Using virtual reality technology to simulate oral English teaching and training environment, we need to rely on the actual teaching and training environment, use 3D scanning technology to scan the real image in a full range, measure the real image data, parameterize the measured real scene data, take the 3D scanning point as the original coordinate point, and look for the mapping point with the real environment in the virtual environment.

Assuming that the coordinate system of the real environment is aligned with the coordinate system in the virtual environment, the real environment is regarded as a rotation matrix $R$ and a translation vector t. The virtual number q is used to represent the virtual environment corresponding to the real environment, w is a scalar, v = $(x, y, z)$ is a vector, q Sitting marked as $(w, v)$, then q satisfies $|q|=\sqrt{w^2 + x^2 + y^2 + z^2} = 1$. Then there are:

$$p = p_m(\Theta) = K[q|qt] \tag{5}$$

In formula (5), $p$ is the matrix from the real environment to the virtual environment, $\Theta$ is the parameter vector, $p_m$ is the matrix function of the parameter vector $\Theta$ converted into the virtual environment, and $K$ is the matrix calibration [9]. If (7) is brought into the equation, then:

$$\begin{cases} x = wt + x^2 \\ y = vt + y^2 \\ z = kt + z^2 \end{cases} \tag{6}$$

Through the calculation of formula (6), the coordinate points for transforming the real environment into the virtual environment can be obtained, and a point model of the virtual environment is generated, so as to construct a virtual scene by virtualizing the real world.

At this time, the operator can walk freely in the virtual environment through unique equipment, or observe the objects in the virtual environment by changing the visual position by operation, or further operation, so as to have the feeling of being in the real world. The virtual environment operation process is shown in Fig. 3.

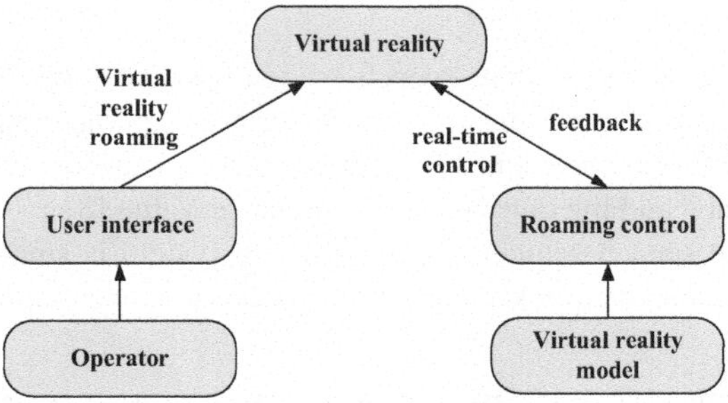


**Fig. 3.** Virtual environment operation process

According to the operation process of virtual environment shown in Fig. 3, the virtual environment can be adjusted in real time on the server according to the training content of oral English teaching, so that the virtual environment can be more in line with the training content of oral English teaching and improve the efficiency of distance teaching.

### 3.3 Setting up a Dynamic Vocabulary for Oral English Teaching and Training

At present, sphinx4 thesaurus is used in the spoken language training system. Its decoding operation module has strict requirements for the format of thesaurus. It provides six original thesauri for users to choose, namely discrete digital thesaurus TI46, continuous digital thesaurus tidigits, mini thesaurus an4, medium thesaurus RMI, large thesaurus WSJ, and super large Thesaurus hub4 [10].

However, the recognition process of sphinx4 depends on the hidden Markov model and speech model of each phoneme in the standard pronunciation in the dictionary, so the recognizer must load the selected dictionary before each recognition. The data contained in it is read into the memory, but this process takes a lot of time. The larger the capacity of the lexicon, the longer it takes to load the lexicon to start recognition. It takes about

2 s to load the RM1 thesaurus on a computer with an Intel Pentium 4 processor and a memory capacity of 2G. It takes about 5 s to load WSJ, and about 12 s to load HUB4, considering the user's computer configuration It is relatively low, and the loading of the thesaurus takes too long, which will require users to wait for a long time, which seriously affects user experience.

Therefore, the design of spoken English distance teaching training system thesaurus, choose to set the dynamic thesaurus, is to take out the vocabulary in the thesaurus, according to the words of the teaching system to dynamically rewrite thesaurus. The basic teaching module of College English teaching system is based on units. There are about 30 words to learn in a unit, so at the beginning of each unit, we will find the words to learn one by one, find the corresponding standard pronunciation and phonetic model of these words in hub4, and read these data into the dynamic new thesaurus. In this way, only the dynamic vocabulary needs to be loaded in each recognition process. The dynamic lexicon workflow is implemented by the system client, and the specific implementation of this design is shown in Fig. 4.

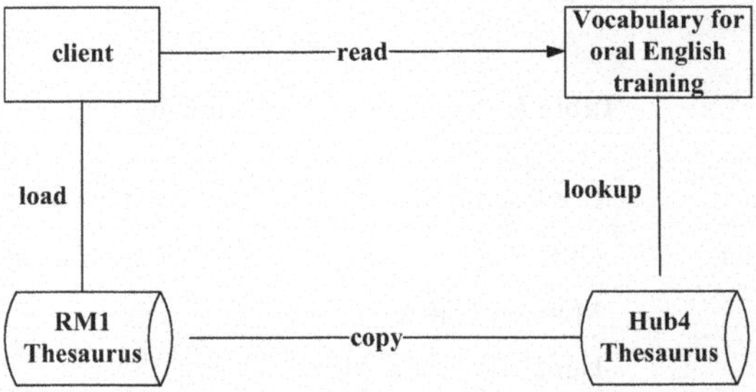


**Fig. 4.** Workflow of dynamic Thesaurus

### 3.4 Formulate Training Rules for Spoken English Distance Teaching

The user and the user should log in to the system and judge whether the students need the training together. When the user is an illegal user, the user needs to log in again; when the user is a legal user, the teacher sets up the virtual teaching environment of distance teaching, and the corresponding oral English teaching content, such as text, image, video, etc., for oral English teaching. According to the teacher's requirements, students make corresponding operation, record the spoken language training pronunciation, and compare it with the standard pronunciation. The teacher judges the result of oral English training in distance teaching and sets the corresponding teaching process.

The spoken English remote teaching training system designed this time is equipped with voice recognition function, simulating the remote teaching environment, setting up a dynamic oral English teaching training vocabulary, increasing the system vocabulary, improving the efficiency of oral English training, and formulating the training rules for oral English remote teaching. Promote the system to have the function of distance teaching and training of spoken English. At this point, the above content is converted into system coding, which completes the design of the training system for spoken English distance education.

# 4 System Testing

To test the spoken English distance teaching training system designed this time, a comparative experiment will be used to verify the spoken English distance teaching training system designed this time. In this system test experiment, the designed spoken English distance teaching training system was recorded as system A; the two traditional spoken English distance teaching and training systems were recorded as system B and system C respectively.

## 4.1 Experimental Preparation

Test the design of spoken English distance teaching training system, set the system test environment, as shown in Table 1.

**Table 1.** System test environment

| Test environment | Configuration | Parameter |
|---|---|---|
| Hardware environment | CPU | Pentium Quad Processor |
| | Memory Capacity | 2G |
| | Hard drive capacity | 250G |
| | Graphics card | Intel Integrated Graphics |
| Software environment | Operating system | Window XP SP2 |
| | Programming language | Java |

Based on the system test environment shown in Table 1, the test tools used to test whether the system can run normally are as follows: 1. Use LoadRunner performance test tool to test three groups of system performance and judge the system server performance; 2. Use winrunner auxiliary function test tool to check whether the system business function is correct; 3. Use TestDirector to monitor the system test process System testing process, tracking detection.

Use the three system detection tools shown above to detect the normal operation of the system. The detection process is as follows: 1. Login detection. Log in to the system and check whether the system's normal login status is consistent with the system's normal status; 2. Page detection. Test the system function interface, check whether the linked page is in a normal associated state; 3. Function detection. Check the function buttons on the page to confirm the execution result of each function button; 4. Interface detection. Check whether the system interface design is consistent with the user's usage habits and operating specifications; 5. Input processing monitoring. Check the input search function of the system, the system makes logical processing and judgment accuracy according to the input keywords; 6. Abnormal state detection. The system detects and prompts abnormal users; 7. Business process detection. System business process execution sequence and requirements description.

Based on the above design of the system detection process, the system test experiment is detected and three groups of test systems are selected. The test results show that: in this test experiment, the selected three groups of test systems, such as login status, page display, button link, interface display, input query, abnormal status prompt, business process and other basic performance of the system, are in normal state, and can be used for system test comparative experiment.

## 4.2 Experimental Result

### 4.2.1 System Performance Test

Based on the experimental design of the system test running environment, as well as the system test experimental object, the first group of system performance test experiments are carried out. Because the oral English distance teaching training system needs to record and store a large number of English words, there is a large number of visits and so on, which needs to bear more pressure and load. Therefore, in the running performance test experiment of the system, the LoadRunner performance test tool is used to generate virtual users to carry out oral English distance teaching training and test the system performance. In this group of experiments, a total of 600 virtual users were used to perform real-time operation on the three groups of systems. The initial virtual users were set to 200, and 100 virtual users were added every 20 min. The average response time, application server utilization rate and the number of system errors of the three groups of systems were compared. And let the LoadRunner performance test tool generate the system running performance test report. The comparison results are shown in Table 2.

**Table 2.** System operation performance test report

| Method | Number of concurrent users | Average response time | Application server usage | Number of system errors |
|---|---|---|---|---|
| A system | 200 | 0.003 s | 1% | 0 |
| | 300 | 0.02 s | 3% | 0 |
| | 400 | 0.12 s | 7% | 0 |
| | 500 | 0.30 s | 12% | 0 |
| | 600 | 0.42 s | 20% | 0 |
| B system | 200 | 0.011 s | 2% | 0 |
| | 300 | 0.05 s | 7% | 0 |
| | 400 | 0.26 s | 10% | 1 |

(*continued*)

**Table 2.** *(continued)*

| Method | Number of concurrent users | Average response time | Application server usage | Number of system errors |
|---|---|---|---|---|
| | 500 | 0.34 s | 15% | 1 |
| | 600 | 0.58 s | 26% | 2 |
| C system | 200 | 0.013 s | 2% | 0 |
| | 300 | 0.07 s | 5% | 0 |
| | 400 | 0.20 s | 9% | 0 |
| | 500 | 0.41 s | 18% | 1 |
| | 600 | 0.55 s | 24% | 1 |

As can be seen from Table 2, when the virtual users are between 200 and 600, the operation response time of the three groups of systems is also maintained between 0.003 and 1 s. However, the utilization rate of application server in system B reaches 26%, and when the virtual number of users reaches 400, there will be a system operation error, so the operation performance of system B is the worst; although the operation performance of system C is better than that of system B, the utilization rate of application server also reaches 24%. When the number of virtual users reaches 500, system operation error occurs; The average response time performance of system a is the worst. Although the response time continues to extend with the increase of the number of users, it is obviously the lowest among the three groups of systems. The utilization rate of application server has been maintained below 20%, and with the increase of the number of virtual users, there is no system error. It can be seen that the design of spoken English distance teaching training system, with a faster running speed, lower server utilization, can support more users and use the system at the same time.

### 4.2.2 Hardware Performance Comparison of System Server

On the basis of the first set of experiments, the third set of experiments was carried out. In the first set of experiments, the number of virtual people shown in Table 2, the average response time, application server utilization rate, and the number of system errors caused by the virtual number of people in the first group of experiments were counted. The Loadrunner performance test tool is used to test the system hardware performance, and TestDirector is used to track the test process of the test system. The comparison result of the server hardware performance is shown in Fig. 5.

As can be seen from Fig. 5, system B has the lowest utilization rate of server hardware resources. When the number of virtual users reaches 330, the server resource utilization rate reaches the highest, which affects the running speed of server hardware. When the number of virtual users reaches 250, the memory presents a horizontal line. Therefore, the server hardware of system B can only bear 250 people. Once the number of virtual users exceeds this number, a curve will appear The server hardware resource utilization ratio of system C is stronger than that of system B. However, when the number of virtual

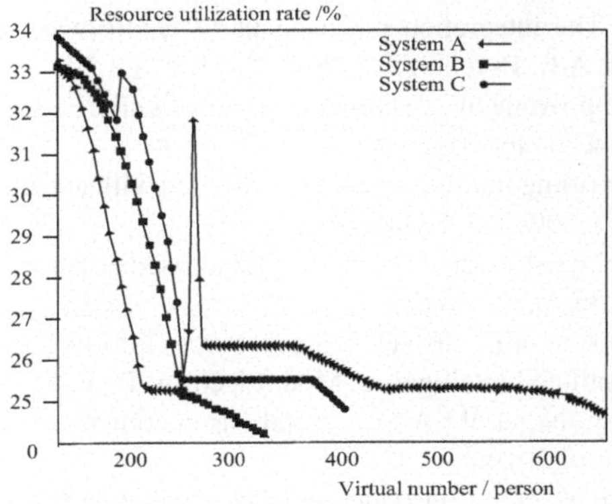


**Fig. 5.** Server hardware performance comparison chart

users exceeds 390, the memory line decreases, and the server resource utilization rate increases, which affects the operation speed of server hardware. Only when the number of virtual users is less than 390, the memory presents a horizontal line, which is normal In the running state, the maximum number of responders supported by system B is 390; while for system a, when the number of people exceeds 600, the memory line tends to decline, and the occupancy rate of server hardware shows an increasing state. Therefore, the maximum number of responders supported by system a is 600. From this, we can see that the number of people who visit the English system at the same time is the lowest.

## 5 Concluding Remarks

"Virtual reality" is a kind of computer system that can create and experience the virtual world. The various virtual environments generated by this system act on the user's vision, hearing and touch, and make the user feel immersive. The so-called virtual world is a collection of virtual environments or given simulation objects. Virtual reality is a new technology developed in recent years, At present, it has been widely used in many fields. Therefore, the design of oral English distance teaching training system, make full use of virtual reality technology, improve the system training students' oral English effect. However, the design of oral English distance teaching training system, has not been in-depth design of virtual reality scene changes, as well as its interactive function. Therefore, in the future design, we need to further design the virtual reality scene changes, as well as its interactive function, to further improve the popularity of the system, to help users overcome various difficulties in oral English learning.

## References

1. Li, L., Liu, B.: Design of oral English training system based on human-computer interaction. Mod. Electron. Tech. **43**(14), 135–137 (2020)
2. Lin, H.: Study on AI virtual English speaking training system for SELL corpus. Microcomput. Appl. **36**(7), 126–129 (2020)

3. Cai, X., Zhang, Q.: The integration mechanisms of feedforward and feedback control in speech motor system. Adv. Psychol. Sci. **28**(4), 588–603 (2020)
4. Wang, X., Ma, F.: Improvement of scoring system for children speaking English based on DNN. Inf. Technol. **44**(9), 46–50 (2020)
5. Fu, C., Xu, D.: A bus riding training system for children with autism based on virtual reality. Comput. Simul. **36**(6), 209–213, 231 (2019)
6. Wang, X.: Design of English aided instruction system based on personalized recommendation. Microcomput. Appl. **35**(5), 35–38 (2019)
7. Sang, H., Sun, X.: Design of English teaching resources information integrated management system of based on artificial intelligence. Mod. Electron. Tech. **43**(10), 173–175 (2020)
8. Liu, S., Bai, W., Zeng, N., et al.: A fast fractal based compression for MRI images. IEEE Access **7**, 62412–62420 (2019)
9. Liu, S., Li, Z., Zhang, Y., et al.: Introduction of key problems in long-distance learning and training. Mob. Netw. Appl. **24**(1), 1–4 (2019)
10. Liu, S., Glowatz, M., Zappatore, M., Gao, H., Jia, B., Bucciero, A. (eds.): eLEOT 2018. LNICSSITE, vol. 243. Springer, Cham (2018). https://doi.org/10.1007/978-3-319-93719-9

# Design of Online Education Decision Support System Based on Machine Learning

Shao-lin Liang[1(✉)] and Huan-wei Liang[2]

[1] College of Mathematics, Sichuan University of Arts and Science, Dazhou 635000, China
uhdsfd545@sina.com

[2] Huali College Guangdong University of Technology, Guangzhou 511325, China

**Abstract.** In view of the increase in the number of users in the traditional online education decision-making system, it is difficult to maintain a high level of practicality in long-distance communication. For this reason, the design of an online education decision support system based on machine learning is proposed. In the hardware design, the embedded SRAM is designed as the Cache of the system chip, and RS232 is used as the main communication chip; in the software design, based on the online education of multiple users, the online education support relationship model is designed, and the multi-objective online education decision-making is realized based on this model stand by. The experimental results show that the designed online education decision support system based on machine learning has stable long-distance communication, high maximum resource utilization, and its practicability has been improved.

**Keywords:** Machine learning · Online education · Decision support · Educational resource management

## 1 Introduction

The decision support system is a comprehensive computer system and related toolkits that assist managers in making decisions and solving problems. It is a PC application management system with a human-computer interaction interface and a semi-structured body with decision-making properties [1]. Its ultimate purpose is to improve the decision-making process by providing specific information needed for management, and it is an advanced information management system produced by the development of a management information system to a higher level [2].

Today, when information technology is widely used in the field of education, managers, teachers and learners who are responsible for decision-making are experiencing the experience of being submerged by the ocean of data, including education statistics, student statistics, and various social For surveys, examinations and assessment of information, decision makers "submerge in a sea of data, yet endure the thirst for information." A decision support system that integrates data mining technology can provide some help to solve this problem.


W. Fu et al. (Eds.): eLEOT 2021, LNICST 389, pp. 515–526, 2021.
https://doi.org/10.1007/978-3-030-84383-0_44

At present, the auxiliary decision-making system is developing rapidly abroad, which has attracted the special attention of foreign experts, especially educational scientists, who have invested a lot of effort in research, and some important academic groups have attached great importance to this system. For example, the International Information Federation not only organizes special academic conferences to discuss this topic, but also organizes and publishes special conference proceedings and sets up a special working group. In foreign universities, for example, the information retrieval system developed by the Technical University of Berlin not only uses fuzzy information processing methods to classify and queue retrieval objects, but also provides an interface for users to evaluate retrieval results and use the results as a basis. A new retrieval and sorting method is formed and stored in the system, which can be used directly next time [3].

In domestic distance education, decision support plays a very important role in online education. At this stage, many schools have applied online education decision support systems to meet their own needs, solving many problems in teaching management [4]. However, with the rapid development of information today, traditional online education decision support systems can no longer meet the actual needs of colleges and universities. With the increase in the number of students and the shortage of educational resources, traditional web-based online education decision support systems and cloud computing-based When the number of users increases, the online education decision support system is difficult to maintain a high level of communication quality, the resource utilization rate in decision support tasks is insufficient, and its overall practicality is relatively poor [5]. Therefore, an online education decision support system based on machine learning is proposed. The software design of the online education decision support system is realized through the design of embedded SRAM applications and communication functions, the online education support relationship model is designed, and the machine learning algorithm is used to achieve multiple Target online education decision support.

## 2 Hardware Design of Online Education Decision Support System Based on Machine Learning

The hardware design of the online education decision support system based on machine learning mainly includes two parts: the design of the embedded SRAM application program and the design of the communication function module. The following two parts are leased and designed.

### 2.1 Embedded SRAM Application Design

Embedded SRAM can greatly reduce the data exchange behavior between the embedded microprocessor and the off-chip memory, which not only speeds up the processor fetching instructions and data, but also reduces the number of times to access the external memory, thereby improving the overall system performance. Embedded SRAM applications in system chips can be roughly divided into two categories, one is as an on-chip cache (Cache), and the other is as a temporary memory Scratch-Pad memory (SPM) [6].

The access of the embedded microprocessor to the memory bank is not arbitrary and random, but has obvious regional characteristics. The analysis of a large number of typical program operation conditions shows that in a short time interval, the program addresses are usually concentrated in a small range. This is because the distribution of instruction addresses is originally continuous, and in addition, the cycle program segment and subprogram segment must be Repeated operation for many times, the access to these addresses must have a tendency of centralized distribution in time [7]. Therefore, in a small space-time range, the next instruction to be executed and the data to be processed are most likely to be in the vicinity of the previous instruction or data. This frequent access to the memory in the local range is called program/data Locality of the visit. Based on the principle of locality, a composite storage system can be constructed, including an on-chip memory with a small capacity but fast speed and a main memory with a large capacity but slow speed [8]. The small but fast on-chip memory is Cache, which can automatically save copies of instructions and data frequently used by the processor. The effectiveness of Cache depends on the spatial and temporal locality of the program. Cache and its control components and main memory together constitute an efficient Cache-main memory composite memory. In the Cache-main memory composite memory, programs and data are stored in the main memory. Cache only stores a copy of some programs and data blocks in the main memory. This block-based storage method is also based on the locality of program access [9]. The programs and data blocks in the Cache make most of the information that the embedded microprocessor needs to access have been stored in the Cache, and the read and write operations of the embedded microprocessor are mainly carried out between the embedded microprocessor and the Cache. When the embedded microprocessor accesses the storage level, it must determine whether there is a copy in the Cache. If there is a copy, it is called a hit, otherwise it is called a miss. When the Cache hits, read and write operations to the Cache immediately; when it does not hit, the embedded microprocessor directly turns to access the main memory. Cache is often used in conjunction with write buffer (write bui)er. The write buffer is a very small first-in first-out (FIFO) memory located between the Cache and the main memory. Its purpose is to free the processor core and Cache from slower main memory write operations.

The SPM is directly connected to the processor through the on-chip high-speed bus, occupies an address space exclusively, and stores some instructions and data. When the processor needs to read instruction data, it first determines the address space to select SPM or SDRAM. The former operates directly, while the latter requires access to SDRAM through an external memory interface module, which requires time sequence waiting and off-chip bus drive, which greatly affects system performance. Compared with SPM, Cache is more suitable for use in online education decision support systems.

## 2.2 Communication Function Design

In the system hardware design, the communication circuit is mainly designed and other parts are optimized for anti-interference. In the design of the remote communication function, RS232 is used as the main communication chip, which can be used at a data transmission rate of 0 to 20000 bps, while ensuring good communication quality [10]. For common control lines such as CTS, DTR, RTS, DSR, etc., the chip has an effective signal range between +3 V and +15 V. RS232 connector generally has three kinds of DB-9, DB-25 and DB-15 [11]. The DB-9 connector is used in the system remote communication, and the definition of each pin is shown in Table 1.

**Table 1.** RS232 pin definition

| Pin number | Function description | Abbreviation |
|---|---|---|
| 1 | Data carrier detection | DCD |
| 2 | Receive data | RXD |
| 3 | Send data | TXD |
| 4 | Data terminal | DTR |
| 5 | Signal ground | GND |
| 6 | Data equipment | DSR |
| 7 | Request to send | RTS |
| 8 | Clear to send | CTS |
| 9 | Ring indicator | BELL |

The serial communication protocol is mainly adopted in the system communication process to unify the data format and transmission parameters of both parties to ensure that the communication between the two parties is effective. The main parameters to be set are baud rate and data bits [12].

With the support of the RS232 serial port, the CAN communication implementation plan is designed. The core chip of the communication module is SN65HVD230, which mainly realizes the transmission and reception of data and signals. The device has good anti-interference ability [13]. Its pin arrangement and logic functions are shown in the Fig. 1 shown.

The device has good transceiver performance and different working modes at different speeds. The working modes are mainly divided into three types: high speed, slope and waiting. In actual work, the adjustment of the working mode can be achieved through the level of the Rs pin. The control logic of SN65HVD230 is shown in Table 2.

In the table, "?" means undecided state, Z means high resistance state, and X means irrelevant. In order to ensure that the communication maintains a high level and high quality even when the impedance is not continuous, two resistors are connected at both ends of the CAN bus to match the bus impedance with a resistance value of 120 [14].

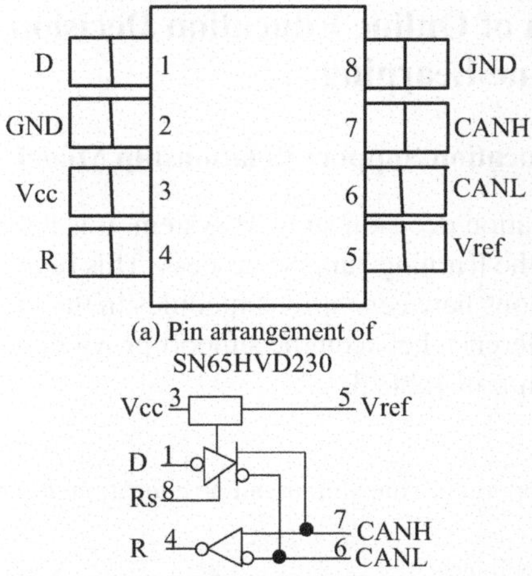


(a) Pin arrangement of SN65HVD230

(b) The logic function of SN65HVD230

**Fig. 1.** SN65HVD230 pin arrangement and logic function diagram

**Table 2.** Control logic of SN65HVD230

| Send | | | | | Receive | | |
|---|---|---|---|---|---|---|---|
| EnterD | Rs | Output | | Bus state | Differential input | Rs | OutputR |
| | | CANH | CANL | | | | |
| L | VRs ≤ 1.2V | H | L | Dominant | VID ≥ 0.9V | X | L |
| H | | Z | Z | Recessive | 0.5V < VID < 0.9V | X | ? |
| OPEN | X | Z | Z | Recessive | VID ≤ 0.5V | X | H |
| X | VRs ≥ 0.75VCC | Z | Z | Recessive | OPEN | X | H |

The reliability of communication is determined by many factors. For the improvement of anti-interference performance, certain anti-interference measures are taken in the power supply [15]. Because different modules within the system require different voltages, the required voltage is provided by a voltage regulator chip, and a switching power supply is used to power the system. On the one hand, it suppresses the noise that the load motor may generate, and on the other hand, it suppresses the instantaneous interference caused by the sudden change of the AC grid load. On this basis, add a filter at the power input to reduce noise or other interference. So far, the design of the hardware part of the system is completed, and the software part of the system is designed according to the actual needs of the user for the system.

# 3 Software Design of Online Education Decision Support System Based on Machine Learning

## 3.1 Design Online Education Support Relationship Model

In the entire online education decision support system, it is necessary to clarify several support relationships in the learning support process. This relationship will be the basis for establishing connections between various modules in the system.

According to the difference between the support provider and the recipient, we can get the support relationship in Table 3.

**Table 3.** Support classification in online education decision support

| Provider | Recipient | Support type |
|---|---|---|
| Subject teacher | Student | Subject support |
| Manager | Student | Non-disciplinary support |
| Student | Student | Subject support |
| School institution | Subject teacher management staff | Meta support |
| Support students | Support staff | |
| Student | Subject teacher management staff | Backfeeding support |

Subject teachers' support to students. This kind of support relationship is called subject support in the literature of distance education, and it has always been the focus of study support research.

Support for students from teaching management staff. In the distance education literature, this type of support is called non-disciplinary support. Due to the humanization of distance education in recent years, this type of support relationship has also received attention in recent years.

Mutual support between students. This type of support relationship is rarely discussed in traditional learning support theories, and it is probably more troublesome to realize this type of support relationship in the previous form of distance education. However, with the development of network communication technology, the realization of this type of support relationship appears to be very simple. At the same time, with the development of collaborative learning theory, the importance of this type of support has begun to emerge, and this type of support is also very concerned in this research. Support relationship.

School-running institutions provide support for subject teachers and teaching administrators. This type of support relationship is called "meta-support". It does not directly support students. However, modern distance education practices show that the necessary training should be provided for teachers and teaching administrators who directly provide learning support. It is an important part of improving the quality of learning support.

Support among supporters. We can classify this type of support as "meta-support". It is the experience of mutual exchange of learning support between people who provide learning support, and it is also conducive to the improvement of the quality of learning support.

Students' "backfeeding" to subject teachers and teaching administrators. This kind of support relationship is very peculiar. Its support direction is exactly the opposite of the traditional learning support direction. Its actual situation is that subject teachers and teaching administrators have learned some relevant things from students. According to these five support relationships, a relationship model for online education decision support can be obtained.

### 3.2 Multi-objective Online Education Decision Support

Based on the above-mentioned decision support relationship model, a multi-objective multi-objective decision-making model is established. Assuming that the set of decision-making methods for a certain problem of online education is $W = \{W_1, W_2, \ldots, W_n\}$, its purpose is to select the best plan from the $n$ plans, and set the attribute of the essential characteristics of the response plan to $\alpha$, with multiple levels, each level is the current The attributes of the level, the evaluation index of the next level, the attribute set of the first level is $G = \{G_{\alpha 1}, G_{\alpha 2}, \ldots, G_{\alpha n}\}$, and the attribute set of the next level is:

$$\begin{cases} G_{\alpha 1} = \{g_1, g_2, \ldots, g_n\} \\ \ldots\ldots \\ G_{\alpha n} = \{g_1, g_2, \ldots, g_n\} \end{cases} \tag{1}$$

By analogy, the attribute values at all levels of the multi-objective decision-making scheme are obtained. In the decision-making process, a group of experts composed of $m$ experts scored plan set $W$, and the experts' scores on each attribute of the $n$ plans were obtained, and the decision attribute matrix $U$ of each expert for $n$ plans was obtained:

$$U = \begin{bmatrix} U_{1m_1} & U_{1m_2} & \ldots & U_{1m_n} \\ U_{2m_1} & U_{2m_2} & \ldots & U_{2m_n} \\ \ldots & \ldots & \ldots & \ldots \\ U_{nm_1} & U_{nm_2} & \ldots & U_{nm_n} \end{bmatrix} \tag{2}$$

Matrix $U$ is a multi-level, multi-attribute multi-objective decision-making judgment matrix. When solving the decision problem, the decision matrix $W$ is normalized to $R = \left(r_{ij}\right)_{mn}$, namely:

$$R_{ij} = \begin{bmatrix} R_{11} & R_{12} & \ldots & R_{1n} \\ R_{21} & R_{22} & \ldots & R_{2n} \\ \ldots & \ldots & \ldots & \ldots \\ R_{m1} & R_{m2} & \ldots & R_{mn} \end{bmatrix} \tag{3}$$

In the above matrix, $R_{ij}$ is the attribute of the plan set. According to the normalized matrix obtained, the multi-objective comprehensive evaluation value of each decision plan is calculated, and the ranking is based on the score to obtain the best decision plan result. So far, the design of an online education decision support system based on machine learning is completed.

# 4 Experimental Research on Online Education Decision Support System

## 4.1 Experimental Platform Construction

In the experimental research on the online education decision support system, the CloudSim simulation platform was selected as the online education project simulation platform, and the designed machine learning-based online education decision support system, the traditional web-based online education decision support system and The online education decision support system based on cloud computing manages educational resources and supports decision-making, verifying the actual performance of different decision support systems under the same experimental conditions. The basic process of CloudSim simulation platform is shown in Fig. 2.

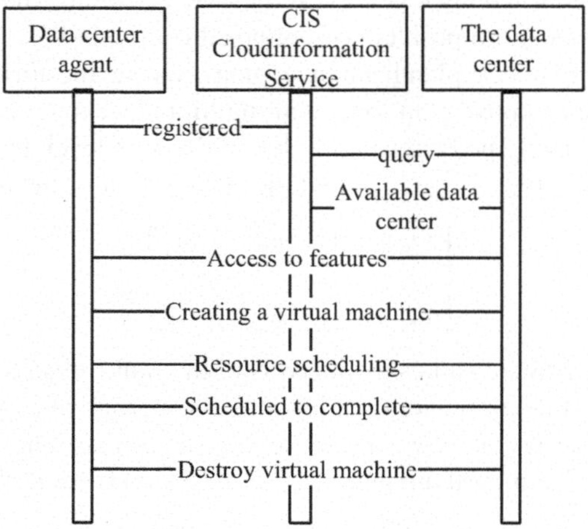


**Fig. 2.** CloudSim simulation platform construction process

Set the relevant parameters of the experiment before performing the experiment.

## 4.2 Experimental Parameter Settings

The virtual machine resource related parameter settings in the CloudSim simulation platform are shown in Table 4.

**Table 4.** Virtual machine resource parameter setting table

| Numbering | Processor | RAM (MB) | Bandwidth (Kbps) | Security level |
|---|---|---|---|---|
| 000 | 4 | 2048 | 500 | {3, 5, 2} |
| 001 | 2 | 2048 | 1000 | {5, 3, 1} |
| 002 | 1 | 2048 | 1000 | {1, 2, 5} |

*(continued)*

**Table 4.** (*continued*)

| Numbering | Processor | RAM (MB) | Bandwidth (Kbps) | Security level |
|---|---|---|---|---|
| 003 | 4 | 1024 | 800 | {2, 3, 4} |
| 004 | 4 | 1024 | 500 | {4, 4, 5} |
| 005 | 1 | 1024 | 600 | {3, 4, 5} |
| 006 | 2 | 512 | 700 | {3, 4, 5} |
| 007 | 1 | 1024 | 600 | {3, 4, 5} |
| 008 | 2 | 512 | 700 | {2, 4, 5} |
| 009 | 1 | 2048 | 1000 | {1, 2, 5} |

In the experiment, an online education decision support example is used to illustrate the actual performance of the designed decision support system and to verify its maximum resource utilization rate and communication signal stability. The resource parameters of each task of the electronic engineering project simulated by the experiment are shown in Table 5.

**Table 5.** Online education decision support resource parameter settings for each task

| Task number | User number | Emergency task | Resource demand per unit time |
|---|---|---|---|
| S | 249 | – | (0, 0, 0) |
| A | 193 | S | (4, 5, 7) |
| B | 157 | S | (2, 3, 4) |
| C | 56 | A | (4, 5, 6) |
| D | 89 | S | (1.1.2) |
| E | 182 | A, B | (3, 3, 4) |
| F | 261 | G, H | (4, 4, 6) |
| G | 308 | F | (2, 2, 3) |
| H | 409 | C, E | (3, 2, 6) |

After completing the above parameter settings, run different decision support systems to perform tasks, and compare the actual performance of different decision support systems with the goal of completing the communication stability and maximum resource utilization of the decision support tasks.

### 4.3 Remote Communication Experiment Results and Analysis

Use third-party software to monitor the communication process of different decision support systems, and output the signals generated by the system during the execution of decision support tasks to the interactive interface. The specific results are shown in Fig. 3.

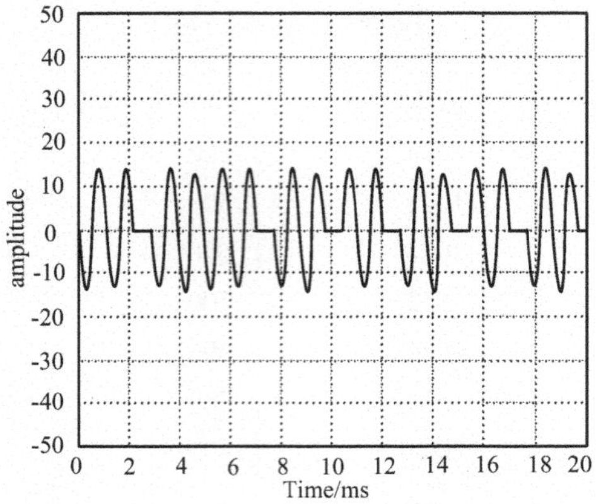


(a)Experimental results of web-based decision support system

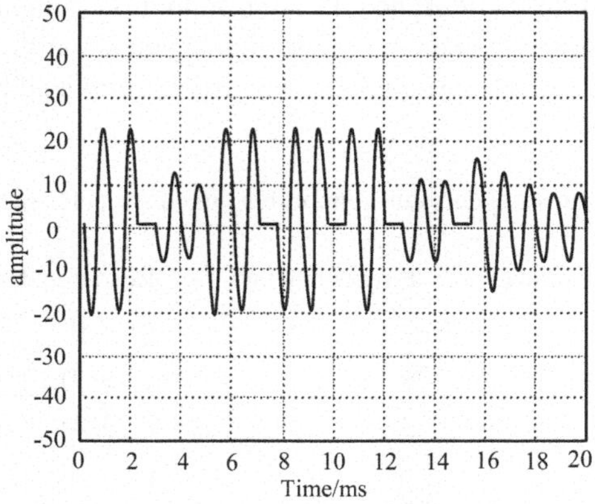


(b)Experimental results of decision support system based on cloud computing

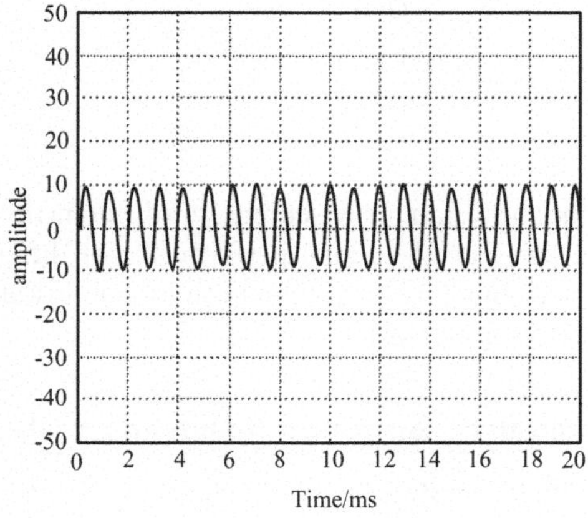


(c)Experimental results of decision support system based on machine learning

**Fig. 3.** Experimental results of communication stability of different decision support systems

Comparing the results in the observation graph, it can be seen from Fig. 3(a) that the signal is not continuous within the effective experimental time, and there is a short stagnant hole in the middle; the result in Fig. 3(b) shows that the signal is not only discontinuous, but the amplitude The size change is not stable; the result in Fig. 3(c) shows that the signal amplitude changes within a fixed range, and is always continuous and uninterrupted. In summary, the designed online education decision support system based on machine learning has more stable signals and better communication effects in long-distance communication.

### 4.4 Experimental Results and Analysis of Maximum Resource Utilization

According to the above results, the maximum resource utilization of different methods is calculated, and the calculation results are shown in Table 6.

**Table 6.** Calculation results of maximum resource utilization

| Method | Number of tasks in parallel | Maximum resource utilization |
|---|---|---|
| Web-based online education decision support system | 6 | 54.92% |
| Online education decision support system based on cloud computing | 7 | 69.36% |
| Online education decision support system based on machine learning | 10 | 99.62% |

It can be seen from the calculation results of the maximum resource utilization rate in the table that the designed decision support system has a large number of concurrent tasks and a high maximum resource utilization rate. Combining the above experimental results, it can be seen that the designed online education decision support system based on machine learning has stable long-distance communication, which can ensure that all resources are fully utilized in resource decision-making and avoid resource waste. The system is superior to traditional online decision-making systems.

## 5 Conclusion

This paper studies and designs an online education decision support system based on machine learning. After the design is completed, a number of comparative experiments have proved that the designed decision support system is more practical and solves the problems existing in traditional decision support systems. It provides certain technical support for future online education.

**Fund Projects.** "Excel application in finance" as the first-class online and offline undergraduate course in Sichuan Province in 2019; (2020KCC005) "Excel application in financial management" as the first-class course of Sichuan University of Arts and Sciences in 2020 (2020KCC005).

## References


1. Qian, D., Luo, A., Gu, Y.: Research on the design of provincial education science decision support system under the background of big data. Res. Educ. Dev. **38**(05), 68–74 (2018)
2. Zhu, Q., Wei, K., Diang, L., et al.: Count judgment decision support system based on text-mining and machine learning. Chinese J. Manag. Sci. **26**(01), 170–178 (2018)
3. Tang, X., Chen, H., Lu, Y.: Research on university data analysis and decision-making support system based on OLAP. Modern Electron. Tech. **42**(02), 155–158 (2019)
4. Zhong, W., Li, Z.: Research on network education system based on machine learning. J. Commun. **39**(S1), 135–140 (2018)
5. Sun, Z., Li, T., Xing, L., et al.: Design and implementation of high performance SIMT processor storage system for machine learning. Microelectron. Comput. **36**(08), 72–76 (2019)
6. Song, K., Li, C., Zhang, S.: Design and implementation of a lightweight distributed machine learning system. Comput. Eng. **46**(01), 201–207 (2020)
7. Chen, J., Wang, Z., Chen, J.-y., et al.: Design and research on intelligent teaching system based on deep learning. Comput. Sci. **46**(S1), 550–554+576 (2019)
8. Li, S., Li, R., Yu, C.: Evaluation model of distance student engagement: based on LMS data. Educ. Res. **24**(01), 91–102 (2018)
9. He, W.: Research on online educational resource crowdfunding based on knowledge-modeling diagram and its application in smart learning environment. E-educ. Res. **40**(04), 59–67 (2019)
10. Peng, Q.: Emergency decision support system demand data self-service mining simulation. Comput. Simul. **36**(08), 329–332 (2019)
11. Liu, S., Li, Z., Zhang, Y., et al.: Introduction of key problems in long-distance learning and training. Mobile Netw. Appl. **24**(1), 1–4 (2019)
12. Liu, S., Bai, W., Zeng, N., et al.: A fast fractal based compression for MRI images. IEEE Access **7**, 62412–62420 (2019)
13. Liu, S., Lu, M., Li, H., et al.: Prediction of gene expression patterns with generalized linear regression model. Front. Genet. **10**, 120 (2019)
14. Rodríguez, G.G., Gonzalez-Cava, J.M., Pérez, J.A.M.: An intelligent decision support system for production planning based on machine learning. J. Intell. Manuf. **31**(5), 1257–1273 (2020)
15. Saito, T., Watanobe, Y.: Learning path recommendation system for programming education based on neural networks. Int. J. Distan. Educ. Technol. **18**(1), 36–64 (2020)

# Design of Financial Management Teaching System Integrated with Online Micro Class

Zhen Li(✉) and Min Luo

SIAS University, Zhengzhou 451150, China

**Abstract.** In order to further improve the teaching quality of financial management courses in colleges and universities, the micro-class teaching system has been introduced. As a new type of curriculum resources, micro-course has the characteristics of simplicity and simplicity, which has injected new vitality into the development and development of education and teaching. Based on the characteristics of micro-course construction, this paper designs an open and interactive micro-course teaching system for financial management courses, including design objectives and principles, architecture, SQLServer2012 database, functional module design and so on. The test results show that under the application of the system, the function and performance can meet the teaching requirements, realize the multi-interactive sharing centered on teachers and students, and effectively improve the creativity and effectiveness of teaching activities in colleges and universities.

**Keywords:** Micro course · Financial management course · Teaching system

## 1 Introduction

With the continuous development of digital learning, multimedia has been widely used in traditional classrooms, and blended learning, which combines online learning with traditional classroom learning, has gradually become a learning trend. The characteristics of the network teaching system are that it can fully reflect the students' autonomous learning ability, can run through the concept of "autonomous learning" in the teaching process, provide a communication platform for teachers to "teach" and students to "learn", and become a "dual master" platform for students' autonomous learning with teachers as the main creator; in addition, it has good versatility, and can be suitable for the teaching of various disciplines; regardless of the user any knowledge of computer should be easy to use and safe enough. In order to ensure the correctness and security of the data and realize the distribution of time and space, the website content released to the outside world should adopt protection measures such as identity authentication and upload content authentication [1]. These characteristics make the network teaching system and micro class can be well combined, using the network teaching system as the support platform of micro class. As a mode of blended learning, micro class integrates traditional classroom learning and online learning. The implementation of micro class


W. Fu et al. (Eds.): eLEOT 2021, LNICST 389, pp. 527–540, 2021.
https://doi.org/10.1007/978-3-030-84383-0_45

should be based on technical tools and information resources. So the network teaching system is used as the teaching platform of micro class. Through the network teaching system to provide learning support for micro class.

As an important professional basic course of business administration, financial management has not been taught online. The 21st century is an information and learning society. The Internet based distance learning will become a main way for people to learn. Therefore, it is necessary to carry out computer-aided instruction based on the Internet, give full play to the educational function of network, and reform the teaching methods. Therefore, a teaching system for financial management course integrated with online micro class was designed. The online teaching system of financial management course can not only provide students with distance learning, but also provide teachers with auxiliary teaching in the network classroom. It not only realizes the browsing of static web page, but also realizes the dynamic and interactive web page.

## 2 General Objectives and Principles of System Design

### 2.1 Overall Objective

The overall goal of this system design is to build a system platform suitable for multi course teaching for financial management micro course. As the basic platform for the implementation of financial management micro course, the network teaching system has the following functions:

(1) Help teachers organize and present curriculum and teaching resources effectively. Classroom learning needs to provide teaching videos and other available learning resources [2].
(2) Create a personalized learning environment. The system can record information about students' learning process, such as online learning time, practice right and wrong. So that teachers can quickly understand the students' learning situation and difficulties, and then can design effective teaching activities in the classroom can give students targeted guidance.
(3) Create a collaborative environment for interaction and communication. The system can expand the interaction in the classroom to the network space, so as to increase the time and effect of teacher-student interaction. Relying on the network teaching system, students can easily establish a learning community and cooperate to complete the learning task.

### 2.2 System Design Principles

Students are the main body, teachers are the leading principle. Constructivist learning theory holds that learning is an active process of learning to construct knowledge. Therefore, when building the system platform, we need to design the system based on the roles of students and teachers, which reflects the dominant position of students' autonomous learning. At the same time, we should also emphasize the leading role of teachers in blended learning and the identity of organizers and instructors [3]. Teachers can better provide help for students' active learning and improve the efficiency of teaching.

Teachers guide and help the learning process by organizing learning materials, tutoring, answering questions and evaluating.

The principle of network openness. The system supports students and teachers to access the network system platform through a variety of network access ways, and also supports teachers and administrators to manage teaching through the Internet at any time and place with their user name and password.

Support a variety of teaching strategy principles. The micro teaching of financial management is different from the traditional classroom teaching of transmission and acceptance, and also different from the network course of completely autonomous learning. The development and design of network teaching system for financial management micro course should be able to reflect these new ideas and methods, and support exploratory and research-based learning, collaborative learning, debating learning, etc. The teaching system should not only support the teaching strategies of network learning, but also support the teaching strategies of class teaching, and provide the relevant tools to implement these teaching strategies [4].

The principle of user interaction. The system should be able to provide students with high-quality video, but also provide rich interaction. Students can know right and wrong in practice before class, and get tips and help in difficult situations. The teacher answers the students' difficult questions online, reviews the students' homework online and feeds back the results to the students.

The principle of simplicity is applied. The interface design should be clear and easy to operate. Because the use of the object is mainly by primary and secondary school students, especially primary school students, complex operation will affect their learning attention, even unable to continue learning. Through synchronous data access technology, reduce the client's access to the database, so that users feel convenient and fast in operation.

# 3 System Architecture Design

## 3.1 B/S Architecture

Before building the teaching system of financial management course, we must make clear the development architecture of the system, which determines the technology choice. The current development architecture includes B/s and C/S, and different types have different application scope. The system based on B/S is easy to maintain, and the system based on C/S mode needs to develop client, which is difficult to develop, but the advantage is stable performance. B/S structure is mainly through the network to achieve business processing, and the browser as the client, do not need to develop a separate client, while C/S structure is mainly applied in the LAN, need to develop an independent client, the workload is relatively large.

B/S structure and C/S structure have different application scope and characteristics

(1) Compared with C/S structure, the application of B/S structure is more flexible, and the business processing is more convenient. For users, the system built under B/S structure is easier to use, and there is no need to install another client. You can directly use the browser to complete the business processing.

(2) After the system based on B/S structure provides services through the network, any user can connect to the network for business processing without additional installation of clients, which can reduce the burden of users. Compared with B/S architecture, C/S architecture system is not without advantages, its processing speed is slow, and the stability is relatively high, can better manage the client. However, the defects are also obvious, the development costs and maintenance cost are relatively high, and the subsequent maintenance will cost more energy [5].

As for the financial management course teaching system integrated into online micro class, there is a perfect network environment inside the school. In the school, the content is processed through the LAN, while outside the school, users use the browser to process the teaching management business through the network. Based on the above characteristics, the teaching system of the financial management course is based on a B/S structure, which helps to improve the teaching quality of the school.

### 3.2 J2EE Platform

Java EE is a set of enterprise application platform specifications developed and launched by Sun company, full name: Java Platform Enterprise Edition, its previous version is called J2EE. It integrates web services, component models, management and communication APIs, and can help us quickly develop and deploy portable, robust, scalable and secure server-side Java applications. It is often used to implement enterprise level service-oriented architecture (SOA) and web applications. The typical Java EE specification defines four levels, namely customer layer, web layer, enterprise component EJB layer, and enterprise resource layer [6, 7].

(1) Client layer: J2EE platform can be used to build the current mainstream application system based on B/S mode and C/S mode. The client layer is mainly used to develop the system of C/S mode. In order to build the system of C/S mode, the client layer of J2EE platform provides swing components.
(2) Web layer: web layer is mainly used to build the system of B/S mode, which provides HTML and JSP technology. The web system built before usually needs to embed Java code in the HTML page. This mode is not only inefficient in development, but also difficult to maintain. Later, it is optimized and improved to separate the two, and the web layer focuses on accepting requests.
(3) Business layer: the business layer is the core, which is mainly used to process various business requests. The technology used in this layer is Java. All business requests need to be processed by the business layer. After the processing, all the results have two directions. The first is to transmit to the web layer or the client layer for display, and the other is to store to the database. At present, there are many boxes in the business layer Shelf technology is used to improve efficiency, such as spring framework.
(4) EIS layer: EIS layer is mainly used to store data and information, which supports the information system to use various types of databases, such as MySQL database and Oracle database.

### 3.3 Framework Design

This project adopts a typical B/S architecture to design, and uses J2EE multi-layer architecture design to realize online teaching system. In this way, the cohesion and integrity between modules are strengthened, the scalability and portability of the system are greatly improved, and the maintenance cost is reduced [8, 9]. In the web interface, Zhongwei users present an efficient, concise and good operation interface. The system architecture of the system is shown in Fig. 1.

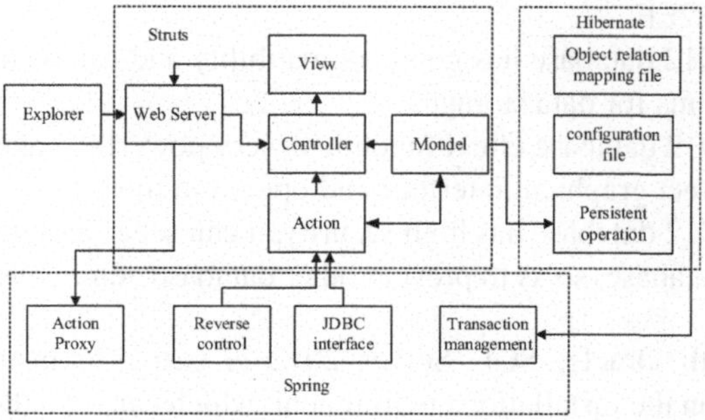


**Fig. 1.** System architecture chart

As can be seen from Fig. 1, the overall architecture of the system adopts struts as the framework basis, which is mainly responsible for the separation of model view controller. Hibernate provides persistence services, while spring is responsible for transaction processing and working logic. The whole design adopts the idea of object-oriented, according to the needs of the system to get the basic objects, and then make the corresponding Dao implementation for each object to achieve the function of accessing the database. Finally, spring completes the work logic and transaction processing.

## 4 SQL Server 2012 Database

SQL Server 2012 is a relational database management system management system (RDBMS) is designed and developed by Microsoft. Because of its powerful functionality, flexibility and rich application programming interface, it is deeply loved by free software lovers and commercial software developers, and has become one of the most popular relational database management systems [10, 11]. Benefited from its extremely sophisticated system structure and index design, the data is stored in different tables instead of centralized storage in a big data warehouse, which greatly improves the speed of data access and improves the flexibility. SQL Server 2012 database still uses the international standard query language (SQL for short), but it also provides many kinds of storage engines to support the application needs of different users. At present, it is divided into community version and commercial version. Because of its small size, faster speed, lower cost, especially its open source characteristics, it is widely used in the current Internet application development. Based on the above characteristics, this topic chooses SQL Server 2012 database as the data storage platform of online teaching system.

SQL Server 2012 database has many advantages compared with other databases, as follows:

(1) SQL Server 2012 database does not need high-performance server as support, although it consumes a small amount of memory, but its performance is outstanding.
(2) SQL Server 2012 database has a good openness. At present, the widely used technologies can be used with SQL Server 2012 database to build the system, including C++, C # and J2EE.
(3) SQL Server 2012 database has good compatibility and can be deployed in various operating systems for data storage.
(4) SQL Server 2012 database client function is very powerful, easy to use, the system provides a perfect graphical interface and operation tips.
(5) SQL Server 2012 database has high security, it can set access permissions for each independent database, so as to prevent other database administrators from viewing data directly.
(6) Compared with Oracle, SQL Server 2012 is easier to install and has lower requirements on the installation environment, which can save the deployment cost.
(7) SQL Server 2012 has a good interface design, easy to use, users can master the use of the database in a short time.

It can be seen from the above description that SQL Server 2012 has many characteristics which are consistent with the requirements of building a financial management course teaching system. Based on the above reasons, the financial management course teaching system integrated into online micro class uses SQL Server 2012 database to store teaching resource information and personnel information.

# 5 Functional Module Design

The financial management course teaching system integrated into online micro class includes comprehensive business process and detailed functions. According to the current situation, through the full investigation of teachers, students and various departments involved in teaching, the functional requirements are formed, including data entry, modification, query, generation and so on. The system provides a visual window with powerful data query function [12]. From a macro point of view, the financial teaching system is a set of classroom teaching, simulation training and teaching management functions as one of the teaching system.

## 5.1 System Setup Function Module

**User login**

The user login interface is mainly used to manage the basic information of the user, including the registration of the user and the login permission. For the users who have no permission to log in, they need to register to get the permission to log in and use the system.

The interface consists of two text boxes and two buttons. The text box is used to input the user name and password. The user's identity information such as account number and password can be verified by comparing with the information accessed in the database. If it is correct, the information can be browsed and operated. If it is incorrect, that is to say, the system does not have the user information, you need to register the user. If the user name and password are verified successfully, you can directly enter the system for operation.

The key of the user login interface is to verify the user registration information such as user name and password. The modification function can be realized by calling the recorded information in the database to compare with the login information.

**Password Management**

The system provides the function of user password management. The password is saved in the binary file after a certain algorithm. Even if you use the software to edit the file, you can't find that the password module has no clear output. Therefore, you must verify the user's identity information before you can change the original password by clicking the change password button. In addition, if the user forgets the original password, the password can be retrieved through the password protection problem set when registering the user.

The password management interface is mainly used to modify and retrieve the password. The user can modify the password by changing the original saved information in the database through the change request.

**System User Management**

The system user management is to manage the user information and authority of the whole system. This function module can realize the operation of adding, deleting and modifying user information. At the same time, it can set the authority of corresponding users, and it can set different permissions of different subsystems.

(1) Add: add a new user and add the permission of an existing user. This permission can only be completed by the system administrator.
(2) Delete: delete the existing users and delete the permissions of the existing users. This permission can only be completed by the system administrator.
(3) Modify: change the information of existing users and update the permissions of existing users. This update is operated according to the permissions of different users.

## 5.2 Teaching Function Modules

The teaching function of the system can improve the learning flexibility of financial management major, and teachers can make teaching plans according to the talent training plan before class. Through this function, teachers and students can interact in class, choose courses, exchange homework, upload and download courseware.

Teachers and students need to register before using the system, input the basic information, and complete the information, then the registration is successful. Each teacher and student has a unique number in the system, which is convenient for the administrator to manage. They can only use the unique identity and password to log in to the system. Teacher users can add, delete courses, set courses; query students who choose courses; teachers initiate classroom interaction, put forward discussion topics and reply to students' questions; teachers upload learning resources such as adding, deleting and querying courseware to view students' homework. Student users can enter the selected course learning, enter the teacher's classroom interactive topic, answer the teacher's questions, or ask the teacher for answers; students can query and download the courseware uploaded by the teacher; complete the homework.

(1) Classroom interaction
The system has the classroom interaction function between teachers and students. According to the psychological characteristics of students, it is convenient for students to put forward problems in time and effectively in the process of learning and interacting with teachers. It is conducive to teachers to find students' shortcomings in class and improve them. Teachers can initiate questions and manage them. Students can participate in them and submit their own opinions [13].
(2) Course selection
Teachers can use the system to add courses and manage them. They can modify and delete the courses. Students can get credits after completing the corresponding study by selecting courses, adding courses and learning.
(3) Homework exchange
Teachers can issue assignments and notices, students can browse assignments and notices, teachers and students, students and students communicate and discuss with each other and other intelligent management.
(4) Courseware upload and download

The teaching function provides teachers with the function of uploading and downloading courseware, and timely updating. Teachers can use corresponding resources in classroom teaching, such as classroom presentation slides. At the same time, teachers can also modify and delete the resource. Student users can only download, not add or delete.

### 5.3 Financial Management Practice Management Module

Financial management business training management module as the core of the system, mainly through the integration of real cases, with a listed company's three-year financial data as the background, combined with the brief introduction of the enterprise, the main production products, enterprise production capacity and market conditions, enterprise organizational structure, enterprise human resource status, corporate governance structure, enterprise financial personnel organizational structure, corporate governance structure, enterprise financial personnel organizational structure Risk response plan, enterprise accounting policies, guidelines, financial system and three years of various financial statements, so that students can carry out "on-site financial management" according to these detailed information.

(1) Financial environment: it mainly realizes the setting of financial environment in different situations, makes users familiar with the financial environment, and provides the basis for subsequent decision-making according to the financial environment.
(2) Financial analysis: it mainly realizes the function of analyzing all kinds of report data, including balance sheet analysis, income statement analysis and cash flow statement analysis, and provides analysis models of other indicators.
(3) Financial forecast in planning period: according to the enterprise background and report data, make long-term financial budget for the enterprise through specific analysis and decision-making.
(4) Fund raising management: according to various background information of the enterprise, it can reasonably determine the fund gap, formulate dividend policy, and finally determine the capital demand. Combined with current asset management and enterprise working capital raising policy, it can analyze various capital costs and advantages and disadvantages of short-term and long-term financing channels, and finally give the most appropriate financing decision of the enterprise.
(5) Project investment management: according to the enterprise financial objectives and fund-raising situation, put forward a number of project investment plans, and carefully analyze the plans, and finally make decisions.

### 5.4 Information Management Function

Through the system, teaching administrators can master college information, professional information, teacher information, class information, student information, achievement information, news information, etc. Assist the school teaching development center and each professional teaching and research section to formulate the corresponding teaching plan to meet the basic business work.

(1) College Information Management
Administrators can add college information and manage it. Establish the information of each college, with a unique number for each college, and add the college name, establishment date, Dean's name, contact number, etc. To facilitate future queries, in the college information management, you can query the corresponding college information. Only administrators can add, modify and delete college information. Teachers and students can only join the selected college.
(2) Professional information management
Administrators can add professional information and manage it. Establish the information of each specialty, and add each specialty number, specialty name, college, establishment date, contact person, contact number, etc. In the specialty information management, you can query and filter the corresponding specialty information. Only administrators have the authority to add, modify and delete professional information. Teachers and students can only join the selected professional learning.
(3) Teacher information management
Administrators can add teacher information and manage it. Establish the electronic file of each teacher, and add teacher information: name, gender, date of birth and other basic information. Each teacher has a unique number. Only administrators can add, modify and delete teacher information.

(4) Class information management
Administrators can add class information and manage class information. Establish the information of each class, and add each class number, class name, major, establishment date, head teacher, contact number, etc.; administrators and teachers can add, modify and delete class information, and students can join the class for learning.
(5) Student information management
Administrators can add student information and manage it. Establish the electronic file of each student, and add the student's number, name, gender, class, date of birth and other basic information; administrators and teachers can add, modify and delete the student's information, and train the students in groups.
(6) Achievement information management

The administrator can add and manage the score information. Add student's grade information, student's name, course grade score and evaluation, etc.; administrators and teachers can add, modify and delete grade information to query and filter student's grade information.

# 6 System Testing and Analysis

System testing is an essential part in the process of system development. After the completion of the system design, before it is put into use, it needs to carry out system testing. Through repeated system testing and system modification, the final design of the system is completed.

The purpose of system testing is to find the deficiencies of the system and verify whether the system meets the initial requirements analysis. After finding out the shortcomings of the system, they modify it, then continue to test the system, test and modify it repeatedly, and finally improve the system to meet the needs of users. The quality and stability of the teaching platform of financial management course depend on the design and implementation of the system. Whether the designed system is easy for students to learn,

To be able to facilitate the use of teachers in teaching, these are issues to be considered. Therefore, in the testing stage, we should focus on these aspects of testing, to improve.

## 6.1 System Operating Environment

(1) Server:

- Minimum hardware requirements
  CPU: PIII 450.
  Memory: 256M.
  Hard disk space: 500M.
- Software requirements
  Operating system: Windows 2000 Server.
  Web Service: IIS 5.0
  Database: MS SQL Server 7.0
  (2) Client:

- Minimum hardware requirements
  CPU: P166.
  Memory: 64M.
  Hard disk space: 100M.
- Software requirements

  Operating system: Windows 95 / 98 / NT / 2000.
  Browser: ie 4.0 or above.

### 6.2 System Test Topology

The system test topology is shown in Fig. 2.

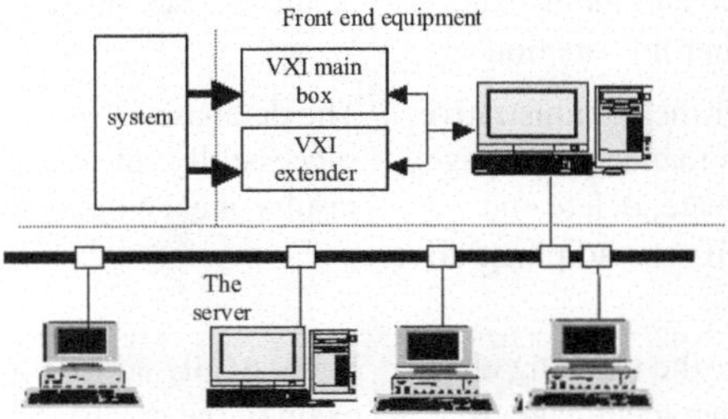


**Fig. 2.** Topology of System Test

### 6.3 Test Methods

Function testing is mainly manual testing. First of all, we need to analyze the functional requirements of online teaching systems, and build test cases according to the functional characteristics. In the test stage, there are different test methods. This paper uses the black box test method. The advantage of black box test method is that it doesn't need to understand the internal logic of the function, just need to know whether the input data can get the corresponding results. This test method is simple and effective.

Performance testing can not be handled manually, so we must borrow performance testing tools to simulate user operating system in order to complete performance testing. Especially when simulating large-scale users for stress testing, the method of increasing the number of concurrent users can be adopted until the performance target is achieved. In the performance test, we need to focus on the response speed of the system, CPU utilization, in order to get the final test results.

### 6.4 Functional Test Results

The information management function module is selected for the function test, and the function test results are shown in Table 1.

It can be seen from Table 1 that the expected results of the function are met.

**Table 1.** Test results

| Test title | Educational administration | Test results | Are the expected results met |
|---|---|---|---|
| Participation roles | Administrators and teachers | The database successfully saved the information results after the operation | Yes |
| Test object | Educational administration page | The database successfully saved the results of each operation | Yes |
| Testing procedure | Enter the teacher management page to add, delete and modify the teacher information | The database successfully saved the results of each operation | Yes |
| | Enter the administrative class management page to create, delete and modify the administrative class | The database successfully saved the results of each operation | Yes |
| | Enter the teaching class management page to create, delete and modify the administrative class | Successfully added an exam to the database | Yes |
| | Enter the test management page to add, delete and modify the test | The parameters of the system have been changed successfully | Yes |
| | Enter the examination management page and add an examination | Test results | Yes |
| | Enter the system parameter setting page to add basic system parameters | The database successfully saved the information results after the operation | Yes |

### 6.5 Performance Testing

In the process of testing, LoadRunner software is mainly used for simulation testing. According to the performance requirements, it needs to meet 500 users to complete concurrent access within 3S. The test results are shown in Table 2.

It can be seen from Table 2 that 500 users have completed concurrent access within 3S, meeting the system performance requirements.

**Table 2.** System performance test results table

| User | Response time (s) |
|---|---|
| 50 | 1.34 |
| 100 | 1.44 |
| 200 | 1.54 |
| 250 | 1.54 |
| 300 | 1.58 |
| 350 | 1.72 |
| 400 | 1.97 |
| 450 | 2.10 |
| 500 | 2.34 |

## 7 Conclusion

In the traditional teaching method of financial management course, there are some problems that students have difficulty understanding some principles and concepts at the beginning stage, which leads to the problems of poor learning effect and insufficient practice time under the premise of setting the total class time. Therefore, this paper introduces the micro-course into the financial management course teaching system, makes the students' learning process more colorful, realizes the multimedia, information, interactive and efficient teaching of financial management, makes the financial management teaching process more interesting and vivid, increases the students' fun in the learning process, promotes the teacher's teaching, and improves the classroom quality. The next step is to apply this system to more types of courses to further improve and optimize the existing system.

## References

1. Lee, S., Kim, T., Han, G., et al.: Design of 20 Nm3/h class liquid organic hydrogen carrier system integrated with electrolyzer and fuel cell. ECS Trans. **96**(1), 149–156 (2020)
2. Wang, R., Yu, C., Wang, J.: Construction of supply chain financial risk management mode based on Internet of Things. IEEE Access **7**(99), 110323–110332 (2019)
3. Zhiwu, S., Xiangping, Z., Cheng, L., et al.: Design of micropipette system with high precision for small enzyme immunoassay analyzer. J. Shanghai Jiaotong Univ. (Sci.) **24**(5), 605–615 (2019)
4. Chen, X., et al.: Thermodynamic and economic assessment of a PEMFC-based micro-CCHP system integrated with geothermal-assisted methanol reforming - ScienceDirect. Int. J. Hydrogen Energy **45**(1), 958–971 (2020)
5. Karimi, M.H., Chitgar, N., Emadi, M.A., et al.: Performance assessment and optimization of a biomass-based solid oxide fuel cell and micro gas turbine system integrated with an organic Rankine cycle. Int. J. Hydrogen Energy **45**(11), 6262–6277 (2020)
6. Qing, T., Duan, X., et al.: Teaching expansion analysis based on computer assisted diversified teaching. Cluster Comput. **22**(6), 13739–13744 (2019)

7. Fu, W., Liu, S., Srivastava, G.: Optimization of big data scheduling in social networks. Entropy **21**(9), 902 (2019)
8. Sutil, F.J.S., la Casa Hernández, J.D., Ortega, A.C.: Power factor compensation using teaching learning based optimization and monitoring system by cloud data logger. Sensors **19**(9), 2172 (2019)
9. Alshehri, A., Rutter, M.J., Smith, S.: An Implementation of the UTAUT model for understanding students' perceptions of learning management systems: a study within tertiary institutions in Saudi Arabia. Int. J. Dist. Educ. Technol. **17**(3), 1–24 (2019)
10. Liu, S., Li, Z., Zhang, Y., et al.: Introduction of key problems in long-distance learning and training. Mob. Networks Appl. **24**(1), 1–4 (2019)
11. Shahzad, A., Zafrullah, M., Islam, M.K.: Design and simulation of double side band optical carrier suppression (DSBSC) based millimeter wave system using optical sub carrier multiplication. J. Opt. **49**(2), 155–162 (2020)
12. Liu, S., Glowatz, M., Zappatore, M., et al. (eds.): e-Learning, e-Education, and Online Training, pp. 1–374. Springer, Cham (2018). https://doi.org/10.1007/978-3-319-49625-2
13. Tamburri, D.A., Casale, G.: Cognitive distance and research output in computing education: a case-study. IEEE Trans. Educ. **62**(2), 99–107 (2019)

# Design of Online Teaching System for Financial Management Course Based on Cloud Platform

Min Luo(✉) and Zhen Li

SIAS University, Zhengzhou 451150, China

**Abstract.** The traditional online teaching system of financial management courses can only be two-way contact between teachers and students. It is difficult to realize the rich teaching resources shared in modern society, and it is also difficult to give play to the subjective initiative of students' learning, so the online teaching system of the financial management course is designed based on the cloud platform. Design the hardware of online teaching system of financial management course, including the main controller power circuit and analog-to-digital conversion module. Based on the cloud platform, the online teaching system software of financial management course is designed, the cloud platform database module in the system deployment is improved, and the courseware on demand system with cloud service as the center is designed. Design experiments to test the function of the online teaching system, and check the completion of its online management function, online teaching management function, authority management function and online examination function. And test the network data security of the teaching system, the ability of different numbers of users online at the same time, the response time in the process of login, communication and teaching.

**Keywords:** Cloud platform · Financial management course · Online teaching · Teaching system

## 1 Introduction

In order to enrich students' vision, increase students' learning resources, and give play to students' subjective initiative, the cloud platform is applied to the online teaching system of financial management course. Through the teaching system, teachers can share teaching resources, optimize the allocation of teaching resources and improve teaching efficiency. The system is built on the cloud platform, which combines private cloud and public cloud to provide stable services for students and teachers [1]. The system introduces database connection pool technology and video on demand cloud technology. Database connection pool technology can ensure that students and teachers can use the teaching system in PC, mobile devices or desktop computers; video on demand cloud technology can ensure the fluency and intelligence of courseware on demand on the website. The system provides teachers with system management, performance management, student management, class management, curriculum management, examination


W. Fu et al. (Eds.): eLEOT 2021, LNICST 389, pp. 541–552, 2021.
https://doi.org/10.1007/978-3-030-84383-0_46

management, homework management, professional management, online Q & A and other functions, and provides students with online learning, online examination, online homework, online communication functions. According to the data information required by the whole digital teaching platform, the specific database table structure is designed to form a systematic and standardized relational database, which can record the changes of data in real time and complete the data persistence operation.

## 2 Design the Hardware of Online Teaching System for Financial Management Course

### 2.1 Design the Main Controller Power Circuit

In the main controller, using single-chip microcomputer as the power supply facilities of the power supply circuit has the advantages of short development cycle, small volume, strong control function, low power consumption, strong adaptability to the environment, flexible expansion and convenient use [2]. In this paper, the minimum system of single chip microcomputer is used as the system device of the main controller. Stc89 MCU minimum system mainly includes MCU, clock circuit, reset circuit and power supply. From the perspective of the design of the online teaching system, the understanding of the minimum system of a single chip microcomputer is the basis of learning a single chip microcomputer. Through the minimum system, we can understand the most basic principle of the system. The stc89 microcontroller and other compatible microcontrollers all have a function: after the microcontroller is reset, the program starts from the ooooh address of the internal ROM; when it is connected to the low level, the program starts from the ooooh address of the external ROM directly after reset [3]. Because when using this series of MCU, the user program of MCU is written in the ROM of MCU, so the pin is connected to high level in the minimum system.

SCM power supply is a very important module, the stable work of power supply is an important guarantee for the stable operation of SCM. Because there are many 220 V switching power supplies on the market and the price is low, in order to save the cost, the online teaching system design in this paper does not design the power circuit in the system, but through a 220 V power interface, as shown in Fig. 1.

Most single-chip microcomputer and related systems use regulated power supply, which can meet the needs of the stable work of the system. Therefore, it is very necessary to design a DC regulated power supply for single-chip microcomputer. For the online teaching system designed in this paper, the required voltage is 220 v. The online teaching system designed in this paper does not include the previous design of rectifier and 220 V voltage regulator, but this part of hardware facilities is essential in the real teaching process, otherwise there will be stuck, flashback and other phenomena [4].

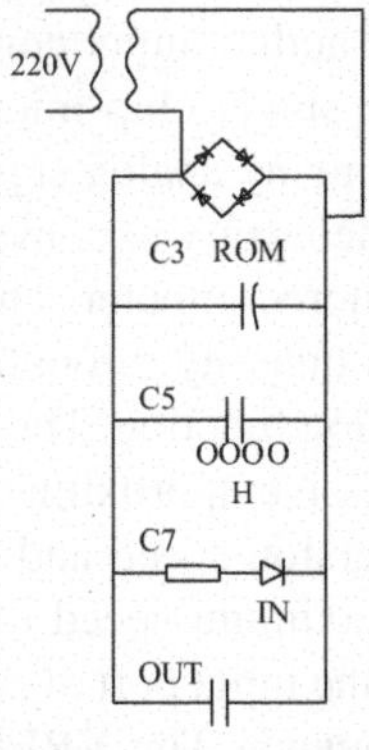


**Fig. 1.** Schematic diagram of power supply principle

## 2.2 Design A/D Conversion Module

The chip of A/D and D/A conversion in the online teaching system of financial management course designed in this paper is pcf8591. The hardware circuit of A/D and D/A conversion in this system is shown in Fig. 2.

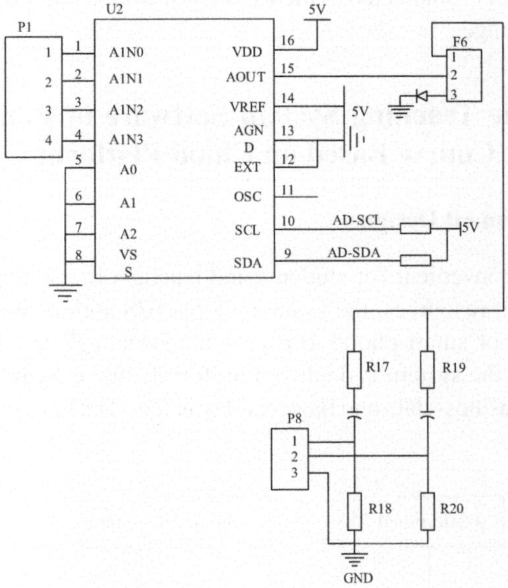


**Fig. 2.** Schematic circuit diagram of pcf8591

As shown in Fig. 2, pcf8591 is a chip with two functions of A/D and D/A conversion. In the experiment of A/D module, the analog voltage input in the schematic diagram is not connected, so the potential within the acquisition range can be connected for acquisition. The results of A/D acquisition can be observed through LCD and other display devices. The LED light and audio output connected to the D/A output port can verify the experimental effect. The single chip microcomputer system can't read the analog signal directly, but there are many analog signals in engineering projects [5, 6]. In order to read analog signal, it is necessary to convert analog signal into digital signal which can be read by single chip microcomputer. The purpose of A/D conversion is to convert analog quantity into digital quantity through a certain circuit. This paper uses pcf8591 chip to realize A/D conversion function. The chip has four 8-bit A/D conversion inputs. A/D converter adopts successive approximation conversion technology, which has the characteristics of fast conversion speed and high precision. The speed of A/D conversion is determined by the maximum speed of IIC bus communication. In A/D conversion operation, a1n0-a1n3 is the input port of A/D, which can simulate the change of analog voltage through potentiometer. The VREF reference voltage of the chip is directly connected to the power supply, so the resolution of A/D is 220 V/256. The interface of SDA and SCL is connected to MCU I/O to realize the communication between A/D conversion chip and IIC bus of MCU.

In order to control some analog parameters, MCU needs to output analog parameters. In order to solve this problem, we need to use D/A conversion technology. In this paper, the D/A conversion function is also realized by pcf8591 chip, which has one 8-bit D/A conversion output. About is the D/A conversion output port of the chip. The hardware configuration of related implementation is the same as A/D conversion. In the D/A output experiment, the output is connected to the LED lamp, and the output change is observed through the lamp change.

## 3 Design Online Teaching System Software of Financial Management Course Based on Cloud Platform

### 3.1 System Deployment Design

In order to make it convenient for students and teachers to use the system to manage learning and teaching resources, the system adopts B/S architecture design, and users can use PC browser or smart phone to access the system [7–9]. The whole server is located in the cloud, the system is deployed uniformly, the reusability is good, and the coupling degree of business data and page display is low. The system deployment design is shown in Fig. 3.

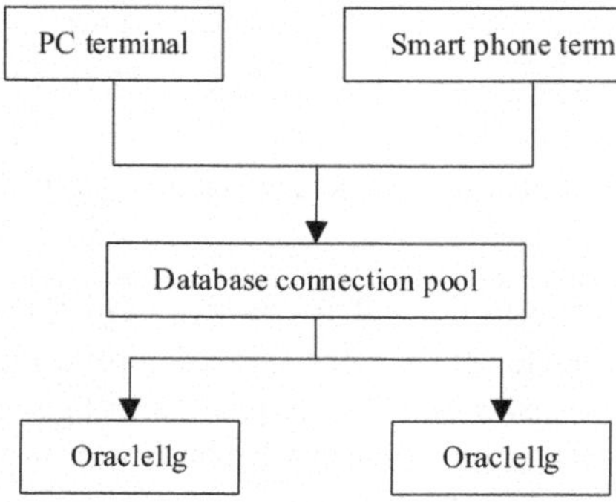


**Fig. 3.** System deployment design

As shown in Fig. 3, the system can be deployed and designed, including database connection pool. This system uses Oracle LLG database, with 119 database tables, which stores organization information, function information, permission information, role information, student information, teacher information, class information, course information, courseware information, examination information, homework information, professional information, etc. With auth_ The first table stores function information, permission information, role information, user role and authority information_ The table at the beginning stores class related information; KC_ The table at the beginning stores the information of courses, courseware and handouts_ The table at the beginning stores the information of exam, paper, question and student's exam result_ The table at the beginning stores the information of students' learning process_ The table at the beginning stores user information. The system adopts connection pool technology to manage database to cope with high concurrent access [10, 11]. In order to optimize the concurrent access processing capability of the database, the server dynamically adjusts the maximum and minimum connections of the connection pool to ensure the optimal performance of the system. The minimum and maximum connections are two important parameters of the database connection pool technology.

### 3.2 Design Courseware on Demand Program Based on Cloud Platform

The system adopts B/S structure, and users can access the system by PC browser, mobile phone, iPad and other devices. Due to the diversity of access channels, in order to ensure that the courseware can be played smoothly on various devices, it is necessary to decode the uploaded courseware. The decoded courseware can be played smoothly on various devices, and users can choose different definition videos to play according to their own network conditions. Due to the different amount of user visits in each period, the network bandwidth occupied by on-demand courseware is different. When the user visits are very concentrated, the bandwidth will be occupied. In order to ensure the fluency of user play, the system adopts the technology of on-demand automatic cloud. To ensure that the courseware can be played on various devices, the system needs to use the courseware decoding technology to transcode the audio and video uploaded by teachers into a format suitable for playing on PC or mobile terminal. Because the decoding speed depends on the playing time of the courseware, the decoding speed is relatively slow, so the system is equipped with three video decoding servers and one learning record server, which are respectively used for audio and video decoding and recording the learning time of students. Courseware decoding is divided into super clear, high-definition, standard definition of these three kinds of definition of video, in the play interface, students choose the definition according to the current network environment [8]. In the case that users do not have centralized access to the system, the bandwidth is sufficient; however, when major activities are held, the bandwidth will be occupied, and the later login users will not be able to order the courseware. Considering the existing resources and user experience, the strategy of on-demand automatic cloud is adopted. According to the preset strategy, the students' learning requests are automatically scheduled to provide the fastest route and on-demand service. First, the system needs to judge the user's network operator, then obtain the corresponding line occupation, and judge the platform used by students when applying the teaching system according to the set network conditions. The whole process flow chart is shown in Fig. 4

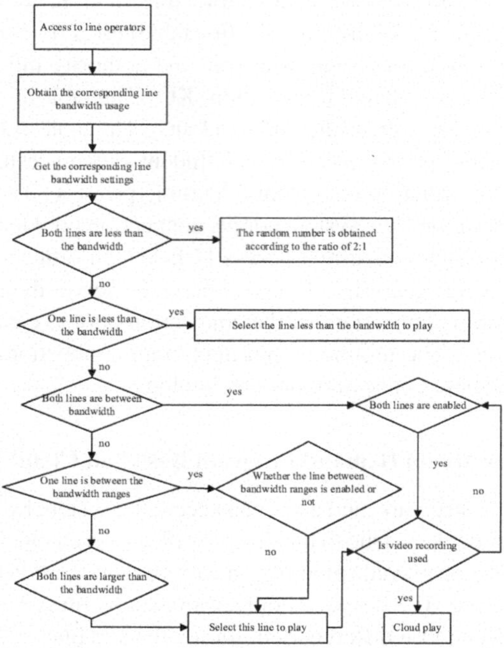


**Fig. 4.** Flow chart of courseware on demand system strategy

As shown in Fig. 4, through the courseware on demand strategy, we can determine whether an audio or video belonging to the current cloud platform in advance can be played by the courseware on demand system. If it can be played, we can choose the appropriate line. If it cannot be played, we will give a prompt [12, 13].

# 4 Experimental Study

## 4.1 System Test Environment

Before the system test, the hardware facilities and software environment of this experiment need to be set, and the specific parameters are shown in Table 1.

After setting up the above experimental environment, we can start to test the systems' function and system performance (Table 2).

**Table 1.** Hardware parameters

| | Name | Parameter |
|---|---|---|
| Processor | CPU | Intel Core I3 CPU M 390@2.67 GHz (dual core 4 threads) |
| | A main board | HP 1667 (Intel HM55) |
| | Memory | 2 GB, DDR3 |
| | Graphics card | Intel HD graphics (ironlake), 256 MB |
| | Hard disk | Wdsooobevt-60aort0400 rpm, 500 GB |
| Peripheral | Monitor | TLC6 |
| | Network card | Rising semiconductor RTL8101/2/3 family fast Ethernet NIC |
| | Sound card | Intel 5 Series/34x0 chipset PCH audio device controller |

**Table 2.** Software environment

| | Software | Name |
|---|---|---|
| Data | System platform | Windows 10 |
| | Web server | Apache |
| | Database server | MySQL |
| | Database management tools | SQL Manager for MySQL and phpMyAdmin |
| Beautify | Web art and image processing | Adobe Photoshop |
| | System diagram drawing tool | Microsoft Office Vision |

### 4.2 System Function Test

Function test is the most basic test in system test. No matter how the software is implemented internally, it only verifies whether the functions of the product meet the requirements according to the requirements specification and test requirements list. It mainly tests the following aspects: first, whether the functions are fully realized and whether there are omissions; second, whether the functions meet the needs of users and the hidden needs of system design. Third, whether the input can be correctly accepted and the correct results can be given [10]. It mainly includes students' learning and teachers' management of classes and courses. For students and teachers online management function, teaching online management function, authority management function, online examination function, the specific test situation is shown in Table 3, 4, 5 and Table 6.

As shown in Table 3, 4, 5, and Table 6, the test results show that each function can be used normally, and the function is perfect, the interface is friendly, and the interaction is good.

**Table 3.** User management function test

| | View user information | Edit user information |
|---|---|---|
| Process | Click user management to view user information | Add, modify and delete user information |
| Expect | Display user information, including: user name, user's gender, user's phone, user's picture information | Add, modify and delete user information according to relevant operation |
| Result | Success | Success |

**Table 4.** Online teaching function test

| | View online information | Edit online information |
|---|---|---|
| Process | Click online teaching management to view the relevant information about online teaching | Add, modify and delete online teaching information |
| Expect | Display online teaching information, including: course name, teacher name, teaching interface, student information, etc | Add, modify and delete online teaching information according to relevant operation |
| Result | Success | Success |

**Table 5.** Function test of authority management

| | View permission information | Edit permission information |
|---|---|---|
| Process | Click authority user management to view the relevant information about authority | Add, modify and delete permission information |
| Expect | Display permission information, including permission name, permission content, permission specific meaning and other information | Add, modify and delete permission information according to relevant operation |
| Result | Success | Success |

### 4.3 System Performance Test

As a web system of B/S architecture, the network teaching system not only needs beautiful page, practical function, but also has strong security requirements, otherwise it will lead to data loss and system paralysis. Because the system is directly facing Internet users, it may be threatened by more network attacks, so it is necessary to test its security. The goal of security testing is to find out the security defects of the system design as much as possible, and then repair them as necessary. The security test of the system includes testing whether there are security vulnerabilities in the login of the system,

**Table 6.** Function test of online examination

| | View test information | Edit exam information |
|---|---|---|
| Process | Click online examination management to view the relevant information of online examination | Add, modify and delete online examination information |
| Expect | Display the online examination information, including: examination name, examination subject, examination content, examination score setting and other information | Add, modify and delete online examination information according to relevant operation |
| Result | Success | Success |

testing whether there are security vulnerabilities in the script program of the server, testing whether the system management code is secure, preventing users from bypassing the program to directly access the background program, testing whether the security settings of the Tomcat system server platform are appropriate, etc.

Taking security as the evaluation index of a teaching system and the basis of analyzing system performance, this paper carries out a system classification performance test and analyzes the integration ability of different systems for information resources. The formula for computing the security of online teaching system of financial management course based on cloud platform is as follows:

$$P = \sum_{t}^{N} a_t(i) \tag{1}$$

Where, $P$ represents the probability of the teaching system being invaded by malicious data; $N$ represents the number of samples in the data set; $a_t$ represents the number of data samples currently running. If we want to extract the characteristic quantity of the security performance of the teaching system, we need to go through the following calculation:

$$G_{m,n} = \begin{bmatrix} C_r^b(q_{k+1}) & 0 \\ 0 & C_r^b(q_{k+1}) \end{bmatrix} \begin{bmatrix} r_a \\ r_m \end{bmatrix} + \begin{bmatrix} v_{k+1}^a \\ v_{k+1}^m \end{bmatrix} \tag{2}$$

In the formula, $C_r^b(q_{k+1})$ is the sequence probability value of the illegal intrusion of the online teaching system of financial management course based on the cloud platform; $q_{k+1}$ is the matching coefficient of the security performance of the online teaching system; in the above formula, the influence of the running module and the non networking data is usually divided into $2 * 2$ boards, and $v_{k+1}^a$ and $v_{k+1}^m$ are expressed as the coefficient components of the network dynamic characteristics. According to the above calculation formula, we can get a schematic diagram of the evaluation results of cloud and local data security performance with the increase of the number of data operations in the process of teaching system interconnection.

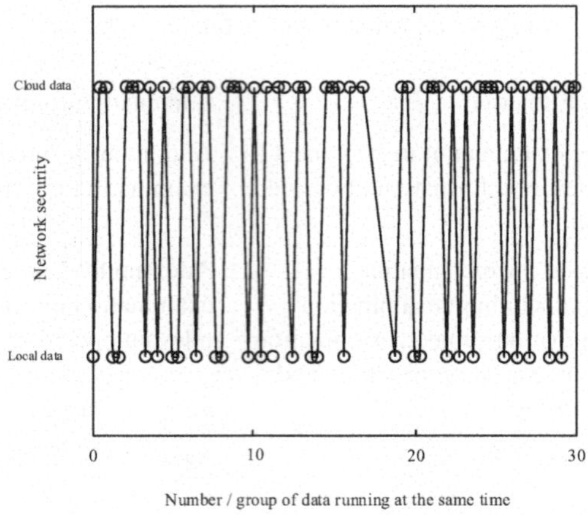


**Fig. 5.** Data security performance evaluation conclusion

As shown in Fig. 5, with the increase in the amount of running data, the network security of the teaching system fluctuates to a certain extent. Compared with cloud data, local data is more secure. But in general, before the number of data running does not exceed 15 groups, the risk is still within the scope of affordability, so the same user needs to ensure that the data opened at the same time does not exceed 15 groups when using the teaching system.

Besides the security, it can also test the response time of teaching system and the ability of users to be online at the same time. Testing the online ability of the users of the teaching system at the same time is to provide guarantee for the big classroom, while the response time of the teaching system ensures the synchronization of data transmission. After testing, we can get the schematic diagram of the online capability test for different numbers of users at the same time, as shown in Fig. 6.

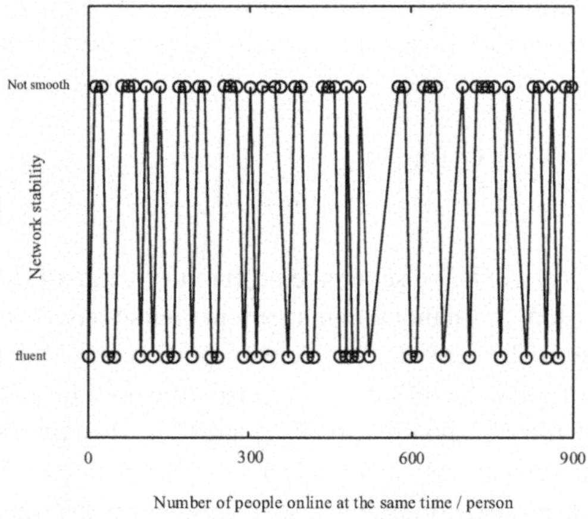


**Fig. 6.** Online capability test for different number of users at the same time

As shown in Fig. 6, if the number of online users is less than 600 at the same time, the online teaching system of financial management course based on cloud platform can ensure smooth operation. But when the number of people online is more than 600, the whole online teaching system of financial management courses based on cloud platform will become stuck with naked eyes.

The response time of the teaching system can be tested by increasing the number of concurrent data. The test can be divided into three aspects: login, online communication and online teaching. The specific test results are shown in Table 7.

**Table 7.** Response time test results

| Operation | Concurrent number | Maximum business time (s) | Average network usage |
|---|---|---|---|
| Login online | 10 | 1.02 | 69 |
| | 20 | 1.23 | 75 |
| | 30 | 1.35 | 88 |
| | 40 | 3.14 | 93 |
| Online communication | 10 | 1.21 | 102 |
| | 20 | 1.42 | 134 |
| | 30 | 1.69 | 159 |
| | 40 | 4.15 | 177 |
| Online teaching | 10 | 2.35 | 314 |
| | 20 | 3.56 | 456 |
| | 30 | 4.97 | 728 |
| | 40 | 12.38 | 1034 |

As shown in Table 7, the maximum time consumption of the three operations with the same number of concurrent services is different. The larger the average network traffic, the longer the time consumption. With the increase of concurrency, business time and network traffic are also increasing. When the concurrency number reaches 40, the increase rate suddenly becomes larger, then we can know that the system can achieve maximum business efficiency when the concurrency number is less than 40.

## 5 Conclusion

This paper designs an online teaching system for financial management course based on the cloud platform, and through the test of the teaching system in the experimental link, it proves that the software has complete design function, a friendly man-machine interface and simple use. It is safe and reliable in the running process, and has good use effect. It can be accessed with different mainstream browsers. It has good cross platform security, and basically achieves the expected goal. However, due to the limited time and energy, some of the design functions of the system are not perfect, which will continue to improve in the later stage. In addition, the interface needs to be further beautified to meet the needs of students in each stage.

## References


1. Yaxian, Z.: A research on the instructional system design ability of enterprise teachers in school-enterprise cooperation. J. Hulunbeier Universities **28**(4), 135–139 (2020)
2. Dai, X.: Design of Japanese teaching system from the perspective of intelligent media. Techniques Autom. Appl. **39**(6), 163–165,172 (2020)
3. Li, P., Song, Z.: Design of English long-distance multimedia teaching system based on virtual reality. Modern Electron. Technique **43**(14), 161–163,169 (2020)
4. Zhang, T., Xu, M., Liu, C.: Design of physics multimedia assisted teaching system based on concept network. Modern Electron. Technique **43**(20), 119–121,125 (2020)
5. Xi, L.I.: Design of MOOC idea based teaching resource sharing system for digital film and television production. Modern Electron. Technique **43**(16), 115–118 (2020)
6. Fu, W., Liu, S., Srivastava, G.: Optimization of big data scheduling in social networks. Entropy **21**(9), 902 (2019)
7. Zhang, J., Li, C., Zhu, Y.: Massive video teaching resource management system based on cloud platform. Modern Electron. Technique **43**(21), 151–155 (2020)
8. Li, J., Zhang, J., Su, J.: Design and realization of teaching system based on cloud platform. Exp. Technol. Manage. **36**(6), 176–180 (2019)
9. Chen, L., Du, S., Huang, C., et al.: Design and implementation of teaching cloud platform based on distributed file system. wuxian hulian keji **07**(08), 94–96 (2019)
10. Ying, F.A.N., Meng, L.I.U.: Design and research of online education course resource sharing based on cloud platform. Mod. Electron. Technique **43**(1), 175–178 (2020)
11. Li, Q., Yao, X.: Study on the construction of "Curriculum Ideology and Politics" in financial management course of agricultural colleges and universities. jiaoyu jiaoxue luntan (25), 88–90 (2020)
12. Liu, S., Li, Z., Zhang, Y., et al.: Introduction of key problems in long-distance learning and training. Mob. Networks Appl. **24**(1), 1–4 (2019)
13. Liu, S., Glowatz, M., Zappatore, M., et al. (eds.): e-Learning, e-Education, and Online Training, 1–374. Springer, Cham (2018). https://doi.org/10.1007/978-3-319-49625-2

# Construction of Network Teaching Information Interactive Platform of Traditional Music in New Media Era

Jun Zhou(✉), Liang Lu, and Yang-bo Wu

Xinyu University, Xinyu 338000, China

**Abstract.** In order to optimize the online teaching effect of traditional music, the interactive information platform of online teaching of traditional ethnic music is constructed. In view of the existing network information interaction platform in the actual operation, the logic of teaching information interaction is chaotic, which leads to too many times of delay generated by the platform. Aiming at this problem, this paper constructs a kind of national traditional music network teaching information interaction platform in the new media era. After constructing the interactive logical relationship of network teaching information, the collected interactive data of teaching information is taken as the processing object, and the platform architecture is built. The data involved in the teaching of national traditional music is outlined by using digital communication technology to realize the real-time interaction of teaching information. After building the platform test environment, we use a traditional interactive platform, the interactive platform in literature [5] and the interactive platform designed in this paper to carry out experiments. The results show that the interactive platform designed in this paper has the least time delay and is suitable for practical use.

**Keywords:** New media era · National traditional music · Network teaching information · Interactive platform

## 1 Introduction

"Traditional music" is a concept that has emerged only recently and in the modern age. Before the Opium War, it was collectively referred to as "Chinese music". After the Opium War, works created or adapted from the acceptance of Western musical theories are referred to as "new music". And the definition of "traditional music" refers to "music created by the Chinese people in the intrinsic forms of their own nationalities by using the intrinsic methods of their own nationalities and with the characteristics of their own nationalities, including not only ancient works produced in history and handed down from generation to generation, but also musical works created by the contemporary Chinese people in the intrinsic forms of their own nationalities and with the characteristics of their own nationalities." It is obvious that traditional music does not include new music, while "Chinese music" includes both "traditional music" and "new music".


W. Fu et al. (Eds.): eLEOT 2021, LNICST 389, pp. 553–565, 2021.
https://doi.org/10.1007/978-3-030-84383-0_47

Traditional music categories are related to their social and cultural attributes, each with its own unique characteristics and content [1]. Understanding the classification of Chinese traditional music is helpful to the selection of teaching contents and the effective implementation of traditional music teaching. Traditional Chinese music contains five thousand years of Chinese history and culture, and precipitates the unique etiquette, custom, spirit and temperament of the Chinese nation. The implementation of traditional music teaching in colleges and universities is conducive to the healthy development of college students' body and mind, and is of great significance to maintaining national culture, inheriting and carrying forward the spirit of the Chinese nation, and enhancing national pride and patriotism.

The Chinese traditional music has a long history, is extensive and profound, and is a huge treasure in our country's cultural treasure-house. This inexhaustible and long-standing source of culture and art should be protected and spread from depth to width. But the fact is not ideal, in more than 100 years of social unrest and change, the traditional culture has been turbulent, experienced too many subversive shocks, spread has not been so deep in people's imagination, so bright. The change of social form, the social adaptability of politics and economy and the emergence of their contradictions lead to the change of social culture as superstructure [2]. In the past one hundred years of the 20th century, the following social factors have exerted a great influence on the traditional music education and inheritance in China.

Therefore, more and more experts begin to pay attention to the problem of information interaction in online teaching of ethnic traditional music. Literature [4] proposed a scheme of "smart phone+Moodle platform" to construct interactive feedback system for teaching. Taking university Chinese classroom teaching as an example, this paper discusses the implementation method, application mode and practical effect of IRS system based on smart phone applied to classroom teaching. The results show that using students' personal smart phones to build interactive teaching feedback system has the advantages of simple and effective, powerful function, low cost and so on. Literature [5] explored three application strategies for Mousemischief to support interactive classroom teaching through teaching experiments, namely class mode, group mode and individualized mode, and pointed out that the process of applying Mousemischief to classroom teaching design can be divided into three stages: front-end analysis, teaching process implementation and teaching evaluation. Finally, the application effect is analyzed through on-site observation, classroom record analysis, interview, questionnaire survey and other methods. However, the above traditional methods have a large number of attacked nodes, a high CPU utilization rate and a serious delay problem when the platform runs.

In order to solve the above problems, build a new media era ethnic traditional music network teaching information interactive platform.

# 2 Construction of Network Teaching Information Interactive Platform of Traditional Music in New Media Era

## 2.1 Constructing Interactive Logical Relationship of Network Teaching Information

According to the composition structure of network teaching information, traditional ethnic music is divided into different nodes and contained equipment according to the teaching lines. According to the topological relationship between the wires where the nodes are located, the data of network teaching information interaction is collected. For traditional ethnic music in the new media era, the information interaction index of current network teaching is calculated. The calculation formula is as follows:

$$C_p = \sum_{i=1}^{n} R_i \cdot I_i \tag{1}$$

$R_i$ represents the number of people participating in information teaching, $I_i$ represents traditional music parameters, $i$ represents the interactive point of network teaching, and $n$ represents the number of nodes obtained by division. Assuming that the external teaching environment is not considered and the information nodes are not affected [3], according to the principle of new med $I_a$ dissemination, the loss of teaching information is reduced as much as possible, and the control of information loss ia can be expressed as:

$$I_a = \frac{(C_p - C_\Delta)}{\sum_{i=1}^{m} R_m} \tag{2}$$

$C_\Delta$ represents the reduced network data information, and $m$ represents the actual network teaching information. In the case of the above control information, according to the reality of national traditional music, the omission of knowledge points generated in the process of interaction can be expressed as:

$$I_b = \frac{\min(\mathrm{I}_a t)}{k} \tag{3}$$

Among them, $t$ represents the time of online teaching, and $k$ represents the number of people participating in online teaching. Take the time data obtained from the above processing as an independent variable, and delimit the change of information loss in the process of interaction, as shown in the following figure (Fig. 1):

In the process of information loss shown in the above figure, the data of network teaching information is continuously collected, and the interaction process between teaching information forms the following influence relationship, and the numerical value can be expressed as follows:

$$C_x = \frac{dlr}{\lambda} \tag{4}$$

Among them, $d$ represents the actual interactive teaching data, $l$ represents the interactive time, $r$ represents the data loss caused by network teaching, and $\lambda$ represents the

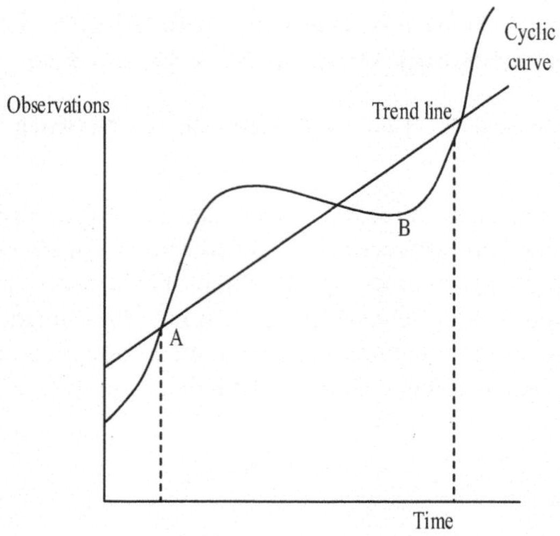


**Fig. 1.** Information loss process

parameter of line failure. According to the interaction frequency $\rho$ generated in network teaching, an information suppression process is constructed, which can be expressed as:

$$C_d = \frac{r_d \rho}{\gamma} \tag{5}$$

In which, $r_d$ represents the information effectiveness generated in unit time, and $\gamma$ represents the failure rate. Synthesize the data obtained from the above control as the processing object of the interactive platform, and build a preliminary interactive platform architecture [4].

## 3 Construction of Platform Architecture

The interactive big data collected above is taken as the processing object, B/S architecture is adopted as the basic structure of the architecture, server is taken as the core processing part of the architecture, and Web server, database server and software application server are integrated into an overall architecture structure, which is shown in the following figure (Fig. 2):

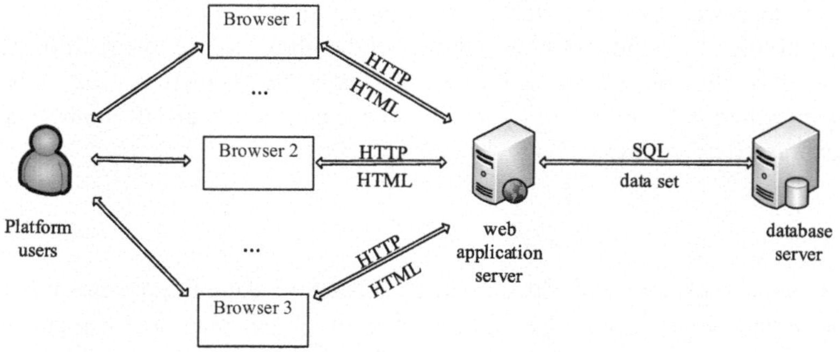


**Fig. 2.** B/S architecture used

Under the architecture shown in the above figure, the collected big data of teaching information is integrated into a SQL data set, and two browsers of different management types are connected by using HTTP and HTML protocols. Combined with the program structure in J2EE framework, the interactive data processing is supported [5]. In order to enhance the running speed of the information interactive platform, Flex technology is used to create the processing function of the information interactive platform, and the program generated by the function is run in the browser containing Flash Player to ensure the data interaction of the interactive platform in different browsers, and the inherent technical framework of Flex technology is adopted, as shown in the following table (Table 1):

**Table 1.** Technical framework of Flex technology

| Serial number | Name | Frame name |
|---|---|---|
| 1 | Scripting language | ECMA specification |
| 2 | Program interface | XML language |
| 3 | Service type | Instant service |
| 4 | Matching library | Powerbuilder foundation class,powerbuilder |
| 5 | Streaming media | Support |
| 6 | Application | Asynchronous call, No interface refresh, Browser compatibility |
| 7 | Ground floor | Callability |
| 8 | Programming language object | As3 programming language |
| 9 | Running framework | Flash playerbe compatible linux |

With the support of the technical framework shown in the above table, the running framework is in the form of Flash player compatible with linux, combined with the basic server-side tasks of J2EE middleware in processing engineering cost, and adopts the state of high-level intermediate component management platform architecture, which reduces the amount of code written by developers under the control of as3 programming language [6]. With the participation of application programs, the logical data of interactive instructions are coded to eliminate the influence of various data in the teaching information database. Under the influence of the adjustability of the bottom layer of the architecture, the platform can integrate the management software only once.

After building the framework of interactive platform, according to the relationship between teaching information and data, Message message is taken as the thread core, and Message Queue mainly adopts FIFO principle to manage the messages sent by Handler. Each message queue needs to have a one-to-one correspondence with Handler. Handler sends messages to the message queue in sendMessage or post mode . The messages sent by these two methods will be arranged at the end of the message queue, but the execution methods are different: what is sent by sendMessage method is the message object processed by handleMessage () function; And what is sent out through the post method is a runnable object that must be executed in person. The logical relationship formed is shown in the following figure (Fig. 3):

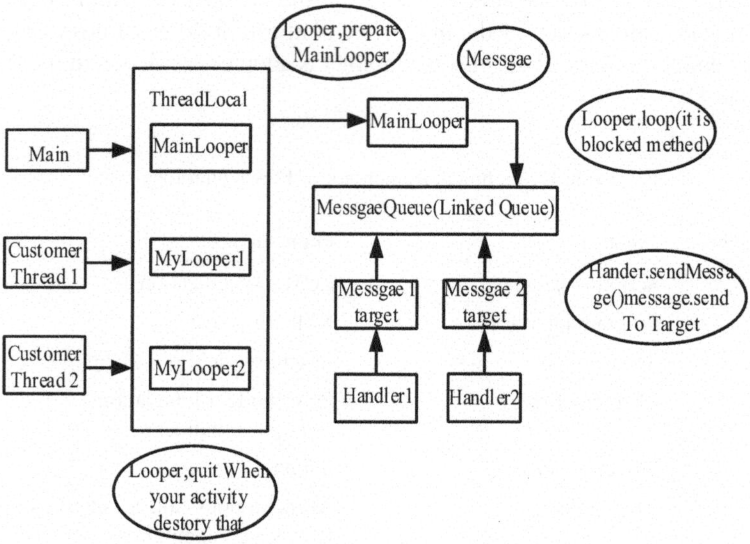


**Fig. 3.** Thread logical relationship

Under the logical relationship shown in the above figure, the network teaching function is realized by JAVA programming, and information exchange is carried out in real time.

## 4 Platform Function Realization

When building a virtual scene, the data involved in the teaching of national traditional music are used to outline the digital scene. According to the requirements of the teaching system, texture mapping and environment mapping are used to map the scene data in online teaching. Using a B/S structure, the built virtual scene is expressed as the front-end presentation layer, and a portal technology is used in the presentation layer to realize the inflow and outflow of various data of national traditional music teaching information [7], and finally form the structure of the virtual scene, as shown in the following figure (Fig. 4):

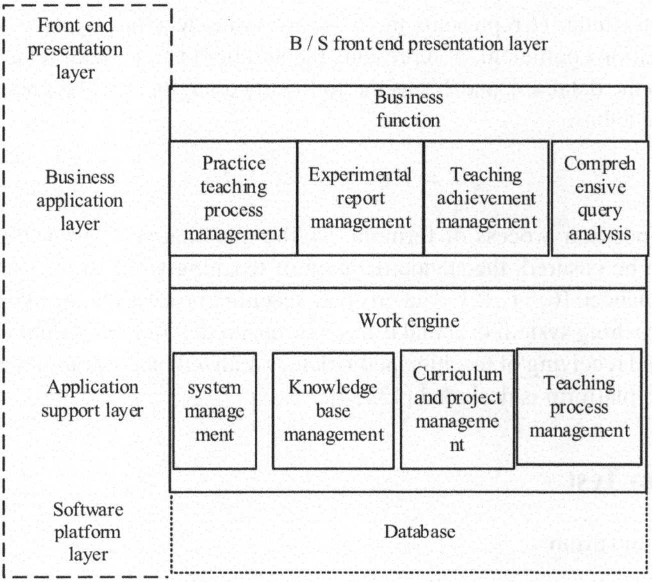


**Fig. 4.** Virtual scene structure

As shown by the scene structure shown in the above figure, each virtual scene is refined into the basic information of different national traditional music in the business application layer, and a work engine is set in the application support layer, which is responsible for managing the users of the simulation teaching system and the access rights of the system. The software platform layer contains the database of national traditional simulation teaching, and different databases always correspond to different simulation teaching objects [8–10].

Considering the universality of the network teaching system, the database specification is established according to the actual needs of the teaching system. Assuming that the set of teaching databases is $F$, the functional dependency set of $F$ is established by BCNF decomposition method. For any sub-database $\alpha \subseteq R$ and $\beta \subseteq R$, given a functional dependency for a given $R$ teaching relational database, the database can be decomposed into:

$$\begin{cases} \alpha \cup \beta \\ (R - (\beta - \alpha)) \end{cases} \tag{6}$$

The formula (6) is used to decompose the pattern and eliminate the dependence on the functional relationship in the database. The decomposition process can be expressed as follows:

$$U \to wR_1(U_1), R_2(U_2), \ldots, R_N(U_N) \tag{7}$$

In the above formula, $U$ represents the database in the teaching system, $w$ represents the decomposition coefficient, $N$ represents the number of functional relationships corresponding to the database, and $U$ has the following quantitative relationship with each decomposed database:

$$U = U_1 \cup U_2 \cup \ldots \cup U_N \tag{8}$$

In the decomposition process of formula (7), the quantitative relationship of formula (8) above can be ensured, the standardization of teaching simulation system in actual use can be enhanced [6, 11, 12], data errors in teaching process can be avoided, and the accuracy of teaching system in actual use can be ensured. After the virtual scene is built, the sending and receiving of teaching audio data is realized by programming, and finally the interactive platform is designed [13, 14].

# 5 Platform Test

## 5.1 Test Preparation

Prepare interactive platform development tools, and the parameters of the development tools are shown in the following table (Table 2):

**Table 2.** Development tool parameters

| Serial number | Tool name | Parameter |
|---|---|---|
| 1 | Source code interactive tool | SVN |
| 2 | Develop application server | Windows2007Server |
| 3 | Documentation | Office2007, visio2003 |
| 4 | Code development tools | Eclipse Jee3.5, Weblogic Server Plugin, SVN Plugin |
| 5 | Data model design | Power Designer 12.5 |
| 6 | JAVA Environmental Science | JDK 1.5 |
| 7 | Web Program container | WebLogic9. 2 |
| 8 | Database | IBMDB2 9. 7 |

Under the control of the parameters shown in the above table, the platform test environment is built as shown in the figure below (Fig. 5):

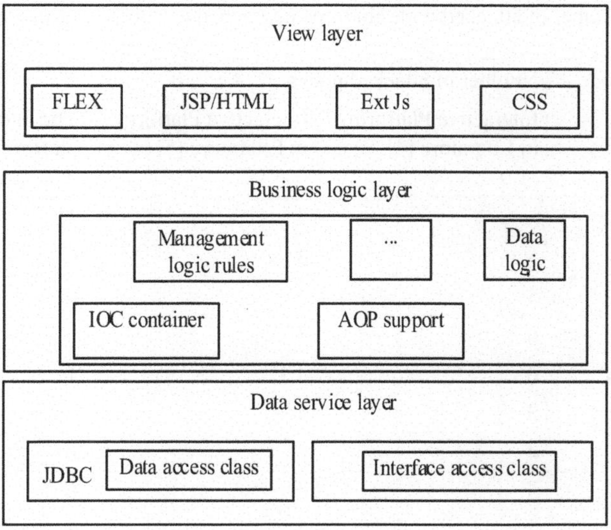


**Fig. 5.** Build the platform test environment

In the test environment built in the above figure, we use the Struts2.0 technology framework to communicate the data between the national traditional music teaching data and the interactive platform, and use the MVC development mode built in the platform to realize the interaction between the teaching data and the traditional music teaching information data. After debugging the software function in the platform test environment, we use the traditional interactive platform, the cost interactive platform in literature [5] and the cost interactive platform designed in this paper to carry out experiments, and compare the performance of the three interactive platforms.

## 6 Test Results and Analysis

Based on the above experimental preparation, the interactive data generated by the teaching at the network teaching node of national traditional music is taken as SYN message, which is transmitted to three interactive platforms through the open port of TCP communication of the platform. The nodes in the whole area are divided into 10 areas containing topological nodes. The SYN ACK message is taken as the attack of the platform, and whether the data of the network teaching node is attacked is taken as the statistical index, and the attack resistance performance of the three interactive systems is compared. The results are shown in the following table (Table 3):

**Table 3.** Number of attacked nodes in three interactive teaching information platforms

| Test topology node area | Number of attacked nodes | | |
|---|---|---|---|
| | Interactive Platform in Literature [4] | Interactive Platform in Literature [5] | The interactive platform designed in this paper |
| Zone 1 | 5 | 3 | 1 |
| Zone 2 | 5 | 3 | 0 |
| Zone 3 | 5 | 4 | 0 |
| Zone 4 | 6 | 3 | 0 |
| Zone 5 | 6 | 4 | 1 |
| Zone 6 | 5 | 4 | 1 |
| Zone 7 | 4 | 3 | 0 |
| Zone 8 | 5 | 4 | 0 |
| Zone 9 | 7 | 3 | 0 |
| Zone 10 | 7 | 3 | 0 |

When running three different information interactive platforms in the same teaching structure, there are the same data nodes in the node division area. From the results of the node data attack shown in the above table, it can be seen that when the traditional interactive platform is attacked, the number of cost data nodes in the topology structure is between 4 and 7, and the security performance of the interactive platform is poor. The number of nodes attacked in the interactive platform in literature [5] is between 3 and 4, and the security performance of the interactive platform is higher than that of the traditional interactive platform. Compared with the two existing interactive platforms, the interactive platform designed in this paper has higher security performance.

Under the above experimental environment, taking the CPU utilization rate of the host when the platform is attacked as a comparison index, calling the task interactors of the interactive hosts in different regions, and counting the CPU utilization rate generated by the three interactive platforms when attacking the topological node structures in different distribution network regions, the results are shown in the following table (Table 4):

It can be seen from the CPU utilization results shown in the above table that when dealing with the same external attack, the CPU utilization rate generated by the traditional interactive platform is the largest, and most of the CPUs of the running host are used for the operation of the interactive platform, which is not suitable for practical use. The CPU utilization rate generated by the interactive platform in reference [4] and reference [5] in the host is relatively small, which can basically provide CPU utilization space for other operations. However, the CPU utilization rate of the interactive platform designed in this paper is about 45%, and the host can provide space for other operations of the interactive platform.

Keep the above experimental environment unchanged, take the interactive data of teaching information uploaded by the interactive platform terminal as the experimental

**Table 4.** CPU utilization rate of three interactive platforms when running

| Test topology node area | CPU Usage/% | | |
|---|---|---|---|
| | Interactive Platform in Literature [4] | Interactive Platform in Literature [5] | The interactive platform designed in this paper |
| Zone 1 | 79.99 | 56.67 | 47.28 |
| Zone 2 | 79.24 | 58.66 | 45.43 |
| Zone 3 | 75.28 | 59.43 | 49.52 |
| Zone 4 | 78.69 | 56.58 | 48.63 |
| Zone 5 | 75.49 | 59.49 | 49.85 |
| Zone 6 | 77.84 | 58.08 | 48.46 |
| Zone 7 | 77.87 | 58.43 | 47.03 |
| Zone 8 | 79.75 | 55.81 | 48.66 |
| Zone 9 | 77.26 | 59.29 | 46.88 |
| Zone 10 | 76.61 | 56.29 | 46.78 |

object, count the number of time delays generated by the three interactive platforms under the same bandwidth numerical control, and take it as the platform data transmission performance. The data transmission performance results of the three interactive platforms are shown in the following figure (Fig. 6):

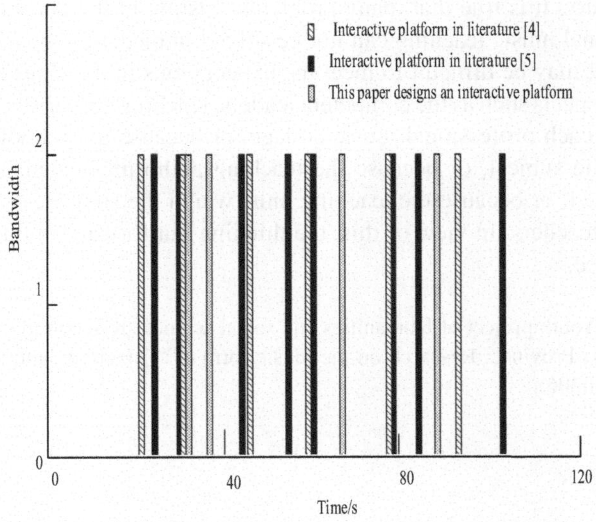


**Fig. 6.** The results of the number of time delays produced by three interactive stations

It can be seen from the results of the times of delay shown in the above figure that when the bandwidth of the three interactive platforms is set at 2 Kbit/s, interactive Platform in Literature [4] generates more times of delay under the same experimental time, and the platform generates six times of delay altogether. The interactive platform in the literature [5] has the most time delay, which is 8 times in the test time of 120 s. However, the interactive platform designed in this paper has the least number of time delays, with a total of four time delays. Based on the above experimental results, it can be seen that the interactive platform designed in this paper is suitable for information interaction, with the least number of nodes attacked by external, the least CPU utilization and the least number of delays. According to the above experimental results, the number of attacked nodes of the platform designed in this paper is less, and the CPU occupancy of the platform is lower when running, which is not easy to cause delay. This is mainly because the platform of this paper uses digital communication technology to form various data involved in the teaching of traditional ethnic music into digital scenes, which avoids unnecessary time consuming in the process of information interaction and makes the goal more clear.

## 7 Conclusion

The problems in the curriculum setting of Chinese traditional music teaching, though seemingly ordinary, do not seem to affect the normal enrollment and talent training of a professional music college, but it is related to how to build its own relatively perfect teaching system in the future development of Chinese traditional music teaching, so as to continuously promote the improvement of Chinese traditional music in teaching mode and teaching method, and make it a subject that attracts more attention from the world in the 21st century. It is true that many problems existing in the curriculum setting of Chinese traditional music teaching can not be solved immediately by any professional music college. It may be difficult to meet the expectations in the short term because it involves many aspects such as the competent leaders, teaching authorities, teaching units and teachers of each professional music college, or because the school leaders attach importance to the subject, or because the teaching authorities calculate the teaching cost of the subject, or because the teaching units weigh the subject, or because of the replacement of teachers. In view of this, the thinking put forward in this paper is only for your reference.

**Fund Projects.** Youth project of Humanities and social sciences research in Colleges and universities of Jiangxi Province: Research on the music form of "Quanfeng lantern" in Northwest Jiangxi (NO. YS20206).

## References

1. Wang, Y.: The cultural logic of the construction of ethnic traditional music culture. Guizhou Ethnic Stud. **40**(02), 94–97 (2019)
2. Li, D.: The construction of national traditional music inheritance mode under the background of cultural consumption. Guizhou Ethnic Stud. **40**(02), 107–110 (2019)

3. Li, H., Zhang, X.: Visualization of National Culture by Minority Music Deduction. Guizhou Ethnic Stud. **40**(04), 78–81 (2019)
4. Shenglan, X.: Design and application of interactive response system based on intelligent mobile phone. China Educ. Technol. **7**, 45–56 (2017)
5. Zheng, L., Zhang, J., Chen, P.: Application research on multipoint-based mouse mischief: a classroom interaction teaching platform. China Educ. Technol. (10), 93–98 (2009)
6. Li, Z., Pu, X., Lin, X.: The online video platform access strategy of content provider based on two-sided markets theory. Manage. Rev. **32**(05), 180–191 (2020)
7. Liu, S., Lu, M., Li, H., et al.: Prediction of gene expression patterns with generalized linear regression model. Front. Genet. **10**, 120 (2019)
8. Liu Ziqiang, X., Haiyun, L.R.: Research on scientific and technological interaction patterns based on topic relevance analysis. J. China Soc. Sci. Tech. Inf. **38**(10), 997–1011 (2019)
9. Fu, W., Liu, S., Srivastava, G.: Optimization of big data scheduling in social networks. Entropy **21**(9), 902 (2019)
10. Luo, G., Chen, H., Liu, J., et al.: Design and implementation of mobile learning platform system based on JavaEE and Android. J. Inner Mongolia Normal University (Nat. Sci. Ed.) **48**(01), 75–81 (2019)
11. Huang, W., Pan, Z.: Load scheduling simulation of cloud platform resource multi-layer service information transmission. Comput. Simul. **36**(06), 364–367+479 (2019)
12. Liu, S., Liu, D., Srivastava, G., et al.: Overview and methods of correlation filter algorithms in object tracking. Compl. Intell. Syst. (2020). https://doi.org/10.1007/s40747-020-00161-4
13. Xing, J., Wang, H., Wu, Z.: Construction of art database for nou mask in Hunan province under the guidance of cultural creativity. Pack. Eng. **40**(24), 77–81 (2019)
14. Zhao, W., Xiao, X., Zheng, Y., et al.: Network operation platform architecture and control strategy of distributed energy storage systems high voltage. Engineering **45**(10), 3256–3262 (2019)

# Design and Development of Online Distance Learning System for Electrical Automation Technology Specialty

Quan-wen Chen(✉) and Shan Jiang

School of Information and Control, Shenyang Institute of Technology, Shenfu demonstration zone, Shenyang 113112, China

**Abstract.** In order to improve the response speed of distance learning system for electrical automation technology specialty, a new online distance learning system for electrical automation technology specialty is designed. In the hardware part, mainly through the selection of microprocessor, power supply mode and download circuit, built-in memory module, external memory module and communication module design to complete the system hardware design; on this basis, mainly through the login process, system management process and database design to achieve system software design. The experimental results show that the response speed of the online distance learning system of electrical automation technology is fast, and the students' performance has been significantly improved after the application of the system.

**Keywords:** Electrical automation technology · Online distance learning · Microprocessor

## 1 Introduction

Electrical engineering and automation is an emerging discipline in the field of electrical information. It is closely related to people's daily life and industrial production. It has developed very rapidly, and it is relatively mature. It has become an important part of the high-tech industry, widely used in industry, agriculture, national defense and other fields, and is playing an increasingly important role in the national economy. Its tentacles extend to all walks of life, ranging from the design of a switch to the research of aerospace aircraft. Students of this major are able to work in the fields of system operation, automatic control, power electronic technology, information processing, experimental technology, research and development, economic management, and electronic and computer technology applications related to electrical engineering. They are a wide-caliber "composite" advanced engineering and technical personnel. There is a great demand for high-level talents in this field. It is estimated that with the entry of large foreign companies, there will be a large gap in this professional field, and there is likely to be a shortage of talents at that time.


W. Fu et al. (Eds.): eLEOT 2021, LNICST 389, pp. 566–578, 2021.
https://doi.org/10.1007/978-3-030-84383-0_48

At present, the construction of teaching network for electrical automation technology has been gradually improved, and the process of teaching informatization is also gradually promoted. Computer technology and network technology have been applied to the process of online education. With the rapid expansion of contemporary information technology in vocational education, with the application of multimedia computer in education and teaching becoming more and more common, the online distance learning system of electrical automation technology specialty has achieved further development, Therefore, it is of great significance to design an online distance learning system for electrical automation technology specialty.

## 2 Hardware Design of Online Distance Learning System

The hardware framework of the online distance learning system for electrical automation technology in this research is as follows (Fig. 1):

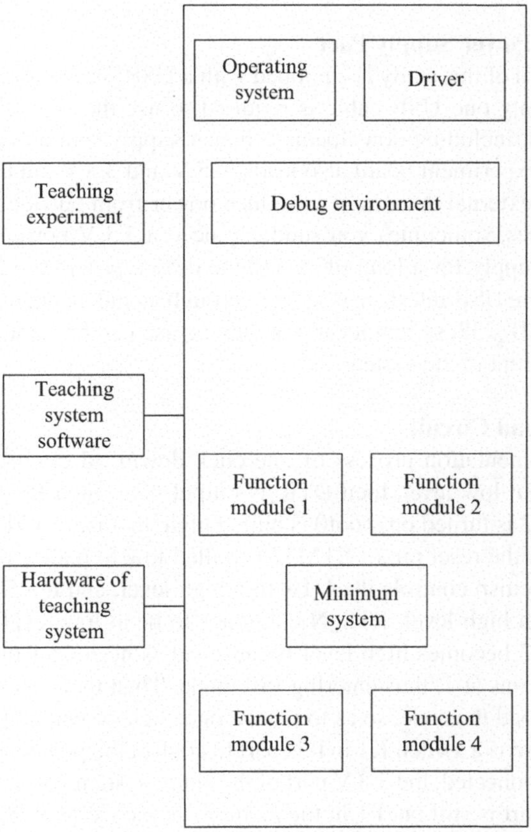


**Fig. 1.** Hardware framework of online distance learning system for electrical automation technology major

## 2.1 Microprocessor Selection

Cortex-M3 adopts ARMV7 architecture, which not only supports Thumb-2 instruction set, but also has many new features [1]. Compared with ARM7TDMI, Cortex-M3 has many advantages, such as stronger performance, higher code density, bit band operation, nested interrupt, low cost and low power consumption.

This paper chooses STM32F103ZET6 as MCU. There are many models of STM32F103. The reason why we choose this one is that we value its cost performance. As a low-end development board, choosing STM32F103ZET6 is the best choice. 128KFLASH, 20KSRAM, 2 SPI, 3 serial ports, 1 USB, 1 CAN, 2 12 bit ADC, RTC, 51 available IO pins [2], such a configuration is very good no matter where it is put. What's more important is its price. The batch price of less than 13 yuan is enough to kill many other chips, so it is chosen as the main chip.

## 2.2 Power Supply Mode and Download Circuit

### Circuit Design of Power Supply Part

The teaching system of this study is equipped with a USB serial port [3] and is powered by USB, so that only one USB cable is required to use the ALIENTEKMiniSTM32 development board, including downloading, power supply, and debugging. The power supply part of the experiment board also leads to 5 V and 3.3 V pin headers, which can provide power for external devices or introduce power from outside [4], which is very useful in many cases, sometimes you suddenly need a 3.3 V power supply, But there is no such power supply for a long time, and the device provides 3.3 V, 5 V power to external devices. The USB interface is led out through an independent MiniUSB header, not shared with USB_232, so that it can not only be used at the same time, but also can provide greater current to the system.

### One Click Download Circuit

The specific implementation process of one click download circuit [5]: first, mcuisp controls DTR output low level, then DTR_N output high, then RTS set high, RTS_N output is low, so Q2 is turned on, boot0 is pulled high, that is, BOOT0 is set to 1, Q1 is also turned on, and the reset pin of STM32 is pulled low to realize reset. Then, after a delay of 100ms, mcuisp controls the DTR to a high level, and the DTR_N output low level, RTS maintain high level, RTS_N continues to be at low level. At this time, the reset pin of STM32 becomes high level because Q1 is no longer on. STM32 ends to reset, but boot remains at 1, thus entering ISP mode. Then mcuisp can start to connect STM32 and download the code, so as to realize one click download [6].

In addition, there is a switch K1 in this part to control the power supply of the entire system. If it is disconnected, the 3.3 V part of the entire system will be powered off. The power of the 5 V part is still on. F1 in the picture is a recoverable fuse, used to protect the USB. In addition, this experiment board also adds two TVS tubes, D4 and D5, to protect the development board and prevent external high-voltage pulses/static electricity from damaging the components on the development board [7].

**Button and LED Display Circuit**
There are three buttons and three LED in the development board, and the schematic diagram is as follows (Fig. 2):

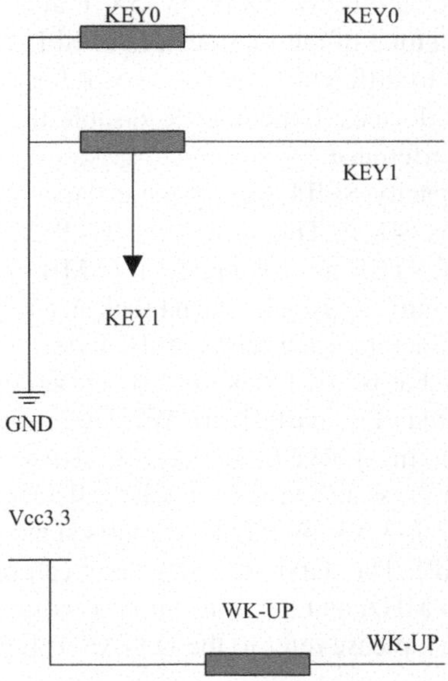


**Fig. 2.** Button circuit

KEY0 and KEY1 are used as common key inputs, which are connected to PA13 and PA15 respectively. They are all connected to JTAG related pins (KEY0 is also connected to SWDIO). In this way, when using KEY0 and KEY1, JTAG can not be used for debugging, which should be noted when using. KEY0 and KEY1 are also shared with DAT and CLK lines of PS/2. They both provide pull-up through pull-up resistor of JTAG. WK_The up key is connected to PA0 (WKUP pin of STM32), which can be used as a wake-up input of STM32 in addition to ordinary input key [8]. This button is triggered by high level. PA0 is also the input pin of DS18B20, so pay attention when using it.

## 2.3 Built-in Storage Module Design

**EEPROM**
In EEPROM, A0–A2 are all grounded. For 24C02, the address bit is set to 0. Pay attention to this when writing programs. IIC_SCL connected to PC12 of MCU, IIC_SDA is connected to PC11 of MCU, but it is not connected to IIC of STM32, because IIC of STM32 is chicken ribs! If you want to use the hardware IIC on the ALIENTEKMiniSTM32 development board, you can also use the hardware IIC by setting pc11 and

PC12 as floating inputs, and then connecting PB10 and PB11 (IIC2) or PB6 and PB7 (IIC1) to PC11 and PC12 through flying wires.

**SPIFLASH**

This development board is equipped with SPIFLASH chip W25X16. The chip has a capacity of 2M bytes, which is at the same level as AT45DB161. The price of ATMEL products has been very unstable recently. Therefore, we have chosen a stable price, good supply, and strong versatility. W25X16. W25X16 also shares SPI1, and F_CS is connected to PA2. So far, a total of the four devices of SPI1 have been introduced, and their CS are all connected to different IO ports (except for the two wireless modules), so when using one of the devices, remember to disable the CS pin of other devices, otherwise there will be interference.

W25Q64 is a high-capacity SPIFLASH product launched by Huabang company. The capacity of W25Q64 is 64MB. This series also has W25Q80/16/32 and so on. The W25Q64 selected by ALIENTEK has a capacity of 64MB, that is, 8M bytes. W25Q64 divides the capacity of 8M into 128 Blocks, each block size is 64K bytes, and each block is further divided into 16 Sectors, each sector is 4K bytes. The minimum erasing unit of W25Q64 is one sector, that is, 4K bytes must be erased each time. In this way, we need to open up a buffer area of at least 4K for W25Q64, so the SRAM requirement is relatively high, and the chip must have more than 4K SRAM to operate well.

W25Q64 has up to 10W erase and write cycles, has a data retention period of 20 years, and supports a voltage of 2.7–3.6 V. W25Q64 supports standard SPI, and also supports dual-output/quad-output SPI. The maximum SPI clock can reach 80 MHz (double the output is equivalent to 160 MHz, and the four-output is equivalent to 320M). For more information about W25Q64, please refer to the DATASHEET of W25Q64.

## 2.4 External Memory Module

This development board contains a standard SD card interface, with this interface, you can expand the capacity of storage devices, can be used to record data. The schematic diagram is as follows:

SD card we use SPI mode communication, the SPI interface of SD card is connected to SPI1 of STM32, SD_CS is connected to PA3, and SPI1 on ALIENTEKMiniSTM32 development board is shared by four peripherals: SD card, NRF24L01 wireless module, JF24C wireless module and W25X16. They can be time-sharing multiplexed by different chip selection signals.

## 2.5 Communication Module

The embedded teaching experiment development board contains two wireless module interfaces, NRF24L01 module and JF24C/D module. They are all wireless modules of 2.4G communication, and have the characteristics of high cost performance. The maximum communication rate of NRF24L01 is 2 Mbps, and that of JF24C/D is 1Mbps. With these two interfaces, wireless communication can be realized.

NRF24L01 wireless module adopts NRF24L01 chip [9]. The main features of the chip are as follows:

1) 2.4G global open ISM frequency band, license-free use.
2) The highest operating rate is 2Mbps, efficient GFSK modulation, and strong anti-interference ability.
3) 125 optional channels to meet the needs of multipoint communication and FM communication.
4) Built-in CRC error detection and point-to-multipoint communication address control.
5) Low working voltage (1.9–3.6 V).
6) Automatic response can be set to ensure reliable data transmission.

The chip communicates with external MCU through SPI, and the maximum SPI speed can reach 10 MHz. The module we use in this chapter is NRF24L01 produced by Shenzhen Yunjia technology, which has been widely used by many companies, and its maturity and stability are quite good.

The voltage range of VCC pin of the module is 1.9–3.6 V. It is recommended not to exceed 3.6 V, otherwise the module may be burnt out. Generally, 3.3 V is suitable. In addition to VCC and GND pins, other pins can be directly connected with the IO port of 5 V MCU. It is precisely because it is compatible with the IO port of 5 V MCU that it has great advantages in use.

# 3 Software Design of Online Distance Learning System for Electrical Automation Technology Major

## 3.1 Login Process Design

Login system gives students and teachers the management authority to use the system, and provides different services for different objects to achieve detailed user authority management. The main functions are as follows:

(1) It provides an interface for teachers and students to log in to the education system, which is convenient for teachers and students to input their account numbers and passwords;
(2) Teachers and students can register their account and password through the registration page, and the system will automatically obtain the MAC of the login device of teachers or students record the address and check whether the account and password have been registered. If the account and password have been registered, you will be prompted to return to login without registering again. If you forget the password, you need to check with the administrator and retrieve the account and password. If the registration is successful, you will be prompted to register successfully and return to the login page. You can log in to the system on the login page.
(3) Verify according to the input of teachers and students. If teachers and students log in to the system and input the account and password at the time of registration, the verification will pass and enter the corresponding system page. If it is not correct, they will not be able to get permission through verification to enter the system, and they will return to the login page and prompt to re-enter [10]. The specific function flow chart is as follows (Fig. 3):

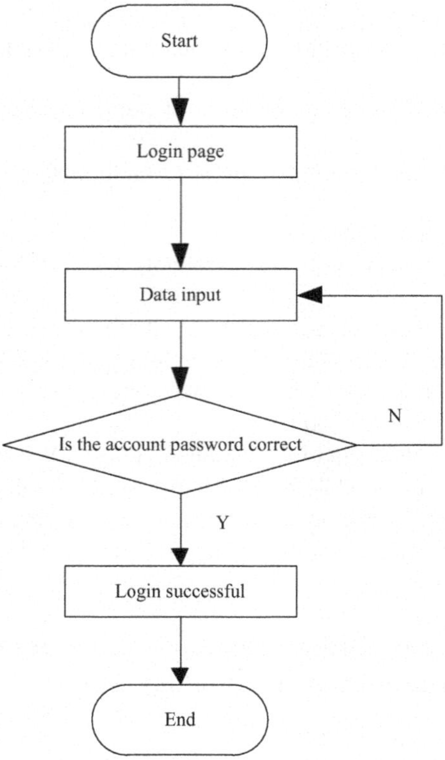


**Fig. 3.** Flow chart of login system function design

### 3.2 System Management Process Design

Teacher management system is one of the most important parts of the whole online education system. It is mainly composed of five modules: information management, class process, online video, submission of materials and message reply. Teachers can realize the basic functions of online teaching through these five modules [11, 12].

Information management module: the information management module mainly refers to the students connected to the teacher's classroom, understanding the basic information of students and managing the information of students, including deletion and modification.

Class process module: the class process module is mainly for teachers to chat and guide the students who have entered their own classroom in real time, and to answer the students' problems in time, which is interactive and timely, and can improve the students' learning enthusiasm [13]. The flow chart of function design is as follows (Fig. 4):

Video management module: video management module is mainly to achieve online video playback, teachers can upload teaching video materials through the module, and manage, classify and delete the uploaded video materials, while students can only watch online video through the online video module of student management system [14].

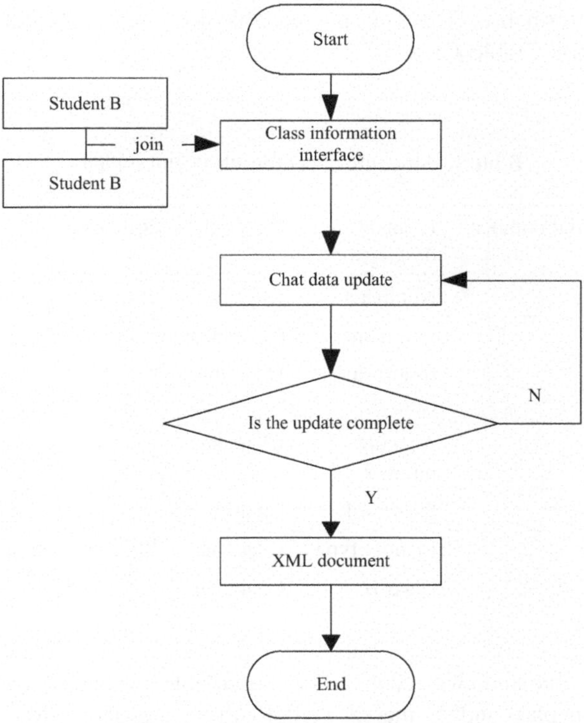


**Fig. 4.** Function design flow chart of class process

Message reply function module: the message reply function is mainly for teachers to display and reply to their own classroom students' after class messages, so that students can provide a questioning module for the questions that they did not think of in time in the process of class, and teachers can reply to the messages after seeing them.

Upload data module: upload data module is mainly for teachers to upload some teaching materials for students to download and learn. Teachers can upload less than 100MB of materials through this module, including review materials such as exercises after class. You can delete the uploaded data.

### 3.3 Database Design

According to the setting of the data storage structure, the data of the technical school online education system can be divided into three tables to store, but the teacher-based information is relatively small, and the student data can be stored together in an xml document, so they are designed separately the two data tables of teacher and student information data table and chat record table are as follows.

(1) Teacher-student information data sheet. The teacher-student information data sheet is mainly used to record the teacher's account, password, name, class ID and the student's name, identity, account number, password, class ID, registration time

and other information [15]. The specific table the structure design is shown in the following table (Table 1):

**Table 1.** Structure data of teachers and students

| Serial number | Element description | Data type | Remarks |
|---|---|---|---|
| 1 | Number | Character | Primary key |
| 2 | Full name | Character | |
| 3 | Registration time | Date time | |
| 4 | Account number | Character | |
| 5 | Password | Character | |
| 6 | Identity type | Character | Teacher/student |
| 7 | Class ID | Character | |

Chat record table and chat record information table are mainly used to record the chat record during class and the message record after class. The following tag elements are applied, and the specific table structure is designed as follows: (Table 2)

**Table 2.** Chat record data table

| Serial number | Element description | Data type | Element length |
|---|---|---|---|
| 1 | Message main element | | |
| 2 | Full name | Character | 10 |
| 3 | Message text | Character | 300 |
| 4 | Message reply | Character | 300 |
| 5 | Main elements of online chat | | |
| 6 | IP address and port | Character | 20 |
| 7 | Text message of online chat | Character | 300 |

At the same time, when storing system data, it was decided to use XML technology, combined with the call of the PHP programming language, to realize data storage and reading, and to abandon large databases such as SQL to increase the speed of data reading.

Mainly use the SIMPLEXML function in PHP. SIMPLEXML is a new feature extension in PHP. The SIMPLEXML extension provides a simple way to get the names, tags and text of XML elements. Compared with other parsers such as DOM, SIMPLEXML can read and write text data from XML elements with just a few lines of code, which is easy to recognize and remember. SIMPLEXML can convert XML documents or XML strings into objects. For example, elements are converted into single attributes of SIMPLEXMLELEMENT objects. When there are multiple elements on the same level, they will be placed in the array. Properties are accessed by using associative arrays, where the index corresponds to the property name. The text inside the element is converted to a string. If an element has multiple text nodes, they are arranged in the order in which they are found. SIMPLEXML is very fast to use when performing basic tasks such as reading/extracting data from XML files/strings, editing text nodes or attributes.

SIMPLEXML extension is a tree based parser, which stores the whole document as a tree data structure. It needs to load the whole document into memory to work. Its structure is shown in the following figure (Fig. 5):

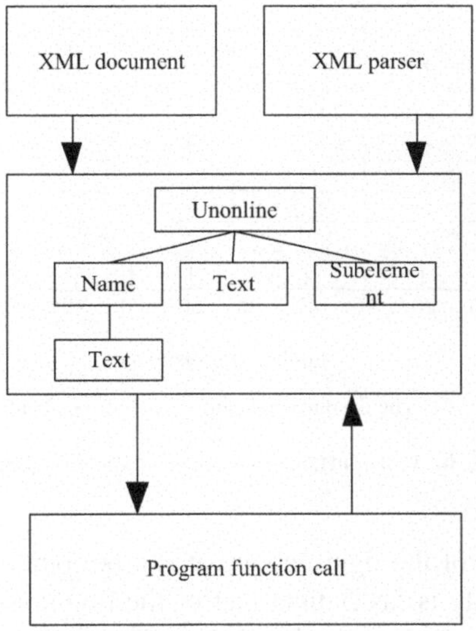


**Fig. 5.** XML reading and writing process

In this way, the design of the system software is completed through the above process.

## 4 Experiment

In order to verify the effectiveness of the designed online distance learning system for electrical automation technology specialty, the experimental analysis is carried out, and the traditional online distance learning system based on information technology is compared with the research system, and the effectiveness of the two systems is compared.

In this paper, the experimental test is carried out under the environment of Intel Xeon Gold6254@3.10 GHz(X2)CPU, 768Gbram, 2× Teslav100GPU, WindowsServer2019 and Matlab. The experimental objects of this paper are the system designed in this paper and the traditional system. By setting the experimental environment and objects, the scientific nature and reliability of the experimental results can be improved.

### 4.1 System Response Speed Comparison

The results of response speed comparison between the research system and the traditional system are shown in the figure below (Fig. 6).

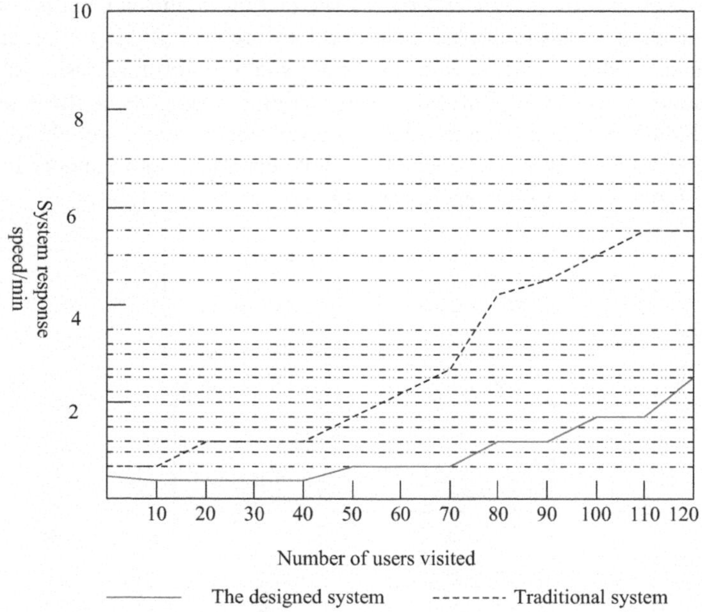


**Fig. 6.** Comparison of system response speed

Through the analysis of the figure above, it can be found that the response speed of the system in this study is faster than that of the traditional system. Although the response speed of the two systems is reduced due to the increase of concurrent users, the system in this study is less affected and has better application effect and faster response speed than the traditional system.

### 4.2 Student Achievement Comparison

Comparing the students' academic performance after applying this system and the traditional system, the comparison results are as follows (Table 3):

Through the above table, we can find that the students' academic performance is significantly higher than that of the traditional system, which proves the effectiveness of the research system.

**Table 3.** Comparison of student performance

| Student | Student scores/points after applying this system | Student | Student grades/points after applying the traditional system |
|---|---|---|---|
| 1 | 98 | 1 | 85 |
| 2 | 95 | 2 | 86 |
| 3 | 98 | 3 | 84 |
| 4 | 97 | 4 | 81 |
| 5 | 98 | 5 | 80 |
| 6 | 95 | 6 | 78 |
| 7 | 98 | 7 | 75 |
| 8 | 96 | 8 | 70 |
| 9 | 95 | 9 | 72 |
| 10 | 98 | 10 | 70 |

## 5 Concluding Remarks

According to the educational needs of an institution, based on the realization of the basic teaching functions of the system, with the main goal of improving the response time and speed of the website, the module function design of the system through research and analysis, and the key technologies to realize each module are researched and tested, build an online education system with students and teachers as the main service objects, design a new teaching model for electrical automation technology education, innovate the teaching model of a school, share a large number of teaching resources, and promote teaching in a technical school Education is advancing with the times. The work done mainly includes:

Firstly, combine the educational and teaching needs of the electrical automation technology professional online education system, including the technical school online education login system, teacher management system, and student management system. It is divided into personal information, class process, online video, and posting messages, Submit documents and other related modules for detailed design;

Secondly, use XML technology to replace database technology for data storage to increase data storage speed, reduce system burden, and improve response speed.

Therefore, the system can be applied to the teaching process of electrical automation technology, in order to solve the shortcomings of traditional learning mode, improve the teaching quality of electrical automation technology, and promote the further development of modern education.

Because this paper does not test the other performance of the system in the experimental part, more experiments are needed in the future to further optimize the performance of the online distance learning system for electrical automation technology specialty, so as to improve the applicability of the system.

## References

1. Efkolidis, N., Garcia-Hernandez, C., Huertas-Talon, J.L., Kyratsis, P.: Sustainability and distance learning: technical universities sharing high cost resources. Int. J. Eng. Educ. **33**(5), 1664–1671 (2017)
2. Gauld, C., Whatley, P.: Distance learning for information professionals: a practical, reality-driven model for postgraduate education. Educ. Inf. **33**(2), 121–133 (2017)
3. Marek, M.W., Wu, W.C.V., Chew, C.S.: Teacher experiences in converting classes to distance learning in the covid-19 pandemic. Int. J. Dist. Educ. Technol. **19**(1), 40–60 (2021)
4. Hsu, C.C., Kung, C.H., Jheng, J.J., Chang, C.Y.: Unsupervised distance learning for extended self-organizing map and visualization of mixed-type data. Intell. Data Anal. **23**(4), 799–823 (2019)
5. Bagattini, N., dos Santos, A.M., Juk, J., Soares, R., Toscano, C.: Vp83 health economics distance learning for healthcare workers in brazil. Int. J. Technol. Assess. Health Care **35**(1), 94–94 (2019)
6. Zeichner, O.: The relationship between extrovert/introvert attributes and feedback on students' achievements. Int. J. Distan. Educ. Technol. **17**(2), 1–17 (2019)
7. Goumopoulos, C., Nicopolitidis, P., Gavalas, D., Kameas, A.: A distance learning curriculum on pervasive computing. Int. J. Contin. Eng. Educ. Life-Long Learn. **27**(1), 122–146 (2017)
8. Dong, H., Gong, S., Liu, C., Ji, Y., Zhong, S.: Large margin relative distance learning for person re-identification. IET Comput. Vis. **11**(6), 455–462 (2017)
9. Zhang, G.: Study on the construction method of the adult distance learning support service system. Boletin Tecnico/Tech. Bull. **55**(20), 516–521 (2017)
10. Omheni, N., Kalboussi, A., Mazhoud, O., Kacem, A.H.: Recognition of learner's personality traits through digital annotations in distance learning. Int. J. Distan. Educ. Technol. **15**(1), 28–51 (2017)
11. Fushun, L.: Design and implementation of distance education system based on computer technology. Pract. Electron. **40**(18), 68–69+81 (2020)
12. Yani, S.: Design of the online examination for distance education based on B/S structure. Tech. Autom. Appl. **37**(07), 48–51,54 (2018)
13. Shuang, L., Rongqin, L., Chen, Y.: Evaluation model of distance student engagement: based on LMS data. Educ. Res. **24**(1), 91–102 (2018)
14. Wei, M.: Research on online teaching system evaluation of distance education. Microcomput. Appl. **35**(11), 127–130 (2019)
15. Wu, H.: Analysis of online examination system of Distance Education under computer network environmen. Digit. Commun. world **84**(04), 276–279 (2020)

# Design of Online Teaching Platform for Packaging and Printing Course Based on Joint Image Denoising

Jia Wang[1(✉)] and Ming Yue[2]

[1] Mechanical Engineering College, Yunnan Open University, Kunming 650500, China
[2] Luliangfu Brand Color Printing Co., Ltd., Qujing 655600, China

**Abstract.** With the development of modern technology, online teaching platform began to appear, but the traditional design of the platform function is not perfect, resulting in the presence of noise when the platform displays teaching images, affecting students' interaction in the platform, so the design of online teaching platform for packaging and printing course based on joint image denoising. This design plans the overall design scheme in advance, sets the corresponding teaching interaction function according to the results of the basic module division of the platform, and optimizes the packaging and printing teaching information combined with image denoising method. Experimental results: compared with the traditional platform, the design of the platform in the display of teaching images, image peak signal-to-noise ratio is higher, clear teaching images stimulate students' learning enthusiasm, so as to strengthen the communication and interaction in the teaching platform.

**Keywords:** Joint image denoising · Packaging and printing course · Online teaching platform

## 1 Introduction

As the basic technology platform of online learning, online teaching platform supports the development of distance learning, a variety of online learning activities and informal learning [1]. The main function of online teaching platform for packaging and printing course is to provide a channel for teaching interaction and teaching resource sharing between teachers and students. With the development of information technology, the teaching resources of packaging and printing course become more and more diverse, but generally speaking, it mainly includes the following two kinds of teaching information: first, packaging and printing course information. It includes course introduction, syllabus, teaching results, teaching calendar, reference materials, timetable and teacher information. Second, packaging and printing classroom resource information. Including coursewares, exercises, assignments and micro course videos [2]. From the traditional learning management system to the large-scale open online course platform, the network teaching platform is also constantly adapting to the development and requirements of


W. Fu et al. (Eds.): eLEOT 2021, LNICST 389, pp. 579–591, 2021.
https://doi.org/10.1007/978-3-030-84383-0_49

information technology and learning environment. Therefore, aiming at the basic content of packaging and printing course, a new online teaching platform is designed based on the joint image denoising method [3]. Based on the way for students to obtain and download the information of packaging and printing course resources: mobile client and browser, the interactive classroom teaching activities are constructed. The activity is divided into two levels. Firstly, the designed platform should be combined with the Android mobile phone client software used by students to realize students' interaction in class; Secondly, the designed platform is combined with campus platform such as web forum to realize students' interaction after class.

## 2 Overall Design of Online Teaching Platform for Package Printing Course

Therefore the platform shares the packing printing curriculum teaching material, first needs to organize the document, organizes the document form from the student user end. Student users can use the Android mobile client and browser to access or download information based on the course and the modules below, which is straightforward and convenient for users. Considering the convenience and shortcut in the organization of server files, we need to set up the corresponding course directory. Among them, the folder "00 _ course" stores package printing course materials, including course introduction, teaching results, teaching calendar and other information. The second level catalogue under "01 _" is the name of the teacher, and the third level catalogue is the courseware corresponding to the teacher. 02 ~ 09 are the corresponding project files under the course, and their three-level directories are the corresponding files under their respective directories. The "10 _ pictures" are some of the teaching files used in the course for packaging and printing pictures. By strictly prescribing the organization form of course materials, the server side can add new course contents, put the new course resource files according to the catalog mode above, and save the catalog of the files to the database conveniently, so that the teaching platform has a good expansibility. Online packaging printing teaching platform, mainly through the use of browsers to complete specific operations, so a dual-mode online teaching platform, taking full account of mobile Internet and intelligent terminal equipment, in teaching plays a good interactive and promotive role, and enhance the enthusiasm and initiative of students. The overall architecture of the mobile Internet-based online teaching platform for packaged print courses is shown in Fig. 1 [4–6].

The server of teaching platform is mainly composed of three parts: network server, application server and database server. The IIS server on Windows platform has the functions of both network server and application server. Teaching platforms target two categories of users: Android mobile clients and PC browsers. The former accesses the teaching platform through mobile client software and the latter accesses the teaching platform through browser software installed on the computer. The design of the online teaching platform, requires the design of two major functions: one is the packaging printing course teaching materials sharing function, and the other is the packaging printing course student interaction function. Classroom interaction is mainly classroom questioning and online testing functions. According to the overall design framework, design a new online teaching platform.

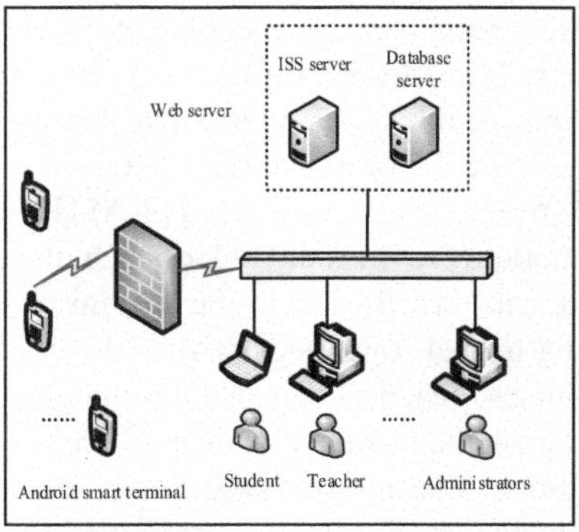


**Fig. 1.** Framework diagram of package printing teaching platform

# 3 Design of Online Teaching Platform for Package Printing Course Based on Joint Image Denoising

## 3.1 Partition Platform Basic Modules

The teaching platform of packaging and printing course adopts modular design method. The modular design mentioned here is different from the software module design, which refers to modularizing the code with relatively independent functions in the software design of an application system to facilitate code reuse, such as user interface module, data access module, etc. Here the modular design, is to consider the teaching function, the entire system layered modular design. Such as the presentation of teaching resources, can be divided into text presentation module, video, audio presentation module; communication can be divided into online communication, non-online communication module. Each function module is closely related to the target, design method and layered model of the platform design, which is helpful for the flexible operation in the actual development and meeting the specific requirements. Reduce the complexity of platform design. First, the teaching information module is designed. Teaching Information provides all kinds of information about packaging and printing courses, including the latest packaging and printing design concepts, the latest teaching documents issued by the school, computer classroom scheduling announcements, practice course schedule adjustment information announcements, etc. Packaging printing consultancy for learners to provide the latest design concepts, in addition to provide students with packaging printing course knowledge introduction, expand students' extra-curricular knowledge. Teaching information provides management service information such as undergraduate teaching plan, textbook receiving and dispatching, course arrangement, result inquiry, etc.

Next designs the teaching resources module. One of the characteristics of the teaching resources module is the rich and diverse forms of expression, which helps to stimulate students' interest in learning. Another characteristic is that the resource design is comprehensive, systematic and logical. For a practical operation, students can not only find video resources in the classroom video, but also find FLASH animation in the animation. The resource navigation module provides the link of each university's package printing teaching system. Students can directly log in the system to select the corresponding practical courses according to their own needs. After the course, students can inquire about the results of the courses. Teachers can also through the link, enter the packaging printing teaching system, view the students' choice of classes, input students' practice course test results. In addition, the link of visual communication and design network platform of some domestic universities is also established to let teachers and students share excellent teaching resources of other schools. Using this module to provide students with comprehensive information in the form of text and pictures, it helps students to understand the objectives and specific contents of packaging printing course.

At the same time design download area module. The practice report is a comprehensive summary of the practice course. It is the basis for the teachers to evaluate the students' mastery of the course of package printing. Students can download printed test reports in the Downloads section. In order to unify the format of students' study report and facilitate teachers' correcting the practice report, the paper provides a standard and representative student's practice report as a reference template. Packaging and printing teaching module, mainly to encourage teachers to learn all kinds of application software, because the construction of resources is a huge project, for teachers familiar with packaging and printing teaching, if they can master these software, the construction of resources will play a considerable role. Certainly these software students may also carry on the click download, carries on the expansion study. Package Printing Course Test Paper: This section is not the main resource of the platform and is available to students for the Theory Course of Package Printing.

Finally, the interactive space module is designed. Interactive space has many functions, such as communication, cooperation and message. It is an interactive environment between students and teachers, students and students, teachers and teachers. Give full play to the initiative of both teaching and learning, give play to the initiative and creativity of students. In this module set up online Q&A, which is the communication module between teachers and students, students can raise questions in practice class or outside the practice class. Answering questions can be divided into in-class answering questions and after-class answering questions. Teachers can either synchronize answers or respond to questions when they have time. The Package Printing Course Forum provides a space for students and teachers to communicate and discuss. The discussion and exchange of the forum is not limited to the content of the learning topic, but can express opinions, discuss experience, exchange and learn from each other. Students in the forum can search by packaging and printing designer, topic and category, and can also participate in the

Q&A. You can also add topics of interest to your favorites. The forum will rank the posts with replies to questions.

### 3.2 Setting up Interactive Functions of Teaching Platform

There are mainly three participants in the interactive teaching platform: students, teachers and administrators. In the design of students' activities, students can use the learning function provided by the platform to assist learning. Students can check the homework after the teacher assigns the homework, submit the package printing picture design homework, and then use the platform to judge and feedback the results to students. Students review their history assignments, review key design topics, and check the problem sets to see how they operate. Using the statistical function of the platform, students can get the statistical results of the recent course of packaging and printing, and arrange the learning plan better. Students use the cloud storage space to save excellent learning attachments on the platform and share them with other users. In the process of using the platform, students can enter the chat room, communicate with other teachers and students in real time, and solve the puzzles in the course of packaging and printing through the wisdom of the group. In the design of teacher's activity function: realize the teacher's online editing function, input high-quality questions into the question bank. The teacher selects the test questions in the question bank, publishes these questions by the assignment form to the student end, guides the student to study [7–10]. Teachers can view the history of homework and homework statistics, the number of students to complete each task and error steps to understand, so as to more targeted adjustment package printing teaching. Teachers use cloud storage space to share learning attachments with other users. At the same time, teachers can also enter the chat room to communicate with the students in the room. In order to ensure the quality of the cloud learning resources, the administrator should audit the questions edited by the teachers online, and then these questions can be input into the question bank. Therefore, the design of the online editing platform, the library to the different categories of teaching materials management packaging printing materials, and packaging printing materials under the database for basic operation. When the administrator maintains the basic information of the whole platform users, he or she has the right to input the topic directly into the item bank.

Through the above steps, the characteristics of the activities of the three participants in the platform are analyzed, and the functions of the platform are set up. Homework management module provides teaching space for teachers and students. Teachers spread the knowledge of packaging and printing by assigning homework. Students think independently by doing homework. At the same time, teachers look at the history of homework, the students have done homework analysis to understand the correct rate of students to complete the homework. But the student then inspects in the packing and printing work the operation mistake part, strengthens to the knowledge which is easy to omit. The question bank management module provides teachers with the scene of designing learning tasks, teachers edit the questions and input the high-quality questions into the questions bank. Administrators to review the subject to ensure the quality of the subject. Also asked to manage the packaging and printing of teaching materials, including the updating and elimination of teaching materials, teaching materials corresponding to the problem of real-time maintenance. The platform management module helps administrators to manage the users of the platform, modify user permissions and roles. The resource management module provides a learning attachment sharing platform for teachers and students. Teachers upload packaging and printing learning attachments to the platform, students download attachments and save them to personal space. At the same time online chat module for teachers and students to provide a platform for instant messaging, students in the process of using the platform, access to online chat rooms, and online teachers and students at the same time, to exchange packaging and printing design process difficulties and skills [11].

According to the storage form of teaching interactive platform resources, known learning attachments are mainly Word, PDF, PPT and other documents, and there are also a small number of video files, intelligent extraction of resource features, documents can be printed by packaging the main word frequency of teaching content, statistics of main features, but video and other streaming media files can not be extracted. Since intelligent extraction is difficult and inaccurate, it is necessary to design a matching model by combining the features of resources with student users to ensure that resources are valuable to students. Therefore, the platform resource management module uses content-based push technology to establish a student resource model:

$$\lambda q = (x_0, x_1, x_2, x_3, x_4, x_5) \tag{1}$$

In the formula: $\lambda$ represents the value of students' knowledge depth; $q$ represents the value of resource knowledge depth. The calculation method of matching parameters of each index can refer to the following equations:

$$\begin{cases} x_0 = (u_0, u_1, u_2, \ldots, u_n) \\ x_1 = (v_0, v_1, v_2, \ldots, v_n) \\ \ldots \\ x_5 = (z_0, z_1, z_2, \ldots, z_n) \end{cases} \tag{2}$$

In the formula: $x_0, x_1, x_2, x_3, x_4, x_5$ respectively represent the subject content involved in the packaging and printing course; $(u_0, u_n)$, $(v_0, v_n)$以及$(z_0, z_n)$ respectively represent the value of knowledge points covered by each packaging and printing teaching course, these values are 0 or 1, where 0 means that the knowledge point is not included, and 1 means that the knowledge point is included. Through the vector group, the knowledge breadth matching model of students and resources is established, and the resource push problem is concretely transformed into the matching degree calculation of students' knowledge model and resource knowledge model. For the similarity calculation between two vectors, this paper uses the angle cosine formula to calculate the similarity between two vectors. If the breadth of knowledge of students and resources is set to sum, there are three problems.

$$\cos\alpha = \frac{AB}{|A||B|} \tag{3}$$

When the angle is larger and the cosine value is smaller, the matching degree between students and resources is lower, so as to set the interactive function of teaching platform [12–16].

## 3.3 Optimization of Packaging and Printing Teaching Information by Combined Image Denoising Method

According to the wavelet coefficients corresponding to the image information and noise, the joint image denoising method performs image denoising on different decomposition scales. From a mathematical point of view, the denoising problem of joint image denoising method can be regarded as a function approximation problem. This method uses certain technology to process the wavelet coefficients of noisy image signal in wavelet domain, filter out the wavelet coefficients corresponding to noise as much as possible, and retain the wavelet coefficients corresponding to image signal as much as possible In order to achieve the purpose of image de-noising, inverse transform reconstruction is used. In this process, the main purpose is to make the denoised packaging printing image as much as possible to achieve an optimal estimation of the original packaging printing image. Its formula expression can be described by the following formula:

$$\begin{cases} s = s_1 + s_2 \\ \beta_{opt} = \arg\min(\|\beta(s) - s_1\|) \\ s_{opt} = \beta_{opt}(s) \end{cases} \tag{4}$$

In the formula, $s$ represents the noisy image information, $s_1$ is the original image information, $s_2$ is the noise, $\beta$ is the mapping from the actual image information space to the wavelet function space, and the optimal solution [17]. The joint image denoising method can be regarded as finding the best mapping The conventional median filtering method is effective for impulse noise denoising, but it is greatly influenced by the size of filter window. When the filter window is small, the image edge feature can be well protected, but the denoising ability is limited. When the filter window is large, the denoising ability can be strengthened, but the protection of image edge feature is weakened. Therefore, there are some contradictions between the ability of protecting image details and denoising, especially when there is a lot of impulse noise. According to the existing research data, when the intensity of impulse noise is more than 0.2, the effect of conventional median filter is poor. In order to solve the problem that the conventional median filter window is fixed and invariant, resulting in the contradiction between the denoising ability and the protection of image details, the joint image denoising method is used to continuously adjust the size of the filter window, and when the current image pixel value is determined as noise, the median value is used to replace it; when the current image pixel value is determined as noise, it remains unchanged, until the teaching platform is designed [18–20].

# 4 Experimental Research

In this experiment, the system is divided into three parts: Hadoop cloud processing platform; HBase distributed massive information database, as well as teaching management control system, using the above system to build the experimental test environment. The test environment is supported by JDK and Tomcat. Download jdk-7u80-linux-i370.bin and apache-tomcat-9.0.17.tar.gz. Configure the IP address and host name of each test machine, and install openssh server to ensure the normal operation of the system program. At the same time, Download hadoop-1.8.1tra.gz installation package to build the running environment of packaging and printing online teaching platform. After completing the above operation, we need to install and configure HBase database. In this step, we need to download the hbase-0.94.12.tar.gz installation package, distribute it to all stages of the cluster, implement the decompression program, and then modify the configuration information of hbase-env.sh. Select the corresponding packaging and printing test image for the teaching platform, which is mainly website image, to test whether different online teaching platforms can improve the signal-to-noise ratio to more than 75%. In order to facilitate comparative analysis, two groups of traditional platforms are selected as the control group. Traditional platform a is designed based on binary method, and traditional platform B is designed based on clustering mining algorithm. Using the way of comparison, according to the different signal-to-noise ratio of three groups of methods, test the noise reduction effect of different platforms for images, so as to demonstrate the interaction of students using the platform under different signal-to-noise ratio conditions.

## 4.1 Noise Reduction Effect Test

In order to test the denoising effect of different teaching platforms, 256 * 256 images are selected as the test objects, and impulse noise is added according to the image resolution (Fig. 2).

**(a)** Original image

**(b)** Noisy image

**Fig. 2.** Experimental test conditions

The designed teaching platform is taken as the test object of the experimental group, and the two traditional teaching platforms are taken as the test objects of the control group A and the control group B respectively. Set the noise density to 0.2, use three teaching platforms to display the teaching image of printing and packaging course, test and analyze the display effect of the same packaging printing image in the three platforms. There are five groups in the experiment. Because the test results are highly similar, only one group of images is given denoising effect, as shown in Fig. 3 below.

**(a)** Experimental group

**(b)** Control group A

**(c)** Control group B

**Fig. 3.** Display effect of teaching pictures on different platforms.

In Fig. 3 the image denoising effect of the experimental group platform is better than the feedback effect of the control group. It can be seen that the experimental group platform has a good denoising ability, which can maximize the retention of image details, make the image clearer and meet the teaching requirements. The peak signal-to-noise ratio (PSNR) of 5 packaging and printing design images in the three platforms is calculated. The results are shown in Table 1 below.

**Table 1.** Statistical table of image peak signal to noise ratio

| Picture number | Experience group | Control group A | Control group B |
|---|---|---|---|
| 01 | 76.0073 | 70.4535 | 68.4624 |
| 02 | 76.0521 | 70.3699 | 68.4547 |
| 03 | 76.0329 | 70.4641 | 68.4439 |
| 04 | 76.0094 | 70.4659 | 68.4528 |
| 05 | 76.0225 | 70.3882 | 68.4525 |

By calculating the average PSNR of the three test groups, it is found that the experimental group is 5.5965 db and 7.5715 db higher than the two control groups respectively.

### 4.2 Teaching Effect Test

In order to further verify the teaching ability of the teaching platform, 100 students were randomly selected to use three groups of teaching platforms for online learning of daily packaging and printing course. The interactive effect of students in the platform is shown in Fig. 4 below.

Figure 4 shows the design of the teaching platform, students on the platform to exchange the number of discussions significantly higher than the two control groups, that the performance of the platform is better, to meet students' learning needs for packaging printing courses, students with a more positive attitude to complete learning tasks, at the same time in a more active state, online interaction with other students and teachers on the platform, packaging printing courses to the implementation of the teaching. In the two control groups, the teaching image of package printing was not clear, which directly affected students' learning enthusiasm and reduced the number of interactions.

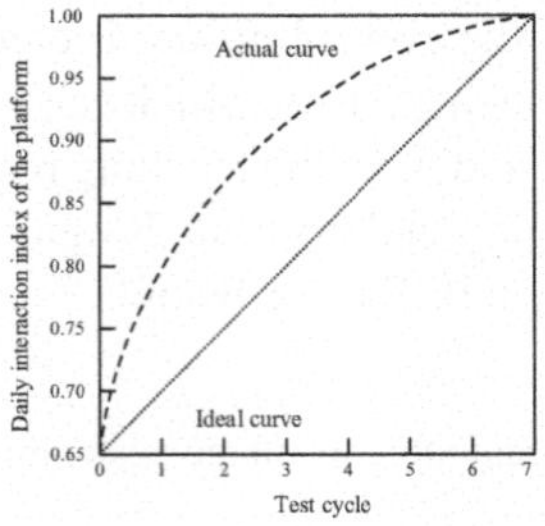


**(a)** Experimental group

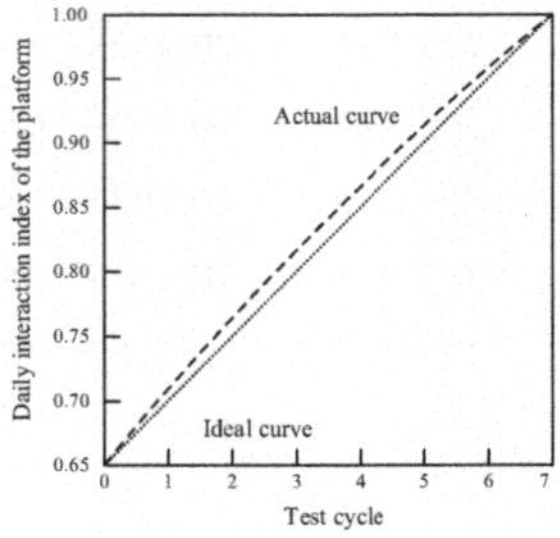


**(b)** Control group A

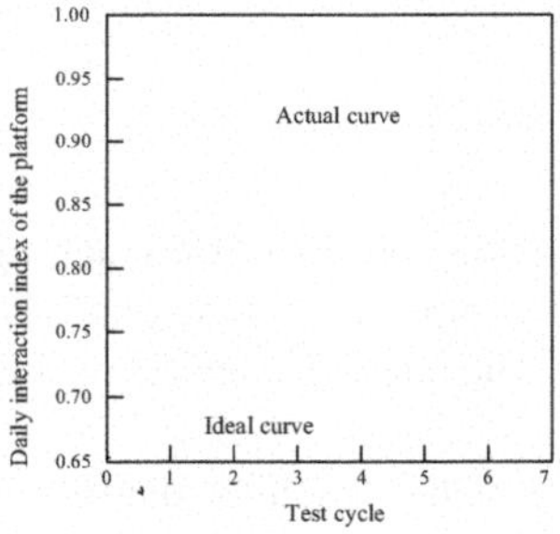


**(c)** Control group B

**Fig. 4.** Student interaction with different platform applications

## 5 Concluding Remarks

The design of the platform in the division of the basic modules, this part can be explained again in the future, through more detailed module division, for the package printing course online teaching, provide a more perfect teaching platform, provide more advanced technology for students to learn.

## References


1. Chen, Y., Hu, C.: Design and management of WeChat learning platform in campus environment. J. Hubei Correspondence University **31**(23), 35–37 (2018)
2. Tong, Y., Tian, Z., Deng, H.: Design and application of the mobile learning platform of college physics based on android. College Phys. **39**(04), 48–52+72 (2020)
3. Li, X., Zhang, Y., Wang, X.-H.: Construction and implementation of professional curriculum system under the transformation and upgrading of packaging and printing industry. Jiaoyu Jiaoxue Luntan (17), 351–352 (2020)
4. Yaping, Z.: Design of network assisted teaching platform based on MOOC+SPOC. J. Tonghua Normal University **39**(02), 8–11 (2018)
5. Wei, L., Erhu, Z., Yajun, C., et al.: Exploration and practice of traditional teaching combining online learning platform for scientific English. Res. Teach. **42**(05), 62–67 (2019)
6. Wei, T., Junqing, C.: The design and implementation of practice teaching platform for college students based on mobile internet. Softw. Eng. **21**(05), 31–33 (2018)
7. Tong, D., Hu, C., Zhu, L., et al.: Construction of multi-dimensional platform for implementing student-centered online teaching of green chemistry. University Chem. **35**(05), 197–204 (2020)
8. Xin, Z., Xiaojie, Z.: Design of APP learning platform for digital electronic technology course based on HTML5. China Mod. Educ. Equipment **11**, 4–7 (2018)
9. Liu, J.: Construction of real-time interactive mode-based online course live broadcast teaching platform for physical training. Int. J. Emerging Technol. Learn. (iJET) **13**(06), 73 (2018)
10. Li, C., Han, C., Han, B., et al.: Construction and practice of "integrated, three-platform and multi-module" experimental teaching system. Acad. Periodical Farm Prod. Processing (01), 83–84+87 (2019)
11. Tao, C., Ming, Y., Ping, M., et al.: Design of comprehensive integrated platform for system modeling and simulation experiment teaching and evaluation. Exp. Technol. Manag. **36**(06), 136–139 (2019)
12. Na, L., Jie, W.: Research on the construction of blended teaching mode based on WeChat public platform—taking law teaching as an example. Mod. Inf. Technol. **4**(14), 179–182 (2020)
13. Fu, W., Liu, S., Srivastava, G.: Optimization of big data scheduling in social networks. Entropy **21**(9), 902 (2019)
14. Liu, S., Bai, W., Zeng, N., et al.: A fast fractal based compression for MRI images. IEEE Access **7**, 62412–62420 (2019)
15. Qing, L., Jiarui, C., Yang, X., et al.: Cloud-sight interactive platform for practical teaching based on continuous quality improvement of china engineering education accreditation. Res. High. Educ. Eng. **12**(4), 99–106 (2020)
16. Jingli, J., Li, G., Hao, L., et al.: Spatial entities matching technology of multi-source spatial vector data for spatial association. Sci. Surveying Mapp. **45**(4), 183–191 (2020)
17. Wentu, M., Youyi, J., Xiao, L., et al.: Denoising method combining non-local mean and wiener filter in wavelet domain. Beijing Surveying Mapp. **33**(9), 1020–1024 (2019)
18. Zhang, S., Wang, L., Chang, C., et al.: Image denoising based on 3D shearlet transform and BM4D. J. Shandong University (Eng. Sci.) **50**(2), 83–90 (2020)
19. Xiao, W., Tang, Z., Liu, J.-p., et al.: Stability characteristics-based zinc-flotation froth image denoising fusing spatial-temporal information. Control Theory Appl. **37**(4), 721–730 (2020)
20. Ma, W., Jiang, Y., Li, X., et al.: Denoising method combining non-local mean and wiener filter in wavelet domain. Beijing Surveying Mapp. **33**(9), 1020–1024 (2019)

# Design of Online Teaching Platform for Printing Color Course Based on Visualization Technology

Jia Wang(✉)

Mechanical Engineering College, Yunnan Open University, Kunming 650500, China

**Abstract.** Due to the unclear entity relationship logic of the traditional online teaching platform, the security of the platform is insufficient in practical application. Therefore, the design of online teaching platform for printing color course based on visualization technology is proposed. The platform architecture is designed based on B/S mode and PHP web development framework. With the support of the architecture, the database is designed to provide data support for the retrieval function of the design, meet the operation needs of users for teaching resources, and intuitively display the required teaching information to users through the designed visual page or interactive device. So far, the design of online teaching platform is completed. The experimental results show that: the designed online teaching platform of printing color course based on visualization technology has low memory leakage probability, fast response time and high fault tolerance rate, and its overall security performance is better than the traditional online teaching platform.

**Keywords:** Visualization technology · Printing color course · Online teaching · Information retrieval

## 1 Introduction

With the rapid development of computer communication technology and mobile terminal technology, the spread speed, breadth, target and efficiency of knowledge have been greatly improved, and people have more ways to learn and receive knowledge. According to relevant statistics, the number of Chinese websites and Internet penetration rate in the past three years have shown an upward trend [1]. The development of network technology has promoted the learners' learning form from a single traditional teaching to a mixed learning mode which combines classroom teaching and network learning. Traditional teaching mode can not meet the diversified learning needs of learners. In this context, web-based education, which is based on an online teaching platform with personalized, autonomous, interactive and other characteristics, has become an indispensable form of education [2, 3].

With the help of network technology, online teaching makes it easier for learners to share learning resources and to interact with each other through forums and chat rooms [4]. Because of the low cost and high profit of network teaching, many colleges


W. Fu et al. (Eds.): eLEOT 2021, LNICST 389, pp. 592–603, 2021.
https://doi.org/10.1007/978-3-030-84383-0_50

and universities in our country have begun to use online teaching platform to carry out teaching activities. With the help of the effective online teaching platform, the high-quality digital learning resources designed and developed are pushed to students in a way that students are willing to accept, and the pace of information construction in colleges and universities is accelerated [5].

Therefore, we need to combine the characteristics of professional resources in Colleges and universities, with the help of relevant platforms, strive to build a digital resource library and build an online teaching platform. From the research at home and abroad, the construction of online teaching platform and website has entered a new stage of development, which is reflected in: the online teaching environment has formed a scale, and the functions of online teaching platform are constantly enriched and improved [6]. These online teaching platforms basically include the following systems: online teaching system, online educational administration management system and online course development system, which respectively complete the functions of web teaching implementation, web teaching management and web course development [7]. In addition, some network teaching platforms also include online teaching resource management system, which includes test database, case database, network courseware database, literature database, etc. Now many products in the market are developed from one of these aspects. After years of accumulation and expansion, they have become a comprehensive platform that can support web-based teaching delivery, teaching management and curriculum development. However, the online teaching platform developed is more for common and popular majors, and some unpopular majors are not used too much. Especially in the teaching of printing color course, in addition to the basic theoretical teaching resources, the teaching of printing color also needs intuitive visual experience, which puts forward higher requirements for the online teaching platform and the security of the platform. The teaching method of early printing color course is more based on theoretical knowledge. As a kind of design major, teachers teach the relevant content to students. With the help of information technology, multimedia technology is used to teach the course. The design of the relevant online teaching platform is only based on the mature teaching platform of other majors, There are still some restrictions on the teaching of printing color course, and many practical operations still need offline teaching. Therefore, the design of online teaching platform of printing color course based on visualization technology is proposed to solve the problems existing in the previous online teaching platform of printing color course.

## 2 Design of Online Teaching Platform for Printing Color Course Based on Visualization Technology

### 2.1 Design Platform Architecture Based on B/S Mode and PHP Web

The online teaching platform is based on the open source platform for architecture and secondary development. In order to standardize the development process and improve the development efficiency, the overall structure of the online teaching platform adopts B/S structure design, and the PHP WEB development framework of the Symfony2 Web Framework realizes the design objectives of the platform [8, 9]. The top layer does not need to rely solely on the implementation details of the bottom layer, and changing the structure of the top layer will not affect the bottom layer, making the code more concise, thus meeting the coupling requirements of the various modules of the platform [10–15].

The View layer of the teaching platform is implemented using the Symfony2 Web Framework framework. Using the Symfony2 Web Framework template tag to implement PHP code functionality, for some complex functions can be directly used PHP tag code to achieve, and finally through the Symfony2 Web Framework template engine to convert the template to PHP files, and then through the caching mechanism to improve access efficiency; the access control layer is implemented through the Symfony2 Web Framework controller, through module mechanism and namespace to distinguish the controller of different modules; the model layer can use the model of the Symfony2 Web Framework, or can directly use the custom model to achieve. The data access layer is implemented by the ORM mechanism of Symfony2 Web Framework, which reduces the complexity of writing data access statements and improves the efficiency of development [16–18].

When the server receives the request of the user to visit the page, it first loads the global configuration file, initializes to load the core framework such as data operation, route, security and so on, schedules the controller and the action according to the route configured by YML, requests the business logic layer and the data layer to load the data, and renders the data to the HTML page, thus completing the whole process of the request operation, and then renders the data to the HTML page. The overall architecture of the online teaching platform is shown in Fig. 1.

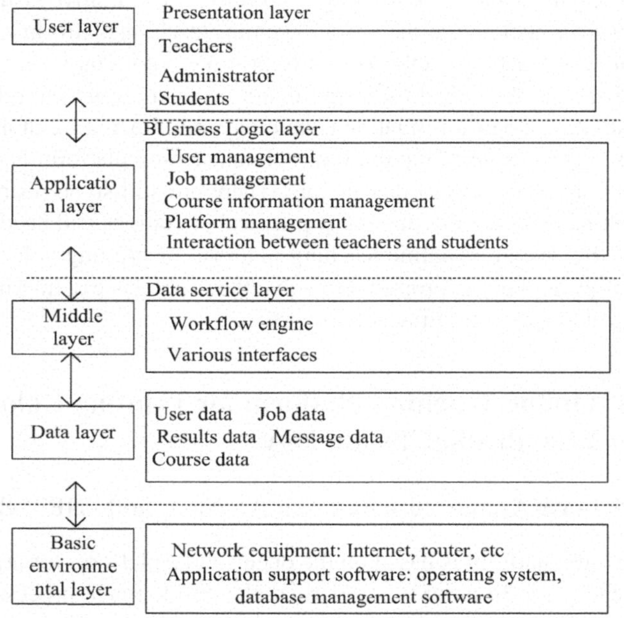


**Fig. 1.** Overall architecture of online teaching platform

The online teaching platform is designed with hierarchical tree structure. Its business logic layer can be divided into 5 modules: user management, course information management, teacher-student interaction, operation management and system management [19–22]. According to the actual functions of the five modules, a database supporting the operation of the platform is designed.

## 2.2 Design of Operational Database Based on Platform User Requirements

Design the key data tables in the database considering the interconnections between the platform users. Identify entity-attribute relationships before designing database key data tables.

The properties of an administrator include the serial number, name and password; the properties of a student user include the serial number, name, password, student number, grade, and selected course number; the properties of a teacher include the serial number, name, password, teacher number, major, course number, and uploaded video number; the properties of a course include the serial number, course name, course classification, course video, class time, teacher name, and student name; the properties of a course examination include the serial number, examination time, examination arrangement, student name, and teacher name; the properties of a student user's message after class include the serial number, student name, teacher name, question content, question time, reply content, reply time, and status; the properties of a score record include the serial number, student name, course title, teacher's score, and answer time; the properties of a course video include the serial number, video name, course title, teacher name, and video description; from the above contents, the users of the platform mainly include administrators, students and teachers, The basic user information data sheet is shown in Table 1.

**Table 1.** Basic information of platform users

| Form serial number | Field name | Type | Length | Describe |
|---|---|---|---|---|
| 001 | A_seq | Int | 8 | Administrator serial number |
| | A_name | Char | 8 | Administrator name |
| | A_pwd | Char | 8 | Administrator login password |
| | A_id | Int | 8 | Primary key, unique |
| 002 | S_id | Int | 8 | Primary key, unique |
| | S_name | Char | 8 | Student name |
| | S_pwd | Char | 8 | Student login password |
| | S_seq | Int | 8 | Student serial number |
| | S_grade | Char | 4 | Student grade |
| | S_cid | Int | 8 | Course number selected by students in the platform |
| 003 | T_id | Int | 8 | Primary key, unique |
| | T_seq | Int | 8 | Teacher serial number |
| | T_name | Char | 8 | Teacher's name |
| | T_pwd | Char | 8 | Teacher login password |
| | T_cid | Int | 8 | Course number offered by teachers |
| | T_vid | Int | 8 | Course video ID uploaded by teacher |

The number format in Table 1 is the standard format of database, all of which are integers. In the database, the relationship between entities is as follows: administrator manages several students, and the relationship between administrator and students is one to many; several students choose several teachers, and the relationship between students and teachers is many to many; a teacher can open several courses, and the relationship between teachers and courses is one to many; a student has several achievement records, and the relationship between students and achievement records is many It is a one to many relationship; a course examination has several students to participate in, students can participate in multiple examinations, the relationship between course examination and students is many to many; a student puts forward a message after class, a message after class is replied by a teacher, and a teacher can reply to multiple messages, the relationship between message after class and students is many to one, message after class and teacher There are many to many relationships between teachers and students; there are many to many relationships between homework and students; there are many to one relationships between homework and teachers; a course is like a course video, a teacher publishes several course videos, there are many to one relationships between course videos and courses, and there are many to one relationships between course videos and teachers. The key data table diagram of the system is shown in Fig. 2.

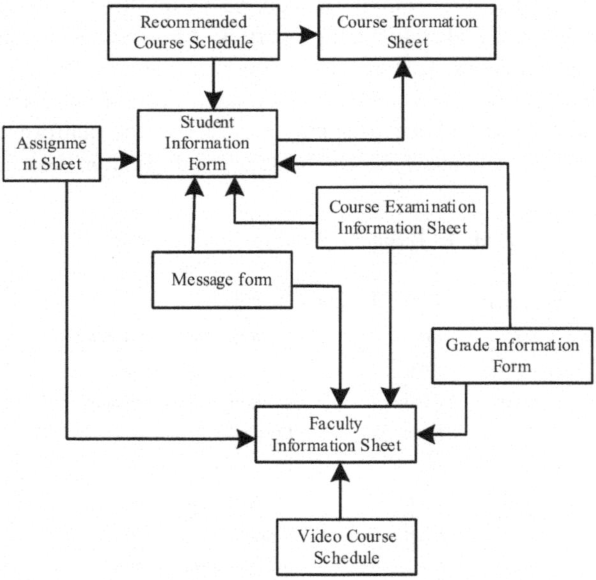


**Fig. 2.** Key data table diagram of database

Through the above design, the following needs can be met: users have different identities, student user information records student information, teacher information records ordinary teachers, educational administrators information and authority information; student users can register and log in, online learning, learning resources have online course information, online video information, learning progress information, a student can choose more than one In online learning, a student corresponds to his own learning progress, and a tutorial corresponds to the learning progress of different students according to the chapter directory; in online evaluation, there are many information, such as online homework, examination question bank, performance report and so on; a student submits many assignments he has completed, and a student corresponds to an exam organized in a certain period, which has the success rate of the exam Performance report; online communication has questions (messages) and other information. A student can ask many questions.

### 2.3 Retrieval Function Design

The retrieval function is to facilitate users to query information, through the user's manual input of vocabulary, and the platform database vocabulary data correlation calculation, and finally present the information needed by users in the platform page.

Assuming that the user manually enters $I$ word and $J$ word in the database, the basic form of the similarity $\kappa(I, J)$ calculation formula is as follows:

$$\kappa(I, J) \approx \sum_{e \in I} \alpha(e, I)\alpha(e, J) \tag{1}$$

Where $e$ represents the term, $\alpha(e, I)$ represents the weight of $e$ in $I$, and $\alpha(e, J)$ represents the weight of $e$ in $J$. Since vocabulary $I$ has been determined, its weight can be ignored in calculation. The weight of $e$ is defined as $\alpha_e = \log \frac{N}{N_e}$, and combined with the weighting function value of the term, it is brought into Formula 1 to get formula 2:

$$\kappa(I, J) = \sum_{e \in I} \alpha(si)e \log \frac{N}{N_e} \tag{2}$$

The formula $\varepsilon(si)e$ represents the weighted value of the node $e$ corresponding to the term and the importance of the term. In order to prevent the influence of the importance of words $si$ on the similarity calculation, log processing is done to get the basic formula of similarity calculation of information retrieval model based on weighted network.

$$\kappa(I, J) = \sum_{e \in I} \log(\alpha(si)e) \log \frac{N}{N_e} \tag{3}$$

Through the above calculation, the similarity between the manually input words and the words in the database is calculated, and the results with large similarity are displayed on the platform page.

### 2.4 Visual Page Design

The visualization of online teaching platform is to present the related data of printing color courses to the users of the platform. The visualization process treats the data as streaming media on the pipeline.

The visualization model is mainly used to process the fitted data and generate the geometry that can be drawn. It includes the processing object and the data object. Data objects are used to represent various types of data. Processing objects act on filters and are used to manipulate data objects and generate new data objects.

There are two basic objects in the data flow in the visualization pipeline: process objects and data objects. The data object has many data types, its parent class is a DataSet class, and the data structure has a standard format. The data types supported by visualization pipeline are structured grids, structured points, polygon data, unstructured grids and unstructured points, etc. Process objects operate on data objects using system-level algorithms for data to generate new data objects. Process objects can be divided into mapping objects (Mapper), filter objects (Filter) and source objects (Source) depending on their role.

The data for the Source object can be either known read in or obtained programmatically. The filter will process the data object through the Source object to generate a new data object. The newly generated data object enters the mapper, maps the color data to a geometric image, and then binds to the presentation object, where the user can set the properties of the presentation object (such as text, color, etc.). After setting properties such as light and camera, the renderer adds the presentation object to the renderer window to draw and display the printing object. Interactive devices provide human-computer interaction (such as scaling, rotation and text display) for demonstration objects.

## 3 Experimental Research on Online Teaching Platform of Printing Color Course Based on Visualization Technology

### 3.1 Database Parameter Settings

In the experiment, contrast experiment is the main method, which includes the visualization based online teaching platform, the spark based online teaching platform and the web based online teaching platform. The contrast experiment is based on the security performance of online teaching platform. Two groups of experiments are designed, one is the platform page operation experiment and the other is the memory leak probability experiment. In order to ensure the impartiality of the experimental results, a unified experimental configuration is set up, which is shown in Table 2.

The setting of experimental parameters is to ensure the fairness of the experiment. Different data types, different acquisition time and different interfaces will have different effects on the attribute and size of the data. For online teaching platform, the change of data size affects the internal data transmission. The larger the data, the longer the transmission time, It will also increase some unnecessary burden and certain data risk for the platform. Therefore, in order to avoid the change of data size affecting the security experimental results of the platform, the same parameters are set.

**Table 2.** Data acquisition field configuration table

| Field name | Field description | Is it required | Remarks |
|---|---|---|---|
| Source tag specification | Source point name | | Node name |
| Source system type | Source system type | Yes | If the node type is calculated point or manual point, select local |
| Source tag type | Source point type | Yes | Numerical type |
| Source tag attribute | Source point properties | Yes | VALUE |
| Source tag unites | Source point unit | | If not, it will be consistent with the target unit |
| Collector name | Interface name | Yes | Select a specified interface name defined in RDI |
| Scan frerquency | Acquisition frequency | Yes | 120 |
| Scan timestamp unit | Acquisition timestamp unit | | S |
| Tolerance, type | Tolerance, type | | |

The experiment is mainly carried out in the local area network, through a switch to test the connection of the experimental environment network, all the platform experiments are carried out in the local area network, try to eliminate external interference, to ensure a closed experimental environment. The experimental environment for deployment is shown in Fig. 3.

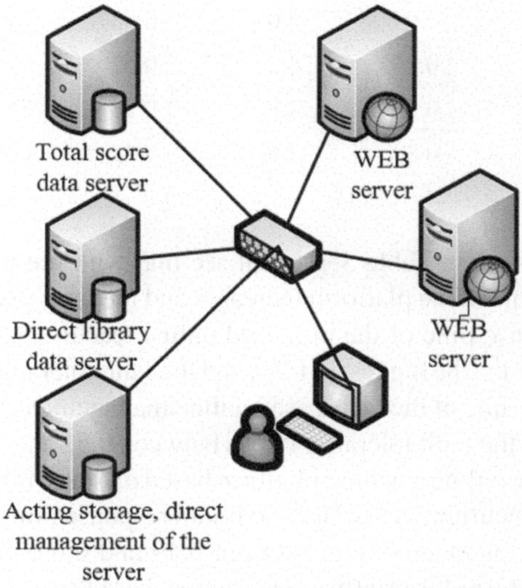


**Fig. 3.** Experimental environment deployment diagram.

Based on the experimental parameters in the table, the energy-saving performance of different databases is tested under the same experimental conditions.

### 3.2 Experimental Results and Analysis of Platform Page Operation

We set the same task for different platforms, and use external plug-ins to calculate the page response time and fault tolerance rate of different platforms. The response time of the page is based on the access time that the user can accept under the normal network. In the experiment, the limit is 2 s. The time below 2 s is the acceptable time, and the time above 2 s is the unacceptable time. The fault tolerance rate mainly determines whether the platform can recover from non serious errors by itself, and its value is between 0 and 1. The closer the value is to 1, the better the fault tolerance rate is, and the platform has a high level of performance Self recovery ability. The experimental results of the two platforms are shown in Table 3.

**Table 3.** Experimental results of platform response time and fault tolerance

| Concurrent visits | An online teaching platform based on visualization technology is proposed | | Online teaching platform based on Web | | Online teaching platform based on spark | |
|---|---|---|---|---|---|---|
| | Response time/s | Fault tolerance | Response time | Fault tolerance | Response time | Fault tolerance |
| 20 | 0.1 | 0.98 | 3.4 | 0.75 | 4.2 | 0.69 |
| 50 | 0.1 | 0.97 | 3.6 | 0.72 | 4.3 | 0.67 |
| 100 | 0.2 | 0.95 | 3.7 | 0.67 | 4.3 | 0.62 |
| 200 | 0.3 | 0.93 | 4.0 | 0.65 | 4.5 | 0.59 |
| 400 | 0.5 | 0.93 | 4.2 | 0.62 | 4.7 | 0.55 |
| 800 | 0.8 | 0.90 | 4.3 | 0.58 | 5.1 | 0.53 |
| 1000 | 1.2 | 0.89 | 4.6 | 0.52 | 5.6 | 0.49 |

Comparing the results in Table 3, we can see that with the increase of concurrent access, the response time of the platform increases and the fault tolerance rate decreases. In this case, the response time of the proposed online teaching platform is always less than 2 s, the lowest is 0.1 s, the highest is 1.2 s, and the fault tolerance rate is between 0.89 and 0.98; the response time of the web-based online management platform is up to 4.6 s, the lowest is 3.4 s, and the fault tolerance rate is between 0.52 and 0.75 with the increase of concurrent visits; the online teaching platform based on spark is between 0.52 and 0.75 with the increase of concurrent visits The maximum response time is 5.6 s, the minimum is 4.2 s, and the fault tolerance rate is between 0.49 and 0.69. To sum up, the design of online teaching platform for printing color course based on visualization technology has less response time, high fault tolerance rate, and high security performance with the increase of concurrent pressure.

### 3.3 Experimental Results and Analysis of Memory Leak Probability

In the experiment of memory leak probability, the leakcanary automatic test tool is used to automatically analyze the memory leak when the platform performs tasks and calculate the memory leak probability. Memory leakage refers to the wrong reference of objects in the platform, which leads to the object occupying the heap resources can not be recycled, and the memory space is seriously wasted. Serious memory leakage will lead to the internal data loss of the platform.

The leakcanary tool is used to automatically detect the internal memory leakage of the platform. The dependency library is introduced into build.gradle to initialize the global configuration. After the initialization configuration, an application named leaks is installed locally to record the log information. If the internal memory leakage is detected, the error information will be sent to the notice and recorded in the leaks. In the actual teaching process, teachers and students need to share courseware or homework and other teaching resources. The size of these shared resources is an important factor affecting the security. In order to verify the relationship between the two, the third-party security plug-in is used to verify.

The probability of memory leakage is closely related to the security of the platform, and its data accuracy is high. Therefore, the experimental results are accurate to two decimal places based on the percentage. The experimental results are shown in Table 4.

**Table 4.** Experimental results of memory leakage probability of different sharing platforms

| Shared resource size/M | An online teaching platform based on visualization technology is proposed | Online teaching platform based on Web | Online teaching platform based on spark |
|---|---|---|---|
| 500 | 9.93% | 9.24% | 0.52% |
| 1024 | 19.24% | 15.62% | 1.26% |
| 5012 | 33.69% | 29.45% | 2.31% |
| 10240 | 41.42% | 36.22% | 5.62% |
| 20480 | 56.35% | 47.85% | 9.41% |

By comparing the results in Table 4, we can see that with the increase of the amount of shared resource data, the memory leakage probability of online teaching platform increases gradually. When the amount of shared resource data is the largest, the memory leakage probability of traditional online teaching platform based on Web and spark is about 50%, which is a relatively high level. The design is based on visualization technology The probability of memory leakage of the online teaching platform is low, which is in line with the actual requirements of the normal online teaching platform. Combined with the experimental results of the platform page operation, we can see that the designed online teaching platform of printing color course based on visualization technology has low memory leakage probability, stable operation of the platform page, and higher security performance.

## 4 Conclusion

According to the actual needs of teachers and students for online learning and teaching in printing color course teaching, this paper studies and designs an online teaching platform based on visualization technology. While realizing the basic function module of the online teaching platform, the secondary development of the teaching platform is carried out, with the addition of homework management, video recommendation and other related functions. The application of online teaching platform provides convenient teaching means for teachers, provides more abundant teaching resources for students, and meets students' personalized, diversified and interactive learning needs. At the same time, it will also promote the construction of informatization and digital campus. In order to achieve the construction of this platform, after the completion of the design, a large number of experiments were carried out to verify the feasibility and effectiveness of the online teaching platform. Of course, the platform is not perfect, there are some problems, the overall design is still rough, the function is still lacking. Due to the limitation of time and personal experience, the functions of the website, the composition and design of page elements are not fully considered, and the development tools are relatively simple. In the follow-up research, we will carry out in-depth research and development from this aspect. After further improving the teaching platform, we will put it into the printing color course teaching of university design major, and realize comprehensive online teaching from theory to practice. It can not only save human and material resources, but also greatly reduce the learning time, so that students have more time to review and practice, Improve teaching efficiency.

## References

1. Wang, J., Wang, X., Yan, M.: Design and implementation of 3D visualization platform based on World Wind . Modern Electron. Tech. **43**(08), 15–18 (2020)
2. Zhou, C.: Visual teaching design of hydrolysis of salts based on IrYdium chemistry lab. Chinese J. Chem. Educ. **40**(03), 75–79 (2019)
3. Hong, D., Li, F., Yao, L., et al.: Design and implementation of a fast data visualization framework for e-learning behavior analysis. Microelectron. Comput. **35**(07), 6–12 (2018)
4. Yang, H., Zhang, Z., Yang, M., et al.: Design and development of online visualization platform for meteorological grid data. Comput. Eng. Appl. **55**(18), 207–211+255 (2019)
5. Tan, Z., Jiang, X.: Interaction design of e-learning platform based on the fogg's behavior model. Packag. Eng. **41**(04), 189–194 (2020)
6. Liu, J.: Construction of real-time interactive mode-based online course live broadcast teaching platform for physical training. Int. J. Emerg. Technol. Learn. (iJET) **13**(06), 73 (2018)
7. Fu, W., Liu, S., Srivastava, G.: Optimization of big data scheduling in social networks. Entropy **21**(9), 902 (2019)
8. Liu, S., Bai, W., Zeng, N., et al.: A fast fractal based compression for MRI images. IEEE Access **7**, 62412–62420 (2019)
9. Sun, L., Liang, Y., Wang, W.: Blended teaching design and preliminary exploration of Environmental Microbiology based on SPOC+Problem orientation. Microbiol. **46**(05), 1226–1234 (2019)
10. Xie, Y., Song, Z., Fu, J.: Design and realization of SE/AIP training simulator based on simulation platform. Comput. Simul. **37**(07), 20–22 (2020)

11. Wei, X., Gu, Q., Luo, Y., et al.: The reform of computer experiment teaching based on O2O model. Comput. Appl. Eng. Educ. **27**(1), 102–111 (2019)
12. Zhao, L., Chen, L., Liu, Q., et al.: Artificial intelligence-based platform for online teaching management systems. J. Intell. Fuzzy Syst. **37**(1), 45–51 (2019)
13. Wei, W., Durbadal, M., Ahmed, F., et al.: Research on the construction of teaching platform of drama film and television literature based on IoT. J. Intell. Fuzzy Syst. **37**(3), 3417–3424 (2019)
14. Peng, F., Hoshang, K., Balas Valentina, E., et al.: Application of deep learning and cloud data platform in college teaching quality evaluation. J. Intell. Fuzzy Syst. **39**(4), 5547–5558 (2020)
15. Wu, D., Shen, H., Lv, Z., et al.: An artificial intelligence and multimedia teaching platform based integration path of IPE and IEE in colleges and universities. J. Intell. Fuzzy Syst. **40**(2), 3767–3776 (2020)
16. Jing, L., Bo, Z., Tian, Q., et al. Network education platform in flipped classroom based on improved cloud computing and support vector machine. J. Intell. Fuzzy Syst. **39**(2), 1793–1803 (2020)
17. Karen, H., Tracie, K., Uyen, L.-J., et al.: Preparing students to be ready for practice: An innovative approach to teaching advanced physical assessment skills online. J. Am. Assoc. Nurse Pract. **31**(11), 640–647 (2019)
18. Fatani Tarah, H.: Student satisfaction with videoconferencing teaching quality during the COVID-19 pandemic. BMC Med. Educ. **20**(1), 396 (2020)
19. Leticia, R., Marco Antonio, M.A., Juvenal, R.R., et al.: Teaching challenges in COVID-19 scenery: teams platform-based student satisfaction approach. Sustainability **12**(18), 7514 (2020)
20. Murray, H., Walker, M., Dawson, J., et al.: Maggio. Teaching evidence-based medicine to medical students using wikipedia as a platform. Acad. Med. **95**(95), 382–386 (2020)
21. Xu, J., Wang, J., Wang, X., et al.: iTest: a novel online testing system based on the WeChat platform. Comput. Appl. Eng. Educ. **27**(4), 885–893 (2019)
22. Marco Antonio, Z.A., Juvenal, R.R., Leticia, R.S., et al.: Analysis of emergency remote education in COVID-19 crisis focused on the perception of the teachers. Sustainability **13**(7), 3820 (2021)

# Design of Online Teaching System of Real Estate Operation and Management Course Based on Cloud Model

Yi-pin Yan(✉) and Qian Peng

Faculty of Management, Chongqing College of Architecture and Technology, Chongqing 400000, China

**Abstract.** In order to improve the performance of the online teaching system for real estate operation and management courses, a cloud model-based online teaching system design for real estate operation and management courses is proposed. The cloud model is applied to the network architecture design of the online teaching system of real estate operation and management courses, and the real estate operation and management courses are realized by designing online management modules, training management modules, course resource management modules, exam resource management modules, and remote video modules Online teaching system design. The test results show that the online teaching system of real estate operation and management courses based on the cloud model has higher performance and speeds up the system's response speed.

**Keywords:** Cloud model · Real estate operation and management · Online teaching · Teaching system

## 1 Introduction

In recent years, with the rapid development of the Internet and the development of multimedia, not only the network resources are abundant, but the application of computer combined with multimedia in education has become more and more extensive [1]. According to my country's Ministry of Education, the construction of a national online learning system consists of three parts: the first part is to establish digital learning content; the second part is to reduce the digital gap between urban and rural areas in primary and secondary schools; the third part is to establish a lifelong learning network platform. In addition, the Ministry of Education actively promotes the nine-year consistent curriculum, and one of its nine-year consistent basic concepts is lifelong learning. Lifelong learning includes: active inquiry, problem solving, and the use of information and world languages. Therefore, the rapid development of the Internet has highlighted the importance of students using Internet resources for learning.

With the development of information technology and the enrichment of network resources, China is committed to the development of digital learning, whether in industry or education Since, e-learning has been officially listed as a national plan and vigorously


W. Fu et al. (Eds.): eLEOT 2021, LNICST 389, pp. 604–616, 2021.
https://doi.org/10.1007/978-3-030-84383-0_51

promoted. The contents include: describing the promotion and planning of China's e-learning environment, the application and Prospect of China's government's e-learning, China's e-learning academic research, the current situation and development of China's e-learning market, and China's e-learning vision and direction. It can be seen that e-learning has become an important factor in the development of national industry or academic education [2]. At present, the teaching methods of integrating information technology into teaching can be divided into three ways. Method 1: the teacher electronizes the textbook, then uses the projector and notebook computer in front of the classroom, and then cooperates with the network in the electronic classroom to teach. This teaching method combining network and self compiled textbook is better than the early school teachers who only use chalk to write blackboard Our teaching environment, whether in the visual or auditory aspects, has more perfect equipment assistance, which is of great help to teachers and listeners [3, 4]. Method 2: the teacher can set the computer screen of the student seat as the implementation screen of the teacher's computer broadcast teaching. The teacher can let the students clearly participate in the classroom teaching through the computer screen in front of each student. At present, this method is mostly used in information class teaching. Method 3: using the TV and computer equipment in the classroom, the network resources of the classroom will be directly broadcast by the TV through the adapter. With the development of modern science and technology and the enrichment of network resources, the whole teaching mode is no longer a single traditional face-to-face teaching in the past, but changes with the application of teachers. According to the research results, whether or not there is computer-assisted teaching or which computer-assisted teaching mode to choose, the degree that really affects students' learning effectiveness and attitude should be related to the students themselves And teachers in the classroom to create a learning environment, so a teacher how to make good use of existing resources in the teaching mode to do the most effective teaching, is a very important topic [5, 6].

At present, the commonly used online teaching system mainly includes the online teaching system based on data mining and the online teaching system based on B/S architecture. But in the practical application, it is found that the application effect of the above system is not ideal. Based on the above background, this paper designed an online teaching system of real estate operation and management course based on cloud model. Under the cloud model environment, it built an online management module, training management module, course resource management module, examination resource management module and remote video module.

## 2 Network Architecture Design of Online Teaching System for Real Estate Operation and Management Course

In order to improve the performance of the system, the database server and system server are deployed on two different servers in the online teaching system of real estate operation and management course [7]. In real estate operation and management course online teaching system server front-end deployment firewall, and then connect the server to the available user access to the LAN. In the early stage of the system operation, the operation mode of single server is adopted temporarily. When a single server can not meet the system requirements, the system runs slowly and crashes, we add a separate database server to specially manage and process the system data After one server can not meet the system requirements, it can also add multiple database servers, separate the data reading and writing from multiple internal program processing servers, and request the client to rotate to the internal server for processing.

In this system, the database server is used to process the data, the Web server is used to provide online information browsing service, and the backup server is used to store and backup the data information. At the same time, the system is connected with the Internet through the hardware firewall. The topology of online teaching system for real estate operation and management courses is shown in Fig. 1.

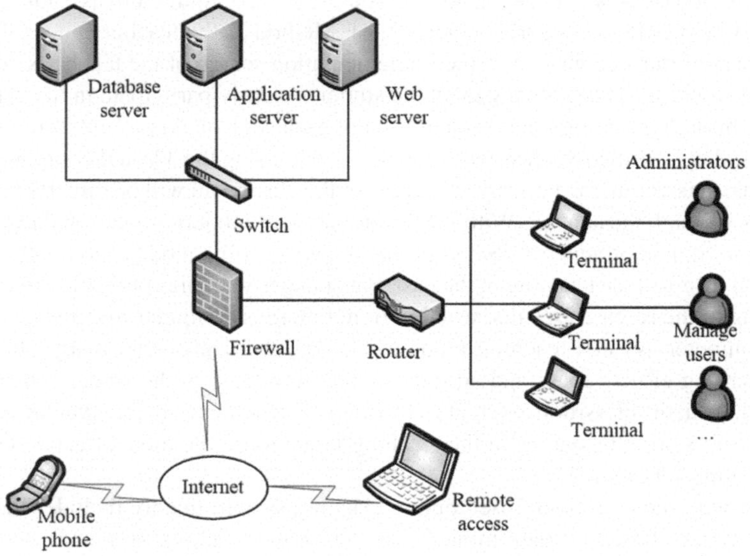


**Fig. 1.** Network topology

The online teaching system server of real estate operation and management course adopts Windows Server 2008 operating system, and the hardware configuration is 8-core CPU, 16 g memory and 250 g hard disk space. Tomcat 6.0 is the server middleware used in distance education system. The database server adopts Windows Server 2008 operating system, and the hardware configuration is 8-core CPU, 16 g memory and 250 g hard disk space. The database adopts my SQL.

## 3 The Functional Module Design of Online Teaching System for Real Estate Operation and Management Courses

In the online teaching system component module of real estate operation and management courses, the main users are system administrators and ordinary users [8–10].

### 3.1 Online Management

Through the administrator to manage the basic information of real estate operation and management online teaching system, such as: student management, role management, portal information management, post qualification classification management, post and post management, etc. Ordinary users can maintain some personal information. As shown in Fig. 2.

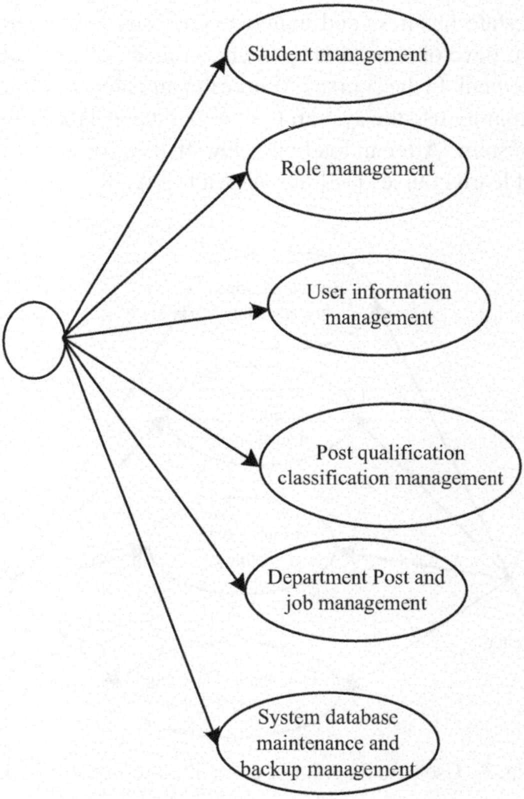


**Fig. 2.** Use case diagram of distance education system

### 3.2 Training Management

Training management is mainly divided into two roles: administrator and ordinary user. Management has the right to manage and maintain the system.

An ordinary user can only view it. For example, in the learning point management system, for an ordinary user, he can only see how much his current learning points are and what level he currently belongs to.

However, the administrator can set the corresponding points rules in the background or modify the points and levels of ordinary users [11, 12]. As ordinary customers, students need to apply for an account and password after completing the student registration, and then learn on the system according to the issued teaching plan. But at the same time, in order to ensure the safety of data, every administrator's operation will be recorded in the database for future audit.

### 3.3 Course Resource Management

Curriculum resource management is one of the important modules of the online teaching system of the real estate business and management course, including course material management, course development management, course content editing, and learning and teaching management. In the course resource management module, the administrator and ordinary users mainly use the system to communicate. The administrator performs operations on the system. After uploading relevant files, ordinary users log in to the system to select and learn courses [13]. As shown in Fig. 3.

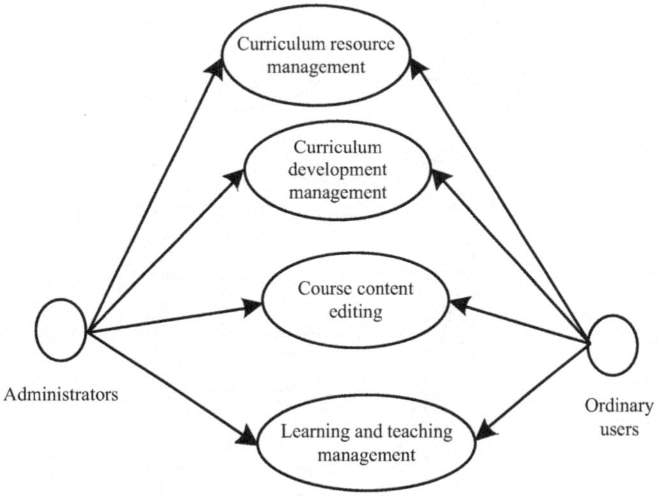


**Fig. 3.** Use case diagram of curriculum resource system

### 3.4 Examination Resource Management

Examination is an important standard for online education and training. The exam resource module is one of the modules of the online teaching system for real estate management and management courses, including question bank management, test paper management, online test management, process monitoring management, scoring management, and score management [14]. The entire examination resource management process involves many aspects. In this process, based on past experience in distance education and training, the original operation process is integrated and the above design method is changed, as shown in Fig. 4.

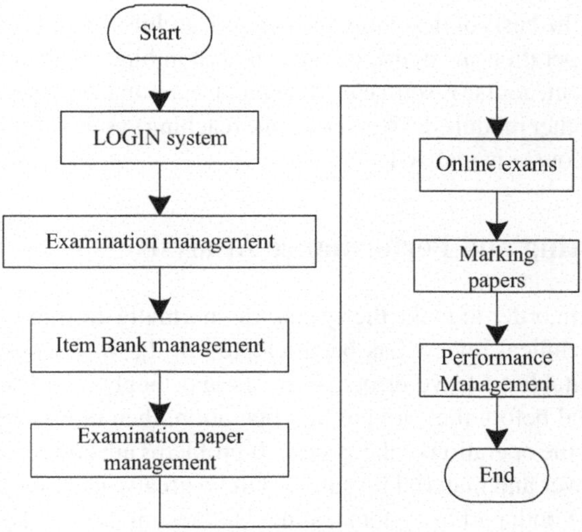


**Fig. 4.** Flow chart of examination management resource system

### 3.5 Remote Video

The remote video module is one of the important modules of the online teaching system of real estate management and management courses, including online teaching management, online learning seminars. Students first log in their user names and passwords on the interface to search, browse and download courseware. They can also watch online videos at any time to make up for their own shortcomings. After forgetting the login password, students can follow the system prompts to retrieve the password, and the operation is quick and convenient, and they will not be unable to log in to the system because they have forgotten the password [15]. As shown in Fig. 5.

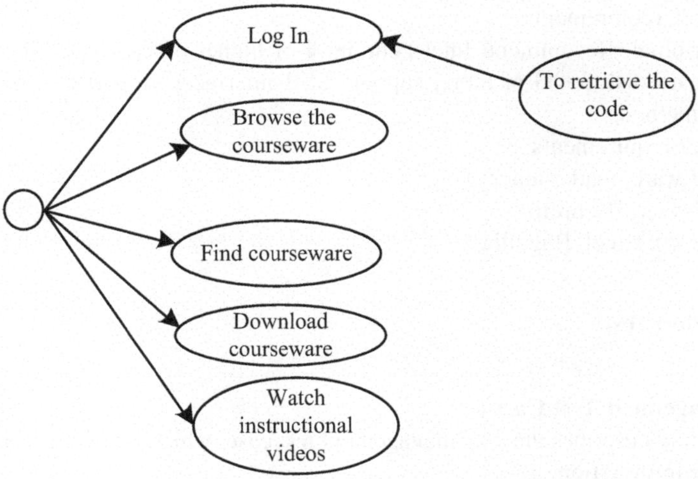


**Fig. 5.** Use case diagram of remote video system

To sum up, on the basis of designing the network architecture of online teaching system of real estate operation and management course, combined with online management, training management, course resource management, examination resource management, remote video and other module design, the online teaching system of real estate operation and management course is realized.

## 4 System Testing and Performance Analysis

A perfect system, in order to make the system run normally, testing is an essential part. Although strict technical review has been adopted in the whole system development process, it is inevitable to leave errors. If errors and loopholes in the system are not found and corrected before they are put into operation, then these loopholes and errors will directly affect the operation of the system. If problems are corrected after they occur, the cost of manpower and material resources will be greatly increased. Unit testing and function testing are both part of system testing. Unit testing is to make developers know that the code is being executed correctly, and the goal of function testing is to verify whether the code plays a given role. Unit tests are written from a developer's perspective. The goal of each test is that the output we get is what we want when we input. It is called function test, which is written for users. The purpose of the test is to make the system run in line with the requirements of users. The so-called software testing mainly focuses on the function and performance. According to the process plan and related testing tools, the results are analyzed and solved. To sum up, in order to improve the quality of software, many related software detection is indispensable.

### 4.1 Testing Environment

The test requirements of the system mainly include hardware requirements and software requirements. The specific configuration is as follows:

1. Hardware requirements
   Test terminal: Recommend Intel Pentium 4 or higher processor, 8GB memory or more, hard disk 300G or more, support USB interface, support multiple network access methods.
2. Software requirements
   Test software: loaderunner
   Test browser: IE, firefox
   Test record: excel, Bugzilla

### 4.2 Function Test

**User Management Test Cases**
Table 1 mainly describes the user management test case, which focuses on viewing and editing user information.

**Table 1.** User management test cases

| Test case description | View user information | Edit user information |
|---|---|---|
| Operation process and data | Click user management to view user information | Add, modify and delete user information |
| Expected results | Display user information, including: user name, user's gender, user's phone, user's picture information | Add, modify and delete user information according to relevant operation |
| Result | √ | √ |

**Permission Management Test Case**
Table 2 mainly describes the permission management test case, which mainly includes viewing user information and editing permission information.

**Table 2.** Permission management test cases

| Test case description | View permission information | Edit permission information |
|---|---|---|
| Operation process and data | Click authority user management to view the relevant information of authority | Add, modify and delete permission information |
| Expected results | Display permission information, including permission name, permission content, permission specific meaning and other information | Add, modify and delete permission information according to relevant operation |
| Result | √ | √ |

**Online Teaching Test Cases**
Table 3 mainly describes the online teaching test case, which mainly includes viewing user information and editing the online teaching information.

**Table 3.** Online teaching test cases

| Online teaching test cases | View online teaching | Editing online teaching |
|---|---|---|
| Operation process and data | Information | Information |
| expected outcome | Click online teaching management to view the online teaching content | Add, modify and delete online teaching information |
| Result | √ | √ |

**Online Test Case**

Table 4 mainly describes the online test case, which consists of the following two parts: viewing user information and editing online test information. The operation process and expected results of these two parts are described in detail in Table 4.

**Table 4.** Online exam test cases

| Test case description | View online exam | Edit online exam |
|---|---|---|
| Operation process and data | Information | Information |
| expected outcome | Click online exam management to view the online exam | Add, modify, and delete online exam information |
| Result | √ | √ |

**Survey Management Test Cases**

Table 5 mainly describes the survey management test cases, which mainly include two parts: viewing user information and survey information. Table 5 describes the operation process and expected results of these two parts in detail.

**Table. 5** Survey management test cases

| Test case description | View survey information | Edit survey information |
|---|---|---|
| Operation process and data | Click Survey Management to view related information about the survey | Add, modify, and delete survey information |
| expected outcome | Display survey information, including: test survey | Follow related operations to add, modify, |
| result | √ | √ |

## 4.3 Performance Testing

In order to better test the performance of the system under high load, the system uses the Loader Runner tool to create multiple groups of different numbers of users to perform simultaneous operations and record the system's response time.

The items tested in this test are: login to the system, online communication, and online teaching.

The test results are shown in Tables 6, 7 and 8.

**Table 6.** Login system test

| Login system test case | | | |
|---|---|---|---|
| Precondition | In the normal login interface | | |
| Test target | Understand the performance of the system under simultaneous login of multiple users | | |
| method | Use LoadRunner tools to simulate multi-user login scenarios and execute test scripts | | |
| Number of concurrent tests | Average time to complete business(s) | Maximum time-consuming business completion(s) | Average use of network packets |
| 30 | 1.045 | 2.345 | 67 |
| 60 | 4.231 | 6.892 | 68 |
| 200 | 5.123 | 9.352 | 100 |

**Table 7.** Online communication test

| Online communication test cases | | | |
|---|---|---|---|
| Precondition | Normal login system | | |
| Test target | Understand the performance of the system in simultaneous online communication with multiple users | | |
| Method | Use the LoadRunner tool to simulate multi-user online communication scenarios and execute test scripts | | |
| Number of concurrent tests | Average time to complete business(s) | Maximum time-consuming business completion(s) | Average use of network packets |
| 30 | 1.235 | 2.231 | 64 |
| 60 | 3.123 | 6.234 | 66 |
| 200 | 5.123 | 11.233 | 79 |

### 4.4 Test Conclusion

After unit testing and functional testing of the online teaching system, the system has reached the standard of design requirements. The system has stable speed and good performance under the condition of less than 200 users, but when there are more than 200 users online at the same time, the system efficiency is low and the response is slow. At present, it has been optimized by adopting the following methods:

**Table 8.** Online teaching test

| Online teaching test cases | | | |
|---|---|---|---|
| Precondition | Normal login system | | |
| Test target | Understand the performance of the system under simultaneous online teaching by multiple users | | |
| Method | Use LoadRunner tools to simulate multi-user online teaching scenarios and execute test scripts | | |
| Number of concurrent tests | Average time to complete business(s) | Maximum time-consuming business completion(s) | Average use of network packets |
| 30 | 1.892 | 3.123 | 72 |
| 60 | 5.122 | 8.213 | 75 |
| 200 | 6.781 | 13.112 | 129 |

1. Database access performance optimization
   Establishing, opening and closing links is a common operation method for users to access database resources. In the process of these operations, information exchange is necessary to ensure that the database can pass the authentication. When users open and close such operations, hibernate can use the connection pool to change the impact of these operations on the system. The user's database connection is stored in the connection pool. The user can take it out when needed and put it back when not needed, and then wait for the customer to use and request it again. However, the carrying capacity of connection pool is also limited. If it is still required to be used when the connection pool is running at full load, it will have a great impact on the function of connection pool.
2. Data caching
   Hibernate has some simple mechanisms to store them when there is no need to dynamically calculate page output or data for each page request. In addition, sorting out cached pages and data requests can improve the efficiency of these pages.
3. Tomcat server optimization

Tomcat 7.0 server is a common web server, which is widely used in web applications. However, the server needs to be optimized according to different scenarios to ensure the best use effect. In order to improve the response speed of the system, the system can be optimized as follows:

Memory Optimization
Because the business logic processing of the web server is put into the memory, the insufficient memory will lead to the data need to be put into the hard disk. When necessary, it will be taken out from the hard disk and put into the memory. In order to improve the hit rate of the memory, the system improves the Tomcat server's memory configuration

to 4G. Since this web server has 8g of memory, the 4G memory overhead is completely affordable.

Connector Optimization
In the Tomcat server, a thread needs to be opened for each request to serve it. When there are too many users, due to the limited number of threads, it is necessary to wait for the completion of other business processing before continuing to use the thread, which results in slow user response. In order to ensure that the system is connected quickly, it is necessary to first recommend a connection pool with sufficient number of connections. This pool can well support the requirement of 1000 people online at the same time. Therefore, the system defines the number of connection pools as 1000, which is much more than The original 800, but from the test results, it does solve the current problem of tight connection threads.

Enable Tomcat7.0 Compression (HTTP Compression) Function
In order to reduce the amount of data during system transmission, this system uses HTTP compression, which can greatly reduce the number of HTTP packets and improve the response speed of web pages. Specific compression algorithms can include GZIP, etc., which are supported by current browsers.

After using it, it can be clearly seen that the browsing performance of the browser is improved by more than 4 times after using the page cache.

## 5 Conclusion

In this paper, based on the real estate business and management courses online teaching system architecture, from the online management, training management, curriculum resource management, resource management, exam remote video, etc., the design based on cloud model of the real estate business and management courses online teaching system, and through the experimental results show that the performance of the system is good.

## References

1. Özyurt, Ö., Özyurt, H., Baki, A.: Design and development of an innovative individualized adaptive and intelligent e-learning system for teaching–learning of probability unit: details of UZWEBMAT. Expert Syst. Appl. **40**(8), 2914–2940 (2013)
2. Winzker, M., Schwandt, A.: Teaching embedded system concepts for technological literacy. IEEE Trans. Educ. **54**(2), 210–215 (2011)
3. Khairurrijal, Munir, M.M., Suhendi, A., et al.: An AT89S52 microcontroller-based single board computer for teaching an instrumentation system course. Comput. Appl. Eng. Educ. **15**(2), 166–173 (2010)
4. Zhu, J.: Multimedia music teaching system application. Key Eng. Mater. **474–476**, 1903–1908 (2011)
5. Kaznacheeva, A.O.: Teaching system for training specialists in the development and operation of magnetic resonance tomographs. Meas. Tech. **53**(4), 459–462 (2010)
6. Yang, H., Lin, S.: The application of improved fuzzy comprehensive evaluation method in practice teaching quality evaluation system. Int. J. Technol. Manage. **8**, 60–64 (2013)

7. Li, Y., Zhang, D., Guo, H., et al.: A novel virtual simulation teaching system for numerically controlled machining. Int. J. Mech. Eng. Educ. **46**(1), 64–82 (2018)
8. Fu, W., Liu, S., Srivastava, G.: Optimization of big data scheduling in social networks. Entropy **21**(9), 902 (2019)
9. Liu, S., Glowatz, M., Zappatore, M., et al. (eds.): E-Learning, E-Education, and Online Training, pp. 1–374. Springer, Cham (2018)
10. Liu, S., Li, Z., Zhang, Y., et al.: Introduction of key problems in long-distance learning and training. Mob. Netw. Appl. **24**(1), 1–4 (2019)
11. Jiang, Y.Y.: Research on SPOC and flipped classroom teaching mode based real estate operation and management. China Educ. Technol. Equipment (20), 102–104 (2018)
12. Fan, Y., Liu, M.: Design and research of online education course resource sharing based on cloud platform. Mod. Elec. Tech. **43**(01), 175–178 (2020)
13. Luo, L.L.: Design of online and offline hybrid intelligent assistant teaching system. Microcomput. Appl. **35**(08), 105–108 (2019)
14. Deng, Y.: Design and implementation of multimedia teaching platform based on cloud computing. Electron. Des. Eng. **26**(08), 162–167 (2018)
15. Zhang, H.W., Wang, H.X., Guo, J.F., et al.: Online teaching of embedded system based on Tencent classroom and virtual simulation technology. Exp. Technol. Manag. **37**(12), 170–174 (2020)

# Design of a Flipped Classroom Platform for Online Music Education in Colleges and Universities Based on the Internet

Hui Lin[1](✉) and Yang-bo Wu[2]

[1] Xinyu University, Xinyu 338000, China
[2] College of Mathematics and Computer, Xinyu University, Xinyu 338000, China

**Abstract.** Online music education is one of the important contents of college education. However, the traditional education mode is too old to cultivate students' innovative consciousness and music practice ability. With the development of Internet technology, great changes have taken place in various fields, and the curriculum system and the mode of music education in colleges and universities have also been affected. Based on the background of "Internet", this paper constructs the classroom platform of online music education in colleges and universities, and puts forward clear provisions on education contents, teaching methods and teacher training. The research proves that the designed platform can effectively improve the quality of classroom teaching, provide high ability compound talents for the society, and has a very good application prospect.

**Keywords:** Internet background · College music · Music education · Education platform

## 1 Introduction

The forms of video and broadcasting in online teaching are carried out in real time, which can effectively improve the learning efficiency of learners. Therefore, online video has become an indispensable learning method in the field of Internet education [1, 2].

The 21st century is the network information age, the Internet gradually infiltrates into each profession, and is playing the key role, is playing the important role in the education profession [3]. This paper designs the overturning classroom platform of online music education in colleges and universities under the background of Internet. The external and internal resources of the Internet constitute the basic resource module. Different sub-layer modules constitute the logical layer of the platform. The service application layer, security layer and data layer constitute the resource operation service module. The construction process of the system is completed. This process clarifies the concept of overturning classroom, analyzes the path of education development, and proves that the overturning classroom platform can effectively cultivate music talents, improve teaching quality, and meet the rapid development of economic level and social needs [4].


W. Fu et al. (Eds.): eLEOT 2021, LNICST 389, pp. 617–630, 2021.
https://doi.org/10.1007/978-3-030-84383-0_52

Based on the above research background, this paper designs a new college music online education reversal classroom platform from the structure and operation of the Internet platform, and validates its effectiveness.

## 2 Internet-Based Classroom Platform Mode for Online Music Education in Colleges and Universities

Although online music education in colleges and universities can take the most traditional way of classroom teaching, but the effect is not good [5]. Traditional teaching methods pay more attention to theoretical explanation, lack of practical teaching, students understand it very difficult [6]. The Internet can be built on the network to help students learn at any time, anywhere [7], while the network can expand a lot of resources together, the introduction of state-of-the-art music education courses, students can intuitively learn music master lectures [8]. Internet teaching is also more diversified in learning methods, whether online tutoring or offline practice, can improve the learning effect of students, pay more attention to the ability to test in the assessment, not limited to theoretical knowledge.

The Internet has a profound impact on music curriculum, changing the structure of the classroom and curriculum content, the current music education curriculum can not leave the Internet. Music courses can be divided into modules according to the students' musical skills, including: music initiation course, music case course, music practice course and music competition. The teaching structure adopts online and offline simultaneous teaching, which is not equivalent to the traditional professional courses, public courses, elective courses and expansion courses. The teaching mode under the Internet completely trains the students' abilities, exercises the students' thinking mode and enables them to have better music skills [9].

Traditional music online education flip platform is composed of self-built infrastructure. Because its server occupies a large amount of memory, flip classroom platform will happen when the number of users exceeds the limit, Karton and automatically exit the platform [10]. Some illegal personnel will make use of platform loopholes to steal classroom resources on the platform, there is no guarantee to reverse the intellectual property rights of classroom resources. In order to solve this problem, a new online music education turnover platform is designed based on the Internet. The platform is composed of resource infrastructure module, resource operation service module and resource access output module. The Internet-based College Music Online Education Reversal Classroom Platform Module is shown in Fig. 1 below:

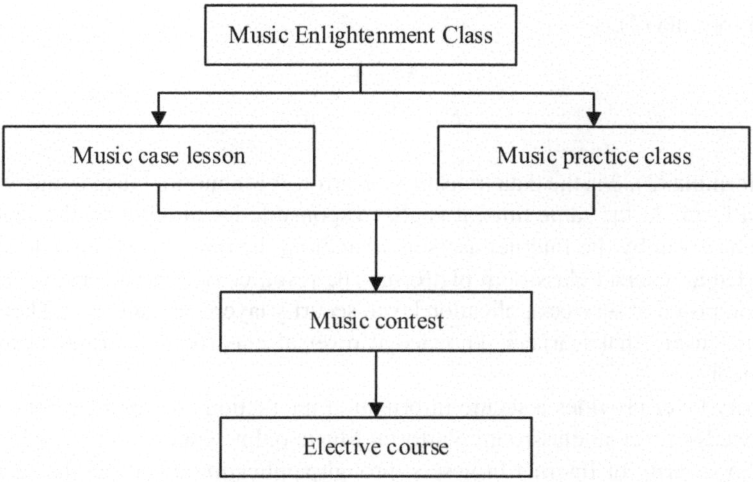


**Fig. 1.** Internet-based classroom platform for online music education in colleges and universities

The core of the resource infrastructure module is the processing method of cloud computing resources. It can logically classify all the data entered on the music online education reverse platform. There is a logic layer and a presentation layer in the resource infrastructure module. The resource base module is used to identify data, and the specific process is shown in Eq. (1).

$$G = \frac{\sum_{i=1} f_i u}{A} - \lambda \tag{1}$$

In formula (1), $A$ represents the total amount of data to be processed. $u$ stands for data transmission speed. The size of the $n$ data in the data is $f_i$ The advantage of the cloud computing resource processing model is that it can identify and analyze data, quickly determine the type of data, use the least time and space to analyze the corresponding data and finally classify the data for storage [11].

The logical layer of the resource infrastructure module is composed of many different sub-layer modules. These sub-layer modules are the places where different types of materials in the music online education flip platform are stored. Each sub-layer module has a unique function to facilitate learners to use the Internet. Easy to call. After a lot of data investigation, all knowledge resources are related and there is no hierarchical relationship, so all sub-layers are in a cooperative relationship to form a complete resource infrastructure block. The task of the presentation layer is to extract and express resources by receiving remote call signals from learners.

The resource operation service module is the main module for regulating and controlling the online music education reversal platform, and its main task is to prevent external lawbreakers from stealing knowledge resources by real-time monitoring the operation of the knowledge reversal classroom platform. The specific control process is shown in formula (2).

$$F = \frac{\sum_{i=1} f_i \vartheta}{G} - \partial \tag{2}$$

AIn formula (2), $\partial$ is the data transmission error. $\vartheta$ is abnormal data in the operation of the platform. At the same time, it is also responsible for monitoring the scheduling instructions given by the Internet users and handling the opinions of some learners on the knowledge reversal classroom platform. The resource operation service module is mainly composed of service application layer, security layer and data layer. The security layer is to ensure that learners' knowledge reversal classroom platform is in a safe environment.

Security layer provides a secure information interaction environment for browsers and knowledge reversal classroom platform. Music online education reversal platform detects the security of Internet browsers through application layer and the security of data resources inside the reversal classroom platform through application layer. The service application layer mainly provides the ordering and inquiry service for some paid resources in the process of Internet to learners [12]. At the same time, when the music online education platform updates new functions, the service application layer will investigate and give reasonable feedback according to the learning tendency of different learners [13]. Compared with the data layer of the traditional inversion classroom platform, the data layer of the online music education inversion platform based on the Internet has a prominent improvement. The data layer of the resource application service block also verifies the collected learning resource data, prevents some unscientific information from entering the formal overturning classroom platform, disturbs the learning cognition of the Internet users, and increases the reliability of the Internet-based overturning platform for online music education.

The resource access module is to collect learning resources from different aspects through multiple ways, and then access the resources legally based on the Internet-based online music education reversal platform within the reversal classroom platform, expand the field of knowledge reversal classroom platform and absorb the external resources of the resource infrastructure block [14]. Compared with the traditional Flip Platform of Music Online Education, the Flip Platform of Music Online Education in this paper sets up an additional resource terminal, which ensures the real-time and high efficiency of the Flip Platform resources. If the application layer collects better learning resources, the original resources will be destroyed through the resource terminal when the resources enter the Flip Platform.

## 3 Construction of Internet-Based Classroom Platform for Online Music Education in Colleges and Universities

Many people think that the music platform is to "train musicians" and "solve the employment problem", which is a wrong understanding of the music platform, and this way of understanding will cause the education platform to become a platform for individual students. At present, there are many problems in college education [15]. Although the teachers can understand the teaching goal before teaching, they only pay attention to "passing on knowledge" and "passing on skills", but ignore whether the students can achieve the teaching goal and really master the knowledge passed on by the teachers [16]. Today, with the rapid development of science and technology, the market competition is becoming more and more fierce. Education should not remain in the teaching of book knowledge, but should take into account students' personal feelings, interests and hobbies. Besides "teaching and solving puzzles", it is also necessary to help students establish a correct outlook on life and values, grasp students' ideological trends and emotional changes, and improve students' comprehensive quality.

In the teaching method, the innovation music education platform must be more diverse. Teachers should make full use of available tools to convey information to students. Teaching should not stay on textbooks, chalk or blackboards. The Internet era provides a lot of resources for students, but also provides more convenient teaching means for teachers [17]. Electronic teaching plans, multimedia courseware, network courses, distance learning, video and other means should all become the mainstream teaching means of the Internet era. Through these new means to attract students' attention, thus achieving the goal of effective communication of information. Only in this way can students and the whole teaching system make common progress. Teachers can help students understand music opportunities through the music process of typical social enterprises, and clarify how to manage, laying the foundation for future music practice. Many famous colleges abroad will apply the teaching method of combining practice with theory [8]. Baisen Business School of famous business school has abandoned the traditional teaching method when developing the students' musical practice ability. They let the students understand the music spirit through on-the-spot teaching, and use the visit to music companies to cultivate the students' musical enthusiasm. The above teaching method of combining interest with knowledge can effectively stimulate the students' enthusiasm for learning.

Teachers are one of the factors that can not be ignored in constructing innovative music education platform in colleges and universities. Innovative music courses are a combination of theory and practice. Teachers with rich professional knowledge and strong teaching ability are required to teach them [18]. In addition to a solid foundation of knowledge, the teachers of the College must always contact with enterprises and elites in investment, music, management, etc., to master the latest music information, and to promote students' progress through the support of enterprises. Schools shall integrate excellent teachers, set up innovative music teaching and research offices, set up a number of teachers with high level and strong ability, carry out special training on a regular basis, vigorously cultivate young backbone teachers [19], provide opportunities for teachers to exchange and visit schools, and encourage teachers to visit excellent music enterprises and learn about music practice experience. The establishment of an assessment system, the inclusion of innovative achievements in music education in the indicators for the assessment of teachers' professional skills, the implementation of a reward and punishment mechanism, and the commendation and encouragement of teachers with excellent performance and outstanding ability may enhance the enthusiasm of teachers and encourage more teachers to make continuous progress by improving their treatment and paying bonuses [20]. Besides the teachers, the school can also invite investors, celebrities, musicians, experts and scholars from all walks of life to come to the school to give lectures regularly and use their own experience to teach and explain to the students. Innovative Music Education Architecture as shown in Fig. 2:

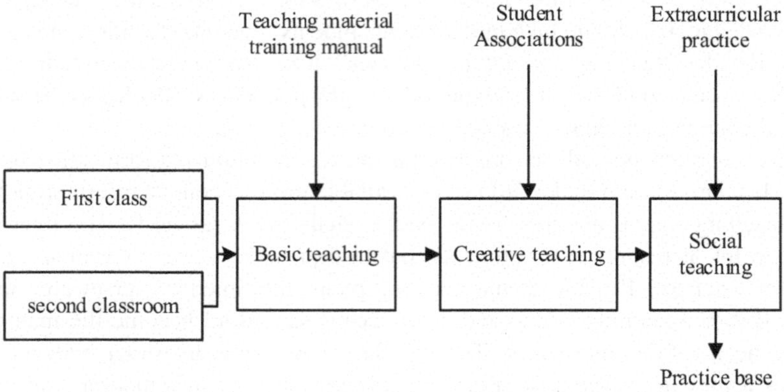


**Fig. 2.** Innovative music education architecture

With the deepening of the curriculum reform, many colleges and universities have included innovative music education into the scope of education and teaching reform, and have made some efforts. Although great progress has been made through various efforts, there are still many problems, such as: the reform of innovative music education form is still too single, lack of overall control, and lack of systematic. Therefore, it is necessary to have a complete classroom system, linking the contents of each class, forming a perfect curriculum system, so as to gradually enhance the students' musical practice ability. In the music course, The musical thinking of college students should be cultivated. Through other courses, students can have a superficial understanding of the framework of music knowledge. Students have a keen understanding of music and establish a basic understanding of music. Colleges and universities can encourage students to participate in a series of elective courses such as music fundamentals and music programs through credits to learn more about music [21]. When setting up elective courses, the professional platform may be set up according to the characteristics of the colleges and universities, and compulsory requirements shall be adopted for students to take at least one elective course, so as to encourage students to expand the scope of knowledge and actively participate in various extracurricular practices while learning the basic knowledge. Schools can organize mass organizations, create a musical atmosphere, strengthen the construction of campus culture, improve students' comprehensive level and enhance students' social adaptability.

Teaching links can not be a single simple. The principle from simple to in-depth should be followed. The interconnection between the various links is guaranteed. On the premise of ensuring that students can have enough learning space, teach students knowledge to the greatest extent. The music education may carry on the pointed teaching according to student's individual characteristic, the development consults the service, helps the university student to answer questions [22]. In addition, schools can actively carry out various lectures, face-to-face teaching, students can interact with the lecturer, through this way to solve the problems faced by students, while enhancing students' interest in learning. The teaching system should be perfected and innovated from four aspects: basic teaching, creative teaching, social teaching and cooperative teaching (Fig. 3).

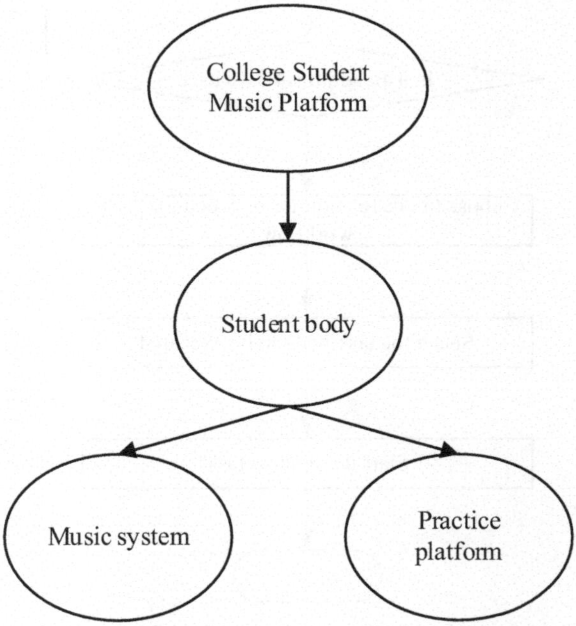


**Fig. 3.** Innovative music education practice platform

The establishment of innovative music education practice platform is of great significance to the development of students' innovative ability. The degree of grasping theory depends on practice, and practice is the only means to test the truth.

## 4 Workflow Design of Music Online Education Turnover Platform Based on Internet

Because the traditional knowledge reversal classroom platform adopts the method of recording and broadcasting, the internal learning data of the platform may change with the change of time, which will lead to some misunderstandings to the learners. The complete process task execution process diagram is shown below (Fig. 4):

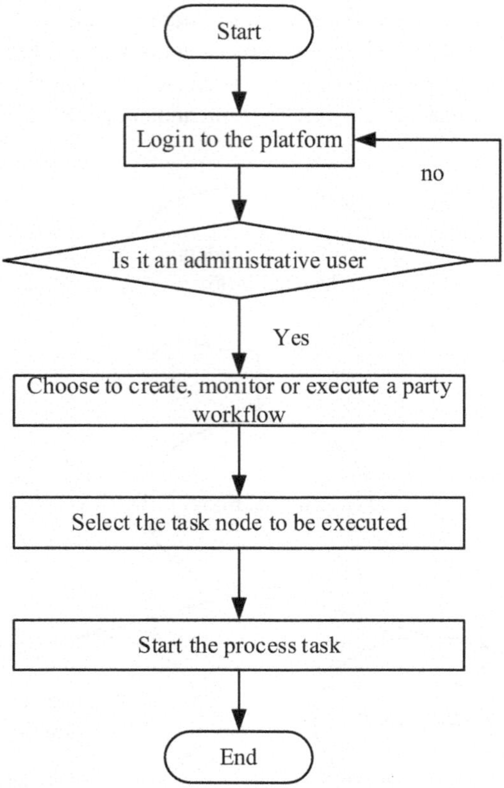


**Fig. 4.** Flowchart of online education flip platform based on Internet music

Although the process task management step is to carry out some simple commands of the learning user, such as searching for courses, the core function of the knowledge reversal classroom platform is still to communicate with other users or lecturers. In order to improve the problem that the Internet can not monitor the state of users in real time, the task management of the Knowledge Reversal Classroom Platform in this paper will input the task points of this study in advance before the users study, and these task points will regularly remind the learners to complete the learning task, and facilitate users to review and summarize the task through the recording function. Enhance the sensitivity of the platform to keywords, once there are keywords, you can quickly lock the direction of resources, reduce the learning knowledge to reverse the running time of the classroom platform. If the Internet-based knowledge reversal platform fails, the task management inside the platform must determine the cause of the failure according to the type of the failure, and quickly resume the normal operation of the reversal platform. The task management process of the online music education turnover platform based on the Internet has its own special working components. Special working groups can assist in-house staff in the maintenance of the Music Online Education Rollover Platform. But through the task management process designed in this paper, these three aspects can cooperate with each other to create a stable operation of the source of learning music online education turnover platform. The internal levels of task management are as follows (Fig. 5):

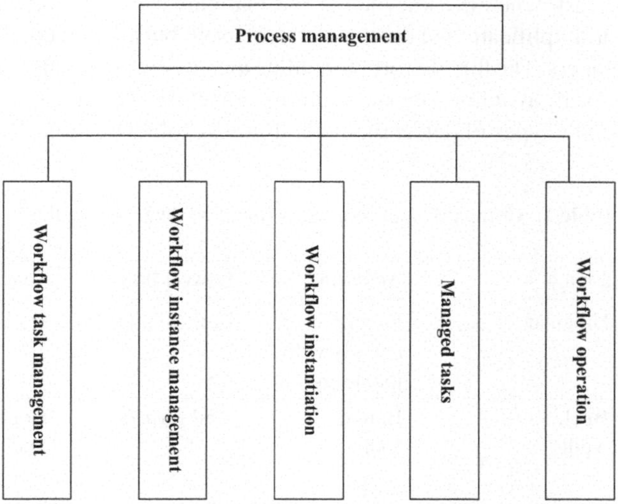


**Fig. 5.** Internal hierarchy of task management

Because of the rapid development of the Internet, data is easy to be lost and stolen in the process of transmission, and related to knowledge resources, can not be simplified, so the knowledge turnover platform designed in this paper adds the steps of rights management in the work, so as to better protect user privacy. Users on the Internet-based Music Online Education Flip Platform can set their own browsing records visible, can also set everyone visible, can also delete any one of the browsing records. Only the same identity will appear on the user's experience side. The resources with identity on the Internet based music online education reversal platform are as if they are locked, unless the system is automatically removed, or the attributes can not be changed. After the above operation, if the Flip Classroom Platform receives the user's command, the Internet-based Music Online Education Flip Platform creates a process instance that matches the command.

Process Instance Management is a step to manage the user's upcoming operation. While transmitting the user's instructions, the Music Online Education Reversal Platform of the Internet will also provide the user with the resources he wants, and the platform will automatically detect the instance command. If there is any risk degree, the user's learning on this platform will be terminated immediately. Jbpm4, Osworkflow and Shark are all similar, but Jbpm4 occupies a lot of memory space and consumes a lot of resources and time when running. Osworkflow does not support transaction management mechanism, which makes the platform of this structure selective for learning resources and unsatisfactory for learners.

The advantage of the method is that it adapts to the online music education reversal platform of the Internet as high as 95%. In addition, it also has good continuity and connects with the resources of the outside world. If a new word appears in the resource field, the Actiti5 command detection method will actively input the resources. The Actiti5 command detection method increases the visualization ability of the music online education reversal platform based on propagandist learning, and alleviates the sudden system crash when the knowledge reversal classroom platform is overloaded. This is not only a simplification of the flip platform itself, but also a reduction of the work of internal developers. The flip platform for online music education will find out the internal glitches by itself, avoiding labor-consuming detection. The functional comparison tables of the specific types of detection methods are as follows (Table 1):

**Table 1.** Comparison of four user command detection methods

| Name | Jbpm4 | Activiti5 | Osworkflow | Shark |
|---|---|---|---|---|
| Database persistence | Hibemate | Failure to comply with jpa norms | Built-in plug-ins | Dods |
| Process definition language | Bpel, Xpdl | Bpma2 Jpdl | Xml format | Compliance with xpdl norms |
| Support database | Support most databases | Support most databases | Support most databases | Support most databases |
| Process definition tools | Eclipse graphical plug-ins and web designers | Eclipse graphical plug-ins and web process designers | Manual writingxml | Jawe tools |
| Open source | Open source | Open source | Open source | Open source |
| Application deployment | Embedded or standalone deployment | Embedded or standalone deployment | With application collections | Flushbonading |
| Enlarge | Flexible expansion | Flexible expansion | Super stretch | Easier to extend |
| Monitoring content | Process definition/instance creation | Various log information of task schedule and execution status process, statistical analysis of process data | Part of the process information, complex processes need to customize the regulatory approach | Process definition, instance creation |
| Management mechanisms | Jat-based things management mechanism | Mybatis things management mechanism | Non-support for business management mechanisms | Adopt jutm things management mechanism |

Responsibility management process is one of the important processes in the work of Internet-based music online education overturning platform. The task of Responsibility management process is to control the structure modules of Internet-based knowledge overturning platform. When receiving the command from a user, it can find the task of each structure block reasonably and quickly. The clear responsibility relationship between the structure blocks is very important. If the right and responsibility relationship is not clear, the resource output speed of the user in the Internet-based music online education overturning platform will be slow, and the learning efficiency will decrease. So the path of the work flow inside the knowledge reversal classroom platform is clear, which can improve the efficiency of users' tasks and save the memory inside the knowledge reversal classroom platform.

# 5 Experimental Research

## 5.1 Experimental Purposes

In order to verify the operation effect of the Internet-based online music education reversal platform designed in this paper, the experiment is compared with the traditional knowledge reversal classroom platform. In order to ensure the authenticity and scientificity of the experiment, the final evaluation result of this paper integrates the results of the user's experience and the use rate of the two platforms in a certain time.

## 5.2 Experimental Procedure

The experimental operation and the analysis of the experimental results are as follows:

(1) Before the experiment, the staff shall respectively test whether the online music education reversal platform and the traditional knowledge reversal classroom platform on the Internet are smooth, and if there is any fault, timely repair the loophole to avoid affecting the final test results. After the preparation of the experiment, 100 users were selected randomly according to the data of the hottest popular science learning platform to determine the user experience of the final experiment.
(2) After the experimental users are selected, each group is divided into 10 groups to experience the rollover platform for online music education. Each user is required to use the two platforms for an hour, immediately after the use of the platform test satisfaction and opinions. Until the last one is completed, the two staff on the spot results of statistics, as part of the final experimental results;
(3) While 100 randomly selected test users experience, the login status of learning users in the same time of the two remote platforms is calculated, and the online learning time is another part of the final experimental results;
(4) The on-site staff shall calculate the final results of the experiment at the ratio of 6 to 4 by using the experimental results of 100 randomly selected testers and the statistical test results of the computer background.

### 5.3 Analysis of Experimental Results

The result of the experiment is scientific, which not only integrates the experience of the learners, but also integrates the use of two different learning methods to avoid the chance of the result. The testers selected in this paper are those with learning ability and learning ideas, which avoids the occurrence of zero evaluation of individual test results and maintains the authenticity of the experimental results. The statistical tables of the specific experimental results are as follows (Table 2):

**Table 2.** User test satisfaction questionnaire for two Internet knowledge flip classroom platforms

| User | Traditional music online education flip platform | Internet-based knowledge flipping classroom platform |
|---|---|---|
| Group I | Ordinary | Satisfy |
| Group II | Not bad | Satisfy |
| Group iii | Negative comment | Satisfy |
| Group iv | Negative comment | Satisfy |
| Group v | Good | Satisfy |

The results of the statistical experiments are as follows (Table 3):

**Table 3.** Experimental results

| Type/user | Traditional Music Online Education Flip Platform | Internet-based knowledge flipping classroom platform |
|---|---|---|
| Number of high praise | 64 persons | 99 persons |
| Number of poor judges | 30 persons | 1 person |
| Computer background computing platform usage | 30% | 80% |

Comparing the user experience results of the two platforms, It can be seen that the use rate of the platform is higher than that of the traditional one, and the satisfaction rate is as high as 98%, and the poor rate is as low as 1%.

The reason for the above results is that the Music Online Education Turnover Platform designed in this paper has a unique resource operation module structure, in which the service application layer and the security layer coordinate with each other, logically collect knowledge resources and processing resources, and provide a secure and stable Music Online Education Turnover Platform. In addition, the security layer is a safe data circulation station of two knowledge reversal classroom platforms, which reduces the interference rate of bad information to the learners to a certain extent, and creates a safe learning environment for the Internet-based music online education reversal platform;

on the other hand, because the workflow of the Internet-based music online education reversal platform is cohesive, the control and scheduling of various resources form a unified management, the function confusion of the Internet-based reversal classroom platform will not occur, so that the learners have a good learning mood and improve the learning efficiency.

## 6 Conclusion

Through the scientific experiment, it is confirmed that the user experience of the music online education turnover platform based on Internet is better than that of the traditional one, and the learner can absorb more knowledge and improve learning efficiency. I believe that with the continuous upgrading of the Internet, the Internet will become the mainstream of learning mode, and the Internet-based music online education platform will be more convenient with the development of science and technology, the public life.

## References

1. Teng, Y., Jiang, P.X., Wang, K.: Moral education teaching in colleges and universities based on the application of multimedia technology. Int. J. Electr. Eng. Educ. 2020:002072092094059 (2020)
2. Thai, N.T.T., De Wever, B., Valcke, M.: The impact of a flipped classroom design on learning performance in higher education: looking for the best 'blend' of lectures and guiding questions with feedback. Comput. Educ. **107**, 113–126 (2017)
3. Li, D.-H., Li, H.-Y., Wei, L., et al.: Application of flipped classroom based on the Rain Classroom in the teaching of computer-aided landscape design. Comput. Appl. Eng. Educ. **28**(2), 357–366 (2020)
4. Jing, L., Bo, Z., Tian, Q., et al.: Network education platform in flipped classroom based on improved cloud computing and support vector machine. J. Intell. Fuzzy Syst. **39**(99), 11 (2020)
5. Usai, F., Neil, K.O., Newman, A.J.: Design and empirical validation of effectiveness of LANGA, an online game-based platform for second language learning. IEEE Trans. Learn. Technol. **1** (2018)
6. Tsai, C.W., Shen, P.D., Chiang, Y.C., et al.: How to solve students' problems in a flipped classroom: a quasi-experimental approach. Univ. Access Inf. Soc. **16**(1), 1–9 (2017)
7. Valery, T., Shayan, S., Ksenia, D.: Design optimization and tolerance analysis of a spot-size converter for the taper-assisted vertical integration platform in InP. Appl. Opt. **57**(13), 3586 (2018)
8. Sanchez-Azqueta, C., Cascarosa, E., Celma, S., et al.: Application of a flipped classroom for model-based learning in electronics. Int. J. Eng. Educ. **35**(3), 938–946 (2019)
9. Estriegana-Valdehita, R., Barchino Plata, R., Medina-Merodio, J.A.: Educational technology in flipped course design. Int. J. Eng. Educ. **33**(4), 1199–1212 (2017)
10. Shiau, S., Kahn, L.G., Platt, J., et al.: Evaluation of a flipped classroom approach to learning introductory epidemiology. BMC Med. Educ. **18**(1), 63 (2018)
11. Fu, W., Liu, S., Srivastava, G.: Optimization of big data scheduling in social networks. Entropy **21**(9), 902 (2019)
12. Liu, S., Li, Z., Zhang, Y., et al.: Introduction of key problems in long-distance learning and training. Mob. Networks Appl. **24**(1), 1–4 (2019)

13. Liu, S., Glowatz, M., Zappatore, M., et al. (eds.): e-Learning, e-Education, and Online Training, pp. 1–374. Springer, Cham (2018). https://doi.org/10.1007/978-3-319-49625-2
14. Kaw, A., Clark, R., Delgado, E., et al.: Analyzing the use of adaptive learning in a flipped classroom for preclass learning. Comput. Appl. Eng. Educ. **27**(3), 663–678 (2019)
15. Murillo-Zamorano, L.R., Sanchez, J.L., Godoy-Caballero, A.L.: How the flipped classroom affects knowledge, skills, and engagement in higher education: Effects on students' satisfaction. Comput. Educ. **141**, 103608.1–103608.18 (2019)
16. Rathner, J.A.: The impact of flipped classroom andragogy on student assessment performance and perception of learning experience in two advanced physiology subjects. Adv. Physiol. Educ. **44**, 80–92 (2020)
17. Henbest, G.: Dissecting the flipped classroom: using a randomized controlled trial experiment to determine when student learning occurs. J. Chem. Educ. **97** (2020)
18. Brandon, D.T.: Unflipping the flipped classroom: balancing for maximum effect in minimum lead-time in online education. J. Chem. Educ. **97**(9) (2020)
19. Slivka, J.: A framework for teaching security design analysis using case studies and the hybrid flipped classroom. ACM Trans. Comput. Educ. **19** (2019)
20. Isherwood, G., Taylor, K., Burnside, G., et al.: Teaching orthodontic emergencies using the "flipped classroom" method of teaching—a mixed methods RCT. Eur. J. Dent. Educ. **24**(1), 53–62 (2020)
21. Rubio-Fernández, A., Muñoz-Merino, P.J., Delgado Kloos, C.: A learning analytics tool for the support of the flipped classroom. Comput. Appl. Eng. Educ. **2019**(1) (2019)
22. Kelliann, C., Fee-Schroeder, et al.: Flipped classroom strategy: an accessible, application-driven approach to genomics education. Clin. J. Oncol. Nurs. (2019)

# Function Design of Music Online Education Network Virtual Classroom Platform

Yang-bo Wu[1](✉), Hui Lin[2], and Wei-hua Zhu[2]

[1] College of Mathematics and Computer, Xinyu University, Xinyu 338000, China
[2] Xinyu University, Xinyu 338000, China

**Abstract.** Music online education network virtual classroom platform has diversified theoretical basis, emphasizing open development and interaction between teachers and students. The music teaching videos spread on the Internet spread the music teaching resources to the outside, which has the characteristics of open, extensible, flexible and quasi permanent separation of distance teaching.According to the theories of education system cybernetics and constructivism, this paper puts forward the function of music online education network virtual classroom platform by using the methods of literature analysis and case study. This paper answers how to build a music micro class distance education platform, expounds the conditions to realize the music education platform, and analyzes the obstacles and Countermeasures to realize the music education platform.

**Keywords:** Music education · Online education · Virtual classroom · Platform function

## 1 Introduction

As an important aspect of quality education in higher education, music appreciation has also been included in the curriculum of humanistic quality education in many colleges and universities. As a kind of culture, music has a long history and a vast horizon [1]. It has an extremely important effect on the quality of talents. Through the process of music appreciation, we can improve the ability of image thinking and abstract thinking, promote the balanced development of the brain, improve the ability of memory and coordination, and stimulate creative emotions. However, how to make students grasp the profound connotation of music and improve their appreciation of music art in a short time has always been a problem that the music education circles strive to solve, and the key to solve the problem is targeted education for students [2]. Among them, the collection and collation of music appreciation materials has become particularly important. Therefore, the design and development of an online music education platform to meet the needs of art college is an effective way to promote students' music education [3].

With the rapid development of network education in China, distance education based on network, as a new form of education, has become one of the hot issues in distance education. Literature [4] uses the theory of collaborative work (CSCW) to virtual the


W. Fu et al. (Eds.): eLEOT 2021, LNICST 389, pp. 631–643, 2021.
https://doi.org/10.1007/978-3-030-84383-0_53

teaching function of traditional classroom and provide a sharing and cooperative classroom learning environment for online teachers and students who are geographically dispersed. Literature [5] proposed a functional design method of network virtual classroom platform. Using the remote virtual classroom system which combines physical classroom and virtual classroom, this paper analyzes and studies the system from the aspects of technicality and practicability, and discusses how to improve the interaction and effectiveness of distance education under the system environment.

Although network education has made a lot of achievements and experience, there are also many unsatisfactory aspects, mainly reflected in the following two aspects: First, the importance of distance learning platform is not fully understood. The traditional concept often only attaches importance to the development of a single network course or network courseware, and ignores the role of information-based teaching platform. As a mature network teaching platform, it should have the important functions of network course development, teaching implementation, network teaching management and student learning support services. Second, the teaching mode is single and lacks support for teaching activities. At present, the common problem of network teaching is that it pays more attention to the presentation and explanation of teaching content than the design of teaching environment and teaching activities, especially the lack of efficient design of teaching interactive activities and single form of teaching content. One of the most prominent contradictions is that the network teaching using new teaching technology still uses the old teaching ideas and teaching methods, leading to the network teaching does not play its due efficiency and potential.

## 2 Summary

According to the current situation of network teaching, this paper designs and develops a multi-functional network teaching platform based on three modes, specifically from the following aspects. First of all, this paper analyzes the current common network teaching mode from the theoretical point of view, synthesizes its advantages, disadvantages and scope of application, and puts forward the design idea of combining the teacher led teaching mode, autonomous learning mode and problem-based inquiry mode, and applying them together on the network teaching platform, so as to make it the guiding theory of the teaching platform; Secondly, design and construct a network teaching platform based on the above three teaching modes. The platform has three user roles, three teaching modes, six functional modules and several sub functions of corresponding roles. The framework involves curriculum development, teaching implementation and teaching management; Finally, using ASP + SQL Server, a specific network teaching platform is developed, and its teaching effect is verified.

## 3 Integration of Teaching Mode

At present, there are many commonly used teaching modes in the network environment, including teaching mode, individual counseling mode, exploratory learning mode, collaborative learning mode, discussion network teaching mode, etc. Most of them come from the traditional teaching mode and combine with the modern network technology.

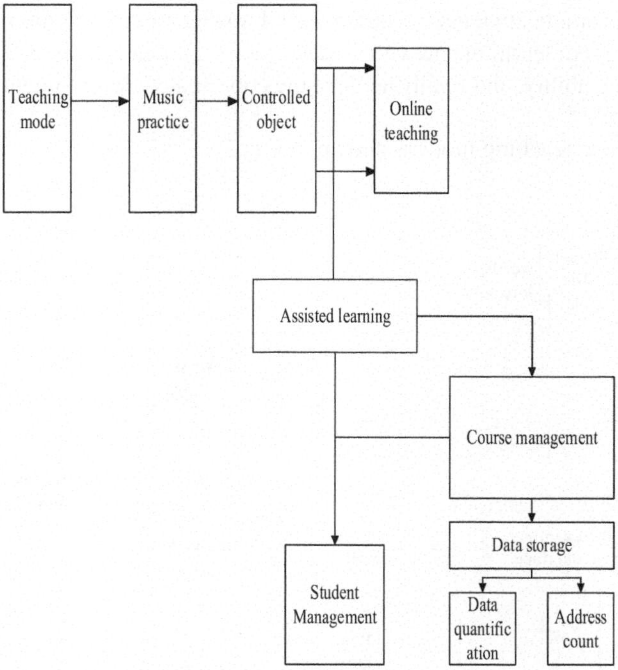


**Fig. 1.** Framework of music online education network virtual classroom platform

They not only have the advantages of the traditional mode, but also have the characteristics of information teaching to a certain extent. With the intervention of network multimedia technology, it provides us with more personalized choices and richer teaching methods. Although there are many kinds of network teaching modes in common use at present, according to the different dominant position and emphasis of teachers and students in the teaching process, the network teaching modes are divided into three categories: There are three teaching modes: teacher led mode, students' autonomous learning mode and inquiry teaching mode. These three models comprehensively summarize most of the characteristics and advantages of common models, and integrate them to meet the needs of learners with different levels and backgrounds. The teacher led mode is a teaching mode based on teacher's lecture, which is the transformation of the traditional transmission acceptance mode (Fig. 1).

This mode emphasizes the leading role of teachers. It mainly stores the prepared teaching materials on the server on the platform, and presents the teaching content in a certain order according to the organization form of online courses. It has the advantages of carrying large amount of information and relatively flexible learning time; its disadvantages are poor interaction and lack of personality guidance [6].

Resource based autonomous learning mode refers to the learning support service system provided by students in the network environment, which can learn actively, independently and exploratively. This model reflects the cognitive and emotional characteristics of students' learning, such as subjectivity, initiative, support and strategy. In the whole cognitive process, the teacher's main role is to effectively organize and guide students' autonomous learning, and timely evaluate whether students complete the learning task. So as to promote students to acquire new knowledge through their own learning, and in the process of learning new knowledge timely "internalize" knowledge, form and develop learning ability, and finally achieve the coordinated development of knowledge and ability [7, 8].

The integrated teaching mode is shown in Fig. 2.

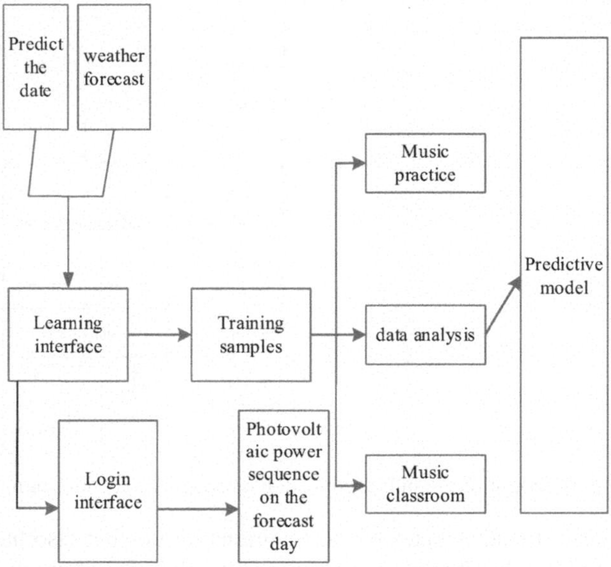


**Fig. 2.** Integrated teaching mode

The problem-based inquiry mode is a learning mode that learners solve the problems through mutual cooperation, learn the scientific knowledge hidden behind the problems, promote learners to form critical thinking, acquire the skills of autonomous learning and collaborative learning, and effectively solve problems. Its main characteristics are problem-based, learner centered, group based and teacher-oriented. Its purpose is to cultivate learners' ability to solve problems, master knowledge flexibly, develop self-study ability and lifelong learning ability.

## 4 The Framework of Multifunctional Teaching Platform

Based on three main teaching modes, a comprehensive teaching platform with multiple user roles, multiple teaching modes, and multiple functions is designed and constructed, which integrates the functions of curriculum development, teaching implementation and teaching management. The role of the platform includes administrator, teacher and student. Administrators have the authority to manage courses and users, teachers have the authority to manage teaching content, students can use a variety of learning modes to learn. In general, according to different types of functions, the platform is divided into six modules, which are user management module, course teaching management and

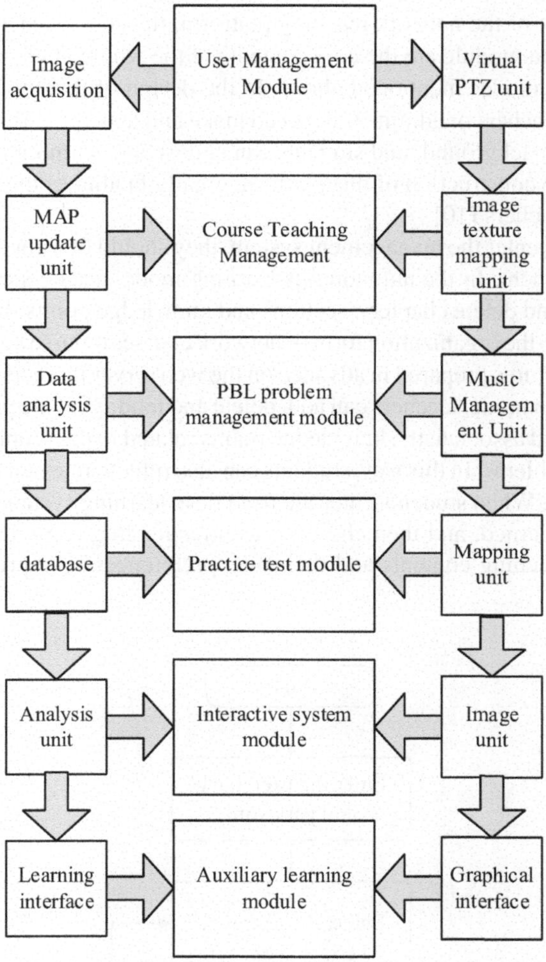


**Fig. 3.** Multi function teaching platform module

PBL problem management module, practice test module, interactive system module, auxiliary learning module and monitoring and evaluation module.

According to Fig. 3, each module is divided into two parts foreground and background. The background is mainly designed for administrators and teachers, providing functions including curriculum management and curriculum development. The front desk serves students and provides various learning mode interfaces. Two problems can be illustrated in the figure. One is that the online course is a modular organizational structure, each module has functions designed for each different role, and the module has permission control inside; Second, the network course is organized in the form of modules, which is extensible. If you want to add other functions, you don't need to change other modules, just need to replace or modify, and don't affect the functions of other modules [9].

In the structure of the network teaching platform, the course teaching management and PBL discussion module are the core contents of the whole platform, which realizes the three teaching modes mentioned above. In the design of this module, for different teaching modes, teachers or administrators can make and manage various types of teaching content in the background, and students can choose any learning method according to their needs. The construction of this platform greatly facilitates the network teaching of students and teachers [10].

When teachers enter the management system, they should first choose a course as the object of management. In the autonomous learning mode, teachers can create courses and add, modify and delete chapters, sections and knowledge points. In the presentation mode, according to the organization form of network courses (courseware), teachers store the multimedia lectures prepared in advance on the web server in a certain order [11, 12]. For PBL discussion mode, teachers can add, delete and modify all the problems that need to be discussed, and associate the knowledge points related to the problem in the process of adding PBL problems. In this way, students can also refer to relevant knowledge points when they discuss. When students enter the front desk learning system, they first choose the course to be learned, and then choose the corresponding learning mode according to the different teaching contents and their own preferences. The process is shown in Fig. 4.

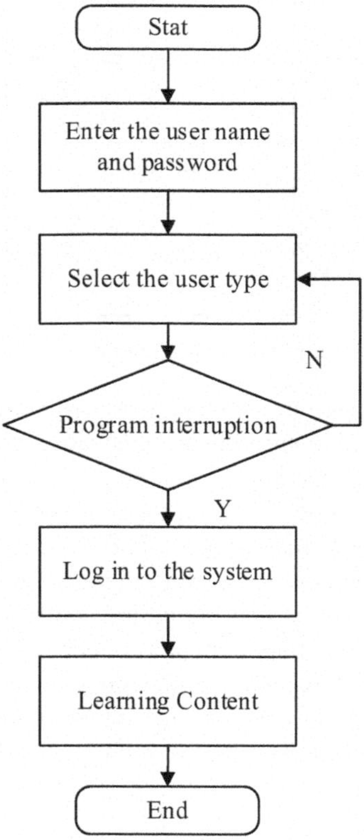


**Fig. 4.** Management process

## 5 Implementation Technology of Network Teaching Platform

The platform uses ASP + SQL Serve: as the implementation tool and windows IIS as the server environment. The platform has the following characteristics in technical implementation: using MDS encryption technology, the user password is stored in the database by fixed length encryption to ensure the security of the system; Through the relationship between SQL Server tables, entity integrity is automatically maintained to ensure that there is no redundant data in the database; The stored procedure and trigger function of SQL SERVE are widely used to improve the system performance; Modularize the functions of paging and database connection to maximize the reusability of the program [13, 14].

This paper summarizes and extracts three representative teaching modes from the common network teaching modes, optimizes and combines them, designs a network teaching platform with multiple functions, and develops a set of practical and effective network teaching platform under the guidance of the design idea.

In order to design and develop an online music education platform to meet the needs of music teachers and students in art college, we must first study the basic principles of music on demand system. At present, general music-on-demand systems adopt a system three-tier structure model, that is, a three-tier structure model of Browser, Application Server, and Database Server. In the music on demand system, the client can use the ordinary PC to operate, as long as the installation of IE browser, the client video player can install related plug-ins for online music appreciation. At present, the traditional Client/Server two-tier application development mode has been gradually replaced by the three-tier application development mode. The three-tier development mode is the most popular development mode at present, which has superior manageability and maintainability. This development method minimizes the application of the client to only need a web browser, so as to reduce the amount of maintenance, reduce the difficulty of program modification and upgrade, and reduce the hardware and software requirements of the client. In the development of Web application system based on Internet, the three-tier architecture mode has been very common at home and abroad, and the development technology and design ideas used in the implementation of VOD system are becoming more and more mature and advanced. In the current web application, this three-tier architecture mode is still the main mode of computer application information system based on network [15].

The basic framework of the education platform is shown in Fig. 5:

Among them, on the server side, there is a large capacity storage device used to store audio and video resources or compressed audio and video resources. In addition, there are some audio and video coding equipment, publishing and management unit and other related streaming media control unit. The compression and format conversion of original audio and video resources or other multimedia resources or animations are mainly completed by encoding devices. The publishing unit is mainly to provide a list or list of programs to the user terminal, mainly in the form of a web interface, and the user performs on-demand operations by clicking the program name. The user management, program management, user authentication, timing and billing are handled by the program management unit. The on-demand control of streaming media is mainly realized by the

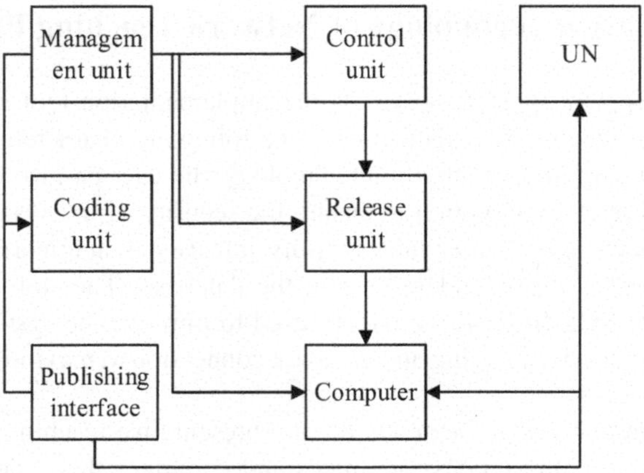


**Fig. 5.** Basic framework of education platform

streaming media control unit, which also includes the core work of system concurrency control.

# 6 Test the Effect of Platform Function Realization

The application performance and ability of virtual classroom functional platforms of different platforms were tested through information recall rate, and the results were shown in Fig. 6.

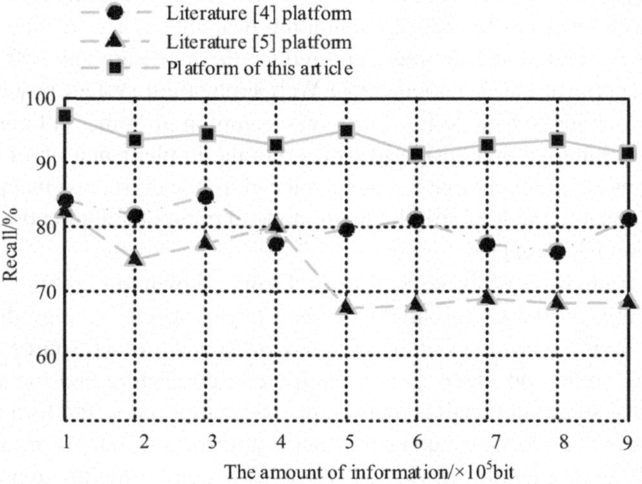


**Fig. 6.** Comparison of virtual classroom information recall rates on different platforms

As can be seen from Fig. 6, with the increase of information in virtual classroom, information recall rates of different platforms are also changing constantly. Only when the amount of information is $4 \times 105$, the information recall rate of the literature platform [4] is higher than that of the literature platform [5], and the lowest information recall rate of the literature platform [5] is below 70%. However, the information recall rate of the platform in this paper is always higher than 92%, indicating that the recall effect of the platform in this paper is obvious because of the two comparison platforms.

## 7 Function of Music Online Education Network Virtual Classroom Platform

In the functional design of this platform, there is a user registration module. Only registered and audited users or students imported by the college management can log in to this system. Legitimate users who log in to the system can use all the resources on the system to search for music, listen online and download songs. The basic function modules of the system include: music online browsing and appreciation module, music search module, music recommendation and collection module, music review module, user information management module, music masters, album management module, information release module, music download management module, etc. The overall functional structure is shown in Fig. 7.

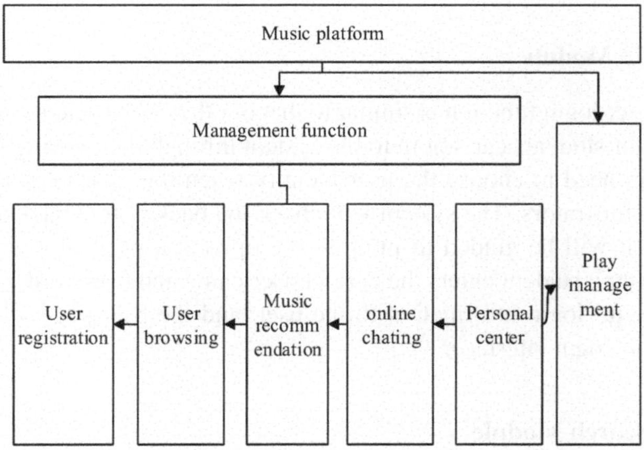


**Fig. 7.** General function structure diagram

### 7.1 Main Functions of Front Desk

The main function modules and basic function flow of the front desk are shown in Fig. 8. After students register and become legal users, they can enjoy music online, download songs, search songs, collect songs, recommend, share and exchange music appreciation experience with other users or teachers.

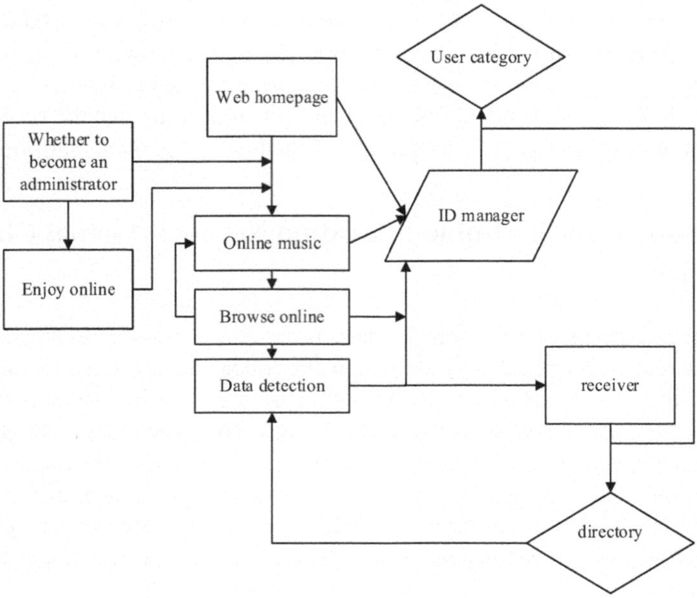


**Fig. 8.** Main function modules of front desk

### 7.2 User Login Module

The design of user login function is similar to that of other web systems. Registered and approved users or students can log in to the system through the existing user name and password. Users need to choose the user identity when they log in, such as teachers, students or administrators. The system will check the background database. If the user is a legal user, it will be guided to jump to the operation page of relevant authority. For example, after a student enters the correct user name and password, the system will assign a successful login information to the user, and the user page will jump to the "online audition" main interface.

### 7.3 Website Search Module

Search is designed for users to quickly find or locate music resources. With the search function, users can find the music resources they need in the massive music library. The search function is generally designed in the appropriate position of the system home page. After students or teachers log in, they can not only browse music resources by category, but also use the search function to search music. There are many kinds of search criteria for the search function, including search by song name, search by famous musician name, search by album name, etc. In the actual operation, users only need to choose a suitable search method, they can quickly query, and the query results will be displayed on the corresponding page.

### 7.4 Online Appreciation Module

After users log in to the system, they can choose the right songs to enjoy, and at the same time, they can evaluate, share and recommend the songs.

### 7.5 Main Functions of Background

In addition to the rights of ordinary members, administrators can also manage songs, albums and users. When adding new music, they can upload files, modify login accounts and passwords, and log off.

The main functions of the module include: music information management, celebrity management, music classification management, song management (including music upload, delete, update, etc.), user management, comment management, etc. After the administrator logs in as an administrator and passes the verification, the system will enter the interface of relevant operation authority and enter the management home page. The basic function flow is shown in Fig. 9.

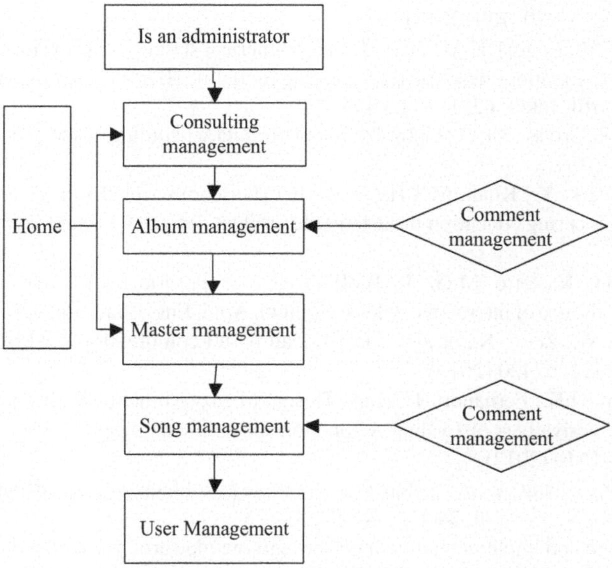


**Fig. 9.** Main function flow chart of background

## 8 Conclusion

According to the rapid development of domestic music and the lack of education platform, this paper takes the music virtual classroom as an example to put forward the design scheme of virtual education platform, and discusses in detail the production and collection of music micro class, the classification, arrangement and release of music education, and the remote management of music education platform. The hardware and software, team cooperation and other conditions needed to realize the design scheme are demonstrated, especially how to solve the problems of shortage of funds, technical difficulties, waste of teaching resources and so on. Music platform can be used as an integral part of the National University micro course platform to provide a method and a way of thinking for building a comprehensive education platform. When looking forward to the future development trend of music education and even the whole education, we need to consider it in a distance education environment. The integrable ware combination platform based on Web browser may become the mainstream direction of the development of educational software platform. Integrable ware has an important impact on the development of education, and education can be regarded as an integral part of integrable ware.

## References


1. Zhang, G., Ge, J.: Design and implementation of the home-school-community synergy online education platform based on mobile information technology. Revista de la Facultad de Ingenieria **32**(2), 720–726 (2017)
2. Ferreira, E.F.M., Rego, P.H.M., Neto, J.V.F.: Numerical stability improvements of state-value function approximations based on RLS learning for online HDP-DLQR control system design. Eng. Appl. Artif. Intell. **63**, 1–19 (2017)
3. Fu, W., Liu, S., Srivastava, G.: Optimization of big data scheduling in social networks. Entropy **21**(9), 902 (2019)
4. Raoufi, K., Park, K., Khan, M.T.H., et al.: A cyberlearning platform for enhancing undergraduate engineering education in sustainable product design. J. Cleaner Prod. **211**, 730–741 (2019)
5. Granjo, J.F.O., Rasteiro, M.G.: LABVIRTUAL—a platform for the teaching of chemical engineering: the use of interactive videos. Comput. Appl. Eng. Educ. **26**(5), 1668–1676 (2018)
6. Liu, S., Bai, W., Zeng, N., et al.: A fast fractal based compression for MRI images. IEEE Access **7**, 62412–62420 (2019)
7. Liu, C., Lam, H.K., Fernando, T., et al.: Design of fuzzy functional observer-controller via higher order derivatives of Lyapunov function for nonlinear systems. IEEE Trans. Cybern. **47**(7), 1630–1640 (2017)
8. Liu, S., Li, Z., Zhang, Y., et al.: Introduction of key problems in long-distance learning and training. Mob. Netw. Appl. **24**(1), 1–4 (2019)
9. Ge, G.: Design and implementation of online learning platform based on massive open online courses education model. C e Ca **42**(6), 2542–2546 (2017)
10. Wang, L., Wang, Z.: Research on the system design and development of online teaching platform based on ASP.NET. Boletin Tecnico/Technical Bull. **55**(7), 539–546 (2017)
11. Blaine, A.M.: Interaction and presence in the virtual classroom: an analysis of the perceptions of students and teachers in online and blended advanced placement courses. Comput. Educ. **132**, 31–43 (2019)
12. Ruthotto, I., Kreth, Q., Melkers, J., et al.: Lurking and participation in the virtual classroom: the effects of gender, race, and age among graduate students in computer science. Comput. Educ. **151**(3), 103854 (2020)
13. Parsons, T.D., Duffield, T., Asbee, J.: A comparison of virtual reality classroom continuous performance tests to traditional continuous performance tests in delineating ADHD: a meta-analysis. Neuropsychol. Rev. (2) (2019)

14. Daly, D., Rasmussen, A.V., Dalsgaard, A.: Learning about midwifery in another country from a distance: evaluation of a virtual classroom learning session. Nurse Educ. Today **75**, 47–52 (2019)
15. Stamps, A., Opton, L.L.: Utilizing VoiceThread technology to foster community learning in the virtual classroom. J. Nurs. Educ. **58**(3), 185 (2019)

# Design of Online Teaching Platform for Accounting Informatization Course Based on Cloud Computing

Qi-feng Wu(✉)

Guangxi Science and Technology Normal University, Laibin 546199, China

**Abstract.** In order to solve the problems of low success rate and low performance of traditional online teaching platform, cloud computing technology is used to optimize the design of online teaching platform of accounting informatization course from three aspects of hardware, database and software. The hardware part is mainly combined with cloud computing technology to refit and optimize the CPU, memory and network structure. Collect the course information of accounting informatization, store it in the platform database, and use the internal logic between the data to realize the construction of the platform database. With the support of hardware equipment and database, the optimization design of online teaching platform software function of accounting information course is realized from three aspects of teachers, students and platform administrators. Through the platform test experiment, a conclusion can be drawn: compared with the traditional teaching platform, the function running success rate of the designed teaching platform is improved by 9.3%, and the average response time of the platform is shorter when multiple users are online at the same time, that is, the running performance of the platform is better.

**Keywords:** Cloud computing · Accounting informatization · Informatization courses · Online teaching · Teaching platform

## 1 Introduction

Accounting informatization is the combination of accounting and information technology. It is a new requirement of the information society to the enterprise financial information management, and a necessary measure for the enterprise accounting to comply with the information tide. It is the main channel for enterprise leaders to obtain information under the network environment, which helps to enhance the competitiveness of enterprises, solve the "isolated island" phenomenon of accounting computerization, and improve the decision-making ability of accounting management and enterprise management level. In order to provide enterprises with a large number of accounting professionals, accounting confidence flower course is set up. Accounting information teaching method is an extension of traditional accounting teaching method. Accounting teaching not only takes place in the classroom, but also integrates into students'


W. Fu et al. (Eds.): eLEOT 2021, LNICST 389, pp. 644–656, 2021.
https://doi.org/10.1007/978-3-030-84383-0_54

daily life through information means [1]. The foundation of students' cultural courses in higher vocational schools is relatively weak, so they will have great difficulties in accepting accounting theoretical knowledge. There will be problems in the understanding of books and the answers to exercises. In addition, many students are lack of perseverance and are easy to give up when they encounter difficulties. Therefore, higher vocational accounting teaching must change the teaching mode and improve students' enthusiasm. Only by strengthening their understanding of theoretical knowledge, can they apply it better. The information-based teaching method is more vivid and specific than the traditional teaching method. Teachers can teach accounting knowledge through the setting of teaching situation, teaching video and other aspects, which avoids the inflexibility of the traditional teaching method and enlivens the classroom atmosphere to a great extent, In addition, these courseware can be directly transmitted to students' computers, tablets, mobile phones, etc., which is conducive to students' review after class, strengthening the understanding of classroom knowledge, and improving students' autonomy in accounting learning.

At present, in order to break the time and space boundaries of accounting informatization course, colleges and universities at home and abroad have designed and developed the corresponding online teaching platform, which provides auxiliary tools for the development of the course. However, the current platform used in colleges and universities has some problems, such as low efficiency in updating accounting teaching resources, single teaching methods, etc. these problems are mainly due to the low performance of traditional system data processing, so cloud computing technology is introduced.

Cloud computing is a type of distributed computing, which refers to the process of decomposing huge data computing processing programs into countless small programs through the network "cloud", and then processing and analyzing these small programs through a system composed of multiple servers to obtain results And return to the user. In the early days of cloud computing, to put it simply, it was simple distributed computing, solving task distribution, and merging calculation results. The application of cloud computing services in the field of education has significant advantages, which are mainly reflected in the profound impact on the reform of teaching methods [2]. First of all, the school will no longer need to spend a lot of financial resources on the purchase of mainframes and high-performance machines, greatly reducing the hardware cost of its teaching resources. In the cloud computing environment, all kinds of cloud resources can be effectively used only by configuring general computer terminal equipment. Second, cloud computing can provide a data storage center with high security performance to ensure the security of all data. Teachers and students do not need to worry about the loss of data caused by viruses and hacker attacks, and can conduct interactive teaching on the network platform anytime and anywhere. Finally, in the cloud computing environment, the resources of each school can be shared, which is conducive to the balanced distribution of teaching resources and greatly improves the utilization of teaching resources in each college. In view of the application advantages of the above-mentioned cloud computing technology, it is applied to the design of the online teaching platform of accounting information courses in order to enhance the application value of the teaching platform.

For this reason, this paper designs the software and hardware parts of the teaching platform under the cloud computing environment. The centerless topology is used to construct the architecture of the network platform. Design cloud server based on TCP/IP protocol. Complete the hardware part of the platform with central processing unit, cloud storage, encoder, timer and counter. The MySQL database is used as the system database. The software part of the system is divided into teacher function module, student function module and administrator function module. In this way, the teaching function of the platform is realized.

## 2 Design of Online Teaching Hardware Platform for Accounting Information Course

The main task of the online teaching platform of accounting information courses is: the administrator manages various resources through the management background, and the teachers and students achieve the purpose of teaching and learning through their respective spaces. Therefore, users on the platform can be divided into three roles: teacher, student, and administrator, and different roles can perform different functions. According to the above design goals, the online teaching platform of accounting informatization courses should reflect the three characteristics of integration, interaction and networking, from the three aspects of hardware, software and database, in terms of the principle of advancement, characteristic and modularity, Compatibility principle and reliability principle, use cloud computing technology to realize the optimization design of the online teaching platform of accounting informatization courses.

### 2.1 Cloud Computing Platform Network Architecture

The use of a centerless topology as the cloud computing platform network topology solves the single point of failure problem existing in many service providers and provides good services to customers of heterogeneous terminals distributed in different geographical locations. Figure 1 shows the basic network topology of the cloud computing platform.

The DHT protocol is introduced in the network topology of Fig. 1, that is, a DHT mechanism for nodes and service programs is designed. This mechanism makes full use of the distributed management characteristics of P2P to integrate the nodes in the topology and the applications deployed on the nodes. They are all regarded as the objects of DHT, manage the server group through the agreement, and locate and use services. The introduction of the DHT mechanism not only makes the overall realization of decentralization, but also eliminates the necessity of overall traffic balancing and load balancing [3]. At the same time, the DHT mechanism separates the management of computing tasks, and each node is likely to act as a calculator and a manager at the same time, so that the risk of system crash is greatly reduced and then distributed to different nodes. In the topological results in Fig. 1, the proxy server of the cache framework for multimedia service awareness is deployed, which brings a better user experience for heterogeneous terminals, especially mobile terminals.

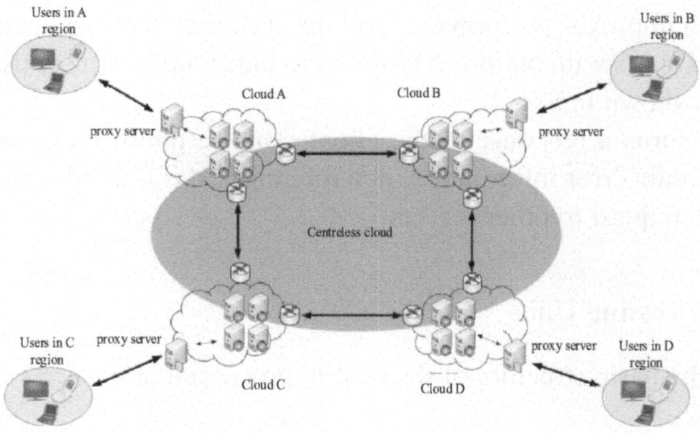


**Fig. 1.** Basic network topology diagram of cloud computing platform

## 2.2 Cloud Server

The cloud server protocol is an application layer protocol based on the client/server model and running on top of TCP/IP. One or more cloud servers form a cloud directory tree. The cloud server is composed of three modules: directory service module, copy service module and management module. The service module is mainly composed of two parts: the front-end part is responsible for the normal network communication between the client and the server, and completes the protocol analysis and analysis; the back-end part is responsible for the management of the directory database.The replication service module is responsible for the directory data replication between cloud servers. The management module is responsible for catalog informatization management to ensure that users obtain accurate catalog information at the expected response time, integrity, safety and consistency. The client connects to a cloud server and sends operation requests to it, and is responsible for performing necessary operations on the directory. Once the server has completed these operations, it returns a result or error response to the requesting client, or points to another cloud server by referring to a redirection mechanism.When the directory item requested by the client does not exist on the local server, the server returns a reference to other servers to the client, and the client completes subsequent

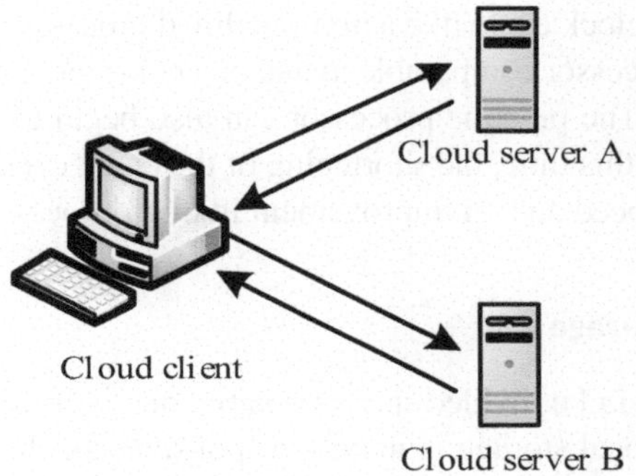


**Fig. 2.** Schematic diagram of client access to cloud server

operations, which improves performance and the ability of distributed applications. The operation process starts with binding The client to the cloud server sends an information query request, as shown in Fig. 2.

The server returns a response to the client. This response may contain the query result, or may contain error information, or a reference; if it is a reference, return to step 1 and send a new request to other servers.

## 2.3 Central Processing Unit

Figure 3 shows the basic structure of the central processing unit.

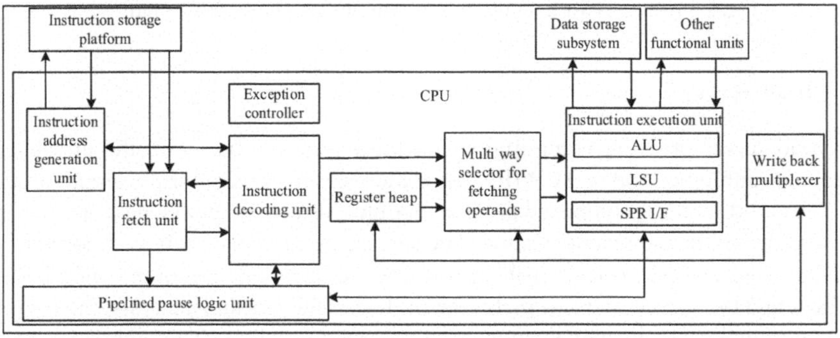


**Fig. 3.** Central processor structure diagram

The processor uses instruction pipelining to accelerate the execution of instructions. In essence, instruction pipeline decomposes the instruction cycle into several consecutive stages, such as fetching instructions, decoding instructions, determining operand addresses and fetching operands, executing instructions and writing back result operands [4]. The next instruction is executed as soon as the instruction completes the first stage. The instruction moves forward through these segments so that different instructions can work on each segment at the same time. Instructions only need to pass through one stage of the pipeline in each clock cycle. It is not necessary for instructions to pass through the entire data path in one clock cycle like a non-pipelined processor. This makes the clock cycle of a pipelined processor comparable to that of a non-pipelined processor The clock cycle is much shorter. The pipeline processor can also begin to execute an instruction in each clock cycle. At this time, the shortening of the clock cycle means an increase in instruction execution speed and an improvement in microprocessor performance.

## 2.4 Cloud Shared Storage

Cloud shared storage can be divided into two parts, one is local storage and the other is cloud storage. The local storage is mainly responsible for the storage of local data. When the node cannot communicate with the host or relay node, the collected The data is temporarily stored in the local storage, and when the communication is normal, the locally stored data is transmitted. The chip selected for local storage is 24LCXXB, which is a series of FLASH memory chips. Their packages and pin numbers are exactly the same. The "XX" in the chip represents the capacity of the chip. You can choose according to the amount of data in use. The actual chip model used [5]. The cloud storage is based on the LINUX shared memory mechanism and is implemented in the user layer of the system, so it has good portability. In the cloud storage structure, a distributed shared memory segment may have cached copies on multiple machines. The cache technology can solve the memory access delay and network delay, making the access time close to the local memory access time. The copy of each distributed shared memory segment is mapped into a local LINUX shared memory segment by the LINUX shared memory mechanism.

### 2.5 Encoder

The main function of the encoder is to encode the teaching resources in the online teaching platform of accounting informatization courses, including video resources, audio resources and courseware resources, to ensure the normal upload and download of related teaching resources. The encoder is mainly composed of encoding control, source encoding, video multiplexing encoding, and transmission buffer. In the optimized teaching platform, a gain control module and an analysis filter module are added. The gain control module is a polyphase quadrature filter., Gain detection and gain modification composition. Polyphase quadrature filtering divides its input signal into four frequency bands. Except for the lowest frequency band without gain control, the other frequency bands use gain detection and gain modification to control and attenuate energy. Because it can do a certain degree of control and attenuation of the sound signal, making the energy range of the original signal smaller. After the above-mentioned gain control, the energy of its attenuation change must be converted into gain control parameters, and finally this parameter is passed to the decoding end [6]. In addition, the analysis filter module uses an improved discrete cosine transform to transform the input audio data in the time domain into a frequency domain signal. Discrete cosine transform adopts time-domain aliasing cancellation technology, which can completely eliminate aliasing in theory. The expression of discrete cosine transform is:

$$X(k) = 2\sum_{n=0}^{N-1} x(n)w(n)\cos\left(\frac{2\pi}{N}(n+n_0)\left(k+\frac{1}{2}\right)\right) \tag{1}$$

Where $w(n)$ is the window function, and $n_0$ is a fixed time offset.

The sine window enables the filter bank to better separate the adjacent spectral components, which is suitable for signals with small spectral component spacing, and KBD window is used when the spectral component spacing is wide. AAC allows continuous and seamless switching between the sine window and the KBD window.

### 2.6 Timer/Counter

Two 32-bit registers are set up in the timer, namely the mode register and the counting register. The specific description of the mode register is shown in Table 1.

**Table 1.** Pattern register domain description

| Domain | Illustration | | |
|---|---|---|---|
| Ttmr [29] | Timer interrupt enable | | |
| ttmr [28] | Timer interrupt | | |
| Ttmr [27:0] | [medical] timing cycle | | |
| Ttmr [31:30] | Counting mode | 00 | Timer banned |
| | | 01 | When the count register matches the timing period, the count register restarts |
| | | 10 | When the count register matches the timing period, the count register stops counting |
| | | 11 | When the count register matches the timing period, the count register does not stop counting |

## 3 Database Design of Online Teaching Platform for Accounting Informatization Course

Using MySQL database as the system database, because the database is open source, it can reduce the cost of system development, and the database is convenient for data processing, so using MySQL database as the system database is a low-cost and efficient development method [7]. To design the database, the first step is to carry out the logical design of the database, generate the table structure of the database, and physically implement the table structure in MySQL. The educational administration courses used by the online teaching platform are shown in Table 2.

**Table 2.** Description of storage field for accounting informatization course

| Field name | Field description | Data type | Major key |
|---|---|---|---|
| ID | Course ID | uniqueidentifier | Yes |
| JXKCMC | Course title | nvarchar(200) | No |
| SSKC | Course of study | uniqueidentifier | No |
| FMT | Course cover | nvarchar(200) | No |
| KCJJ | Course Introduction | nvarchar(500) | No |
| KCZT | Course Status | int | No |
| JLCJR | Course teachers | uniqueidentifier | No |
| JLCJSJ | Course creation time | datatime | No |

In the same way, it can be concluded that other database tables in the online teaching platform database of accounting informatization courses, combined with the logical relationship between each database data, realize the link between the database tables.

# 4 Design of Online Teaching Software Platform for Accounting Informationization Courses

## 4.1 Teacher Function Module

In the teacher space, teachers can compile electronic teaching plans and publish, modify, and delete electronic teaching plans according to the actual teaching situation for students to learn. Teachers can organize Q&A discussions, assign homework and other teaching activities, publish news, manage personal data and information, etc. Administrators and teachers as users can also enter the student space for browsing, but have no right to modify student information. In the student space, students can carry out learning activities such as course study, course discussion, and completion of homework, as well as post messages and manage personal data and information [8]. The administrator can manage system announcements, users, forums, teaching and resources in the administrator studio.

During the operation of the teacher's teaching function, the user issues instruction on-demand instruction on the interface. The interface calls the server-side method according to the user's operation to realize the playback of specific resource streams, while the client needs to realize the resource content through the streaming media resource player. Show. In the multimedia teaching platform, the teaching on-demand information of the relevant content on the multimedia teaching server is stored in the database server and can be read at any time. These data are the basis for resource allocation. During the playback process, the user controls the playback progress by operating the progress bar and volume adjustment control on the interface. In addition, the teacher's processing and management process of the accounting informatization course exercises is shown in Fig. 4.

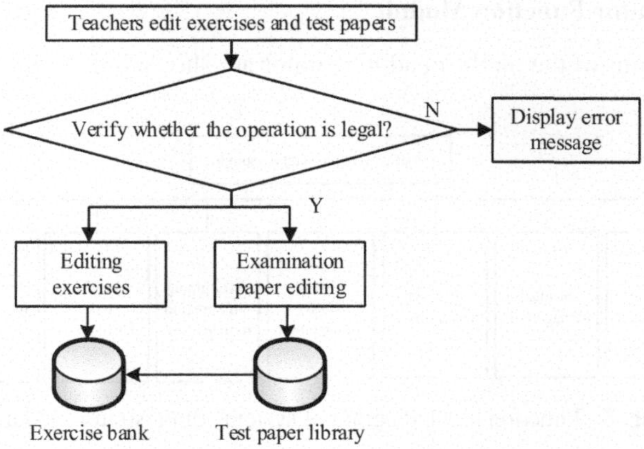


**Fig. 4.** Flowchart of teacher management exercises

## 4.2 Student Function Module

According to functional needs, the system is divided into modules such as online learning, online examination, online classroom, skill map, study group and personal space. The system is divided into modules. Students can study network resources, such as video, OFFICE, PDF, SCORM, and online simulation test of question bank. Through the study of resources, interactive learning is reflected, such as learning record tracking, learning reminders, notes, questions and answers, Comments, site letters, concerns, collections, etc. According to the operation of the platform navigation bar, you can realize the jump of the platform interface and realize the online learning function of students' accounting informatization courses.

After a stage of study, students can perform the question bank test function, select a category according to the category of the existing test paper, and then click to view all test papers under that category, select the test paper to be tested, and click to start the mock test, The user enters the examination interface [9]. In the test interface, the system will automatically write the reminders contained in the test paper at the top of the test paper. The user can answer in categories or in order. At the same time, when the user enters the test paper, the system starts to enter the test time statistics status. On the right side of the side timing mark, there are "pause" and "do it next time". Users can control the answering speed according to their own schedule. In the course of the user's answering paper, if you encounter a test question, you can choose to mark the test question individually or bookmark it, and there will be a record in the user's personal center in the future, which is convenient for viewing at any time. After completing the answer, click to submit the test paper, and the system will automatically enter to modify the paper and automatically pop up the user's test score. In addition, students can realize the functions of course inquiry, course preview, course material download, questioning, and feedback information inquiry in the online teaching platform of accounting informatization courses, so as to realize the information exchange and sharing of the platform.

## 4.3 Administrator Function Module

The basic functions of the platform administrator are shown in Fig. 5.

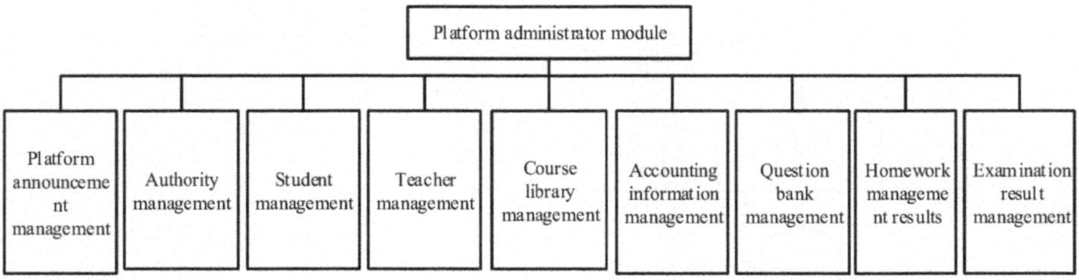


**Fig. 5.** Function block diagram of system administrator module

System administrators can manage user information and user rights, and maintain and manage the teaching platform [10]. The system administrator opens an account for the teacher, and then the teacher adds a new class, then imports the student's information and adds the list of elective students to start accounting training and teaching.

## 5 Platform Test

In order to test the operating function and application performance of the designed online teaching platform of accounting informatization courses based on cloud computing, the platform test experiment was designed, and the traditional teaching platform and the teaching platform based on big data analysis were set as the two comparison platforms of the experiment. Develop and run in the same experimental environment to ensure the uniqueness of the platform test experimental variables.

### 5.1 Build Platform Development and Testing Environment

The accounting informatization course teaching platform in the cloud computing environment is a typical distributed system. In order to realize the simple deployment of the client, the system adopts a browser/server-based development model. The specific technology used is Microsoft's ASP.NET technology. With Silver light technology, the integrated development environment is Visual Studio 2012, the platform support required for development is.NET Framework 4.0, and the operating system based on development is Windows 7.For any system, relying solely on personal manual testing is far from achieving the ideal performance test state. Therefore, with certain testing tools, the platform mainly uses two testing tools: one is the performance testing tool LoadRunner and the defect management tool BugFree. Among them, LoadRunner is a load testing tool that predicts system behavior and performance. Mainly by simulating tens of millions of users to implement concurrent load and real-time performance monitoring to confirm and find problems, LoadRunner can test a wide range, including the entire enterprise architecture.Therefore, LoadRunner will be the first choice for performance testing in enterprises, which can minimize testing time, optimize performance and accelerate the release cycle of application systems. It is also an automatic load testing tool suitable for various architectures, which can predict system behavior and evaluate system performance. BugFree is a bug management system written independently using PHP + MySQL based on Microsoft's R&D process and bug management concept. In the process of testing the online teaching platform of accounting informatization courses, LoadRunner is used as a testing tool for platform operating performance, and BugFree is used as a testing tool for platform operating functions.

### 5.2 Determination of Test Methods and Content

The platform principle is to provide the basis for the tester, to restrain the defects and problems, and to promote the online implementation of the software. The main principles used in testing are as follows: testing should trace back to original requirements. The requirement analysis document is the most intuitive embodiment of the user's initial requirements, and the most serious problem for user-oriented software is that it can not meet its needs. The test is carried out by an independent third party. Software testers should not be developers. Only independent third parties can ensure the objective and fairness of the results to the greatest extent. The platform's operating function selects the white box test method, that is, running the platform with known results, and observing whether the platform's operating results are consistent with the set known results, so as to judge the success of the platform function. Prepare users with three different roles respectively, and import relevant user information into the platform environment, and set test content and standard output results for different users. The specific settings are shown in Table 3.

**Table 3.** Platform test sample setting table

| User role | Student | Teacher | Manager |
|---|---|---|---|
| User name | UserName1 | UserName2 | admin |
| Test Type | 48000029 | 48000029 | 48000037 |
| Number of user samples | 500 | 500 | 500 |
| Input content | Course selection, download course resources, ask questions, upload assignments, query course information, play course video, accounting informatization course examination, query test results | Set up accounting informatization course, inquire student information, upload course resources, answer student questions, issue examination questions, correct examination papers, issue examination results | Grant user rights, course resource scheduling, issue course announcement |

In addition, the performance test of the platform is mainly to test the product under various pressure and extreme conditions, and to test the endurance and stability of the system.

### 5.3 Platform Function Test Analysis

Different users operate on different platform environments according to their own learning habits, enter corresponding content, and observe the implementation of platform functions. In order to avoid the impact of a single experiment on the experimental results, the method of averaging multiple experiments is selected to obtain the test results of the platform functions, as shown in Table 4.

It can be seen from Table 4 that the function operation success rates of the three teaching platforms are 89.1%, 95.2%, and 98.4%, respectively. In contrast, the function of the online teaching platform of the cloud computing-based accounting informatization course is successfully operated The rate is higher.

**Table 4.** Test results for platform functionality

| User number | Number of functional tasks | Traditional teaching platform | | Teaching platform based on big data analysis | | Design of accounting informatization course online teaching platform | |
|---|---|---|---|---|---|---|---|
| | | Number of successful tasks/number | Number of failed tasks/number | Number of successful tasks/number | Number of failed tasks/number | Number of successful tasks/number | Number of failed tasks/number |
| 1 | 55 | 48 | 7 | 52 | 3 | 54 | 1 |
| 2 | 29 | 25 | 4 | 27 | 2 | 28 | 1 |
| 3 | 38 | 34 | 4 | 36 | 2 | 38 | 0 |
| 4 | 42 | 38 | 4 | 40 | 2 | 41 | 1 |
| 5 | 57 | 51 | 6 | 53 | 4 | 55 | 2 |
| 6 | 51 | 46 | 5 | 50 | 1 | 50 | 1 |
| 7 | 46 | 42 | 4 | 45 | 1 | 46 | 0 |
| 8 | 44 | 39 | 5 | 42 | 2 | 44 | 0 |

### 5.4 Platform Operation Performance Test Analysis

The main performance indicators of platform operation are the concurrent use of the platform by multiple users, the concurrent amount of access to the system database, the response speed of the system and the processing performance of the database server when the number of users accessing data gradually increases. According to the current business conditions, the equipment support system requires that the largest number of users be online at the same time. The response time test result is shown in Fig. 6.

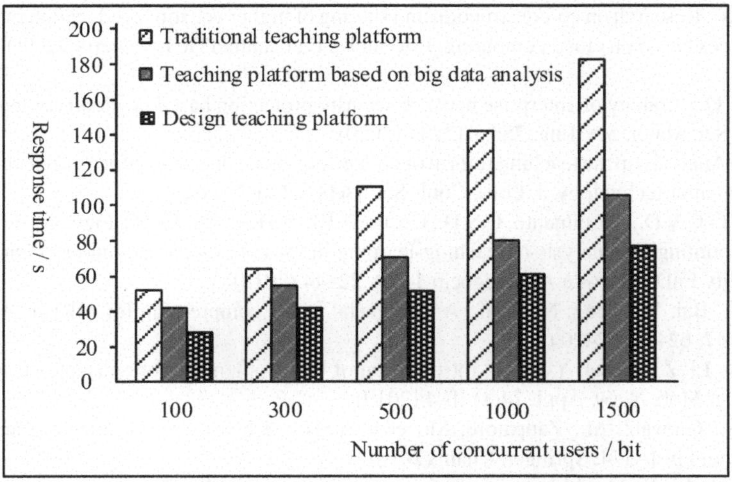


**Fig. 6.** Comparison results of platform response time test

It can be seen from Fig. 6 that as the number of users on the platform increases, the response time for login increases. The platform can meet the basic requirements of users when each user is concurrent. After horizontal comparison, it can be seen that compared with the two comparison platforms, the average response time of the design platform is shorter, and there are no abnormal phenomena, which proves that the designed teaching platform has higher operating performance.

## 6 Conclusion

The method in this paper designs the hardware part and software part of the online teaching platform based on cloud computing. The teaching effect is optimized. The construction and application of an online teaching platform for accounting informatization courses based on cloud computing is a requirement for the rapid development of accounting and information technology, as well as a requirement for continuous improvement of open education itself. Through the continuous deepening of accounting practice teaching, a more comprehensive practice teaching system will be gradually established, which will play a key role in imparting knowledge, cultivating abilities, and improving quality. Follow-up research will improve the core literacy of the accounting profession through informatization teaching.

## References

1. Xin, C., Wang, X.: Research on the application of college physical education teaching mode in the cloud computing environment. J. Phys. Conf. Ser. **1624**(2), 022068 (2020). (4pp)
2. Zhang, Z., Min, H.: Analysis on the construction of personalized physical education teaching system based on a cloud computing platform. Wirel. Commun. Mob. Comput. **2020**(3), 1–8 (2020)
3. Tian, X.: Research on co-construction and sharing of higher vocational education information resources based on cloud computing. Revista De La Facultad De Ingenieria **32**(11), 984–989 (2017)
4. Wang, Q.: Strategy of enterprise network security protection based on cloud computing. IOP Conf. Ser. Mater. Sci. Eng. **750**, 012234 (2020)
5. Li, S.: Analysis on the teaching reform of college physical education informationization based on computer technology. J. Phys. Conf. Ser. **1648**, 032042 (2020)
6. Melo, G.C.V.D., Nascimento, C.S.D., Costa, W.P.L.B.D., et al.: Technology and the teaching of accounting: an analysis of teaching-learning in the courses of accounting sciences in the modality EaD. Custos e Agronegocio **14**(1), 22–44 (2018)
7. Liu, S., Bai, W., Zeng, N., et al.: A fast fractal based compression for MRI images. IEEE Access **7**, 62412–62420 (2019)
8. Liu, S., Li, Z., Zhang, Y., et al.: Introduction of key problems in long-distance learning and training. Mob. Netw. Appl. **24**(1), 1–4 (2019)
9. Liu, S., Glowatz, M., Zappatore, M., et al. (eds.): e-Learning, e-Education, and Online Training, pp. 1–374. Springer, Cham (2018)
10. Luo, Y.J., Li, Y., Liu, M.L., et al.: Reform and application of biochemistry teaching based on formative evaluation of mobile network platform. J. Phys. Conf. Ser. **1533**, 022037 (2020)

# Online Video Learning Design of Civil Engineering and Architecture Education in Higher Vocational Education Based on Streaming Media Technology

Yu Liu(✉)

School of Road Bridge and Architecture, Chongqing Vocational College of Transportation, Chongqing 402247, China

**Abstract.** The streaming media online video education model is comprehensively promoting the reform of college education, and the construction of online video learning courses is in full swing. Based on this, the design method of online video learning for education based on streaming media technology is summarized. Taking civil engineering majors and graduates of higher vocational colleges as objects, the research is carried out, and the necessity and common problems of the current online video learning design of civil engineering education based on streaming media technology are analyzed, and targeted Solution. Finally, a questionnaire survey was conducted. Based on the analysis and summary of the survey data, we explored suitable ways of constructing quality online courses in civil engineering in higher vocational colleges in order to design more high-quality and practical online courses.

**Keywords:** Streaming media technology · Higher vocational colleges · Civil engineering and construction · Education online video

## 1 Introduction

With the continuous development of science and technology, streaming media technology has become a new form of education in the field of Internet line vision teaching. Online video course is a typical one. The Ministry of Education encourages higher education institutions to actively carry out the construction of excellent online courses, and promote the construction of online open courses and platforms suitable for China's national conditions. In recent years, educational online video learning has sprung up in various Internet platforms. The construction of online video course of civil and Architectural Education in higher vocational colleges is to play a better role in teaching and avoid being mere formality. Targeted selection of the online video learning mode of civil engineering majors in higher vocational colleges for quality education provides more reasonable reference and support for the construction of quality online courses in civil


W. Fu et al. (Eds.): eLEOT 2021, LNICST 389, pp. 657–667, 2021.
https://doi.org/10.1007/978-3-030-84383-0_55

engineering in higher vocational colleges, so as to make higher vocational colleges high-quality, advanced and Convenient online courses. Due to the poor effect of traditional online video learning in Higher Vocational civil and architectural education, this paper designs an online video learning in Higher Vocational civil and Architectural Education Based on streaming media technology. Firstly, it analyzes the current situation of online video learning in Higher Vocational civil and architectural education, and then according to the analysis results, combined with streaming media technology, it provides more understandable video learning resources for online learners, Design the online video learning mode of education, and realize the online video learning of civil architecture education. Finally, the effectiveness of the design is verified by simulation.

## 2 Current Situation of Online Video Learning in Civil and Architectural Education in Higher Vocational Colleges

The production of online courses is reflected in the visual effects of learners. There are many forms, such as PPT + screen recording, classroom recording, physical demonstration, studio recording, production animation, white paper + mobile phone recording, etc. Teachers should choose suitable production methods for different professional courses and content. Online video learning for civil engineering education in higher vocational education is not a movie. It does not require full production, but a practical and applicable form. Too much attention to visual effects will not only increase production costs, but also distract learners from irrelevant aspects [1, 2]. The length of the online video learning and production of civil engineering education in higher vocational education should be moderate. Too short will make the learner have not mastered the knowledge. If the online video learning time of higher vocational civil engineering education is too long, it will make the learner easily distracted, and it is not conducive to anytime and anywhere Do fragmented learning. Teachers should make a comprehensive decision according to the characteristics of network video learning, the level of learners and the content of knowledge points. Mainly people appear on the camera, sound on the camera, or a combination of the two.

In recent years, the construction of online courses in China has made remarkable achievements. Video is the main form of online courses. The design and development of high-quality video learning resources has always been the primary task of online course construction. However, there are still some potential problems to be solved in the current situation of resource application and design.

The online video learning of civil engineering education in higher vocational education is carried out by learners independently on the Internet, and no teachers can communicate face to face [3]. This will make it easy for learners to lose focus and lose concentration. Therefore, teachers can increase the teaching effect by adding some interaction in the curriculum. Common interactive methods for online courses include online exercises, homework after class, online exams, study forums, etc. However, if the frequency of interaction is too frequent, it will increase the pressure and time of the learner, and if it is too small, the corresponding effect will not be achieved. As an intermediary of communication between teachers and learners in the online learning environment, the online video learning resources of civil engineering and construction education in higher vocational education are important nodes to break through the bottleneck of informatization teaching.

The current design and application of video learning resources can not meet this demand. Video learning resources are mainly used in face-to-face teaching environment, and teachers are used as the "intermediary" between students and video learning resources. Under this teaching mode, video is an application object or tool in teaching activities. With the construction of online open courses, online learners will directly face the video learning resources. Teachers have retired from the intermediary position to the auxiliary position, and carry out teaching activities indirectly through video learning resources [4]. Without the teacher's on-site guidance and intervention, students can still complete the whole learning process only through online video, and teachers can also complete all teaching tasks through online video.

Online video learning resources for civil engineering and architectural education in higher vocational education have become an extension of teachers in the online teaching environment, and gradually replace teachers' face-to-face guidance and intervention functions for students. In the face of this situation, the actual demand for online video learning resources of civil engineering education in higher vocational education will also change. Not only must we undertake the mission of explaining online video learning content of civil engineering education in higher vocational education, but also need to consider the understanding process of students. The design quality of online video learning for civil architecture education will directly affect the final understanding effect [5]. Therefore, the current video learning resources should not only be a single, static video concept in the general sense, nor a simple, linear content organization, but should be a three-dimensional design generated according to learners' understanding rules. Multi-dimensional learning resources include the necessary links in the learning process such as learning content presentation, learning activity design, and learner interaction. Therefore, the design of video learning resources that integrates students' understanding process is the goal pursued by the development of information education.

Under the guidance of traditional theories, we still regard "learning resources" and "learning process" as two independent research areas. In the past, the design of learning resources is less related to learning process. In teaching practice, video is also an auxiliary tool used by teachers in the teaching process. Therefore, the role of video in the past classroom teaching is very limited [6]. However, today's online video learning resources of civil and Architectural Education in higher vocational colleges are endowed with broader connotation and value by the times, and the online video learning of Higher Vocational civil engineering education and the learning process of students have become an integral whole [7]. However, the design perspective of online video learning designers of civil engineering and architecture education in higher vocational colleges has not changed in time and conform to the trend. They do not realize the teaching value of video learning resources. They still keep unchanged and adapt to changes. They regard video as a traditional sound transmission tool and fail to redesign it in combination with teaching process.

Some online learning videos are just copies of face-to-face classroom teaching, and do not really consider the difference between online and offline learning environments. The content is still based on traditional lecture-based teaching, which is difficult to fully integrate with the learning process of online learners [8]. Most of these online videos of civil engineering and construction education in higher vocational colleges are still formal videos, that is, they simply record live classroom situations and upload them to the website. However, there are very few "content videos" resources to assist students and promote learning, and the quality of teaching videos is uneven. The content design of many video learning resources has problems such as focusing on teaching results, focusing on the learning process, knowledge transfer, and students' understanding. They only care about mechanical methods instead of teaching process design. They only focus on the expansion of the number of videos and ignore the improvement of video quality.

The design and development of online video learning resources for civil and Architectural Education in higher vocational colleges has always been the historical mission of educational technology discipline. Throughout the research status of video resource design and tracing the root of this work, there is a lack of a set of reasonable design theoretical guidance, and the research on the understanding of video learning resources is even less [9]. As a result, a lot of resource construction work is like a blind man feeling an elephant. Only by constantly exploring and experimenting in practice can we see the whole picture of resource design theory. The lack of online video learning design theory in Higher Vocational civil engineering education will lead to the disorder and weakness of practical work. The contradiction between the teaching value of video learning resources and the current application situation urgently needs the guidance of new ideas and new ideas of resource design theory.

## 3 Optimization of Online Video Learning Design Method for Civil and Architectural Education

### 3.1 Design of Educational Online Video Learning Resources

The design of online video resources for civil engineering and construction education in higher vocational education should emphasize the role of video learning resources in connecting teachers and students in the learning process, and combining streaming media technology to provide online learners with more easy-to-understand video learning resources. The structure of higher vocational civil engineering education and teaching usually consists of three elements: teachers, students and teaching resources.

Under the streaming media technology, teachers can transfer teaching ideas to students through teaching resources such as teaching materials, coursewares and test paper assignments. Teachers can also skip these teaching resources and directly talk with students to promote knowledge understanding in face-to-face communication. At present, the mediating role of teaching resources in the whole process of understanding is gradually weakened, and seems to be a "dispensable" existence. The design goal of online video learning course of Higher Vocational civil engineering education focuses on "online video watching of Higher Vocational civil engineering education" and "online video interpretation of Higher Vocational civil engineering education", which guides students from learning, learning to learning, and achieving a good state [10–12]. Among them, the learning in the online video of Higher Vocational civil engineering education is not simple, but purposeful.

Online video learning for civil engineering and construction education in higher vocational colleges requires the support of certain basic knowledge of visual culture, and on this basis, the ability to learn and do well can be improved. In other words, the knowledge goal is the foundation and the key goal. The learner's understanding of the basic knowledge of the online video learning theory of civil engineering education in higher vocational education is the key basis for further study and interpretation. Based on this, optimize the design of the online video teaching resource management function of higher vocational civil engineering education, as shown in the Fig. 1.

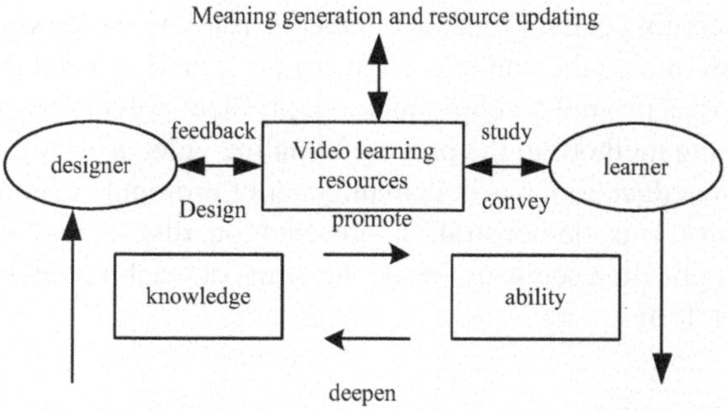


**Fig. 1.** Online video teaching resource management module

Different from traditional face-to-face teaching, the hermeneutical relationship between "designer-video learning resource-learner" in the online learning environment is more clear.

Through the design and development of online video learning resources for higher vocational civil and architectural education to achieve the teaching process, the intermediary role of online video resources of Higher Vocational civil and architectural education has been highlighted unprecedentedly. In online learning, video learning resources are used for indirect dialogue. Learners can feed back their understanding views to designers through resources, and designers can also send feedback to students through resources, so as to promote the communication and sharing of views between teachers and students under the media effect of video learning resources, and stimulate the fusion and collision of vision of both sides. Generally speaking, enriching the online video learning resources of civil engineering education in Higher Vocational Colleges and meeting the personalized needs of learners is only a way to improve the learning effect, not the ultimate goal. The ultimate goal of network video course resource design of civil architecture education in higher vocational colleges is to promote the improvement of knowledge and ability. Through the form of video to promote learners' knowledge understanding, and on this basis to promote the improvement of ability, which in turn promotes the further deepening of knowledge.

## 3.2 Educational Online Video Learning Model Design

Teaching method is the general name of the methods and means used by teachers and students in the teaching process in order to achieve the common teaching goal and complete the common online video learning task of civil engineering education. According to Professor Li Bingde's classification and summary of the teaching methods commonly used in the teaching activities of primary and secondary schools in China, online video learning of civil and architectural education can be divided into teaching class, question and answer class, inspiration class, discussion class, demonstration class, practice class, experiment class, performance class, autonomous learning class, cooperative learning class and inquiry learning class. From the interactive roles of teachers, students, teaching materials and environment, the online video learning of civil and architectural education can be summarized as prompt teaching method, problem-solving teaching method and independent teaching method. In the process of online video learning of civil engineering and architecture education, teachers mainly adopt prompt teaching methods, which mainly include four forms: demonstration, presentation, display and oral narration. The connotation and application scope of these four forms of teaching methods are different, as shown in the Table 1.

**Table 1.** Educational online video learning teaching methods

| Teaching method | Connotation description | Example analysis |
|---|---|---|
| Demonstration | Demonstration is a teaching method that teachers provide students with certain activities, actions and attitudes for students to follow | Teachers demonstrate how to use principles, how to analyze problems, how to grasp the test, how to explain the relationship, how to extract articles, how to use textbooks, etc. for students, the above are all demonstration teaching |
| Oral account | Oral teaching is a teaching method that prompts the course content through language | Oral form includes report, speech, explanation, narration, etc. The act of telling refers to the presentation of oral language by teachers to students. Explain knowledge and make students understand the behavior of knowledge |
| Present | An intuitive teaching method, which can vividly and intuitively present some contents that are difficult to grasp only by language description and students' imagination with the help of various static teaching methods | Use such as wall charts, models, specimens, drawings, etc. |

(*continued*)

**Table 1.** (*continued*)

| Teaching method | Connotation description | Example analysis |
|---|---|---|
| Exhibition | Exhibition is a method of teaching by presenting the process and process of things and phenomena intuitively and dynamically | Demonstrate experiments, watch software operation, listen to literature or music tapes, reproduce the process and process of things and phenomena, and visit the scene, so that students can actually observe Wang's live phenomenon in progress: the display is different from presentation, the display is dynamic, it is the observation of movement, it requires students to focus on observation |

The above online video learning methods of civil engineering education are mainly based on classroom teaching, and the classification is detailed. Generally, the online video learning resources of civil engineering education are prone to overlap due to excessive details. Therefore, according to the teaching method of teaching micro video, the teaching micro video can be divided into oral teaching micro video and operation demonstration online video learning.

### 3.3 Realization of Online Video Learning in Civil Engineering Education

The main process of online video learning design for civil engineering education in higher vocational education is: selecting courses → selecting knowledge points → writing teaching plans, making courseware, writing exercises → course production → course release → interactive reflection and perfection. There are many factors that need to be considered in the selection of its construction method, including course preparation, publishing platform, production format and duration, teaching method, interactive method and frequency, etc. The key to the effect of online video learning in civil engineering education is the teacher's teaching content, teaching design and teaching level. Develop from the perspective of the learner. Teachers then select and decompose course knowledge points according to the goals, and write lesson plans, courseware and scripts.

The expression content of online video learning resources of civil engineering and architecture education needs to have the enlightening effect of the text. It not only enables learners to correctly understand the designer's intention, but also stimulates learners' thinking, so as to provide a broader discussion space for all online participants and open up more meaningful fields. From the perspective of hermeneutic understanding, a new form of resource design to promote understanding is formed, and an understanding oriented online video learning resource design framework for civil architecture education is constructed, as shown in the Fig. 2.

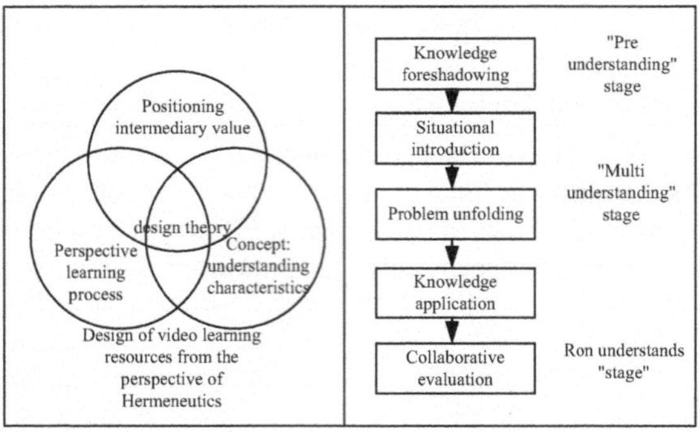


**Fig. 2.** Educational online video learning resource design framework

The design framework puts forward three stages of the content design of online video learning resources for civil and Architectural Education: pre understanding, multi understanding and integrated understanding. At the same time, the learning content is divided into five parts: knowledge foreshadowing, situation introduction, problem deployment, knowledge application and collaborative mutual evaluation.

Explain the application path of the design framework through a specific teaching case, and according to the later questionnaire feedback and interview investigation, it is shown that the case video can promote students' understanding. Teaching understanding focuses on the teaching process, and each link in the teaching process can be described through diagrams.

By analyzing the structure of knowledge points, we can test the learners' mastery of "required knowledge". Through the concept discrimination, the students will have a simple review of the concept of friction and review the old to learn the new. Students with wrong answers will give detailed explanation of wrong answers and review the definition and knowledge points of friction concept. Like the teaching design of other types of teaching resources, the online video learning of civil engineering education also needs to effectively design the online video learning objectives, learning content, learning process, teaching strategies, media selection, etc. around the characteristics of learners, such as knowledge level, learning style, learning ability, etc.

According to the characteristics of online video learning in civil and architectural education, based on working memory theory, cognitive load theory, multimedia learning cognitive theory, constructivism, and learning objective classification theory, some principles are proposed for the instructional design of micro-class videos in order to give Learners provide a good learning experience. When choosing the teaching content of the online video learning of civil engineering and construction education, avoid multiple teaching contents in the online video of civil engineering and construction education, and design the teaching content as a unit of knowledge points.

When designing and producing the online video of civil and architectural education, it is the most important link to determine the learning objectives. First of all, the teaching content of online video of civil engineering education is based on knowledge points, and the teaching objectives should be layered according to the teaching content, and the corresponding teaching objectives should be designed according to the specific teaching content. Secondly, the level of teaching objectives should be adapted to the level differences among learners. When determining the teaching objectives of online video of civil and architectural education, we can refer to Bloom's classification method of teaching objectives to establish the cognitive $D_s$, motor skills $D_p$ and emotional learning objectives $D_e$ that match the teaching content and learners.

$$\rho = \left(D_s, D_p, D_e\right) \tag{1}$$

The constructivist view of learning believes that the learning process is a process in which students actively construct knowledge. Learners select, process and process external information based on their own learning experience and existing knowledge structure. Students construct knowledge meaningfully through adaptation and assimilation in a specific learning situation. Therefore, when designing the specific teaching process in the civil and architectural education online video, we should combine the teaching content and the actual situation of the learner, and strive to create a learning situation to promote the learner's processing, memory and transfer of knowledge.

## 4 Analysis of Experimental Results

In order to explore the construction mode of online video learning course for civil and architectural education, this paper designs questions from the above six factors and conducts a questionnaire survey. 132 valid answers are collected, of which 37.88% are reading and 62.12% are graduated. After the completion of autonomous learning based on micro class video, the experimental group and the control group were tested for learning effect. The average score of the experimental group was 97.24, while that of the control group was 83.6. The average score of the experimental group was higher than that of the control group. In order to verify whether the average score difference between the two groups is significant, that is, whether the learning effect of the experimental group is significantly better than that of the control group, this study conducted two independent sample t tests on the test scores of the two groups of students (Table 2).

**Table 2.** Sample test results

| Test results | | Suppose the variances are equal | Suppose the variance is not equal |
|---|---|---|---|
| Levete test of variance equation | F | 2.908 | 0.096 |
| | Sig | | |
| Test of mean value equation | T | 6.184 | 6.184 |
| | Dt | 38 | 33 |
| | Sig | 0.00 | 0.00 |
| | Mean difference Standard | 13.750 | 13.750 |

*(continued)*

**Table 2.** (*continued*)

| Test results | | Suppose the variances are equal | Suppose the variance is not equal |
|---|---|---|---|
| | Error value | 2.223 | 2.223 |
| | Lower limit | 9.248 | 9.248 |
| | Upper limit | 18.251 | 18.750 |

The results in the table are divided into two parts. The first part is Levene's variance homogeneity test to judge whether the overall variance of the two groups is homogeneous, where $f = 2.908$, $P = 0.096$, the significance level $\alpha$ is 0.05, and the probability p value is greater than 0.05, so the variance is homogeneous, that is, there is no significant difference between the two groups; the t test of homogeneity of variance is selected, where $t = 6.184$, $P = 0$, $P < 0.05$, reaching a very significant level of 0%, so there is a significant difference between the experimental group and the control group, that is, the test scores of the experimental group are significantly higher than those of the control group.

Further investigate and record the experience of civil engineering students on online video teaching, and conduct statistics to obtain the following information:

Among the interactive (multiple choice) options, "online exercises" accounted for 62.88%, and "Learning Forum" accounted for 48.48%. In the preference of interaction frequency (single choice question), 46.21% chose "interaction of each class"; 32.58% chose "interaction of each chapter". In addition, online learning forum is set up for learners to discuss with each other, solve questions and answer doubts. Teachers can answer questions online in the forum at a fixed time every week. In the multi topic "for civil engineering courses, which courses do you need to make into online (Network) courses for learning?" Among them, BIM modeling, engineering CAD, reinforcement calculation, measurement and pricing ranked the top four, with more than 50% of the choices, and BIM modeling was as high as 77.27%. From this analysis, learners have a strong demand for professional courses with strong practical operation, but a low demand for theoretical courses (such as engineering laws and regulations) (28.79%).

In the multiple-choice questions in the form of video learning and production, 90 people chose "PPT + screen recording"; 68 people chose "Physical Demonstration"; 58 people chose "Classroom Recording"; and "Studio Recording" only had 14 choices. From this analysis, when students majoring in civil engineering choose online courses, they do not pursue gorgeous visual effects, but prefer the simple and simple form of "PPT + screen recording" that is commonly used. The civil engineering course is highly professional, and it is necessary to integrate practice and apply what you have learned. The combination of "in-kind demonstration" when teachers teach will be more popular with learners, and the teaching effect will be better.

## 5 Conclusion

In order to improve the learners' learning effect and subjective satisfaction, we should follow certain teaching design principles and picture design principles in the design and production of online video learning for civil and architectural education. It should be noted that the overall optimization of the teaching design and picture design of the online video of civil and architectural education needs the cooperation of teachers and professional producers. Further promote the in-depth integration of information technology and higher education, and provide high-quality learning resources for students. Because this paper does not consider the efficiency of online video learning when studying the online video learning of civil architecture education in higher vocational colleges, in the future research, it can improve the online video learning effect of civil architecture education in Higher Vocational Colleges in the shortest learning time.

## 6 Fund Projects

No. 203683, Project Name: Research and Application of Teaching System and Method of Construction Engineering Management Specialty Based on BIM Technology.

## References

1. Al-Jabri, K.S., Diouri, A., Boukhari, A., et al.: Research on the use of Ferro-Chrome slag in civil engineering applications. MATEC Web Conf. **149**(4), 01017 (2018)
2. Xie, M., Meng, F., Feng, W., et al.: Education reform of theoretical mechanics for civil engineering in big data era. J. Phys. Conf. Ser. **1624**(3), 032037 (2020). (5pp)
3. Ma, Z., Liu, S.: A review of 3D reconstruction techniques in civil engineering and their applications. Adv. Eng. Inf. **37**, 163–174 (2018)
4. Moravej, H., Chan, T.H.T., Nguyen, K.D., et al.: Vibration-based Bayesian model updating of civil engineering structures applying Gaussian process metamodel. Adv. Struct. Eng. **22**(16), 3487–3502 (2019)
5. Scott, R., Vidakovic, M., Chikermane, S., et al.: Encapsulation of fiber optic sensors in 3D printed packages for use in civil engineering applications: a preliminary study. Sensors **19**(7), 1689–1690 (2019)
6. Tekkumru-Kisa, M., Stein, M.K., Coker, R.: Teachers' learning to facilitate high-level student thinking: impact of a video-based professional development. J. Res. Seci. Teach. **55**(4), 479–502 (2018)
7. Granjo, J.F.O., Rasteiro, M.G.: LABVIRTUAL—a platform for the teaching of chemical engineering: the use of interactive videos. Comput. Appl. Eng. Educ. **26**(5), 1668–1676 (2018)
8. Liu, S., Bai, W., Zeng, N., et al.: A fast fractal based compression for MRI images. IEEE Access **7**, 62412–62420 (2019)
9. Liu, S., Li, Z., Zhang, Y., et al.: Introduction of key problems in long-distance learning and training. Mob. Netw. Appl. **24**(1), 1–4 (2019)
10. Liu, S., Glowatz, M., Zappatore, M., et al. (eds.): e-Learning, e-Education, and Online Training, pp. 1–374. Springer, Cham (2018)
11. Polloth, B., Schwarzer, S., Zipse, H.: Student individuality impacts use and benefits of an online video library for the organic chemistry laboratory. J. Chem. Educ. **97**(2), 328–337 (2020)
12. Kaw, A., Clark, R., Delgado, E., et al.: Analyzing the use of adaptive learning in a flipped classroom for preclass learning. Comput. Appl. Eng. Educ. **27**(3), 663–678 (2019)

# Author Index

An, Li I-86, I-205

Cai, Hong II-39, II-241
Chen, Cheng-zhao II-477
Chen, Mei I-405
Chen, Quan-wen I-381, I-566, II-441
Chen, Wei II-599
Chen, Xi I-71, II-103
Chen, Yong-ming I-99, I-322
Chen, Zheng II-477
Cheng, Ling I-254, II-365

Dai, Mei-li I-205
Dai, Xin II-16
Dong, Lian-shi I-181, II-50
Dong, Li-na II-75, II-252
Duan, Ping I-266, I-278
Duan, Xiao-xiao I-266, I-278

Feng, Zhi-xin I-3, I-23
Fu, Jun I-194, II-165
Fu, Shuai II-502

Gao, Fei II-205, II-218
Gong, Ping I-381
Guo, Lu II-430, II-441

Han, Pei-jun II-103
Hao, Rui-can I-3, I-15, I-23
He, Jie II-415
He, Lin I-110, II-392
He, Wei I-442, II-491
Hou, Wei II-16
Huang, Xiao-feng I-134
Hui, Sun II-291

Ji, Rou-jia II-277, II-415
Jiang, Guang-min II-16, II-354
Jiang, Hong-bing I-167, II-514
Jiang, Qian I-110, II-392
Jiang, Shan I-566, II-430, II-441
Jiang, Yi I-122, II-403
Jiang, Yi- huo II-403
Jiang, Yi-huo I-122

Kang, Ying-jian I-405

Li, Ang I-146
Li, Dong-rui I-134
Li, Hui II-538
Li, Jiang II-218
Li, Jun-mei I-464, II-3
Li, Liu II-341
Li, Ming-sheng II-193, II-303
Li, You-xin II-477
Li, Zhen I-527, I-541
Liang, Huan-wei I-32, I-515
Liang, Shao-lin I-32, I-515
Lin, Hui I-617, I-631
Lin, Ying I-418, II-118
Liu, Fang I-332, I-344
Liu, Hua-gang I-3, I-23
Liu, Ji-wei II-75, II-252
Liu, Li I-289, II-538, II-599
Liu, Li-ting II-205
Liu, Xin-bo II-599
Liu, Yan I-243, II-291
Liu, Yu I-476, I-657
Liu, Yu-xiang I-311, I-502
Lu, Jiang-lin I-231, I-367
Lu, Liang I-553, II-527
Luo, Min I-527, I-541
Luo, Qing-yue II-599
Lv, Xin-yu I-405, II-502

Ma, Jin-ru I-15
Ma, Lei I-405, II-502
Ma, Ran II-205
Men, Yu-feng II-39, II-241
Mi, Fa-li I-355, II-562

Peng, Qian I-604, II-230
Peng, Zhi-hua II-538

Qi, Mei-bin I-301, I-489
Qiao, Jun-hao II-264, II-550
Qin, Ming I-194, II-165
Qin, Nan II-576, II-588

Sha, Zhi-li I-311, I-502
Shang, Yi-jia I-453, II-130
Shen, Shu-tao I-99, I-322
Sun, Hui I-243
Sun, Tong II-143, II-154
Suo, Dong-dong I-453, II-130

Tang, Jie II-538, II-599
Tang, Xin II-264, II-550
Tang, Yana II-465
Tang, Ya-na II-61
Tao, Guang II-277, II-415
Tian, Hong-wei II-325, II-452

Wang, Dan I-181, II-50
Wang, Hong-gang I-218, II-25
Wang, Jia I-579, I-592
Wang, Sen-wei II-291
Wang, Shang I-3, I-15, I-23
Wang, Tian-hui I-146
Wang, Tian-Hui I-57
Wang, Yan I-86
Wang, Ying II-50
Wei, Ying II-430
Wei, Yu-hui I-23
Wu, Qi-feng I-155, I-644
Wu, Qi-xiang II-392
Wu, Sheng-bin I-134, II-313
Wu, Yang-bo I-418, I-442, I-553, I-617, I-631
Wu, Yangbo II-118
Wu, Yang-bo II-491, II-527

Xi, Ying-di I-418, II-118
Xia, Guang-hui I-3
Xiao, Jing-qiong I-181
Xu, Li-tang I-218, II-25

Yan, Hui-ying I-254, II-365
Yan, Ru I-395, II-176
Yan, Yi-pin I-604, II-230
Yan, Yong-lan I-464, II-3
Yang, Xiao-tian II-218
Yang, Ying I-134, II-313
Yin, Jin-tian II-538, II-599
Yuan, Jia-wei I-355, II-562
Yue, Ming I-579
Yun, Li-jun II-193, II-303

Zhang, Cai-ming I-289, II-341
Zhang, Cheng-hui I-442, II-491
Zhang, Jie-lan I-430, II-90
Zhang, Li-min I-43, II-379
Zhang, Shu-Yang I-71
Zhang, Shu-yang II-103
Zhang, Yu-juan I-301, I-489
Zhang, Zheng I-57, I-146
Zhao, Dan II-354
Zhao, Jing II-61, II-465
Zheng, Chun-ni I-395, II-176
Zhou, Jun I-553, II-527
Zhu, Wei-hua I-631

The manufacturer's authorised representative in the EU is Springer Nature Customer Service Centre GmbH, Europaplatz 3, 69115 Heidelberg, Germany. If you have any concerns regarding our products, please contact ProductSafety@springernature.com

Printed and bound by CPI Group (UK) Ltd, Croydon, CR0 4YY
30/09/2026
02225688-0010